Introduction to Law Enforcement and Criminal Justice

Third Edition

Introduction to Law Enforcement and Criminal Justice

Third Edition

Henry M. Wrobleski

Normandale Community College
Bloomington, Minnesota

Kären M. Hess

Normandale Community College
Bloomington, Minnesota

Criminal Justice Series

West Publishing Company
St. Paul • New York • Los Angeles • San Francisco

Text Design: Adapted from design by David Farr, Imagesmythe, Inc.
Copyeditor: Laura Beaudoin
Composition: Carlisle Communications
Photo Credits:

Section 1. **xxiv** James Shaffer. *Chapter 1.* **2** The Granger Collection, New York; **9** Historical Pictures Service, Chicago; **18** The Granger Collection, New York. *Chapter 2.* **22** Minnesota Historical Society; **26** J. D. Stinchcomb; **36** Courtesy of the Federal Bureau of Investigation; **41** Courtesy of U.S. Secret Service; **47** Scott Harr. *Chapter 3.* **58** The Granger Collection, New York; **69** The Granger Collection, New York; **72, 92** Bill Powers, Frost Publishing; **86, 88, 90, 95** Library of Congress. *Chapter 4.* **100** AP/Wide World Photos. *Chapter 5.* **134** AP/Wide World Photos; **136** UPI/Bettmann Newsphotos; **146, 147** Sergeant David Indrehus/Minneapolis Police Department. *Section 2.* **156** Tony O'Brien, Frost Publishing. *Chapter 6.* **158** AP/Wide World; **190** Courtesy of Hennepin County Sheriff's Water Patrol; **193** Tony O'Brien, Frost Publishing. *Chapter 7.* **202** James Shaffer; **209, 218** Scott Harr; **216** UPI/Bettmann Newsphotos. *Chapter 8.* **222** Tony O'Brien, Frost Publishing; **232** Scott Harr; **233, 237** Bill Powers, Frost Publishing; **235** James Shaffer; **236** Courtesy of Hennepin County Sheriff's Water Patrol. *Chapter 9.* **251** Frost Publishing; **271** James Shaffer. *Chapter 10.* **276** James Shaffer; **281** UPI/Bettman Newsphotos; **290, 291** West Publishing. *Chapter 11.* **300** AP/Wide World. *Chapter 12.* **322** James Shaffer; **333** Tom Grill, Comstock; **350** James Shaffer. *Section 3.* **358** UPI/Bettman Newsphotos. *Chapter 13.* **360** UPI/Bettman Newsphotos; **366** West Publishing; **371** Paul Brou, The Picture Group; **374** AP/Wide Word. *Chapter 14.* **381** West Publishing Company; **393** Bill Powers, Frost Publishing; **398** UPI/Bettmann Newsphotos, **399** James Shaffer. *Chapter 15.* **402** Arnaud Borrel, Liaison; **408** Comstock; **421, 429** UPI/Bettman Newsphotos; **422** James Shaffer. *Chapter 16.* **432** Jeffrey D. Smith, Woodfin Camp & Associates; **445** Jim Anderson, Woodfin Camp & Associates. *Chapter 17.* **449** Dave Healey, Liaison. *Chapter 18.* **462, 478** James Shaffer; **472** Frost Publishing. *Section 4.* **482** Library of Congress. *Chapter 19.* **484** Russ Kinne; **500** Library of Congress; **507** John Maher, EKM-Nepenthe; **514** UPI/Bettman Newsphotos. *Chapter 20.* **522** Michael Hayman, Stock Boston; **527** Library of Congress; **543** James Shaffer; **549** Steve Starr, Picture Group; **551** J. D. Stinchcomb; **552** Bernard Pierre Wolff, Photo Researchers. *Chapter 21.* **558** Frost Publishing; **575** Yves Gellie, Liaison; **582** Scott Harr.

A student workbook has been developed to assist students in mastering the concepts presented in this text. The workbook reinforces concepts by presenting them in a concise format with self-testing exercises. An examination copy is available to instructors by contacting West Publishing Company at the address below. Students can purchase the workbook from the local bookstore under the title *Student Workbook to Accompany Introduction to Law Enforcement and Criminal Justice, Third Edition,* prepared by Henry M. Wrobleski and Kären M. Hess.

Library of Congress Cataloging-in-Publication Data

Wrobleski, Henry M., 1922-
   Introduction to law enforcement and criminal justice / Henry M.
Wrobleski, Kären M. Hess. — 3rd ed.
      p.   cm. / — (Criminal justice series)
   ISBN 0-314-59950-9
   1. Law enforcement—United States. 2. Crime—United States.
I. Hess, Kären, 1939-   . II. Title. III. Series.
HV8138.W76   1990
363.2'3'0973—dc20

89-22764
CIP

About the Authors

Henry M. Wrobleski, LLB, is coordinator of the Law Enforcement Program at Normandale Community College. He is a respected author, lecturer, and consultant with 30 years of experience in law enforcement. He is also Dean of Instruction for the Institute for Professional Development, holds a LLB degree and is a graduate of the FBI Academy.

Kären M. Hess, PhD, has written extensively in the field of law enforcement. She is a member of the English department at Normandale Community College as well as the president of the Institute for Professional Development.

Henry M. Wrobleski

Kären M. Hess

Contents in Brief

Contents

FIGURES

TABLES

Table of Cases

Preface

The future of our lawful, democratic society depends in large part upon those of you currently in the field of law enforcement and those of you preparing to enter this field. The law enforcement officer is responsible for assisting those in distress, providing services to persons who request them, preserving peace and order in the community, preventing unlawful acts, and apprehending those who violate the law. These complex responsibilities must be met under constantly changing conditions and in a manner that assures the rights of the individual. Increased technology, industrialization, urbanization, and mobility have brought new problems to law enforcement, requiring the law enforcement officer to be knowledgeable in a wide variety of areas.

Introduction to Law Enforcement and Criminal Justice provides basic information that should serve as an overview of the entire field as well as a solid foundation for future course work. The content in each chapter could easily be expanded into an entire book or course, but the basic concepts in each area have been included.

You will be introduced to the history of law enforcement, including how our laws have evolved and the basic rights all American citizens have. You will also look at the distinction between criminal and civil offenses.

Then you will look at police operations as they exist in the 1990s, including the roles and responsibilities of the modern law enforcement officer. Next you will look at the specific problems and people involved, including crime, criminals, gangs, and victims.

The text concludes with a discussion of the total criminal justice system, the role of the courts and corrections, the juvenile justice system, and some critical issues and challenges facing law enforcement in the 1990s.

Important court cases and decisions are presented throughout the text rather than isolated in a single chapter. Likewise, modern advancements in law enforcement are integrated into chapters rather than presented as a separate subject. The content of the text is based on fifteen years of classroom research among law enforcement officers and preservice students as to what subject matter is most important and useful to the future police officer. The text itself has been classroom tested and reviewed by several experts in the field.

HOW TO USE THIS BOOK

Introduction to Law Enforcement and Criminal Justice is more than a textbook; it is a learning experience requiring your active participation to obtain the best results. You will get the most out of the book if you first familiarize yourself with the total scope of law enforcement: read and think about the Contents and what is included. Then follow these steps as you read each chapter:

> *1.* Read the objectives at the beginning of each chapter:

DO YOU KNOW

■ *What the basic instrument of government is?*
Think about your current knowledge on each question.
What preconceptions do you hold?

> *2.* Read the chapter (underlining or taking notes if that is your preferred study style).
>   a. Pay special attention to all information between rules:

The United States Constitution is the basic instrument of government and the supreme law of the United States.

>   The key concepts of each chapter are emphasized in this manner.
>   b. Look up unfamiliar words in the glossary at the back of the text.
>
> *3.* When you have finished reading the chapter, reread the list of objectives given at the beginning of the chapter to make certain you are able to give a response to each question. If you find yourself stumped, find the appropriate material in the chapter and review it.
> *4.* Finally, read the Discussion Questions, think about possible responses, and be prepared to contribute to a class discussion.

Good reading and learning!

ACKNOWLEDGMENTS

We would like to thank the following individuals and organizations for their contributions to *Introduction to Law Enforcement and Criminal Justice.*
        Thank you to Larry Gaines, Eastern Kentucky University; Professor George Green, Mankato State University; Robert Ingram, Florida International University; Glen Morgan, Lincolnland Community College; Profes-

sor Frank Post, Fullerton College; Jack Spurlin, Missouri Southern State College; and Larry Tuttle; Palm Beach Junior College for their helpful reviews of the manuscript and their suggestions for changes. A special thank you to Professor Post for his valuable additions, particularly in the areas of law enforcement agencies and the police career.

For their valuable suggestions for the third edition of *Introduction to Law Enforcement and Criminal Justice,* thank you to Robert Ives, Rockford Police Department; Sergeant James Walsh, Mount San Jacinto College; Paul H. Johnson, Murry State University; Roger Brown, Golden Valley Lutheran College; Dr. Jack Taylor, Oscar Rose Junior College; Lt. David A. Wilson, Turmbull Police Department; Professor Joseph Polanski, Sinclair Community College; Dr. David G. Epstein, Burnswick Junior College; Professor Kenneth Bowser, Westfield State College; Myron Utech, University of Wisconsin at Eau Claire; Dr. Steven Brown, East Tennessee State University; James Stinchcomb, Miami Dade Community College; Daniel Gunderson, Chippewa Valley Technical College; and Tim Vieders, Niagara County Community College.

Thank you to the administration and staff of Normandale Community College for their assistance and support during the classroom testing of the manuscript, to the students in Law Enforcement 050 for providing ideas and suggestions, and to Pamela Reierson, media specialist, for her invaluable assistance in locating sources and information.

Thank you to the Department of Justice; the Federal Bureau of Investigation; the Federal Drug Enforcement Administration; the International Association of Chiefs of Police; the Minnesota Attorney General's Office, Civil Service Department, County Attorney's Association, Governor's Commission on Crime Prevention and Control, and State Highway Department; the National Safety Council; and police departments of Minneapolis, Philadelphia, San Diego, and St. Louis Park; Keith Rodgers, Chief of the Criminal Investigation Training Division of the IRS; and the publishers for permission to include their materials in our text.

Thank you also to Susan Tubb and to Mélina Brown-Hall, our editors, for their patience, their attention to detail, and their encouragement and support. It is largely through their efforts that this third edition has a new look.

Finally, thank you to our families and collegues for their support and assistance during the development of *Introduction to Law Enforcement and Criminal Justice.*

SECTION ONE
Law Enforcement in Context

Our system of law enforcement did not magically appear. It has a rich heritage as well as a very complex system of laws on which it is based. The origins of law enforcement, from primitive and ancient times up through developments in English law enforcement, are the focus of chapter 1. Chapter 2 traces the evolution of law enforcement in the United States, from the time the colonists arrived, bringing with them their European customs and laws, up through the creation of our various levels of local, county, state, and federal governments.

Chapter 3 discusses the foundation of our law enforcement system, our Constitution and Bill of Rights, which are the supreme law of this country and which have a profound effect on how law enforcement is practiced. In addition to constitutional law, police officers must also be familiar with the vast array of local, state, and federal statutes that have developed over the years. Chapter 4 looks at the various kinds of laws that have evolved and then focuses on the two most relevant to law enforcement, criminal law and civil law. The elements of specific crimes such as murder, assault, rape, robbery, burglary, larceny/theft, auto theft, and arson are discussed. The chapter concludes with a look at the various areas frequently resulting in law enforcement officers being sued.

Everything a law enforcement officer does must be done with the realization that the profession is governed by laws and that all citizens, even if they are committing illegal acts, have certain rights that cannot be violated. Citizens , however, also have the right to be protected from those who would harm them—a precarious balancing act. As one yellowed piece of paper taped to the wall of a police roll-call room said:

The policeman, he told us, is a mercenary: Society tries to make us out to be the Jolly Green Giants of the community. We're not. We're the barbed wire separating the wolves from the lambs.

The section closes with a discussion of the police profession in the 1990s (chapter 5), including the process of becoming a police officer and some of the challenges involved.

CHAPTER ONE

A Brief History:
The Evolution of Law
and Law Enforcement

History is a vast early warning system.—Norman Cousins

DO YOU KNOW

What a law is?

When and why law enforcement began?

The origins of features of our law enforcement system such as:
The offices of constable, sheriff, and justice of the peace? General alarms and citizen's arrests? Separation between enforcing laws and judging offenders? Local responsibility for law enforcement? Division of offenses into felonies and misdemeanors? Jury by peers and due process? Paid law enforcement officers? Women in law enforcement?

The significance of the tithing system, the Frankpledge system, Leges Henrici, the Magna Carta, the Parish Constable system, and the Watch and Ward system?

How law enforcement has traditionally responded to increased crime?

What significant contributions to law enforcement were made by Sir Robert Peel?

Where and when the first police department was established in England and what it was called?

Introduction

Chapter 1

A brief look into the history of laws and law enforcement will give you answers to many of the preceding questions. The heritage of law enforcement is a source of pride as well as a guide to avoiding mistakes in the future. Specific dates and events are not as important as acquiring a sense of the sequence or chronology of how present-day laws and our system of law enforcement came into existence.

Law is a body of rules for human conduct that are enforced by imposing penalties for their violation. Technically, laws are made and passed by the legislative branches of our federal, state, county, and city governments. They are based on customs, traditions, mores, and current need.

Law refers to all the rules of conduct established and enforced by the custom, authority, or legislation of a group, community, or country.

Notice that law implies both prescription (rule) and enforcement by authority. It might seem that the term *law enforcement* is redundant since law refers to both the rules and their enforcement. But, in the United States, those who enforce the laws are *not* the same as those who make them. This has not always been true.

PRIMITIVE AND ANCIENT LAW

Even cave dwellers had certain rules they were expected to follow or face death or banishment from the tribe. The customs depicted in early cave-dwelling drawings may well represent the beginning of law and law enforcement.

The prehistoric social order consisted of small family groups living together as tribes or clans. Group living gave rise to certain customs that everyone was expected to observe. The chief of the tribe had executive, legislative, and judicial powers and often appointed members of the tribe to perform special tasks such as serving as a bodyguard or enforcing edicts. Crimes committed against individuals were handled by the victim or the victim's family. The philosophy of justice was retaliatory, that is, punish the offender. A person who stole the game from a neighbor's traps could expect to pay for the crime by being thrown into a pot of boiling oil or a cage of wild beasts. Other common punishments for serious offenses were flaying, impalement, burning at the stake, stoning, branding, mutilation, and crucifixion.

A system of law and law enforcement began earlier than 2000 B.C. as a means of controlling human conduct and enforcing society's rules.

The earliest record of ancient people's need to organize and standardize rules and methods of enforcement to control human behavior dates back to approximately 2300 B.C. when the Sumerian rulers Lipit-shtar and Eshumma set forth standards on what did and did not constitute an offense against society. A hundred years later, the Babylonian King Hammurabi established rules for his kingdom that designated not only offenses but punishments as well. In fact, Hammurabi established the oldest known building code. Although the penalties prescribed were often barbaric by today's standards, the relationship between the crime and the punishment are of interest.

The Code of Hammurabi consisted of three hundred legal provisions concerning such matters as false accusations, witchcraft, military service, land and business regulations, family laws, tariffs, wages, loans, and debts. The main principle of the code was that "the strong shall not injure the weak." The code also established a social order based on individual rights. Hammurabi originated the legal principle of *lex talions*—an eye for an eye.

Egypt

The first accounts of a developing court system came from Egypt in approximately 1500 B.C. The sophisticated court system was presided over by judges appointed by the Pharaoh. About 1000 B.C. in Egypt,

If a builder builds a house for a man and does not make its construction firm and the house collapses and causes the death of the owner of the house—that builder shall be put to death. If it causes the death of a son of the owner—they shall put to death a son of that builder. If it causes the death of a slave of the owner—he shall give the owner a slave of equal value. If it destroys property he shall restore whatever it destroyed and because he did not make the house firm he shall rebuild the house which collapsed at his own expense. If a builder builds a house and does not make its construction meet the requirements and a wall falls in—that builder shall strengthen the wall at his own expense.

Source: Masonry Institute, 55 New Montgomery Street, San Francisco, Cal. 94105.

Figure 1–1   **From the Code of Hammurabi (2200 B.C.)**

public officers performed police functions. Their weapon and symbol of authority was a staff topped by a metal knob engraved with the king's name. The baton carried by the modern police officer may have its origin in that staff.

Greece

Solon, the ancient lawgiver of Athens (638 to 559 B.C.) was asked to name the essential ingredient of the ideal community. His answer could be memorized by every law enforcement professional: "When those who have not been injured become as indignant as those who have."

The Greeks had an impressive form of law enforcement called the *epohri*. Each year at Sparta a body of five epohrs was elected and given almost unlimited powers. They were the highest executive power in the land, being investigator, judge, jury, and executioner. These five men also presided over the Senate and Assembly, assuring that their rules and decrees were followed. One problem with this system, however, was that it promoted corrupt enforcement.

From the Greek philosopher Plato, who lived from 427 to 347 B.C., came the idea that punishment should serve a purpose rather than just being retaliation. Note the similarity between this concept and the relationship between the crimes and punishments set forth by Hammurabi in 2200 B.C. This relationship is the basis of equity and the basis of law in America, as will be discussed later.

Rome

Like the Greeks, the Romans had a highly developed system for the administration of justice. The Twelve Tables were the first written laws of the Roman Empire. Drawn up by ten of the wisest men in Rome in 451 and 450 B.C., the Twelve Tables were fastened to the speakers' stand in the Roman Forum. The tablets dealt with legal procedures, property ownership, building codes, marriage customs, and punishment for crimes.

About the time of Christ, the Roman emperor Augustus chose members from his military to form the Praetorian Guard to protect the palace and the Urban Cohort to patrol the city. Augustus also established the Vigiles of Rome. Initially assigned as fire fighters, they were eventually also given law enforcement responsibilities; consequently, they are sometimes referred to as the first integrated police-fire service. As the first civilian police force, the Vigiles sometimes kept the peace very ruthlessly. It is from these Vigiles that we derive the word *vigilante*.

In the Roman Empire during the first century A.D., public officials (called *lictors*) acted as bodyguards for magistrates (judges). When the magistrate ordered, the lictor would bring criminals before him and carry out the magistrate's prescribed punishments, even the death penalty. Their symbol of public authority was a *fasces*, a bundle of rods tied by a red thong around an axe, which represented their absolute authority of life and limb. Within the city of Rome itself, however, the fasces had no

Source: Drawing by Ione Bell.
Figure 1–2 **Fasces**

axe because there was a right to appeal a capital sentence (Hall 1974, p. 119).

Another important contribution from the Roman Empire was the Justinian Code. Justinian I, ruler of the Eastern Roman Empire from A.D. 527 to 565, collected all the existing Roman laws. They became known as the Corpus Juris Civilis, meaning body of law. The Corpus Juris Civilis consisted of all Roman laws and legal principles, illustrated by cases, as well as explanations of new laws under proposal.

ENGLISH LAW AND LAW ENFORCEMENT

The early beginnings of just laws and social control were destroyed during the Dark Ages as the Roman Empire disintegrated. Hordes of Germanic invaders swept into the old Roman territory of Britain, bringing with them their own laws and customs. These German invaders intermarried with conquered English, the result being the hardy Anglo-Saxon.

Anglo-Saxons—The Tithing System

The Anglo-Saxons grouped their farms around small, self-governing villages that policed themselves. When criminals were caught, the punishment was often severe, as in ancient times. Sometimes, however, the tribe would let an offender prove innocence through battle. And sometimes they allowed testimony by other tribespeople willing to swear that the accused was innocent. In addition, the practice of allowing a criminal to pay a fine for committing a crime or to work off the debt was beginning to come into vogue.

As time went on, the informal grouping of families became more structured. Alfred the Great (A.D. 849 to 899) first set down the guideline that all freemen should belong to an association that binds them with a certain group of people. The idea was that if one person in the group committed a crime and was convicted, all people in the group were responsible for the person's fine. Consequently, all members of the group were very careful to see that no one in the group broke the law. Every male, unless excused by the king, was enrolled for police purposes in a group of ten families known as a **tithing.** To maintain order in the tithing, they had a leader or chief tithingman who was the mayor, council, and judge all in one. Society was so basic at this time that they needed to enforce only two laws: laws against murder and theft.

The tithing system established the principle of collective responsibility for maintaining local law and order.

Any victim or person who discovered a crime would put out the "Hue and Cry," for example, "Stop, thief." Anyone who heard the cry would stop any activity and help capture the suspect. This may be the forerunner of both the general alarm and the citizen's arrest.

The Hue and Cry may be the origin of the general alarm and the citizen's arrest.

When capture was made, the suspect was brought before the chief tithingman, who determined innocence or guilt plus punishment. Theft was often punished by civil restitution or working off the loss by bondage or servitude—the basis for civil law, restitution for financial loss (Lunt 1938).

If a criminal sought refuge in a neighboring village, that village was expected to return the criminal for punishment. This cooperation among villagers eventually resulted in the formation of *hundreds*, which were groups of ten tithings. The top official of the hundred was called a reeve.

The hundreds also elected a constable to lead them in pursuit of any lawbreakers. The constable was the first English police officer and, as such, had charge of the weapons and horses of the whole community. Finally the hundreds were consolidated into shires, or counties. The head of the shire was called, quite logically, the shire-reeve, which is the forerunner of our county sheriff.

Constables on duty during Anglo-Saxon times.

The shire-reeve acted as both police officer and judge for the territory, traveling from hundred to hundred. The shire-reeve had the power of *posse commitatus*, meaning he could gather all the men of a shire together when he needed assistance in pursuing a lawbreaker. This is the forerunner of our posse.

The Norman Frankpledge System

In 1066, William the Conqueror, a Norman, invaded and conquered England. As king of a conquered nation, William was too concerned about national security to allow the tithings to keep their own system of home rule. He established fifty-five military districts each headed by a Norman shire-reeve who answered directly to the crown. William also decided that shire-reeves should not try cases but should serve only as police officers. He selected his own judges who traveled around and tried cases. These were the forerunners of our circuit judges. Even more important, however, is that this separated the law enforcement and judicial roles.

Under William the Conqueror, the shire-reeves were limited to law enforcement and separate judges were appointed to try cases.

William established a highly centralized bureaucracy that also unified the country's law enforcement. He introduced the curfew, requiring that all fires be extinguished or covered during the night; and he developed a doomsday book, a tax roll listing the landowners and the extent of their land. The doomsday book was also a legal code with penalties for infractions—an idea formulated by King Alfred the Great 150 years earlier.

In addition, the Normans modified the tithing system into the Frankpledge system, which refers to the guarantee for peace maintenance that the king demanded from all free Englishmen.

The Frankpledge system required loyalty to the king's law and mutual local responsibility in maintaining the peace.

The Twelfth Century

William's son, Henry I, who ruled England from 1100 to 1135, also made significant contributions to law enforcement. In fact, he came to be known as Henry the Lawgiver after he issued the **Leges Henrici**, which established certain offenses such as arson, robbery, murder, counterfeiting, and crimes of violence as being against the king's peace. The Leges Henrici set the precedent that for certain crimes a person should be punished by the state rather than by the victim or by peers. It also divided crimes into felonies and misdemeanors.

The Leges Henrici made law enforcement a public matter and separated offenses into felonies and misdemeanors.

Henry I's reign ended in 1135 and was followed by many years of turmoil, which lasted until Henry II became king in 1154. Henry II's greatest contribution to law enforcement was the jury system. Called an inquisition, people were required to give information to a panel of judges, who then determined the guilt or innocence of the accused.

Henry II established the jury system.

For the next hundred years kings appointed enforcement officers to meet their needs but who had no real control over their power. When John became king in 1199, however, he abused his power by demanding more military service from the feudal class, selling royal positions to the highest bidder, and increasing taxes without obtaining consent from the barons— actions all contrary to feudal custom. In addition, John's courts decided cases according to his wishes, not according to law.

In 1213, a group of barons and church leaders met near London to call for a halt to the king's injustices. They drew up a list of rights they wanted King John to grant them. After the king refused to grant these rights on two separate occasions, the barons raised an army and forced him to meet their demands. On June 15, 1215, King John signed the Magna Carta.

The Magna Carta

Our modern system of justice owes much to the Magna Carta, a decisive document in the development of constitutional government in England.

The Magna Carta contained sixty-three articles, most requiring the king to uphold feudal law. The articles initially benefited only the barons and other members of the feudal class, but they later became important to all people. Some articles granted the church freedom from royal interference, and a few guaranteed the rights of the rising middle class. Ordinary freemen and peasants, although making up the great majority of England's population, were hardly mentioned in the charter.

The charter required the king to seek the advice and consent of the barons on all matters important to the kingdom, including taxation. Later such articles supported the argument that no law should be made nor tax raised without the consent of England's Parliament. Article 13 restored local control to cities and villages, a fundamental principle of American law enforcement.

Other articles of the Magna Carta became foundations for modern justice. One article, for example, required that no freeman should be imprisoned, deprived of property, sent out of the country, or destroyed except by the lawful judgment of peers or by the law of the land. The concept of due process of law, including trial by jury, developed from this article.

The Magna Carta, a precedent for democratic government and individual rights, laid the foundation for requiring rulers to uphold the law, forbidding taxation without representation, requiring due process of law, including trial by jury, providing safeguards against unfair imprisonment.

The Next Five Hundred Years

Several interesting developments in law enforcement occurred in the following centuries. The **police des mouers** (police of the puters) was established to regulate prostitution. A register was maintained, and no prostitutes were permitted except in certain parts of the city. Thus, the origin of the **red light district**.

In 1285 King Edward I set up a curfew and night watch program that allowed for the gates of Westminster, then capital of England, to be locked. This would keep the city's occupants in and unwanted persons out. Bailiffs were hired as night watchmen to enforce the curfew and guard the gates. Edward I also mandated that groups of one hundred merchants be responsible for keeping peace in their districts, thus making law enforcement a local responsibility. This system of law enforcement, called the **Watch and Ward**, provided citizens protection twenty-four hours a day. The term "Watch and Ward" originated from the name of the shifts, with the day shift called "ward" and the night shift "watch."

With an ever-increasing population and a trend toward urbanization, society in England became increasingly complex. Law enforcement became truly a collective responsibility. If a man's next-door neighbor broke the law, the man was responsible for bringing the lawbreaker before the shire-reeve. This prompted the development of a system under which the hundred would decide yearly who would be responsible for maintaining law and order. Responsibility rotated among community members. It was inevitable that some people, not wanting to serve their turn, would seek other members of the hundred to serve in their place for pay. This was the beginning of the system of paid deputies appointed to be responsible for law and order. The paid deputy system was then formalized so that those whose turn it was to pay met and appointed the law enforcers. The abuse of citizen duty to serve as watchmen was pervasive, however, and led to the dregs of society, such as petty thieves and town drunks, serving as watchmen.

During the fourteenth century the office of justice of the peace was established to replace the shire-reeve. The justice of the peace was assisted by the constables and by three or four men knowledgeable of the country's laws. At first the justice of the peace was involved in both judicial matters and law enforcement, but later his powers became strictly judicial. He was responsible for settling matters of wages, prices, and conditions of labor and for pretrial hearings to determine if there was enough evidence to keep a man in jail to await trial. The justice of the peace eventually became the real power of local government (Lunt 1938).

During the fourteenth century, the shire-reeve was replaced by the justice of the peace.

With the passing of feudal times and the rise in the power of the church, the unit of local government in rural areas progressed from the hundred to the parish, that is, the area in which people lived who worshipped in a particular parish church. Once each year the parish appointed a person to be **parish constable** and to act as their law officer. This system of maintaining law and order in rural Britain lasted from the Middle Ages until the eighteenth century.

During the Middle Ages, the Parish Constable system was used for rural law enforcement; the Watch and Ward system was used for urban law enforcement.

Developments in urban England required a different system of law enforcement. With urbanization came commerce, industry, and a variety of buildings usually made of wood since England was primarily forest land. For purposes of fire prevention, the town guild appointed men (Watch and Ward) who patrolled at night on fire watch. They assumed the coincidental responsibility of preventing people from breaking into houses and shops.

In 1689, after numerous attacks on personal liberty, the English Parliament forced King James II to abdicate his throne. In addition, Parliament produced a Bill of Rights that contained the following provisions (Gardner 1985, p.26):

> *Suspending laws . . . without consent of Parliament is illegal. Keeping a Standing Army within the Kingdom in Time of Peace unless it be with Consent of Parliament is against the law. Election of Members of Parliament ought to be free. Freedom of Speech . . . ought not to be impeached or questioned.*

In 1692, in response to steadily increasing crime, a system of *monetary reward* was instituted to encourage people to help apprehend thieves and bandits. The result was disappointing, however, for it led only to a great deal of blackmail and false accusations.

Although the Watch and Ward system was primitive and not too effective, it was adequate until the Industrial Revolution (1750) began. About the same time famine struck the rural areas, and large numbers of people moved from the country into the towns seeking work in weaving and knitting mills and in factories. Many, however, failed to find work, and England experienced much unemployment, poverty, and crime.

In addition, political extremists often aroused mobs and incited them to march upon Parliament. These mobs were usually unruly, destructive, and indifferent to the safety of local residents and their property. The government had no civil police force to deal with mob violence, so they ordered a magistrate to read the "riot act," which permitted the magistrate to call the military to quell the riot.

The use of a military force to repress civil disobedience did not work very well. Soldiers hesitated to fire on their own townspeople, and the townspeople, who actually paid the soldiers' wages, resented being fired on by soldiers they had hired to protect them. Consequently, when the riot act was read and the military were called into action, citizen unrest usually mounted.

In addition to unemployment, poverty, and resentment against use of military force, the invention of gin and whiskey in the seventeenth century and the subsequent increase in the liquor trade also caused a great rise in violent crimes and theft.

The government responded to the increase in crime by improving street lighting, hiring more watchmen, and greatly increasing the severity of punishment for all kinds of crimes.

In 1736 a law was passed requiring every gin and whiskey seller and manufacturer to purchase exorbitantly priced licenses. This law did not stop the flow of gin and whiskey but instead greatly increased the corruption of the constables. Since the constables were often employed in the liquor trade, it was impossible for them to honestly enforce the regulations governing taverns and inns. Additionally, the London watch-men who were responsible for regulating the morals of the townspeople were highly susceptible to bribes and payoffs.

Henry Fielding and the Bow Street Runners

Around 1750 Henry Fielding, an English magistrate and novelist (author of *Tom Jones*), was instrumental in establishing the **Bow Street Runners,** the first detective unit in London and an indicator of the increasing problems faced by law enforcement officials.

The Bow Street Runners, first called "Thief-takers," were specially chosen men with reliable characters who were paid a weekly wage so they would not be tempted by bribes. Known for their incorruptibility, physical strength, and tenacity, they soon became the terror of all street gangs. Because of their skill and reputation, other agencies from throughout England often hired them. The most famous runner was Townsend, who was hired to guard the royal family and became a close friend of the king.

When these runners proved successful, other units were organized. Foot patrols of armed men guarded the city's streets during the day and a horse patrol combatted highway robbery on the main roads up to twenty-five miles from Bow Street.

Although the Bow Street Runners and patrols greatly improved control in the Bow Street area of London, other parts of London were overwhelmed by the impact of the Industrial Revolution. Machines were taking the place of many jobs, causing unemployment and poverty. The cities were developing into huge slums and the crime rate soared. Children were often trained to be thieves, and for the first time in England's history, juvenile delinquency became a problem. Citizens began to carry weapons, and the courts used long-term prison sentences, resulting in overcrowding in the jails and prisons. Punishments were also severe, with over 160 crimes punishable by death.

The Rookeries of London

As noted by Brantingham and Brantingham (1984, p.298) the **rookeries** of London were dilapidated and teeming places:

> London and other nineteenth-century English cities were marked by notorious criminal areas, some of which had been in place for centuries. These rookeries were slum criminal quarters, known to public and police alike as neighborhoods in which the homes of prostitutes, beggars, thieves, and killers were intermixed with those of the desperate urban poor. They were mazes of squalid hovels and houses carved into warrens of tiny rooms connected by secret doors, tunnels, catwalks, dark passages, and dank lanes. The rookeries sustained criminal social systems that provided schooling in crime for the young or the new-comers, fencing systems to purchase and resell stolen goods, and a protective code of silence in the face of police inquiries. . . .
>
> By the nineteenth century, the boundaries of the imperial metropolis lay far behind the ancient City limits: the City was just one of a number of municipalities that together formed Greater London. Differences in the quality and character of public administration and the jealous way in which the different municipal constituents of the metropolis guarded their perogatives and liberties from encroachment by any of the others go far toward explaining this pattern.

Despite the rampant crime, however, most Londoners resisted an organized police force, seeing it as restricting their liberty. They had

Source: Tobias, J.J. *Crime and Industrial Society in the 19th Century.* London: B.T. Batsford Limited, 1967, p. 133. Reprinted with permission.

Figure 1–3   **Distribution of the principle London rookeries**

fought long and hard to overcome the historical abuse of military power by the English kings and resisted any return to centralized military power.

Then, in 1819 and 1820, two contrasting incidents occurred that helped people change their minds. The first incident was an attack by armed *soldiers* on a meeting of unemployed workers that left eleven people dead and hundreds injured. This incident, known as the Peterloo Massacre, was a vivid example of the result of using soldiers to maintain peace. In contrast, in the second incident the Bow Street Runners were able to break up a conspiracy to murder a number of government officials. When the conspirators were executed, people were well aware that actions by a group of professional peacekeepers could prevent a major insurrection.

In addition to rampant crime, Parliament was also justifiably concerned about poverty, unemployment, and general conditions. Five parliamentary commissions of inquiry met in London between 1780 and 1820 to determine what should be done about the public order. It was not until Sir Robert (Bobbie) Peel was appointed Home Secretary that the first really constructive proposal was brought before Parliament.

Peelian Reform

Sir Robert Peel, often referred to as the "father of modern policing," proposed a return to the Anglo-Saxon principle of individual community responsibility for preserving law and order. He proposed that London have a body of civilians appointed and paid by the community to serve as police officers. Parliament agreed and passed the Metropolitan Police Act of 1829, creating the Metropolitan Police of London.

The name *police*, introduced into England from France is derived from the Greek word *polis* meaning "city." Originally, in continental Europe, the term included all state activities that had not been segregated into special administrative branches. By the middle of the eighteenth century, the scope of police activity had narrowed to two main classifications: security police, charged with preserving individuals from dangers threatening person or property, and welfare police, charged with fostering the public welfare by promoting interests beneficial to society.

Many of the fundamental principles of Peelian Reform are as applicable today as they were in 1829.

- Police must be stable, efficient, and organized militarily.
- Police must be under governmental control.
- The distribution of crime news is essential.
- The deployment of police strength by both time and area is essential.
- No quality is more indispensable to a policeman than a perfect command of temper; a quiet, determined manner has more effect than violent action.
- Good appearance commands respect.
- The securing and training of proper persons is at the root of efficiency.

- Public security demands that every police officer be given a number.
- Police headquarters should be centrally located and easily accessible.
- Policemen should be hired on a probationary basis.
- Police records are necessary to the correct distribution of police strength.

In addition, one of Peel's first steps was to introduce reform that abolished the death penalty for over one hundred offenses.

Although most of these principles make sense to us in the twentieth century, they were not readily accepted in nineteenth-century England. During the first few years of Peelian Reform, strong opposition was encountered. In addition to this opposition, Peel was faced with the problem of finding a building for the newly created London Police. He chose an abandoned building that had been built many years before for the Scottish nobility to use when they visited London. This building housed the London Metropolitan Police, and it became known the world over as Scotland Yard, as immortalized by A. Conan Doyle in his Sherlock Holmes mysteries.

Peel eventually became a national hero, and his reforms led to increased status and prestige for all who entered a career in law enforcement. His principles also became the basis of police reform in many large cities in America.

Peel's principles for reform called for local responsibility for law and order; appointed, paid civilians to assume this responsibility; and standards for these individuals' conduct and organization. His proposals resulted in the organization of the Metropolitan Police of London in 1829.

London Metropolitan Police (1829)

The London Metropolitan Police were uniformed for easy identification—top hats, three-quarter-length royal blue coats, and white trousers—and were armed only with truncheons. They were obviously not soldiers as they had no guns. They were (and still are) called "Bobbies" after Sir "Bobbie" Peel.

Unfortunately, the London Metropolitan Police were not popular. Soon after the force went on street duty in 1829, a London mob assembled, prepared to march on Parliament. A police sergeant and two constables asked the mob leaders to send their people home. The police, trained to be courteous but firm, did their job properly; however, the mob did not disperse. Instead they attacked the sergeant and constables, killing the sergeant and critically injuring the constables. A jury of London citizens,

Scotland Yard headquarters, 1890.

after hearing evidence clearly indicative of a cold, brutal murder, returned a verdict of justifiable homicide. In time, however, the effect of the police officers discharging their duties with professional integrity created a respect for the law that still exists in England.

City and Borough Police Forces (1835)

Broad public use of the steam engine and railways and better roads helped move many criminals from London to provincial cities such as Birmingham, Liverpool, and Manchester. Soon the citizens of these cities demanded some police organization similar to that of London. In 1835 Parliament enacted permissive legislation allowing (but not requiring) every city or borough (unincorporated township) over 20,000 people to form a police force. The act called for the town council, a body of elected representatives who administered the city's affairs, to appoint from its members a watch committee to (1) appoint a chief of police, (2) appoint the officers of the force, and (3) administer the force.

County Police Act (1839)

The counties had no collective system of local government larger than the individual parish, yet they, too, felt the need for an organized police force. This prompted Parliament to pass the County Police Act (1839) giving magistrates the responsibility to fix the strength of the force and to appoint and dismiss the chief constable. Unlike the borough counterpart, the parish magistrate, once appointed, had absolute rights of appointment over subordinates. The new force was paid for by citizens' taxes.

The County Police Act produced an uneven response. Only fifteen of the fifty-two counties had adopted it by the end of 1840. Reluctance to implement the legislation came from several sources, the most important being financial interests. The decision rested with the magistrates, the principal landowners in each county, and they had a vested interest in keeping taxes down.

Women Enter Law Enforcement

In 1883 the London Metropolitan Police appointed two women to supervise women convicts. Their numbers and functions later expanded. In 1905 a woman was attached to the London Metropolitan Police force to conduct inquiries in cases involving women and children. Each year an increasing number of police matrons were hired.

Around 1914 considerable public concern arose in favor of employing women police as part of the organization to prevent and detect crime. The Penal Reform League passed a resolution urging the appointment of women police constables with powers equal to those of men constables in all county boroughs and the metropolitan boroughs of the County of London (Chapman and Johnston 1962).

Soon after, the Criminal Law Amendment Committee and the National Vigilance Association sent delegates to interview the secretary of state on the subject. Delegates were then appointed by the Women's Industrial Council to serve on the Parks Committee of the London Council.

Early in World War I, two separate movements for women police began. The Women Police Volunteers was formed and later came to be called the Women Police Service. In 1920 the group split into the Women's Auxiliary Service and the Women Patrols of the National Union of Women Workers of Great Britain and Ireland. The present official women police are largely a direct continuation of the Women Patrols (Chapman and Johnston 1962).

In 1883 the London Metropolitan Police appointed two women to supervise women convicts. Their numbers and functions later expanded.

SUMMARY

Our current laws and the means by which they are enforced have their origins in the distant past, perhaps as far back as the cave dwellers. Law refers to all the rules of conduct established and enforced by the custom, authority, or legislation of a group, community, or country. A system of law and law enforcement began earlier than 2000 B.C. as a means of controlling human conduct and enforcing society's rules. Many features of our present system of law enforcement are borrowed from the Greeks, Romans, and particularly the English.

The English tithing system (groups of ten families) established the principle of collective responsibility for maintaining local law and order. If a law was broken, the Hue and Cry sounded. The Hue and Cry may be the origin of the general alarm and the citizen's arrest.

The constable was the first English police officer and, as such, had charge of the weapons and horses of the whole community. In response to a need for more regional law enforcement, the office of shire-reeve was established. The shire-reeve was the law enforcement agent for an entire county.

In 1066 William the Conqueror invaded England and changed the tithing system to the Frankpledge system, requiring loyalty to the king's law and mutual local responsibility for maintaining the peace. Under his rule the shire-reeves were limited to law enforcement, and separate judges were appointed to try cases. In effect, he separated the powers of law enforcement and the courts.

William's son, Henry I, became known as Henry the Lawmaker. His Leges Henrici made law enforcement a public matter and separated offenses into felonies and misdemeanors. Henry II established the jury system.

The next significant development was the Magna Carta, a precedent for democratic government and individual rights. The Magna Carta laid the foundation for

- requiring rulers to uphold the law;
- forbidding taxation without representation;
- requiring due process of law, including trial by jury;
- providing safeguards against unfair imprisonment.

During the fourteenth century, the shire-reeve was replaced by the justice of the peace. Later, during the Middle Ages, the Parish Constable system was used for rural law enforcement; the Watch and Ward system was used for urban law enforcement. The government responded to an increase in crime by improving street lighting, hiring more watchmen, and greatly increasing the severity of punishment for all kinds of crime.

Of great importance to English law enforcement were the contributions of Sir Robert (Bobbie) Peel. Peel's principles for reform called for local responsibility for law and order; appointed, paid civilians to assume this responsibility; and standards for these individuals' conduct and organization. His proposals resulted in the organization of the first police force in England, the Metropolitan Police of London, established in 1829. In 1883 the London Metropolitan Police appointed two women to supervise women convicts. Their numbers and functions later expanded.

Discussion Questions

1. What common problems have existed throughout the centuries for people in law enforcement?

2. How have these common problems been approached at different points in history?

3. Why was there no law enforcement during the daytime for many centuries?

4. Why did it take so long to develop a police force in England?

5. What parts of the Code of Hammurabi would not be applicable or accepted in contemporary society?

6. In today's society how has the power of the Posse Commitatus assisted and how has it worked against law enforcement?

7. The police des mouers was established to regulate prostitution. What methods do we use to control prostitution today?

8. At present, how does the government respond to increased crime in the United States in comparison to the responses in the 17th century?

9. The Rookeries of London can be compared to what areas of cities in the United States today?

10. How many of Peel's principles still exist in today's police departments?

References

Brantingham, P., and Brantingham P., *Patterns in Crime*. New York: Macmillan, 1984.

Chapman, S.G., and Johnston, Colonel T.E. St. *The Police Heritage in England and America*. East Lansing, Mich.: Michigan State University, 1962.

Gardner, T. J. *Basic Concepts of Criminal Law, Principles and Cases*,3d ed. St. Paul, Minn.: West Publishing Company, 1985.

Hall, J. *Dictionary of Subjects and Symbols in Art*. New York: Harper & Row, 1974.

Lunt, W.E. *History of England*. New York: Harper & Brothers, 1938.

The Evolution of Law Enforcement in the United States

The execution of the laws is more important than the making of them.—Thomas Jefferson

DO YOU KNOW

What systems of law enforcement were brought from England to colonial New England and the South?

When and where the first modern American police force began and what it was modeled after?

When and how state and federal law enforcement agencies originated in the United States?

What effect the spoils system had in the 1900s?

What law enforcement organizational systems have been tried and have been most successful?

What the Pendleton Act accomplished?

What the five levels of law enforcement are?

Who the chief law enforcement officer at the federal and state level is?

What services the FBI provides?

What state agencies are involved in or offer assistance to law enforcement?

What functions state police often serve?

What two main types of county law enforcement are?

How public and private law enforcement differ?

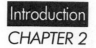

CHAPTER 2

When the English colonists came to America, they brought with them many traditions, including traditions in law enforcement. From the beginning they were concerned with avoiding anarchy. As noted by Gardner (1985, p. 26):

> As the Mayflower rode at anchor off Cape Cod, some of the passengers threatened to go out on their own, without any framework of government. To avoid this threat of anarchy, the Mayflower Compact [1620] agreed that: "We . . . doe . . . solemnely and mutually . . . covenant and combine our selves together into a civil body politike for our better ordering and preservation . . . and by vertue hereof to enact . . . such just and equall lawes . . . unto which we promise all due submission and obedience."

EARLY LAW ENFORCEMENT IN THE UNITED STATES

The early colonial American settlements relied heavily on self-policing to assure the peace. Communal pressure rather than formal policing was the backbone of law enforcement. The colonists were of similar background, most held similar religious beliefs, and there was actually little worth stealing. The seeds of vice and crime were present, however, as noted by political scientist David Perry (1973, p. 24):

> These colonists were far from the cream of European society; in many cases they represented the legal and religious castoffs. (Persons found guilty of criminal or religious offenses who were banished from Europe and exported to the New World.) Their migration served the dual purpose of removing socially undesirable persons from the Mother country and providing manpower for the outposts of imperial expansion. The governors of the new colonies were responsible for keeping such people in line.

Many features of British law enforcement were present in early American colonial settlements. In New England, where people depended on commerce and industry, the night watchman or constable served as protector of public order. In the South, where agriculture played a dominate role, the office of **sheriff** was established as the means of area law enforcement. Most watchmen and sheriffs were volunteers, but many were paid to serve in the place of others who were supposed to patrol as a civic duty.

New England adopted the night watchman or constable as the chief means of law enforcement; the South adopted the office of sheriff.

Many different types of law enforcement were tried in many different parts of the country. Almost all used some kind of night watch system, with little or no protection during the day. As might be expected, the fastest growing municipalities were the first to organize legal forces.

Creation of the Boston Police

In 1631 the Boston court ordered a six-man force to be established to guard the city from sunset to sunup. This was the first night watch in colonial America. In 1636 a town watch was created. This watch consisted of a group of citizens appointed by the town council and stayed in effect for over two hundred years. During this time the services performed by the watch changed significantly. At first the primary function was to ring a bell in case of fire. In 1702 the police were to patrol the streets in silence; in 1735 they were required to call out the time of day and the weather.

In 1801 Boston became the first city in the United States to acquire a permanent night watch. These men were paid fifty cents a night. In 1807 the first police precincts were formed, and in 1838 a day force was created to supplement the night force.

Creation of the New York Police

The first colonists in New York, then called New Amsterdam, were the Dutch. They settled on Manhattan Island's south end and were governed by Peter Minuit, director general of New Netherlands. In 1624 Minuit established the office of sheriff attorney to enforce the laws of the Dutch West India Company. The sheriff attorney was both police officer and prosecutor and was responsible for both civil and military laws. In 1632 Wouter van Tiller succeeded Minuit. Van Tiller instituted the whipping post from which lawbreakers were suspended to deter criminal activity.

In 1643 a "burgher guard" was formed to protect the colony. Then, in 1653 New Amsterdam became a city (population, eight hundred). The burgher guard was changed to a rattle watch, a group of night patrolling citizens armed with rattles to call for help. In 1658 the rattle guard was replaced by eight night watchmen who were paid to guard the city. These men were the first police force (Bailey 1989, p. 346).

In 1664 the British took over New Amsterdam and renamed it New York. Thirty years later the first uniformed police officers replaced the nighttime rattle watch, and four years after that New York's streets were lighted. In 1700 the mayor created a constable's watch.

The system of watchmen was very ineffective. Often the person on watch was sentenced to be a watchman as a form of punishment for a misdemeanor. In addition, citizens could avoid watch duty by hiring someone to take their places. This practice had its problems. Wealthy citizens came to rely on hiring others, and the men they hired were then hesitant to invoke their authority against the well-to-do. According to Richardson (1970, p. 10), by the mid-1700s New York City's night watch was described as follows:

[a] *parcel of idle, drinking, vigilant snorers, who never quell'd any noc-*
turnal tumult in their lives; . . . but would, perhaps, be as ready to join in
a burglary as any thief in Christendom.

Due to a continuing increase in crime during the daytime, New York City hired an assortment of watchmen, fire marshals, and bell ringers to patrol during the day and night. In 1844 a paid day watch was established, consisting of sixteen officers appointed by the mayor. At this time the night watch consisted of 1,100 watchmen and was completely separate from the day force. As might be expected, friction existed between the day and night forces, and it became an impossible arrangement, totally incapable of combatting the growing lawlessness in the city.

Legislators from New York City visited the London Metropolitan Police Department and were so highly impressed that, in 1844, New York City followed the pattern set in England fifteen years earlier by Sir Robert Peel and established a round-the-clock, paid police force.

In 1844 New York City established the first modern American city police force,
modeled after London's Metropolitan Police Department.

Soon other police forces similar to that in New York developed, including forces in Chicago, Cincinnati, New Orleans, Philadelphia, Boston, Baltimore, and San Francisco.

In 1856 New York adopted a full uniform for each ward.

In spite of patterning themselves after the London Metropolitan Police, New York police officers vigorously protested against wearing uniforms. Not until twelve years later did the New York police adopt a full police uniform and become the first uniformed law enforcement agency in the country. Likewise, although Henry Fielding established the Bow Street Runners (the first detective unit) in 1750, it was over a hundred years later before American police agencies recognized a need for detective units. In 1866 Detroit established the first detective bureau, followed by New York in 1882, and Cincinnati in 1886.

Creation of the Los Angeles Police

In 1850 California became a state and Los Angeles incorporated as a city with a population of 1,610. During its first year the city elected a mayor, a city marshal, and a sheriff. According to Bailey (1989, pp. 310–16):

The duties assumed by the sheriff and marshal included the collection of local taxes. The sheriff's obligations required him to traverse a vast area on horseback, fighting bands of Indians and marauding desperadoes. Lacking paid assistants, the marshal was permitted to deputize citizens whenever necessary to maintain order.

In 1853 the city council established a police force of one hundred volunteers, the first official police officers, and called them the Los Angeles Rangers. Four years later they were replaced by the Los Angeles City Guards, who were charged with maintaining the peace. Finally, in 1869, the police force changed from a voluntary organization to a paid department.

The first mounted police force was formed in 1875, headed by Chief Jacob F. Gerkins. Bailey (1989, p. 310) described the duties of Chief Gerkins and his patrol officers as the following:

The enforcement of laws prohibiting the grazing or herding of cattle in the streets, the sale of opium except for scientific or medical purposes and the speed of steam trains at more than six miles an hour within city limits. Officers were also instructed to pick up loose paper blown about the streets, lest it cause horses to run away.

Evolution of the City Police

When city police were first established, their only contact with their departments was face-to-face meetings or messengers. During the 1850s, however, telegraph networks linked police headquarters directly with their districts, making unnecessary the daily meetings between the captains and the commissioners. Several decades later a modified telegraph system linked the patrol officers directly to the station. A fire alarm system, first introduced in Boston, was adopted for police use. Call boxes placed on city street corners became a common sight. These boxes were equipped with a simple lever that signaled the station that the officers were at their posts. A bell system was then added that allowed the patrol officers to use a few simple signals to call an ambulance, a "slow wagon" for routine duties, or a "fast wagon" for emergencies. The introduction of a special "Gamewell" telephone into the call box in 1880 made this a truly two-way communication system, greatly improving the contact between the patrol officers and their station houses.

The Civil War brought new problems of social control. Municipal forces tried to meet these problems by organizing new divisions and specializing the force. As centers of population became increasingly urbanized and fringe areas became incorporated suburbs of the hub city, a trend developed to add forces to the police organization rather than to centralize or consolidate them. Consequently, newly developed fringe cities had their own forces, which fostered complex, uncoordinated relationships, compartmentalization, and inefficiency.

Establishment of State Law Enforcement Agencies

In 1835, when Texas was still a republic, the Texas provisional government established the Texas Rangers. The Texas Rangers were actually a military unit, established into three companies responsible for border patrol. The apprehension of Mexican cattle rustlers was a primary task (Folley 1980, p. 88).

In 1874 the Texas Rangers were commissioned as police officers in Texas. At that time there were 450 Rangers, and their duties included tracking down murderers, robbers, smugglers, and mine bandits.

The Texas Rangers were the first agency similar to our present-day state police.

Massachusetts was next to establish a state law enforcement agency by appointing a small force of state officers in 1865 to control vice within the state. The state also granted them general police powers; therefore, Massachusetts is usually credited with establishing the first law enforcement agency with general police authority throughout the state.

Establishment of Federal Law Enforcement Agencies

Several federal law enforcement agencies were created by Congress to meet demands created by the changing conditions of the nation.

The oldest federal agency is the United States Marshals Office, created in 1789. Thirteen United States Marshals were assigned to President George Washington's attorney general. As the nation began to grow westward, the United States Marshals were the main law enforcement in the territories. When the Civil War ended (1865) and most of the territories had become states, the United States Marshals became the bailiffs of the United States District Courts, where violations of federal crimes are tried.

The Justice Department established other federal law enforcement agencies such as the Immigration and Naturalization Service (1891), of which the Border Patrol is a well-known division.

The Treasury Department established federal law enforcement agencies that are still well known today. The Secret Service was created in 1865 to control the flood of counterfeit currency bankrupting the war effort. After President McKinley was assassinated in 1901, the Secret Service was authorized to protect the president and his family.

Another well-known federal agency established within the Treasury Department was the Internal Revenue Service (1862). Its famous Intelligence Division agents' income tax evasion cases brought long prison sentences to such infamous criminals as Al Capone, Vito Genovese, and many others.

Among the earliest federal law enforcement agencies were the United States Marshals Office, the Immigration and Naturalization Service, the Secret Service, and the Internal Revenue Service.

The Problem of Corruption

As in other countries, corruption became a problem in United States law enforcement. One primary factor underlying this corruption was the prevelant **spoils system,** whose motto, "To the victor go the spoils," resulted in gross political interference with policing. The winning party felt that its members should be immune from arrest, given special privileges in naming favorites for promotion, and assisted in carrying out vendettas against their political opponents. This system led politicians to staff many of the nation's police forces with incompetent people as rewards for support, "fixing" arrests or assuring that arrests were not made, and securing immunity from supervision for certain establishments or people.

The spoils system encouraged politicians to reward their "friends" by giving them key positions in police departments.

As noted by Walker (1983, p. 7):

The quality of American police service in the 19th century could hardly have been worse. The police were completely unprofessional and police work was dominated by corruption and inefficiency. The source of these problems was politics. Local government was viewed primarily as a source of opportunity—for jobs, for profit, for social mobility, for corrup-

tion. . . . Selection standards for police personnel were nonexistent. Officers obtained their jobs through political contacts. . . . In 1880 most big cities paid their police $900 a year; a factory worker could expect to earn only about $450 a year.

Reform movements began early but moved slowly against the solidly entrenched political "untouchables." Cities sought to break political control by a variety of organizational techniques, including the election of police officers and chiefs, administering forces through bipartisan lay boards, asking states to assume local policing, and instituting mayor–council or council–city manager municipal government.

The election of the municipal **chief of police** was common with the establishment of local departments. Remembering the corrupt officials who served as long as they pleased the king, the people elected police officials to serve short terms so they would not have time to become too powerful or corrupt. But this system had its drawbacks. Not only were the officials not in office long enough to become corrupt, they were not in office long enough to gain proficiency in their jobs. In fact, officials would just get to know their own officers and have enough experience to run the police department when their terms would expire. Additionally, since terms were so short, officials kept their civilian jobs and generally devoted most of their time to them, giving only spare time to running the police force. This system lacked professionalism; the position of police chief became a popularity contest. Therefore, it was decided that a permanent police chief, with experience and ability, was the best way to have effective law enforcement. Today the elected police chief system remains in only a few cities.

In the mid-1800s administrative police boards or commissions were established. These boards were made up of judges, mayors, and private citizens and served as the head of the police department with the police chief following its orders. The rationale was that the chief of police should be a professional and keep the job continuously, but that civilian control was necessary to maintain responsibility to community needs. This system lasted many years, but it had serious weaknesses. The board members often proved more of a hindrance than a help, and the system fostered political corruption.

As a reaction against local boards, and in an attempt to control corrupt police agencies, state control of local agencies was developed in some areas of the country. It was believed that if the state controlled local agencies, citizens would be assured of adequate and uniform law enforcement. While some cities still operate within this framework, most cities and states found this was not the answer to the problem because the laws were not equally enforced. In some areas the laws were underenforced and in other areas overenforced. The system also lacked responsiveness to local demands and needs. Therefore, control was again given to the local government in most instances.

The next system to be tried was the commission government charter. Commissioners were elected and charged with various branches of city government. This sytem, also on the decline, was as inadequate as the administrative police board.

The most efficient and prevalent current local system is the mayor–council or council–city manager government. The former is very efficient when the mayor is a full-time, capable administrator. The latter assures more continuity in the business administration and executive control of the overall operations because a professional, nonpolitical administrator manages the affairs of the community. Either way the chief of police is selected on the basis of merit.

Cities sought to break political control by a variety of organizational techniques, including the election of police officers and chiefs, administering forces through bipartisan lay boards, asking states to assume local policing, and instituting mayor–council or council–city manager municipal government—which has proved to be the most effective thus far.

In 1883, a major step toward reducing corruption within the police department occurred when Congress passed the Pendleton Act. Prior to this act, most government positions were filled by political appointment. Frequently the people appointed were incapable of performing their tasks well. One government worker who was going to be replaced by President Garfield shot and killed the president. This incident caused a public outcry and resulted in passage of the Pendleton Act. The act established a Civil Service Commission to enforce its provisions. The new laws called for a test open to all citizens and for new workers to be hired on the basis of who had the highest grades. The act also made it unlawful to fire or demote workers for political reasons and relieved government workers from any obligation to give political service or payments.

The Pendleton Act created the civil service system for government employees and made it unlawful to fire or demote a worker for political reasons.

DEVELOPMENTS IN THE EARLY 1900s

In the early 1900s state and federal law enforcement agencies continued to emerge, and national attention began to focus on police work as a profession.

Development of State Law Enforcement Agencies

Most state police agencies established before the twentieth century were created in response to a limited need such as the control of vice. This was not the case in Pennsylvania.

The first modern state police agency was the Pennsylvania Constabulary, which originated in 1905 to meet several needs. As noted by Folley (1973, p. 66), the **Pennsylvania Constabulary** (1) provided the governor an executive arm to assist him in accomplishing his responsibilities, (2) provided a means to quell riots occurring during labor disputes in the coal regions, and (3) improved law enforcement services in the rural portions of the state where county officials were generally ineffective. Governor Pennypacker vividly describes the rationale for such a state agency (Mayo 1917, pp. 5–6):

> In the year 1903, when I assumed the office of chief executive of the state, I found myself thereby invested with supreme executive authority. I found that no power existed to interfere with me in my duty to enforce the laws of the state, and that by the same token, no conditions could release me from my duty so to do. I then looked about me to see what instruments I possessed wherewith to accomplish this bounden obligation—what instruments on whose loyalty and obedience I could truly rely. I perceived three such instruments—my private secretary, a very small man; my woman stenographer; and the janitor. . . . So I made the state police.

Humorous as it may sound, there was a large element of truth in the governor's thinking. Further, the labor riots were real and had to be faced. Perhaps most important, however, was the emphasis on rural law enforcement and the establishment of a uniformed mounted force offering protection in even the most remote areas of Pennsylvania. Although they were organized originally for the purpose of and functioned as strike-breakers, the Pennsylvania state police served as a model for other states and heralded the advent of modern state policing.

The first modern state police agency was the Pennsylvania Constabulary, which originated in 1905 to meet several needs.

Development of Federal Law Enforcement Agencies

The world-famous Federal Bureau of Investigation (FBI) was created by Congress in 1908. In 1924 J. Edgar Hoover was appointed director, and he completely reorganized the bureau. Shortly thereafter it reached national stature. The importance of the FBI as well as other federal and state agencies is discussed in detail later in the chapter.

The most important federal law enforcement agency created in the twentieth century is the Federal Bureau of Investigation, better known as the FBI.

The Wickersham Commission and Police Professionalism.   In 1929 President Herbert Hoover appointed the national Commission on Law Observance and Enforcement to study the American criminal justice system. The commission, named after its chairman, George Wickersham, devoted two of its fourteen reports to the police. Report 11, *Lawlessness in Law Enforcement*, delineated the problem of police brutality. The report concluded that "the third degree—the inflicting of pain, physical or mental, to extract confessions or statements—is extensively practiced." Report 14, *The Police*, concentrated on police administration and called for expert leadership, centralized administrative control, and higher personnel standards; in short, police professionalism.

THE EVOLUTION OF MODERN LAW ENFORCEMENT

Largely because of civil service and a grassroots-inspired groundswell of general reform, most police forces have shaken the influence of corrupt politics. In contrast to conditions at the turn of the century, appointment to the forces and police administration generally is vastly improved. Police recruitment, discipline, and promotion have been removed from politics in most cities.

Communications involving police service have also greatly improved. The radio and patrol car transformed the relationship between the police and the public and offered increased protection for everyone. The continuous expansion of the telephone in the 1960s and 1970s made it easier for people to call the police. Police dispatchers were added to tie radio systems directly into telephone networks. The use of fingerprint systems and the increased employment of women as police officers as well as many other advances occurred at an accelerated pace.

Despite advanced technology, which greatly improved police officers' abilities to respond to requests for aid and increased their mobility, the basic strategy of police has not altered. Crime waves in metropolitan areas prompt cities to improve their street lighting, increase the number of police officers on the streets, and demand more severe punishment for the convicted criminals.

In the last three decades, the human factor has assumed greater importance as police agencies cope with the tensions and dislocations of population growth, increasing urbanization, developing technology, the civil rights movement, changing social norms, and a breakdown of traditional values. These factors have enormously complicated law enforcement, making more critical the need for truly professional police officers.

Today's local police officers must be law enforcement generalists with a working knowledge of federal, state, county, and municipal law, traffic law, criminal law, juvenile law, narcotics, liquor control, and countless other areas. But this accounts for only approximately 10 percent of what a modern police officer does. Today's police officers spend 90 percent of their time providing a variety of services while protecting life, property, and personal liberty. They must be aware of human factors and understand the psychological and sociological implications of their work for the community. They must deal with all citizens, rich and poor, young and old, in ways that maintain the community's support and confidence. This is no small responsibility.

Although law enforcement is primarily a local responsibility, criminal activities frequently do not remain localized; they may extend throughout a county, a state, or across the country. This is particularly true of organized crime. In such instances local authorities benefit from the assistance of other law enforcement agencies. Conversely, since the actual crimes are committed in a specific place, federal and state officials rely on the cooperation of local law enforcement officers. Each can provide valuable assistance to the other.

American police forces may be classified according to the level of government that each serves, but no uniform pattern of police administration exists at any of the five levels of government, and no mechanism exists to coordinate the activities and goals of the agencies, which differ greatly in size, jurisdiction, and operational methods.

The five levels of government authorized to have law enforcement agencies result in the presence of (1) township and special district police, (2) municipal police, (3) county police, (4) state police, and (5) federal police.

FEDERAL AGENCIES

Federal law enforcement agencies were created by Congress to meet the needs of a dynamic, rapidly growing democracy. Federal agents fulfill important responsibilities. Intelligence agents produce and disseminate information on foreign and domestic areas which affect national security. Investigative agents conduct investigations to determine compliance with federal laws. They carry guns, make arrests, and are usually enforcement oriented. Most federal agencies are attached to specific departments of the executive branch of government and have duties confined to the interests of the parent department.

The Department of Justice

The Department of Justice is the largest law firm in the country, representing the citizens in enforcing the law. It plays a significant role in protecting citizens through its efforts for effective law enforcement, crime prevention, crime detection, and prosecution and rehabilitation of offenders. It also conducts all suits in the Supreme Court that concern the United States.

The attorney general is head of the Department of Justice and the chief law officer of the federal government.

The Department of Justice's law enforcement agencies include the Federal Bureau of Investigation, the Federal Drug Enforcement Administration, United States Marshals, the Immigration and Naturalization Service, and the Bureau of Prisons.

The Federal Bureau of Investigation (FBI)   Created as the Bureau of Investigation, this agency was renamed the Federal Bureau of Investigation in 1935. Its national headquarters in Washington, D.C., maintains field offices in strategic cities in the United States and its possessions.

The FBI is the primary investigative agency of the federal government. Its special agents have jurisdiction over more than 200 federal crimes. They are responsible for general investigations, both criminal and civil, and for domestic intelligence dealing with the internal security of the nation. FBI agents are not subjected to the same demands for service that local police officers are: they do not handle drunks, answer domestic calls, respond to medical emergencies, or deal with deviant persons, which are the most frequent local problems of the community.

The Federal Bureau of Investigation's responsibilities include investigating espionage, interstate transportation of stolen property, kidnapping; unlawful flight to avoid prosecution, confinement, or giving testimony; sabotage, piracy of aircraft and other crimes aboard aircraft; bank robbery and embezzlement; and enforcement of the Civil Rights Acts.

The FBI's four investigative priorities are organized crime, foreign counterintelligence, white-collar crime, and terrorism. In addition to previous responsibilities, the FBI has been given further obligations under the Foreign Corrupt Practices Act of 1977, the Foreign Intelligence Surveillance Act of 1978, and the highly publicized Parental Kidnapping Prevention Act of 1980. Under this federal statute, the FBI's traditional jurisdiction over crimes involving unlawful flight to avoid prosecution has been extended to include parental kidnappers.

In 1982 the United States Attorney General assigned the bureau jurisdiction to investigate federal drug offenses. This significantly increased the FBI's involvement in major narcotic investigations and provided assistance to the Drug Enforcement Administration in a massive effort to deal with the serious drug problems in the United States.

In addition to these numerous responsibilities, the FBI provides valuable services to law enforcement agencies throughout the country.

The *Identification Division* was established in 1924 as a result of the tremendous value of fingerprint identification data. The FBI is the central repository for fingerprint information; over 22,000 agencies contribute to and may obtain information from it.

Data from the identification records are furnished to law enforcement and governmental agencies at the federal, state, county, and local levels for official use only. Wanted notices, periodically distributed by the FBI at the request of other law enforcement agencies, frequently result in the apprehension of dangerous criminals. The Identification Division is not restricted to criminal matters, however; many missing persons have been located, and victims of amnesia and homicides have been identified.

The Identification Division also maintains a disaster squad to assist in identifying victims of disasters such as explosions, storms, and plane crashes in which fingerprints are often the only means of identifying victims.

The *FBI Laboratory*, established in 1932, is the largest, most effective criminal laboratory in the world. Its facilities are available without cost to any city, county, state, or federal law enforcement agency in the country. Physical evidence obtained in a criminal investigation is examined not only to support evidence against a suspect but also to establish the innocence of accused persons. Included in the laboratory's services are

A technician inspects bomb components at the FBI crime laboratory.

identification of firearms, shoe prints, and tire prints; mineral analyses; and examination of blood, documents, hairs, fibers, and poisons.

The *National Crime Information Center (NCIC)*, established in 1967, is a complex, computerized, electronic data exchange network developed to complement computerized systems already in existence and those planned by local and state law enforcement agencies.

Records on file in the NCIC concern wanted persons, stolen vehicles, vehicles used in the commission of felonies, stolen or missing license plates, stolen guns, and other stolen items that are serially identifiable such as television sets, boat motors, and so on. The reservior of scientifically stored data on criminal activities gathered by federal, state, and local law enforcement agencies gives the street officer of any law enforcement agency in any part of the country up-to-the-minute information upon request in a matter of seconds.

Uniform Crime Reports is another service provided by the FBI. Since 1930, by an act of Congress, the FBI has served as a national clearinghouse for United States crime statistics. States report their monthly crime statistics to the FBI, which in turn releases information semiannually and annually regarding all crimes reported to them.

Crimes are categorized by their seriousness and their frequency. Part I crimes consist of murder, forcible rape, aggravated assault, robbery, burglary, larceny/theft, arson, and motor vehicle theft. Part II crimes consist of forgery, prostitution, narcotics, and the like. Uniform Crime Reports give law enforcement administrators valuable information related to crime rates in similar communities, the number of arrests, and clearance rates. The FBI reports are valuable in assessing needed workers, equipment, and budget increases.

The FBI Uniform Crime Reports seek to (1) measure the reporting trends of serious crime, (2) record the volume of crime, and (3) determine significant police matters related to crime such as number of employees per thousand capita, the number of officers assaulted each year, the number of officers killed each year, and the types of action that caused the assaults or deaths.

The diverse character of the bureau's work makes it necessary to have regular contact with police at every level of government.

Federal Drug Enforcement Administration (FDEA)   Before 1973, many fragmented government agencies pursued various courses of action in combating dangerous drugs. In 1973 the Bureau of Narcotics and Dangerous Drugs (BNDD), the Office for Drug Abuse Law Enforcement, the Office of National Narcotics Intelligence, and the drug and investigative and intelligence units of the Bureau of Customs were merged into the Federal Drug Enforcement Administration.

Narcotics agents seek to stop the flow of drugs at their source, both domestic and foreign, and to assist state and local police in preventing illegal drugs from reaching local communities. They become involved in surveillance, raids, interviewing witnesses and suspects, searching for evidence, and seizure of contraband goods.

The FDEA is charged with the full responsibility for prosecuting suspected violators of federal drug laws. They have liaison with law enforcement officials of foreign governments and highly trained agents stationed in all major United States cities and in thirty countries throughout the world. The FDEA also regulates the legal manufacture of drugs and other controlled substances under the Controlled Substances Act of 1970.

The FDEA maintains six regional laboratories throughout the country to accumulate up-to-date information regarding drugs under its jurisdiction. This information is distributed to law enforcement agencies, allowing them to better cope with drug abuse problems and their related effects.

The federal government recognized the existence of a drug problem in this country nearly sixty-five years ago. Early government response, embodied in the Harrison Narcotic Act of 1914, was directed exclusively at controlling the supply of dangerous drugs. The Harrison Act established federal control over the supply, distribution, and use of narcotics. But almost no attention was given at the federal level to treating and rehabilitating drug users until the early 1930s, when the United States Public Health Service Hospitals at Lexington, Kentucky, and Fort Worth, Texas, were established to treat drug addicts.

The United States Marshals   In 1789 Congress created the office of United States Marshal. United States Marshals are appointed by the president with the approval of the Senate, as recommended by the attorney general, for a period of four years. The first marshals were appointed by President George Washington.

Each marshal's office has a staff of deputy marshals to carry out its functions and responsibilities. The functions of most deputy marshals are more enforcement than investigative. They are responsible for (1) seizing property in both criminal and civil matters to satisfy judgments issued by a federal court, (2) providing physical security for United States courtrooms and protection for federal judges, jurors, and attorneys, (3) transporting federal prisoners to federal institutions when transferred or sentenced by a federal court, and (4) protecting government witnesses whose testimony might jeopardize their safety. Such witnesses are protected by the government by being salaried, relocated in other cities, and provided with new identities.

Immigration and Naturalization Service (INS)   The Immigration and Naturalization Service has border patrol agents who serve throughout the United States, Canada, Mexico, Bermuda, Nassau, Puerto Rico, the Philippines, and Europe. They conduct investigations, detect violations of immigrant and nationality laws, and determine whether aliens may enter or remain in the United States. It also has immigration inspectors who are responsible for detecting people who violate immigration and nationality laws. They work with border patrol agents and other investigators to determine if an applicant can enter the United States.

The extensive activities of the border patrol have resulted in many arrests for smuggling contraband and aliens into the United States.

Searches for smuggled aliens are often made of automobiles, airplanes, and boats. The border patrol uses primarily airplanes, boats, and vehicles to deter illegal smuggling. Air-to-ground operations and searches of freight trains traveling between the United States and Mexico are common.

The Bureau of Prisons   The Bureau of Prisons is an integral part of the federal criminal justice system. It is responsible for the care and custody of persons convicted of federal crimes and sentenced to federal penal institutions. Correctional officers coordinate work assignments, enforce rules and regulations within institutions, and carry out plans developed for correctional treatment and modification of inmates' attitudes. The Bureau operates a nationwide system of maximum, medium, and minimum security prisons, halfway houses, and community program offices.

The Department of the Treasury

The Department of the Treasury also has several agencies directly involved in law enforcement activities. Law enforcement agencies under the jurisdiction of the Department of the Treasury include the Bureau of Customs, the Internal Revenue Service, the Secret Service, and the Bureau of Alcohol, Tobacco, and Firearms Tax.

The Bureau of Customs   The Bureau of Customs has agents stationed primarily at ports of entry to the United States, where people and/or goods enter and leave. Customs agents investigate frauds on customs revenue and the smuggling of merchandise and contraband into or out of the United States. Customs agents have authority to conduct investigations and searches on all ships registered under United States laws.

Customs is active in suppressing the traffic in illegal narcotics and works in close cooperative with the Federal Drug Enforcement Administration. Customs patrol officers maintain uniformed and plainclothes surveillance at docks and airports.

The Internal Revenue Service (IRS)   The Internal Revenue Service, established in 1862, is the largest bureau of the Department of the Treasury. Its mission is to encourage the highest degree of voluntary compliance with the tax laws and regulations. Internal Revenue Service agents investigate willful tax evasion, tax fraud, and the activities of gamblers and drug peddlers.

The bureau has three divisions: Examination, Collection, and Criminal Investigation. Examination staff selects and audits tax returns of individuals and corporations. Collection staff includes revenue officers and field workers who contact delinquent taxpayers. Criminal Investigation staff includes special agents who conduct investigations, make arrests, provide armed escorts, protect other employees as well as government property, and assist Secret Service agents in protecting the president and other public officials.

The United States Secret Service   The Secret Service was established in 1865 to fight currency counterfeiters. In 1901 it was given the responsibility of protecting the president of the United States, the president's family members, the president-elect, and the vice-president.

The Secret Service has two major law enforcement functions: to suppress counterfeiting and to suppress forgery of government checks and bonds. It has other duties, too, such as investigating United States financial institutions. In their efforts to suppress counterfeiting and forgery, agents rely heavily on scientific investigation. To aid the agents, the Bureau of Engraving and Printing in Washington maintains a laboratory with modern scientific crime detection equipment. From the examinations conducted at the laboratory, the Secret Service gets valuable information that often leads its agents to the successful conclusion of cases.

The Secret Service is also responsible for investigating threats against the president. In 1976 the Secret Service became responsible for protecting presidential candidates as a result of threats against several of them and the actual shooting of presidential candidate, Governor George Wallace of Alabama.

In addition to Secret Service special agents, two uniformed groups are under the control and direction of the service: the Secret Service Uniformed Division and the Treasury Police Force.

The *Secret Service Uniformed Division* protects the executive mansion and its grounds. Officers assigned to the Secret Service Uniformed Division are highly trained in techniques for identifying potential threats to the president and in self-defense tactics.

The *Treasury Police Force* protects the Treasury Building and the Treasury Annex in Washington. The Treasury Building has 475 rooms and covers the greater part of two city blocks. Beneath this building are safety vaults where the nation's money and valuable papers are kept. The Treasury Police Force is assigned to the continuous protection of the immense sums in the United States Treasury.

The Bureau of Alcohol, Tobacco, and Firearms Tax (BATF)   The Bureau of Alcohol, Tobacco, and Firearms Tax, an enforcement arm of the Department of the Treasury, is primarily a licensing and investigative agency involved in federal tax violations.

The Firearms Division enforces the Gun Control Act of 1968, which deals with the manufacture, sale, transfer, and possession of restricted firearms in the United States, including the illegal possession of automatic weapons, machine guns, and submachine guns by persons other than antique collectors.

The bureau also regulates interstate commerce in all types of guns to or from foreign countries. In addition, they collect the taxes of United States importers, manufacturers, and dealers of firearms. The bureau maintains a close relationship with other federal, state, and local enforcement agencies so that gun control laws are rigidly enforced.

The objectives of its criminal enforcement activity are to eliminate illegal possession and use of firearms, destructive devices, and explosives; to suppress the traffic in illicit distilled spirits; to enforce the criminal violation and forfeiture aspects of the federal wagering laws; and to

The United States Secret Service protecting President Bush during the inaugural parade.

cooperate with state and local enforcement agencies to reduce crime and violence (Office of the Federal Register 1976).

Other Federal Law Enforcement Agencies

Although the majority of federal law enforcement agencies are within the Department of Justice and the Department of the Treasury, other federal agencies are also directly involved in law enforcement activities such as the United States Postal Inspectors, the Coast Guard, military police of the armed forces, and investigators and intelligence agents and security officers for other federal agencies.

United States Postal Inspectors enforce federal laws pertaining to mailing prohibited items such as explosives, obscene matter, and articles likely to injure or cause damage. Any mail that may prove to be libelous, defamatory, or threatening can be excluded from being transported by the postal service. Postal inspectors protect the mails and recipients of mail. They also investigate any frauds perpetrated through the mails such as chain letters, gift enterprises, and similar schemes. The postmaster general is also authorized to prevent the delivery of mail to persons who might be using the mails to conduct a fraudulent business.

The *United States Coast Guard* assists local and state agencies that border the oceans, lakes, and national waterways. They have been actively involved in preventing the smuggling of narcotics into this country.

The *armed forces* also have law enforcement responsibilities. The uniformed divisions are known as the Military Police in the Army, the Shore Patrol in the Navy, and the Security Police in the Marine Corps and Air Force. Military police are enlisted personnel and officers; civilians do not serve in the uniformed military police units. Usually, these military police must not only meet all enlistment requirements of the service but also must show an aptitude for police work, must score well on the entrance examination, and must meet certain physical requirements. The military police are primarily concerned with the physical security of the various bases under their control. Within each operation, the security forces control criminal activity, court martials, discipline, desertions, and the confinement of prisoners. In time of war they are responsible for prisoners of war as well as custodial care and movement of refugees.

The Law Enforcement Assistance Administration (LEAA)

In 1968 Congress enacted the Omnibus Crime Control and Safe Streets Act; Title 1 of this act established the Law Enforcement Assistance Administration. When the act was amended in 1970 the LEAA program was expanded. The Crime Control Act of 1973 further strengthened the agency and extended its authorization through 1976. The Crime Control Act of 1976 extended the program through September of 1979.

Pursley (1984, p. 165) notes:

> Although the *Law Enforcement Assistance Administration (LEAA)* was never a federal law enforcement agency, it deserves special attention because it may well have brought about the most important developments in the annals of American criminal justice. During its relatively brief period of existence, no other American crime control agency appears to have produced the far-ranging improvements that LEAA brought to American criminal justice.

LEAA worked in partnership with state and local governments, which have historically assumed the primary responsibility for crime reduction and law enforcement. Congress affirmed this historical responsibility in the Omnibus Crime Control and Safe Streets Act: "Crime is essentially a local problem that must be dealt with by state and local governments if it is to be controlled effectively."

On the other hand, as noted by Richard W. Velde, former LEAA administrator: "Crime control is everyone's business. It is not just the business of the criminal justice system—of police, courts, and corrections—but of all citizens who want to live in harmony and peace."

Realizing the national significance of the crime problem, Congress created the LEAA to join state and local law enforcement agencies in their efforts to combat crime. Under the anticrime partnership, the federal government supplied financial resources, technical advice, and leadership; however, states and localities set their own crime control priorities, devised specific action programs, and allocated LEAA funds according to their carefully developed plans.

LEAA awarded more than $9 billion to state and local governments to improve police, courts, and correctional systems; to combat juvenile delinquency; and to finance innovative crime-fighting projects.

Major Achievements Every state and locality felt the impact of LEAA's nationwide anticrime program. Tens of thousands of programs and projects were supported with LEAA funds, and millions of hours were applied to identify effective, efficient, economical ways to reduce crime and improve criminal justice. Projects were developed to reduce crime and improve criminal justice, to improve the management and administration of courts, to deploy police officers more effectively, to find jobs for ex-offenders, to sharpen the skills of criminal justice personnel, to give prosecutors better tools to fight crime, and to break the jail-street-crime-jail cycle of the drug addict.

The Demise of LEAA Richard D. Lamm (1978), governor of Colorado, notes that LEAA "endured a very troubled history," due in part to extremely unrealistic and high expectations that led to inevitable excesses and failures. In the program's early years, the Nixon "law and order" administration exerted great pressure to get money out into the field without allowing states sufficient time to properly plan for use of the funds. In addition, LEAA's management was unstable; it had five administrators in seven years, each with his own philosophy. Finally, frequent delays in publishing the guidelines for the annual planning cycle hampered the states' ability to plan properly.

STATE AGENCIES

Many of the federal agencies have state counterparts.

State agencies with law enforcement responsibilities include state bureaus of investigation and apprehension and state fire marshal divisions as well as departments of natural resources, driver and vehicle services divisions, and departments of human rights.

Office of the State Attorney General

The attorney general is the chief legal counsel for the state. This office provides representation and advice to agencies in the executive branch of state government. The attorney general proposes and drafts legislation on a variety of subjects and assures that all state laws are adequately and uniformly enforced. This office also supervises district attorneys and sheriffs.

In addition to an antitrust division and a consumer protection division, the attorney general's office has a criminal division, which conducts criminal appeals, advises local prosecutors on the conduct of criminal trials, and helps develop and prosecute certain criminal cases, particularly those of organized crime and white-collar crime.

The attorney general's opinions office provides information to state and local officials on effects and requirements of state laws when laws either appear to conflict or are unclear in their application.

The state attorney general is the chief law enforcement officer at the state level. This office usually includes an antitrust division, a consumer protection division, a criminal division, and an opinions office.

State Bureau of Investigation and Apprehension

States vary in the organization and function of agencies that offer support to other law enforcement agencies in the state. They usually are organized to assist local law enforcement officials. The Bureau of Investigation and Apprehension places investigators throughout the state to help investigate major crimes and organized criminal activities; help investigate the illegal sale or possession of narcotics and prohibited drugs; conduct police science training courses for peace officers; provide scientific examination of crime scenes and laboratory analysis of evidence; and maintain a criminal justice information and telecommunications system. The bureau also provides statistical information on crimes and crime trends in the state.

State Fire Marshal Division

Designated state fire marshals investigate suspicious and incendiary fire origins, fire fatalities, and large-loss fires; tabulate fire statistics; and provide education, inspection, and training programs for fire prevention.

The *Fire Prevention Section* provides information on the state's Uniform Fire Code, removal of combustible materials, correction of fire hazards, fire prevention, and general information on smoke/heat detectors, fire alarms, fire extinguishers, and other fire protection appliances.

The *Inspection and Investigation Section* organizes investigation of all fires of suspicious and incendiary origin, large-loss fires, and fire fatalities. The section also conducts ongoing inspection of public and private schools, state hospitals, convalescent and other special purpose homes, hotels, rooming houses and other multiple dwellings, dry-cleaning establishments, motion picture theaters, places of assembly, and all installations where petroleum products, liquified petroleum gas, and natural gas are manufactured, stored, or distributed.

The *Fire Prevention Awareness Section* identifies problem fire areas, inspects fires and buildings to guarantee fire safety standards, conducts public awareness programs, and maintains contact with local fire departments.

State Department of Natural Resources (Fish, Game, and Watercraft)

Some states combine fish, game, and watercraft under one division, a Department of Natural Resources, which enforces all laws and rules under its jurisdiction including hunting, fishing, and trapping laws and licenses and laws on the operation of watercraft. In some states the department is responsible for the firearms training laws. The division may hold auction sales to dispose of furs, firearms, and hunting, fishing, and trapping equipment confiscated from violators of fish and game laws.

Conservation officers investigate complaints about nuisance wildlife, misuse of public lands and waters, violations of state park rules, and unlawful appropriation of state-owned timber. Conservation officers also dispose of big game animals struck by motor vehicles, assist state game managers on wildlife census projects, enforce wild-rice harvesting rules, and assist in identifying needed sites for public access to lakes and streams.

The department also issues resident and nonresident boat licenses and licenses for hunting, fishing, and trapping.

Driver and Vehicle Services Division

The *Motor Vehicle Section* of the Driver and Vehicle Services Division registers motor vehicles, issues ownership certificates, answers inquiries, returns defective applications received through the mail, licenses motor vehicle dealers, supplies record information to the public, and in some states, registers bicycles.

The *Driver's License Section* tests, evaluates, and licenses all drivers throughout the state; maintains accurate records of each individual driver including all violations and accidents occurring anywhere in the United States and Canada; interviews drivers whose record warrants possible revocation, suspension, or cancellation; records the location of every reported accident; assists in driver education efforts; and administers written and road tests to applicants.

The Department of Human Rights

The Department of Human Rights enforces the Human Rights Act, which prohibits discrimination on the basis of race, color, creed, religion, national origin, sex, marital status, status with regard to public assistance or disability in employment, housing, public accommodations, public service, and education. It is also responsible for current affirmative laws. It investigates and conciliates discrimination complaints. When conciliation is not possible, it settles the complaint through legal proceedings.

State Police and State Highway Patrol

The most visible form of state law enforcement is the state police, who often have general police powers and enforce all state laws, and state highway patrols, who focus their attention on the operation of motor vehicles on public highways and freeways.

Each state police agency differs, depending on its history and evolving law enforcement needs. From the Texas Rangers in 1835 to the present, new agencies have been formed and old agencies reorganized to meet the changing requirements of the states.

Some state police enforce all state laws; others enforce only traffic laws on highways and freeways and are usually designated as state highway patrol.

Usually *state police agencies* do not work within municipalities that have their own forces, except on request. These state forces generally do not enter local labor, political, or other mass disturbances or potentially disastrous situations unless asked by the local sheriff or police chief.

Most *highway patrol agencies* enforce state traffic laws and all laws governing operation of vehicles on public highways in the state. They usually operate in uniform, drive distinctively marked patrol cars and motorcycles, and engage in such activities as (1) enforcing laws regulating the use of vehicles, (2) maintaining preventive patrol on the highways, (3) regulating traffic movements and relieving congestion, (4) investigating traffic accidents, and (5) making surveys and studies of accidents and enforcement practices to improve traffic safety (Adams 1980).

The Michigan State Police and the Pennsylvania State Police are examples of agencies with general police powers. In contrast, Florida's Highway Patrol deals with traffic, while the Florida Department of Law Enforcement conducts investigations. Similarly, the Minnesota Highway Patrol directs its primary attention to enforcing traffic laws, while the Minnesota Bureau of Criminal Apprehension limits its function to investigative and enforcement functions at the state level.

In California, the Department of the California Highway Patrol is responsible for enforcing traffic laws, investigating traffic accidents, and rendering aid to motorists on the state and interstate highways. The California State Police are responsible for protecting only state property. They protect the state capital and grounds as well as other state government buildings located throughout the state.

In addition, some highway patrol agencies coordinate the activity and maintain records on commercial vehicle enforcement, maintain public scales on the highways, inspect all school buses, and investigate

The Minnesota Highway Patrol began using high-tech Mustangs to patrol its highways.

accidents involving school buses throughout the state. Licensing or registration of official smog-control devices or headlights and other safety equipment installations, as well as inspection stations, may also be functions performed by state highway patrol.

A governor may send state highway patrol or state police personnel to a locality to preserve the peace. This occurred in Mississippi and other southern states during mob actions prompted by efforts to racially integrate public schools. On two such occasions (Little Rock, Arkansas, in 1957 and Oxford, Mississippi, in 1962), National Guard units and regular United States Army military personnel were ordered by federal authorities to help state and local police maintain civil order.

The increasing responsibilities of state police are considerable. They often work in cooperation with the National Guard to restore order in mass disturbances. They have assumed responsibility from county sheriffs for policing traffic on major highways, and they assist the sheriff or small-town police officer in solving crimes requiring the use of specialized equipment. Further, many state police or highway patrol organizations administer the duties of the state fire marshal's office.

COUNTY AGENCIES

The two main types of county law enforcement agencies are the county sheriff and the county police.

The County Sheriff

Many state constitutions have designated the sheriff as the chief law enforcement officer of the county. The sheriff is usually elected locally for a two- or four-year term. Qualifications are set by state law, and the salary is usually set by the legislature or the county board. As Folley (1980, p. 228) notes:

> The office of sheriff is probably the most obvious example of mixing police and politics. This office was integrated into the American police system with little change from what it was in England. Today the office of sheriff is subject to popular election in almost all counties throughout the United States . . . when a new sheriff is elected he will repay political debts by appointing new deputies and promoting others already employed. . . . This constant change of leadership and manipulation of the heirarchy has not been conducive to the provision of efficient police services.

The sheriff's powers and duties are also established by state law. Each sheriff is authorized to appoint deputies and, working with them, to assume responsibility for providing police protection as well as a variety of other functions including (1) keeping the public peace, (2) executing civil and criminal process throughout the county (such as serving civil legal papers and criminal warrants), (3) keeping the county jail, (4) preserving the dignity of the court, and (5) enforcing court orders.

The sheriff operates freely in the unincorporated portions of the county and works with the municipal police departments in incorporated areas. The sheriff also works closely with the state police or highway patrol and township personnel in unincorporated portions of the county.

The sheriff appoints deputy sheriffs to assist in fulfilling responsibilities. The hundreds of sheriff's departments vary greatly in organization and function. In some states the sheriff is primarily an officer of the court; criminal investigation and traffic enforcement are delegated to state or local agencies. In other states, notably in the south and west, the sheriff and deputies perform both traffic and criminal duties.

The sheriff's staff ranges in size from one (the sheriff only) to several hundred, including sworn deputies as well as civilian personnel. Likewise, a wide range of technical proficiency and expertise also occurs among a sheriff's personnel. Some departments have little equipment; others have fleets of patrol vehicles, airplanes, helicopters, and lavishly equipped crime laboratories.

Holten and Jones (1978, p. 98) cite a major difference between sheriffs' offices and municipal police departments as "a greater emphasis by sheriffs on civil functions and operation of corrections facilities. There are often, for example, separate divisions or bureaus within sheriffs' departments for performing the civil functions of process serving and/or operating the county jail and caring for prisoners."

There are an estimated 3,340 county sheriff departments in the United States.

The County Police

The county police, not to be confused with the county sheriff and deputies, are often found in areas where city and county governments have been merged, such as in Florida. County police departments are headed by a chief of police, usually an administrator appointed from within the department, who is accountable to a county commissioner, prosecutor, manager, or director of public safety.

There are about seventy-five such county police departments in the United States. Pursley (1984, p. 169) states: "Many counties that have adopted the county police department have given this agency full authority and responsibility to perform all law enforcement functions."

Overlap Between the County Sheriff and County Police

Pursley goes on to note that when county police departments are established, they are often forced to retain the sheriff. He cites Georgia as an example of a state that recognizes the sheriff as a constitutional officer yet allows counties to establish independent police agencies. Pursley suggests:

> This duplication is costly, and people do not know whether to call the sheriff's department or the county police. A great deal of political acrimony has also been apparent between the heads of these two agencies as well as among political supporters and elected officials who either side with the sheriff or the county police. This results in charges and countercharges of incompetence, poor service, corruption, and a host of other claims being leveled at one agency by supporters of the other.

The Coroner or Medical Examiner

Another officer of the county is the coroner or medical examiner. Adams (1980, p. 150) points out that the office of coroner has a history similar to that of the sheriff and comes to modern law enforcement from ancient times. The principal task of the coroner is to determine the cause of death and to take care of the remains and personal effects of deceased persons. According to Adams: "The coroner is required by law to investigate and sign the death certificate in all circumstances where a violent death has occurred, a sudden or unusual death, an unattended death, and any death that may have suspicious circumstances surrounding it whether it be associated with a crime, a public hazard, or a disease."

The coroner need not be a medical doctor or have any legal background to be elected; in some jurisdictions, however, the coroner has been replaced by the medical examiner, a doctor of medicine and usually a pathologist who has studied forensic science.

In some states the coroner or medical examiner is, by statutory provision, the chief law enforcement officer of the county. When this occurs, a sheriff's department usually has the traditional combination of criminal and civil duties to perform. In Illinois, for example, the coroner is the only one who can serve subpoenas on the sheriff. If the sheriff becomes incapacitated and cannot function, or if the sheriff is arrested (which can be done only by the coroner), the coroner becomes sheriff until one is elected.

LOCAL AGENCIES

Township and Special District Police

The United States has approximately 19,000 townships, which vary widely in scope of governmental powers and operations. Most townships provide a very limited range of services for predominately rural areas. Some townships, often those in well-developed fringe areas surrounding a metropolitan complex, perform functions similar to municipal police.

Not all townships have their own police forces. Many rural townships have few law enforcement problems and purposely avoid appropriating funds for local police protection, relying instead on the sheriff or state police (or both) for preventive patrol and criminal investigation.

When small, essentially rural townships enter the policing field, a variety of difficulties arise. In addition to jurisdiction conflicts and the resulting diffusion of responsibility, a general lack of coordination results from having two or more government agencies, at different levels, actively policing the same area. The small township department, with its limited financial support, cannot offer complete police services, provide specialized services, nor police the area continually, but if there is a township police force, regardless of its adequacy, township residents and officials cannot exert as much pressure on the county governing body to expand the sheriff's force to bring about better general county police protection.

Many townships have only a one-person police force similar to the resident deputy system frequently found in sheriff's departments in which one person must police vast, sparsely populated regions. This person serves as a "jack-of-all-trades" and is on emergency call day and night. This individual's home may serve as headquarters.

The Constable

Approximately twenty states have established the office of constable, especially in New England, the South and the West. The constable is usually an elected official who serves a township, preserving the peace and serving processes for the local justice court. The constable may also be the tax collector or be in charge of the pound, execute arrest warrants, and transport prisoners. In some jurisdictions, the constable is under the direction of the sheriff.

Municipal Police

The United States has over 40,000 police jurisdictions and approximately 450,000 police officers, all with similar responsibilities but with limited geographical jurisdictions. The least uniformity and greatest organizational complexity is found at the municipal level due to local autonomy, that is, the independence of local governmental units to control their own police departments.

The majority of these police forces consist of fewer than ten officers, who provide resident deputy-type police service rather than emergency-oriented service. Some personnel of very small forces are appointed with little attention to their mental or physical fitness for the work, and many such personnel have never received any formal police training and lack proper supervision and discipline.

In contrast are police agencies in large metropolitan areas such as New York City, which have over 30,000 officers highly qualified and trained to perform demanding duties. Likewise, many suburban areas are now hiring career-minded, progressive police officers who bring with them dedication, education, and a high degree of competency in human relations and technical skills.

Suburban police departments have different policing problems than small towns and large cities, just as a small-town police department is far different from that of a city of several million people in terms of organization, structure, and discipline.

The Marshal

In some parts of the United States, a marshal serves as an officer of the court, serving writs, subpoenas, and other papers issued by the court and escorting prisoners from jail or holding cells in the courthouse to and from trials and hearings. The marshal also serves as the bailiff and protects the municipal judge and people in the court. In some jurisdictions the marshal is elected; in other jurisdictions the marshal is appointed.

OVERLAP

Police agencies of the five governmental levels can be found operating in any given spot in America. For example, you can find (1) several federal police establishments operating as much as 4,000 miles from Washington, D.C., (2) one or more statewide police services, (3) the county sheriff and county police force, (4) the township constables and town police constables or marshals, (5) village police or marshals, (6) city police forces that range in size from 10 to 39,000 officers, (7) special park and turnpike police, (8) special district police, (9) independent state and county detectives, identification, communication, and records agencies, and (10) numerous others of less direct relationship to the official police function.

Overlapping jurisdictions and potential competition when two (and often many more) forces find themselves investigating the same offense pose serious problems to law enforcement and highlight the need for education and professionalism. In addition, private security personnel may sometimes be involved, further complicating jurisdiction.

PRIVATE SECURITY FORCES

Private security forces include guards, patrols, investigators, armed couriers, central alarm respondents, and consultants. These private security officers perform many of the same functions as public law officers: controlling entrances and exits to facilities; preventing or reporting fires; promoting safety; safeguarding equipment, valuables, and confidential material; and patrolling restricted areas. Businesses and educational, industrial, and commercial organizations frequently hire private security guards to protect their premises and investments.

There are, however, important differences between private and public security forces. Public police officers are salaried with public funds. They are responsible to a chief of police and ultimately to the citizens of the community. Technically they are on duty twenty-four hours a day and have full authority to uphold the law, including the authority to make arrests and to carry a concealed weapon.

Still, the public police officer cannot be everywhere. Therefore, many businesses and organizations have elected to hire special protection. Basically, two different types of private security may be hired: private patrols and private guards.

As the name implies, private patrols operate both on and off the premises of their employers and may have several customers to check periodically during a specified time period. Private guards, however, stay on the property to safeguard the premises at all times.

A further distinction exists between a security officer employed by a large industrial concern and a night guard employed by a small firm. The former are usually carefully screened, well paid, and trained to perform specific duties. In contrast, the night guard is frequently retired from a regular job (sometimes as a public police officer), needs only temporary work, or is simply supplementing a regular income by taking on a second job.

From 200,000 plant guards in World War II, to over one million private security personnel today, the private security force is experiencing tremendous growth and has expanded to include private investigators, armed couriers, central alarm respondents, and consultants. Hemphill (1979, p. 279) notes that in the 1980s private security was a multibillion-dollar-a-year business that in the past decade grew 10 to 12 percent annually.

Private security forces differ from public security forces in several ways. They are salaried with private funds. They are responsible to an employer. They have limited authority and then only on the premises that they were hired to guard. They have no authority to make arrests except as a citizen's arrest, unless deputized. They have no authority to carry a concealed weapon. Their uniform and badge must not closely resemble that of a regular police officer.

The Complementary Roles of Private and Public Officers

Private and public security forces frequently engage in similar activities and have similar goals, including crime prevention (Hess and Wrobleski, 1988, p. 40). However, private security officers also perform functions that cannot be performed by public law enforcement officers, which makes their roles complementary. As noted by Kakalik and Wildhorn (1977, p. 90):

> With few exceptions guards perform work that the regular police cannot perform because of legal constraints or because of resource limitations. The public police typically can not be spared to prevent or investigate certain suspected crimes such as employee pilferage, and by law they must refrain from most crime-prevention activities on private property unless asked to do so by the owner. The public police are not legally charged with enforcing privately established rules and regulations. When specific private citizens, businesses, or institutions desire protection not offered by the public police, they must draw upon private sources. Typically, private guards perform functions that complement those of public police.

The International Association of Chiefs of Police (IACP) and the American Society for Industrial Security (ASIS) have been working together to improve the interactions of private and public officers so vital to successful crime prevention.

Unfortunately, however, friction often exists between private and public officers. The Law Enforcement/Private Security Relationship Committee of the Private Security Advisory Committee found the following barriers to an effective relationship between the two sectors: lack of mutual respect; lack of cooperation; lack of two-way communication; lack of knowledge by law enforcement of the function, mission, and problems of private security; the failure of private security to speak with a unified professional voice; and the need for better formulated and articulated standards of professionalism on both sides (National Advisory Committee on Criminal Justice Standards and Goals, 1976, p. 19).

Because of the preceding factors, in 1974 the Private Security Council established a standing committee to study the law enforcement/ private security relationship, to outline proposals to improve understanding and cooperation between them, and to develop guidelines for cooperation (National Advisory Committee on Criminal Justice Standards and Goals, 1976, p. 207). Promoting cooperative interaction between private and public police officers is of utmost importance, as noted by a past LEAA administrator, Richard Velde:

> There is so much to be done in the area of crime prevention that I can think of no reason for competition between the police and private security in this area. In fact, I visualize a comprehensive program of modern, effective crime prevention in which private security and police departments cooperate with each other, exchange information, and utilize common bases of expertise and know-how. This will require, or course, mutual respect for each other's talents and capabilities.

SUMMARY

The early American settlers brought with them several features of English law and law enforcement including those found in Leges Henrici, which made law enforcement a public matter, and in the Magna Carta, which provided for due process of law. Law enforcement in colonial America was frequently patterned after England's Watch and Ward system and later after the London Metropolitan Police and the principles for reform set forth by Sir Robert Peel. The first modern American police force, modeled after London's Metropolitan Police, was the New York City Police Department, established in 1844.

Although law enforcement was generally considered a local responsibility, the early beginning of state law enforcement agencies occurred with the establishment of the Texas Rangers and the early beginning of federal law enforcement agencies with the establishment of United States Marshals. After the turn of the century other state agencies, notably the Pennsylvania Constabulary, and other federal agencies, notably the Federal Bureau of Investigation, were established.

The spoils system encouraged politicians to reward their friends by giving them key positions in police departments. Cities fought to break political control by a variety of organizational techniques, including the election of police officers and chiefs, administering forces through bipartisan lay boards, asking states to assume local policing, and instituting mayor–council or council–city manager municipal government—which has proved to be the most effective thus far. In addition, in 1883 the Pendleton Act created the civil service system for government employees and made it unlawful to fire or demote a worker for political reasons.

Law enforcement in the United States is a cooperative effort among local, county, state, federal, and private law enforcement officers. Each has something to offer and to gain from the other.

At the federal level several law enforcement agencies are under the jurisdiction of the Departments of Justice and the Treasury. The United

States Attorney General, as head of the Department of Justice, is the chief federal law enforcement officer. Within this department are the Federal Bureau of Investigation, the Federal Drug Enforcement Administration, United States Marshals, the Immigration and Naturalization Service, and the Bureau of Prisons.

The FBI, in addition to its numerous investigative responsibilities, provides assistance to law enforcement agencies throughout the country through its Identification Division, the FBI Laboratory, its National Crime Information Center, and its Uniform Crime Reports.

Law enforcement agencies within the Department of the Treasury include the Bureau of Customs, the Internal Revenue Service, the Secret Service, and the Bureau of Alcohol, Tobacco, and Firearms Tax.

Other federal law enforcement agencies include the United States Postal Inspectors, the Coast Guard, and the military police of the armed forces.

State law enforcement agencies include state bureaus of investigation and apprehension, state fire marshals divisions, state departments of natural resources, driver and vehicle services divisions, departments of human rights, state police, and state highway patrol.

At the county level, the two main types of law enforcement agencies are the county sheriff and the county police.

In addition, private security officers provide special protection for businesses and educational, industrial, and commercial organizations. They perform many of the same functions as public law officers, but they also differ in several important ways.

Discussion Questions

1. Why did it take so long to develop a police force in the United States?

2. Should police chiefs be appointed or elected?

3. What demands are made on the modern police officer that were not present twenty or thirty years ago?

4. How do different law enforcement agencies relate to each other?

5. Which departments have jurisdiction over other departments?

6. Why aren't all the federal law enforcement agencies under the Department of Justice?

7. What major differences are there between a private security officer and a public law enforcement officer?

8. What state law enforcement agencies do you have? Which are most important in assisting your local law enforcement agency?

9. What form of county law enforcement do you have?

10. Where is your regional FBI office? What facilities and services does it offer?

References

Adams, T. F. *Introduction to the Administration of Criminal Justice*, 2d ed. Englewood Cliffs, N.J.: Prentice-Hall, 1980.

Bailey, W. G. (Ed.) *The Encyclopedia of Police Science*. New York: Garland Publishing, 1989.

Folley, V. L. *American Law Enforcement.* Boston: Allyn and Bacon, 1980.

Gardner, T. J. *Basic Concepts of Criminal Law: Principles and Cases,* 3d ed. St. Paul, Minn.: West Publishing Company, 1985.

Hemphill, C. F., Jr. *Modern Security Methods.* Englewood Cliffs, N.J.: Prentice-Hall, 1979.

Hess, K. M., and Wrobleski, H. M. *Introduction to Private Security* 2d ed. St. Paul, Minn.: West Publishing Company, 1988.

Holten, N. G., and Jones, M. E. *The System of Criminal Justice.* Boston: Little, Brown, 1978.

Kakalik, J. S., and Wildhorn, S. *The Private Police.* New York: Crane Russak (The Rand Corporation), 1977.

Lamm, R. D., "Evaluating LEAA—Is It Worth Continuing?" *Security Management,* 22:1 (January 1978): 33–35, 66.

Mayo, K. M. *Justice to All: The Story of the Pennsylvania State Police.* New York: G. P. Putnam's Sons, 1917.

National Advisory Committee on Criminal Justice Standards and Goals. Report of the Task Force on Private Security. *Private Security.* Washington, D.C.: U.S. Government Printing Office, 1976.

Office of the Federal Register, National Archives and Records Service, General Sevices Administration. *U.S. Government Manual: 1976–77* (Revised 5-1-76). Washington, D.C.

Perry, D. C. *Police in the Metropolis.* Columbus, Ohio: Charles E. Merrill, 1973.

Pursley, R. D. *Introduction to Criminal Justice.* New York: MacMillan, 1984.

Richardson, J. F. *The New York Police.* New York: Oxford University Press, 1970.

Walker, S. *The Police in America: An Introduction.* New York: McGraw-Hill, 1983.

CHAPTER THREE

The American Quest for Freedom and Justice: Our Laws

We hold these truths to be self-evident: that all men are endowed by their creator with certain unalienable rights; that among these are life, liberty, and the pursuit of happiness.—Thomas Jefferson

DO YOU KNOW

What civil rights and civil liberties are?

What the Declaration of Independence says about civil rights and civil liberties?

How to define and differentiate law, social or moral law, common law, case law, and statutory law?

What law takes precedence if two laws conflict?

What equity is?

What the basic instrument of government and the supreme law of the land is?

What the Bill of Rights is?

What specific rights are guaranteed by the First, Second, Fourth, Fifth, Sixth, Eighth, Thirteenth, and Fourteenth Amendments?

Where police get their power and authority and what restrictions are placed on this power and authority?

When changes in our institutions and statutes are necessary?

Introduction
Chapter 3

The Europeans' original immigration to the New World was heavily motivated by a desire to escape the religious, economic, political, and social repressions of traditional European society. North America was seen as a land where individuals could get a new start, free to make of themselves what they chose.

Sometimes, however, reality did not fully coincide with the **American creed** of individual freedom, as seen in the treatment of native Americans, the importation of slaves, the establishment of state churches, and the repressiveness involved in episodes such as the Salem witchcraft trials. Nevertheless, the spirit of liberty and justice remained strong. As noted by Gunnar Myrdal (1944): the American creed is the national conscience; a body of beliefs about equality, liberty, and justice which most Americans believe in, in spite of the fact that America has, and always has had, multiple wrongs.

In the 1760s the British began taking away rights that Americans had come to feel were naturally theirs, and the American Revolution resulted. In effect, the United States was born out of a desire for—indeed, a demand for—civil rights and civil liberties.

Civil rights are those claims that the citizen has to the affirmative assistance of government. Civil liberties are an individual's immunity from governmental oppression.

Civil rights and civil liberties are recurring themes in America's development. Our initial institutions reflected an intense concern for the individual human spirit. Our founding fathers showed strong commitments to postively guarantee those rights that Americans had fought and died to protect in the American Revolution. These values were forcefully stated in our most basic document: The Declaration of Independence.

THE DECLARATION OF INDEPENDENCE

The Declaration of Independence is not only a statement of grievances against England, but it is also a statement of alternative basic premises underlying human freedom. As Thomas Jefferson phrased it in the Declaration, the United States was demanding "the separate and equal station to which the laws of nature and of nature's God entitle them." In powerful rhetoric, Jefferson asserted:

> We hold these truths to be self-evident:—That all men are created equal; that they are endowed by their Creator with certain unalienable rights; that among these are life, liberty, and the pursuit of happiness. That, to secure these rights, governments are instituted among men, deriving their just powers from the consent of the governed; that, whenever any form of

government becomes destructive of these ends, it is the right of the people to alter or to abolish it, and to institute new government.

In other words, the purpose of government is to secure the people's unalienable rights, including life, liberty, and happiness—on an equal basis, since "all men are created equal."

The Delcaration of Independence asserts that all individuals are created equal and are entitled to the unalienable rights of life, liberty, and the pursuit of happiness. It further asserts that governments are instituted by and derive their power from the governed.

The Declaration of Independence was an idealistic statement of philosophy. It broke our ties with England, but it did not establish how the United States should be structured or governed. As you saw in chapter 2, each colony developed its own means of policing and protecting itself. The colonists relied heavily on laws they had brought with them from their homelands, England in particular.

TYPES OF LAW

Folley (1980, p. 12) notes: "To fully appreciate the significance and complexities of law and to place the police role in proper perspective, familiarity with several types of law is important." Recall that this book began with a discussion of what law is: Law is a body of rules for human conduct that are enforced by imposing penalties for their violation. Laws define social obligations and determine the relations of individuals to society and to each other. The purpose of law is to regulate the actions of individuals to conform to the way of life that the people's elected representatives or the community consider essential.

Social or Moral Law

Often obedience to law is obtained through social pressure— ridicule, contempt, scorn, or ostracism. Such methods are called moral or social sanctions, and the laws they enforce are called moral or social laws.

Moral or social laws are laws made by society and enforced solely by social pressure.

Moral or social laws include laws of etiquette, "honor," and morality. When moral laws break down and social sanctions fail to obtain conformity, other laws may be enacted and enforced.

Precedents: Common Law and Case Law

The beginnings of law are found in social habit or custom. Custom is simply precedent—doing what has been done before. In early times custom, religion, morals, and the law were intermingled. Some early customs have, over the centuries, become law.

Some customs were enforced physically rather than morally, and the violator was expelled from the community, sacrificed to the gods, or hanged. Other violations of custom that were not felt to be harmful to the whole community were punished by the injured group or the injured individual with the aid of the family (self-help, vengeance, feud). As long as such acts of vengeance, although regarded as right by the victim, might lead to retaliation, the sanction behind the rules of custom were still purely moral. But when the community began to protect those who had taken *rightful* vengeance, these persons became agents of the community. This kind of self-help met early society's needs when the right to take vengeance or redress was clear. It did not provide a way to settle controversies. Therefore courts were established to interpret customs and settle controversies.

Custom was replaced by judicial precedent. Legally, however, precedents or decisions are not law, but only evidence of the law. Even if the precedent or decision is written, the law in them is "unwritten."

In England, **common law** was the term applied to the laws and customs of the realm applied by the royal courts. It was defined as the customary law of England set by the judges as disputes rose. This was in contrast to local custom, equity, or ecclesiastical (church) law. When Parliament supplemented and modified the existing legal principles, the term *common law* was used to describe the law in force before, and independent of, any acts of the legislature.

Common law refers to the precedents set by the judges in the royal courts in England.

The common law brought to the United States by the early settlers and established in the various colonies forms the basis of modern American law. The common law of the states has one exception, Louisiana, which established and kept the system of French civil law.

In a nontechnical sense, common law describes the precedent generally followed in the absence of a specific law. In the United States this has come to be known as **case law.**

Case law refers to judicial precedents; no specifiic law exists, but a similar case serves as a model to be followed.

According to Oran's *Dictionary of the Law:* "Case law summarizes how statutes and constitutional problems have been interpreted by judges in cases coming before them." When cases not covered by the law come before the courts, the judges' rulings on previous similar cases will, for all practical purposes, be treated as law.

Statutory Law

In an advanced society, legislation becomes an increasingly important agency of legal development. The United States, as well as many other countries, has largely succeeded in replacing common law (unwritten law) with **statutory law** (legislated and written law.). Much of our law still rests upon judicial precedent, however; that is, common law and case law.

Statutory law is law passed by the legislature. It may be passed at the federal or state level, and at either level it includes constitutional and ordinary law.

Federal constitutional law is based on the United States Constitution, its amendments, and interpretations of the Constitution by the federal courts, as discussed shortly. Law enforcement officers must comply with constitutional law, which places numerous restrictions on their actions. Ordinary federal law consists of acts of Congress, treaties with foreign states, executive orders and regulations, and interpretation of the preceding by federal courts.

State constitutional law is based on the individual state's constitution, its amendments, and interpretations of them by the state's courts. State ordinary law consists of acts of the state legislatures, decisions of the federal courts in interpreting or developing the common law, executive orders and regulations, and municipal ordinances.

In addition, in most states, each county and city is given the right to make and pass laws for its local jurisdiction, providing the law does not conflict or preempt the state's laws. The basis of the local ordinances (laws) are primarily enacted to protect the individual community.

Order of Authority of Law

If two laws conflict, a set order of authority has been established.

The order of authority of law is the federal Constitution, treaties with foreign powers, acts of Congress, the state constitutions, state statutes, and finally, common law or case law.

Equity

Before leaving the general discussion of laws, one other concept is important; that is, the concept of **equity.**

Equity means to resort to general principles of fairness and justice whenever existing law is inadequate.

Neither the Roman praetors nor the English chancellors made rigid rules like legislators; instead they found law in the decisions of single cases as judges do. They did not, however, regard themselves bound by precedents. The new rules were not regarded as law at first but rather as arbitrary assertions of governmental power. Both in Rome and in England, however, equity, following its own precedents, soon developed a new body of judicial custom recognized as law. In England and in the United States today, equity is recognized as judge-made law, that is, a legal ruling by a judge based on fairness. In the United States, equity describes a system of rules and doctrines supplementing common and statutory law and superseding laws that are inadequate for fair settlement of a case. In other words, equity requires that the "spirit of the law" take precedence over the "letter of the law."

As noted by Ferguson and Stokke (1976, p. 64): "The rule of thumb in construing penal statutes is that criminal statutes are not to be strictly construed, but rather should be interpreted so as to promote fairness and justice. When construing penal statues, one must take into consideration the 'spirit of the law, not the letter of the law.' " This imperative to justice is echoed by Germann, Day, and Gallati (1972, p. 16): "In order that justice might prevail, the strict letter of the law is not always satisfactory; often equity must be considered, and legal justice corrected or suplemented by reference to the spirit of the law rather than to the letter of the law."

Equity demands that the law change as society changes. In fact, our law has been called a "living law." Laws that once made good sense now appear ridiculous. Consider, for example, the following laws:

- An old law in Truro, Massachusetts, states that a young man may not marry until he has killed either six blackbirds or three crows.
- In Gary, Indiana, it is illegal to go into a theater within four hours of eating garlic.

- An old Minnesota law requires that men's and women's underwear may not be hung on the same clothesline at the same time.
- In Pine Island, Minnesota, a man must tip his hat to every passing cow.
- In Gurnee, Illinois, a two-hundred pound woman is not allowed to wear shorts when riding a horse.

Obviously, if every locality and state were left alone, our legal system would be in a terrible state. Fortunately, our founding fathers foresaw this danger and wrote the Constitution of the United States, a carefully drafted document to establish the workings of a democracy.

THE UNITED STATES CONSTITUTION

The **Constitution** was drafted by the Constitutional Convention of 1787 and, following its ratification by conventions in two-thirds of the states, became effective in 1789. It is the basic instrument of government and the supreme law of the United States.

The Constitution states that the legislative, executive, and judicial departments of government should be separated as far as is practical, and that their respective powers should be exercised by different individuals or groups of individuals. The legislature makes the laws, the executive branch, of which law enforcement is a part, enforces the laws, and the judicial branch determines when laws have been violated.

The Constitution is the basic instrument of government and the supreme law of the United States.

When the first Congress of the United States convened on March 4, 1789, it had before it 103 amendments to the Constitution submitted by the states, forty-two amendments proposed by minority groups within the states, and bills of rights submitted by two states. After deliberating on these proposed amendments, Congress reduced them to twelve to submit to the states for ratification. Two failed to be ratified; the others became the first ten amendments. They went into effect on December 15, 1791, and are known as the Bills of Rights.

THE BILL OF RIGHTS

The Constitution organized the government of the new nation but contained few personal guarantees. Consequently, some states refused to ratify it without a specific bill of rights. In 1791 ten amendments, with personal guarantees included, came into effect. They became known as the **Bill of Rights,** a fundamental document describing the liberties of the people and forbidding the government to violate these rights.

The Bill of Rights protects a person's right to "life, liberty, and the pursuit of happiness." It forbids the government to violate these rights.

Humans are considered to have inborn rights of which a government may not deprive them. Government has only limited powers, which are delegated by the people.

Individual constitutional rights are clearly specified in each amendment. Some are of more relevance to individuals in law enforcement than others. Of special importance are the First, Second, Fourth, Fifth, Sixth, Eighth, Thirteenth, and Fourteenth Amendments.

The First Amendment

Congress shall make no law respecting an establishment of religion, or prohibiting the free exercise thereof; or abridging the freedom of speech or of the press; or the right of the people peaceably to assemble and to petition the government for a redress of grievances.

The First Amendment guarantees:

- *freedom of religion;*

- *freedom of speech;*

- *freedom of the press;*

- *freedom of peaceable assembly;*

- *freedom of petition.*

Freedom of Religion   Two guarantees of religious freedom are provided: (1) no law can establish an official church that all Americans must accept and support or that favors one church over another, and (2) no law is constitutional that prohibits the free exercise of religion. In short, citizens are guaranteed freedom to worship as they see fit.

The First Amendment clearly separates church and state and requires that the government be neutral on religious matters, favoring no religion above another. The first guarantee of this amendment, called the Establishment Clause, was made applicable to the states in *Cantwell v. Connecticut* (1949) and *Murdock v. Pennsylvania* (1943).

The second guarantee of the First Amendment is called the Free Exercise Clause and is very closely related to the freedom of speech portion of the First Amendment. Important cases related to this law are as follows (Pritchett 1977, p. 391):

- *Pierce v. Society of Sisters* (1925) struck down an Oregon law requiring all children to attend only public schools for the first eight grades.
- *Lovell v. Griffin,* (1938) protected the right of Jehovah's Witnesses to sell the sect's literature door to door without a permit, on free-press grounds.
- *Cantwell v. Connecticut* (1940) held that a state statute requiring approval of a county official for any person to solicit from house to house for religious or philanthropic causes amounted to "a censorship" of religion.
- *Murdock v. Pennsylvania* (1943) ruled that municipal license fees on transient merchants or book agents could not be applied to Jehovah's Witnesses who went door to door offering religious tracts for sale.
- *Niemotko v. Maryland* (1951)reversed the conviction of some Jehovah's Witnesses who had been arrested for making speeches in a public park without a permit.
- *Kunz v. New York* (1951) invalidated a New York ordinance requiring a police permit for public worship meetings on city streets.

Freedom of Speech   The Supreme Court has ruled that the First Amendment does not protect all forms of expression. Highly inflammatory remarks spoken to a crowd, which advocate violence and clearly threaten the peace and safety of the community, or present a "clear and present danger" to the continued existence of the government, are not protected.

Schneck v. United States (1919) established the "clear and present danger" doctrine and serves as a guide to the constitutionality of government restrictions on free speech (and free press). The Court held that: "The most stringent protection of free speech would not protect a man in falsely shouting fire in a theatre causing a panic. . . . The question in every case is whether the words are used in such circumstances and are of such a nature as to create a clear and present danger that they will bring about the substantive evils that Congress has a right to prevent."

Chaplinsky v. New Hampshire (1942) also established that use of "fighting words" likely to cause violence will not be tolerated. The Court ruled in this case that the states can ban the use of those "personally abusive epithets which, when addressed to the ordinary citizen, are, as a matter of common knowledge, inherently likely to provide violent reaction" (Lewis and Peoples 1978, p. 1074).

The ban on "fighting words" and words presenting a "clear and present danger" is counterbalanced by the concept of "pure speech," a theory created by the Supreme Court. Pure speech is speech without any accompanying action. In *Watts v. United States* (1969) the Court reversed the conviction of a defendant who told a discussion group that he was not going to report for military induction and that: "If they ever make me carry a rifle, the first man I want to get in my sights is L.B.J." Watts was originally convicted under the federal law against knowingly and willfully threatening the president. When it was proved that Watts had no real intention of killing the president, the Court held Watts was exercising his right to free speech and that his statement was "political hyperbole" rather than a true threat. Another example of pure speech is the Americanism "Kill the umpire," heard throughout the country during the baseball season.

Unlike pure speech, a second type of speech called "speech plus" is not protected by the First Amendment. An example of speech plus is the action taken by people in a labor strike picket line. If the striking employees physically prevent other people from entering or leaving a commercial building, the police may be called upon to assure that those who wish to enter or exit the building are allowed to do so.

Courts have also recognized that "symbolic speech," involving tangible forms of expression such as wearing buttons or clothing with political slogans or displaying a sign or a flag, is protected by the First Amendment.

Tinker v. Des Moines School District (1969) upheld the right of an individual to wear a black armband as an antiwar emblem. *Stromberg v. California* (1931) held the burning of a red flag as symbolic opposition to organized government to be an activity protected under the First Amendment. In contrast, *United States v. O'Brien* (1968) held that burning a draft card in protest of the Vietnam War violated a constitutional statute and was not permissible. The Court reasoned here that the government had a substantial interest unrelated to the free speech issue and that this issue far outweighed the defendant's right to freedom of speech. As noted by Klein (1980, p. 131): "The relative weights of the individual's constitutional rights are thus placed theoretically on a scale of values. The right which the Supreme Court holds to be the most weighty at a given time becomes the law of the land."

Finally, the courts have frequently condemned censorship by requiring official approval or a license in advance of speaking. While citizens are free to make speeches on the public streets, they may be prevented from doing so when they use a loud, raucous amplifier in a hospital zone or when the location chosen for the address is likely to interfere with traffic. Thus, freedom of speech is not an absolute.

Freedom of the Press   The First Amendment also guarantees the right to express oneself by writing or publishing one's views. The founding fathers recognized the importance of a free interplay of ideas in a democratic society and sought to guarantee the right of all citizens to speak or publish their views, even if they were contrary to those of the government or the society as a whole. Accordingly, the First Amendment generally forbids censorship or other restraint upon speech or the printed word.

As with speech, freedom to write or publish is not an absolute right of expression. The sale of obscene or libelous printed materials is not protected. The Supreme Court has ruled, however, that public figures cannot sue for defamation unless the alleged libelous remarks were printed with knowledge of their falsity or a reckless disregard for the truth.

Andrew Hamilton defends John Peter Zenger in the famous libel case of 1735.

Broadcasting, including radio, television, and motion pictures, receives the protection of the free press guarantee and is subject to its limitations.

As Klein (1980, p. 141) notes: "The right of freedom of expression has come to a head-on collision with those proponents of pornographic literature, movies, and photos. The police are in a dilemma in enforcing statutes designed to inhibit or control this activity. . . . The Supreme Court has not been too helpful in offering precise guidelines as to what is constitutional and what is unconstitutional behavior." Several Supreme Court decisions have attempted to define obscenity.

Roth v. United States (1957) held that obscenity is not within the area of constitutionally protected freedom of speech or press and that the standard to be employed is "whether to the average person, applying contemporary community standards, the dominant theme of the material, taken as a whole, appeals to prurient interest, that is, having a tendency to excite lustful thoughts."

In *Memoirs v. Attorney General of Massachusetts* (1966) the Court stated that for material to be obscene it must be shown that (1) the dominant theme of the material taken as a whole appeals to a prurient interest in sex, (2) the material is patently offensive because it affronts contemporary standards for the description or representation of sexual matters, and (3) the material is utterly without redeeming social value.

Mishkin v. New York (1966) held that the First Amendment was not violated by a state criminal obscenity statute that covered only "hard-core pornography"—that definition being more stringent than the definition required by federal constitutional standards. The case of *Miller v. California* (1973) set forth the following guidelines to determine whether a particular material was obscene: (1) whether the average person, applying contemporary community standards, would find the work, taken as a whole, as appealing to prurient interests; (2) whether the work depicted or described, in a patently offensive way, sexual conduct specifically prohibited by the applicable state law; and (3) whether the work, taken as a whole, lacked serious literary, artistic, political, or scientific value. This case held that the "utterly without redeeming social value" test and the "national standards" test were no longer applicable. In essence, the Court held that local community standards determine what is obscene, and that a work having "some redeeming social value" could no longer be used as a defense.

Finally, *Jenkins v. Georgia* (1974) stated that in state obscenity prosecutions, juries could properly be instructed to apply "community standards" of obscenity without specifying which community.

Other Supreme Court cases have dealt with private use of obscene materials, using the mails to send obscene materials, and laws protecting minors from obscene material. Among the most important of such cases are the following:

- *Bantam Books v. Sullivan* (1963) stated that it was unconstitutional for a commission created by a state legislature to notify distributors that certain books and magazines were obscene or objectionable for youths under age eighteen.
- *Freedman v. Maryland* (1965) found a state motion picture censorship statue to be unconstitutional because it failed to provide adequate safeguards against undue inhibition of expression protected by the First Amendment.
- *Ginzburg v. United States* (1966) affirmed the conviction for mailing obscene materials even though the literature was not obscene on its face.
- *Ginsburg v. New York* (1968) stated that it was constitutional for state criminal statutes to prohibit the sale of obscene material to minors.
- *Stanley v. Georgia* (1969) held that an individual possessing and viewing an obscene film in the privacy of his or her home is protected by the First Amendment.
- *Hamling v. United States* (1974) found that a federal statute prohibiting use of the mails for sending obscene material or advertisements was not in violation of the First Amendment.

One other area in which police officers may confront problems related to freedom of the press is during political elections. *Branton v. State* (1949) held that a statute forbidding candidates to distribute ballots used in the election to instruct voters to vote for them was constitutional. This problem should diminish, however, as use of voting machines becomes more common.

Freedom of Peaceable Assembly   Americans have the right to assemble peaceably for any political, religious, or social activity. Public authorities cannot impose unreasonable restrictions on such assemblies, but they can impose limitations reasonably designed to prevent fire, health hazards, or traffic obstructions. The Supreme Court has emphasized that freedom of assembly is just as fundmental as freedom of speech and press. Thus, while no law may legitimately prohibit demonstrations, laws or governmental actions may legitimately restrict demonstrations to certain areas or prohibit the obstruction and occupation of public buildings.

Picketing has also been protected under the free speech guarantee; however, it may be reasonably regulated to prevent pickets from obstructing movement onto and from the involved property. Picketing on private property has been upheld but only where the property is open to the public and the picketing relates to the business being conducted on the property. Klein (1980, p. 137) points out the following:

> *Police problems involving labor disputes are similar in some respects to that of the Parade Regulation. There are two competing constitutional rights that the police officer is confronted with: those who are on strike have a constitutional right to peacefully picket and those who may wish to go to work who have a constitutional right to peacefully conduct their business. . . . The police administrator is often confronted with the problem of maintaining order when groups unlawfully and without applying for a permit take over the streets, parks, or public buildings. . . . The prevailing rule now appears to be that so long as the gathering is reasonably orderly, notwithstanding the fact that the police may validly enforce a constitutional limitation, the demonstration is permitted in order to avoid a confrontation which might result in loss of life or injury to persons or property.*

Supreme Court decisions related to balancing the rights of people who wish to assemble and those who want to pursue their normal routine include *Poulos v. New Hampshire* (1953). This case stated that a group of demonstrators cannot insist on the right to blockade a street or entrance to a public or private building and allow no one to pass who did not agree to listen to their exhortations. *Walker v. Birmingham* (1967) stated that the First Amendment does not give people the right to trespass and disrupt the normal operations of business and government during the course of social protest, while *Cameron v. Johnson* (1968) held that taking over buildings for the purpose of demonstration is not protected by the First Amendment.

Freedom of Petition   The right of petition is designed to allow citizens to communicate with their government without obstruction. When citizens exercise their First Amendment freedom to write or speak to their senator or representative, they partake of "the healthy essence of the democratic process."

The Second Amendment

A well-regulated militia being necessary to the security of a free state, the right of the people to keep and bear arms shall not be infringed.

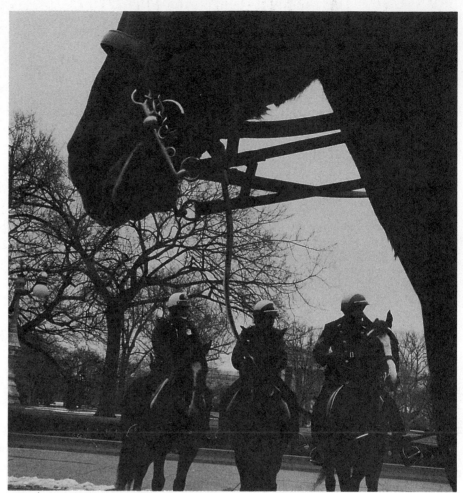

Officers on horseback maintain order.

The Second Amendment guarantees the right to bear arms.

Citizens are guaranteed the right to protect themselves from disorder in the community and attack from foreign enemies. This right to bear arms has become much less important in recent decades as well-trained military and police forces have been developed to protect citizens. No longer do citizens need to rely on having their own weapons available, yet attempts to limit this right are strenuously opposed by many citizens, as evidenced in the current gun control controversy. No matter what police officers' views are on gun control, they are obliged to enforce the laws passed by Congress.

The Supreme Court has ruled that state and federal governments may pass laws that prohibit the carrying of concealed weapons, require the registration of firearms, and limit the sale of firearms for other than military use. Thus, it is illigal to possess certain types of "people-killing" weapons such as operable machine guns and sawed-off shotguns of a certain length.

The right of the states to pass laws regulating firearms rests in the interpretation of the Second Amendment by the Supreme Court. In *United States v. Cruickshank* (1876) the Court stated that the amendment protected only the right of the states to maintain and equip a militia, and that unless a defendant could show that the possession of a firearm in violation of federal statutes had "some reasonable relationship to the preservation or efficiency of a well-regulated militia," that individual could not challenge a gun control statute on Second Amendment grounds. The American Bar Association has stated: "Every Federal court decision involving the amendment has given the amendment a collective, militia interpretation and/or held that firearms control laws enacted under a state's police power are constitutional" ("Handgun Facts"). The basic issue of gun control is discussed in chapter 21.

The Third Amendment

No soldier shall, in time of peace, be quartered in any house without the consent of the owner, nor in time of war but in a manner to be prescribed by the law.

Before the Revolution, American colonists were frequently forced to provide food and lodging for British soldiers. The Third Amendment prohibited continuing this practice.

The Fourth Amendment

The right of the people to be secure in their persons, houses, papers, and effects, against unreasonable searches and seizures, shall not be violated, and no warrants shall issue but upon probable cause, supported by oath or affirmation, and particularly describing the place to be searched, and the persons or things to be seized.

The Fourth Amendment requires probable cause and forbids unreasonable searches and seizures.

In some countries, even today, police officers may invade citizens' homes, seize their property, or arrest them whenever they see fit. In the United States such actions are prohibited by the Fourth Amendment, which protects individuals and their property from unreasonable search and seizure by law officers.

In most instances a police officer is not allowed to search the homes of private citizens, seize any of their property, or arrest them without first obtaining a court order—a **warrant.** Before a warrant will be issued, the police officer must convince a magistrate that there is **probable cause**— good reason—to believe either that the individual involved has committed a crime, or that the individual has in possession evidence related to a crime. Even with a warrant, police cannot typically break into a private home without first demanding entrance, unless such action is permissible under a "no-knock" statue, which authorizes such entry if it is reasonable to expect the evidence will be destroyed.

The courts have ruled that in some instances it is permissible to arrest a person or conduct a search without a warrant. For example, if a felony is committed in the presence of a police officer, the officer has the right to arrest the criminal immediately, without an arrest warrant. If police officers make such an arrest, they may search the suspect and a limited area surrounding the suspect to prevent the suspect from seizing a weapon or destroying evidence. Any evidence in plain view may also be seized.

The courts have permitted the police to search certain vehicles without a warrant on the grounds that the vehicle may be miles away by the time a police officer returns with a warrant.

The courts have frequently faced the problem of determining what constitutes probable cause for a search or an arrest. Generally speaking, the criterion has been common sense: On the available evidence, would a reasonable person consider there was a good basis to believe that the person to be arrested had committed a crime or that the place to be searched contained evidence of a crime?

The Supreme Court, in considering whether a police officer who stopped and frisked a citizen with reason to believe that individual had committed a particular crime, ruled that the Fourth Amendment did not prohibit such a search if it was reasonable on the basis of the police officer's experience and the demeanor of the individual who was frisked (*Terry v. Ohio*, 1968).

Listening in on a telephone conversation by mechanical or electronic means and electronic bugging are considered search and seizures under the Fourth Amendment, and, therefore, they also require probable cause, reasonableness, and a warrant for their use. Congress has passed legislation that limits the use of wiretapping and bugging to the investigation of specific crimes and restricts those officials permitted to authorize them. *Berger v. New York* (1967) established that electronic evesdropping was prohibited by the Fourth Amendment, but that under specific conditions and circumstances it could be permitted. *Katz v. United States* (1967) also established that evidence of conversations overheard through electronic surveillance of a telephone booth was inadmissible because the proper authorization had not been obtained.

Evidence secured by means of an unlawful search and seizure cannot be used in either a state or federal prosecution. Thus, the phrase "innocent until proven guilty" in practice means "innocent until proven guilty by evidence obtained in accordance with constitutional guarantees."

Numerous Supreme Court cases have interpreted restrictions imposed by the Fourth Amendment. For example, in *Boyd v. United States*

(1886), the Court held that the Fourth Amendment applied "to all invasions on the part of the government and its employees of the sanctity of a man's home and the privacies of life. It is not the breaking of his doors, and the rummaging of his drawers, that constitutes the essence of the offense; but it is the invasion of his indefensible right of personal security, personal liberty and private property." The findings in *Boyd* clearly suggest that evidence gathered in violation of the Fourth Amendment should be excluded from Federal criminal trials and, consequently, contributed to the development of the Exclusionary Rule some thirty years later.

In *Weeks v. United States* (1914) the Court, considering evidence seized unconstitutionally, concluded:

> *If letters and private documents can thus be seized and held and used in evidence against a citizen accused of an offense, the protection of the Fourth Amendment declaring his right to be secure against such searches and seizures is of no value, and, so far as those thus placed are concerned, might as well be stricken from the Constitution. The efforts of the courts and their officials to bring the guilty to punishment, praiseworthy as they are, are not to be aided by the sacrifice of those great principles established by years of endeavor and suffering which have resulted in their embodiment in the fundamental law of the land.*

The *Weeks* case established that "in a federal prosecution the Fourth Amendment bars the use of evidence secured through an illegal search and seizure."

Mapp v. Ohio (1961) established that the Exclusionary Rule must be applied at the state level as well as the federal level—that any evidence seized in violation of the Fourth Amendment guarantees was not admissible in state criminal prosecutions.

Other important Supreme Court cases related to the Fourth Amendment include several related to searches:

- *Burdeau v. McDowell* (1921) held that evidence obtained by a government agency from an unlawful search and seizure conducted by a private citizen can be used in government prosecution, provided the government had not "connived" in the unlawful search and seizure.
- *Abel v. United States* (1960) found that there was no invasion of privacy if an abandoned room or property was searched.
- *Stoner v. California* (1964) established that a guest in a hotel room was entitled to constitutional protection against unreasonable search and seizure, and that evidence obtained without a warrant, even with the consent of the desk clerk, was not admissible.
- *Michigan v. Tyler* (1978) held that entry by police and fire officials to investigate fire-damaged private property was subject to the Fourth Amendment, but that no warrant was required in an emergency to enter a burning structure to extinguish the fire.
- *Nix v. Williams* (1984) adopted what is now known as the "inevitable discovery exception to the Exclusionary Rule."

Supreme Court cases concerning searches related to arrests include *Henry v. United States* (1959), which found that if police did not have reasonable cause to believe a crime had been committed at the time they stopped a defendant, any search incidental to arrest was not legal. *Beck v. Ohio* (1964) held that in determining the validity of a warrantless arrest, the court must first determine if the facts available to the officer at the time would cause a person of "reasonable caution" to believe a crime had been committed.

In *Terry v. Ohio* (1968) it was established that if police officers believe a suspect is armed, they can stop and frisk that person as a safety precaution, and *Chimel v. California* (1969) held that a warrantless search incidental to lawful arrest must be limited to the suspect's immediate surroundings to prevent the suspect from obtaining a weapon or destroying evidence. Any search beyond this limit was unconstitutional.

Five other Supreme Court decisions relate directly to searches of automobiles:

- *Carroll v. United States* (1925) established that since automobiles and other conveyances were highly mobile, they could be searched without a warrant if they were suspected of containing contraband.
- *Chambers v. Maroney* (1970) held that police could search a vehicle at the police station after they had arrested the driver. They did not have to search it at the time of the arrest.
- *Coolidge v. New Hampshire* (1971) found that a warrantless search of a suspect's car parked in the driveway at the time the suspect was arrested inside the house was not constitutional; a warrant should have been obtained.
- *South Dakota v. Opperman* (1976) established that a routine search of vehicles impounded for traffic violations was constitutional.
- *United States v. Ross* (1982) held that the police may search a car, including containers, without a warrant as long as they have probable cause to believe contraband is somewhere in the car.

Strict interpretation of the Fourth Amendment frequently results in evidence being excluded from a trial and may greatly limit the police's investigatory powers. Consequently, support for the strict interpretation of the amendment has declined. In *Go-Bart Import Company v. United States* (1931), and in *United States v. Rabinowitz* (1950), the Court held that "what is a reasonable search must be resolved in the facts and circumstances of each case." In effect, the Court assumed the responsibility of deciding on a case-by-case basis whether the Fourth Amendment was violated. This has resulted in numerous exceptions to the warrant requirement implied by the Fourth Amendment.

The search and seizure provisions of the Fourth Amendment are critical to law enforcement officers and will be discussed in depth in chapter 12.

The Fifth Amendment

No person shall be held to answer for a capital or otherwise infamous crime unless on a presentment or indictment of a grand jury, except in cases arising in the land or naval forces, or in the militia, when in actual service, in time of war or public danger; nor shall any person be subject for the same offense to be twice put in jeopardy of life or limb; nor shall be compelled in any criminal case to be a witness against himself; nor be deprived of live, liberty, or property, without due process of law; nor shall private property be taken for public use without just compensation.

The Fifth Amendment guarantees:

* *due process—notice of a hearing, full information regarding the charges made against him, the opportunity to present evidence in his own behalf before an impartial judge or jury, and to be presumed innocent until proven guilty by legally obtained evidence;*

* *just compensation when private property is acquired for public use.*

  The Fifth Amendment prohibits:

* *double jeopardy;*

* *self-incrimination.*

Grand Jury   The Fifth Amendment requires that before individuals are tried in federal court for an "infamous" crime, they must first be indicted by a **grand jury.** The grand jury's duty is to assure that there is probable cause to believe the accused person is guilty. This prevents a person from being subjected to a trial when insufficient proof exists that he or she has committed a crime.

An "infamous" crime is a felony (a crime for which a sentence of more than one year's imprisonment can be given) or a lesser offense that can be punished by confinement in a penitentiary or at hard labor.

An indictment is not required for a trial by court-martial or by other military tribunals. Also, the constitutional requirements of grand jury indictment do not apply to trials in state courts.

Due Process   The words *due process of law* express the fundamental ideas of American justice. A due process clause is found in both the Fifth and Fourteenth Amendments as a restraint upon the federal and state governments respectively.

The due process clause protects against arbitrary, unfair procedures in judicial or administrative proceedings that could affect a citizen's personal and property rights. Due process requires notice of a hearing or trial that is timely and that adequately informs the accused persons of the charges against them. It also requires the opportunity to present evidence in one's own behalf before an impartial judge or jury, to be presumed innocent until proven guilty by legally obtained evidence, and to have the verdict supported by the evidence presented.

The due process clauses of the Fifth and Fourteenth Amendments provide other basic protections to prevent the state and federal governments from adopting arbitrary, unreasonable legislation or other measures that would violate individual rights. Thus, constitutional limitations are imposed on governmental interference with important individual liberties such as the freedom to enter into contracts, to engage in a lawful occupation, to marry, and to move without unnecessary restraints. Governmental restrictions placed on one's liberties must be reasonable and consistent with due process to be valid.

The United States Supreme Court has not given a precise definition of due process. Justice Frankfurter, in *Rochin v. California* (1952), stated: "Due process of law, as a historic and generative principle, precludes defining, and thereby confining, these standards of conduct more precisely than to say that convictions cannot be brought about by methods that offend a sense of justice."

Lewis and Peoples (1978, p. 19) suggest: "Due process can be operationally defined as law in the regular course of judicial proceedings that is in accordance with natural inherent and fundamental principles of justice. Thus one could argue that due process simply means that a defendant must receive all the substantive and procedural protections that the law presently provides." They also note: "In general, substantive due process protects all persons against unreasonable, arbitrary, or capricious laws and acts as a limitation against arbitrary governmental actions so that no court or governmental agency may exercise powers beyond those authorized by the Constitution."

In contrast, procedural due process deals with notices, hearings, and gathering of evidence. The vast majority of due process cases are in the area of procedural due process. Because the Fifth Amendment is so vague, hundreds of cases have been heard. Important Supreme Court cases involving due process include *Brady v. Maryland* (1963), which held that the suppression of evidence favorable to an accused by the prosecution violates due process. *In Re Gault* (1967) established that juvenile court proceedings must also meet the requirements of due process, and *United States v. Russell* (1973) found that it was not entrapment for an undercover agent to have supplied the defendant with a scarce ingredient required to manufacture an illicit drug.

In *Hampton v. United States* (1976) the court held that it was not entrapment for undercover agents to be both providers and purchasers of drugs involved in the case. *Manson v. Brathwaite* (1977) established that eyewitness identification could be made from a single photograph if "the totality of circumstances" made it reliable.

Double Jeopardy   The Fifth Amendment also guarantees that citizens will not be placed in double jeopardy; that is, they will not be tried before a federal or state court more than once for the same crime. A second trial can occur, however, when the first trial results in a mistrial, for instance, when the jury cannot agree on a verdict, or when a second trial is ordered by an appellate court.

Double jeopardy does not arise when a single act violates both federal and state laws and the defendant is prosecuted in both federal and state courts. Nor does a criminal prosecution in either a state or federal court exempt the defendant from being sued for damages by anyone who is harmed by the criminal act. Further, a defendant may be prosecuted more than once for the same conduct if it involves the commission of more than one crime. For instance, if a person kills three victims at the same time and place, he or she can be tried separately for each slaying. *Benton v. Maryland* (1969) stated that the double jeopardy clause also applies to state prosecutions.

Self-Incrimination   In any criminal case every person has the right not to be a witness against himself or herself; that is, individuals are not required to provide answers to questions that might convict them of a crime. Such questions may be asked at the very earliest stages of an investigation; therefore, the Supreme Court has ruled that when an individual is interrogated in the custody of the police, the guarantees of the Fifth Amendment apply. Custodial interrogation can extend to questioning outside the police station and has even included police questioning of a defendant in his or her own bed.

In ancient times, self-incrimination was a standard means of justice. People convicted of crimes were put to various inhumane tests that few could pass. Those who did not pass were determined to be guilty. As noted by Klotter and Kanovitz (1985, p. 335): "Before the year 1236 the accused in a criminal case was required to be sworn, but there was no questioning by the judge. The act of taking the oath was a ritual, and the decision of guilt or innocence was determined not on what was said, but on the correct pronunciation of the oath."

In 1236 this changed when the ecclesiastical courts required an accused to answer specific questions under oath. In seventeenth-century England all ecclesiastical courts were forbidden to administer any oath whereby people might be obliged to accuse themselves. As the original states developed their constitutions, the principle that individuals could not be compelled to witness against themselves was entrenched in the common law.

To insure against self-incrimination the Court ruled, in the well-known *Miranda* decision, that citizens must be warned prior to custodial interrogation of their right to remain silent, that what they say may be used against them in court, and that they have a right to counsel, which will be furnished them. If these warnings are not given, any statements obtained by the questioning are inadmissible in later criminal proceedings.

Although accused persons may waive their rights under the Fifth Amendment, they must know what they are doing and must not be forced to confess. Any confession obtained by force or threat is excluded from the evidence presented at the trial. Further, if defendants or witnesses fail to invoke the Fifth Amendment in response to a question when on the witness stand, such a failure may operate as a waiver of the right, and they will not be permitted to object to a court's admitting their statement into evidence.

Courts have ruled that the guarantee against self-incrimination applies only to testimonial actions. Thus, handwriting samples, blood tests, and appearance, including repeating words in a police lineup, do *not* violate the Fifth Amendment.

Courts have also ruled that the Fifth Amendment prohibits both federal and state prosecutors and judges from commenting on the refusal of defendants to take the witness stand in their own defense. The refusal of witnesses to testify to matters that could subject them to criminal prosecutions at a later date has also been upheld. The courts have recognized, however, a limited right of the government to question employees about the performance of official duties and have upheld the dismissal of employees who refuse to answer such questions.

Important Supreme Court cases regarding self-incrimination include the following:

- *Rochin v. California* (1952) held that pumping a defendant's stomach without a search warrant to obtain contraband was a denial of due process.
- *Escobedo v. Illinois* (1964) said that when the investigative process shifts to accusatory, the adversary system starts to operate and the suspect must be allowed to consult with an attorney.
- *Schmerber v. California* (1966) established that taking physical evidence such as blood samples despite the accused's objections did not violate the Fifth Amendment, and that the evidence was admissible.
- *Miranda v. Arizona* (1966) held that suspects must be told of their right to remain silent, of the possibility of using what is said against them in court, and the right to a lawyer. Unless a suspect is advised of these rights, any statements, admissions, or confessions are not admissible in court.
- *Gilbert v. California* (1967) established that requiring a suspect to give a handwriting sample without an attorney present did not violate the Fifth Amendment.
- *Cupp v. Murphy* (1973) held that police may take incriminating samples from the fingernails of a suspect without a warrant where there was probable cause to arrest.
- *Carter v. United States* (1981) stated that defendants who do not choose to testify in their own defense have the right to ask the judge to instruct the jury not to infer guilt because of this refusal to testify.
- *New York v. Quarles* (1984) established a new public safety exception to the Exclusionary Rule in that in certain cases police may question a subject in custody without first advising of the right not to self-incriminate.

Creamer (1980, p. 367) contends the following:

The public sees the Fifth Amendment invoked by people they don't like and who they presume are dishonest—or worse. People perceive that crime by government officials and other white-collar types is a serious problem, and they assume that too many such criminals are hiding behind the Fifth Amendment. The rising use of the Fifth Amendment has brought with it a rising outcry that the Fifth isn't worth the trouble it causes. This shallow notion is appealing on the surface, but in substance it is a dangerous idea, much like setting fire to one's home in order to rid the house of termites.

No principles of law are more misunderstood by Americans than those which encompass the Fifth Amendment. From the old Red-baiting days through the postwar anti-racketeering era and the anti-war dissent period and the Watergate age, the myth has grown that justice and virtue have been continually frustrated by public enemies hiding behind the Fifth.

To the contrary, the history of the Fifth Amendment is the history of humankind's attempts to become civilized. In its origins it was a rejection of government tortue as a means of solving governmental problems. Today it is all that stands between a citizen and our government's unlimited right to ask questions and demand answers.

The Fifth Amendment serves as a declaration of our centuries-old American distrust of public officials. That this distrust has been well founded is especially evident now, when we are still recovering from overzealous governmental assaults on war protesters, black militants and political dissidents coupled with government-sponsored burglaries, illegal wiretaps and illegal mind control experiments, all committed in the name of law and order. . . . The right to silence has long been with us. It stands for human dignity and self-respect. It prevents the government from probing the secrets of our conversations or our innermost thoughts. Former Supreme Court Justice William O. Douglas once observed, "The crucial point is that the Constitution places the right of silence beyond the reach of government."

The Sixth Amendment

The Sixth Amendment establishes requirements for criminal trials. It guarantees the individual's right:

- *to have a speedy public trial by an impartial jury;*
- *to be informed of the nature and cause of the accusation;*
- *to be confronted with witnesses against him or her;*
- *to subpoena witnesses for defense;*
- *to have counsel for defense.*

In all criminal prosecutions, the accused shall enjoy the right to a speedy and public trial, by an impartial jury of the state and district wherein the crime shall have been committed, which districts shall have been previously ascertained by law, and to be informed of the nature and cause of the accusation; to be confronted with the witnesses against him; to have compulsory process for obtaining witnesses in his favor, and to have the assistance of counsel for his defense.

The right to speedy and public trial requires that the accused be brought to trial without unnecessary delay and that the trial be open to the public. Intentional or negligent delay has been grounds for dismissal of charges. The Supreme Court has ruled that delay in prosecution is not justified by the defendant's confinement on an earlier conviction; the defendant should be temporarily released for trial on the later charge.

The requirement that the jury have twelve members and that the twelve members must reach a unanimous verdict was derived from common law, not from the Constitution. The Supreme Court has ruled that state juries need not have twelve members and has approved state statutes that require only six. Moreover, the Court has ruled that jury verdicts in state courts need not necesssarily be unanimous.

The right to jury trial does not apply to trials for petty offenses, that is, those punishable by six months' confinement or less; examples are shoplifting or some traffic violations.

In all jury trials the jury members must be impartially selected. No one can be excluded from jury service because of race, class, or sex.

The Sixth Amendment requires that accused persons must be told how it is claimed they have broken the law so they can prepare their defense. The crime must be established by statute beforehand so all persons know it is illegal before they act. The statute must clearly inform people of the exact nature of the crime.

Genearlly, accused persons are entitled to have all witnesses against them present their evidence orally in court. Hearsay evidence cannot be used in federal criminal trials except in certain instances. Moreover, those accused are entitled to the court's aid in obtaining their witnesses. This is usually accomplished by **subpoena,** which orders into court as witnesses persons whose testimony is desired at the trial.

Finally, the Sixth Amendment provides a right to be represented by counsel. For many years this was interpreted to mean that defendants had a right to be represented by a lawyer only if they could afford one. The Supreme Court held in 1963, in *Gideon v. Wainwright,* however, that the amendment obligated the federal and state governments to provide legal counsel at public expense for those who could not afford it even for petty offenses if a jail sentence might result. The indigent have such a right at any "critical stage of the adjudicatory process," including the initial periods of questioning, police lineups, and all stages of the trial process.

In addition, indigents have the right to a free copy of their trial transcript for purposes of appeal of their conviction. Congress enacted the

Criminal Justice Acts of 1964 and 1970 to implement this right to counsel by establishing a federal defender system to represent those defendants who could not afford legal counsel. Most state legislatures have enacted similar measures.

The Supreme Court's first modern ruling on the right to counsel was *Powell v. Alabama* (1932), a case involving nine young black males, ages thirteen to twenty-one, charged with raping two white girls. The trial was held in Scottsboro, Alabama, where community sentiment was extremely hostile toward the defendants. Although the trial judge appointed a member of the local bar to serve as defense counsel, no attorney appeared on the day of the trial, so the judge appointed a local lawyer who reluctantly took the case. The defendants challenged their conviction on the grounds that they did not have a chance to consult with their lawyer or prepare a defense, and the Supreme Court concurred.

Another Supreme Court case seems to fly in the face of the Sixth Amendment right to a lawyer. That is the case of *Faretta v. California* (1975) in which the Supreme Court held that defendants could reject appointed counsel and could, instead, represent themselves. Justice Potter Steward stated: "It is one thing to hold that every defendant, rich or poor has the right to the assistance of counsel, and quite another to say that a state may compel a defendant to accept a lawyer he does not want."

Other important Supreme Court cases related to the Sixth Amendment include the following:

Right to a Speedy Trial

- *Klopfer v. North Carolina* (1967) held that the right to a speedy public trial applies to the states.
- *Barker v. Wingo* (1972) found that whether or not a defendant has been denied the right to a speedy trial must be determined by considering the length of delay, the reason for the delay, and any prejudice resulting from the delay.

Right to an Impartial Jury

- *Parker v. Gladden* (1966) stated that the right to trial by an impartial jury applies to the states.
- *Duncan v. Louisiana* (1968) held that the states are bound by the Sixth Amendment requirement of a jury trial in criminal cases but not in cases involving petty offenses.

Right to Confront Witnesses

- *Pointer v. Texas* (1965) found that the right to confront witnesses applies to the states.
- *Illinois v. Allen* (1970) stated that the Sixth Amendment right to be present during the trial can be lost by a defendant who, despite warnings, disrupts the trial.

Right to Counsel

- *Massiah v. United States* (1964) stated that an indicated person cannot be questioned or otherwise persuaded to make incriminating remarks without the presence of counsel.
- *United States v. Wade* (1967) found that an accused's right to counsel included having counsel present during a lineup identification because the suspect had been indicted and it was a critical stage in the prosecution.
- *Kirby v. Illinois* (1972) held that there is no right to counsel during a police lineup for identification if a suspect has not been formally charged with a crime.
- *Argersinger v. Hamlin* (1972) stated that no person can be imprisoned for any offense, even a misdemeanor, unless represented by counsel at trial, or unless this right was knowingly and intelligently waived.
- *United States v. Ash, Jr.* (1973) found that a suspect is not entitled to counsel during postindictment display of photographs used for identification.
- *Brewer v. Williams* (1977) reaffirmed the Massiah rule that once defendants are formally charged with a criminal offense, they have the right to have a lawyer present when being interrogated.
- *Scott v. Illinois* (1979) held that a state defendant has the right to a state-paid attorney, if necessary, only in cases that lead to imprisonment, not in all cases where imprisonment is possible.

The Eighth Amendment

Excessive bail shall not be required, nor excessive fines imposed, nor cruel and unusual punishments inflicted.

The Eighth Amendment forbids excessive bail, excessive fines, and cruel and unusual punishments.

Bail   Bail has traditionally meant payment by the accused of an amount of money, specified by the court based on the nature of the offense, to insure the presence of the accused at trial. An accused released from custody and subsequently failing to appear for trial forfeits bail to the court.

The Eighth Amendment does not specifically provide that all citizens have a right to bail, but only that bail will not be excessive. A right to bail has, however, been recognized in common law and in statute since 1791. In 1966 Congress enacted the *Bail Reform Act* to provide for pretrial release from imprisonment of indigent defendants who could not afford to post money for bail, and who were, in effect, confined only because of their poverty. The act also discouraged the traditional use of money bail by requiring the judge to seek other means as likely to insure that defendants would appear when their trial was held.

The leading Supreme Court decision on excessive bail is *Stack v. Boyle* (1951) in which twelve community leaders were indicted for conspiracy and bail was fixed at $50,000 per defendant. The defendants moved to reduce this amount on the ground that it was excessive, and the Supreme Court agreed. Chief Justice Fred M. Vinson stated that in the opinion of the Court:

> *This traditional right to freedom before conviction permits the unhampered preparation of a defense, and serves to prevent the infliction of punishment prior to conviction. . . . Unless this right to bail before trail is preserved, the presumption of innocence, secured only after centuries of struggle, would lose its meaning.*
>
> *The right of release before trial is conditioned upon the accused's giving adequate assurance that he will stand trial and submit to sentence if found guilty. . . . Bail set at a figure higher than an amount reasonably calculated to fulfill this purpose is "excessive" under the Eighth Amendment.*

The following spring, in *Carlson v. Landon* (1952), the Court held that the Eighth Amendment did not guarantee the right to bail.

Cruel and Unusual Punishment   Whether fines or periods of confinement are cruel and unusual must be determined by the facts of each particular case. Clearly excessive practices such as torture would be invalid. The Supreme Court has held the death penalty itself to be cruel and unusual in certain circumstances if it is not universally applied. This issue is discussed in chapter 21.

The clause also applied to punishment for a condition that the criminal had no power to change. For example, a law making narcotics addiction illegal was struck down by the Supreme Court as cruel and unusual since it punished a condition beyond the accused's control. Some courts have held laws punishing public drunkenness to be cruel and unusual when applied to homeless alcoholics, since they cannot usually avoid public places.

The Supreme Court has heard numerous cases concerning cruel and unusual punishment, including the following:

- *Furman v. Georgia* (1972) stated that the death penalty does violate the Eighth Amendment if the sentencing authority has the freedom to decide between the death penalty and a lesser penalty.
- *Gregg v. Georgia* (1976) held that the death penalty for murderers is not per se cruel and unusual punishment.
- *Proffitt v. Florida* (1976) reaffirmed the *Gregg* decision.
- *Jurek v. Texas* (1976) also reaffirmed the *Gregg* decision, refusing to declare the death penalty unconstitutional in all circumstances.
- *Roberts v. Louisiana* (1977) ruled that the statute requiring the death penalty for murdering a police officer engaged in performing

Gas Chamber

Guillotine

Military Execution

Electric Chair

These forms of execution were introduced to make capital punishment more humane.

his or her duty, with no consideration of mitigating circumstances, was unconstitutional.

- *Coker v. Georgia* (1977) stated that the death penalty for a person convicted of rape was cruel and unusual punishment.
- *Lockett v. Ohio* (1978) invalidated Ohio's death penalty for murder because it limited too strictly the factors that could be considered in the decision whether or not to impose the death penalty.

- *Rummel v. Estelle* (1980) rules that a mandatory life sentence required by a state habitual offender statue was not cruel and unusual punishment.

The Ninth Amendment

The enumeration in the Constitution of certain rights shall not be construed to deny or disparage others retained by the people.

The Ninth Amendment emphasizes the founding fathers' view that powers of government are limited by the rights of the people, and that it was not intended, by expressly guaranteeing in the Constitution certain rights of the people, to recognize that government had unlimited power to invade other rights of the people.

Griswold v. Connecticut (1965), a case involving the Ninth Amendment, addressed the issue of whether the right to privacy was a constitutional right, and, if so, whether the right was reserved to the people under the Ninth Amendment or was only derived from other rights specifically mentioned in the Constitution.

Courts have long recognized particular rights to privacy that are part of the First and Fourth Amendments. Thus, freedom of expression guarantees freedom of association and the related right to be silent and free from official inquiry into such associations. It also includes the right not to be intimidated by the government for expressing one's views. The Fourth Amendment's guarantee against unreasonable search and seizure confers a right to privacy because its safeguards prohibit unauthorized entry onto property and tampering with a citizen's possessions or property including his or her very person.

The Court in *Griswold* ruled that the Third and Fifth Amendments, in addition to the First and Fourth, created "zones of privacy" safe from governmental intrusion, and, without resting its decision upon any one of these or on the Ninth Amendment itself, simply held that the right of privacy was guaranteed by the Constitution.

The Tenth Amendment

The powers not delegated to the United States by the Constitution, nor prohibited by it to the states, are reserved to the states respectively, or to the people.

The Tenth Amendment embodies the principle of federalism, which reserves for the states the residue of powers not granted to the federal government or withheld from the states.

ADDITIONAL AMENDMENTS

Since the ratification of the first ten amendments (the Bill of Rights), other amendments have been passed.

The Thirteenth Amendment

Neither slavery nor involuntary servitude . . . shall exist within the United States or any place subject to their jurisdiction.

The Thirteenth Amendment abolished slavery.

Before the Civil War slaves were considered property. Article IV, Section 2 provided that slaves were to be counted as three-fifths of a person when determining representatives to the lower house of Congress (Klotter and Kanovitz 1985, p. 493). Even the Supreme Court placed its stamp of approval on slavery in the infamous Dred Scott decision (*Dred Scott v. Standford*, 1856). Chief Justice Taney proclaimed that the dark race as a class was inferior and altogether unfit to associate with the white race, either in social or political relations, and whether enslaved or emancipated, the Negro could not be a citizen (Klotter and Kanovitz 1985, p. 495).

After the Civil War, in 1865, the Thirteenth Amendment was enacted, emanicipating the slaves. According to Klotter and Kanovitz (1985, pp. 493—95):

> *Hostile Southern legislatures responded to the Thirteenth Amendment with the enactment of Black Codes which were designed to compel the newly freed slaves to return to the service of their former masters. . . . A period of racial turbulence and violent unrest followed as terrorist organizations like the Ku Klux Klan and the Knights of the White Camelia sprang up in numerous local communities.*

The Thirteenth Amendment was enacted after the Civil War, while Abraham Lincoln was president.

To protect the newly emancipated slaves, Congress ratified the Fourteenth Amendment. Klotter and Kanovitz (1985, pp. 493—95) suggest: "The immediate object of the Fourteenth Amendment was to protect the newly freed slaves from arbitrary and unequal treatment at the hands of hostile state and local government officials.

The Fourteenth Amendment

1. *All persons born or naturalized in the United States, and subject to the jurisdiction thereof, are citizens of the United States and of the state wherein they reside. No state shall make or enforce any law which shall abridge the privileges or immunities of citizens of the United States; nor shall any state deprive any person of life, liberty, or property without due process of law, nor deny to any person within its jurisdiction the equal protection of the laws. . . .*

* * *

5. *The Congress shall have power to enforce by appropriate legislation the provisions of this article.*

The Fourteenth Amendment requires each state to abide by the Constitution and the Bill of Rights. It guarantees due process and equal protection under the law.

Due Process   The Fourteenth Amendment limits the states' infringement upon the rights of individuals. The Bill of Rights does not specifically refer to actions by states but applies only to actions by the federal government.

Thus, state and local officers could proceed with an arrest without any concern for the rights of the accused. The Fourteenth Amendment, in essence, duplicates the Fifth Amendment, except it specifically orders state and local officers to provide the legal protections of due process.

Some important Supreme Court cases related to the Fourteenth Amendment include *Brown v. Mississippi* (1936), which stated that a criminal conviction based on a confession obtained by brutality was not admissible under the Fourteenth Amendment due process clause. In *Gideon v. Wainwright* (1963) the Court held that the Fourteenth Amendment requires states to provide indigent defendants with counsel in criminal cases, whether the offense is capital or noncapital. Finally, *Malloy v. Hogan* (1964) found that the Fourteenth Amendment gives state prosecutors the same privileges against self-incrimination as provided to federal prosecutors under the Fifth Amendment.

Equal Protection   The Fourteenth Amendment also prohibits denial of the "equal protection of the laws." A state cannot make unreasonable, arbitrary distinctions between different persons as to their rights and

The Bill of Rights as originally proposed contained 12 amendments to the Constitution.

privileges. Since "all people are created equal," no law could deny red-haired men the right to drive an automobile, although it can deny minors the right to drive. The state can make reasonable classifications; however, classifications such as those based on race, religion, and national origin have been held to be unreasonable. Thus, racial segregation in public schools and other public places, laws that prohibit sale or use of property to certain races or minority groups, and laws prohibiting interracial marriage have been struck down.

The Supreme Court has further held that purely private acts of discrimination violate the equal protection clause if such acts are customarily enforced throughout the state, whether or not there is a specific law or other explicit manifestation of action by the state.

The equal protection clause also means that citizens may not arbitrarily be deprived of their right to vote, and that every citizen's vote must be given equal weight. Therefore, state legislatures and local governments must be apportioned strictly in terms of their populations in a way that accords one person one vote.

POLICE POWER

Without means of enforcement, the great body of federal, state, municipal, and common law would be empty and meaningless. Recall that the term *law* implies not only the rule but also enforcement of that rule. It has been said: "Common to all forms of society are the requisites of authority and power. *Authority* is the right to direct and command. *Power* is the force by means of which others can be obliged to obey" (Germann, Day, and Gallati 1972, p. 9).

Police power is a term used to describe the power of the federal, state, or municipal governments to pass laws regulating private interests, to protect the health and safety of the people, to prevent fraud and oppression, and to promote public convenience, prosperity, and welfare.

Police power is derived from the United States Constitution, United States Supreme Court decisions, federal statutes, state constitutions, state statutes, state court decisions, and various municipal charters and ordinances.

Section 5 of the Fourteenth Amendment provides the authority for much of the civil rights legislation passed by Congress in the 1960s.

Police power was defined by the United States Supreme Court in 1887 as "embracing no more than the power to promote public health, morals, and safety" *(Mugler v. Kansas)*. Others have defined police power as the force used by the state to preserve the general health, safety, welfare, and morals.

For example, narcotics laws are passed to preserve the people's health. Individuals who abuse narcotics or drugs by taking them without medical prescription and in proper dosage jeopardize their own mental and physical health. Traffic laws are passed to preserve the general safety and to make the highways safe for the motoring public. Gambling laws are passed by the legislature to protect the individual and the family from financial loss. Likewise, juvenile laws are passed to protect juveniles from parents, guardians, relatives, or other people who would place the youths' physical and mental welfare in danger. Finally, legislation prohibiting prostitution and obscenity is passed to protect the public's morals.

All levels of government grant their legislative branches the right and power to make laws. The executive branches of government are created to enforce these laws, while the judicial branches interpret what the laws mean and how they are to be enforced.

The police power of the federal government is based on authority granted by the United States Constitution. The general grants of power, such as the power of Congress, the legislative branch of government, to provide for the general welfare of the United States by law, are restricted by other provisions of the Constitution taken from the English Bill of Rights or from the political experience of England and America.

The police power of the states is delegated to them by the federal government in the Bill of Rights. The Tenth Amendment of our Bill of Rights gives the states those powers not delegated to the federal government. Since the power to organize police forces is not delegated to the federal government, this authority is given to the individual states and their subdivisions, that is, their cities, counties, and townships. Therefore, police power ultimately rests with the people, since their elected representatives create the laws that the police enforce.

Because each state is responsible for its citizens' health, safety, and general well-being, the usual procedure has been to assign these functions to municipal police departments in the cities and to sheriffs and constables in the rural areas of the state. Within the limits established by state constitutions, state legislatures may define the powers and duties of police officers in the state. However, police officers' authority and powers cannot conflict with the provisions in the Fourteenth Amendment of the Constitution, which guarantees citizens equal protection by due process of law. Therefore, police officers can exercise only the powers and authority specifically granted by legislative enactment.

The authority, powers, duties, and limits of the police officer are usually determined by each state for all police officers—state, municipal, and rural. Most states fulfill their responsibilities for preserving the public peace, detecting and arresting offenders, and enforcing the law by giving cities the authority to appoint municipal police officers. Although these municipal officers are concerned with enforcing city ordinances, enforcing state statutes is their most important job.

Police authority and power are broad in scope and include maintaining the peace, licensing trades and professions, regulating public

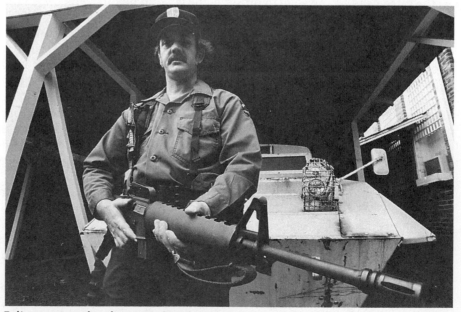

Police power and authority are broad in scope.

service corporations' rates, and enforcing health regulations such as quarantines, compulsory vaccinations, and segregation of people with contagious diseases. State laws and judicial decisions also determine the civil and criminal liability of police officers who step beyond their legal powers in discharging the duties of their office.

Although the state legislature passes laws, the courts, the judicial branch of government, decide the purpose and character of the statutes as well as whether or not these statutes conflict with the Constitution or are contrary to proper public policy. Since the courts continuously review laws, police authority and power cannot easily be corrupted or controlled by private interests.

The courts determine what police authority and power is appropriate. Acceptable police power requires that the regulations are (1) reasonable, (2) within the power given to the states by the Constitution, and (3) in accord with due process of law.

Police power is restricted by the Constitution, by the Fourteenth Amendment, and by the courts.

PRINCIPLE VERSUS PRACTICE

There is a vast difference between stating ideals and goals and achieving them. Our Constitution and the Bill of Rights were written on the premise that all people would obey the law. Time has shown that this is not always true. The ideals set forth in our Declaration of Independence, our Constitution, and our Bill of Rights have not been achieved automatically.

Civil rights and civil liberties must be consciously and actively sought and protected if the documents on which our government is founded are to be more than elegant words. Laws and institutions must parallel our goals and ideals of liberty, freedom, equality, justice, human dignity, individual self-determination, freedom from tyranny, and freedom of conscience.

These goals have motivated Americans since they first came to the New World. These same goals carried American pioneers west, looking for a new life, a Utopia. These goals have led men and women of all races and creeds, from all parts of the country, to invest tremendous energy in the civil rights movement, to risk their lives confronting violently irate traditionalists, in an effort to obtain new levels of human decency and equality and new levels of freedom and justice for millions of Americans who belong to minority groups.

In many respects the history of civil rights and civil liberties in the United States has been a fight for the attainment of the abstract values that our nation claims it is committed to achieving.

The history of civil rights and civil liberties is not simply struggle, confrontation, marching, picketing, and demanding; it is holding the government responsible for the principles that are its central purpose for existence. From the beginning, our institutions, our statutes, and our legal process were means to obtain fundamental civil liberties central to the American purpose: freedom of speech, freedom of the press, freedom of assembly, freedom of religion, due process of law, the right to privacy, the right to a fair trial, the right to vote and have that vote counted fairly, and the right to equal opportunity, education, housing, and employment.

The history of civil rights and civil liberties has been dynamic, reflecting constant change as new challenges emerged in the shift from a simple, homogenous, agrarian, rural society to an advanced, highly complex, industrial, urban society. Although our principles have remained the same, our institutions and laws have continually changed. Thomas Jefferson recognized the necessity for such change in a letter he wrote in the nineteenth century:

> I am certainly not an advocate for frequent and untried changes in laws and constitutions. I think that moderate imperfections had better be born with because we accommodate ourselves to them and find practical means to correct their ill effects, but I know also that laws and institutions must go hand in hand with the progress of the human mind, as that becomes more developed, as more discoveries are made, new truths disclosed, and manners and opinions change with the changing circumstances, institutions must advance also, and keep pace with the times. We might as well require a man to wear still the coat which fitted him as a boy as civilized society to remain ever under the regiment of their barbarous ancestors.

Our institutions and laws must change as our society changes.

The history of civil liberties has not always been a pleasant one, nor does it show Americans in their best light. It is painfully clear in American history that at certain times and under certain circumstances individuals and groups have been deprived of their liberties and denied fundamental freedoms under the rationalization that such denial was in the public interest.

Granted, liberty is not license; if an individual abuses freedom, takes advantage of society, corrupts justice, or poses a threat to law and order, society has the right to take action on its own behalf. The problem is to know when and where to draw that line. When have the limits of freedom been exceeded? Conversely, when have the essential social controls of free society been imposed too arbitrarily? Does the majority have the right to temporarily suspend the rights of the minority in order to preserve liberty?

Examples of attempts to suspend the rights of members of minority groups are, unfortunately, recurrent in our history. Aliens, for example, have faced this problem since the Alien and Sedition Acts of 1798. In the turbulent years of the 1840s, Catholic immigrants were often treated with intolerance and as second-class citizens. The lack of equality in the treatment of native Americans, slaves, free blacks following the Civil War, and women is also evident in the treatment of labor agitators and political and economic radicals with allegedly dangerous ideas. Pacifists and conscientious objectors encounter great difficulties during war years. And we have had not only arguments, but also public policy, that calls for placing American Communists in a deprived legal status.

The treatment of the Japanese-Americans during World War II is an example of the complexity of civil rights and civil liberties. After the attack on Pearl Harbor many Americans honestly believed the Japanese-Americans posed a serious national threat. Some 110,000 Japanese, the majority of whom were American-born citizens, were forced by government order to sell their homes and businesses and were herded into temporary barracks (internment camps).

Although at the time it was claimed that Japanese-Americans were a threat to national security, if one group of citizens can be so treated during a period of national emergency, a precedent is created that should disturb every American. From the standpoint of civil liberties, the episode has

A military policeman supervises the transport of Japanese-Americans to a relocation center during World War II.

long-range implications, for the denial of one individual's rights is a direct threat to the rights of all Americans.

In the 1930s the United States Supreme Court began to question whether justice was being attained for large numbers of Americans as a result of the federal policy of keeping "hands off" local law enforcement. After careful examination, begun in 1932 and continuing for forty years, it was gradually and consistently concluded that local justice was *not* true justice. Often local courts offered no true justice for a black person in the South. Likewise, there was often little justice for a stranger accused of a crime in a community. Local standards were often biased, prejudiced, and intolerant. Therefore, the Court came to insist that uniform national standards be applied in local courts and in police procedures. The Supreme Court, charged with interpreting our laws, established uniform national standards to be applied to local justice.

Unfortunately, however, value systems such as prejudices and resistance to change cannot be legislated out of existence

SUMMARY

Just as our current methods of enforcing the laws have slowly evolved, so have the laws themselves. In the beginning most laws were set by a ruler or were moral or social laws, enforced by social pressure. This was followed by common law—law based on precedent. In the United States common law became known as case law. Statutory law has replaced most common and case law. Statutory law consists of laws passed by federal and state legislatures regarding both constitutional and nonconstitutional (ordinary) matters.

The history of civil rights and civil liberties reflects our values, national purpose, the American experience with government, and the need for flexibility within stability. If the fundamental values of our society are to be preserved and extended, citizens must understand and support those institutions and statutes that, in practice, reflect the principles set forth in the Declaration of Independence, the Constitution, and the Bill of Rights.

These documents established not only each citizen's civil liberties—freedom from government oppression—but also each citizen's civil rights—claims to affirmative assistance from the government.

To achieve the goals set forth in the Declaration of Independence, the United States Constitution was drafted, the basic instrument of our government and the supreme law of the land, which was signed in 1789.

Some states refused to ratify the Constitution if it did not contain personal guarantees. Ten amendments to the Constitution containing such guarantees were passed in 1791 and became known as the Bill of Rights. The Bill of Rights protects a person's right to "life, liberty, and the pursuit of happiness" and forbids the government to violate these rights:

- The First Amendment guarantees freedom of religion, freedom of speech, freedom of the press, and freedom of assembly and petition.

- The Second Amendment guarantees the right to bear arms.
- The Fourth Amendment forbids unreasonable searches and sei-zures and requires probable cause.
- The Fifth Amendment guarantees due process and just compen-sation when private property is acquired for public use; it prohib-its double jeopardy and self-incrimination.
- The Sixth Amendment guarantees the individual's rights in a criminal trial.
- The Eighth Amendment forbids execessive bail, excessive fines, and cruel and unusual punishments.

Since the Fifth Amendment was directed to federal officials, an additional amendment was later ratified, the Fourteenth Amendment, which requires each state and locality to abide by the Constitution and the Bill of Rights.

Without means of enforcement, the great body of federal, state, and municipal law would be meaningless. To ensure enforcement, police have been given power and authority from local, state, and federal sources; but they are also restricted in their use of this power by the Constitution, the Fourteenth Amendment, and the courts. They have the power to enforce the laws so long as they do not violate the civil rights and liberties of any individual.

Although the principles of civil rights and civil liberties do not always prevail in practice, they remain the cornerstone of our democracy and our American creed. These principles directly affect how law enforcement officers fulfill their responsibilities. In addition, as our society changes, our institutions and laws must change accordingly.

Discussion Questions

1. What specific restrictions are placed on the police officer by the Bill of Rights?

2. Why has the Supreme Court said that state and federal governments can pass laws against carrying weapons when the Second Amendment specifically guarantees the right to bear arms?

3. Why were black people considered "unequal" until Lincoln was president? The Constitution existed; why did it not apply to black people?

4. What is the basic difference between civil rights and civil liberties?

5. In what well-known cases has the Fifth Amendment been repeatedly used?

6. What does police power and authority consist of?

7. The Declaration of Independence states that all people are created equal. Does this mean all people have the same opportunities?

8. Why is the general public so adamant about upholding the rights stated in the Fifth Amendment?

9. Should we do away with the jury system and replace it with a panel of professional judges to determine guilt or innocence in a trial?

10. Should Fourth Amendment rights be extended to include general searches?

0

References

Creamer, J. S. *The Law of Arrest, Search and Seizure*, 3d ed. New York: Holt Rinehart & Winston, 1980.

Ferguson, R. W., and Stokke, A. H. *Concepts of Criminal Law*. Boston: Holbrook Press, 1976.

Folley, V. L. *American Law Enforcement*. Boston: Allyn & Bacon, 1980.

Germann, A. C.; Day, F. D.; and Gallati, R. B. *Introduction to Law Enforcement and Criminal Justice*. Springfield, Ill.: Charles C. Thomas, 1972.

"Handgun Facts." A pamphlet distributed by Handgun Control, Inc. (n.d.).

Klein, I. J. *Constitutional Law for Criminal Justice Professionals*. North Scituate, Mass.: Duxbury Press, 1980.

Klotter, J. C., and Kanovitz, J. R. *Constitutional Law*, 5th ed. Cincinnati, Ohio: Anderson Publishing, 1985.

Lewis, P. W., and Peoples, K. D. *The Supreme Court and the Criminal Process: Cases and Comments*. Philadelphia: W. B. Saunders, 1978.

Myrdal, G. *The American Dilemma*. New York: Harper & Brothers, 1944.

Pritchett, C. H. *The American Constitution*. New York: McGraw-Hill, 1977.

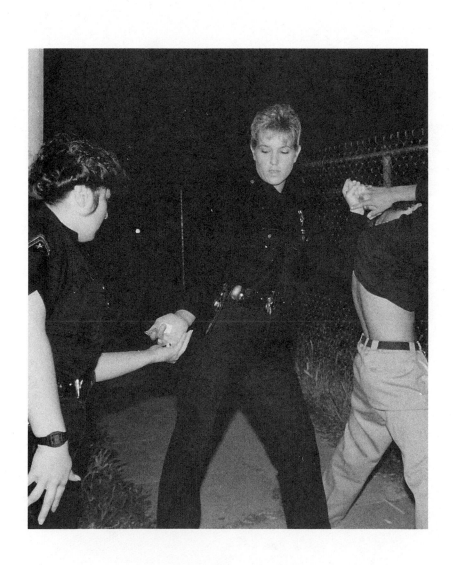

Criminal and Civil Offenses: An Important Distinction for Law Enforcement

There is no man so good, who, were he to submit all his thoughts and actions to the laws would not deserve hanging ten times in his life.—Montaigne

DO YOU KNOW

What criminal law does?

The difference between a felony and a misdemeanor?

How crime is defined?

What is usually necessary to prove that a crime has been committed?

What strict liability crimes are?

What the eight Index Crimes are?

How to define the following violent crimes against persons: murder, assault, rape, and robbery?

How to define the following crimes against property: burglary, larceny/theft, motor vehicle theft, and arson?

What civil law refers to?

What a tort is?

What the basic differences are between a crime and a tort?

What Section 1983 of the United States Code stipulates?

Introduction

Chapter 4

To assure each United States citizen the right to "life, liberty, and the pursuit of happiness," society has established laws that all are expected to obey. In chapter 3 you were introduced to the supreme law of the land—the United States Constitution and its Bill of Rights.

Beyond that, however, each city, state, and the federal government has continued to pass laws governing citizen behavior. Our system of laws is extremely complex and may be classified as follows:

- *Type*— written or common law
- *Source*—constitutional, statutory, case
- *Parties involved*—public, private
- *Offense*—criminal, civil

The criminal/civil distinction is of most interest to law enforcement officers, for they must learn to deal with those who break criminal laws but at the same time not violate the "criminal's" civil rights. Officers who do not deal legally with criminal matters may find themselves the target of a civil lawsuit.

In addition, it is important that law enforcement officers be able to tell the difference between a criminal and a civil offense because they are responsible for investigating only criminal matters. Civil offenses are not within their jurisdiction.

Consider first criminal law and its importance for police officers.

CRIMINAL LAW

Criminal law defines crimes and fixes punishment for them. Criminal law includes rules and procedures for investigating crimes and prosecuting criminals; regulations governing the constitution of courts and the conduct of trials; and the administration of penal institutions.

American criminal law has a number of unique features. In establishing criminal law, the federal government and each state government are sovereign within the limits of their authority as defined by the Constitution. Therefore, criminal law varies from state to state. Although there are many differences, most of them have a tradition derived from English common law. There is no federal common law jurisdiction in criminal cases, however (*United States v. Hudson*, 1812).

Criminal law defines crimes and fixes punishments for them.

The statutes that define what acts constitute social harm are called substantive criminal law, for example, a statute defining homicide. A substantive criminal law not only defines the offense but also states the punishment. The omission of the punishment invalidates the criminal law.

In most countries crimes and punishments are expressed in statutes. Punishments include removal from public office, fines, exile, imprisonment, and death. Unless the act of which a defendant is accused is expressly defined by statute as a crime, no indictment or conviction for the commission of the act is legal. This provision is important in establishing the difference between government by law and arbitrary dictatorial government.

Criminal law in the United States generally defines seven classes of crimes. It includes offenses against (1) international law, (2) the dispensation of justice and the legitimate exercise of governmental authority, (3) the public peace, (4) property, (5) trade, (6) public decency, and (7) persons.

And, like English law, American criminal law also classifies crimes with respect to their gravity as treason, felonies, and misdemeanors. **Felony** refers to serious crimes, generally those punishable by death or by imprisonment for more than one year in a state prison or penitentiary. The court may inflict a lesser punishment. **Misdemeanor** is a term applied to any minor offense, generally punishable by a fine or a short imprisonment, usually not to exceed one year, in a jail or workhouse.

No crime is a felony unless made so by statute, or unless it is a felony under common law. Formerly a felony was a crime punishable by forfeiture of the criminal's lands, or goods, or both. In addition, other punishment might be added, according to the degree of guilt. In England for a long time most felonies were punishable by death.

Felony refers to serious crimes, generally those punishable by death or by imprisonment for more than one year in a state prison or penitentiary. The court may inflict a lesser punishment.

The criminal codes of the states vary in their classification of offenses that are considered misdemeanors. Examples of crimes usually defined as misdemeanors include libel, assault and battery, malicious mischief, and petty theft.

Misdemeanor is a term applied to any minor offense, generally punishable by a fine or a short term, usually not to exceed one year, in a jail or workhouse.

In some states the distinction between felonies and misdemeanors is practically discarded, the punishment for each particular crime being prescribed by statute.

The same situation existed under common law. Although under common law a crime was generally classified as treason, felony, or misdemeanor, many offenses could not be defined exactly, so the rule was adopted that any immoral act harmful to the community was, in itself, a crime, punishable by the courts. Crimes were classified as *mala in se* (bad in itself), based to a large degree on religious doctrine, or as *mala prohibita* (bad because it is forbidden). A *mala in se* crime is one that is so offensive that it is obviously criminal, for example, murder or rape. A *mala prohibita* crime is one that violates a specific regulatory statute, for example, certain traffic violations. These would not usually be considered crimes if no law prohibited them.

A CLOSE-UP ON CRIME—WHAT MUST BE PROVEN

Haskell and Yablonsky (1983, p. *ix*) suggest that "crime exists in all societies. Wherever there are laws or moral prescriptions for behavior, there is always a segment of society that will violate these norms."

The Bureau of Justice Statistics (U.S. Department of Justice 1983, p. 2) defines **crime** as follows: "We define crime as all behaviors and acts for which a society provides formally sanctioned punishment." Crimes are made so by law. State and federal statutes define each crime, the elements involved, and the penalty attached to each.

Crime is defined as any prohibited behavior for which society sanctions a punishment.

Sutherland and Cressey (1978, pp. 12–14) have summarized seven interrelated and overlapping characteristics of crime delineated by Jerome Hall:

1. *A crime has certain external consequences called a harm. Crime has a harmful impact on social interests; mere intention without resulting in such a harm is not a crime.*
2. *The harm must be specifically outlawed in advance.*
3. *Conduct must occur, either intentional or reckless action or inaction, to bring about the harmful consequences.*
4. ***Criminal intent** must be present. Criminal intent must not be confused with motivation. The motive might be "good," but if the intention is to perform an act specifically outlawed, it is still a crime. For example, if a person steals from the rich to give to the poor, his motives are "good," but his intention is still wrong.*
5. *The criminal intent and conduct must be related. For example, a salesperson who enters a home on business and then decides to steal something cannot be charged with breaking and entering.*

6. *A causal relation must exist between the outlawed harm and the intentional act. For example, if a person shoots someone and the victim suffocates while in the hospital recovering from the wound, the causal relation is not clearcut.*
7. *The punishment must be legally prescribed; the action must be punishable by law.*

Another way of looking at crime is presented by Samaha (1983, p. 34), who suggests: "Every crime for which a law has been passed and punishment spelled out is comprised of several essential ingredients called *material elements.*" The five principal material elements are as follows:

- The actual act (*actus reus*—the forbidden act)
- The mental state of mind (*mens rea*—the guilty mind)
- Concurrence—the act and mental state occurring at the same time
- Harmful result
- Surrounding circumstances

All of these most be proven beyond a reasonable doubt for a person to be convicted of a crime.

Law enforcement officers are most responsible for proving that the actual act occurred—establishing the elements of a specific crime, which will be discussed shortly.

Much more difficult to establish is the mental state of the suspect. Gardner (1985 p. 34) suggests that the "mental requirement of criminal intent is embodied in criminal statutes in the following degrees: intentionally (the highest degree of mental fault), knowingly, recklessly, negligently." According to Gardner, "The U.S. Supreme Court has never drafted and announced a doctrine requiring proof of *mens rea* in all crimes . . . therefore, the states are free to create criminal laws that do not require proof of *mens rea* or to create criminal laws requiring different degrees of mental fault or mental guilt." Further, as Gardner notes, "A criminal intent without a criminal act is no crime. . . . To prove a true crime the state must show that the external physical act and the internal mental state essential to that crime occurred at the same time."

When criminal intent *is* an essential element of a crime, it is up to the state to prove it. How law enforcement officers can assist in this is discussed in chapter 10.

To prove a crime has been committed the following are usually necessary:
- *Prove the act itself (actus reus)—the elements of the crime.*
- *Prove the criminal mental state (mens rea)—intent to do wrong.*

In some crimes intent is not an element. These are known as *strict liability crimes*. These offenses generally involve traffic violations, liquor violations, and hunting violations. Individuals who break traffic, liquor, and hunting laws are not considered "criminals," and the penalties involved are usually less.

In strict liability crimes such as violations of traffic codes, hunting regulations, and liquor laws, the defendant is liable regardless of his or her state of mind when the act was committed.

As Gardner (1985 p. 41) notes:

> *A bartender cannot ordinarily use as a defense the fact that the person to whom he sold liquor looked twenty-two when in fact the person was only seventeen. The driver of an overweight truck cannot argue that the company scales were faulty; nor can an adult male, in most, if not all, states, argue that he did not know the age of the fifteen-year-old girl with whom he had sexual intercourse.*

Nor can the speeder claim ignorance of the posted speed limit or claim a faulty speedometer. Intent is not at issue—only the speed.

Intent is *not* to be confused with *motive*. Your motive for doing something is your *reason*. Motive is not an element of any crime, but it can help to establish intent. If police officers can show why a suspect would benefit from committing a certain act, this greatly strengthens the case. Gardner (1985, p. 40) illustrates that "the mother who kills her imbecile and suffering child out of motives of compassion is just as guilty of murder as is the man who kills for gain, since each intentionally takes another human life. Although motive is not relevant to the issue of guilt or innocence, it can be a factor in sentencing."

Another element of a crime that must sometimes be proven is *scienter*. Scienter is a "degree of knowledge that makes an individual legally responsible for the consequences of his or her acts" (Gardner 1985, p. 37). In other words, the person committing the act knew that it was a crime. For example, to be guilty of harboring a felon, the person harboring the felon has to know the person *is* a felon. Or the person who buys stolen property has to know that the property is, indeed, stolen.

Crimes can be categorized in many different ways. You have already seen one such classification—a criminal act can be either a misdemeanor or a felony. Another common classification is to differentiate between violent crimes or crimes against persons and property crimes. Crimes against persons include homicide, rape, assault, and robbery—actions that involve the use of force or the threat of force against a person. In contrast, property crimes do not involve such force. They include larceny, burglary, motor vehicle theft, and arson.

SOURCES OF INFORMATION ON CRIME

The major source of information of criminal activity has traditionally been the FBI's Uniform Crime Reporting Program. Based on information provided by local and state law enforcement programs, the bureau estimates the total number of certain "index offenses" known to law enforcement agencies.

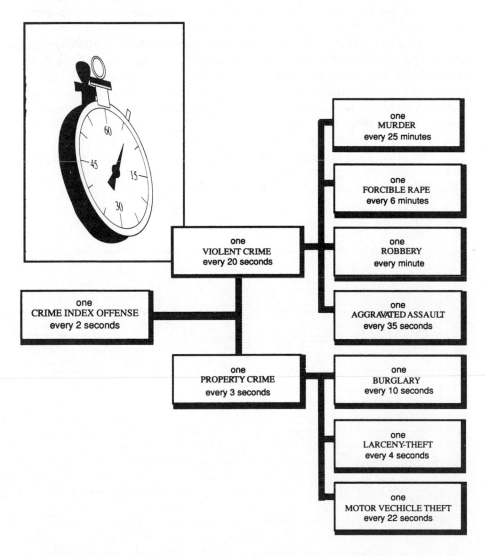

The crime clock should be viewed with care. Being the most aggregate representation of UCR data, it is designed to convey the annual reported crime experience by showing the relative frequency of occurrence of the Index Offenses. This mode of display should not be taken to imply a regularity in the commission of the Part I Offenses; rather, it represents the annual ratio of crime to fixed time intervals.

Source: FBI Uniform Crime Reports

Figure 4–1   Crime Clock 1988

Yearly publications titled *Crime in the United States* contain the results of this process together with a crime index. This index takes into consideration crime rates per 100,000 persons.

As noted by Nettler (1978, p. 55): "The most popular measure of crime is official statistics of offenses 'known to the police.' . . . Crimes known to the police are themselves a result of social processing. . . . Complaints to the police are subject to errors that result from mistakes and from lies." In addition, "Official statistics on crime are imperfect not only because of what is and is not included but also because of imperfections in those who do the counting" (Nettler 1978, p. 63).

This point is reiterated by the Brantinghams (1984, p. 56): "Criminal justice statistics do not enumerate all crimes. They enumerate only those crimes made known to the criminal justice system. A substantial number of crimes are never reported to the police or any other agent of criminal justice. The true number of crimes, called the dark figure of criminality, is unknown." In spite of these difficulties, police departments do make frequent use of the information from the Uniform Crime Reports.

The Uniform Crime Reports divide crimes into Part I and Part II crimes, with Part I crimes being those that are most serious in terms of either their use of violence or the value of the property involved.

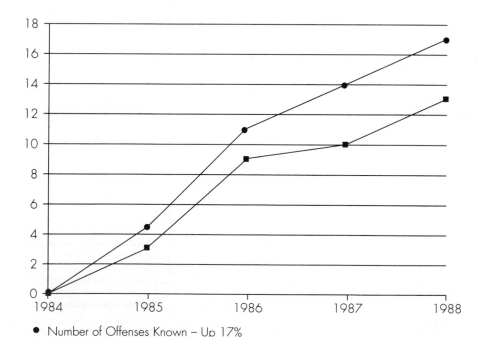

● Number of Offenses Known – Up 17%
■ Rate per 100,000 Inhabitants – Up 13%

Source: FBI Uniform Crime Reports

Figure 4—2   Crime Index Total

The eight Part I crimes are (1) murder, (2) aggravated assault causing serious bodily harm, (3) forcible rape, (4) robbery, (5) burglary, (6) larceny/theft, (7) motor vehicle theft, and (8) arson.

Table 4–1 Number of Crimes and Police Officers per 1,000 Population in Selected Cities

Officers per 1,000 pop.	1987	1980	1971
Atlanta	3.13	2.89	2.32
Cincinnati	2.38	2.60	2.11
Denver	2.59	2.85	2.34
Houston	2.55	1.90	1.59
Kansas City	2.50	2.65	2.36
Milwaukee	3.20	3.22	2.87
Minneapolis	2.03	1.93	1.87
Philadelphia	4.06	4.43	3.75
Phoenix	1.93	2.10	1.77
San Francisco	2.44	2.58	2.76
Seattle	2.27	2.11	2.27
St. Louis	3.54	4.33	3.58
St. Paul	1.92	2.06	1.62
U.S. big cities avg.	2.8	2.7	2.9*
Midwest big cities*	3.3	3.3	3.4

Crimes per 1,000 pop.	1987	1980	1971
Atlanta	156	141	60
Cincinnati	73	86	46
Denver	91	120	73
Houston	94	89	48
Kansas City	119	110	55
Milwaukee	83	65	30
Minneapolis	126	97	56
Philadelphia	57	60	30
Phoenix	90	115	51
San Francisco	75	104	82
Seattle	148	108	51
St. Louis	127	143	71
St. Paul	80	82	47

Crimes included are murder, non-negligent manslaughter, forcible rape, robbery, aggravated assault, burglary, larceny theft and motor-vehicle theft. Although these figures are called uniform, there is some variation in record-keeping from city to city. Many factors other than policing affect levels of crime, so these figures should be used to see trends rather than for direct comparison.
*All U.S. cities over 250,000 population.
*Midwest cities over 250,000 in North and South Dakota, Nebraska, Kansas, Missouri, Iowa, Minnesota, Wisconsin, Illinois, Indiana, Michigan and Ohio.
Source: FBI Uniform Crime Reports

Another source of data compiled every two years that interests the general public as well as criminal justice researchers and educators is the Bureau of Justice Statistics (BJS) document, *Report to the Nation on Crime and Justice.* This document brings together a wide range of data from the BJS's own statistical series, FBI Uniform Crime Reports, the Bureau of the Census, the National Institute of Justice, the Office of Juvenile Delinquency Prevention, and many other research and reference sources. The report presents national data on crime and the criminal justice system and answers questions such as the following:

- How much crime is there?
- Whom does it strike?
- When?
- Where?
- Who is the typical offender?
- What is the government's response to crime?
- How differently are juveniles handled from adults?
- What are the costs of justice and who pays?

Data from both the Uniform Crime Reports and those of the BJS will be used throughout this text.

Figure 4.3 illustrates the types of data collected by the BJS that would not be found in the Uniform Crime Reports.

Now turn your attention to the specific crimes law enforcement officers must deal with. Remember, however, that since definitions of crimes and their penalties vary considerably on the local, county, state, and federal levels, law enforcement officers must be familiar with their area's criminal statutes and ordinances. These statutes and ordinances list specific conditions, called the *elements of the crime*, that must occur for an act to be called a specific kind of crime.

Knowing these elements is essential to a firm base in *substantive* criminal law. Later in the book you will look at *procedural* criminal law—how to lawfully carry out the responsibilities of law enforcement officers. For now, however, concentrate on recognizing the elements of each crime, which is essential to gathering evidence to prove that a crime has, in fact, been committed.

CRIMES AGAINST PERSONS—VIOLENT CRIMES

Murder (Homicide)

Murder is defined in the Uniform Crime Reporting Program as the willful killing of another person. Deaths caused by negligence, suicide, accident, justifiable homicide, attempts to murder or assaults to murder are *not* included.

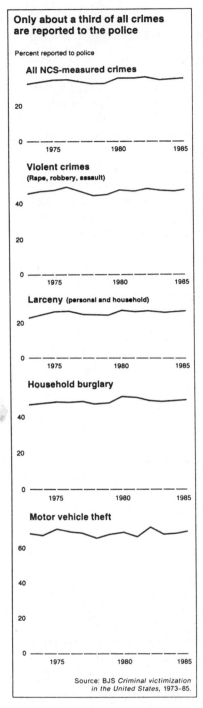

Only about a third of all crimes are reported to the police

Percent reported to police

All NCS-measured crimes

Violent crimes
(Rape, robbery, assault)

Larceny (personal and household)

Household burglary

Motor vehicle theft

Source: BJS *Criminal victimization in the United States,* 1973–85.

The extent to which crime is reported to police has only become known in the past decade

It has long been known that many crimes escape the attention of the police, but it was only with victimization surveys that systematic data were collected on crimes that are not reported—the so-called "dark figure" of crime.

Since 1973 the National Crime Survey has provided yearly findings on the extent to which crimes are reported to the police, the characteristics of crimes that are and are not reported, and the reasons for not reporting.

The decision to report a crime is often based on its seriousness

In 1983 the rate of reporting to the police was higher for—
• violent crimes than for personal crimes of theft (48% vs. 26%)
• female than for male victims of violent crimes (53% vs. 45%)
• older than for younger victims (38% of those 65 or older vs. 22% of those 12–19).

Reporting rates for motor vehicle theft were higher than for burglary and for household larceny

In 1983 the rates of reporting to the police were—
• 69% for motor vehicle theft
• 49% for household burglary
• 25% for household larceny.

Only minor differences occurred in the rates at which whites and blacks reported these three household crimes.

The highest income group was more likely than the lowest income group to report household crimes

	Under $10,000	$30,000 and over
Household burglary	41%	57%
Household larceny	20	29
Motor vehicle theft	62	68

Source: *Reporting crimes to the police,* BJS Special Report, December 1985

Thefts resulting in large losses and serious violent crimes with injury are most likely to be reported to the police

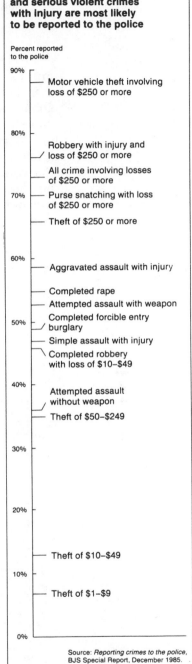

Percent reported to the police

— Motor vehicle theft involving loss of $250 or more

— Robbery with injury and loss of $250 or more
— All crime involving losses of $250 or more
— Purse snatching with loss of $250 or more
— Theft of $250 or more

— Aggravated assault with injury

— Completed rape
— Attempted assault with weapon
— Completed forcible entry burglary
— Simple assault with injury
— Completed robbery with loss of $10–$49

— Attempted assault without weapon
— Theft of $50–$249

— Theft of $10–$49

— Theft of $1–$9

Source: *Reporting crimes to the police,* BJS Special Report, December 1985.

Source: *Report to the Nation on Crime and Justice,* March 1988, pp. 34 and 35.

Figure 4–3   **Most Crimes Are Not Reported to the Police**

Murder (homicide) is the willful killing of a human by another human.

The generally recognized levels of homicide are (1) first-degree murder, (2) second-degree murder, (3) manslaughter (or nonnegligent manslaughter), and (4) negligent homicide. The first three categories, considered to be willful acts, are classified as felonies. Negligent homicide, however, is usually considered a misdemeanor.

First-degree murder is willful, deliberate, and *premeditated* (planned) taking of another person's life. A homicide that occurs during the commission or attempted commission of arson, robbery, rape, or burglary is also usually classified as first-degree murder, even though it was not willful, deliberate, or premeditated. The question of premeditation is always left up to the jury.

Second-degree murder is murder that is *not* premeditated but the intent to kill is present. The charge of murder in the second degree or manslaughter often results from killings that do not involve weapons.

Manslaughter is differentiated from murder in that the element of malice is absent, that is, the death was accidental; there was no original intent, hatred, ill will, or disregard for the lives of others. In many states

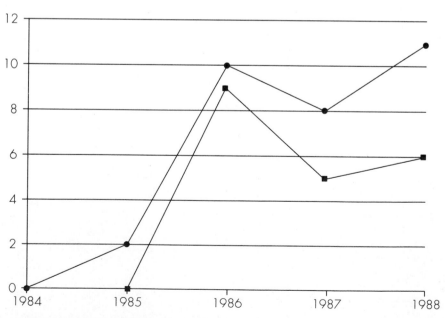

● Number of Offenses Known – Up 11%

■ Rate per 100,000 Inhabitants – Up 6%

Source: FBI Uniform Crime Reports

Figure 4–4   **Murder**

manslaughter is classified as either voluntary or involuntary. *Involuntary* manslaughter involves killing someone while doing some lawful act negligently or while negligently failing to perform some legal duty. Many deaths resulting from automobile accidents are classified as involuntary manslaughter. If there is no malice or intent to harm, and if the activity that led to the death is not a felony and would not usually cause bodily harm, most state statutes define it as involuntary manslaughter. In contrast, *voluntary* manslaughter is intentionally killing someone without previous malice but in the sudden heat of passion due to adequate provocation. For example, a man who kills another man whom he found in bed with his wife would probably be found guilty of voluntary manslaughter. If a store owner kills a robber in his store, his act and many other instances of self-defense are often defined as voluntary manslaughter.

Negligent homicide refers to an accidental death that results from the reckless operation of a motor vehicle, boat, plane, or firearm.

According to the UCR, 20,000 homicides are committed per year. The Bureau of Justice Statistics cites these facts regarding homicide:

- Homicide is the least frequent violent crime.
- Ninety-five percent of the victims were slain in single-victim situations.
- At least 55 percent of the murderers were relatives or acquaintances of the victim.
- Twenty-four percent of all murders occurred or were suspected to have occurred as the result of some felonious activity.

The elements needed for a crime to be called a homicide are as follows:

1. It causes the death of another human being;
2. It is premeditated;
3. Malicious intent exists;
4. Adequately provoked intent results in the heat of passion;
5. It occurs while committing or attempting to commit a felony or a crime not a felony;
6. Force or threat is used;
7. Culpable negligence or depravity exists;
8. There is negligence.

The elements present determine what degree of murder is charged.

Assault

Assault is the unlawful attack by one person on another to inflict severe bodily injury. Aggravated assault is usually accompanied by the use of a weapon or other means likely to produce serious bodily harm or death. Attempts are included since it is not necessary that an injury result when a gun, knife, or other weapon is used that could and probably would result in serious personal injury if the crime were successfully completed.

Assault is attacking a person. It may be aggravated or simple.

Whether an assault is aggravated or simple is determined by the prosecuting attorney and is based on the intent of the attacker. Some states include the term *battery* in their statutes; others omit the term and allow the term *assault* to refer to both the blow and threats of attack. Assaults are frequently committed in conjunction with rape, burglary, and robbery.

Aggravated assault is an unlawful attack on a person to inflict severe bodily injury or death. Assault can safely be classified as *aggravated* if a gun, knife, or other weapon is used and serious personal injury is inflicted. In most states aggravated assault is a felony and carries severe penalties because it would have been murder if the victim died. The intent of the act "appears" to be murder and not simply injury.

Simple assault, the most frequent type of assault, has no intent of serious injury. It may or may not be accompanied by a threat. Hands, fists, or feet are the most frequently used weapons. Most simple assaults result from emotional conflicts and are classified as misdemeanors. The mere pointing of a gun at a person or threatening a person with bodily harm may constitute simple assault in certain situations.

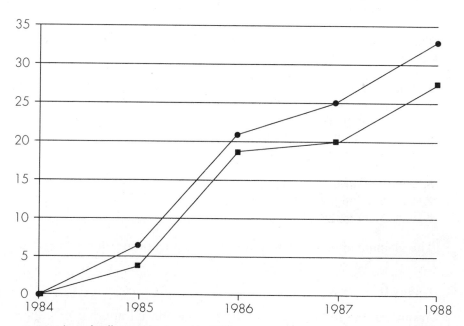

- ● Number of Offenses Known – Up 33%
- ■ Rate per 100,000 Inhabitants – Up 28%

Source: FBI Uniform Crime Reports

Figure 4–5   Aggravated Assault

The UCR estimates that between 800,000 and 900,000 aggravated assaults occur annually. The Bureau of Justice Statistics cites these facts about assault:

- Assault is the most common type of violent crime.
- Simple assault occurs more frequently than aggravated assault.

For a crime to be called aggravated assault, bodily injury must be intentionally inflicted and result in:

- A high probability of death;
- Serious disfigurement; or
- Permanent or protracted loss or impairment of the function of any body member or organ, or other severe bodily harm.

The elements needed for a crime to be called simple are as follows:

1. Intent to do bodily harm to another exists;
2. Present ability to commit the act exists; and
3. An overt act toward carrying out the intention is committed.

Rape

Rape, as defined in the Index Program, is the carnal knowledge of a female through the use of force or the threat of force. Assaults to commit forcible rape are also included in the definition; however, statutory rape (without force) is not.

Rape is having sexual intercourse with a female through the use or threat of force. Rape may be aggravated or simple.

Aggravated rape involves using force, threats of immediate use of force, or taking advantage of an unconscious or helpless woman or a woman incapable of consent because of mental illness or a defect reasonably known to the attacker.

Simple rape involves misleading a victim about the nature of the act being performed; for example, having intercourse under the guise of a medical examination or treatment or knowingly destroying the victim's will to resist by use of a drug or intoxicant.

According to the UCR, between 90,000 and 95,000 forcible rapes occur annually. Rape is a violent crime against the person, yet it is probably one of the most underreported crimes because the victim fears her assailant or is extremely embarrassed. The Bureau of Justice Statistics cites these facts about rape:

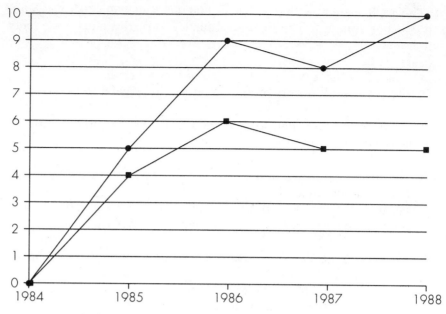

● Number of Offenses Known – Up 10%
■ Rate per 100,000 Inhabitants – Up 5%

Source: FBI Uniform Crime Reports

Figure 4–6   **Forcible Rape**

● Most rapes involved a lone offender and a lone victim.
● About 36 percent of the rapes were committed in the victim's home.
● Fifty-eight percent of the rapes occurred at night between 6 P.M. and 6 A.M.

The elements that constitute the crime of rape are as follows:

1. It is an act of sexual intercourse;
2. It occurs with a female other than a wife;
3. It is committed without the victim's consent; and
4. It is committed against the victim's will and by force.

It should be noted that some states have deleted the word *female* from their rape statutes and substituted the word *person*. This, in effect, includes males as potential victims of rape. Likewise, wives can be considered potential victims of rape. This not only has social significance, but it also indicates a problem with the figures included in the Uniform Crime Reports.

Robbery

Robbery is stealing or taking anything of value from the care, custody, or control of a person by force or by threat of force. Assault to commit robbery and attempts are included in the definition. This violent crime frequently results in injury to the victim.

Robbery is stealing anything of value from the control, care, or custody of a person by force or threat of force.

In 50 percent of the cases, robbery is accompanied by an assault upon the victim. Sometimes labeled as the most brutal and vicious of all crimes, robberies occur in all parts of the country; its victims are people of all ages, incomes, and backgrounds. Robbers may shoot, assault, or torture their victims to find where their valuables are located. Many victims who have refused to cooperate, and even some who have, have been ruthlessly killed. Further, robbery calls are the third-ranking cause of police fatalities.

The favorite weapon of most robbers is the handgun. Other weapons used include knives, acids, baseball bats, and explosives. Armed robbers frequently attack drug stores (often for narcotics), supermarkets, liquor stores, jewelry stores, gas stations, banks, residential homes, cab drivers, and pedestrians.

The classic image of a robber is a masked man pointing a gun at a lone pedestrian in a city street or in a small grocery store at night, but in actuality many do not wear masks or carry guns. Frequently the victims are old people who are robbed of a small amount of money and are knocked to the ground, sometimes suffering permanent injuries or even death.

Robbery produces millions of dollars for criminals and is the most frequently reported crime. Approximately 10 percent of all willful homicides are the result of robbery attempts. But statistics do not reflect the human loss and tragedy often involved in robbery.

Not all robberies are aggravated, however. Some states have a category of simple robbery where no force or threat is used. A usual element of the crime of robbery is force and fear, not stealth. If a thief jostles a victim in a crowd to divert attention and picks his or her pocket, the crime is robbery. A normal pickpocket operation or purse snatching is larceny, not robbery, unless there is resistance or bodily contact.

Nationally about 50 percent of the robberies committed are street robberies. Large cities commonly have twenty to thirty robberies reported in a twenty-four-hour period on Fridays and Saturdays.

According to the UCR, between 500,000 and 550,000 robberies are committed annually. The Bureau of Justice Statistics cites these facts about robbery:

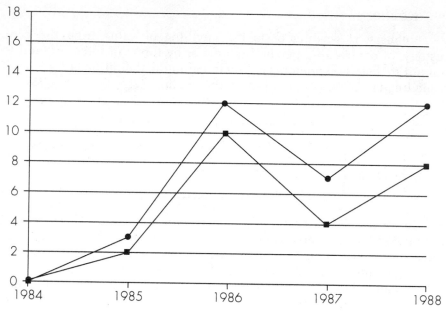

● Number of Offenses Known – Up 12%

■ Rate per 100,000 Inhabitants – Up 8%

Source: FBI Uniform Crime Reports

Figure 4–7   Robbery

● Robbery is a violent crime that typically involves more than one offender (in about half of all cases).
● Slightly less than half of all robberies involved the use of a weapon.
● Less than 2 percent of the robberies reported to the police were bank robberies.

The elements of the crime of robbery are as follows:

1. It is the wrongful taking of personal property;
2. It involves taking property from the person or in the person's presence; and
3. It is committed against the person's will by force or threat of force.

CRIMES AGAINST PROPERTY

Burglary

The Uniform Crime Reporting Program defines **burglary** as the unlawful entry into a structure to commit a felony or theft. The use of force to gain entry is not required to classify the crime as a burglary.

Burglary has three subclassifications: forcible entry, unlawful entry where no force is used, and attempted forcible entry.

Burglary is unlawful entrance into a building to commit theft or other felony.

Many dictionaries have as their first (most common) definition of burglary, "the act of breaking into a house at night to commit theft or other felony." This definition reflects what burglary was historically (under common law)—breaking and entering a dwelling of another in the night. Modern-day statutes reflect numerous changes in that definition, broadening its scope considerably.

Some states, for example, have eliminated the word *breaking* and require only a trespass. Burglaries can occur by forcible or attempted forcible entry, unlawful entry, or without force as when a burglar opens an unlocked door or window or remains in a building without the consent of the person in charge with the intention of committing a crime. Department stores often have been the victims of burglars who hide in the store at closing time and wait until everyone else has left, take what they want, and then break out of the store to escape.

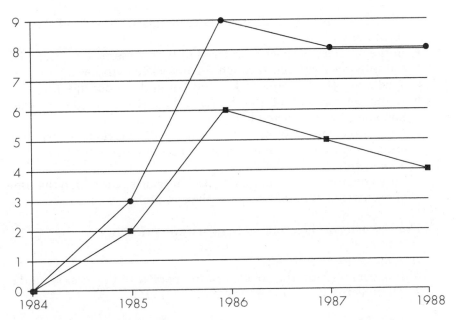

● Number of Offenses Known – Up 8%

■ Rate per 100,000 Inhabitants – Up 4%

Source: FBI Uniform Crime Reports

Figure 4–8 **Burglary**

State statutes often restrict *building* to a dwelling or other structure suitable for human shelter or connected to such a structure. Warehouses, barns, garages, and some types of shelters have also been defined by the courts as dwellings. California defines burglary as the entry of a *structure* for the specific purpose of committing theft or some other felony. A structure is anything having continuous walls, a floor and roof, windows, and doors included.

State statutes also vary as to whether the crime must occur at night to be a burglary. Some states say it may occur at any time of the day or night. If entry occurs during the night, breaking may not be an essential element of the crime.

Punishments are usually most severe if the burglar has an explosive or tool in possession, if the building entered is a dwelling and the burglar has a dangerous weapon when entering, or if the burglar assaults someone while committing the burglary.

Some states have a modified charge of "breaking and entering," which is a lesser charge than burglary. The intricacies in defining burglary are interesting. For instance, if a salesperson pockets a diamond ring while making a sales call in a home, it is not burglary. If a person poses as a salesperson to get into a home and then steals a diamond ring, however, it is burglary in most states.

The UCR estimates between three and three and one-half million burglaries are committed annually. The Bureau of Justice Statistics cites these facts about burglary:

- Forty-five percent of all household burglaries occurred without forced entry.
- In the burglary of more than three million American households, the offenders entered through an unlocked window or door or used a key (for example, a key hidden under a doormat).
- About 34 percent of the no-force household burglaries were known to have occurred between 6 A.M. and 6 P.M.
- Residential property was targeted in 67 percent of reported burglaries; nonresidential property accounted for the remaining 33 percent.
- Three-quarters of the nonresidential burglaries for which the time of occurrence was known took place at night.

The elements of the crime of burglary are as follows:

1. A structure is entered;
2. It occurs without the consent of the person in possession; and
3. There is the intent to commit a crime therein.

Larceny/Theft

Larceny/theft is the unlawful taking or stealing of property or articles without the use of force, violence, or fraud. It includes shoplifting, pocket picking, purse snatching, thefts from motor vehicles, thefts of motor vehicle parts and accessories, and bicycle thefts. The category does not include embezzlement, "con" games, forgery, and passing worthless checks, all Part II crimes. It also does not include motor vehicle theft, which is a separate Crime Index offense.

Larceny/theft is unlawfully taking and removing another's personal property with the intent of permanently depriving the owner of the property.

Larceny/theft may be classified as either a misdemeanor or a felony. It differs from robbery in that it does not involve force, threats of force, or violence. The severity of punishment usually depends on the value and type of property taken, whether it was taken from a building or a person, and the specific circumstances of the case.

Most theft statutes indicate situations where the value of the article is immaterial in determining whether the offense is a felony or misdemeanor. These situations include stealing from the person of another or a grave or a corpse, stealing public records or public funds, looting, and stealing articles representing trade secrets.

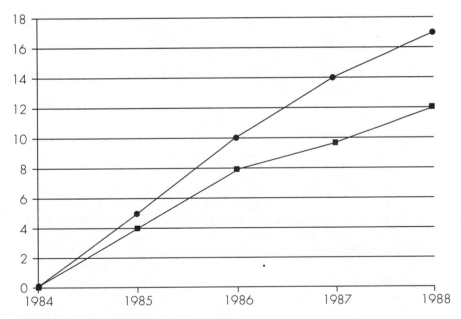

● Number of Offenses Known – Up 17%

■ Rate per 100,000 Inhabitants – Up 12%

Source: FBI Uniform Crime Reports

Figure 4–9   Larceny-Theft

Some states categorize larceny into degrees. Grand and petty larceny are common identifications for value of property taken and punishment. First-, second-, and third-degree larceny also indicate a certain minimum value of the property taken and various degrees of punishment.

The most common type of theft is the theft of items from motor vehicles and motor vehicle parts and accessories. The files of police departments throughout the country are filled with reports of losses such as CB radios, stereo tape decks, clothing, and photographic equipment taken from motor vehicles.

Other common forms of larceny are thefts from buildings such as underground garages where maintenance equipment such as lawn-mowers, snowblowers, lawn hoses, and fertilizers are the target. Bicycles are also a common target for thieves. Because they are easily removed and lack serial number markings, bicycle theft has become big business for many criminals. Police departments find that in some cities dealers specialize in the sale of stolen bicycles.

Thefts from coin-operated vending machines, pocket picking, purse snatching, and shoplifters are other common forms of larceny/theft. Shoplifting accounts for an estimated two billion dollars lost each year. Shoplifters range in age from five to eighty-five. The great majority are amateurs, but there are professional shoplifters (called "boosters") as well as itinerant schools for professionals. The vast majority of shoplifters apprehended are not prosecuted because merchants do not want to alienate good customers or spend the time involved in prosecution, so the customers pay for the shoplifting losses in higher prices.

The UCR estimates approximately seven and one-half million larceny/thefts annually in the United States. The Bureau of Justice Statistics cites these facts about larceny/theft:

- Pocket picking and purse snatching most frequently occur inside nonresidential buildings or on street locations.
- Unlike most other crimes, pocket picking and purse snatching affect the elderly as much as other age groups.
- Most personal larcenies with contact occur during the daytime, but most household larcenies occur at night.

The elements of the crime of larceny/theft are as follows:

1. Felonious stealing, taking, carrying, leading, or driving away of another's goods or property;
2. Value of the property is above (grand) or below (petty) a specified amount;
3. There is an intent to permanently deprive the owner of the property or goods.

Motor Vehicle Theft

In Uniform Crime reporting, **motor vehicle theft** is defined as the unlawful taking or stealing of a motor vehicle, including attempts. This definition excludes taking a vehicle for temporary use by those persons having lawful access to the vehicle. Motor vehicle theft includes automobiles, trucks, buses, motorcycles, motorized boats, and aircraft.

Motor vehicle theft is the unlawful taking or stealing of a motor vehicle without the authority or permission of the owner.

Motor vehicle theft rates show this crime to be primarily a large city problem; the highest rates appear in the most heavily populated sections of the country.

It is difficult to obtain a conviction for auto theft unless witnesses see the person drive the vehicle away and make positive identification later. It is also difficult to prove if the suspect intended to permanently deprive the rightful owner of its use. Therefore, another category of auto theft has been created called "Unlawful Use of a Motor Vehicle," which applies to suspects who merely have possession of a vehicle reported stolen.

Auto thefts represent the greatest monetary property loss—greater than the combined total of all other offenses. The police are not only charged with the recovery of stolen vehicles but with the apprehension of the guilty parties.

Of the many motives for auto theft, joyriding leads the list. Young people steal a car, take it for ride, and then abandon it. Joyriding is often a separate charge where intent to permanently deprive is not in evidence. Autos are also stolen for revenge, for transportation, for commercial use, and for use in committing other crimes such as kidnapping, burglary, and bank robbery. Autos are stolen and stripped for such parts as transmissions, engines, and seats. Sale of stolen auto parts is one of the fastest growing businesses today because of the high cost of replacement parts and the unavailability of parts for foreign-made cars. Automobiles are also stolen, modified, given altered serial numbers and fraudulent titles, and sold to an unsuspecting public.

With the increased number of foreign students attending our universities, a relatively new scheme has caused millions of dollars of losses to American banks. The fraudulent car scheme has accelerated to a new high under the guise of car loans from banks. Foreign students buy new cars, obtain loans on them, and then ship them to foreign countries, which require no proof of ownership. In addition, many vehicles reported as stolen are actually driven into lakes and rivers or buried by their owners to defraud insurance companies.

The UCR estimates over one million motor vehicle thefts are reported annually. The Bureau of Justice Statistics reports the following:

- Motor vehicle theft is relatively well reported to the police because reporting is required for insurance claims, and vehicles are more likely than other stolen property to be recovered.
- About three-fifths of all motor vehicle thefts occur at night.

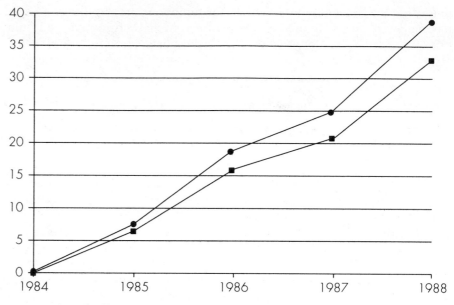

● Number of Offenses Known – Up 39%

■ Rate per 100,000 Inhabitants – Up 33%

Source: FBI Uniform Crime Reports

Figure 4–10   **Motor Vehicle Theft**

The elements of the crime of unauthorized use of a motor vehicle are as follows:

1. There is an intent to take or drive a motor vehicle; and
2. There is no consent of the owner or the owner's authorized agent.

Arson

Arson is intentionally damaging or destroying or attempting to damage or destroy property by means of fire or explosion. It is a felony in all fifty states. It was not until 1978 that Congress made arson a Class I (Part I) crime. Arson has increased over 400 percent in the past ten years (1977–1987). An estimated 1,000 people, including 45 firefighters, die each year in arson fires, and 10,000 people are injured annually. Annual damage estimates are as high as $15 billion. Insurance losses exceed $3 billion. New York's arson task force estimates that New York loses about 300–400 buildings a month by fire, the majority of which are arson.

Arson is intentionally damaging or destroying or attempting to damage or destroy by means of fire or explosion the property of another without the consent of the owner or one's own property, with or without the intent to defraud.

One of the most serious problems often encountered in arson investigations is the joint jurisdiction of firefighters and law enforcement officers. All too frequently this results in duplication of effort and inefficiency.

The Uniform Crime Reports carry only trend and clearance tables for arson, stating that sufficient data is not available to estimate totals for this offense. The Bureau of Justice Statistics states the following regarding arson:

- Single-family residences were the most frequent targets of arson.
- Fifteen percent of all structures where arson occurred were not in use.

The elements of the crime of arson include:

1. Willful, malicious burning of a building or property of another or of one's own to defraud; or
2. Aiding, counseling, or procuring such a burning.

Comparative Statistics for the Part I Index Offenses

Table 4–2 summarizes the number of offenses reported in seven of the Part I Index crimes from 1979 through 1988.

PART II INDEX CRIMES

The Part II offenses consist of several other crimes that can be either misdemeanors or felonies. They are as follows:

- Other assaults (intimidation, coercion, hazing, etc.)
- Forgery and counterfeiting
- Fraud (confidence games, etc.)
- Embezzlement
- Stolen property: buying, receiving, possessing
- Vandalism
- Weapons: carrying, possessing, etc.
- Prostitution and commercialized vice

Table 4–2 Index of Crime, United States, 1979–1988

Population[1]	Crime Index total[2]	Modified Crime Index total[3]	Violent crime[4]	Property crime[4]	Murder and non-negligent man-slaughter	Forcible rape	Robbery	Aggra-vated assault	Burglary	Larceny-theft	Motor vehicle theft	Arson[3]
Number of offenses:												
1979-220,099,000	12,249,500		1,208,030	11,041,500	21,460	76,390	480,700	629,480	3,327,700	6,601,000	1,112,800	
1980-225,349,264	13,408,300		1,344,520	12,063,700	23,040	82,990	565,840	672,650	3,795,200	7,136,900	1,131,700	
1981-229,146,000	13,423,800		1,361,820	12,061,900	22,520	82,500	592,910	663,900	3,779,700	7,194,400	1,087,800	
1982-231,534,000	12,974,400		1,322,390	11,652,000	21,010	78,770	553,130	669,480	3,447,100	7,142,500	1,062,400	
1983-233,981,000	12,108,600		1,258,090	10,850,500	19,310	78,920	506,570	653,290	3,129,900	6,712,800	1,007,900	
1984-236,158,000	11,881,800		1,273,280	10,608,500	18,690	84,230	485,010	685,350	2,984,400	6,591,900	1,032,200	
1985-238,740,000	12,431,400		1,328,800	11,102,600	18,980	88,670	497,870	723,250	3,073,300	6,926,400	1,102,900	
1986-241,077,000	13,211,900		1,489,170	11,722,700	20,610	91,460	542,780	834,320	3,241,400	7,257,200	1,224,100	
1987-243,400,000	13,508,700		1,484,000	12,024,700	20,100	91,110	517,700	855,090	3,236,200	7,499,900	1,288,700	
1988-245,807,000	13,923,100		1,566,220	12,356,900	20,680	92,490	542,970	910,090	3,218,100	7,705,900	1,432,900	
Percent change: number of offenses:												
1988/1987	+3.1		+5.5	+2.8	+2.9	+1.5	+4.9	+6.4	-.6	+2.7	+11.2	
1988/1984	+17.2		+23.0	+16.5	+10.6	+9.8	+12.0	+32.8	+7.8	+16.9	+38.8	
1988/1979	+13.7		+29.7	+11.9	-3.6	+21.1	+13.0	+44.6	-3.3	+16.7	+28.8	
Rate per 100,000 inhabitants:												
1979	5,565.5		548.9	5,016.6	9.7	34.7	218.4	286.0	1,511.9	2,999.1	505.6	
1980	5,950.0		596.6	5,353.3	10.2	36.8	251.1	298.5	1,684.1	3,167.0	502.2	
1981	5,858.2		594.3	5,263.9	9.8	36.0	258.7	289.7	1,649.5	3,139.7	474.7	
1982	5,603.6		571.1	5,032.5	9.1	34.0	238.9	289.2	1,488.8	3,084.8	458.8	
1983	5,175.0		537.7	4,637.4	8.3	33.7	216.5	279.2	1,337.7	2,868.9	430.8	
1984	5,031.3		539.2	4,492.1	7.9	35.7	205.4	290.2	1,263.7	2,791.3	437.1	
1985	5,207.1		556.6	4,650.5	7.9	37.1	208.5	302.9	1,287.3	2,901.2	462.0	
1986	5,480.4		617.7	4,862.6	8.6	37.9	225.1	346.1	1,344.6	3,010.3	507.8	
1987	5,550.0		609.7	4,940.3	8.3	37.4	212.7	351.3	1,329.6	3,081.3	529.4	
1988	5,664.2		637.2	5,027.1	8.4	37.6	220.9	370.2	1,309.2	3,134.9	582.9	
Percent change: rate per 100,000 inhabitants:												
1988/1987	+2.1		+4.5	+1.8	+1.2	+.5	+3.9	+5.4	-1.5	+1.7	+10.1	
1988/1984	+12.6		+18.2	+11.9	+6.3	+5.3	+7.5	+27.6	+3.6	+12.3	+33.3	
1988/1979	+1.8		+16.1	+.2	-13.4	+8.4	+1.1	+29.4	-13.4	+4.5	+15.3	

[1]Populations are Bureau of the Census provisional estimates as of July 1, except April 1, 1980, preliminary census counts, and are subject to change.

[2]Because of rounding, the offenses may not add to totals.

[3]Although arson data are included in the trend and clearance tables, sufficient data are not available to estimate totals for this offense.

[4]Violent crimes are offenses of murder, forcible rape, robbery, and aggravated assault. Property crimes are offenses of burglary, larceny-theft, and motor vehicle theft. Data are not included for the property crime of arson.

All rates were calculated on the offenses before rounding.

Data for 1988 were not available for the States of Florida and Kentucky; therefore, it was necessary that their crime counts be estimated.

- Sex offenses (except forcible rape, prostitution, and commercialized vice)
- Drug abuse violations
- Gambling
- Offenses against the family and children (child abuse, neglect, nonsupport)
- Driving under the influence
- Liquor laws (liquor law violations, bootlegging, etc.)
- Drunkenness
- Disorderly conduct
- Vagrancy
- Curfew and loitering (juveniles)
- Runaway (juveniles)
- All other offenses (abortion, bigamy, contempt of court, the list goes on and on)

CRIMINAL LAW AND CRIME—IN REVIEW

You've looked at what constitutes a crime, at the various classifications of crime, and at the elements of the major crimes. You've also seen statistics on the prelevance of the eight serious Part I Index Crimes. You'll return to the subject of crime later in the book when you look at white-collar crime, organized crime, and the problems of drugs and gangs. Turn your attention now, however, to unlawful acts that are not classified as crimes.

CIVIL LAW AND TORTS

Civil law refers to all noncriminal restrictions placed on individuals. Although laws vary from state to state, generally such actions as trespassing, desertion of family, slander, failure to make good on a contract, or similar actions against an individual would be covered under civil law.

Civil law refers to all noncriminal restrictions placed on individuals. It seeks not punishment, but restitution.

As Prosser notes (1955, p. 7):

A **tort** is not the same thing as a crime, although the two sometimes have many features in common. The distinction between them lies in the interests affected and the remedy afforded by the law. A crime is an offense against the public at large, for which the state, as the representative of the public, will bring proceedings in the form of criminal prosecution. . . . A criminal prosecution is not concerned in any way with compensation of the injured individual against whom the crime is committed. . . . The civil action for a tort, on the other hand, is commenced and maintained by the injured person himself, and its purpose is to compensate him for the damage he has suffered, at the expense of the wrongdoer.

A tort is a civil wrong for which the court will seek a remedy in the form of damages to be paid.

Sutherland and Cressey (1978, p. 8) clarify the distinction between a tort and a crime:

> *The conventional view is that a crime is an offense against the state, while, in contrast, a tort in violation of civil law is an offense against an individual. A particular act may be considered as an offense against an individual and also against the state, and is either a tort or a crime or both, according to the way it is handled. A person who has committed an act of assault, for example, may be ordered by the civil court to pay the victim a sum of $500 for the damages to his interests, and may also be ordered by the criminal court to pay a fine of $500 to the state. The payment of the first $500 is not punishment, but payment of the second $500 is punishment.*

It is important that law enforcement officers recognize when a matter is covered by criminal law and when it is covered by civil law (noncriminal matters). Sometimes police officers are asked to describe a citizen's rights in a noncriminal matter and what legal options are open.

The distinction between crimes and torts are as follows:

Crime
- Public wrong
- State prosecutes
- Seeks to punish
- Criminal intent is required

Tort
- Private wrong
- Individual prosecutes
- Seeks redress for injury
- Intent not necessary

Table 4–3   **Legislative Designations of Crime**

Reasons a Legislative Body Might Designate Specific Conduct as Criminal	Reasons a Legislative Body Might Not Designate Specific Conduct as Criminal
To protect the public from violent or dangerous conduct To protect public health To maintain public order To protect the right of privacy of individuals To protect public morality Because there appears to be no other way in which to promote a desired public policy	It is not within the power of the government to prohibit such conduct. The conduct in question is constitutionally protected. There is no demand by influential public or private groups or individuals for the regulation of such conduct. It would not be economically feasible to enforce a law criminalizing such conduct. It would not be politically popular to pass a law criminalizing such conduct.

Source: Thomas J. Gardner. *Criminal Law, Principles and Cases*, 3d ed. St. Paul, Minn.: West Publishing Company, 1985, p. 6.

THE LAW ENFORCEMENT OFFICER AND CIVIL LIABILITY

According to Harr and Hess (1990, p. 76), "Only naive or deluded police officers believe they would never be sued. The past two decades have produced an unprecedented increase in suits brought against the police. It is presently estimated that over thirty thousand lawsuits are initiated against law enforcement annually (Silver 1986, p. xi)."

One reason for the numerous lawsuits is the current interpretation of Section 1983 of the Civil Rights Act.

The Civil Rights Act (Section 1983)

The United States Code, Statute 42, Section 1983, passed after the Civil War in 1871, states the following:

> *Every person who, under color of any statute, ordinance, regulation, custom, or usage, of any State or Territory, subjects, or causes to be subjected any citizen of the United States or other person within the jurisdiction thereof to the deprivation of any rights, privileges, or immunities secured by the Constitution and laws, shall be liable to the party injured in an action at law, suit in equity, or other proper proceeding for redress.*

Section 1983 of the United States Code stipulates that anyone acting under the authority of local or state law who violates another person's constitutional rights—even though they are upholding a law—can be sued.

The two basic requirements for a Section 1983 action are that (1) the plaintiff must be deprived of a constitutional right and (2) the defendant must deprive the plaintiff of this right while acting under the "color of the law" (*Adickes v. Kress and Co.*, 1970). Like criminal law, civil law has levels of "intent."

- Strict liability—the wrongdoer is liable even if no harm was intended (for example keeping wild animals).
- Intentional wrong—the person knows the act was unlawful but did it anyway.
- Negligence—the person did not set out to do harm but acted carelessly.

The last two categories are the ones law officers most frequently find themselves involved with.

The intentional wrongs that may affect law enforcement include assault, battery, false imprisonment, false arrest, malicious prosecution, intentional infliction of emotional distress, trespass, illegal electronic surveillance, invasion of privacy, and defamation. Later chapters will introduce procedures to be followed to minimize the likelihood of a civil lawsuit for an intentional wrong.

The second category of civil charges frequently filed against law enforcement officers and their agencies is negligence, defined as the failure to use due care to prevent foreseeable injury. The routine police duties that most frequently lead to negligence lawsuits are care of incapacitated persons, duty to render emergency aid, caring for arrestees, aiding private citizens, investigating unusual circumstances, and operating emergency vehicles carelessly, for example, high-speed chases.

Again, procedures discussed elsewhere in this text should help to lessen the probability of a civil lawsuit.

Good Samaritan Laws

Law enforcement officers should be familiar with the "Good Samaritan" laws and which are applicable in their jurisdiction (see table 4–4).

SUMMARY

The law enforcement officer functions in a society where the citizens enjoy great freedom. Sometimes, however, this freedom is viewed by citizens as license to do as they please, to ignore the laws of society. State and federal statutes have defined actions that are not to be tolerated—crimes—and have set specified penalties for each. Although state statutes vary in their definitions of and penalties for crimes, certain generalizations can be made. Generally, a crime is an intentional action that is prohibited by law, and for which punishment is legally prescribed, that directly causes an actual harm.

The crimes most frequently reported to police, the most serious crimes in the nation, are called Part I Index Crimes. They include murder, assault, rape, robbery, burglary, larceny/theft, motor vehicle theft, and arson.

Table 4–4   "Good Samaritan" Laws

Broadly defined, "Good Samaritan" laws include statutes that fall into the following categories:

1. Practically all states have enacted "Good Samaritan" laws that encourage doctors and other health practitioners to aid injured or ill strangers. Such statutes do not encourage acts of heroism or impose a duty to aid, but rather they eliminate fear of malpractice suits that had discouraged doctors and others from rendering assistance to those who had been injured or were ill.

2. Some European countries impose on their citizens a duty to come to the aid of another and to rescue if this can be done without danger or peril to the person. Few states have enacted such statutes. Vermont is one of the exceptions. Failure to come to the aid of another when such aid "can be rendered without danger or peril to himself" is punishable by a fine up to $100 in Vermont.

3. Another form of a "Good Samaritan" law is a statute passed by Maryland in 1982: "Any person witnessing a violent assault upon the person of another may lawfully aid the person being assaulted by assisting in that person's defense" (Art. 27, Sec. 12A). This statute and others authorizing force in self-defense or the defense of another *do not impose a duty* to come to the assistance of another.

Source: Thomas J. Gardner, *Criminal Law, Principles and Cases,* 3d ed. St. Paul, Minn.: West Publishing Company 1985.

Crimes may be classified as felonies or misdemeanors. A felony refers to serious crimes, generally those punishable by death or by imprisonment for more than one year in a state prison or penitentiary. The court may, however, inflict a lesser punishment. A misdemeanor refers to any minor offense, generally punishable by a fine or a short term, usually not to exceed one year, in a jail or workhouse.

To prove a crime has been committed, it is usually necessary to prove the act itself (*actus reus*)—the elements of the crime—and to prove the criminal's mental state (*mens rea*)—intent to do wrong. In strict liability crimes, however, such as traffic violations, the defendant is liable regardless of intent.

Part I Index Crimes are described as follows:

- Murder (homicide) is the willful killing of a human by another human.
- Assault is attacking a person. It may be aggravated or simple.
- Rape is having sexual intercourse with a female through the use or threat of force. Rape may be aggravated or simple.
- Robbery is stealing anything of value from the control, care, or custody of a person by force or threat of force.
- Burglary is unlawful entrance into a building to commit theft or other felony.
- Larceny/theft is unlawfully taking and removing another's personal property with the intent of permanently depriving the owner of the property.
- Motor vehicle theft is the unlawful taking or stealing of a motor vehicle without the authority or permission of the owner.

- Arson is intentionally damaging or destroying or attempting to damage or destroy by means of fire or explosion the property of another without the consent of the owner or one's own property, with or without the intent to defraud.

Civil law refers to all noncriminal restrictions placed on individuals. It seeks not punishment but restitution. A tort is a civil wrong for which the court will seek a remedy in the form of damages to be paid. Section 1983 of the United States Code, states that anyone acting under the authority of local or state law who violates another person's constitutional rights even though they are upholding a law—can be sued.

Discussion Questions

1. If a person's reckless driving of a car injures another person who dies two weeks later as a result of the injuries, could the reckless driver be charged for a crime, sued for a tort, or both? How would the type of charge affect the possible consequences faced by the reckless driver?

2. Why is motor vehicle theft in a different category than larceny/theft?

3. Why are some crimes divided into categories or degrees?

4. Who should investigate arson offenses: the fire department or the police department?

5. Is fear of punishment a deterrent to criminal activity?

6. Would a law making the reporting of all crimes to the police mandatory, be a good deterrent to future criminal activity?

7. Should a mandatory sentence be imposed for all Part I offenses of the Uniform Crime Report?

8. Torts are a civil wrong. What purpose do they serve? Give an example.

9. Should law enforcement officers be immune from tort action?

10. Are the laws police are required to enforce today, adequate for the continuous protection of the general public?

References

Brantingham, P., and Brantingham, P. *Patterns in Crime*. New York: Macmillan, 1984.

Gardner, T. J. *Criminal Law, Principles and Cases*, 3d. ed. St. Paul, Minn.: West Publishing Company, 1985.

Harr, Scott, and Hess, Karen. *Criminal Procedure*. St. Paul, Minn.: West Publishing Company, 1990.

Haskell, M. R., and Yablonsky, L. *Crime and Criminality*. Boston: Houghton Mifflin, 1983.

Nettler, G. *Explaining Crime*. 2d ed. New York: McGraw-Hill, 1978.

Prosser, W. L. *Handbook of the Law of Torts*. 2d ed. St. Paul, Minn.: West Publishing Company, 1955.

Samaha, Joel. *Criminal Law*. St. Paul, Minn.: West Publishing Company, 1983.

Silver, Isidore. *Police Civil Liability*, New York: Matthew Bender, 1986.

Sutherland, E. H., and Cressey, D. R. *Criminology*. 10th ed. Philadelphia: Lippincott, 1978.

U.S. Department of Justice. Bureau of Justice Statistics. *Report to the Nation on Crime and Justice*. Washington, D.C.: U.S. Government Printing Office, 1988.

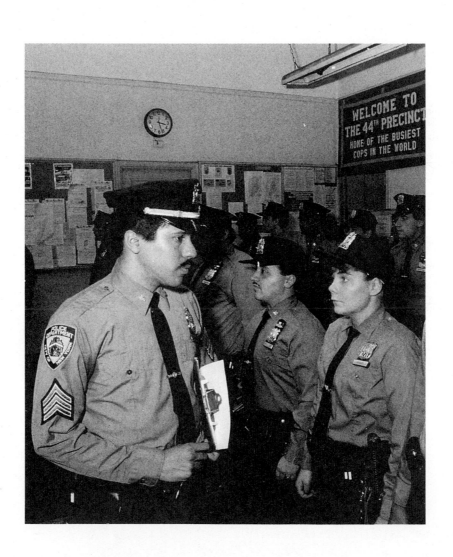

CHAPTER FIVE

A Career in
Law Enforcement:
A Challenging Profession

No one is compelled to choose the profession of a police officer, but having chosen it, everyone is obliged to perform its duties and live up to the high standards of its requirements—Calvin Coolidge

DO YOU KNOW

What qualities are essential for good police officers?

What steps are involved in officer selection?

What qualifications are required of police officers?

What most physical fitness tests are like?

What information is sought during oral interviews?

What is most important in the medical examination?

What occurs during the background investigation?

What the length and purpose of probation are?

What restrictions are sometimes placed on police officers' off-duty employment?

What legal considerations in hiring practices are mandated by the Omnibus Civil Rights Law?

What the benefits of having a police department whose racial makeup reflects that of the community are?

The dominant characteristic of police culture?

How stressful police work may be?

Introduction

Chapter 5

For years society has sought more effective law enforcement and a criminal justice system to meet its needs. Concurrently, criminologists, psychologists, sociologists, police practitioners, and scientists have worked to solve the crime problem in America. Despite some disillusionment and cynicism, progress has been made, and the future offers encoragement.

The most visible signs of progress in the vast criminal justice system have been in the field of law enforcement, and the most notable advancement within this field has been in the professionalization of the police officer.

This is, in part, because 86 to 90 percent of most police agencies' budgets are allocated for personnel, and, therefore, they are demanding higher quality performance from them. This goal is sometimes difficult to achieve, however, because most police departments are understaffed. The attrition rate throughout the country—approximately 100,000 officers per year—compounds this problem and creates a constant demand for training.

An equally important force behind the professionalization of the police officer is the realization that to a large degree the future of law enforcement, its success or failure, is contingent on the quality and effectiveness of its police officers, their status in the community, and their ability to serve its residents. Members of minority groups and women are

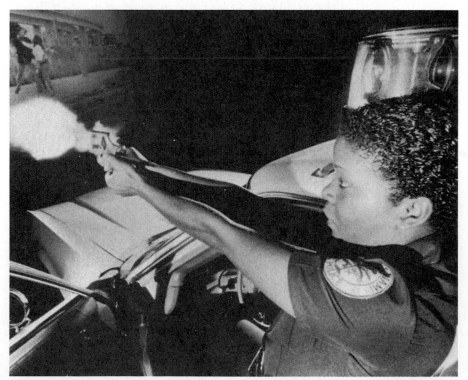

Police officers require a variety of skills. This officer is undergoing stress training in a shooting simulator.

now perceived by most departments as necessary and valuable individuals in the department. Although members of minority groups and women have had a long, difficult battle in achieving equal employment rights, not only in the field of law enforcement but also in most other fields as well, great advancements have been made in the past decade. Today law enforcement offers excellent opportunities for all who are interested in a law enforcement career.

DESIRED QUALITIES OF LAW ENFORCEMENT OFFICERS

If the citizens of a community were asked what traits they felt were desirable in police officers, a compilation of their responses might read something like the following: police officers should be able to work under pressure, to accept direction, to express themselves orally and in writing; they should have self-respect and the ability to command respect from others; they should use good judgment; and they should be considerate, compassionate, dependable, enthusiastic, fair, flexible, honest, humble, industrious, intelligent, logical, motivated, neat, observant, physically fit, prompt, resourceful, self-assured, stable, tactful, warm, and willing to listen and to accept change.

Unfortunately, no one possesses all these traits, but the more of these traits police officers have, the more likely they are to be effective in dealing with not only the citizens of the community but lawbreakers as well.

An LEAA funded study conducted at Indiana University ("Indiana University Develops Police Selection Procedure" 1977, p. 1) identified twelve characteristics that separated good police officers from poor ones:

- Reliability
- Leadership
- Judgment
- Persuasiveness
- Communication skills
- Accuracy
- Initiative
- Integrity
- Honesty
- Ego control
- Intelligence
- Sensitivity

Finding individuals qualified to become police officers is no easy task. The process of recruiting and screening candidates is a continuous and critical function of all police agencies in the country. By examining personnel selection developments over the past years, police administrators can evaluate the effectiveness of their personnel selection procedures.

They can assess the recommendations made by the personnel branch and whether they are implemented, and they can assess whether their procedures conform with federal guidelines and regulations.

Qualities of a good police officer include reliability, leadership, judgment, persuasiveness, communication skills, accuracy, initiative, integrity, honesty, ego control, intelligence, and sensitivity.

EXAMINATION ANNOUNCEMENTS

The most common law enforcement recruitment practice is to place want ads in local newspapers, including minority newspapers to attract more minority candidates. Notices are also sent to colleges and universities inviting students to make application.

When applicants come to the designated place, they are given a fact sheet containing a brief job description, the salary range, fringe benefits, and an application to be filled out and submitted. They are also given a time and place to report for the written examination. Candidates who cannot personally appear may call or write to have the information sent to them.

Most police agencies and civil service commissions accept applications even though no openings are presently listed. The application is placed on file, and when an examination is to be conducted, the applicant is notified by mail or phone.

THE SELECTION PROCESS

Police officer selection usually includes:
- *A formal application.*
- *A preliminary screening.*
  Written examination.
  Psychological examination.
- *A physical agility test.*
- *An oral interview.*
- *A medical examination.*
- *A background investigation.*

Although procedures differ greatly from agency to agency, several procedures are common to most selection processes, such as a formal application, a preliminary screening, written examination, psychological examination, a physical agility test, an oral interview, medical examination, and a background investigation. Failure at any point in the selection process may disqualify a candidate.

The Formal Application—Basic Requirements to Become a Police Officer

Usually anyone who wishes to become a police officer completes a formal application. A careful examination of this formal application shows several factors that are evaluated in a candidate: driving record, any criminal record, visual acuity, physical, emotional, and mental condition, and education.

Most agencies require that a police officer:

- *be a citizen of the United States;*
- *have or be eligible for a driver's license in the state;*
- *not have been convicted of a felony.*

Requirements related to education and residency are also frequently stated.

Education   Opinions differ as to how much education a candidate for police officer should have. Most police agencies require a minimum of a high school education or equivalency certificate. On the other hand, some jurisdictions require at least two years of college and some a four-year degree.

Most police agencies require a minimum of a high school education.

Some administrators use set educational standards to attain professionalism and upgrade the service. However, police chiefs are at odds as to whether education contributes significantly to the fight against crime. Unquestionably, a college-educated police officer contributes significantly to the quality of police service. On the other hand, some police chiefs feel that too much education makes social service officers of personnel who ought to be fighting crime in the streets. Some surveys indicate that the more education police officers have, the less likely they are to become involved in physical confrontations. Others feel that to require a degreed officer to perform such mundane tasks as issuing traffic tickets and parking tickets, making money runs, and carding juveniles in liquor stores is demeaning, and that such routine tasks soon diminish the highly educated officer's interest in law enforcement. Besides, they argue, most police officers see themselves as crime fighters, not social engineers.

Residency Requirements Over the years, cities and municipalities have waived residency requirements to obtain better candidates. Though generally not required, cities are again beginning to accept only candidates who reside within their boundaries.

It is always preferred and sometimes required that police officers live in the community they serve.

Sometimes compromises have been made whereby candidates are given one year to move into the community they serve. City and municipal politicians feel that by living in the community, a police officer becomes more closely identified with that community, more sensitive to its crime problems, and more readily participates in community activities.

The value of living in the community served cannot be disputed. Police officers are better able to understand the problems and needs of the community. They also develop relationships with the professional groups in the community and can better understand the life-style of the citizens. Additionally, politicians' self-interests dictate that their police officers live in the community so they can contribute their fair share of taxes. However, it may be economically unfeasible for police officers to afford to live in the community they serve.

Preliminary Screening Tests

The demands upon police officers are great. Not only are they subjected to emotional and physical stress, but they also are placed in positions of trust and responsibility. Effective screening tests are, therefore, a necessity. Preliminary screening procedures may include examinations that determine adaptability, memory retention, reading comprehension, spelling, and the potential to fit into the present organization.

Most candidates are required to complete a preliminary screening consisting of a written examination and a psychological examination. Standardized tests may be used.

Those candidates who do well on the original preliminary testing or screening procedures of the police agency go on to other testing procedures including physical agility tests, oral interviews, medical examinations, and a thorough background check.

Physical Agility Tests

Physical fitness tests are usually administered to determine a candidate's coordination and muscular strength and to ascertain whether the candidate is in good or poor physical condition. The type of test varies with police agencies throughout the country.

A candidate may be required to run a designated number of yards and while doing so hurdle a three-foot barrier, crawl under a twenty-four inch bar, climb over a four- or six-foot wall with both hands on top of the wall, and sprint the remaning distance—all within a designated time period monitored by a police officer with a stopwatch.

Candidates may also be required to climb ropes or fire ladders, do chin-ups, or push-ups. Other variations of the physical agility test may be required, but usually only a minimum of strenuous activity is obligatory.

Physical agility tests are necessary because they simulate what an offier may have to do on the street—jumping over a fence, climbing a wall, or chasing someone through backyards or streets. Candidates who are considerably overweight rarely pass the physical agility test.

Physical agility tests evaluate a candidate's coordination, speed of movement, and strength. The most common physical agility tests are similar to a military obstacle course, which must be completed in a designated time.

A candidate can prepare for the physical agility test through a regular system of workouts. Running is an excellent general conditioner because it develops endurance and strengthens the legs. Sit-ups, leg-lift exercises, push-ups, and lifting light weights are also helpful in preparing for the physical agility test. Like knowledge, physical fitness does not develop overnight; it develops gradually over an extended period.

The Oral Interview

Oral boards usually consist of three to five skilled interviewers knowledgeable in their fields. They may be staff officers from the agency doing the hiring or from other agencies, psychologists, sociologists, or representatives of a community service organization. The entire interviewing board may consist of members of a police or civil service commission. In smaller jurisdictions, oral boards are sometimes replaced by an interview with the mayor, a member of the council, or the chief of police.

The interviews, whether structured or unstructured, are designed to elicit answers revealing the candidates' personalities and suitability for police work, *not* to determine their technical knowledge in the police field.

The candidate should be prepared to answer questions such as the following:

- Why do you want to be a police officer?
- What have you done to prepare for a career in law enforcement?
- What do you feel are the causes of crime?
- What are your favorite hobbies?
- Have you talked with your wife/husband about this position of police officer?
- What does she/he think about it?
- What is the last book you have read?
- What was your favorite subject in school?
- When did you last get drunk?

The oral interview seeks information about the candidate's personality and suitability for police work.

The oral interview will also test the candidate's ability to use good judgment in specific situations such as the following:

- A person is standing on the corner making a speech regarding the overthrow of the government. He is drawing a crowd, and a certain amount of animosity is being shown toward the speaker, indicating future trouble. How would you handle this situation?
- You are working radar and you clock the mayor going 39 mph in a 30 mph zone. How would you handle this situation?
- You are walking a beat and a juvenile thrusts a stick between your legs causing you to fall to the pavement and tear your pants. What would you do?

The interview usually lasts about thirty minutes. The same questions are asked each candidate to allow comparison of answers. After the interview, the qualifications of each candidate are evaluated. Each candidate is given an overall rating, which is combined with the scores of the other examinations to yield a composite (total) score.

Candidates should prepare themselves both physically and mentally for the oral interview. They should be well groomed and present a professional appearance. They should have considered in advance responses to questions that are likely to be asked. It is critical to be well prepared since the oral interview generally disqualifies more candidates than it qualifies.

The oral interview usually evaluates appearance, ability to present ideas, social adaptability, alertness, judgment, emotional stability, interest in the job, and communication ability.

The Medical Examination

Medical requirements vary from jurisdiction to jurisdiction, but the purpose is the same. With the modern emphasis on health care, more and more importance is being placed on the medical examination. Citizens, concerned about the possibility of early retirements due to poor health, are demanding physically fit officer candidates.

The medical standards usually include a variety of factors with some—vision, hearing, and the cardiovascular-respiratory system—being more important than others.

Good eyesight is of great importance. Candidates who wear glasses that correct their vision to meet the agency's requirements can qualify in some departments. Likewise, candidates who wear hearing aids that correct their hearing to meet the agency's requirements can qualify.

Because of the stress of the job and the hypertension that frequently accompanies it, the cardiovascular system is thoroughly checked. The respiratory and cardiovascular system play a critical role in fitness. To a great degree, endurance, the ability to continue exertion over a prolonged time, is directly related to the capacity of the cardiovascular-respiratory system to deliver oxygen to the muscles.

A physician who feels a candidate has a functional or organic disorder may recommend disqualification of that candidate.

Vision, hearing, and the cardiovascular-respiratory system are of prime importance in the medical examination.

The Background Investigation

The applicant's background is one of the most critical factors considered in recruitment. In most police agencies an applicant must submit a personal history. The background investigation serves two purposes: (1) it examines the past work and educational record of the candidate, and (2) it determines if anything in the candidate's background might make him or her unsuitable for police work. The extensiveness of the background investigation is limited only by the number of candidates being investigated and time available.

Normally all information given by the applicant on the history sheet must be verified. Birth and age records are verified through vital statistics and driving records through the drivers' license bureau. Adverse driving records containing drunken driving, driving after suspension or revocation of license, or a consistent pattern of moving violations may cause disqualification.

Candidates are fingerprinted, and the prints are sent to the Federal Bureau of Investigation in Washington to determine if the candidate has a criminal record. The candidate's criminal record is also checked on the local and state levels, usually through fingerprints, name, and date of birth. Juvenile records are normally discounted unless a person has committed a heinous crime.

Ironically, because of the transient nature of our population, persons wanted on warrants in one part of the country have applied for a police officer's position in another part of the country. The criminal record check has sometimes resulted in the apprehension of such individuals.

Military records are usually checked to verify service and eligibility under the veteran's preference acts of some states. The check also determines if the candidate was involved in any court martials or disciplinary actions.

All personal and professional references listed on the history sheet are interviewed. Interviewing of references is sometimes criticized because candidates obviously will list only those who see them favorably; however, these references may lead to others who know the candidates and have a different view of them. When candidates list out-of-town references, letters or questionnaires are usually mailed.

Neighbors of the candidate, past or present, are an excellent source of information about a candidate's character and reputation. No department wants police officers who have had prior association with the criminal element, who have been addicted to narcotics or drugs, or who abuse alcohol. Their reputation in the community should be high.

Previous employers are contacted to determine the applicant's work record. An inability to hold continuous employment may indicate trouble getting along with supervisors. A high absentee rate may indicate lack of interest or initiative or health problems.

The financial status of the candidate is also determined, usually through a credit records check. Individuals whose expenditures exceed their total incomes may be candidates for bankruptcy or bribery. Good credit indicates the person can live within his or her means and possesses self-control. The candidate may be required to submit a financial statement.

Educational records from high school, college, and any other schools attended are usually checked through personal contact. The education record may indicate interests, achievements, accomplishments, and social life-style while attending school. The scholastic record reflects not only intelligence but also study habits. Any degrees, certificates of achievement, or awards are usually noted.

The use of the polygraph examination as a follow-up to the background investigation is a widely increasing means of verifying the background of a candidate. Although some states have banned its use for preemployment purposes, where it is used to screen police candidates it is necessary to determine why it is being given. Some departments use the polygraph extensively, especially if they have many transient applicants from other parts of the country. Some agencies use it to determine if the candidate has ever engaged in criminal activity and was ever apprehended. Some want to know if the candidate has any sexually deviant behaviors. Others use it to verify the written information the candidate has given on the application and history sheet.

The background investigation includes the following:

- *Verification of all information on the application and history sheet.*
- *Check on driving record.*
- *Fingerprinting and a check on any criminal record.*
- *Check on military records.*
- *Interviews with personal references, acquaintances, past employers, neighbors, and teachers.*
- *Check on financial status.*
- *Check on past performances at school and previous jobs.*

The Final Result

After all required tests are completed, they are analyzed and a composite score is given for each candidate. A list is made of eligible candidates, and they are called as openings occur in the police department. Some larger police departments keep their eligibility lists one to two years, depending on civil service requirements or other requirements mandated by states or municipalities.

PROBATION AND TRAINING

Some states have mandated that recruits must be given from 240 to 400 hours of police training within one year of employment. Coincidentally, this is also usually the length of time the officers are placed on probation.

The probationary period is a trial period, usually one year, during which the officer is observed while obtaining training and applying this training on the streets.

Cadets in the Minnesota Police Department Cadet School, one of the first of its kind, receive academic instruction. The program requires all applicants to have a college degree.

Police officers may obtain their training in a state police academy, a city academy, or a specialized rookie school. The basic training of police officers varies with each jurisdiction and its needs, but most officers will be trained in constitutional law, laws of arrest, search and seizure, and in the various requests for service such as accident investigation, crisis intervention, and first aid.

While in training recruits may be required to return to the department and spend a specified number of hours on street patrol. Some jurisdictions alternate their training periods every two weeks, allowing an officer to apply on the street what was learned in basic recruit school.

While on the street the recruits ride with a trainer, usually a sergeant, who monitors their movements and helps them apply principles learned in rookie school. While in school, the officers are evaluated and tested by their instructors, who periodically send progress reports to the chief of police. After completing training, they continue to ride with one or more training officers who evaluate their street performance.

Following successful completion of the probationary period, they are full-fledged police officers. After probation some states license the person to be a police officer. Legislatures in Texas, Michigan, California, Oregon, Minnesota, and other states have adopted standards for police officers that must be met to satisfy the state's training requirements for licensing.

States have also mandated a certain amount of in-service training to keep the license current. Many of these in-service training requirements revolve around the behavioral sciences so police officers have a better

Police academy cadets doing sit-ups. Physical fitness may make the difference between success and failure on the job.

understanding of the entire criminal justice system. Guest speakers from the corrections system, the court system, and on many occasions from minority groups present their philosophy and objectives to police officers.

SALARY AND BENEFITS

Salaries among police departments in the country have little uniformity. A variety of factors influence a police officer's salary. Of utmost consideration are the community's ability to pay, the cost of living in the area, and the prevailing wages of similar police departments in the surrounding area.

Normally position-classification plans are implemented under a personnel ordinance or department rule book. Steps on the salary scale are established in each position classification. New recruits start at the bottom of the salary scale and receive increment raises after six months and each succeeding year until they reach their maximum salary, usually after three to five years. They obtain more salary only if granted a cost-of-living raise; however, a promotion to the next rank would bring them into a different salary bracket. Sergeants, lieutenants, captains, and chiefs all have minimum and maximum starting levels with the top salary usually reached after three years in the position.

To compensate individuals who do not attain a rank during their police careers, many police departments have adopted longevity plans whereby nonranking officers receive a certain percentage more of their salaries after the tenth year, the fifteenth year, and so on. This seniority system has been attacked, however, on the grounds that is discourages initiative and further education.

When salary schedules are formulated, fringe benefits such as hospitalization and dental plans, insurance, vacation, sick leave, and holidays are all considered. Police officers' indirect benefits from their employers are estimated to be approximately 33 percent, comparable to what business and industry currently allow their employees.

In addition to fringe benefits, most police departments give police officers a yearly clothing allowance to maintain their uniform wardrobe.

Policies vary regarding overtime pay for officers on the job, going to court while on duty, being required to attend training while off duty, and being called back to duty in an emergency. Some departments pay overtime; others give compensatory time off.

Police departments may belong to unions that bargain for them. Usually all conditions of employment are clearly spelled out in their contracts.

OFF-DUTY WORK LIMITATIONS

Moonlighting, working at a part-time job while fulfilling the obligations of a full-time position, has been a source of controversy in the police field for many years. Some administrators allow their officers latitude in the off-duty work performed and the number of hours worked. Other administrators are becoming more conservative as a result of poor work performance by some moonlighting officers and lawsuits against the officer and the city or municipality due to some incident while the officer was working off duty.

Some cities allow their police officers to work off duty in only police-related areas; others allow them to work in only nonpolice-related areas. While there are advantages and disadvantages in allowing police officers to work off duty, most cities and municipalities have some limits on the officer's off-duty time.

Most police departments restrict the type of work that can be done and the number of hours an officer can work while off duty.

FEDERAL GUIDELINES AND REGULATIONS

In 1964 Congress enacted the Omnibus Civil Rights Law. Title VII of this law concerns employment opportunities and prohibits discrimination because of sex, race, color, religion, or national origin. The law also established the Equal Employment Opportunity Commission (EEOC) to administer the law and gave this commission authority to establish guidelines. This law affected only private business, not state and local governments; therefore, it had little impact on police agency practices.

The 1964 Omnibus Civil Rights Law prohibits discrimination in employment opportunities in private business.

In 1972 Congress passed the Equal Opportunity Act, which modified Title VII to include state and local units of government. This law was passed because six years after the EEOC published guidelines for employment and promotion testing, few state or local central personnel selection agencies had taken positive steps to meet the guidelines. Although not legally required to do so, they should have been forward-looking enough to realize that if such guidelines were not voluntarily followed, steps would be taken to assure compliance.

The 1972 Equal Employment Opportunity Act prohibits discrimination due to sex, race, color, religion, or national origin in employment of any kind, public or private, local, state, or federal.

MINORITY GROUP MEMBERS IN LAW ENFORCEMENT

According to the Task Force on the Police of the President's Commission on Law Enforcement and the Administration of Justice (1967), police administrators in most large cities are genuinely interested in attracting more officers from minority groups—Puerto Ricans, Mexican-Americans, Asian-Americans, and African-Americans.

To gain the community's general confidence and acceptance, police department personnel should be representative of the community as a whole. An integrated department helps reduce stereotyping and prejudice. Further, minority officers provide a department with an understanding of minority groups, their languages, and their subcultures, all with practical benefits to successful law enforcement. For example, a police officer with a knowledge of Spanish can help to prevent conflicts between the police and Spanish-speaking residents of the community.

A racially balanced and integrated police department both fosters community relations and increases police effectiveness.

WOMEN IN LAW ENFORCEMENT

Deborah Lancaster (1983, p. 43) notes:

In 1970, women constituted only 1 percent of sworn law enforcement officers. Today that figure is 4 percent and it continues to slowly rise each year. The men who are entering police work today are, for the most part, a new generation. They have been raised in an era of equal opportunity with the idea that women are equal and capable of performing just about any job. As these men rise through the ranks of police departments across the nation, I believe women will continue to enter and rise in the profession as well.

Initially women were restricted to processing female prisoners and to positions as police matrons. Many misconceptions about the female's ability to perform certain "masculine" tasks have been dispelled as a result of changing social attitudes; yet room for improvement remains.

Just before the turn of the century, a movement to employ women as regular police officers gained support. The first woman police officer in the United States was Marie Owen, appointed in 1893 by the Detroit Bureau of Police. In 1910 the first regular policewoman under civil service was appointed in Los Angeles. Shortly thereafter, in 1912, in New York, the first woman chief of police was appointed by the mayor of Milford, Ohio. By the end of World War I, over 220 cities employed policewomen.

A major reason for this relatively rapid acceptance of female peace officers was a change in the public's view of the police function. The acceptance of women paralleled the newly accepted emphasis on citizen protection and crime prevention rather than exclusive concentration on the enforcement of laws and detection of crimes.

THE POLICE CULTURE

Police officers work nights and weekends; they deal with highly confidential material that cannot be shared with friends; they must enforce the law impartially, whether it is a friend or a stranger who violates a law; and they frequently face public hostility, abuse, name calling, and biased reporting in the media. A combination of these factors largely accounts for the existence of a "police culture."

Individuals who become police officers frequently find that they lose their nonpolice friends within a few years. They work different hours—nights and weekends—and they may make some of their friends uneasy, especially their friends who drink and drive or who habitually speed. Police officers' friends often do not understand some of the actions police are forced to take in fulfilling their responsibilities.

Police officers not only frequently lose their nonpolice friends, they may also come to realize that they are now a part of a group that is isolated from the rest of society. Although they are highly visible, they are set apart. They may be feared, disliked, hated, or even assaulted by citizens, thus they keep close ranks for protection and security. The closer they become, the greater the suspicion and fear on the part of the citizens, leading to even tighter ranks, and so the cycle goes. Police officers are expected to take the place of mother, father, church, and school—to be "family"—to those who will not accept them.

The police become the "in group" and everyone else is the "out group." As noted by Skolnick (1967, p. 52), social isolation produces a "we-they" view of the world. To a police officer the world consists of cops and civilians, or perhaps better phrased as cops versus civilians.

This "them versus us" attitude leads to defensiveness exhibited in such ways as reluctance to give up traditional police responsibilities (for example, traffic control on state highways) or reluctance to explain their actions to citizens. Official police silence is sometimes necessary to protect the rights of others or to safeguard an investigation, but sometimes it is, in reality, a defensive response.

The dominant characteristic of the police culture is isolationism. It may result in a "them versus us" situation.

Police officers who isolate themselves from the community and from their nonpolice friends frequently develop a "one-track" life with the central focus being law enforcement. They may have few outside interests, devoting their attention to reading articles and watching programs related to law enforcement and socializing only with other individuals in the law enforcement field.

STRESS AND BURNOUT

No discussion of the real life of a police officer would be complete without recognizing the highly stressful nature of this profession. Police officers deal with crisis on a daily basis, usually that of someone else. Sometimes, however, the demands of the roles and how they are expected to be performed create enough stress to put police officers themselves into a crisis situation.

A police officer's job is highly stressful and may result in a personal crisis for the officer.

Several writers and researchers have stated that police work is, indeed, stressful:

- "Police work is a high stress occupation. It affects, shapes, and, at times, scars the individuals and families involved" (Dash and Reiser 1978, p. 18).

- "Police work has been identified as the most psychologically dangerous job in the world" (Axelberd and Valle 1978, p. 13).
- "Police officers have the highest rate of divorce of all professions and, according to recent research, most of it is due to a combination of the traditional demands imposed on an officer by himself, society, and the organization as well as the social change affecting today's marriages" (Somodevilla, et al., 1978, p. 10).
- "The law enforcement profession is notorious for the incidence of heart problems and in fact runs close to the top of professions in cardiovascular insufficiency and/or impairment" (Somodevilla, et al., 1978, p. 18).

Terry (1981, pp. 61—65) discusses four sets of stressors functioning in police work:

External stressors include frustrations with the criminal justice system, particularly in terms of the apparent leniency of court decisions and the scheduling of court appearances, discontent with unfavorable media coverage, resentment of certain opinions arising out of minority communities, and dislike of the decisions and interests of government and administrative bodies affecting the performance of police work.

Internal stressors cover a large number of problem areas, many of which are organizational, including training that is felt to be inadequate, equipment that is thought to be substandard or in a state of disrepair, poor pay, and ambiguously defined reward structures, as well as inadequate career development guidelines, offensive departmental policies, excessive paperwork, and intradepartmental political favoritism.

Task-related stressors include role conflicts, the rigors of shift work, boredom, fear, danger, being exposed to the miseries and brutalities of life, and work overload.

Finally individual stressors include fears about job competence, individual success, and safety. Discussions of individual stressors also include consideration of stressors arising out of performing police work, particularly health problems, alcoholism, marital problems, divorce, and suicide.

Bennett-Sandler and Ubell (1977, pp. 47–51) state that some departments have hired psychologists or counselors to help their members deal with the symptoms of job-related stress: alcoholism, suicide attempts, and the like. When faced with severe or prolonged stress, many police officers become what has been called "burned-out samaritans" (Maslach 1976, pp. 16–22).

According to Ellison and Genz (1978, p. 3): "A situation is more likely to be stressful and result in crisis reactions if it is unpredictable and if the individual has, or feels he has, little or no control over it." When stress results in "burnout," individuals tend to place themselves at a great distance from the situations in which they are involved: They tend to go by the book rather than by the specific situation; a major symptom of burnout is "the transformation of a person with original thought and creativity on the job into a mechanical bureaucrat" (Maslach 1976, p. 18).

Maslach (1976, p. 18) also describes symptoms that indicate when a person is burning out: "He becomes cynical and develops negative feelings about his clients. He may begin to talk of them as other than human, and to withdraw from contact with them."

According to Ellison and Genz (1978, p. 3): "The reactions described by Maslach are seen all too frequently in police officers." Niederhoffer (1967), too, describes the increasing alienation and cynicism in urban police officers, which are similar to Maslach's example of burnout. In fact, he asserts that the kind of cynicism that is directed against life, the world, and people in general is endemic to police officers of all ranks and persuasion.

Ellison and Genz (1978, pp. 4—5) examine some specific factors that might account for burnout. They first identify two specific types of particularly stressful situations: the first is the wounding or death of a fellow officer, especially one's partner; the second is the maiming or sexual assault of a child. They note that as long as only one kind of basic skill is required in a job, problems are minimal, but that when assignments require different, contradictory skills, problems do arise:

> When the necessity for interaction and sensitivity to human feelings and behavior is combined in an assignment with the necessity for dealing with situations which demand distancing because they [police officers] deal with basic human fears of mutilation, trauma, and death, the officer must attempt to perform the almost impossible balancing act of working appropriately with 'clients' who are undergoing ego-threatening crisis and protecting his own ego.

Ellison and Genz (1978, pp. 4—5) feel that burnout is more of a problem when officers are required to handle large numbers of serious calls or when they are not equipped or trained to handle them. Further, they believe that "job-related stress is exacerbated, and indeed, may be caused by certain traditional police practices. One of the most devastating of these is the indiscriminate use of a military model. This model sees police skills as technological ones. It assumes that every assignment involves skills that do not vary greatly from individual to individual or with the setting. It views discretion as unimportant and inappropriate for all but top brass." Unfortunately, this model simply does not work in many situations.

SUMMARY

The future success (or failure) of our law enforcement system depends in large part on the effectiveness of our police officers. Therefore, valid recruitment, screening, testing, and selection procedures must be used to assure that only well-qualified candidates are hired. Qualities identified in good police officers include reliability, leadership, judgment, persuasiveness, communication skills, accuracy, initiative, integrity, honesty, ego control, intelligence, and sensitivity. Individuals possessing such skills are sought through a careful selection procedure.

Police officer selection usually includes (1) a formal application, (2) a preliminary screening including a written examination and a psychological examination, (3) a physical agility test, (4) an oral interview, (5) a medical examination, and (6) a thorough background investigation. Most agencies require that a police officer candidate be a citizen of the United States, have or be eligible for a driver's license in the state, and not have been convicted of a felony. Additional requirements may specify educational level and residency in the community served.

Once candidates have passed all tests in the selection process, they usually enter a one-year probationary period during which they are observed while obtaining training and while applying this training on the streets. This probationary period allows for evaluation of the selected candidates. After the probation, the officers should continue to receive periodic in-service training to maintain already acquired skills and to achieve proficiency in new ones.

In addition to local and state requirements for recruitment and selection of police officers, certain federal guidelines and regulations must be met. Most important are the 1964 Omnibus Civil Rights Law, which prohibits discrimination in employment opportunities in private business, and the Equal Employment Opportunity Act of 1972, which prohibits discrimination due to sex, race, color, religion, or national origin in employment of any kind, public or private, local, state, or federal. All individuals meeting the specific requirements of the department should be given the opportunity to apply for and successfully compete with other candidates.

Members of minority groups are highly beneficial in a police department. A racially balanced and integrated police department fosters community relations and increases police effectiveness.

Just as members of minority groups have a promising future in law enforcement, so do women. The acceptance of women into law enforcement paralleled the newly accepted emphasis on citizen protection and crime prevention rather than exclusive concentration on the enforcement of laws and detection of crimes.

All police officers, be they white, black, brown, male, or female, are subjected to the hazards of police work, and all are expected to fulfill the responsibilities of the job. Each must be given an equal chance to become a police officer, to be adequately trained, and to be promoted. Each offers the profession an added dimension and one more means of fulfilling its mission.

The dominant characteristic of the "police culture" is isolationism, which may result in a "them versus us" orientation that does little to further good community relations. Stress and burnout are often a problem for police officers.

Discussion Questions

1. What is the most common restriction for off-duty work for a police officer?

2. Where are the United States Civil Service Commission offices in your area?

3. Is a newspaper advertisement placed by a police department that requests that only women apply for a job opening fair?

4. What is the most common reason for rejection during the selection process?

5. What employment opportunities in law enforcement are available locally? In your county? Your state?

6. What is the percentage of minorities and women on your police force? Is this "balanced"? How did this situation come to be?

7. How do police officers deal with their own lives when they spend so much time with the worst of people?

8. What are some societal factors interfering with police work?

9. What is the dominant characteristic of the police culture?

10. Whose problem is it when the police and the community don't get along?

References

Axelbred, M., and Valle, J. "South Florida's Approach to Police Stress Management." *Police Stress* , no. 2, (1978): 13—14.

Bennett-Sandler, G., and Ubell, E. "Time Bombs in Blue." *New York Magazine* (March 21, 1977): 47—51.

Dash, J., and Reiser, M. "Suicide among Police in Urban Law Enforcement Agencies."*Journal of Police Science and Administration* (1978): 18—21.

Ellison, W. K., and Genz, J. L. "The Police Officer as Burned-Out Samaritan. *FBI Law Enforcement Bulletin* (March 1978): 2—7.

"Indiana University Develops Police Selection Procedure." *Target* 6 no. 8 (September 1977): 1.

Lancaster, D. A. "One Woman's Struggle." *Police* 7, no. 9 (September 1983): 42—43.

Maslach, C. "Burned-Out." *Human Behavior* (September 1976): 16—22.

Niederhoffer, A. *Behind the Shield.* New York: Anchor, 1967.

President's Commission on Law Enforcement and Administration of Justice. Task Force Report. *The Police.* Washington, D.C.: U.S. Government Printing Office, 1967.

Skolnick, J. H. *Justice without Trial: Law Enforcement in a Democratic Society.* New York: John Wiley and Sons, 1967.

Somodevilla, S. A.; Baker, C. J.; Hill, W. R.; and the Dallas Police Department. Departmental memorandum prepared by the psychological services unit of the Dallas Police Department, (January 1978).

Terry, W. C. III, "Police Stress: The Empirical Evidence." *Journal of Police Science and Administration* 9, no. 1 (1981): 61—65.

SECTION TWO
Police Operations:
The Twenty-First Century
Law Enforcement Officer

By this point you should have a good understanding of the total context within which present-day law enforcement officers function. They have a rich heritage dating back centuries. They must also enforce a vast array of complex laws while themselves staying within these laws.

This section looks at policing in the 1990s and into the next century. It begins with the roles and responsibilities of the modern law enforcement officer (chapter 6). Police operations can usually be divided into four basic categories: community service (chapter 7), patrol (chapter 8), traffic (chapter 9), and investigation (chapters 10 and 11). Although discussed separately, the four categories have considerable overlap. In some smaller agencies all four functions are performed by a single field service division. In very small agencies they may be performed by a single police officer. Larger agencies, on the other hand, may have divisions within each of the four categories. In addition, larger agencies may have a separate division to deal with juveniles.

The section concludes with a discussion of how police officers search and arrest and still stay within the law (chapter 12).

CHAPTER SIX
Policing in the 1990s: Roles and Responsibilities

The will of the people is the best law—Ulysses S. Grant

DO YOU KNOW

How the police officer's roles relate to the people?

What five basic roles the police officer must play?

What special skills are required of officers?

What two department organizational categories are?

Who the local-level chief law enforcement officer is?

What functions are handled in administration?

How officers receive their information?

What is the main method of transmitting information between headquarters and units in the field?

What types of records are used in law enforcement?

Why centralization of records is encouraged?

What the NCIC is?

What is required by a data privacy act?

What functions are handled in field service?

What tasks occur in patrol? In a traffic division? In investigation? In community relations programs?

What specialized officers or departments may exist?

What basic styles of policing have been identified?

What discretion is and what role it plays?

Introduction

Chapter 6

A quarter of a century ago, in a special report for the president's Crime Commission, Professors Lohman and Misner (1966 p. 50) surveyed the literature and research on police roles and responsibilities and listed the following major activities of a typical law enforcement agency:

- Preventing and repressing crime.
- Maintaining the peace (domestic tranquility).
- Protecting persons and property (security).
- Enforcing laws.
- Detecting crime.
- Recovering lost and stolen property.
- Apprehending offenders.
- Regulating noncriminal conduct.
- Protecting individual rights.
- Controlling traffic.
- Providing miscellaneous public services.
- Preparing cases to present in court.

Much has changed in the past quarter of a century, and the change is likely to continue through the 1990s. Police departments will be taking a more positive philosophy of *social responsibility*. Many people in our society recognize that police agencies will be serving society in ways they formerly were not expected (or trained) to serve. What was formerly second to the last on the list, "providing miscellaneous public services," is likely to replace the responsibility traditionally ranked as top priority, that is, "preventing and repressing crime."

Experience indicates, however, that the police are quite capable of providing emotional first aid or counseling services to people who might not otherwise look for or accept such services. Many communities look to the police for emergency medical care and other services not provided elsewhere on a continuous basis. These expectations are causing concern among law enforcement officers who do *not* see their primary responsibility as that of solving sociological problems. This is consistent with the general theme of most police officers: "We're not social workers; we're crime fighters."

Unfortunately, the police are infused with this narrow perception of their roles and responsibilities by those who preceded them. But, it is a fact that the police *do* perform social work. The general public demands it of them. In fact, they perform more social work than law enforcement activities. Less then 3 percent of police officers' time is spent on dispatches concerning crimes against persons. Lamentably, as social workers, most police officers are poorly trained and incompetent.

What do police officers do? The answer according to many surveys is that they spend more than 50 percent of their time on administrative tasks such as community relations, compiling various types of reports, running errands, attending court, serving warrants, and the like. Spotting and towing abandoned vehicles is a good example of an administrative task. In some cases, such as larceny and burglary, and even in some crimes

SECTION VI
LAW ENFORCEMENT PERSONNEL

Law Enforcement Code of Ethics

As a Law Enforcement Officer, *my fundamental duty is to serve mankind; to safeguard lives and property; to protect the innocent against deception, the weak against oppression or intimidation, and the peaceful against violence or disorder; and to respect the Constitutional rights of all men to liberty, equality and justice.*

I will *keep my private life unsullied as an example to all; maintain coura-geous calm in the face of danger, scorn, or ridicule; develop self-restraint; and be constantly mindful of the welfare of others. Honest in thought and deed in both my personal and official life, I will be exemplary in obeying the laws of the land and the regulations of my department. Whatever I see or hear of a confidential nature or that is confided to me in my official capacity will be kept ever secret unless revelation is necessary in the performance of my duty.*

I will *never act officiously or permit personal feelings, prejudices, animos-ities or friendships to influence my decisions. With no compromise for crime and with relentless prosecution of criminals, I will enforce the law courteously and appropriately without fear or favor, malice or ill will, never employing unnecessary force or violence and never accepting gratuities.*

I recognize *the badge of my office as a symbol of public faith, and I accept it as a public trust to be held so long as I am true to the ethics of the police service. I will constantly strive to achieve these objectives and ideals, dedicating myself before God to my chosen profession . . . law enforcement.*

Source: Reprinted by permission of the International Association of Chiefs of Police.

Figure 6–1 **Law Enforcement Code of Ethics**

against persons such as assault, the police may not be notified for several hours or several days after the incident has happened. In other cases police are assigned administrative duties to report on crimes against persons and property where they, in effect, function as "order takers." Much of what they report is primarily for insurance companies, not for the "fight against crime."

As stated, police officers spend more than 50 percent of their time on administrative tasks, but police departments are among the most poorly managed organizations in our society. No business, public or private, could survive very long without knowing what its responsibilities were and how well they were doing. But the police role is frequently vague. And the only record of activities that most departments maintain is the FBI Uniform Crime Report of the eight index crimes. With this emphasis, is it any wonder that the police come to perceive themselves as crime fighters?

WHAT IS POLICING?

John Webster (n.d., p. 94) points out the difference between what people often think of as the police officer's role and what it is in most instances:

> The cover of a major city's annual police report dramatically shows two police officers reaching for their guns as they burst through the doors of a massive black and white police car which is screeching to a halt . . . the flashing red lights and screaming siren complete the illustration. A less dramatic scene on an inside page of the report shows a police officer talking to a grateful mother whose lost child was returned. Which one of these illustrations most accurately describes the police role? . . . The New York Times reports that policemen like to think of themselves as uniformed soldiers in an extremely dangerous war against crime . . . in fact the police are more social workers and administrator than crime fighter.

What is it about the police officer's role that makes the general public think of the law enforcement aspect of police work more often than the social service aspect when, in fact, approximately 90 percent of a police officers's time is spent in the social service function? According to Egon Bittner (1971), the police, "unlike you and me, bear a very broad right to use coercive force in all sorts of situations that may call for it." Klockars (1983, p. 227) expands on the police officer's role and the right to use coercive force:

> Whether it is catching criminals, enforcing laws, maintaining order, moving pedestrian or vehicular traffic, managing the scene at fires, accidents, deaths, and unanticipated births, picking up lost or runaway children, taking custody of drunk or deranged persons, handling domestic or neighborhood disputes, turning on a fire hydrant on an oppressively hot city summer day, the police officer does these things because doing them may require exercising the right to use coercive force. The work of polic-

ing appears to call far more often for the skills of a social worker or administrator than those of a crime fighter. How do we reconcile Bittner's concept of the right to use coercive force as the core of the police role with the finding that the vast majority of work police are called upon to do requires skills of a social service nature? Bittner's [1974] answer . . . is that while the core of the police role is the right to use coercive force, THE SKILL OF POLICING CONSISTS IN FINDING WAYS TO AVOID ITS USE.

THE POLICE OFFICER AND THE PEOPLE

You learned earlier that **police authority** comes from the people—their laws and institutions. Police officers are ultimately responsible to the public they serve, and they usually recruit their officers from among local citizens.

Although the Tenth Amendment reserves police power for state and local governments, these governments must adhere to the principles of the Constitution and the Bill of Rights as well as to federal and state statutes. Police officers are not only a part of their community, they are also part of the state and federal government, which provides their formal base of authority, as well as a part of the state and federal criminal justice system, which determines society's course in deterring lawbreakers and rehabilitating offenders.

Note that in figure 6–2 the arrows between the citizens, governments, and courts go two ways. Not only are the people ultimately responsible for establishing governments and courts, they also elect the representatives

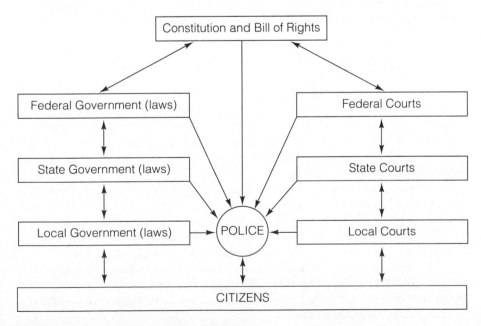

Figure 6–2   **Sources of Police Authority**

who serve there. The citizens also directly influence the police. To a large extent, the specific goals and priorities of the police are established by what the community wants. For example, a community might want more patrols at night, stricter enforcement of traffic regulations during rush hour, or reduced enforcement for certain violations such as speeding.

Priorities are often more influenced by the desires of the policed than by any other consideration. Because the success of the police depends heavily upon public support, the wishes of the citizens must be listened to and considered.

The people largely determine the role of the police and give them their authority to fulfill this role. Their support is vital.

In addition, because the police are highly visible representatives of local government and are on duty twenty-four hours a day, people often call upon them for services that they are not, specifically, required to perform. Other agencies might be providing these services, but people do not know of them. For example, if a woman seeks help in dealing with a drunk husband (he is not abusing her; he is just drunk), a drug counselor, minister, or social worker might be the appropriate person to call. The woman, however, often does not know this. Since the police officers' reactions to requests for help affect the amount of respect received and promote a cooperative relationship with the public, police officers usually respond as helpfully as possible, even when the matter is technically civil and outside their responsibility (and sometimes their expertise).

BASIC ROLES OF THE POLICE OFFICER

Since the citizens of a community have such a great influence on the role of the police within the community, many differences exist in roles performed by police officers in different geographic localities. Generally, however, five basic roles are performed: enforcing laws, preserving the peace, preventing crime, protecting civil rights and civil liberties, and providing services.

These roles often overlap. For example, officers intervening in a fight may not only enforce a law by arresting a suspect for assault, they may also maintain order, prevent others from becoming involved in the fight, protect the civil rights and civil liberties of the suspect, the victim, and the bystanders, and provide emergency service to an injured victim.

Success or failure in fulfilling each role directly affects the success or failure of fulfilling the other roles. Although five roles normally performed by police officers are listed, in reality, policing is a single role comprised of numerous responsibilities.

Five basic roles of most police officers are to:

- *enforce laws;*
- *preserve the peace;*
- *prevent crimes;*
- *protect civil rights and civil liberties;*
- *provide services.*

Law Enforcement—Crime Repression

The term "law enforcement officer" underscores the central importance of this long-accepted responsibility. Historically, enforcement of laws has been the prime responsibility of police officers; however, this long-accepted role has become increasingly complex. Not only must decisions be made as to what laws to enforce, but also the police have become an integral part of the criminal justice system, responsible not only for apprehending offenders but for assisting in their prosecution as well.

Police officers are responsible for enforcing laws and for assisting in the prosecution of offenders.

The stereotype of the police officer emphasizes the role of "crime fighter," often to the exclusion of all others. In enforcing laws, police officers perform many functions: investigating offenses, interrogating suspects, interviewing witnesses, conducting searches, acting upon leads, participating in stakeouts, apprehending suspects, recovering stolen property, testifying in court, suppressing riots, combatting organized crime, and patrolling to discover crimes in progress.

The patrol function is central to law enforcement. Not only may law enforcement officers encounter crimes in progress, they may also encounter "suspicious" circumstances that may be crime related. Questioning a suspicious person might lead to arrests for outstanding warrants, possession of narcotics or concealed weapons, burglary, and other serious crimes.

Because each community and each state have numerous statutes to be enforced and limited resources, full enforcement of all laws is never possible. Even if it were, it is questionable whether full enforcement would be in keeping with legislative intent or the people's wishes. The police can, do, and must exercise discretion in which laws to enforce; that they cannot enforce all laws at all times must be accepted by both the police officer and the public.

Each police department must decide which reported crimes to actively investigate and to what degree, as well as which unreported crimes to seek out and to what degree. The law does not set priorities; it simply defines crimes, classifies them as felonies or misdemeanors, and assesses penalties for them. The police department sets its own priorities, based on citizens' needs.

Usually police departments concentrate law enforcement activities on serious crimes—those that pose the greatest threat to public safety and/or cause the greatest economic losses (the Part 1 Index Crimes). From that point on, priorities are usually determined by past police experience, the wishes and expectations of the citizens, and the resources available.

Engaging in law enforcement activities such as arresting armed robbers and using force when needed are sanctioned by statute and public opinion. On the other hand, if police become involved in conflicts that do not involve a crime, such as loud domestic arguments, their action may be viewed as interference. Even within the traditional role of enforcing laws, decisions must be made as to what is proper and what is not.

Further, the police officer's responsibility does not end with enforcing a law and apprehending a suspect. In effect, when the police arrest an offender, they have initiated the criminal justice process. The offender's guilt must then be determined in court. The police officer plays a key role in assisting the prosecutor in preparing the case and often is called on to present evidence in court (the focus of chapter 19). Unfortunately, since police are in the closest contact with the public, they are often blamed for failures in the criminal justice system. For example, an assault victim whose attacker is found innocent in court may feel resentment not only against the court but against the police.

The release of a suspect from custody for lack of sufficient evidence, the failure of a prosecutor to take a case to trial, or the failure of the corrections system to reform a convict prior to parole or release all directly affect the role police officers must play as well as their public image. And the public image of the police officer is critical when you consider that a large percentage of police work is in direct response to citizen complaints or reports. In fact, members of the community may be the single most important factor in the total law enforcement effort.

Preserving the Peace

The role of preserving the peace has also long been accepted by law enforcement officers. They have the legal authority to arrest individuals for disturbing the peace or for disorderly conduct.

Police are responsible for preserving the peace.

Police are often called upon to intervene in noncriminal conduct such as that which occurs at public events (crowd control), in social relations (domestic disputes), and in traffic control (parking, pedestrians) to maintain law and order. They frequently help people solve problems that they cannot cope with alone.

Often such problems, if unresolved, could result in crime. For example, loud parties, unruly crowds, or disputes between members of a family, business partners, landlord and tenant, or a businessperson and customer might result in bodily harm—assault. Studies indicate that domestic violence frequently leads to homicide. In addition, responses to domestic disputes are a leading cause of serious injury and fatal assaults on police officers.

The police officer's effectiveness in actually preserving the peace will largely be determined by public acceptance of this role. Often if a police officer simply asks a landlord to allow a tenant access to his or her apartment or asks the host of a loud party to turn down the stereo, this is enough. Mere police presence may reduce the possibility of a crime—at least temporarily.

If the citizens respect the police and accept their suggestions, it is likely that police officers will be successful in preserving the peace. On the other hand, if the citizens do not accept this function and do not respect the police, the presence of police may provoke crime and violence. Here, as in the enforcement of laws, public support is vital.

Crime Prevention

Crime prevention is closely related to law enforcement and preservation of the peace. If the peace has been kept, crime has, in effect, been prevented. Crime prevention differs from peacekeeping and law enforcing in that it attempts to eliminate potentially dangerous or criminal situations.

A routine patrol might not only discover a crime in progress, but it might also deter or prevent crimes from being committed. If the police are very visible in a community, it is likely that many crimes will be prevented. This is extremely difficult to prove, however, since we do not know what crimes might have been committed if the police were not present.

Police officers are responsible for attempting to prevent a crime.

Notice the word *attempting*. These efforts will often be unsuccessful. Just as police officers cannot be expected to enforce all the laws at all times, they cannot be expected to prevent all crimes from occurring.

Crime prevention activities frequently undertaken by police officers include working with juveniles, cooperating with probation and parole personnel, educating the public, instigating operation identification programs, and providing visible evidence of police authority. In addition, many of the community services often provided by police departments (discussed in chapter 7) aid considerably in crime prevention.

Protection of Constitutional Rights

The first paragraph of the *Law Enforcement Code of Ethics* concludes with the statement that a law enforcement officer has a fundamental duty "to respect the Constitutional rights of all men to liberty, equality, and justice," described in chapter 3.

As noted by the National Advisory Commission on Criminal Justice Standards and Goals (1973, p. 9): "Any definition of the police role must acknowledge that the Constitution imposes restrictions on the power of the legislatures to prohibit protected conduct, and to some extent defines the limits of police authority in the enforcement of established laws."

The commission goes on to state, however, the following (1973, p. 9): "Concern for the constitutional rights of accused persons processed by the police has tended to obscure the fact that the police have an affirmative obligation to protect all persons in the free exercise of their rights. The police must provide safety for persons exercising their constitutional right to assemble, to speak freely, and to petition for redress of their grievances."

Many citizens are angered when a suspect's rights prevent prosecution of the case. They begin to have doubts about the criminal justice system; however, should these same individuals find themselves in the position of being suspected of a crime, they, doubtless, would expect their rights to be fully protected. (Recall the Magna Carta and how these rights began.) It was Sir John Fortescue who said, "Indeed, one would rather twenty guilty persons should escape the punishment of death than one innocent person should be executed." Countries must guarantee all citizens, even those perceived as unworthy of such protection, their constitutional rights or there is danger of a police state.

The authority, goals, and methods of the police must promote individual liberty, public safety, and social justice. The role of protecting civil rights and civil liberties is perceived by some as the single most important role of the police officer. As a case in point, the National Advisory Commission on Criminal Justice Standards and Goals states (1973, p. 9): "If the overall purposes of the police service in today's society were narrowed to a single objective, that objective would be to preserve the peace in a manner consistent with the freedoms secured by the Constitution."

Police are responsible for protecting citizens' constitutional rights.

Provide Services

In addition to enforcing laws, preserving the peace, assisting in preventing crime, and protecting civil rights and liberties, the police are often called upon to provide additional services to their community.

This role is acknowledged in the first sentence of the *Law Enforcement Code of Ethics:* "As a law enforcement officer, my fundamental duty is to serve mankind." Many police departments have as their motto: "Serve and Protect."

As society has become more complex, however, so have the types of service requested. Many new demands are made on the police because of their authority. Included among the numerous functions the police may perform in providing services are giving information, directions, and advice; counseling and referring; licensing and registering vehicles; intervening in domestic arguments; working with neglected children; rendering emergency medical or rescue services; dealing with alcoholics and the mentally ill; finding lost children; dealing with stray animals; and controlling traffic and crowds. In addition, many police departments provide community education programs regarding crime, drugs, safety, and the like.

Police are often responsible for providing services.

Considerable disagreement exists regarding what type and amount of services the police should provide.

On one hand, individuals like Garmire (1972, pp. 3—7) feel that this role should not be performed by police officers. He contends that to expect police to perform the two conflicting roles of law enforcement and community service is wrong:

> Even if the numbers of policemen were vastly increased, even if their training were improved, and even if their resources were expanded, I still submit that they could not perform both roles—so sharply do they conflict and so different are the skills required. One person simply cannot reasonably be expected to master both roles intellectually and jump psychologically from one to another in an instant's notice. . . . If we are to restore any semblance of faith in the police by the public—and the police themselves—we must begin first by defining the police role very carefully so that it does not distort reality . . . by fostering the belief that police . . . could function as a gigantic surrogate service agency to the community handling all the needs of the people all the time.

Garmire criticizes sharply the view that the police department is a "social agency of last resort—particularly after 5:00 P.M. and on weekends."

On the other hand, many contend that providing social services is critical to perform effectively the other functions expected of police officers, a position supported in the Task Force Report of the President's Commission on Law Enforcement and Administration of Justice (1967, p. 14):

> *Proposals to relieve the police of what are essentially social services have also been lacking in their consideration of the relationship of such services to the incidence of more serious crimes. Domestic disturbances, for example, often culminate in a serious assault or a homicide. The down-and-out drunk is almost a certain victim of a theft if he is left to lie on the street and has any article of value on him. The streetwalking prostitute may, in one sense, be primarily a social problem, but many streetwalkers engage regularly in arranging the robbery of their patrons as a supplement to their income.*
>
> *It might be desirable for agencies other than the police to provide community services that bear no relationship to crime or potential crime situations. But the failure of such agencies to develop and the relationship between the social problems in question and the incidence of crime suggest that the police are likely to remain, for some time, as the only twenty-four-hour-a-day, seven-day-a-week agency that is spread over an entire city.*

Between these two positions regarding the social service function of the police is that of the National Advisory Commission on Criminal Justice Standards and Goals (1973, pp. 14—15). It recognizes that police are often inappropriately asked to perform functions that might better be performed by another agency of the government—usually because they are the only government representatives available around the clock and because they have the resources and the authority to use force if necessary. It also notes, however, that in many small cities and towns, the police services provided (even though considered by some to be inappropriate "social services") could not be provided by any other agencies.

Many police agencies have provided personnel with information to refer persons in need to the proper agency. For example, since New York City began using a citywide 911 emergency number, telephone calls for nonpolice municipal services have decreased dramatically. Police officers in Washington, D.C., use the *Referral Handbook of Social Services*, which indexes available governmental and private services by problem and agency. Police in Milwaukee, Wisconsin, have a comprehensive directory of almost five hundred community agencies and organizations.

What is of primary importance is that people who need help receive it; who provides the help is secondary. Since many people are likely to turn first to the police for help, however, the police officer must be prepared either to provide the help or to refer the person to an agency that can provide it.

REQUIRED PROFICIENCIES

Look again at the two middle paragraphs of the *Law Enforcement Code of Ethics:*

I will keep my private life unsullied as an example to all; maintain courageous calm in the face of danger, scorn, or ridicule; develop self-restraint; and be constantly mindful of the welfare of others. Honest in thought and deed in both my personal and official life, I will be exemplary in obeying the laws of the land and the regulations of my department. Whatever I see or hear of a confidential nature or that is confided to me in my official capacity will be kept ever secret unless revelation is necessary in the performance of my duty.

I will never act officiously or permit personal feelings, prejudices, animosities or friendships to influence my decisions. With no compromise for crime and with relentless prosecution of criminals, I will enforce the law courteously and appropriately without fear or favor, malice or ill will, never employing unnecessary force or violence and never accepting gratuities.

Not only are police officers expected to enforce laws, preserve the peace, prevent crimes, protect constitutional rights, and perform community services, they are also expected to do so in an impeccable, professional manner. As noted by Dwight Dalbey of the FBI (James 1968, p. 104):

We expect of a police officer the wisdom of Solomon in understanding the law, the strength of Sampson in arresting a criminal, the gentleness of St. Francis of Assisi in repelling a riot, the patience of Job in dealing with each of us, and the moral purity of Caesar's wife in a nation whose public and private morals in areas outside police work are sometimes open to legitimate questions.

In spite of these expectations, police officers are human, with emotions, biases, and weaknesses. Their work is sometimes dangerous. They see suffering, injustice, and cruelty. They see people at their best and their worst. They are under constant pressure, even when things are momentarily calm. They must make rapid decisions, often without any guidelines. They frequently lack the necessary equipment and/or training. Their work is further complicated by people's conflicting expectations of them.

Police roles must be carried out skillfully and professionally. This requires mental, intellectual, physical, and personal proficiencies.

To perform in the manner expected by the department and the community, the police officer needs numerous proficiencies. The following list summarizes the results of a University of Chicago study of the behavioral requirements needed to perform police patrol duties. Saunders, Charles B., Jr. *Upgrading the American Police.* Brookings Institution, 1970, pp. 17—18.

Mental   Police officers must:

- Endure a long period of monotony in routine patrol yet react quickly (almost simultaneously) and effectively to problem situations observed on the street or to orders issued by the radio dispatcher (in much the same way that a combat pilot must react to interception or a target opportunity).
- Have the facility to act effectively in extremely divergent interpersonal situations. A police officer constantly confronts persons who are acting in violation of the law, ranging from curfew violators to felons.
- Endure verbal and physical abuse from citizens and offenders (as when placing a person under arrest or facing day-in-and-day-out race prejudice) while using only necessary force in the performance of their functions.
- Tolerate stress in a multitude of forms, such as meeting the violent behavior of a mob, arousing people in a burning building, coping with the pressures of a high-speed chase or a weapon being fired at them, or dealing with a woman bearing a child.

Personal   Police officers must:

- Relate to the people of their beat—businesspeople, residents, school officials, visitors, etc. Their interpersonal relations must range up and down a continuum defined by friendliness and persuasion on one end and firmness and force at the other.
- Exhibit a professional, self-assured presence and a self-confident manner in their conduct when dealing with offenders, the public, and the court.
- Take charge of situations, for example, a crime or accident scene, yet not unduly alienate participants or bystanders.
- Be flexible enough to work under loose supervision in most of their day-to-day patrol activities and also under the direct supervision of superiors in situations where large numbers of officers are required.
- Exhibit personal courage in the face of dangerous situations that may result in serious injury or death.
- Maintain objectivity while dealing with a host of special interest groups, ranging from relatives of offenders to members of the press.
- Maintain a balanced perspective in the face of constant conflict, for example, refrain from accepting bribes or "favors," provide impartial law enforcement, etc.

Intellectual   Police officers must:

- Exhibit initiative, problem-solving capacity, effective judgment, and imagination in coping with the numerous complex situations they are called upon to face, for example, a family disturbance, a potential suicide, a robbery in progress, an accident, or a disaster.

Police officers themselves clearly recognize this requirement and refer to it as "showing street sense."

- Make prompt and effective decisions, sometimes in life-and-death situations, and be able to size up a situation quickly and take appropriate action.
- Demonstrate mature judgment, as in deciding whether an arrest is warranted by the circumstances or a warning is sufficient, or in assessing a situation where the use of force may be needed.
- Demonstrate critical awareness in discerning signs of out-of-the-ordinary conditions or circumstances that indicate trouble or a crime in progress.
- Adequately perform the communication and record-keeping functions of the job, including oral reports, preparation of formal case reports, and the completion of departmental and force forms.
- Be capable of restoring equilibrium to social groups, for example, restoring order in a family fight, in a disagreement between neighbors, or in a clash between rival youth gangs.
- Be skillful in questioning suspected offenders, victims, and witnesses of crimes.
- Gain knowledge of their patrol areas, not only of its physical characteristics but also of its normal routine of events and the usual behavior patterns of its residents.

Physical   Police officers must:

- Exhibit a number of complex psychomotor skills, such as driving a vehicle in normal and emergency situations, firing a weapon accurately under extremely varied conditions, maintaining agility, endurance, and strength, and showing facility in self-defense and apprehension, as in taking a person into custody with a minimum of force.

Few roles in modern society are as demanding as that of the police officer.

THE VITAL ROLE OF WRITING SKILLS

In November of 1987 the Alexandria Technical Institute Law Enforcement Program mailed a questionnaire to all eighty-seven Minnesota county attorneys. The purpose of the survey was to learn the prosecutor's opinions about police reports and how these reports could be improved. Fifty-two county attorneys (60 percent) returned the survey.

Of those responding, 98 percent felt that police reports were either critically important or very important to the successful prosecution of criminal cases. Among their comments were the following:

The police reports are often the first impression a judge or defense attorney has of an officer's competence, both generally and in regard to the specific elements of the offense charged. If the report is weak, defense attorneys and judges are inclined to require officers to testify and to scrutinize carefully the officer's testimony. A well-written report can often result in a settlement of the case without an Omnibus Hearing or trial.

All prosecution is initiated by the reports submitted by the investigating agency. The decision to charge someone with a crime is based upon the police reports, usually alone.

Good police reports help to speed up the entire system. Delays in prosecution often occur because of incomplete reports.

Poorly phrased reports or reports that are too brief have a tendency to blow up in your face at trial time.

If sloppy or incomplete, they will impeach the officer at trial.

A well-written report alone can settle a case.

As noted by Stokes (1987, preface):

Most law enforcement officers submit their reports for prosecution with concern over the outcome, but without much thought about the wheels they've started in motion. This is understandable, for they've done their jobs and many more cases wait to be investigated. But what happens when they haven't really done their jobs—when their reports are distorted or incomplete (as many are) because of poor writing? The results not only cost the taxpayers in wasted man-hours, but they also breed disaster in the courtroom.

To cite an all-too-common example, in one recent criminal case, the reporting officer, using the passive voice, wrote the following in his report: "The weapon was found in the bushes where the suspect had thrown it." He did not clarify this statement elsewhere in his report. Expectedly, the prosecuting attorney subpoenaed the reporting officer to testify at the preliminary hearing. Unfortunately, the reporting officer's testimony revealed that his partner, not he, had observed the suspect's action and had retrieved the weapon. The partner was unavailable to testify on short notice. Without his testimony the necessary elements of the crime could not be established. The case was dismissed and had to be re-filed. The hours expended at the time of the dismissal—by witnesses, secretaries, clerks, attorneys, and the judge—were virtually wasted because the whole process had to be repeated. The reporting officer could have avoided the problem at the onset through use of the active voice, by writing: "Officer Jones found the weapon in the bushes." Sadly, this basic writing error is not an isolated example; such errors slip through the system daily, causing delays in the judicial process and depleting dwindling budgets.

Rutledge (1986, pp. 169—70) says: Given a choice between this:

Dick sees Jane
    and this:
    It should be noted that a male white juvenile subject, identified as subject Dick, in fact visually observes a female white juvenile subject, identified as subject Jane,
    I'll take "Dick sees Jane" anyday.

Rutledge (1986, pp. 169—70) suggests that if police officers write every report in straightforward, factual plain talk, there would most likely be the following:

Less police time writing reports.
More police time in the field.
Less typing time.
Less copying time and expense.
Less filing space and expense.
Less reading time by investigators and supervisors.
More time for investigating and supervising.
Less reading time by prosecutors.
Less confusion as to what the report says.
Less duplicative work.
More factual work.
Better police work.
More reports approved.
Fewer rewrites.
More complaints approved.
More defense motions denied.
Fewer defense motions filed.
Higher sentences on negotiated pleas.
Better police testimony.
Worse defendant testimony.
More convictions.
Fewer trials.
More pleas.
Less court time for officers.

ORGANIZATION OF THE DEPARTMENT

According to Arnold and Brungardt (1983, p. 232): "The organizational features of the United States police department exhibit a great deal of variation. The departments range from small, informally organized, small-town operations to highly bureaucratic metropolitan police departments with many subdivisions and thousands of employees."

The two basic organizational units within most police departments are field services (also called operations or on-line services) and administrative services (also called staff or support services).

Most police departments are organized into two basic units: field services and administrative services. Tasks and personnel are assigned to one or the other.

Field services include patrol, traffic control, community services, and investigation. **Administrative services** include recruitment and training, planning and research, records and communications, crime laboratories, and facilities including the police headquarters and jail. Teamwork is essential within and between field services and administrative services.

The chief of police oversees the operation of the entire department and coordinates the efforts of field and administrative services. Under the chief of police, depending on the size of the department, are captains, lieutenants, sergeants, and police officers.

The chief law enforcement officer at the local level is the chief of police.

A typical department might be organized as illustrated in figure 6–3. The specific organization within a police department is influenced by the department's size, location, and the extent and type of crime with which it must deal. For example, a small police department often combines patrol, traffic, community services, and investigative tasks in a single division; a large police department usually has separate divisions for each. A community with a major freeway running through its business section faces different problems than a community located on a coast or on a border between the United States and Canada or Mexico. Communities with large groups of minorities face different problems than those that are homogeneous. For some communities, traffic control is a major problem; for others gambling, smuggling, or racial unrest may be priorities.

ADMINISTRATIVE SERVICES

Administrative services include records and communications, recruitment and training, and provision of special facilities and services.

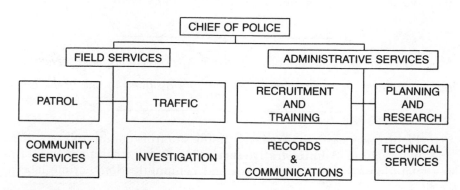

Figure 6–3 Typical Department Organization

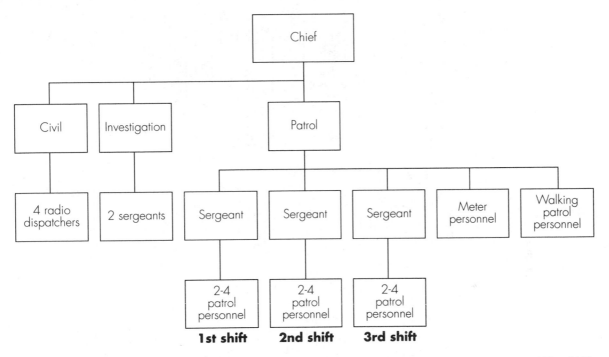

Source: Paul B. Weston, *Police Organization and Management.* Pacific Palisades, Calif.: Goodyear Publishing Co., 1976, pp. 107 and 108.

Figure 6—4   **Organization of a Small Police Department**

Twenty-five to thirty employees. The shift sergeant on duty serves as patrol commander in the absence of the chief.

Administrative services' two areas that most directly affect the efficient provision of field services are communications and records.

Communications

To properly serve the community, police officers must be kept currently and completely informed. They must know how much of each type of crime occurs, such as burglaries, car prowls, malicious destruction of property, and auto thefts. They also have to know where the crimes are occurring.

Current information is usually provided at roll call and by means of radio.

Roll Call   One of the most important functions of the administrative division in its support of the other units of the police department is keeping members informed of daily police operations and providing administrative instructions and special assignments and tasks to be performed. This is usually done at a **roll call** session before the officers on the next shift go out into the street.

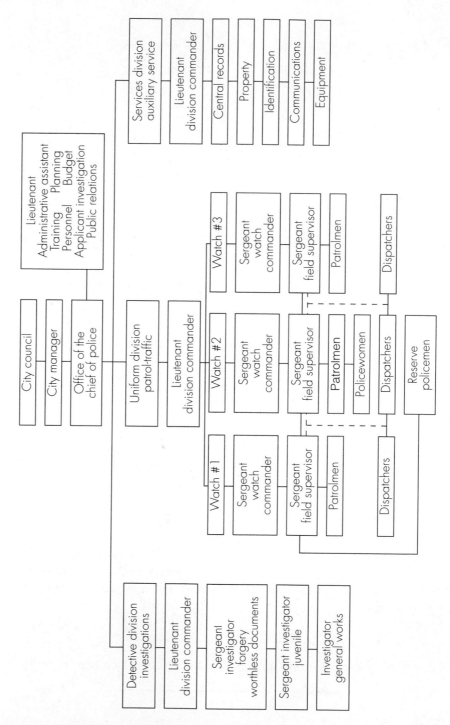

Source: Paul B. Weston, *Police Organization and Management.* Pacific Palisades, Calif.: Goodyear Publishing Co., 1976, pp. 107 and 108.

Figure 6–5   Organization of a Medium-Sized Police Department

Four hundred to six hundred police employees. Note the functional relationship between field supervisors (sergeants) and dispatchers.

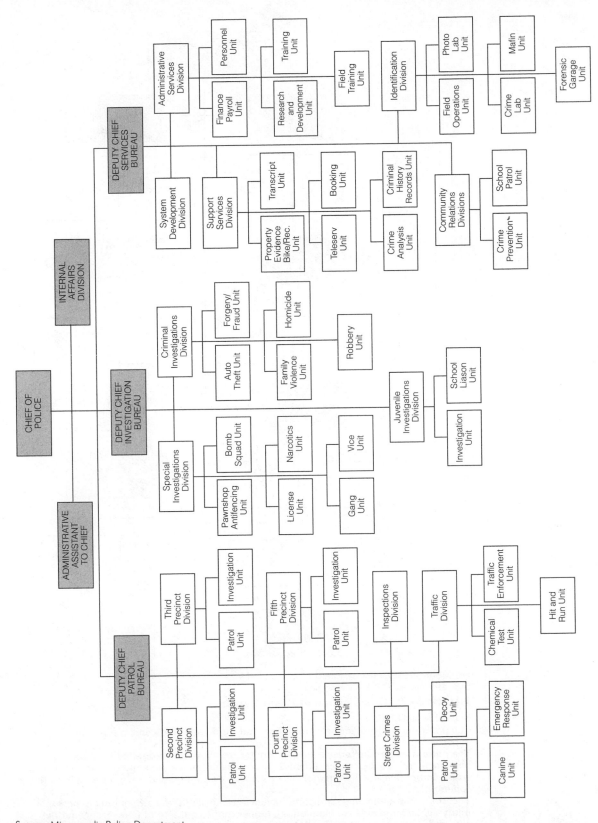

Source: Minneapolis Police Department

Figure 6–6 **Organization of a Large Police Department**

*Number of personnel assigned
Source: Minneapolis Police Department

Figure 6–7 **Organization of Patrol Bureau**

Major Responsibilities:
The patrol bureau provides general patrol and traffic law enforcement functions for the department.
The patrol function includes responsibility for responding to requests for emergency and non-emergency police service, offender apprehension, prevention and deterrence of crime, initial investigation and evidence gathering and maintenance of order within the community.
The traffic law enforcement function includes responsibility for responding to personal injury vehicular accidents, maintaining proper traffic control and flow throughout the city, and the issuance of traffic violation citations to encourage compliance with existing traffic ordinances or laws.

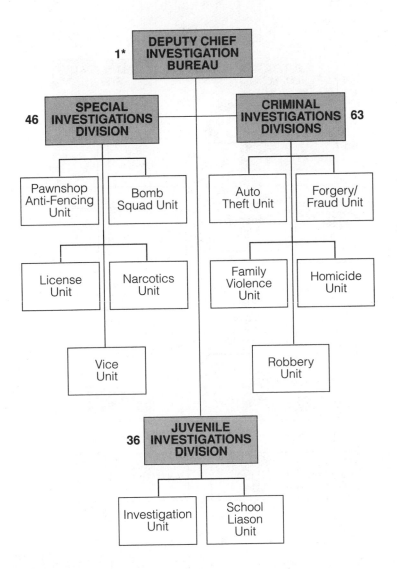

*Number of personnel assigned
Source: Minneapolis Police Department

Figure 6–8   **Organization of Investigation Bureau**

Major Responsibilities: The investigative bureau is comprised of specialized and technical divisions and units providing investigative capability for the department. The investigative function includes responsibility for gathering evidence, identifying and apprehending offenders, preparing cases for trial, and maintaining liaison with prosecutors, courts, corrections, and other law enforcement agencies.

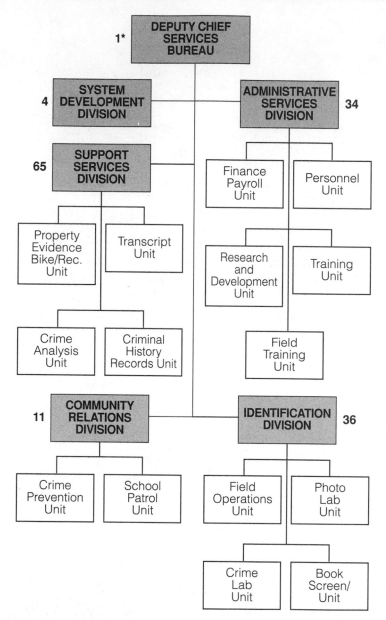

*Number of personnel assigned
Source: Minneapolis Police Department

Figure 6–9   **Organization of Service Bureau**

Major Responsibilities:
The service bureau is comprised of various areas of work specialization providing service or administrative functions for the department.
The service bureau includes the divisions of Community Relations, Administrative Services, Support Services and Identification. Each provide specialized support services.
Major Activities:
Community relations programs.
Neighborhood crime prevention programs.
Selection and training of personnel.
Fiscal control of departmental operations.
Maintenance of central police records.
Provision of criminal identification information.
Statistical analysis of crime trends.
Crime laboratory-criminalistics support.

Up-to-date information is usually provided in a daily bulletin, which contains brief summaries of what has transpired in the previous twenty-four hours. Officers are given a synopsis of each complaint received and acted on as well as descriptions of missing and/or wanted persons, stolen personal property, and stolen autos.

Radio Communications   The information provided at roll call is continuously updated by radio. Data is available to officers in patrol cars or carrying portable radios. This immediate communication has improved the safety of law enforcement officers and has provided for better allocation of resources.

Radio is the primary method of transmitting and seeking information between headquarters and units in the field.

The introduction of the small hand-carried portable police radio and the beeper have extended the communications system so that officers on foot may be reached to assist mobile patrol units and vice versa.

The dependability of radio transmissions has improved steadily over the years and has resulted in a great reduction in response time to calls for service or criminal activity.

A typical radio system has four channels providing the capability of (1) contacting car to car in its own jurisdiction, (2) contacting its own dispatchers, (3) contacting another officer patrolling in a different geographical subdivision through a repeater system, and (4) placing emergency calls. The fourth channel is reserved for such emergencies as roadblocks, disasters, and civil defense messages.

Communications is the lifeline of the police department. The police dispatcher, or in some cases the telephone operator, receives all citizens' requests for police service. In some instances the calls come directly to the dispatcher, who must act upon them and determine their priority. Some agencies have telephone operators screen the calls prior to giving them to the dispatcher to segregate informational calls from service calls.

Dispatchers have the responsibility for dispatching patrol vehicles to requests for service and for knowing what patrol vehicles are ready for assignment. They may also have some records responsibility, for example, making out the original incident complaint report, noting the time the call was received, the time the patrol vehicle was dispatched, the time it arrived, the time it cleared, and the disposition of the call.

In addition, dispatchers may have to handle any walk-in complaints. Some dispatchers also have the added responsibility of monitoring jails through a closed-circuit television hookup. Such a system exists in many smaller and medium-sized departments today.

In larger agencies several dispatchers handle the incoming calls and give them priority according to their seriousness and the availability of officers to respond. Larger agencies may also have direct and complete integration of police radio with regular telephone service. In this system any call to the police emergency number is automatically channeled to the dispatcher who controls squad cars assigned to the area from which the caller is telephoning.

Some cities have a *911 system*. A person who wishes to call the police dials 911 on the phone, and a central dispatching office receives the call directly. The 911 system has been implemented in many cities in the United States. The eventual goal is to have this number as the emergency number to call for police service in any city in the United States.

Records

The quality of records maintained is directly related to the quality of communications and field services provided. To give proper direction, a police agency must have a sound record system as well as an efficient communication system. Police departments throughout the country vary in their reporting systems and their needs in management control and effective operational control. The activities of a police department require keeping records not only of criminal activity but of all essential activities of the department.

Types of Records

Police records may be categorized as (1) administrative records, (2) arrest records, (3) identification records, and (4) complaint records.

Administrative records include inventories of police equipment, department memorandums, personnel records, evaluation reports, and all general information that reflects correspondence or services rendered.

Arrest records contain information obtained from arrested persons when they are booked as well as information about the control and/or release of prisoners and court procedures.

Identification records contain fingerprints, photographs, and other descriptive data obtained from arrested persons.

Complaint records usually contain information related to complaints and reports received by the police from citizens or other agencies as well as any actions initiated by the police. Since police work is public business, it requires accurate records of complaints received and the action taken by the police. Complaints may be criminal or noncriminal in nature; they may involve lost property, damaged property, traffic accidents, medical emergencies, or a missing person. Requests for police assistance may also involve robberies, murders, burglaries, vandalism, or children playing in the streets or cats up in trees. Although most complaints are minor, each must be treated with personal concern to the complainant and as a matter of importance to the police.

Most police agencies have a procedure for recording complaint information either on sheets or data processing cards. Initial complaint records are filled out on all complaints or requests for service received by the dispatcher or a police officer.

Information on the initial complaint record normally shows the complainant, victim, address of each, type of complaint, time of day, day of week, the officer handling the complaint or request, the area of the community where it occurred, the disposition, whether there was an arrest, and whether further follow-up reports or further investigation is justified by the investigative services division.

Benefiits of Efficient Records Systems   Efficient records systems are a vital management tool that aid in assessing department accomplishments, in developing budget justifications, in determining additional work force needs, and in evaluating the performance of officers as well as the attainment of objectives and goals.

Evaluation of carefully kept records will generally reflect needs in training, recruitment, public relations, allocation of resources, and general effectiveness. The continual or periodic evaluation of records by management in planning and research has allowed police agencies to provide better service to the public and, in turn, they have gained public support.

Centralized, integrated, and accurate systems of communications and records increase the effectiveness and efficiency of field services.

Computerized Information   Many informational tools available to police agencies today are the result of the introduction of random-access storage and retrieval systems and computers into the police field. In the future such information can connect all law enforcement agencies in the country in a vast communications network.

A step in this direction was taken in 1967 when the FBI implemented its computerized crime information storage system, the **National Crime Information Center (NCIC).** Under this system, each state has a number of computer terminals that interface with the FBI's main computer in Washington, D.C. The computer contains records of stolen property such as guns, autos, and office machines, and, in some cases, records of persons who are wanted on warrants.

The NCIC computer receives its information from other federal law enforcement agencies and from state and local law enforcement agencies. The NCIC makes it possible for a law enforcement officer in Texas who stops a suspicious person or car from California to contact the dispatcher by radio or teleprinter requesting information. The dispatcher can make an inquiry to the computer in Texas, which, in a matter of seconds, makes an inquiry on the status of the individual and/or the car to the NCIC terminal in Washington. The police officer can be quickly informed if the car has been stolen or if an arrest warrant is outstanding on the individual in the car.

The great volume of information contained in various state and federal computers is another aid given to police officers in maintaining up-to-date records systems.

The National Crime Information Center allows all police agencies in the country to have access to the computerized files of the FBI.

Privacy of Records   The most sensitive aspect of computerized or manual records on persons arrested and related information about them is the possibility of including in the file unsubstantiated information that might contain derogatory, incomplete, or incorrect information—information that disseminated to the wrong person could prove damaging and provide cause for a civil action against the police agency. In addition, police agencies often tend to retain information longer than necessary.

As a result, by authority of the Omnibus Crime Control and Safe Streets Act of 1968, which was amended by the Crime Control Act of 1973, the Department of Justice issued regulations to assure that criminal history record information, wherever it appears, is collected, stored, and disseminated in a way that insures the completeness, integrity, accuracy, and security of such information and that protects individual privacy. The regulations apply to all state and local agencies and individuals collecting, storing, or disseminating criminal history information either manually or by computer.

A data privacy act regulates the use of confidential and private information on individuals in the records, files, and processes of a state and its political subdivisions.

Some law enforcement agencies have expressed dissatisfaction with provisions relating to law enforcement records and with the dissemination of criminal history information, particularly for employment purposes.

Because states have been slow in passing privacy act legislation, a certain amount of confusion often occurs among those who try to abide by the Department of Justice regulations. The effect of some state legislation has been that in the absence of an emergency classification, almost all information or data a police agency has kept on individuals legally must be made available to anyone requesting it. This unfortunate situation has been avoided in other states.

Administrative services are vital to the efficient functioning of any police department. But it must always be remembered that they are *support* for the field services. Without the field services, they would serve no purpose.

FIELD SERVICES

Sometimes field services are performed by one division; sometimes they are performed by separate divisions. They may be further specialized by the type of individual involved: juveniles, gamblers, prostitutes, burglars, drug dealers, and so on; by specific geographic areas (beats); or by specific times when the demand for service is highest, for example, holiday traffic or abnormal conditions such as strikes and protests.

Field services include patrol, traffic, investigation, and community services.

Traditionally, however, police departments have been generalist organization; that is, most of their personnel is assigned to routine patrol and each officer is responsible for providing basic law enforcement services of all types to a specified geographic area. This routine patrol has been and is the backbone of police work in smaller departments. Larger departments tend to be more specialist-oriented.

Patrol

Usually 60 to 70 percent of a department's police officers are assigned to patrol operations. Although other divisions may have more prestige, patrol officers are the first and primary contact between the public and the criminal justice system. They not only initiate the criminal justice system, they strongly influence the public's perception of this system.

Patrol accounts for a major portion of most departments' expenditures, activities, personnel, and visibility. Whether measured by the number of police officers involved, the number of dollars spent, or by the reality that the uniformed police officer is the most visible part of our law enforcement system, patrol is the most vital component of police work. All other units are supplemental to this basic unit.

Patrol provides both crime- and noncrime-related services including preventing or deterring crime, apprehending criminals, recovering stolen property, providing emergency assistance, and giving citizens a sense of community security and confidence in the police.

Patrol is normally performed by uniformed officers in marked vehicles, although some larger departments assign uniformed officers to motorcycle and foot patrol in heavily populated or congested areas. This visibility, in itself, is one way to deter and repress crime. In addition, because the officers are in their vehicles and already moving, patrol allows the officers to respond quickly to calls for crime- and noncrime-related services, for example, to apprehend suspects or to assist in medical emergencies.

Patrol is responsible for providing continuous police service and high visibility of law enforcement. Tasks include crime prevention, response to calls for service, self-initiated activity, and completing administrative functions.

Traffic

Traffic may be a responsibility of patrol, or it may be a separate function. A well-rounded traffic program involves many activities designed to maintain order and safety on streets and highways.

Traffic officers are usually responsible for enforcing traffic laws, directing and controlling traffic, providing directions and assistance to motorists, investigating motor vehicle accidents, providing emergency assistance at the scenes of accidents, gathering information related to traffic, and writing reports.

The most frequent contact between the police and the noncriminal public is through traffic encounters; consequently, the opportunity for improving public relations by how traffic violations are handled must be considered. Although the traffic responsibilities of a police officer may not have the glamour of a criminal investigation, they are critical not only to the safety of the citizens in a community but also to the police image. It should be noted that a great number of criminal arrests result from traffic stops, for example, wanted persons and discovery of contraband.

The primary objectives of most traffic programs are to obtain the best possible movement of vehicles and pedestrians consistent with safety and to reduce losses from accidents. Chapter 9 describes the functions performed by the traffic officer in more detail.

Investigation

Although some investigations are carried out by patrol officers, the investigation services division (also known as the detective bureau) has the responsibility for follow-up investigation. The success of any criminal investigation relies on the cooperative, coordinated efforts of both the patrol and the investigative functions. The primary responsibilities of the investigator are to make certain the crime scene is secure, interview witnesses and interrogate suspects, photograph and sketch the crime scene, obtain and identify evidence, and record all facts related to the case for future reference and testimony in court.

To accomplish a successful investigation, police officers must (1) take their time, (2) use an organized approach that is efficient and methodical, as this may be their only chance to observe the scene, (3) recognize the issues and find facts to settle these issues, and (4) determine if a crime has been committed, and if so, by whom and how. These topics are the focus of chapter 10.

The primary responsibilities of the investigator are to make certain the crime scene is secure, interview witnesses and interrogate suspects, photograph and sketch the crime scene, obtain and identify evidence, and record all facts related to the case for future reference.

Community Service/Community Relations

In essence, every action of a police officer has an effect on community relations—either positive or negative. Many larger departments have established separate community relations divisions or community service divisions to strengthen communication channels between the public and its police department and/or to stress public education programs and crime prevention programs.

Every action of a police officer is, in effect, a part of community relations. Specific community relations or community service divisions seek to improve communications between the police and the public and/or to promote public education and crime prevention programs.

The importance of community relations and community service will be seen throughout the remainder of the book. Chapter 7 focuses on community relations and community service programs and approaches.

Specialized Officers

In addition to the basic divisions that may exist within a police department, larger departments frequently train officers to perform highly specialized tasks.

Members of an underwater recovery unit at work.

Specialized officers may include evidence technicians, identification officers, intelligence officers, juvenile officers, vice officers, canine-assisted officers, and tactical forces officers.

Evidence Technicians   Some police agencies, such as suburban police departments with a complement of forty or more officers, have established the position of evidence technician. The evidence technician is usually a patrol officer who has received extensive classroom and laboratory training in crime scene investigation. In departments that have small detective bureaus and relatively inexperienced officers, this position fills a notable void. The officer has not been relieved of regular patrol duties but may be called upon to conduct a crime scene investigation. Use of evidence technicians provides better coordination of the preliminary investigation of crimes and increases the probability that the investigation will be successful during the preliminary stage because other patrol officers work with the evidence technician as a team.

It is the evidence technician's responsibility to photograph the scene, take all necessary measurements, search the scene for physical evidence, and interview any suspects or witnesses still at the scene.

Evidence technicians carry tools to collect, mark, and identify evidence found at the scene, including cameras, fingerprint equipment, recorders, sketching equipment, and casting or impression material. They may have a vacuum cleaner in the equipment van for gathering evidence from a carpet or the inside of a car.

Through their laboratory training, evidence technicians know precisely what the laboratory can determine from the evidence submitted and its limitations. They do not have the equipment a full-scale crime laboratory possesses, but they do have some equipment to conduct preliminary tests for blood and certain types of narcotics and to identify the classifications of fingerprints.

Evidence technicians' classroom and laboratory training make them valuable assets to the patrol force because when not busy investigating crime scenes, they do regular patrol work.

Identification Officers   Identification officers have had specialized training in taking, identifying, and filing fingerprints. Fingerprint identification is an extremely important form of positive identification used by the police in identifying persons who break the law. Identification officers are highly trained in using scanners and computers in their work.

Intelligence Officers   Most large cities have an intelligence division whose top officer reports directly to the chief of police and whose activities are kept secret from the rest of the police department.

Intelligence units work in two areas. The first area is long-term, ongoing investigations into such criminal activity as illegal sale of guns, payoffs to police officers or politicians, major drug cases, and activities of organized crime. They often work on the same case in cooperation with county, state, and federal investigators.

Intelligence officers obtain information, buy information, infiltrate criminal groups, solicit data, conduct surveillances, and develop sources of information to keep themselves updated on criminal activity in the community. Any factual information that could lead to an arrest is given to the chief of police, who assigns it to another division of the police department for action.

The second area of intelligence work is investigation of fellow police officers in the department. For example, the intelligence unit may investigate a complaint of an officer drinking on duty, corruption, or other activities considered conduct unbecoming to police officers.

Intelligence officers do not wear uniforms or drive marked cars. They may even use assumed names and fictitious identities. To avoid identification problems, some large police agencies use officers who have just graduated from rookie school, as they are less known on the street.

Juvenile Officers   The police officer is often the first contact for a child in legal trouble. Therefore, it is justifiable and logical to have juvenile police specialists to work primarily with juvenile offenders.

Because most juvenile work is informal and includes powers to release, refer, or detain, juvenile officers must be chosen from the most qualified officers in the department. Specialists in handling juveniles should know the goals and functioning of the juvenile justice system because, in reality, they sit as judges of a youngster's actions and also serve the functions of social workers. Officers who work primarily with juveniles should be highly concerned for the welfare of the child, highly trained in the law, and able to recognize the difference between a neglected, dependent juvenile and a juvenile delinquent.

Juvenile officers can provide assistance to all other departments within their own agency when juveniles are involved. Since juveniles commit more than 50 percent of local crimes, all officers are juvenile officers much of the time, and it is the uniformed patrol division that has the most contact with these juvenile offenders.

Vice Officers   Vice problems vary from community to community; for example, some sections of the country allow prostitution, but many sections of the country do not. Vice officers usually concentrate their efforts on illegal gambling, prostitution, pornography, narcotics, and liquor violations. Sometimes their work is coordinated with intelligence officers.

Once vice becomes established in a community, more criminals are frequently attracted to the community. They may either believe that the law enforcement is ineffective in the community or that the police already have so many problems with vice that their operations will go unnoticed. If left uncontrolled, vice operations can create other police problems such as embezzlement, burglary, robbery, and murder. A community that allows vice to flourish is often politically corrupt and frequently has corruption within the police department as well.

Canine-Assisted Officers   Humans have used dogs in a variety of ways for thousands of years. Dogs have been used in police work in the United States, Europe, and throughout the world for more than fifty years. Today canine units exist in more than three hundred towns and cities in the United States.

Today's police dog has had intensive schooling with one officer—the dog's partner. Both spend many weeks under a special trainer. The dog works with only one partner and will respond to his or her commands only. The police dog's use in most cities falls into five categories: search, attack and capture, drug detection, bomb detection, and crime deterrence.

Tactical Forces Officers   Special crime tactical forces are immediately available, flexible, and mobile officers used for deployment against any emergency or crime problem. Tactical units supplement the patrol force and may operate selectively in high-crime areas. They may suppress burglaries, robberies, or auto thefts. They may be used in hostage situations and where persons have barricaded themselves. In such instances, the idea is to negotiate and reason with barricaded subjects, hostage takers, or the mentally disturbed rather than using force. Tactical forces are frequently deployed in sniper situations to protect police

Miami Police Department SWAT team during briefing (above) and in field exercises (below).

officers. In addition, they may perform rescue missions, provide security for visiting dignitaries, and rescue hostages.

Tactical forces are deployed when the regularly assigned patrol forces cannot effectively cope with an emergency situation, based on current crime-pattern analyses or on information received regarding expected crime activity.

Tactical forces officers receive special training in numerous areas including crowd control, patrol maneuvers, investigative techniques, and stakeout tactics. SWAT team members are highly trained in marksmanship, guerrilla tactics, patroling, night operations, camouflage and concealment, and the use of chemical agents. They frequently participate in field exercises to develop discipline and teamwork.

Reserve Officers Some police departments have reserve units to help achieve the department's goals. The reserve officers patrol in uniform and are visible symbols of law enforcement although they cannot write citations. The reserve officers also help in public education programs, informing the public about such things as operation identification, in which valuables are marked for identification in case of theft, drugs, and bike safety. When a crime does occur, the reserves can guard the crime scene while the regular officers continue with their routine or specialized patrol.

You have looked at what policing is, how the police relate to the people they serve, the basic roles of police officers, and required proficiencies and desired qualities of law enforcement officers. You have also been introduced to the organization of typical police departments and the administrative and field services provided. Now turn your attention to something more personal—*how* individual officers interpret their responsibilities and how they carry out their specific roles, that is, officer style in policing.

STYLES OF POLICE WORK

As noted by Senna and Siegel (1984, p. 179):

Policing involves a multitude of diverse tasks, including peacekeeping, criminal investigation, traffic control, and providing emergency medical service. Part of one's socialization as a police officer is developing a working attitude, or style, which is used to confront and interpret these various aspects of policing. For example, some police officers may view their job as well-paid civil service positions that stress careful compliance with written departmental rules and procedures. Other officers may see themselves as part of the "thin blue line" that therefore may use any means to "get their man."

Many studies have looked at styles of policing and have classified these styles into clusters called *typologies.* Although few police officers

Table 6—1   The Typologies of Policing Styles

James Q. Wilson (1968)	Joseph Senna and Larry Siegel (1984)	Robert Pursley (1987)
Legalistic	Law enforcer Crime fighter	Enforcer Zealot
Service style	Social agent	Social service agent
Watchman	Watchman	Watchman

fall completely into a single typology, most tend to exhibit several behaviors that would place them into a specific typology.

The first typology, the "enforcer," according to Pursley (1978, p. 245), "places relatively high value on social order and 'keeping society safe,' and a relatively low value on individual rights and legal due process." Pursley suggests that such officers are highly critical of institutions such as the Supreme Court, of politicians, of police administrators, of minority interest groups, and of others viewed as "corrupt, incompetent, weak, criminal by nature, or simply naive." Enforcers have little time for minor violations of the law, seeing them as a waste of police time and resources.

The crime fighter/zealot is like the enforcer in that a primary goal is to "keep society safe." Officers with this style of policing tend to deal with all laws and all offenders equally. According to Pursley (1987): "This type of officer typically defines his or her role as a general law enforcement agent and is generally less critical than the enforcer. In fact, zealots tend to accept the diverse groups of society for what they are." They also are less critical of the social service aspects of policing than are enforcers.

The third typology, the social service agent, is much more accepting of the social service roles and much more attuned to due process. Frequently officers falling into this category are "young, highly educated, and more idealistic police officers" (Pursley 1987). Like the enforcer and the crime fighter, however, the social service agent is also interested in protecting society but is much more flexible in how this is approached.

The fourth typology, the watchman, is on the opposite end of the spectrum from the enforcer. The watchman is interested in maintaining the status quo, in not making waves. According to Wilson (1968, pp. 140–41):

> The police ignore many common violations, especially traffic and juvenile offenses, to tolerate, though gradually less so, a certain amount of vice and gambling, to use the law more as a means of maintaining order than of regulating conduct, and to judge the requirements of order differently depending on the character of the group in which the infraction occurs.

Basic styles of policing include the following:

- *The enforcer.*
- *The crime fighter/zealot.*
- *Social service agent.*
- *Watchman.*

No individual is purely one type or another and may change from one style to another depending on the situation. And, in any given police department it is likely that a variety of policing styles with some combination of the preceding typologies can be found.

One reason these styles exist within police departments is that police agencies and their officers have a great amount of *discretion* in how they carry out their roles and responsibilities.

POLICE DISCRETION

Just as citizens can decide to obey the laws or not, police agencies and their officers can decide which offenses to actively seek to control and which offenses to simply ignore.

Police discretion is the freedom of an agency or individual officer to make choices as to whether or not to act.

Any speeder who has talked a traffic officer out of issuing a ticket probably thinks that police discretion is good. The person who does receive a ticket, however, probably thinks the officer has erred in spending time chasing speeders rather than catching criminals.

Klockars (1983, pp. 262—67) uses the illustration of the speeding ticket to explain why discretion is necessary. One important reason is that most laws tend to "overreach." A posted speed limit, for example, applies to all situations, including people with valid reasons for exceeding the posted limit such as a volunteer firefighter on the way to a fire or a mother with a seriously injured child on the way to a hospital. As Klockars explains:

> *Every law has the property of overreach, whether it provides penalties for traveling in excess of 35 mph on a certain stretch of road, gambling, assault, burglary, robbery, or the killing of another human being. Police exercise discretion in the enforcement of all these laws and every other law, because each criminalizes more than it intends. From the point of view of*

*the law as written, the single most astonishing fact of police behavior is
the extent to which police do not enforce the law when they have every
legal right to do so.*

A second important reason for the existence of discretion is that
often the stop or confrontation with the law accomplishes its purpose and
the punishment that might follow could be considered too severe.
Klockars cites as examples a person who has never had a speeding ticket
before and faints at the thought of it, the person whose insurance will be
canceled, and the person who teaches driver's education at the local high
school.

A third factor entering into the decision making of police officers is
that they know that people will frequently lie to avoid "punishment" of
any kind.

Yet another factor to be considered is that the police often cannot
reveal their true reasons for issuing a ticket. Klockars says (1983):

> *Imagine a police officer saying . . .*
> > *Sorry, but I've got a quota of arrests to make.*
> > *Sorry, but the city depends on traffic fines for revenue.*
> > *Sorry, but I don't like people like you.*
> > *Sorry, but I don't think your excuse is good enough.*
> > *Sorry, but I don't believe you.*

Any one of the preceding may, in fact, be the underlying reason for the
ticket. But, since the officer cannot give any of these reasons, the most
likely explanation will be: "I don't make the laws, I just enforce them,"
pretending to have no discretion at all.

Klockars (1983) also discusses the range of police discretion. He
notes that it extends to such decisions as the following:

> *Resource allocation: patrol vs. detectives, drugs vs. juvenile aid, police
> academy vs. two officer cars, in-service training vs. internal affairs.
> Whether to use police dogs, or use hollow point ammunition, or carry
> shotguns.
> Whether to wear nameplates or bulletproof vests.
> Whether to be allowed to moonlight.*

Another interesting aspect of police discretion, as noted by Cole
(1983, p. 141) is as follows:

> *Within the police bureaucracy, discretion has a special dimension: It in-
> creases as one moves down the organizational hierarchy. Thus, patrol
> officers, the most numerous and lowest-ranking officers and the ones who
> are the newest to police work, have the greatest amount of discretion.*

Wilson (1968, p. 30) expands on the patrol officer's role, "which is unlike
that of any other occupation . . . working alone, exercising wide discretion in matters of utmost importance (life and death, honor and dishonor)
in an environment that is apprehensive and perhaps hostile."

One of the most important discretionary options police officers have is whether to arrest someone or not. Jacob (1973, p. 27) suggests four factors that influence this decision:

> The characteristics of the crime (some are considered trivial).
> The relationship between the alleged criminal and the victim (domestic disputes may cool and family members may refuse to press charges).
> Relationship between the police and the criminal or victim (a respectful alleged wrongdoer is less likely to be arrested).
> Departmental policies (preferences of the chief and the city administration).

Jacob (1973, p. 27) goes on to note:

> In sum, police officers are street-level bureaucrats, since their encounters with citizens allow for extensive independence. Further, they are not primarily concerned with order-maintenance where the law is not cut and dried and where citizens are often hostile. Because of the situational environment, they must mobilize information quickly and make decisions through the tactics of simplification and routinization in which their perceptions of the clients are based on prior cases and experiences. Such a process often leads to error.

Nonetheless, discretion is and will remain an integral part of policing in the 1990s.

As noted by Reiss (1971, p. 45), discretion is an integral of policing:

> It is incumbent upon a police officer to enter upon a variety of social stages, encounter the actors, determine their roles, and figure out the plot. Often, before they can act, the police must uncover the "plot" and identify the roles and behavior of the actors. This is true even in emergency situations where an officer is expected to assess the situation almost immediately and make judgments as to what he must do.

Sutherland and Cressey (1978, p. 389) call attention to the fact that "although police officers are expected to help make crime dangerous for all, they are to use discretion and to exercise certain judicial functions as they do so. They must decide whether a certain act is in violation of the law, and also whether it probably can be proved that the law has been violated."

Police officers, even those assigned to patrol duties in a large city, are confronted with few serious crimes in the course of a single tour of duty. They tend to view such involvement, particularly if there is some degree of danger, as constituting "real" police work. It is apparent, however, that they spend considerably more time keeping order, settling disputes, finding missing children, and helping with medical emergencies than they do responding to criminal conduct that is serious enough to call for arrest, prosecution, and conviction.

This does not mean that serious crime is unimportant to police officers. Quite the contrary is true. But it does mean that they perform a wide range of other functions that are of a highly complex nature and often involve difficult social, behavioral, and political problems rather than major crimes.

Today's law enforcement officers need a broad background as well as broadening experiences to meet the complex challenges of a modern, changing, multiethnic, and multiracial society. On that point there is near-unanimous agreement.

SUMMARY

The people largely determine the role of the police and give them their authority to fulfill this role. Their support is vital if any law enforcement effort is to succeed.

Police officers must *enforce laws,* federal, state, and municipal, to protect the health and welfare of the community. For example, they enforce highway laws to make the streets safe for driving; they arrest people who unlawfully sell narcotics or who otherwise break the law.

They *preserve the peace* in a professional manner by patrolling troubled areas, intervening in domestic disturbances, and advising people in community disputes.

They *prevent crime* by being highly visible in the community, by educating the public about crime and crime prevention, and by involving them in programs such as operation identification.

They *protect civil rights and civil liberties* by living and enforcing the principles contained in the Bill of Rights.

They also *provide necessary services* such as rendering first aid in medical emergencies, and assisting in community programs.

These roles must be carried out skillfully and professionally, and require numerous mental, intellectual, physical, and personal proficiencies as well as discretion.

Although numerous federal and state agencies are directly involved in law enforcement, the ultimate responsibility is usually at the local level. It is here that the goals of law enforcement are initiated, based on what the citizens of the individual community perceive to be their most pressing needs.

Police officers work within the basic organizational structure of their department, which, most often, is divided into two sections: field services and administrative services. Tasks and personnel to accomplish them are assigned to one of these two sections.

Overseeing the entire police department is the chief of police, the primary law enforcement officer at the local level, who coordinates both the field services and the administrative services.

Administrative services provide support for field services, including records and communications, recruitment and training, and special facilities and services. Most current information is conveyed to police officers at roll call or by radio, the primary method of transmitting and seeking information between headquarters and units in the field.

In addition to direct communication, police officers also rely upon information contained in the department's records. Centralization of these records allows the various line functions to be coordinated. Among the types of records the police officer may use are administrative, arrest, identification, and complaint records. Further, the NCIC provides all police agencies in the country access to the computerized files of the FBI.

Access to information is not always unlimited, however. A data privacy act regulates the use of confidential and private information on individuals in the records, files, and processes of a state and its political subdivisons.

Within the field services provided in a police department are patrol, traffic, investigation, and community service. Sometimes these are specialized departments; sometimes the services are provided by a single department. In addition, many police departments, particularly the larger departments, have specialized officers such as vice officers and juvenile officers.

With the varying roles and responsibilities police officers have, it is not surprising that distinct styles of policing have developed. Four major typologies have been identified: the enforcer, the crime fighter/zealot, the social agent, and the watchman.

Also because of these varying roles and responsibilities, police agencies and their officers exercise a great deal of discretion, that is, they have the freedom to make choices as to whether or not to act—which often means to arrest or not.

Discussion Questions

1. How has communication between the officer in the field and headquarters changed in the last hundred years?

2. What effect does a data privacy act have on investigations of individuals involved in organized crime?

3. How have the roles of police officers changed over time?

4. What services should police officers provide? Which are provided in your community?

5. Why is the support of the people vital to the successful accomplishment of the responsibilities of the modern police officer?

6. Why does Garmire believe it is hard for an officer to change roles? Don't we all play many different roles in our lives? Isn't it harder to be the same all the time?

7. What aspects of the Code of Ethics seem most relevant to the 1990s?

8. What style of policing will you probably lean toward? Why?

9. Have you witnessed firsthand police discretion? Explain.

10. Do you feel police agencies and officers have too little, too much, or just the right amount of discretion?

References

Arnold, W. R., and Brungardt, T. M. *Juvenile Misconduct and Delinquency.* Boston: Houghton Mifflin Co., 1983.

Bittner, E. "Florence Nightingale in Pursuit of Willie Sutton: A Theory of the Police," In *The Potential for Reform of the Criminal Justice System,* edited by Herbert Jacob. Beverly Hills: Sage, 1974.

Bittner, E. *The Function of Police in Modern Society.* Washington, D.C.: U.S. Government Printing Office, 1971.

Cole, George F. *The American System of Criminal Justice.* 3d ed. Belmont, Calif.: Brooks/Cole Publishing Co., 1983.

Garmire, B. L. "The Police Role in an Urban Society." In *The Police and the Community,* edited by Robert F. Steadman. Baltimore: The Johns Hopkins University Press, 1972. (Copyright by the Committee for Economic Development.)

Jacob, Herbert. *Urban Justice.* Boston, Mass.: Little, Brown, 1973.

James, H. *Crisis in the Courts.* New York: David McKay Company, 1968. (Copyright by the Christian Science Publishing Society.) Based on a series of weekly articles in *The Christian Science Monitor,* April to July, 1967.

Klockars, C. B. *Thinking about Police: Contemporary Readings.* New York: McGraw-Hill, 1983.

Lohman, Joseph D. and Misner, Gordon E. *"The Police and the Community"* (Berkley: University of California School of Criminology, 1966), vol. 1, p. 50. Report prepared for the President's Commission on Law Enforcement and Administration of Justice by the School of Criminology at the University of California.

National Advisory Commission on Criminal Justice Standards and Goals. *The Police.* Washington, D.C.: U.S. Government Printing Office (LEAA Grant Number 72–DF–99–0002, and NI 72–0200) 1973.

President's Commission on Law Enforcement and Administration of Justice. *Task Force Report: The Police.* Washington, D.C.: U.S. Government Printing Office, 1967.

Pursley, Robert D. *Introduction to Criminal Justice.* 4th ed. New York: Macmillan, 1987.

Reiss, A. J., Jr. *The Police and the Public.* New Haven, Conn.: Yale University Press, 1971.

Rutledge, Devallis. *The New Police Report Manual,* Sacramento, Calif.: Custom Publishing Company, 1986.

Saunders, Charles B., Jr. *Upgrading the American Police.* Washington, D.C.: The Brookings Institution, 1970.

Senna, Joseph J., and Siegel, Larry J. *Introduction to Criminal Justice.* St. Paul, Minn.: West Publishing Company, 1984.

Stokes, Floyd. *For the Record: Report Writing in Law Enforcement.* Eureka, Calif.: Innovative Systems, 1987, Preface.

Sutherland, E. H., and Cressey, D. R. *Criminology.* 10th ed. Philadelphia: J. B. Lippincott, 1978.

Webster, J. A. "Police Task and Time Study." In *Journal of Criminal Law, Criminology, and Police Science,* Vol. 61. No date.

Wilson, J. Q. *Varieties of Police Behavior.* Cambridge, Mass.: Harvard University Press, 1968.

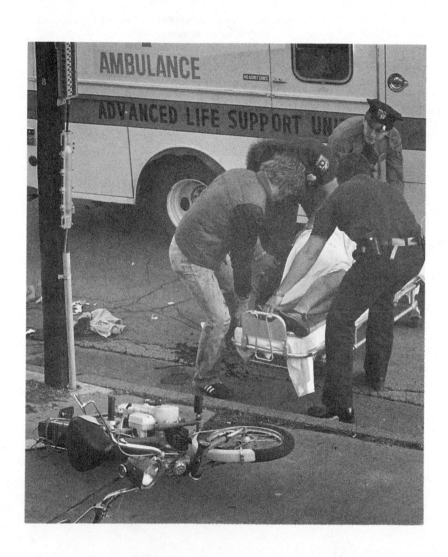

Community Service: To Serve and Protect

The vocation of every man and woman is to serve other people.

—Leo Tolstoi

DO YOU KNOW

What community services the police department may provide its citizens?

What most public relations programs emphasize?

What most community relations programs emphasize?

What factors interfere with good community relations?

What single element is critical for any successful community relations program?

What types of community service programs have been instituted to deter crime?

Introduction

Chapter 7

"Police . . . and communities they serve need to be reminded that police are people dealing with people, that it is people who commit crimes, and it is people who need police assistance" (Radelet 1970, p. 62). The types of assistance provided by the police take a variety of forms. In chapter 6 we discussed the types of service that might be expected from a police department and the controversy as to how much and what types of service are justified.

Police departments provide a wide variety of services including giving information, directions, and advice; counseling and referring; licensing and registering vehicles; intervening in domestic arguments; working with neglected children; rendering emergency medical or rescue services; dealing with alcoholics and the mentally ill; finding lost children; dealing with stray animals; controlling crowds; and providing community education programs on crime prevention, drug abuse, safety, and the like.

Although some police departments have a separate division assigned the responsibilities of community service and some have made community service a responsibility of a patrol team, in reality, community service is a vital part of every police officer's job.

In the interest of economy and professionalism, several departments have turned to the use of civilians for such duties as monitoring parking meters, dispatching, and doing clerical jobs. Certain types of community service are important not only because they fulfill community needs, however, but also because they allow the public to see police officers functioning in a helping way rather than only performing acts related to criminal activity.

PROVIDING EMERGENCY SERVICES

Frequently patrol officers are the first on the scene of a situation requiring emergency services.

Emergency First Aid

Police officers are often the first on the scene of a traffic accident and are responsible for providing first aid to any persons injured in the accident. They may also be called on to assist persons who have been injured in other ways or who become seriously ill. Police officers should be thoroughly trained and certified in CPR as well as in advanced first aid, including measures to stop bleeding and to deal with fractures, shock, burns, and epileptic convulsions. They should also recognize insulin coma and know how to treat it.

Ambulance Service

Closely related to providing emergency first aid, police officers may be required to transport accident victims or other persons who are gravely ill or injured to the nearest medical facility. In fact, in some communities, the police department is the sole ambulance service, and patrol cars are specially equipped to serve as ambulances. This policy of providing ambulance service tends to make the public more appreciative of the police department and may foster citizen cooperation; however, this can place a drain on a police department's resources. Local conditions should determine whether this service is routinely provided.

Fire Control Service

In some departments, police and fire fighting are combined into a public safety department. In such instances, obviously, police officers must be trained in fire suppression techniques. In departments where the police are not primarily responsible for fire suppression activities, they may still be the first to arrive at the scene of a fire and can lend valuable assistance to the fire fighters.

The first action of police officers who come upon an uncontrolled fire is to call the fire department. Only then should any attempts be made to control or suppress the fire. Other functions the police may serve include traffic control, assuring that fire fighting equipment can arrive quickly at the scene, and helping search for and rescue people trapped by the fire. If children are trapped in a home that is burning, rescuers should check under beds and in closets because children frequently try to hide from the smoke and flames. Police officers can also provide crowd control, assist with first aid, transport injured persons to the nearest medical facility, and guard any personal property removed from the burning structure.

Bomb Threats or Incidents

If a bomb threat is made or a bomb is actually found, the police are usually the ones to be notified. In such instances the main responsibility of the police is to assure the safety of persons in the vicinity of the bomb and to call in experts to actually dispose of the bomb. Frequently a bomb disposal unit of a military installation is called in. Larger departments, however, may have their own bomb disposal teams.

In the event of an actual explosion, be it intentional or accidental as in an explosion at an industrial site, the police are usually responsible for crowd control and for investigating the incident.

Natural Disasters

Floods, tornadoes, hurricanes, fires, and earthquakes can produce emergency conditions requiring action on the part of police officers. They may need to provide first aid to victims, provide crowd control, and protect the property of those involved.

Search and Rescue

Many departments are also actively involved in search and rescue operations that may or may not be necessitated by natural disasters.

PRESERVING THE PEACE AND SAFETY OF THE PUBLIC

As part of their role to preserve the peace and safety of the public, police officers may be called to handle disputes and disturbances, to quell civil disturbances, and to maintain order in labor/management disputes and strikes.

Disputes and Domestic Quarrels

One of the most common and most dangerous calls made to the police department is for assistance in settling a dispute, for example, a fight in a bar, or for resolving a domestic situation, for example, a husband beating his wife (or vice versa). Frequently alcohol is involved in such situations. Tempers are short, and the potential for violence is ever present.

As noted by Levine, Husheno, and Palumbo (1980, p.23):

> Diversity within cities creates the potential for all kinds of disputes and disturbances. Parties to traffic accidents get angry with one another; people imbibing at taverns get into fights; young people blasting stereos disturb neighborhood residents. One purpose of the criminal justice system is to moderate these tensions and keep hostilities from escalating. Indeed peacekeeping is one of the primary missions of the police and as important as this goal is, if it is pursued too zealously, the right of the people to be different may be impaired. There is a fine line between obnoxious conduct that intrudes into other people's lives and harmless behavior that merely defies common standards of propriety. Thus, neighbors may be annoyed when teen-agers "hang out" on the streets and use vulgar language, but it is arguable that they have the right to do so if they do not interfere with passersby. Likewise, demonstrators passing out political fliers often disturb people who disagree with their views, and the discarded sheets of paper can cause a mess, but to prohibit such activities would invade the constitutional right of freedom of speech. Too much emphasis on public peace can lead to social repression and an insistence on mass conformity.

Civil Disturbances

The civil disturbances on campuses throughout the country in the 1960s highlighted the role of the police in controlling civil disturbances. Although civil disturbances are not as prevalent, protest demonstrations continue throughout the country, for example, strong antiwar sentiment, disagreement with legislative decisions, strong sentiments for or against abortion, or protests against industries engaged in manufacturing war materials.

In dealing with civil disturbances, police officers must always remember that our Constitution guarantees its citizens the right to *peacefully* assemble. This right must be protected. It is only when the assembly is no longer peaceful that officers have the responsibility to intervene. Determining what constitutes peaceful assembly places a large amount of discretionary power in the hands of police officers.

The primary responsibilities of police officers are to maintain order and to protect lives and assets. In the event of sit-in demonstrations, it may be necessary to forcibly remove participants. In such instances, the minimum amount of force necessary should be used.

Labor/Management Disputes and Strikes

Strikes are legal, but, as with the right to assemble, the strike must be peaceful. If strikers physically restrict others from crossing the picket line, they are acting illegally, and the police may be called to intervene. In such instances, police officers must remain neutral. Their only responsibility is to prevent violence and property damage or loss.

Escort Services

Police may be called upon to provide escort service to individuals who are extremely popular, for example, rock stars, or for those who are extremely unpopular, for example, a politician the public greatly dislikes. They may also provide escort services for dangerous cargoes such as those containing highly inflammable materials, hazardous wastes, and the like or for oversized cargoes.

In addition, police may be asked to provide escort services for funeral processions or for very valuable cargoes such as large sums of cash.

Little agreement exists on when escort services are appropriate or on how they should be provided, that is, should they include red flashing lights and sirens, or proceed as though on routine patrol? Local circumstances will largely determine the answers to these questions. The important thing in the area of escort services is that the department have a clearly established policy on the use of police escorts to avoid any charges of favoritism should a request for such services be denied.

Licensing

The police department is frequently involved in licensing handguns, understandably so since it is to their advantage to know who owns what kind of weapons in their locality. In addition, they are in a position to investigate the applicant for a license and to determine if such a license should be granted. They may also do background investigations on applicants for liquor licenses, for taxi licenses, and for tow truck licenses.

The police department is also frequently involved in other types of licensing such as licenses for holding a parade or for blocking off a street for a community function. When such licensing is provided by the police department, it is also responsible for such activities as blocking off streets and setting up detours, rerouting traffic and the like.

Inspections

Because patrol officers routinely cover the entire area over which the police department has jurisdiction, many decision makers believe they should be responsible for inspections to insure adherence to fire codes, health codes, and building codes. This is another area of controversy because such activities are extremely time consuming. They do present the advantage of familiarizing the patrol officers with the people and buildings on their beats. On the other hand, such activities take patrol officers off the street and into buildings where they are no longer on preventive patrol but rather are serving a function that could easily be carried out by an inspector specifically hired for the job and, usually, at less cost.

In many areas, police are also responsible for checking the weight of trucks. Police are used in this capacity because they must be on the scene anyway to issue tickets to overweight trucks or to stop trucks who bypass the scales completely. Others contend, however, that the patrol officers in the vicinity could be called in for either of the preceding situations and that it might be more practical not to use patrol officers in this capacity.

OTHER COMMUNITY SERVICES

Several other services may or may not be provided by police departments, depending on local policy.

Transporting Civilians in Police Cars

As a general rule, most police officers are not allowed to transport civilians in their patrol cars unless they are on official business, for example, transporting a prisoner from one jail to another, a defendant to court for trial, or a witness to view a suspect.

In some departments, police officers are responsible for chauffeuring public officials and for transporting economically disadvantaged people to the welfare office to obtain assistance. Use of police vehicles for such purposes is usually not good practice; however, instances may arise when the police need to transport civilians in their squads. For example, a patrol officer may come upon a motorist whose car is totally disabled and the weather is extremely inclement. The patrol officer may, in such instances, give the civilian a ride to a service station or home, depending on the circumstances. In such instances, the patrol officer should notify headquarters of the situation.

Persons Locked Out

The police are frequently called to assist people who have locked themselves out of their car or home. In such instances it is usually preferable to have the civilian call a locksmith. If this is not possible, however, police officers should check the identity of the person requesting assistance. Imagine the predicament of a police officer who assists a burglar in breaking and entering.

If the police do assist in gaining entry to a car or home, headquarters should be fully informed prior to the action.

Missing Persons

Television programs have made the missing persons function of the police department seem a routine activity. In actuality, however, unless foul play is suspected or the person missing is retarded, mentally incompetent, or in need of medication, the police do not become involved in missing person cases. If no crime has been committed and the safety of

Officers often assist people who have locked themselves out of their car.

the missing person is not in jeopardy, the police department performs an administrative function, recording the information to be used in helping to identify individuals who are unconscious, who are found wandering (senility), or who are found dead and have no identification on them.

Because of the mobility of individuals in our society, the need for a centralized, computerized system for recording information about missing persons was recognized and acted upon over a decade ago when the National Crime Information Center (NCIC) Advisory Policy Board approved establishing a Missing Person File. This file was added to the nationwide NCIC system in October 1975. The file has four specific categories and criteria for entry (Bishop and Schuessler 1982, p.21):

> *Disability—A person of any age who is missing and under proven physical and/or mental disability or is senile, thereby subjecting himself or others to personal and immediate danger.*
>
> *Endangered—A person of any age who is missing and is in the company of another person under circumstances indicating that his physical safety is in danger.*
>
> *Involuntary—A person of any age who is missing under circumstances indicating that the disappearance was not voluntary, that is, abduction or kidnapping.*
>
> *Juvenile—A person who is missing and declared unemancipated as defined by the laws of his state of residence and who does not meet the entry criteria of the other three categories.*

Damage to Property

Citizens who experience damage to their property are very likely to call the police. The first action of officers responding to such calls is to determine if any danger is inherent in the situation. If danger does exist, the police officers must take action to remove the danger. For example, if a tree has fallen on power lines and hot wires are on the ground, the police should rope off the area and call the power company. If no danger is inherent in the situation, the police officers should determine if the damage is the result of criminal or noncriminal actions. If it is criminal property damage, for example, the work of vandals, the officers should conduct a thorough investigation. If it is a noncriminal (and nondangerous) situation, for example, a tree has fallen on a home, the police officers should advise the complainant of alternatives in taking care of the damage. The complainant should usually also be advised to notify his or her insurance agent.

Lost and Found

People who find valuable property are likely to turn it in to the police department. Conversely, people who have lost items of value are likely to request assistance from the police department. In this situation, also, the police department plays primarily an administrative function, maintaining accurate records of property that has been found or lost. The department is responsible for protecting all found property and for attempting to locate the rightful owners. Of course, the owner also is responsible for checking with the police to see if the property has been found. Any unclaimed property is frequently disposed of through an open auction.

Missing and Stray Animals

Some police departments also have the responsibility for stray animals, especially unlicensed dogs. They may also be called upon to deal with dangerous animals such as bears or with trapped animals such as a raccoon up a chimney of a home. Department policy will determine whether such calls are responded to by the police department. If the department policy is not to handle animal problems other than unlicensed stray dogs (usually in violation of a leash law), officers should be prepared to offer advice to the person seeking assistance, for example, that the person should call the humane society.

PUBLIC RELATIONS PROGRAMS

Public relations programs frequently seek to enhance the image of the police officer by helping citizens gain an understanding and acceptance of the role of the police in the community. The programs are directed to groups or the entire community. The police officer may be portrayed as the friend of young and old, appear at school and church programs, sponsor little league teams or law enforcement days, or hand out bumper stickers encouraging people to support their local police.

The primary emphasis of most public relations programs is to raise the image of the police agency and its officials.

Such programs are usually geared to the needs of the police. Sometimes they are only cosmetic or token efforts to gain community approval; however, public relations is an accepted and healthy form of advertising used very successfully by major corporations and by many law enforcement agencies. There is nothing wrong with a police department using such tactics. The problem arises when a department institutes a special unit to "take care of the public image" and assumes that this is all that is required. No amount of bumper stickers or sponsorships will counteract negative actions by police officers. Respect must be earned; it cannot be bought or commanded. It must always be remembered that the police image is primarily the result of daily contacts between police officers and citizens of the community.

Any public relation program should be realistic in the image it hopes to convey to the public. As Garmire (1972, p.11) states:

> *I do not believe that police officers and the police service can become objects of love and endearment; it is not in the nature of men, particularly Americans, to give such affection to those representatives of authority who directly control their lives. And, no matter how we describe the activities of the police, the business of police is policing. The most we can hope for . . . is respect for the police as professionals, confidence in their integrity, and public conviction that the police will perform their mission.*

Conveyance of such an understanding requires more than public relations programs. It requires, first and foremost, appropriate actions by police officers, and second, sound community relations programs.

POLICE-COMMUNITY RELATIONS PROGRAMS

While public relations programs are a one-way effort directed at raising the image of the police, police-community relations programs seek to provide means for police and citizens to work together to achieve their mutual goal of law and order.

The primary emphasis of police-community relations programs is to provide two-way communication between police and citizens to work toward achieving law and order in the community.

Over twenty years ago the president's 1966 Crime Commission, in *The Challenge of Crime in a Free Society* (1967, p. 100), stated:

> *A community relations program is not a public relations program 'to sell the police image' to the people. It is not a set of expedients whose purpose is to tranquilize for a time an angry neighborhood by, for example, suddenly promoting a few Negro officers in the wake of a racial disturbance. It is a long-range, full-scale effort to acquaint the police and the community with each other's problems and to stimulate action aimed at solving those problems.*

Many people are concerned about the relationship between police and citizens. Many people think they know the answer to the problem. Police officers feel that if citizens would only understand the responsibilities of law enforcement officers and would obey the law themselves, there would be no problem. Citizens, on the other hand, frequently believe that if the police would be more human and understanding, the problem would be solved. Both sides are partly right and partly wrong;

however, their attitudes toward one another frequently interfere with working together to find answers to their mutual problems.

People tend to think in terms of the "ingroup"—the group to which they belong—and the "outgroup." The outgroup is everyone else and usually is perceived as being "bad." If citizens perceive police as members of the outgroup, they will be uncooperative and perhaps even hostile. Nobody wants to tell on a friend or sometimes even a total stranger who is a private citizen like himself or herself.

Group protectiveness interferes with communication and good relations.

Today it is more difficult to get a case through court, more dangerous to walk the streets at night, and more of a strain to get along with neighbors crowded in on all sides. Living in this generation requires more skill, knowledge, patience, and goodwill.

Police work also requires better training and more self-discipline than ever before. Law enforcement is no longer a job. It is a profession. Likewise, citizens must be willing to pay the price for living in this generation. One cost is personal involvement. To stand aside and expect others to carry the load is to default in a primary obligation of citizenship. As the Roman statesman and philosopher Seneca noted: "He who does not prevent a crime when he can, encourages it."

The police and public are bound together in a common destiny. What is good for one is inevitably good for the other. What is bad for one is bad for the other. If police work for low salaries, with inadequate training, or in hostile communities that provide little cooperation and frequent danger, they are not going to operate effectively. Citizens can do something to alleviate these conditions and thereby assure themselves of better and more professional police services.

As long as citizens live in fear of the police, believing them to be unfriendly mercenaries at best and brutal oppressors at worst, they will not provide the environment essential for effective law enforcement. Robert F. Kennedy once said: "Every society gets the kind of criminal it deserves. What is equally true is that every community gets the kind of law enforcement it insists upon."

Approaches to Police-Community Relations

Several approaches have been taken to police-community relations programs. Bureaus have been established within police agencies. Community-wide citizen groups have been formed. Civilian review boards or advisory committees have worked with police agencies in establishing goals and priorities. Large-scale educational programs have been successful when they have promoted dialogue rather than simply conveying information (public relations). As noted by the President's

Commission on Law Enforcement and the Administration of Justice (*The Police*, p. 159):

> *Citizens who distrust the police will not easily be converted by information programs they consider to come from a tainted source. However, even for these groups, long-term education based upon honest and free DIALOGUE between the police and the public can have an effect. Indeed, this is one of the basic goals of the citizen advisory committees. On the other hand, citizens who are neutral or supportive can benefit from increased understanding of the complicated problems and tasks of the police. Informational programs can also generate support for more personnel, salary increases, sufficient equipment, and other resources to improve the efficiency of police work. It can help the cooperative citizen to avoid becoming a victim of crime and show him how to work more effectively with the police. And, to the extent that the police department is genuinely working at improved community relations, dissemination of this information to the press and other media does have a positive effect on community relations.*

The police officer on the street is the community relations officer of the department. The officer's actions, demeanor, appearance, and empathy for people are all accountable for positive or negative community relations.

Community acceptance of crime prevention programs initiated depends on the overall effectiveness of all police operations. Hundreds of programs have aided the police in their efforts toward not only community relations but also improved law enforcement. As police officers' knowledge of the community and its citizens increases, so does their effectiveness as law enforcement officers. Their street contacts and sources of information are also vastly improved.

The police officer on the street is ultimately responsible for the success of police-community relations programs.

Community relations is a responsibility of both the police and the citizen. The police may contribute to improving two-way communication by the following:

- Understanding the problems of citizens and keeping an open mind; using good judgment.
- Paying attention rather than displaying a casual attitude. Police officers should listen attentively. If they disagree on a point, they should do so politely. They should show consideration rather than ignoring citizens. The problems citizens convey to the police may be of utmost importance to them.

- Using courteous words. Sarcasm in either words or attitude is readily apparent to citizens and hampers communication. Tone of voice can be as important as the words used. Tone can incite anger or instill confidence.
- Being patient. Police officers must exercise self-command and self-discipline. Although patience and kindness may be misperceived by some as a sign of weakness, this is not true.
- Giving time. Give citizens time to air their problems. Do not rush them.
- Showing enthusiasm. Officers should approach each contact with enthusiasm, believing in themselves and their communities. A lackadaisical attitude will thwart the objectives of any contact.
- Being helpful instead of hindering. Rendering aid is one of the most important functions of police officers.
- Showing sincerity. Mere words, in themselves, are not proof of sincerity. Police officers must be honest and straightforward in their citizen contacts.
- Being polite and friendly. A smile at the opportune moment is an asset to a police officer. It is hard for anyone to ignore a friendly smile.

COMMUNITY SERVICE PROGRAMS TO DETER CRIME

Many police departments have instituted programs aimed at preventing crime in the community.

Crime prevention programs include store security, home security, operation identification programs, neighborhood or block watch programs, and automobile security.

Store Security

Police departments may assist store owners in their efforts to reduce losses from shoplifting by studying their stores and then recommending action. Recommendations might include hiring store detectives, implementing educational campaigns, installing convex, wide-angle mirrors in isolated areas, installing closed-circuit television cameras to watch shoppers from observation booths, or installing electronic systems using special magnetic or microwave-sensitive tags. The tags require a deactivating device or a special tool to remove them without damaging the merchandise. If a customer leaves an area of the store before a salesperson

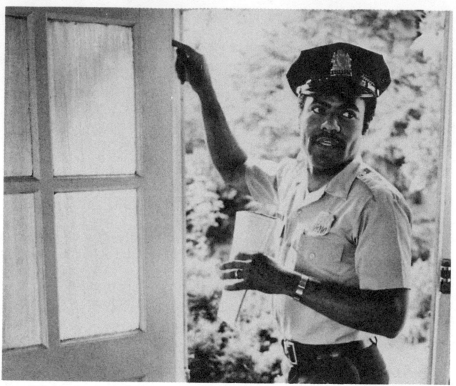

An officer teaches home safety.

removes the tag or deactivates it, a sensor sounds an alarm and store personnel apprehend and detain the suspect for the police.

Home Security

Police departments may also provide home security inspections in which an officer goes to a citizen's home, evaluates its security, and suggests methods for making the home a less inviting target for crime. Recommendations may be made to install deadbolt locks, improve lighting, and so on. In some communities a subsidy is available for half the cost of making recommended changes.

Operation Identification Programs

Police have also implemented operation identification programs in which citizens are provided tools and loaned markers to identify their property with a permanent identification number. If these items are lost or stolen and recovered by the police, the identification number provides a positive method of identifying the rightful owner. If the items are found in the possession of a burglar or thief, the number can aid the police in prosecuting and convicting the suspect.

Source: Courtesy of Minnesota Crime Watch—Department of Public Safety.
Figure 7–1   **Operation I.D. Sticker**

Stickers and decals are furnished those citizens participating so that they can place a warning on their doors and window.

The warning labels and the marking of personal property with a permanent identification number are positive approaches to deter a burglar or thief from attempting to steal that property.

Neighborhood or Block Watch Programs

Block watch programs have been initiated that instruct homeowners to form cooperative block groups to deter burglaries and thefts during the absence of homeowners and to provide places of safety for children who might be threatened on their way to or from school. Such neighborhood watch programs bring neighbors together in an effort to reduce the incidence of crime in their neighborhood. The program involves being aware of who your neighbors are, what their daily routines are, and of suspicious activities or persons in the neighborhood and reporting anything unusual to the police.

With cooperation and involvement of all citizens, such as sharing the responsibility of checking each other's homes when owners are on vacation, the neighborhood is a safer place in which to live. Most programs emphasize that residents should *not* try to apprehend suspects, so programs do not create "vigilante" actions.

Automobile Security

Because of the vulnerability of autos to theft, many antitheft programs and devices have been introduced to make it more difficult for a person to steal a car and more difficult for that person to use or sell it without its stolen nature being detected.

Automobile manufacturers have contributed by making the ignition switch mechanism lock the steering wheel and by having a separate steering post lock key and door lock key. Some police agencies have placed on every parking meter a sticker stating: "Have you locked your car?" and provided dashboard stickers that remind motorists: "Have you taken your keys and locked your car?"

Some cities have encouraged used-car dealers to fence in their lots or chain their entrances and exits. Public education campaigns have also been instituted using newspaper, radio, television, and placard publicity as well as bumper stickers with slogans reminding motorists to lock their cars.

Because 72 percent of the autos stolen are taken by persons under the age of twenty-one, extensive educational campaigns have been launched to educate youth about the seriousness of car theft and its consequences. Law enforcement agencies have also taken stronger measures to assure the immediate processing of persons apprehended.

Other Programs

Programs in the schools, such as lectures and videos about "Children and the Law," have aided police in their fight against vandalism and shoplifting. They reach a segment of society that represents future citizens, informing children of the problem of crime in our society and how they might help reduce this problem.

In addition to community programs to help combat crime, many police departments have instituted programs to promote safety and the general welfare of the public. Most such programs are aimed at children, for example, bike safety programs, drug abuse program, "officer friendly"

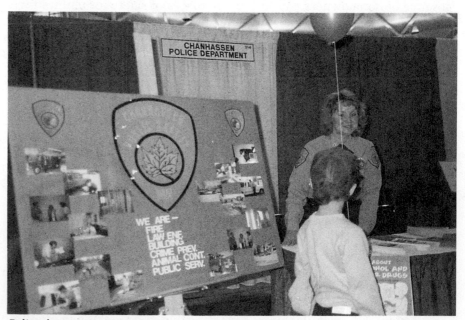

Police department programs on safety are often aimed at children.

programs for elementary school children, and school-police liaison programs.

SUMMARY

Although the type and amount of community service provided by a police department varies from city to city, a certain level of community service is expected everywhere. The services provided include giving information, directions, and advice; counseling and referring; licensing and registering vehicles; intervening in domestic arguments; working with neglected children; rendering emergency medical or rescue services; dealing with alcoholics and the mentally ill; finding lost children; dealing with stray animals; controlling crowds; and providing community education programs on crime prevention, drug abuse, safety, and the like.

Community service should be differentiated from public relations and community relations. Public relations emphasizes building a positive image of the law enforcement officer. Community relations emphasizes improving two-way communication between citizens and the police, with the raising of image an anticipated side effect. Community service, in contrast, emphasizes actual police assistance or efforts to help citizens learn to help themselves in preventing crime and preserving individual safety and well being.

Some police departments attempt to improve their image by instituting public relations programs—programs that emphasize raising the image of the police officer rather than opening channels of communications. Other departments concentrate on community relations programs to provide two-way communication between police and citizens to work toward achieving law and order in the community.

No matter what type of program is instituted, however, the fact remains that the police officer on the street is ultimately responsible for the success of the police-community relations program and for the image of the police held by the citizens of the community.

Several community service programs focus on crime prevention, including store security, home security, operation identification programs, neighborhood or block watch programs, and automobile security.

Discussion Questions

1. What community services are available in your community? Which are most important? Which might be frivolous? Are any necessary services *not* provided?

2. What types of crime prevention programs are used in your community?

3. What types of safety promotion programs are used in your community?

4. Which is the most important: public relations programs, community relations programs, or community service programs? Why?

5. Can you imagine a situation in which a police department placed so much emphasis on public relations that it had the opposite effect than intended, that is, the image of the police was lowered rather than raised?

6. Have you ever personally received service from a police officer? What were the circumstances? How would you evaluate the officer's performance? Have you ever needed a service that was not provided?

7. How might one event serve all three purposes: public relations, community service, and community-police relations?

8. What are the advantages and disadvantages of combining firefighting and law enforcement services?

9. What are the advantages and disadvantages of the police department providing the only ambulance service?

10. For what kinds of individuals should the police provide escort service?

References

Bishop, D. R., and Scheussler, T. J. "The National Crime Information Center's Missing Person File." FBI Law Enforcement Bulletin (August 1982): 20-24.

The Challenge of Crime in a Free Society. President's Commission on Law Enforcement and the Administration of Justice. Washington, D.C.: U.S. Government Printing Office, 1967.

Garmire, B. L. "The Police Role in an Urban Society." In *The Police and the Community*, edited by R. F. Steadman. Baltimore: Johns Hopkins University Press, 1972.

Levine, J. P.; Husheno, M. C.; and Palumbo, D. J. *Criminal Justice: A Public Policy*. New York: Harcourt Brace Jovanovich, 1980.

President's Commission on Law Enforcement and Administration of Justice, *The Police Task Force Report*. Washington, D.C.: U.S. Government Printing Office, 1967.

Radalet, L. A. "Who's in Charge of Law and Order?" In *Police-Community Relations: An Anthology and Bibliography*, edited by W. H. Hewitt and C. L. Newman. Mineola, N.Y.: Foundation Press, 1970.

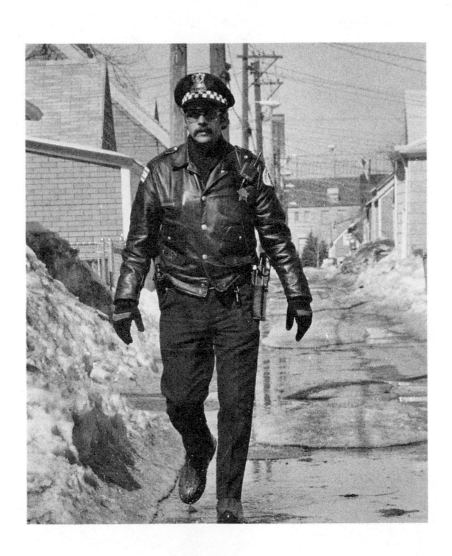

CHAPTER EIGHT

Patrol: The Essence of the Police Function

Your day-by-day—sometimes minute-by-minute—contact with criminals, complainants and citizens alike who are crying, cursing, bleeding, puking, yelling, spitting, biting, fighting, lying, dying, dead, drunk, doped, dirty, scared, scarred, angry, vengeful, irrational, evasive, outlandish, grieving, manipulative, taunting, demanding, defiant, cruel, neurotic, hopeless, and just plain crazy subjects your system to repeated onslaughts of disturbance—Charles Rensberg, *The Tactical Edge*

DO YOU KNOW

What the primary responsibilities of patrol are?

What five specific areas of responsibility are assigned to patrol?

What might be more effective than increasing the level of patrol as a means to reduce crime?

How specialized patrol differs from routine patrol?

What methods of patrol may be used?

What type of shift and beat staffing often lessens the effectiveness of preventive patrol?

What approaches have been tried to improve preventive patrol effectiveness?

What the central features of team policing are?

Whether it is preferable to have one or two officers assigned to a patrol car?

How women on patrol perform compared with men?

Introduction

Chapter 8

Patrol is responsible for providing continuous police service and high-visibility law enforcement, thereby deterring crime. Patrol is the most vital component of police work. All other units are supplemental to this basic unit. Patrol can contribute to each of the common goals of police departments, including preserving the peace, protecting civil rights and civil liberties, enforcing the law, preventing crime, and providing services.

Patrol is responsible for providing continuous police service and high-visibility law enforcement, thereby deterring crime.

In addition, patrol officers must understand the federal, state, and local laws they are sworn to uphold and use good judgment in enforcing them. As noted by the Task Force on the Police (1973, p. 192):

> The patrol officer is the first interpreter of the law and in effect performs a quasi-judicial function. He makes the first attempt to match the reality of human conflict with the law; he determines whether to take no action, to advise, to warn, or to arrest; he determines whether he must apply physical force, perhaps sufficient to cause death. It is he who must discern the fine distinction between a civil and a criminal conflict, between merely unorthodox behavior and a crime, between a legitimate dissent and disturbance of the peace, between the truth and a lie. As the interpreter of the law, he recognizes that a decision to arrest is only the first step in the determination of guilt or innocence. He is guided by, and guardian of, the Constitution.

Unfortunately, however, as noted by this same report (p. 189): "The patrolman is usually the lowest paid, least consulted, most taken for granted member of the force. His duty is looked on as routine and boring."

Despite the lack of status within some police departments, patrol is the backbone of policing. Samuel Walker (1983, p. 103) notes that the "majority of police officers are assigned to patrol and, in that capacity, deliver the bulk of police services to the public. The marked patrol car and the uniformed patrol officer are the most visible manifestations of the police in the eyes of the public."

THE IMPORTANCE OF PATROL

The importance of the patrol function is emphasized by Hale (1981, p. 2):

> In recent years, the police mission in contemporary society has become incredibly varied and complex, and law enforcement agencies are grow-

ing and evolving at a rapid pace. Patrol remains, however, the most important of all police functions. All other police services and activities exist for the exclusive purpose of supporting and enhancing the patrol effort. Patrol is the essence of the police function. Typically, the patrol force is the single largest element in the police organization, and the actions taken by patrol officers have a direct impact on citizen satisfaction and well-being and on the accomplishment of police goals and objectives.

Hale notes that the patrol function is the most visible form of police activity and that individual patrol officers are representatives of the entire police department. Their actions have "far-reaching consequences for the police agency, for the citizenry, and for the quality of justice in contemporary society."

THE CHALLENGE OF PATROL

Not only is patrol exceedingly important to the police function, it is also exceedingly challenging. According to Hale (1981, pp. 37–38):

Police patrol is conducted in a world of contrasts, ranging from the skid row alleys of major cities to the quiet residential avenues of suburbia. . . . In some settings they must be tough and uncompromising, while in others they can afford to be compassionate and relenting. They may be required to take a life one instant and help to bring another into the world the next. In some cases they are feared and mistrusted, while in others they are regarded in high esteem, . . .

Patrol officers often work alone and with little direct supervision . . . . While the good that they do goes unnoticed, their errors frequently do not.

Patrol work can at times be challenging, exciting, emotionally exhausting, and quite satisfying. At other times it can be routine, monotonous, and boring. . . . Patrol officers must learn to expect the unexpected; to respond calmly in the face of danger; to endure undeserved criticism; to show composure during times of crisis and hysteria; and to remain self-possessed when confronted with adversity and hostility.

DUTIES AND RESPONSIBILITIES

The Task Force on the Police (1973, p. 191) notes that no matter what size a police department is, patrol officers have two basic responsibilities: (1) to prevent criminal activity and (2) to provide day-to-day police service to the community. "The specific duties and responsibilities of the patrol officer are innumerable, as varied and complex as the society in which he works. In his multi-purpose role, the patrol officer serves as a protector of public safety, enforcer of law, controller of traffic, and investigator and interpreter of the law."

Patrol officers are responsible for:

- *preserving the peace;*
- *protecting and serving the community;*
- *enforcing the laws;*
- *directing traffic;*
- *investigating crimes;*

As protectors, patrol officers promote and preserve order, respond to requests for services, and attempt to resolve conflicts between individuals and groups. Specific aspects of community service were covered in chapter 7.

As law enforcers, the first duty of patrol officers is to protect constitutional guarantees (as described in chapter 3); the second duty is to enforce federal, state, and local statutes. Patrol officers not only encourage voluntary compliance with the law but also seek to reduce the opportunity for crimes to be committed.

Patrol officers also serve important traffic control functions, described in detail in chapter 9, and important investigative functions, described in detail in chapters 10 and 11.

Finally, as also noted in the Task Force on the Police, patrol officers in any community are the most visible representatives of government, and although they are not supervisors in the organizational sense, they are responsible for the safety and direction of hundreds of people each day.

TYPES OF PATROL

Patrol is frequently categorized as being either routine or specialized. Both routine and specialized patrol seek to deter crime and apprehend criminals as well as to provide community satisfaction with the services provided by the police department. Routine patrol does so by providing rapid response to calls for service; specialized patrol does so by focusing its efforts on already identified problems. Whether routine or specialized patrol is used depends on the nature of the problem and the tactics required to deal with it most effectively.

Routine Patrol

There is nothing "routine" about routine patrol. Its demands and challenges change constantly; the patrol officer may be pursuing an armed bank robber in the morning and rescuing a cat from a tree in the afternoon. It has been said that patrol consists of seven hours and fifty-nine minutes of boredom followed by one minute of sheer panic. As noted previously, routine patrol is the most basic unit of the police department. It is the primary means by which the police department fulfills its responsibility

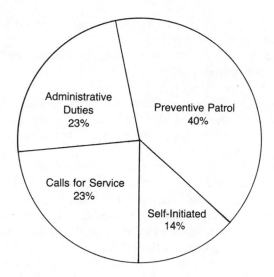

Source: National Institute of Law Enforcement and Criminal Justice, *Improving Patrol Productivity.* Vol. 1, *Routine Patrol,* Washington, D.C.: U.S. Government Printing Office, 1977, p. 3.

Figure 8–1   **Routine Patrol**

to the community. The workload of routine patrol is illustrated in figure 8–1.

Crime Prevention   The theory behind preventive patrol is that the presence of highly visible mobile patrol units will help prevent crime. As noted by the President's Commission on Law Enforcement and Administration of Justice (1967): "Preventive patrol, the continued scrutiny of the community by visible and mobile policemen, is universally thought of as the best method of controlling crime that is available to the police."

Preventive patrol is generally accomplished by uniformed officers moving at random through an assigned area. Since officers usually decide for themselves what they will do while on preventive patrol, this time is sometimes referred to as "noncommitted" time. It comprises between 30 and 40 percent of patrol time, but it is often broken into small segments due to interruptions by self-initiated activities, service calls, and administrative duties.

Often priorities for preventive patrol are identified and/or assigned during roll call. For example, patrol officers may be alerted to the presence of a known escaped criminal sighted in the area to watch for while on patrol.

Although patrol is commonly thought to have a deterrent effect on crime, one important study, the *Kansas City Preventive Patrol Experiment,* suggests this is not the case. Funded by a grant from the Police Foundation, this study was conducted in 1972 and is often referred to as the most comprehensive study of routine preventive patrol ever undertaken. The basic design divided fifteen beats in Kansas City into three different groups:

- Group 1 Reactive Beats—five beats in which no routine preventive patrol was used. Officers responded only to calls for service.

- Group 2 "Control" Beats—five beats maintained their normal level of routine preventive patrol.
- Group 3 Proactive Beats—five beats doubled or tripled the level of routine preventive patrol.

According to Kellings et al. (Klockers 1983, p. 160): "Given the large amount of data collected and the extremely diverse sources used, the overwhelming evidence is that decreasing or increasing routine preventive patrol within the range tested in this experiment had no effect on crime, citizen fear of crime, community attitudes toward the police on the delivery of police services, police response time or traffic accidents."

Klockers (1983, p. 130) asserted that the results of the Kansas City Patrol Experiment indicated that "it makes about as much sense to have police patrol routinely in cars to fight crime as it does to have firemen patrol routinely in fire trucks to fight fire."

Although the Kansas City study found no significant differences in the incidence of crime resulting from varying the *level* of patrol, Goldstein (1977, p. 110) questioned whether the results would have been the same if they had varied the *form* of the patrol. Goldstein asked, "Specifically, would officers produce any different results if the time they devote to patrol was spent in more aggressive and intensive probing of individuals, places and circumstances?"

Given the fact that street-wise criminals study police patrol methods and select targets that are not likely to be detected, and given the fact that many crimes are committed on the spur of the moment, particularly violent crimes such as murder and assault, and given the fact that much crime is committed inside buildings, out of the sight of patrols, Goldstein's question deserves serious consideration.

This sentiment was adopted by Hale (1981, p. 110) when he stated: "It should be the job of the police, then, to carefully analyze crime data, identify those types of crimes that are most likely to be prevented by police efforts, and design patrol strategies accordingly. The preventive efforts of the police must become more crime specific and target oriented."

It may be more effective to vary the form of patrol rather than the level to reduce crime. A more aggressive approach to patrol is part of the form change suggested.

Self-Initiated Tasks   Officer-initiated activities usually result from officers' observations while on preventive patrol; that is, they encounter situations that require their intervention. For example, an officer may see a crime in progress and arrest the suspect. Usually, however, officer-initiated activities involve community relations or crime prevention activities such as citizen contacts or automobile and building checks. Officers may see a large crowd gathered and decide to break it up, thereby preventing a possible disturbance or even a riot. Or they may see a break in a store's security, take steps to correct it, and thus prevent a possible burglary later.

Such self-initiated activities occupy about 14 percent of an officer's patrol time. Officers are sometimes hesitant to get involved in community services and preventive activities because such duties make the officers unavailable for radio dispatches and interfere with their ability to respond rapidly to service calls. Hand-held radios and beepers have allowed patrol officers more freedom of movement and have allowed them to initiate more activity.

Call for Service The two-way radio has made the service call an extremely important element of patrol. It has also made it necessary to prioritize calls. A radio dispatch almost always takes precedence over other patrol activities. For example, if an officer has stopped a traffic violator (a self-initiated activity) and receives a call of an armed robbery in progress, most department policies require the officer to discontinue the contact with the motorist and answer the service call.

Too often little attention is paid to the officer's use of noncommitted time, which is often regarded as having no function other than to ensure the availability of officers to quickly respond to service calls. Frequently noncrime service calls interrupt a patrol officer's self-initiated activity that could prevent or deter crime. Emphasis on rapid response to all service calls has sometimes retarded the development of productive patrol services. Obviously, not all service calls require a rapid response.

Calls for service account for approximately one-fourth of the officer's workload.

Administrative Duties Accounting for another one-fourth of patrol time is administrative work, including preparing and maintaining the patrol vehicle, transporting prisoners and documents, writing reports, and testifying in court. Efforts to make patrol more cost effective have often been aimed at cutting time spent on administrative duties. Some departments have greatly reduced the time officers spend maintaining their vehicles. Other departments have drastically reduced the amount of paperwork required of the patrol officers by allowing them to dictate reports, which secretaries then transcribe.

The types of reports police officers frequently use include Motor Vehicle Reports, Vehicle Recovery Reports, Offense Reports, Continuation Reports, Juvenile Reports, Juvenile Report Summaries, Missing Persons Reports, Arrest/Violation Reports, and Record Checks.

Specialized Patrol

Specialized patrol is designed to handle problems and situations that require concentrated, coordinated efforts. Some patrol officers receive special training to deal with specific problems such as hostage and sniper situations, VIP protection, riot or crowd control, rescue operations, and control of suppressible crimes.

Suppressible crimes are crimes that commonly occur in locations and under circumstances that provide police officers a reasonable opportunity to deter or apprehend offenders. Included in the category of suppressible crimes are robbery, burglary, car theft, assault, and sex crimes. Such problems frequently involve a need for covert surveillance and decoys, tactics that cannot be used by uniformed patrol officers.

Specialized patrol operations are often used to saturate particular areas or to stake out suspects and possible crime locations. Countermeasures to combat street crimes have included police decoys to catch criminals—one of the most cost-effective and productive apprehension methods available. Officers have posed as cab drivers, old women, truck drivers, money couriers, nuns, and priests. They have infiltrated drug circles as undercover agents. Usually operating in high-crime areas, decoy officers are vulnerable to violence and injury. The results are considered worth the risk, however; an attack upon a decoy almost always results in a conviction of the attacker.

Some patrol officers receive special training to deal with specific problems such as hostage and sniper situations, VIP protection, riot or crowd control, rescue operations, and control of suppressible crimes.

METHODS OF PATROL

Williams, Formby, and Watkins (1982, p. 100) note: "Patrol usually refers to the random movement of uniformed officers within a defined area. This random movement may be done on foot, in or on some type of vehicle, or, in some areas, on horseback."

Patrol may be accomplished via foot, automobile, motorcycle, bicycle, horseback, aircraft, and boat. The most commonly used and most effective patrol is usually a combination of automobile and foot patrol.

Foot Patrol   Foot patrol, the oldest form of patrol, has the advantage of close citizen contact. Most effective in highly congested areas, it may help to deter burglary, robbery, purse snatching, and muggings. The 1980s saw a significant trend back to foot patrol. Foot patrol is relatively expensive and does limit the officer's ability to pursue suspects in vehicles and to get from one area to another rapidly. Used in conjunction with motorized patrol, foot patrol is highly effective. Chapman (1970, Introduction) says, "According to one authoritative source, the word 'patrol' is derived from the French word *patrouiller*, which means, roughly, to travel on foot."

Foot patrol was historically the "mainstay of the police patrol effort" according to Heaphy (1978, p. 11). But, Heaphy suggests: "In modern times, however, the scope and methods of police patrol have changed dramatically. Today the foot patrol beat is, in all but the largest cities, a vestige of the past. Nationally less than 10 percent of the total patrol force consists of foot patrol."

This view is not accepted by the National Neighborhood Foot Patrol Center, Michigan State University School of Criminal Justice. According to the center:

> *Foot patrol is an exercise in communication—an attempt to develop rapport between the officer on the beat and the citizens he or she serves. Foot patrol officers constantly interact with the community. They instruct citizens in crime prevention techniques and link them to available governmental services. They are catalysts of neighborhood organizations.*

Foot patrol is *proactive* rather than reactive. Its goal is to address neighborhood problems before they become crimes. The center notes that "motorized patrolling has proven ineffective in certain key areas. Crime rates continue to rise, and even in areas where they are not high, vagrants, abandoned cars, and groups of juveniles on the street create an impression that the environment is violent and uncontrollable."

The center cites a series of experimental programs conducted by criminal justice researchers to see if a modified version of foot patrol could contribute to modern policing. The intent was not to replace motorized patrol but rather to provide a combination of foot and motorized patrol, capitalizing on the strengths of each. One highly successful program was in Flint, Michigan, where in a three-year span crime was down 8.7 percent and calls for service were down 43.4 percent in areas where foot patrol was in force. Clear signs that police/community relations had dramatically improved were also evident. It was in part due to the success of this program that the Charles Stewart Mott Foundation provided funding for the National Neighborhood Foot Patrol Center.

According to Trojanowicz (1982, p. 86), the Flint program was highly regarded by the citizens: "Almost 70 percent of the citizens interviewed during the final year of the study felt safer because of the Foot Patrol Program."

Automobile Patrol   Automobile patrol offers the greatest mobility and flexibility and is usually the most cost-effective method of patrol. It allows wide coverage and rapid response to calls—the vehicle radio provides instant communications with headquarters. The automobile also provides a means of transporting special equipment and prisoners or suspects. The obvious disadvantage of automobile patrol is that access to certain locations is restricted, for example, inside buildings. Therefore, officers may have to leave their vehicles to pursue suspects on foot.

In addition, while patroling in a vehicle, officers cannot pay as much attention to details they might see were they on foot, for example, a door ajar, a window broken, or a security light out. The physical act of driving

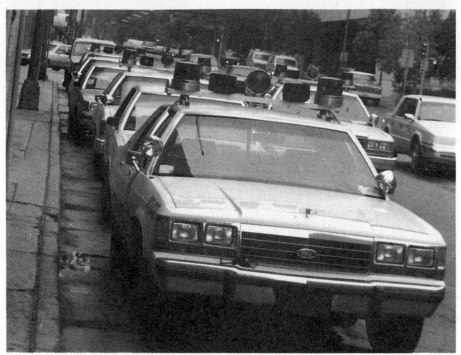

Automobile patrol provides the greatest mobility and flexibility for officers.

may draw attention away from such subtle signs that a crime may be in progress.

Another disadvantage of automobile patrol is a lack of community contact so necessary for effective police work. As one police officer said: "I'm encapsulized in this car, and I'm driving along, usually the windows are probably rolled up because I'm moving, and so I'm in this steel cocoon, and I'm pretty isolated from the outside world" (Conroy 1987, p. 59).

To counteract this isolation, the President's Commission on Crime urged that officers in patrol cars should be considered foot officers who use cars for transportation from one point to another. Many officers, however, do not see it that way.

Many officers resist getting out of their cars to talk to citizens; some even feel it is a degrading type of appeasement. In addition, the practice contradicts the tactical principle of preventive patrol, which requires the continual presence of moving, motorized street patrol. Some departments stress this principle to the extent that department regulations forbid unnecessary or unofficial conversations with citizens.

Recent research on the effectiveness of preventive patrol, however, indicates that a crime prevented by a passing vehicle can, and usually is, committed as soon as the police are gone. In effect, police presence only prevents street crime if the police can be everywhere at once.

Hale (1981, p. 90) suggests: "It is likely that the automobile will continue to be the dominant form of transportation for the patrol officer in the foreseeable future." Hale also notes, however: "The automobile should be regarded as only one form of patrol, even though a dominant one. Other forms of patrol can be combined with automobile patrol to increase the overall effectiveness and scope of the police patrol function."

Motorcycle Patrol   Motorcycle patrol is similar to automobile patrol; however, it foregoes the advantage of transporting special equipment and prisoners to overcome the disadvantage of limited access presented by automobile. The motorcycle is also better suited to maneuver easily through heavy traffic or narrow alleys.

According to Chapman (1970, p. 645):

> *For many years two-wheel motorcycles were used almost exclusively by police departments for the purposes of traffic enforcement, escort, and*

Motor scooters can be used instead of motorcycles.

parade duty. The two-wheel motorcycle, supplemented by the automobile, has traditionally dominated the field of traffic law enforcement, largely due to the fact that the motorcycle offers several distinct advantages over the automobile, including its manueverability in heavily congested areas.

Among the disadvantages of motorcycles are their relatively high cost to operate, their limited use in adverse weather, and the hazards associated with riding them.

In a study conducted in Washington D.C. in 1974, per-mile costs for motorcycles were much higher than for conventional patrol vehicles. As a result of this study, the Metropolitan Police Department switched to less expensive two- and three-wheel motor scooters rather than standard motorcycles. These motor scooters were as maneuverable as motorcycles, and they were less expensive and less hazardous.

Bicycle Patrol   Bicycle patrol is sometimes used in parks and on beaches or in conjunction with stakeouts and surveillance. Although used infrequently, it adds another dimension of patrol available in special circumstances such as in areas that are inaccessible for patrol vehicles and too large to be adequately patrolled on foot.

In addition to mobility, bicycles also provide a "stealth factor" since they can be ridden very quietly and do not attract attention. Yarbrough (1977, pp. 10–13) states:

Bicycles are often used by plain clothes patrol officers for the purpose of conducting surveillance in high-crime areas, such as central parks or shopping districts. It is often is such areas that street crimes, such as mugging, purse snatching, robbery, and sexual assault occur with great frequency. Bicycle patrols have also been found to be highly effective in combatting theft, burglary, and vandalism in residential areas and around schools during evening hours.

Bicycles have some of the same disadvantages as motorcycles. One is that their use is limited by the weather. A second, more important disadvantage is that the officer is very vulnerable while riding a bicycle. Officers should have the proper safety equipment and follow all basic safety precautions while on bicycle patrol.

Mounted Patrol   Mounted patrol is decreasing in the United States, but it is still used effectively in larger cities such as New York City to quell civil disorders and riots, to patrol bridle paths and parks, and to control traffic. Although expensive, this method of patrol has a unique advantage—the size and mobility of the horse is more effective in an unruly crowd than an officer on foot or in a vehicle.

Air Patrol   Air patrol is another expensive yet highly effective form of patrol, especially when large geographic areas are involved, for example, a widespread search for a lost person, a downed plane, or an escaped

An officer on horseback maintains order at a demonstration.

convict. Helicopters and small aircraft are generally used in conjunction with police vehicles on the ground in criminal surveillance and in traffic control, not only to report tie-ups but to clock speeds and radio to ground units. Helicopters have also been used to rescue persons from tall buildings on fire and in other situations such as floods. In addition aircraft is a cost-effective means of transporting prisoners over long distances.

Airplanes were first used by the New York City Police Department in 1930. At this time daredevil pilots were flying all over the city, sometimes crashing in densely populated areas. The New York airborne police unit was created to control reckless flying over the city (Potter 1979, p. 22). In 1947 New York City bought its first helicopter.

During the 1970s and 1980s, many cities and counties added helicopters and fixed-wing planes to their patrol capability. Air patrol does have disadvantages, however, including the high cost of buying, operating, and maintaining planes and helicopters. Another disadvantage is that citizens may complain of the noise when the aircraft are used to patrol residential areas. And, some citizens feel they are being spied on—that the police are literally an "eye in the sky," and it makes them nervous. This disadvantage might be countered by public relations information stressing the purpose of the air patrol.

Boat Patrol   Boat patrol is used extensively on our coasts to apprehend gun and narcotics smugglers. Inland, boat patrols are often used to control river and lake traffic.

Water patrol units are very specialized and are used in relatively few cities in the United States. In those cities with extensive coasts, however, they are a vital part of patrol. Hale (1981, pp. 96–97) lists the following purposes serviced by police marine units:

Sheriff's water patrol at work.

Water safety and protection
Search and rescue
Antismuggling operations
General surveillance
Patrol and operation
Ordinance enforcement

Hale notes that cities with "expansive waterfronts or large marinas" may use police marine units primarily "to guard against theft, burglary, and vandalism."

One disadvantage of water patrol is expense. Boats are expensive to buy, operate, and maintain. In addition, they must be moored, and they must be operated by officers with special boating skills.

Special Terrain Patrol   Some police departments may require special-purpose vehicles to patrol. For example, areas that receive a lot of snow may have snowmobiles as part of their patrol fleet. These vehicles may be especially useful in rescue missions as well as on routine patrol.

At the opposite extreme, police departments operating in desert areas may require vehicles such as trail bikes and dune buggies. Police departments in remote parts of the country may use four-wheel drive vehicles. Departments with miles of beaches to patrol may use jeeps and dune buggies.

Canine-Assisted Patrol   Canine-assisted patrol is a specialized method of patrol usually found only in large departments. It has been used in crowd control, in searching out concealed suspects, and in identifying hidden narcotics. Dogs have also been trained and used extensively in major airports to locate bombs or narcotics on planes. Although expensive, canine-assisted patrol may be cost effective by diminishing the number of officers required for a search.

According to Chapman (1970, p. 656): "Canine or dog units have been used for law enforcement and civil protection purposes for centuries.

Officers and dogs in training for canine-assisted patrol.

After World War II, the use of dogs in police work spread rapidly from England to the United States."

Police dogs are often used in place of a second officer on automobile and foot patrols. As noted by Hale (1981, pp. 94–95): "Properly trained dogs are virtually fearless and totally loyal to their handlers. They also have a significant psychological effect on would-be troublemakers. Officers assigned to high-crime areas have little to fear with a well-trained canine at their side

Like other forms of patrol, canine-assisted patrol also has some disadvantages. A canine program is relatively expensive. In addition, each dog works with only one handler. If that officer is ill or is transferred or promoted, problems can occur. Further, the dogs require special patrol cars.

Combination Patrol   Combination patrol provides the most versatile approach to preventing or deterring crime and apprehending criminals. The combination used will depend not only on the size of the police department but also on the circumstances that arise.

Hale (1981, p. 86) cautions:

> *There is no "single best" or "ideal" patrol method. A variety of patrol methods is available. Some will work exceptionally well in some jurisdictions and not at all in others. There is yet much to be learned about the effectiveness of various patrol methods. Methods of patrol vary by time of day, the size and type of agency concerned, and the nature of the police problems that exist in a given area. In too many cases, police patrol continues to be practiced in a very haphazard and unsystematic manner. Few attempts have been made to fully evaluate new patrol methods or strategies. Tradition and routine have dictated the manner in which patrol operations have been conducted.*

Table 8—1   **Summary of Patrol Methods**

Method	Uses	Advantages	Disadvantages
Foot	Highly congested areas Burglary, robbery, theft, purse snatching, mugging	Close citizen contact High visibility Develop informants	Relatively expensive Limited mobility
Automobile	Respond to service calls Provide traffic control Transport individuals, documents, and equipment	Most economical Greatest mobility and flexibility Offers means of communication Provides means of transporting people, documents, and equipment	Limited access to certain areas Limited citizen contact
Motorcycle	Same as automobile except for transporting individuals and limited equipment	Maneuverability in congested areas and areas restricted to automobiles	Inability to transport much equipment Not used during bad weather Hazardous to operator
Bicycle	Stake-outs Parks and beaches Congested areas	Quiet and unobtrusive	Limited speed
Mounted	Parks and bridal paths Crowd control Traffic control	Size and maneuverability of horse	Expensive
Aircraft	Surveillance Traffic control Searches and rescues	Covers large areas easily	Expensive
Boat	Deter smuggling Water traffic control Rescues	Access to activities occurring on water	Expensive
Special-terrain	Patrol unique areas inaccessible to other forms Rescue operations	Access to normally inaccessible areas	Limited use in some instances
Canine-assisted	Locating bombs, drugs, and concealed suspects	Minimizes officers' risks	Expensive

HIGH VISIBILITY VERSUS LOW VISIBILITY

According to Hale (1981, p. 113): "The theory underlying the high-visibility patrol concept is that *certain* types of crimes can be reduced by increasing the 'aura of police omnipresence' in the community." High-visibility patrol is often used in high-risk crime areas in hopes of deterring criminal activity. In addition, high-visibility patrol gives the citizens of a community a sense of safety, justified or not. Types of high-visibility patrol include foot patrol, especially with a canine partner, mounted patrol, marked police car patrol, and helicopter patrol.

Low-visibility patrol is often used to apprehend criminals engaged in targeted crimes. Many of the specialized patrol operations would fall into this category. Types of low-visibility patrol include unmarked police cars and bicycles.

The relative effectiveness of high-visibility and low-visibility patrol has not been determined. As noted by Hale (1981, p. 113): "The conclusion is that both low- and high-visibility patrol tactics have produced encouraging reductions in the incidence of selected crimes."

STRUCTURE AND MANAGEMENT OF PATROL

Traditionally, patrol officers have been assigned a specific time and a specific geographic location to patrol. Typically, a three-shift structure is implemented and the beats are set up to be of equal geographic size. Such a structure poses obvious problems, because the workload is not the same at all hours of the day or in all areas. For example, as noted by Williams, Formby, and Watkins (1982, p. 101): "Statistics show that the 4 P.M. to midnight shift workload, in terms of calls for service and crimes committed, is about twice as high as that for the midnight to 8 A.M. shift. Where equal shift staffing is used, the amount of preventive patrol time and the workload per officer are doubled, resulting in less preventive patrol to deter crime during times when the crime occurrence is highest." Likewise, some areas of a city or town are likely to have a higher demand for police service than others.

Equal shift and beat size staffing creates major problems and lessens the effectiveness of preventive patrol during certain times and in certain areas.

Several attempts have been made to overcome the problems inherent in equal shift and beat size staffing. Some departments, usually larger ones, assign officers according to the demand for services, concentrating the officers' time where it is most needed. Union contracts, however, sometimes make this difficult.

Another problem with traditional approaches to organizing patrol is how the officers' time is structured. Recall that preventive patrol occupies approximately 40 percent of an officer's time, but it is usually broken up into short intervals of twenty to thirty minutes. Lack of a concentrated effort reduces the effects of preventive patrol.

Several attempts to improve the use of preventive patrol time have been implemented. Four such nontraditional preventive patrol strategies are described by Williams, Formby, and Watkins (1982, p. 101).

Their first example involves the Community-Oriented Policing concept and the Community Manager concept. Both approaches allow an officer to plan ahead for use of noncommitted time through the use of statistics on crime in the officer's allotted time and area. Officers are to use such crime analysis information to work with the community to devise methods to deter crime. Although such programs might be perceived as basically community relations, they do provide one approach to planning for more effective use of preventive patrol time.

A second approach, used primarily in and around New Haven, Connecticut, is the Directed Deterrent Patrol (DDP). Like the preceding example, DDP uses crime analysis information to organize the route and timing of preventive patrol. Officers are given the exact time, route, and duration of each preventive patrol activity, known as a D. run. When a D. run begins, the officers notify the dispatcher. From then until the run is completed, these officers do not receive any routine calls. Upon completion of the D. run, the officers again notify dispatch. This approach provides substantial time to be used for only preventive patrol.

A third example is the approach used in Wilmington, Delaware, called the Directed Apprehension or the Split-Force Patrol. In this approach, part of the patrol force undertakes only directed patrol activities; the remainder of the patrol force answers calls for service and performs traditional patrol activities.

The fourth example is the New York City Street Crime Unit, a unit of specially trained patrol officers using plainclothes surveillance and decoy tactics to apprehend offenders in the act of committing crimes. The officers, disguised as potential victims, patrol high-crime areas, watched by a backup team, also in disguise. Such specialized patrol teams were described earlier in this chapter.

Preventive patrol has used crime statistics to plan shift and beat staffing, providing more coverage during times of peak criminal activity and in high-crime areas.

Other approaches to enhance the effectiveness of patrol include team policing and use of volunteers from the community.

TEAM POLICING

Team policing in the United States, patterned after a unique patrol experiment in Aberdeen, Scotland, in 1948, is designed to deliver patrol, investigative, and community services on a more informal basis. In other words, neighborhood team policing combines the specialized services and equipment of large urban departments with the more personal community contact of small departments.

Police services are decentralized, with a team of officers assigned around-the-clock responsibility for crime control and police services in a specific area. In many programs the officer's responsibilities are expanded to include investigative work as well as community relations services. As departments become decentralized, decision making becomes a product of teamwork, giving officers a voice in planning actions and policies that directly affect them. These features not only increase officer job satisfaction, but they also frequently improve the quality and quantity of police service delivered to the community.

Central features of team policing include the following:

- *Combining patrol, investigative, and community relation services.*
- *Decentralization.*
- *Cooperative decision making.*
- *Permanent assignment to a team and a geographic area.*

Although team policing means different things to different departments, a 1973 study of team policing suggests that most programs have three basic operational elements (Sherman, Milton, and Kelly 1973, pp. 3–5):

Geographic stability of patrol.
Maximum interaction among team members.
Maximum communication among team members and the community.

The authors identify the most basic operational element as geographic stability of patrol. This same study identified common organizational supports in addition to the three basic operational elements: unity of supervision, lower-level flexibility in policy making, unified delivery of services, and combined investigative and patrol functions.

The teams are organized in two different ways: shift teams and area teams. A shift team usually has no formal coordination of the various shifts serving a single area. The supervisor of the shift team reports to a watch commander, who is responsible for only a single shift within a twenty-four-hour period. This approach provides less continuity of service.

Area teams, in contrast, provide law enforcement services twenty-four hours a day. This around-the-clock responsibility allows a single team leader to coordinate all patrol activities in the same area and provides considerable flexibility in deploying officers to meet changing levels of service demands throughout the day.

Area teams have three distinct advantages over shift teams. First, they provide continuity of service to citizens; second, they allow for alteration of schedule; and third, they have a larger pool of officers from which to draw.

Team policing is found in small, medium, and large cities in equal numbers, not just in the big cities. It is found in both urban and suburban communities and in all parts of the country. Most team programs have replaced random roving patrol with objective-based patrol activities. Teams are assigned crime prevention, investigative, and community relations activities to perform when not responding to calls. Some departments place more emphasis on one of these activities than the others, and hence they can be classified by their primary focus.

ONE-OFFICER VERSUS TWO-OFFICER PATROL UNITS

Another controversial organizational decision is whether patrol units should be one-officer or two-officer units. According to Hale (1981, p. 97): "It is a very emotional subject since officer safety is an overriding concern. At the same time, the police administrator must be concerned with the economic aspect of the issue as a result of scarce resources and limited appropriations. . . . It is safe to say that there are a number of valid arguments for both one-officer and two-officer patrol units." Hale points out that sometimes it is necessary to use two-officer units to ensure the officers' safety and to resolve the problem involved satisfactorily; however, usually officer productivity and operational efficiency can be increased by using one-officer patrol units.

Circumstances should determine whether a one-officer or a two-officer unit is more appropriate.

Hale contends that the single-officer unit is the "rule rather than the exception," and that most incidents can be handled by one officer. If two officers are required, two one-officer units can be dispatched to the scene. He feels two-officer units should be restricted to those areas, shifts, and types of activities most likely to threaten the officers' safety, for example, during the evening or in high-crime areas.

Several advantages are obtained by the one-officer unit including cost effectiveness in that the same number of officers can patrol twice the area, with twice the mobility, and with twice the power of observation. In addition, officers working alone are generally more cautious in dangerous situations, recognizing that they have no backup. And, officers working alone are generally more attentive to patrol duties, since they do not have a conversational partner. The expense of two cars compared to one, however, is often a mitigating factor.

In addition, a study conducted by Chapman (1974, p. 145) found that two-officer patrol units did not enhance officer safety; nearly two-thirds of the officers suffering on-duty assaults were assigned to two-officer units; less than 15 percent of the reported assaults occurred with only one officer present.

Another study conducted in the San Diego Police Department (Boydstun et al. 1977), comparing one-officer and two-officer patrol units on several criteria, found the following:

- While overall performance for calls for service and officer-initiated activities were judged to be equal, more traffic citations were issued by two-officer units.

- Overall efficiency of one-officer units was judged to be higher than that of two-officer units, even though the former required most backup support.
- While citizens resisted arrest less frequently when dealing with one-officer units, overall safety was judged to be equal between both types of units. Assaults on officers, officer injuries, and vehicle accidents occurred at the same rate for both one-officer and two-officer units.

Although the San Diego study seems to support using single-officer patrol units strongly, authors of the study stress that the results of the study apply only to San Diego. Departments in other parts of the country should conduct their own studies.

Hale (1981, p. 100) notes: "Police unions have also supported the use of two-officer patrol units and have often managed to include provisions for two-officer units in their contracts with the local jurisdiction. In so doing, the unions have jeopardized the ability of management to make proper use of available resources and to make rational decisions concerning personnel deployment and scheduling."

EFFECTIVENESS OF WOMEN ON PATROL

In 1971 Miami promoted the first woman to sergeant to command a patrol sector of six to ten men from a mixture of ethnic backgrounds. The woman sergeant not only did a highly competent job, she helped change the department's uniform regulations so female officers could wear slacks on duty.

According to Miami Chief of Police Bernard L. Garmire (1974, pp. 11–13), female officers proved to be effective in all phases of police work in Miami. Women officers were well accepted by male officers and by the public. In fact, the classification of policewomen was eliminated with all personnel classified as police officers. As noted by Garmire: "Crime makes no distinction between sexes, and neither should law enforcement in its effort to combat it (p. 13)."

Studies have shown that women perform as well as men in police patrol work.

The LEAA financed a seven-month study in New York City ("Women on Patrol" 1978, p. 43), which found that women generally perform as well as men in police patrol work, although some small differences exist. The study, based on direct observation of 3,625 patrols and 2,400 police-civilian encounters, examined an equal number of men and women. It analyzed the actions required of the officers, their style of patrol, their methods of gaining control, their initiative, physical strength, and the reactions of the public.

The study found that the performance of policewomen is more like that of policemen than it is different, although the women made a better impression on the public. Citizens said women officers were more competent, pleasant, and respectful than the men. The women's performance created a better civilian regard for the New York City Police Department.

The study also found that women were less likely to join male partners in taking control of a situation or jointly making decisions. In the few incidents judged to be dangerous, however, men and women were equally likely to attempt to gain control. Women were neither more nor less likely than men to use force, display a weapon, or rely on a direct order. In addition, the behavior of women who patrolled with women was more active, assertive, and self-sufficient.

Other findings of the study were that women were slightly less physically agile in such activities as climbing ladders or steep stairs. Women took more sick leave than men—consistent with earlier research showing that, in general, women are absent from work more frequently than men, perhaps because they are more likely to stay home when family members are ill.

The report attributed the small but consistent differences to socially conditioned attitudes such as protectiveness, disdain, or skepticism by men and passivity by women. The study concluded: "The results offer little support either to those who hold that women are unsuited to patrol or to those who argue that women do the job better than men. By and large, patrol performance of the women was more like that of the men than it was different."

According to James M. H. Gregg, former LEAA administrator: "This report is another important step toward creating equal opportunities for women in law enforcement. . . . Today's police patrolwomen are pioneering in what has always been a man's world, and there are obstacles to overcome. This report makes it clear that they are being overcome."

In 1972 the Police Foundation funded a comparison study of male and female recruits in Washington, D.C. Completed in 1974, the study concluded that from a performance viewpoint it was appropriate to hire women for patrol on the same basis as men. Among its specific findings were the following (Kiernan and Cusik 1977):

> *Both men and women officers obtained similar results in handling angry or violent citizens. No incidents cast serious doubt on a female officer's ability to patrol satisfactorily.*
>
> *Women made fewer arrests and gave fewer traffic citations. However, they also had fewer opportunities to do so, as they were not given patrol assignments as often as men. Arrests made by women and men were equally likely to result in convictions.*
>
> *Men were more likely to engage in serious misconduct than women, for example, to be arrested for drunk and disorderly conduct while off duty. Women, on the other hand, were more likely to be late for work.*
>
> *A majority of Washington residents approved of the use of women in patrol work, although they were "moderately skeptical" of women's abilities to handle violent suspects.*
>
> *There were no differences between men and women in the number of sick days used, number of injuries sustained, or number of days absent from work because of injuries.*
>
> *Male and female partners shared driving equally, took charge with*

about the same frequency, and were about equal in giving each other in-structions.

Resignation rates were also similar: 14 percent for women and 12 percent for men.

Perhaps the most graphic illustration of the equal role played by men and women on police patrol is that of Gail A. Cobb, who joined the Washington, D.C. Police Department in 1973. She had been assigned to patrol duty for only five months when she responded to her last police call.

Around noon one Friday in September, Officer Cobb was patrolling downtown Washington when she was called to help search for two suspected bank robbers who had exchanged shots with police and then fled. Officer Cobb saw a man dash down a ramp into an underground parking garage and followed him. Then, moments after entering the garage, she was shot in the chest. Only twenty-four years old, Officer Gail Cobb became the first United States policewoman to be killed in the line of duty. As noted by Police Chaplain Reverend R. Joseph Dooley, her death "established the fact that the criminal makes no distinction between the sexes. It is the badge and the blue uniform that makes the difference."

VOLUNTEER PATROLS

The use of volunteer patrols is described in depth by Lawrence W. Sherman in *Crime and Public Policy*. According to Sherman (1983 p. 147):

> *Few developments are more indicative of public concern about crime, and declining faith in the ability of public institutions to cope with it, than the burgeoning growth in private policing. According to a recent Gallup poll, 17 percent of Americans surveyed nationally reported some sort of organized volunteer crime prevention effort in their neighborhoods. The upsurge in private policing bears witness to the persistence in modern life of an age-old, commonsensical conviction about public safety, namely, that "watching" is one key to preventing crime. At the same time, the recent emphasis on voluntary watching efforts suggests a diminishing public confidence in the ability of publicly empowered police to perform this traditional task.*

Sherman goes on to note that questions related to "watching" raise very difficult public policy questions, such as, How much watching do we need? Who should pay for it? How effective is watching by volunteers? Watching as a crime prevention strategy consumes a vast amount of public financing and, in addition, is a controversial strategy because it is reminiscent of dictatorships and oppression.

Nonetheless, the growth of private watching has been resisted by many police executives who view such watchers as lacking competence. In some instances, incidents of volunteer "vigilantism" have reinforced such concerns. It may also be that police executives view such private watchers as a threat to their own job security. In fact, according to Sherman (1983, p. 147): "Public police unions have been called auxiliary police 'scab labor.' . . . The more the police can discourage private watching, the larger the market share they may be able to retain."

One key question yet to be answered is just how effective private watching is. Sherman (1983, p. 147) states: "There is virtually no systematic evidence about the crime prevention effectiveness of private watching in uniform, by commercial uniformed private security guards, uniformed volunteer auxiliary police, or uniformed volunteer patrols such as the Guardian Angels."
Numerous volunteer programs have claimed dramatic reduction in crime. The tendency is for interest in such voluntary watching to gradually decrease, however, and as citizen interest decreases, crime increases.

The limited research on the effectiveness of watching by citizen volunteers from within their own homes is somewhat more encouraging.

EVALUATING POLICE EFFECTIVENESS

Table 8—2   **Some Recommended Measures of Police Productivity**

Police Function Being Measured	Measure Employed
Police patrol operations	1. Number of patrol officers assigned to street patrol in terms of total patrol officers 2. Work-hours of patrol time spent on activities contributing to patrol objectives in terms of total patrol work-hours 3. Number of calls of a given type and response time for answering these calls 4. Arrests resulting from patrol that survive the first judicial screening 5. Felony arrests from patrol surviving the first judicial screening 6. Arrests (felonies and misdemeanors) that result in convictions
Provision of noncrime services	1. Number of noncrime calls for service that are satisfactorily responded to in terms of work-hours devoted to noncrime service calls 2. Medical emergency calls that emergency room personnel evaluate as having received appropriate first aid
Human resource management	1. Number of disciplinary charges filed and number substantiated in terms of total departmental personnel 2. Number of work-hours lost during the year due to illness, injury, or disciplinary action
Miscellaneous considerations	1. Population served per police employee and per dollar 2. Crime rates and changes in crime rates for reported crimes (relative to dollars or employees per capita) 3. Clearance rates of reported crimes (relative to dollars or employees per capita) 4. Arrests per police department employee and per dollar 5. Crime rates, including estimates of unreported crimes based on victimization studies 6. Clearance rates, including estimates of unreported crimes based on victimization studies 7. Percentage of crimes solved in less than x days 8. Percentage of population indicating a lack of feeling of security 9. Percentage of population expressing dissatisfaction with police services

Sources: The National Commission on Productivity, *Opportunities for Improving Productivity in Police Services* (Washington, D.C.: National Commission on Productivity, 1973), pp. 14–28, 49–52; The Urban Institute, *The Challenge of Productivity Diversity: Improving Local Government Productivity Measurement and Evaluation, Part III, Measuring Police-Crime Control Productivity* (Washington, D.C.: The Urban Institute, June 1972). p. 11.

SUMMARY

Of all the operations performed by the police, patrol is the most vital. Patrol is responsible for providing continuous police service and high-visibility law enforcement, thereby deterring crime. Patrol officers are responsible for protecting and serving the community, enforcing the laws, directing traffic, and investigating crimes. Specialized patrol officers concentrate on specific problem such as hostage and sniper situations, VIP protection, riot and crowd control, rescue operations, and control of suppressible crimes.

It may be more effective to vary the *form* of patrol rather than the level to reduce crime. A more aggressive approach to patrol is part of the form change suggested.

Patrol can be accomplished via foot, automobile, motorcycle, bicycle, horseback, aircraft, and boat. The most commonly used and most effective patrol is usually a combination of automobile and foot patrol.

Several factors are important in the structure and management of patrol. Equal shift and beat size staffing creates major problems and lessens the effectiveness of preventive patrol during certain times and in certain areas. Preventive patrol has used crime statistics to plan shift and beat staffing, providing more coverage during times of peak criminal activity and in high-crime areas.

Another approach to enhancing the effectiveness of patrol is use of team policing, especially popular during the 1970s. The central features of team policing include combining patrol, investigative, and community relation services; decentralization; cooperative decision making; and permanent assignment to a team and a geographic area.

An additional factor of importance in the management and structure of patrol is whether one-officer or two-officer patrol units are more appropriate. This is determined by individual circumstances.

Women have been found to be as effective as men on patrol.

Use of volunteers to patrol is another approach to preventing crime, but its effectiveness has not been clearly established.

Discussion Questions

1. What type of patrol is used in your community?
2. What would happen if your police officers went on strike?
3. Why doesn't patrol have as much prestige as investigation?
4. Why is patrol considered a hazardous assignment by some and a "drag" by others?
5. Are volunteers used in your police department? If so, how?
6. Which do you support, a one-officer or two-officer patrol unit? Why?
7. Does visible patrol deter crime?
8. What arguments would you use to support using canine-assisted patrol?
9. What types of administrative support could relieve patrol officers for more street duties?
10. If you had your choice of patrol, what method would you select? Why?

References

Boydstun, E. et al. *Patrol Staffing in San Diego: One- or Two-Officer Units*. Washington, D.C.: Police Foundation, 1977.

Chapman, S. G. "Introduction," *Police Patrol Readings*, 2nd ed. Springfield, Ill.: Charles C. Thomas, 1970.

Chapman, S. G. et al. *Perspectives on Police Assaults in the South Central United States*. Vol. 1. Norman, Okla.: The University of Oklahoma Press, 1974.

Conroy, D. L. *The Prices They Paid: A Phenomenological Study of Police Officers*. Unpublished Ph.D. dissertation, 1987.

Garmire, B. L. "Female Officers in the Department." *FBI Law Enforcement Bulletin* (June 1974): 11–13.

Gay, W. G., and Schack, S. *Prescriptive Package: Improving Patrol Productivity*. Vol. 1, *Routine Patrol*. Washington, D.C.: Office of Technology Transfer, National Institute of Law Enforcement and Criminal Justice, Law Enforcement Assistance Administration, U.S. Department of Justice (Grant Number 76–NI–00–0055), July 1977.

Goldstein, H. *Policing in a Free Society*. Cambridge, Mass.: Ballinger Publishing, 1977.

Hale, C. D. *Police Patrol Operations and Management*. New York: John Wiley and Sons, 1981.

Heaphy, J., ed. *Police Practices: The General Administrative Survey*. Washington, D.C.: Police Foundation, 1978.

Kiernan, M. and Cusik, J. "Women on Patrol: The Nation's Capitol Gives them High Marks." *Police Magazine* (1977): 45–53.

Klockars, C. B., ed. *Thinking about Police: Contemporary Readings*. New York: McGraw-Hill, 1983.

National Neighborhood Foot Patrol Center (pamphlet). East Lansing, Mich.: Michigan State University (n.d.).

Potter, J. "Aviation Units: Are They Worth the Money?" *Police Magazine*, Vol. 2, No. 4, July 1979, p. 22.

President's Commission on Law Enforcement and Administration of Justice. *The Challenge of Crime in a Free Society*. Washington, D.C.: U.S. Government Printing Office, 1967.

Schack, S., and Gay, W. G. *Prescriptive Package: Improving Patrol Productivity*. Vol. II, *Specialized Patrol*. Washington, D.C.: Office of Technology Transfer, National Institute of Law Enforcement and Criminal Justice, Law Enforcement Assistance Administration, U.S. Department of Justice (Grant Number 76–NI–00–0055), July 1977.

Sherman, L. W. "Volunteer Patrols." In *Crime and Public Policy*, edited by James Q. Wilson. San Francisco: Institute for Contemporary Studies, 1983.

Sherman, L. W.; Milton, C. H.; and Kelly, T. V. *Team Policing: Seven Case Studies*. Mineola, N.Y.: Police Foundation, 1973.

Task Force on the Police. National Advisory Commission on Criminal Justice Standards and Goals. *The Police*. Washington, D.C.: U.S. Government Printing Office, 1973.

Trojanowicz, R. *An Evaluation of the Neighborhood Foot Patrol Program in Flint, Michigan*. East Lansing: Michigan State University, 1982.

Walker, S. *The Police in America: An Introduction*. New York: McGraw-Hill, 1983.

Williams, V. L.; Formby, W. A.; and Watkins, J. C. *Introduction to Criminal Justice*. Albany, N.Y.: Delmar Publishers, 1982.

"Women on Patrol," *Minneapolis Police Journal*, 50, no. 1 (February 1978): 43.

Yarbrough, J. L. "Plainclothes Bicycle Patrol: Silent-Preventive-Effective," *FBI Law Enforcement Bulletin*, 46 (May 1977): 10–13.

Traffic: Law Enforcement in Our Mobile Society

Motor vehicle accidents are the leading cause of death for people between the ages of one and forty-five!—Accident Facts

DO YOU KNOW

What the responsibilities of the traffic officer are?

What the primary goal of traffic law enforcement is?

What five actions are included in effective traffic enforcement?

What the Enforcement Index is and how it is used?

What selective enforcement is and what purpose it serves?

What the most basic causes of motor vehicle accidents are?

How frequently alcohol is related to automobile accidents?

What Scandinavian-type drunken driving laws are and when they are effective?

What implied consent laws are?

What specific tasks are performed by the police officer when responding to a traffic accident?

What should be included in a traffic accident report?

What purposes are served by traffic reports? Who makes use of them?

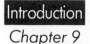

Chapter 9

Traffic is a complex responsibility, involving not only investigation but also service and interrelation with other agencies such as traffic engineering.

According to *Accident Facts* (1988, p. 62):

The first motor-vehicle death in the United States is reported to have occurred in New York City on September 14, 1899. The world's first motor-vehicle death probably occurred in London, England, on August 17, 1896.

Since the first motor-vehicle death in the United States, slightly more than 2,700,000 persons have died in motor-vehicle accidents through the end of 1987. Based on historical figures, the 1,000,000th motor-vehicle death occurred sometime during 1952. The 2,000,000th motor-vehicle death will probably occur in the early 1990s.

THE RESPONSIBILITIES OF THE TRAFFIC OFFICER

As noted by the National Advisory Commission on Criminal Justice Standards and Goals (1973, p. 226):

The role of the police in motor vehicle transportation systems have undergone significant changes through the years. The traditional police function has centered around traffic law enforcement, accident investigation, and traffic direction and control processes. In today's highly complex and mobile society, the police officer's responsibilities have been expanded beyond the restrictive area of traffic supervision and evolved into a more comprehensive service that includes motorist service, public information, motor theft prevention, and other activities vital to the safe and efficient movement of traffic.

A well-rounded traffic program involves many activities designed to maintain order and safety on streets and highways. Although the traffic responsibilities of a police officer may not have the glamour of a criminal investigation, they are critical not only to the safety of the citizens in a community but also to the police image. Traffic is the most frequent contact between police and law-abiding citizens.

Traffic officers are usually responsible for the following:

- *Enforcing traffic laws.*
- *Directing and controlling traffic.*
- *Providing directions and assistance to motorists.*
- *Investigating motor vehicle accidents.*
- *Providing emergency assistance at the scene of an accident.*
- *Gathering information related to traffic and writing reports.*

All uniformed officers should be responsible for enforcing traffic laws and regulations because of the close interrelationship between traffic activity and all other police activities. It is not uncommon, for example, for a routine stop for a traffic violation to result in the arrest of the driver for a serious nontraffic offense. Abandoned vehicles may have served as getaway cars in a robbery or have been stolen for joyriding by teenagers.

The primary objectives of most traffic programs are to obtain the smoothest possible movement of vehicles and pedestrians consistent with safety and to reduce losses from accidents.

Enforcing Traffic Laws   Police officers seek to obtain the compliance of motorists and pedestrians with traffic laws and ordinances as well as driver license regulations and orders. They issue warnings or citations to violators. Traffic officers provide law enforcement action related to operating and parking vehicles, pedestrian actions, and vehicle equipment safety.

Directing and Controlling Traffic   Police officers frequently are called on to direct traffic flow, to control parking, to provide escorts, and to remove abandoned vehicles. They frequently are asked to assist in crowd control at major sporting events. They also are responsible for planning traffic routing, removal of traffic hazards, and emergency vehicle access for predictable emergencies.

Providing Directions and Assistance to Motorists   Police officers provide information and assistance to motorists and pedestrians by patrolling, maintaining surveillance of traffic and the environment, conducting driver-vehicle road checks, and being available when needed.

Investigating Motor Vehicle Accidents   Police officers gather and report the facts about accident occurrence as a basis for preventing accidents and providing objective evidence for citizens involved in civil settlements of accident losses. Police officers investigate accidents, including gathering facts at the scene and reconstructing the accident. They may also prepare cases for court and appear as prosecution witnesses when there has been a violation such as drunk driving.

Providing Emergency Assistance at the Scene of an Accident   At an accident scene the police officer may assist accident victims by administering first aid, transporting injured persons, protecting property in the victim's vehicle, and arranging for towing of disabled vehicles.

Gathering Information Related to Traffic and Writing Reports   The police officer reports on accidents, violations, citations and arrests, disposition of court actions, drivers' cumulative records, roadway and environmental defects, and exceptional traffic congestion. The reports assist the traffic engineer and traffic safety education agencies by providing information useful in their accident prevention programs as well as in planning for traffic movement or vehicle parking. Furthermore, traffic-related records, including registration records, drivers' licenses, traffic citations, and collision reports, may play an important role not only in traffic management but also in criminal investigations.

Sometimes police officers serve unofficially as the city's road inspectors as they discover problems in either road conditions or traffic flow. They may propose corrections to achieve safer, more effective motor vehicle and pedestrian travel and vehicle parking.

The National Advisory Commission on Criminal Justice Standards and Goals (1973, p. 227) defines the traffic law enforcement function as "the total police effort directed toward obtaining compliance to traffic regulations after programs of traffic safety education, driver training, traffic engineering, and similar activities have failed to reach this objective. This function involves all levels of operation within a police organization."

The commission points out that violating traffic laws does not carry the social stigma attached to violation of other laws such as laws against murder and rape. Running a stoplight or speeding is not considered a crime, and people "regularly and without any natural consciousness of wrongdoing violate laws designed to insure safe use of the streets and highways." Recall the distinction between crimes that are *mala in se* (bad in themselves) and *mala prohibita* (bad because they are forbidden). Traffic laws are excellent examples of *mala prohibita* crimes. The commission also states that "The ultimate aim of traffic law enforcement is to produce voluntary compliance with traffic regulations and to provide maximum mobility with minimum interruption."

The primary goal of traffic law enforcement is to produce voluntary compliance with traffic laws while keeping traffic moving safely and smoothly.

A properly administered and executed police traffic law enforcement procedure is probably the most important component of the overall traffic program. If people obey the traffic laws, traffic is likely to flow more smoothly and safely, with fewer tie-ups and accidents. Effective traffic law enforcement usually consists of at least five major actions: on-the-spot instructions to drivers and pedestrians; verbal warnings, written warnings with proper follow-up, citations or summonses, and arrests.

Each of these actions has importance to traffic law enforcement. The circumstances of each individual incident will determine which action is most appropriate. It is up to the traffic officers to decide which action to take, but their decisions will be more impartial and consistent if they have guidelines on which to base them.

Traffic law enforcement may take the form of the following:

- *On-the-spot instructions to drivers and pedestrians.*
- *Verbal warnings.*
- *Written warnings with proper follow-up.*
- *Citations or summonses.*
- *Arrests.*

The question inevitably arises as to how much enforcement is needed to control traffic and reduce accidents. How many traffic citations will constitute the right amount to meet enforcement requirements and still retain public support for the police department? This is a local issue that must be determined for each jurisdiction; however, a nationally approved guide, called the *Enforcement Index,* has been developed to assist in this determination.

The Enforcement Index

The Enforcement Index is calculated by dividing the number of convictions with penalty for hazardous moving traffic violations during a given period by the number of fatal and personal injury accidents occurring during the same period.

For example, if during January a city had 25 fatal or personal injury accidents and the police departments had 300 convictions for hazardous moving traffic violations, you would divide 300 by 25 and arrive at an index figure of 12—below the recommended level. This city should have from 500 to 625 convictions for hazardous moving violations rather than 300.

$$\text{Enforcement Index} = \frac{\text{number of convictions for hazardous moving traffic violations}}{\text{number of fatal and personal injury accidents}}$$

Recommended Index Figure: 20 to 25

While not conclusive, this index provides one means of measuring the quantity of enforcement. The International Association of Chiefs of Police and National Safety Council, through statistical research, have suggested that an index of twenty to twenty-five is both obtainable and effective for most cities. In other words, for each fatal and personal injury accident there should be twenty to twenty-five convictions for hazardous moving traffic violations.

To attain an effective traffic program, the index value may have to be raised in some cities and lowered in others. The index is simply a management tool designed to measure general compliance of the motorists in the community.

In addition, any strategy that makes use of indexes or quotas must also take into account the "human equation," that is, the possibility that officers may fill the quota as quickly as possible and then do no more until the next period of evaluation. Effective supervision can eliminate this problem of substituting quantity for quality.

Selective Traffic Law Enforcement

Because numerous traffic violations occur every hour of every day, police departments cannot enforce all traffic regulations at all times. It is impossible to achieve 100 percent and almost always unwise to try to do so. Selective enforcement emphasizes giving citations for hazardous violations that cause accidents, for example, excessive speed around a school yard or playground where young children are present.

Selective enforcement is not only logical, it is practical, since most police departments' limited work forces require them to spend time on violations that contribute to accidents. Enforcement personnel, such as officers on motorcycles or assigned to a radar unit, are usually the officers assigned to selective traffic enforcement. The officers' activity is directed to certain high-accident areas, during certain days of the week and certain hours of the day or night.

Selective enforcement places officers in preselected locations where high rates of vehicle and pedestrian accidents and traffic law violations require patrol saturation.

Studies in city after city have proven a definite relationship between accidents and enforcement. In analyzing accident reports, one finds at the top of the list year after year the same traffic violations contributing to accidents and the same group of drivers being involved. Accidents will be discussed in greater detail later in the chapter.

Selective enforcement is based on thorough investigation of accidents, summarization, and careful analysis of the records. Adequate records are essential to the overall effectiveness of the selective enforcement program.

Quantity and quality of traffic law enforcement go hand in hand in any community. Many police departments have found that without quality, selectivity, or direction, their desired objectives in traffic supervision programs simply will not work. The public resents quantity goals that cause a police officer to issue many traffic citations and the court dockets to become overloaded with "not guilty" pleas. In departments where quality is emphasized, the public usually complies with safe driving techniques and acknowledges and supports safety programs.

Almost everyone has heard in exhaustive detail a friend's version of getting an "unfair" speeding ticket. The person will tell several people about it. In terms of quality and selective enforcement, this has the effect of informing the general public that the police are doing their job. It may also prevent others from speeding.

High-quality enforcement is not only supported by the public, it has an important effect on the would-be traffic violator. When the public is informed of the police department's enforcement program and it is understood and believed to be reasonable and fair, the public will usually accept and support it.

Traffic and Patrol

Detecting traffic violations is no different for a patrol officer than detecting vandalism, auto theft, burglary, or trespassing. The officers know general police methods, they appreciate the functions they have to perform while on patrol, and they know traffic laws and the department's traffic policies. A thorough knowledge of the department's overall traffic program, its objectives and operations, will make the patrol officers assigned to traffic responsibilities more effective.

While on patrol, police officers may also inspect buildings, detect hazardous road situations, and note locations where traffic control signs may be needed. In addition, they are readily available to respond to accident calls.

Public Education Programs

The police also seek to educate the public in traffic safety. Although it is not one of their primary functions, they often participate in local school programs, private safety organizations, local service clubs, and state safety councils. The police are in a position to know why these programs are important and how they can contribute to the good of the community.

Traffic safety education also has high public relations value. An officer on the school grounds supervising the school crossing guards (patrols) or teaching youngsters bicycle safety contributes much to the police officers' image. It reflects their concern for the safety and welfare of the community's youth. Since safety education is a community responsibility, however, community agencies should assume their share of work and not rely solely on the police department for the entire effort.

TRAFFIC ACCIDENTS

As noted at the beginning of this chapter, motor vehicle accidents are a leading cause of death for people ages one to forty-four. During the hour in which you are reading this chapter there have probably been two hundred traffic accidents resulting in injury and five resulting in death. Billions of dollars are lost annually through motor vehicle accidents, and the cost in human suffering and loss is impossible to estimate.

Of the vehicles involved in fatal accidents in 1987, approximately 62 percent were passenger cars, 27 percent were trucks, and only 7 percent were motorcycles. (Unless otherwise noted, all statistics, tables, and figures in this chapter are from Accident Facts, 1988 edition, a National Safety Council Publication.)

Age of Driver

Twenty-five percent of the 162,000,000 licensed drivers in the nation in 1987 were in the twenty-five to thirty-four-year-old age group and accounted for 28 percent each of the drivers involved in fatal and all motor vehicle accidents. The figures in the last two columns at the right in table 9.5 indicate the frequency of accident involvement. The fatal accident involvement rates (per 100,000 drivers in each age group) ranged from a low of 22 for drivers fifty-five to sixty-four years of age to a high of 61 for drivers twenty-one to twenty-four and seventy-five or more years of age. The all accident involvement rates (per 100 drivers in each age group) ranged from a low of 12 for drivers forty-five to fifty-four, fifty-five to sixty-four, and sixty-five to seventy-four years of age to a high of 37 for drivers under twenty years of age.

Deaths		48,700
Disabling injuries		1,800,000
Cost		$64.7 billion
Motor vehicle mileage		1,909 billion
Death rate per 100,000,000 vehicle miles		2.55
Registered vehicles in the U.S.		186,137,000
Licensed drivers in the U.S.		161,975,000

Accident totals	Number of accidents	Drivers (vehicles) involved
Fatal	43,300	59,000
Disabling injury	1,200,000	1,900,000
Property damage and nondisabling injury	19,600,000	31,000,000
Total (rounded)	20,800,000	33,000,000

Source: National Safety Council

Figure 9–1   **Motor Vehicle Accidents, 1987**

Table 9–1   Motor Vehicle Deaths by State, 1984–1987

Motor-Vehicle Deaths by State, 1984-1987
(Population Death Rates for 1987 by place of accident are shown on page 64)

State	Motor-Vehicle _Traffic_ Deaths (Place of Accident)				_Total_ Motor-Vehicle Deaths[a] (Place of Residence)			
	Number		Mileage Rate[b]		Number		Population Rate[b]	
	1987	1986	1987	1986	1985[c]	1984	1985	1984
Total U.S.[a]	48,700	48,300	2.6	2.6	45,901	46,263	19.2	19.6
Alabama.	1,116	1,086	3.2	3.2	1,013	1,035	25.2	25.5
Alaska	76	101	2.0	2.5	126	117	24.1	23.2
Arizona.	933	1,002	3.9	4.4	869	875	27.2	28.5
Arkansas	638	603	3.5	3.4	583	572	24.7	24.4
California	5,500	5,222	2.4	2.4	5,291	5,324	20.1	20.6
Colorado	590	602	2.3	2.3	619	645	19.1	20.2
Connecticut	451	455	1.8	1.9	481	481	15.2	15.2
Delaware	147	138	2.5	2.4	119	132	19.1	18.6
Dist. of Col.	56	45	1.7	1.4	56	84	9.0	13.4
Florida	2,891	2,874	3.2	3.3	2,805	2,739	24.7	24.8
Georgia	1,604	1,542	2.7	2.7	1,440	1,448	24.1	24.8
Hawaii	138	117	1.9	1.7	129	136	12.3	13.1
Idaho	262	258	3.3	3.3	257	236	25.6	23.6
Illinois.	1,685	1,617	2.2	2.2	1,752	1,726	15.2	15.0
Indiana.	1,056	1,038	2.6	2.5	1,066	992	19.4	18.1
Iowa	491	441	2.3	2.2	523	483	18.2	16.6
Kansas.	491	500	2.5	2.5	518	562	21.1	23.0
Kentucky	849	808	2.9	2.8	731	755	19.6	20.3
Louisiana	827	932	2.9	3.1	991	963	22.1	21.6
Maine	228	208	2.1	2.1	211	234	18.1	20.2
Maryland	830	790	2.3	2.2	766	666	17.4	15.3
Massachusetts.	690	752	1.7	1.8	810	772	13.9	13.3
Michigan	1,622	1,632	2.2	2.3	1,684	1,634	18.5	18.0
Minnesota	530	572	1.6	1.7	676	676	16.1	16.2
Mississippi	757	766	4.0	4.0	688	703	26.3	27.1
Missouri.	1,057	1,143	2.5	2.7	945	984	18.8	19.7
Montana.	234	222	3.1	2.9	210	232	25.5	28.2
Nebraska.	297	290	2.4	2.3	261	285	16.3	17.8
Nevada	262	233	3.0	2.9	214	211	22.8	23.0
New Hampshire.	179	172	2.1	2.2	176	189	17.6	19.3
New Jersey	1,023	1,039	1.9	1.9	1,015	974	13.4	13.0
New Mexico.	568	499	4.1	3.8	504	468	34.7	32.8
New York	2,327	2,114	2.4	2.2	2,176	2,191	12.3	12.3
North Carolina.	1,598	1,645	3.0	3.1	1,518	1,489	24.2	24.1
North Dakota.	101	100	1.7	1.8	103	122	15.0	17.8
Ohio.	1,772	1,673	2.1	2.1	1,657	1,673	15.4	15.6
Oklahoma	608	711	1.9	2.3	775	887	23.4	26.8
Oregon.	618	619	2.7	2.7	610	612	22.7	22.9
Pennsylvania	2,006	1,928	2.5	2.5	1,823	1,880	15.4	15.8
Rhode Island	100	114	1.8	2.1	112	109	11.6	11.3
South Carolina.	1,087	1,059	4.0	3.7	924	946	27.7	28.6
South Dakota.	134	134	2.2	2.1	147	158	20.8	22.4
Tennessee	1,248	1,230	3.2	3.1	1,137	1,160	23.9	24.5
Texas	3,261	3,568	2.3	2.4	3,799	4,005	23.2	24.9
Utah	297	313	2.4	2.6	342	309	20.8	19.0
Vermont	120	109	2.4	2.3	108	104	20.2	19.6
Virginia.	1,022	1,118	1.9	2.2	998	1,007	17.5	17.9
Washington	790	714	2.1	2.0	797	835	18.1	19.2
West Virginia	469	437	3.6	3.3	443	436	22.9	22.3
Wisconsin.	815	757	2.1	2.0	773	859	16.2	18.0
Wyoming	129	168	2.5	3.1	130	148	25.5	28.8

Source: Motor-Vehicle _Traffic_ Deaths from state traffic authorities; _Total_ Motor-Vehicle Deaths from National Center for Health Statistics.
[a] Includes both traffic and nontraffic motor-vehicle deaths. See definitions of traffic and nontraffic accidents on inside of back cover.
[b] The mileage death rate is deaths per 100,000,000 vehicle miles; the population death rate is deaths per 100,000 population. 1987 mileage death rates are National Safety Council estimates.
[c] Latest year available.

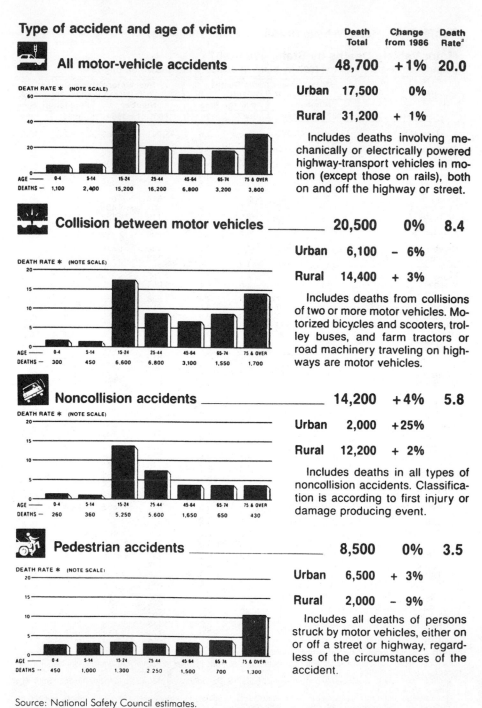

Source: National Safety Council estimates.

Figure 9–2 **How People Died in Motor-Vehicle Accidents, 1987**

Collision with fixed object _____

	Death Total	Change from 1986	Death Rate²
	3,400	**– 8%**	**1.4**
Urban	**1,900**	**– 10%**	
Rural	**1,500**	**– 6%**	

Includes deaths from collisions in which the first harmful event is the striking of a fixed object such as a guardrail, abutment, impact attenuator, etc.

Collision with pedalcycle _____

	1,400	**+8%**	**0.6**
Urban	**900**	**0%**	
Rural	**500**	**+ 25%**	

Includes deaths of pedalcyclists and motor-vehicle occupants from collisions between pedalcycles and motor vehicles on streets, highways, private driveways, parking lots, etc.

Collision with railroad train _____

	600	**0%**	**0.2**
Urban	**100**	**0%**	
Rural	**500**	**0%**	

Includes deaths from collisions of motor vehicles (moving or stalled) and railroad vehicles at public or private grade crossings. In other types of accidents, classification requires motor vehicle to be in motion.

Other collision _____ **100   0%** (b)

(animal, animal-drawn vehicles, street cars)

Includes deaths from motor-vehicle collisions not specified in other categories above. Most of the deaths arose out of accidents involving animals or animal-drawn vehicles. Death from accidents involving street cars are not yet known for 1987.

*Deaths per 100,000 population in each age group.

Deaths per 100,000 population.
ᵇDeath rate was less than 0.05.

Source: National Safety Council estimates.

Figure 9–2 How People Died in Motor-Vehicle Accidents, 1987 (*Continued*)

Table 9–2   Age of Drivers—Total Number and Number in Accidents, 1987

| Age Group | All Drivers | | Drivers in Accidents | | | | | |
| | Number | % | Fatal | | All | | Per No. of Drivers | |
			Number	%	Number	%	Fatal[a]	All[b]
Total	162,000,000	100.0%	59,000	100.0%	33,000,000	100.0%	36	20
Under 20	14,100,000	8.7	8,200	13.9	5,200,000	15.8	58	37
20-24	16,900,000	10.4	10,300	17.5	5,800,000	17.6	61	34
25-34	39,800,000	24.6	16,300	27.6	9,100,000	27.6	41	23
35-44	33,200,000	20.5	9,500	16.1	5,400,000	16.4	29	16
45-54	23,400,000	14.5	5,600	9.5	2,900,000	8.8	24	12
55-64	18,500,000	11.4	4,000	6.8	2,200,000	6.6	22	12
65-74	12,500,000	7.7	2,900	4.9	1,500,000	4.5	23	12
75 and over	3,600,000	2.2	2,200	3.7	900,000	2.7	61	25

Source: Drivers in accidents based on reports from 10 state traffic authorities. Number of drivers by age are National Safety Council estimates based on reports from state traffic authorities and research groups.
[a]Drivers in Fatal Accidents per 100,000 drivers in each age group.
[b]Drivers in All Accidents per 100 drivers in each age group.

Sex of Driver

Of the estimated 162,000,000 drivers in 1987, about 84,100,000 are males and 77,900,000 are females. Males are involved in more accidents than are females, as shown in table 9.6. The difference is due at least partly to differences in the amount of driving done by the members of each sex and to differences in time, place, and circumstance of the driving.

CAUSES OF MOTOR VEHICLE ACCIDENTS— AN OVERVIEW

"In most accidents, factors are present relating to the driver, the vehicle, and the road, and it is the interaction of these factors which often sets up the series of events which culminates in the mishap" (*Accident Facts* 1984, p. 48).

Table 9–3   Sex of Driver Involved in Accidents, 1973–1987

| Year | Drivers in Fatal Accidents | | | | Drivers in All Accidents | | | |
| | Male | | Female | | Male | | Female | |
	No.	Rate[a]	No.	Rate[a]	No.	Rate[b]	No.	Rate[b]
1973	55,900	63	11,400	27	20,200,000	227	7,900,000	189
1974	48,000	55	9,800	24	17,800,000	205	7,300,000	177
1975	46,500	52	9,600	22	19,100,000	212	8,400,000	195
1976	48,100	51	10,900	24	19,600,000	206	8,800,000	191
1977	51,900	53	11,800	25	20,600,000	209	9,300,000	193
1978	51,500	50	15,500	30	21,700,000	209	9,800,000	192
1979	52,700	52	12,500	25	20,600,000	202	9,100,000	180
1980	56,100	56	12,200	24	20,100,000	200	9,700,000	192
1981	53,200	52	11,800	23	20,500,000	200	9,500,000	183
1982	48,800	47	11,500	22	20,600,000	198	9,900,000	186
1983	46,300	43	11,700	21	20,400,000	187	10,300,000	184
1984	47,600	42	13,300	23	21,800,000	192	11,200,000	190
1985	46,800	40	12,700	21	21,400,000	185	11,600,000	191
1986	46,400	41	13,100	18	22,100,000	196	12,900,000	177
1987	45,500	42	13,500	16	20,700,000	192	12,300,000	148

Source: Accidents and Drivers—National Safety Council estimates based on reports from state motor-vehicle departments and Federal Highway Administration. Mileage—National Safety Council estimates.
[a]Number of drivers in fatal accidents per 1,000,000,000 miles driven.
[b]Number of drivers in all accidents per 10,000,000 miles driven.

Table 9–4 Improper Driving Reported in Accidents, 1987

Kind of Improper Driving	Fatal Accidents			Injury Accidents			All Accidents[a]		
	Total	Urban	Rural	Total	Urban	Rural	Total	Urban	Rural
Total.................	100.0%	100.0%	100.0%	100.0%	100.0%	100.0%	100.0%	100.0%	100.0%
Improper driving.........	**62.0**	**60.6**	**62.6**	**70.9**	**71.9**	**69.2**	**67.3**	**67.7**	**66.4**
Speed too fast[b]............	27.2	25.7	28.0	24.2	21.4	28.9	18.8	16.2	24.3
Right of way	10.8	15.7	8.7	22.0	26.8	13.8	20.2	23.3	13.5
Failed to yield	*7.0*	*10.0*	*5.8*	*15.5*	*18.2*	*11.0*	*15.2*	*17.0*	*11.2*
Passed stop sign...........	*1.4*	*1.4*	*1.4*	*1.4*	*1.6*	*1.1*	*1.0*	*1.1*	*0.8*
Disregarded signal	*2.4*	*4.3*	*1.5*	*5.1*	*7.0*	*1.7*	*4.0*	*5.2*	*1.5*
Drove left of center........	8.5	3.7	10.5	2.8	1.1	5.8	2.2	1.0	5.0
Improper overtaking.........	3.9	3.3	4.1	1.8	1.4	2.3	2.2	2.0	2.7
Made improper turn	0.3	0.4	0.2	1.4	1.7	1.0	2.4	2.8	1.4
Followed too closely.........	0.7	0.7	0.7	5.0	6.0	3.5	5.4	6.0	3.9
Other improper driving.......	10.6	11.1	10.4	13.7	13.5	13.9	16.1	16.4	15.6
No improper driving stated	**38.0**	**39.4**	**37.4**	**29.1**	**28.1**	**30.8**	**32.7**	**32.3**	**33.6**

Source: Based on urban and rural reports from 6 state traffic authorities.
[a]Principally property damage accidents, but also includes fatal and injury accidents.
[b]Includes "speed too fast for conditions."

Improper Driving

Table 9–4 relates just to the driver and shows the principal kinds of improper driving that were factors in accidents. Correcting these improper practices could have an important effect on accident occurrences. This does not mean that road and vehicle conditions can be disregarded.

The basic causes of motor vehicle accidents are human faults, errors, violations, and attitudes; road defects; and car defects.

Vehicle defects account for approximately 5 percent of all accidents. The most common defect is worn or smooth tires. The second most common defect is faulty brakes.

The National Safety Council notes that improper driving is the most common factor by far in fatal and nonfatal accidents. The most common type of improper driving is speeding. The second most common type of improper driving is failing to yield the right of way. Drinking is indicated to be a factor in at least half of the fatal motor vehicle accidents. Problems mount when the drinking age varies from state to state. In such instances, some teenagers may drive to neighboring states with lower drinking ages than their own and come home, usually during the late night hours, driving under the influence of alcohol. Overall, however, a study by the Insurance Institute of Highway Safety *Status Report*, September 23, 1981, reports that, on the average, a state that raises its drinking age can expect about a 28 percent reduction in nighttime fatal crash involvement among drivers to which the law change applies.

Alcohol is a factor in at least 50 percent of fatal motor vehicle accidents.

Another driver-related factor is failure to wear seat belts. The National Highway Traffic Safety Administration studies show that safety belts are 50 percent to 65 percent effective in preventing fatalities and injuries, meaning 12,000 to 16,000 lives could be saved annually if all passenger car occupants used safety belts at all times.

Good driving attitudes are more important than driving skills or knowledge, a fact frequently overlooked in driver education programs. Drivers who jump lanes, try to beat out others as they merge from cloverleafs, race, follow too closely, or become angry and aggressive account for many of our serious motor vehicle accidents. Negative driver behavior, such as illegal and unsafe speed, failure to yield the right of way, crossing over the center line, driving in the wrong lane, and driving while under the influence of alcohol, increases the number of accidents and causes traffic statistics to rise year after year.

And year after year the same group of drivers cause the most frequent accidents: male drivers ages twenty to twenty-nine. Although males are involved in more accidents than females, males also do more driving.

Thus far, causes of motor vehicle accidents resulting in personal injury or fatality have been discussed. Also of concern, however, are those accidents that involve property damage. The United States Department of Transportation undertook an extensive study of traffic accidents from 1972 through 1977 (Treat et al. 1979). This $1.5 million project found that human factors were cited by the in-depth team as probable causes in 92.6 percent of the accidents investigated. The major human direct causes were improper lookout, excessive speed, inattention, improper evasive action, and internal distraction.

Environmental factors were cited as probable causes in 33.8 percent of the accidents, with view obstructions and slick roads leading the list of causes.

Vehicular factors were identified as probable causes in 12.6 percent of the accidents with brake failure, inadequate tread depth, side-to-side brake imbalance, underinflation, and vehicle-related vision obstructions being among the leading causes.

Vision and personality (especially poor personal and social adjustment) were also found to be related to accident involvement. Interestingly, knowledge of the driving task was not shown to be related.

Alcohol and Accidents

Special studies indicate that drinking is a factor in 50 to 55 percent of fatal motor vehicle accidents. According to 1985 data from the National Highway Traffic Safety Administration National Accident Sampling System, alcohol was a factor in 8 percent of property damage accidents and 27 percent of serious injury accidents. In other words, in 1987 alcohol was a factor in 22,000 fatal accidents, 320,000 injury accidents, 1,600,000 property damage accidents. The estimated cost of alcohol-related motor vehicle accidents is about $13 billion.

It is encouraging, however, that alcohol-related fatalities and fatal accidents are declining. Studies show that the proportion of all drivers estimated to be legally intoxicated when involved in fatal accidents has steadily declined from 30 percent in 1982 to 26 percent in 1986. The total number of drivers involved in fatal accidents increased 8 percent from 1982 to 1986.

Holidays and Alcohol

About 58 percent of holiday fatalities in 1986 were alcohol related compared to 52 percent during nonholidays, according to estimates made by the National Highway Traffic Safety Administration (NHTSA). The proportion of alcohol-related deaths varied from 50 percent on New Year's Eve to 64.7 percent on New Year's Day. The proportion of traffic deaths due to persons with a BAC of .10 percent or more, that is, legally drunk, was also consistently higher on holidays than on nonholidays. For four of the seven holidays, the proportion was also greater than the normal weekend alcohol involvement.

About 8 percent of all traffic deaths in 1986 occurred during holiday periods. Table 9–5 shows the percent distribution of holiday fatalities by blood alcohol concentration (BAC) for the major holidays in 1986 and comparison periods. The days assigned to each holiday are those on which NHTSA assumed that most holiday travelers were on the road.

Law Enforcement and the Drunk Driver

Ross (1981, p. 632) contends:

The problem of crashes caused by drivers influenced by alcohol has pre-occupied public opinion and the law ever since the invention of the auto-mobile in the late nineteenth century . . . . Vehicle codes initially forbade driving "while under the influence of intoxicating liquor," driving in an

Table 9–5   Holiday Alcohol-Related Fatalities, 1986

Holiday or Other Period	Per Cent of Deaths by BAC			
	Total	.00%	.01%–.09%	.10% or more
Total fatalities	**100.0%**	**47.9**	**11.1**	**41.0**
New Year's Day (Wed., Jan. 1, 1986)	100.0%	35.3	10.4	54.3
Memorial Day (Friday-Monday)	100.0%	41.2	12.6	46.2
Fourth of July (Friday-Monday)	100.0%	38.2	14.1	47.6
Labor Day (Friday-Monday)	100.0%	40.7	12.9	46.4
Thanksgiving (Wednesday-Sunday)	100.0%	45.3	11.9	42.8
Christmas (Wednesday-Monday)	100.0%	46.6	10.1	43.3
New Year's Eve (Wed., Dec. 31, 1986)	100.0%	50.0	8.3	41.7
Nonholidays	100.0%	48.4	11.0	40.6
Friday-Monday average	100.0%	43.3	11.7	45.0

Source: National Highway Traffic Safety Administration. (March 1988). *Fatal Accident Reporting System 1986,* DOT HS 807 245. Washington, DC: U.S. Department of Transportation.

"intoxicated condition," or simply "drunk driving." These "classical" laws were directed against obviously blameworthy conduct and prescribed traditional criminal penalties and procedures.

Such laws were extremely difficult for police officers to enforce unless an accident resulted, and even then obtaining a conviction was difficult.

In the 1930s a new approach to drinking and driving emerged as a result of widespread dissatisfaction with existing laws. This approach, called the **Scandinavian-type law,** reflected the Scandinavian tendency at that time toward temperance. The Scandinavian-type laws prohibited driving with blood alcohol concentrations exceeding specific levels relative to body weight. According to Ross (1975, p. 633):

Enforcement required chemical tests: a preliminary breath test that could be demanded by a policeman who suspected a driver of committing the offense, and an evidentiary quantitative blood test for those failing the first test. Penalties for violating the laws included license suspension and confinement in prison; the latter was made mandatory for blood alcohol concentration exceeding .05 percent in Norway and .15 percent in Sweden. In short, the Scandinavian laws introduced objective, nonclinical definitions of the drinking-and-driving offense, employing novel scientific criminal procedures and severe penalties. After World War II these laws were widely adopted throughout the developed, automobile-dependent world.

The effectiveness of Scandinavian-type laws in deterring drunk driving has been studied in England, France, and Canada, with the conclusion usually being that such laws are initially effective in deterring drunk driving, but that the effect eventually dissipates. The United States Department of Transportation conducted several campaigns called Alcohol Safety Action Projects, which all found that declines in the frequency of drinking and driving were limited to the period covered by the campaigns.

In addition to enforcement campaigns, punishment campaigns have also been attempted, greatly increasing the severity of the penalty for driving under the influence of alcohol. Such campaigns have been largely unsuccessful; however, an increased public perception of the likelihood of punishment *does* appear to deter drinking and driving. Unfortunately, it has been estimated that the chances of a drunk driver being apprehended in the United States under a Scandinavian-type law are between 1 in 200 and 1 and 2,000 (Beitel, Sharp, and Glauz, 1975).

Scandinavian-type drinking and driving laws prohibit driving with blood alcohol concentrations exceeding specific levels and establish severe penalties for doing so. Such laws are effective if they are widely publicized and if the likelihood of punishment for noncompliance is high.

Ross (1981, p. 635) concludes:

The deterrent effect on drinking and driving that is apparently achieved by the adoption and enforcement of Scandinavian-type laws affords some encouragement to those who advocate deterrence as a means of dealing with this problem. However, the universal experience of a declining and vanishing deterrent effect suggests the need for great caution. In the future, policies using deterrence to control drinking and driving might aim at increasing the genuine likelihood of punishment to such an extent that important and permanent changes in public perception are achieved.

Implied Consent

Since so many fatal automobile accidents involve drivers who have been drinking alcohol, legislators and law enforcement agencies have tried to find a valid way to determine if drivers are under the influence of alcohol. In 1953 New York enacted the first implied consent statute.

Implied consent laws state that any person driving a motor vehicle is deemed to have consented to a chemical test of the alcohol content of his or her blood if arrested while intoxicated, or refusal to take such a test can be introduced in court as evidence.

The alcohol content in a person's body can be determined through breath, urine, or blood tests. The courts have held that this is not a violation of a person's Fifth Amendment privilege against self-incrimination.

One of the first cases to test the constitutionality of forcibly taking blood from an arrested person was *Breithaupt v. Abram* (1957). In this case the conviction was upheld.

Then, in 1966, in the landmark case of *Schmerber v. California* the issue was greatly clarified. The United States Supreme Court upheld the conviction and stressed that taking a blood sample was not a violation of the privilege against self-incrimination:

We hold that the privilege protects an accused only from being compelled to testify against himself, or otherwise provide the state with evidence of a testimonial or communicative nature, and that the withdrawal of blood and use of analysis in question in this case did not involve compulsion to these ends.

The Court did caution that the blood sample should be taken by medical personnel in a medical environment.

The Court also ruled that the blood test did not violate the Fourth Amendment even though there was no warrant. The Court reasoned that the blood alcohol content might have dissipated if the officer had been required to obtain a warrant before taking the test.

Illegal per se versus Presumptive Levels   Statutes often define two kinds of blood alcohol concentrations (BAC): illegal per se and presumptive levels, with the presumptive levels generally lower and requiring a different burden of proof.

According to the Bureau of Justice Statistics (1983):

> *Across the States, illegal per se blood alcohol levels cluster around .10, but several States define it as low as .08 and others as high as .15. Presumptive levels for DWI or DUI may range from .05 and up but also cluster at the .10 level. The President's Commission on Drunk Driving has recommended that a presumptive BAC of .08 be enacted by State legislatures.*

A BAC level above .05 is described as "driving while impaired" by the National Institute on Alcohol Abuse and Alcoholism Clearinghouse on Alcohol Information.

Blood alcohol concentration can be influenced by many factors including physiological differences, food consumption, the amount of ethanol ingested, and the time elapsed between drinking and testing.

Speed and Accidents

Legislation passed in April 1987 allowed states to raise the speed limit to 65 mph on interstate highways passing through areas with populations under 50,000. In 1987 thirty-eight states had implemented the 65 mph limit. The National Highway Traffic Safety Administration assessed the impact of the speed limit increase on highway safety and made the following conclusions in their May 1988 interim report:

> *For the first thirty-seven states that raised rural Interstate speed limits, 1987 rural Interstate fatalities were 23 percent higher during the period after the speed limits were increased through September than for the identical period in 1986. In comparison, 1987 fatalities for the period from January 1 to the time the speed limit was raised, increased 10 percent over the identical 1986 period.*
>
> *In the first twenty-eight states that raised the speed limit, rural Interstate fatalities increased 18 percent during January to March 1987 versus 1986. In states that did not raise the speed limit, rural Interstate fatalities were stable January to March and increased 16 percent June to September.*
>
> *Four states, Arizona, California, Louisiana, and New Mexico, accounted for about 70 percent of the total 1987 increase in rural Interstate fatalities in the states that raised their rural Interstate speed limit.*
>
> *A survey conducted by Motor Vehicle Manufacturers Association shows the relationship between speed limits and traffic deaths in selected countries.*

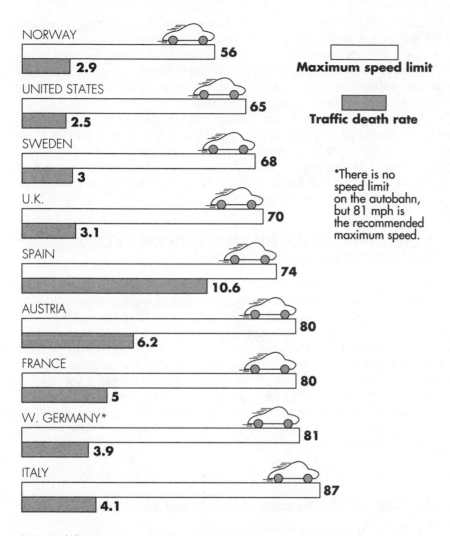

NORWAY 56
2.9

UNITED STATES 65
2.5

SWEDEN 68
3

U.K. 70
3.1

SPAIN 74
10.6

AUSTRIA 80
6.2

FRANCE 80
5

W. GERMANY* 81
3.9

ITALY 87
4.1

☐ **Maximum speed limit**

▨ **Traffic death rate**

*There is no
speed limit
on the autobahn,
but 81 mph is
the recommended
maximum speed.

Source: InfoGraphics
Data: Motor Vehicle Manufacturers Association

Figure 9–3 **Speed Limits and Traffic Deaths**

Occupant Restraints and Accidents

According to National Highway Traffic Safety Administration studies, safety belts are 45 percent effective in preventing fatalities, 50 percent effective in preventing moderate to critical injuries, and 10 percent effective in preventing minor injuries. As of July 1, 1988, thirty-one states and the District of Columbia have enacted mandatory safety belt use laws. Five years before, in 1983, only New York had a mandatory seat belt law. All fifty states and the District of Columbia have mandatory child safety seat laws.

In a nineteen-city observation survey by the National Highway Traffic Safety Administration, driver restraint use was estimated to be 42 percent in 1987, a significant increase over the 11 percent observed using safety belts in 1982. Still, more than half the drivers in the United States are not wearing seat belts. Child safety seat use was estimated at 80 percent in 1987, up from 23 percent in 1982.

The University of Michigan Transportation Research Institute evaluated the effects of *mandatory safety belt use laws* on motor vehicle fatality rates. The study showed a statistically significant decrease of about 9 percent in the fatality rates per vehicle mile traveled in the first eight states with seat belt laws. (The study was a time series analysis of fatalities occurring between January 1976 and June 1986.)

RESPONSIBILITIES OF THE OFFICER CALLED TO THE SCENE OF AN ACCIDENT

Frequently police officers are the first persons to arrive on the scene of a traffic accident who are equipped, trained, and legally responsible for providing services—perhaps lifesaving services if they act quickly and effectively. In addition to rendering first aid to accident victims, police officers have several other duties to perform such as protecting victims from further harm, reducing to the extent possible the involvement of other cars as they arrive on the scene, summoning emergency service for victims and, if needed, towing services for the vehicles involved, protecting the victims' personal property, locating witnesses, securing evidence and in other ways investigating the accident, and keeping traffic moving as though no accident had occurred.

The officer called to the scene of an auto accident should:

- *proceed to the scene rapidly but safely;*
- *park safely and conveniently;*
- *administer emergency first aid if required;*
- *interview all persons involved as well as all witnesses;*
- *provide needed assistance to victims;*
- *accurately observe and record all facts related to the accident;*
- *clear the scene as soon as possible to restore traffic flow.*

It is important that all facts related to the accident are accurately observed and recorded. The time of day should be noted, as a setting or rising sun might have temporarily blinded one of the drivers. All marks on the road should be measured and recorded. The condition of the road should be noted: wet or dry; muddy, dusty, or sandy; dirt, asphalt, or cement. The width of the street and any obstruction to vision should also be noted.

Officers noting details at the scene of an accident.

Traffic accident reports should include all relevant details, including information about the drivers, their actions, their vehicles, the type of accident, the manner of collision, the type of street, weather conditions, road conditions, light conditions, and existing traffic control.

IMPORTANCE OF ACCIDENT REPORTS

Accident reports provide important imformation for enforcement of laws, traffic engineering, and educational activities. Report writing is critical to a good traffic program. The best possible investigation serves little purpose if it is not accurately and completely reported.

Accident reports by police officers provide a guide for many other department activities as well as a guide for other agencies involved in traffic and safety.

Accident reports provide important information for:
- *enforcement of laws;*
- *traffic engineering;*
- *educational activities.*

In addition, a host of other agencies involved in traffic make use of the information contained in traffic accident reports. Public information agencies such as newspapers, television, and radio disseminate information about traffic, traffic conditions, road conditions, and traffic accidents. Attorneys and the courts use traffic accident reports in determining the facts in traffic accidents that result in lawsuits. The state motor vehicle department or state department of public safety, which has the power to suspend or revoke drivers' licenses, also uses information contained in these reports. Legislative bodies in each state may rely on traffic accident reports when they plan for providing funds, equipment, and personnel to effectively enforce traffic safety programs and when they determine what laws must be passed to control traffic.

Traffic accident reports may be used by engineers, both federal and state, who research ways to improve highway systems and by the National Safety Council and state safety councils that compile statistics related to accidents: Who is having them? Where? When? How? The reports may be used by insurance companies that base their automobile insurance rates on the accident record of the community.

Traffic accident reports serve as the basis of traffic law enforcement policy, accident prevention programs, traffic education, legislative reform of traffic laws, traffic engineering decisions, and motor vehicle administration decisions.

In addition to effective reporting, police departments need an efficient traffic accident records system to evaluate the effectiveness of highway safety measures. Compilation of traffic statistics and records on major moving violations and frequent locations and causes of traffic accidents is also critical if a department is going to institute selective patrol and enforcement techniques.

In some smaller police departments, a police officer might be assigned to work with public works departments or city engineers in traffic engineering. Although not involved in the technical design, construction, or maintenance decisions and problems, the officer contributes information beneficial to mechanical operations such as routine maintenance by calling in hazardous road situations encountered while on routine patrol; inspecting facilities and making recommendations for the erection of traffic control signs, needed painting of street lines, crosswalks, and curbs; and performing similar activities of a nontechnical nature.

Although large cities usually have special traffic engineers, police officers still contribute expertise to those who make the final decisions. Police officers' most important contribution to traffic engineering is the research they compile related to accidents and congested streets. They further report hazardous conditions that need attention. In return, traffic engineers often furnish the police with advice and information to further their traffic supervision policies. This relationship can result in increased accident prevention and attainment of traffic control goals and objectives.

ACCIDENT RECONSTRUCTION

A relatively new technique used to establish the facts of accidents and of help in lawsuits, insurance cases, and vehicular criminal cases is accident reconstruction using videotape.

In video reconstruction scale models of the vehicles are used, often with a photo or video of the accident scene itself as the background. Speed calculations are made from the reporting officer's diagram and notes. Using time/distance equations, the accident can be shot in segments of one-thirtieth of a second or one frame at a time. The only facility currently having the technology to do such accident reconstruction is the Minnesota State Patrol's Training Center.

SUMMARY

Traffic is a major problem in most cities. Many hours are spent in traffic-related police work. Traffic officers have numerous responsibilities to fulfill and specific tasks to perform including enforcing traffic laws, directing and controlling traffic, providing directions and assistance to motorists, investigating motor vehicle accidents, providing emergency assistance at the scene of an accident, gathering information related to traffic, and writing reports.

The laws the officers enforce, the services they provide, and the information they compile are important to the total police department traffic program as well as to the image conveyed to the public.

The primary goal of traffic law enforcement is to produce voluntary compliance with traffic regulations and to provide maximum mobility with minimum interruption. Traffic law enforcement may take the form of on-the-spot instructions to drivers and pedestrians, verbal warnings, written warnings with follow-up, citations or summonses, or arrests. The type of enforcement may be guided by the Enforcement Index and by use of selective enforcement principles.

In spite of a highly effective traffic program, motor vehicle accidents will occur. The three basic causes of such accidents are (1) human faults, errors, violations, and attitudes, (2) road defects, and (3) car defects.

Drinking alcohol is indicated to be a factor in at least half of the fatal motor vehicle accidents. One attempt at reducing the problem of the drunk driver has been establishing Scandinavian-type drinking and driving laws that prohibit driving with blood alcohol concentrations exceeding specific levels and establishing severe penalties for doing so. Such laws are effective if they are widely publicized and if the likelihood of punishment for noncompliance is high.

An officer called to the scene of an accident must proceed to the scene rapidly but safely, park safely and conveniently, administer emergency first aid if required, interview all persons involved as well as all witnesses, provide needed assistance to victims, accurately observe and record all facts related to the accident, and then clear the scene as soon as possible to restore normal traffic flow. The accident report should include all relevant details including information about the drivers, their actions, their vehicles, the type of accident, the manner of collision, the type of street, weather conditions, road conditions, light conditions, and existing traffic conditions.

It is important that accident reports be accurate and complete as they provide information for enforcement of laws, traffic engineering, and educational activities. They may also serve as the basis of traffic law enforcement policy, accident prevention programs, traffic education, legislative reform of traffic laws, traffic engineering decisions, and motor vehicle administration decisions.

The responsibilities of the traffic officer in a mobile society are numerous, demanding, and vital.

Discussion Questions

1. How should an officer approach an accident scene and what should be done first?

2. Have you ever been involved in a traffic accident? How would you evaluate the performance of the officer(s) responding to the call?

3. What can the public do to make the traffic officer's job easier?

4. Does your police department use an Enforcement Index?

5. How does an officer determine who gets a verbal or written warning and who gets a ticket (citation)?

6. Is the idea of selective enforcement a good one? When and where should it be used?

7. What should be top priority for a traffic program?

8. Does your state have a seat belt law? If so, when was it passed and what kind of penalty does it impose?

9. How does your police department typically handle people who drive under the influence of alcohol?

10. When do you think police officers should issue warning tickets rather than citations for people who are speeding?

References

Accident Facts. 1983 and 1984 eds. Chicago: National Safety Council, 1988.

Adams, T. F. *Police Field Operations.* Englewood Cliffs, N.J.: Prentice-Hall, 1985.

Beitel, G. A.; Sharp, M. C.; and Glauz, W. D. "Probability of Arrest while Driving under the Influence of Alcohol." *Journal of Studies of Alcohol 36* (1975): 109–16.

Bureau of Justice Statistics, Special Report Drunk Driving, Washington, D.C.: U.S. Department of Justice, November 1983.

Insurance Institute for Highway Safety. *Status Report.* Vol. 16, No. 14 (September 23, 1981).

National Advisory Commission on Criminal Justice Standards and Goals. *The Police.* Washington, D.C.: U.S. Government Printing Office, 1973.

Ross, H. L. *Deterrence of the Drinking Driver: An International Survey.* National Highway Traffic Safety Administration Technical Report, DOT HS-805 820. Washington, D.C.: U.S. Government Printing Office, 1981.

Ross, H. L. "Drinking and Driving." *Encyclopedia of Crime and Justice.* New York: The Free Press, 1983.

Ross, H. Laurence. "The Scandinavian Myth: The Effectiveness of Drinking-Driving Legislation in Sweden and Norway." *Journal of Legal Studies* 4 (1975): 285–310.

Treat, J. R. et al. *Tri-level Study of the Causes of Traffic Accidents: Executive Summary, Final Report.* National Highway Safety Administration Technical Report, DOT HS-805 099. Washington, D.C.: U.S. Government Printing Office, 1979.

U.S. Department of Transportation, National Highway Traffic Safety Administration, Interim Report on the Safety Consequences of Raising the Speed Limit on Rural Interstate Highways, May 1988, Washington, D.C.

Wagenaar, A. C., Maybee, R. B., and Sullivan, K. P. "Mandatory Seat Belt Laws in Eight States: A Time-Series Evaluation. *Journal of Safety Research* (Summer 1988): 19 (2).

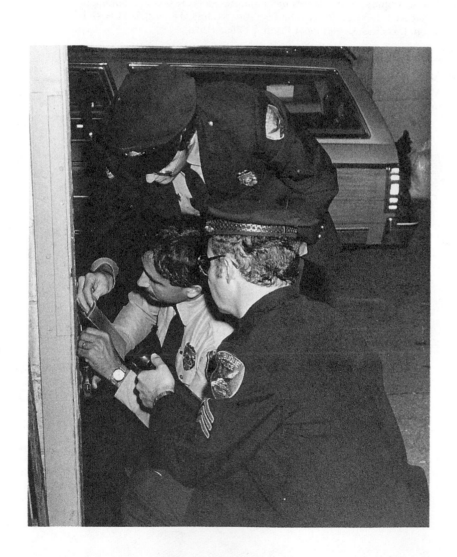

CHAPTER TEN

Investigation: Processing the Crime Scene

Every fact that is learned becomes a key to other facts.—E. L. Youmans

DO YOU KNOW

What the primary characteristic of an effective investigator is?

What the primary responsibilities of the investigator are?

What questions the investigator must seek answers to?

Why both sketches and photographs of a crime scene are usually needed?

How the investigators must deal with evidence?

What types of evidence are likely to be found at the scene of a crime?

What DNA fingerprinting is?

Introduction

Chapter 10

A large part of an investigator's role centers around obtaining information and **evidence.** The successful investigator obtains proof that a crime has been committed as well as proof that a particular person (the suspect) committed the crime. Investigators do *not* determine the suspects to be guilty; they remain objective in their investigation.

A primary characteristic of an effective investigator is objectivity.

The investigator seeks to find the truth, not simply to prove suspects guilty. As stated in Article 10 of the *Canons of Police Ethics* (International Association of Chiefs of Police):

> *The law enforcement officer shall be concerned equally in the prosecution of the wrong-doer and the defense of the innocent. He shall ascertain what constitutes evidence and shall present such evidence impartially and without malice. In so doing, he will ignore social, political, and all other distinctions among the persons involved, strengthening the tradition of the reliability and integrity of an officer's word.*
>
> *The law enforcement officer shall take special pains to increase his perception and skill of observation, mindful that in many situations his is the sole impartial testimony to the facts of a case.*

Walton (1979, p. vii) points out that investigation is a line function and traditionally a task for patrol, but at times the type and frequency of crimes may require a specialized organization component, commonly called the investigative or detective division. He goes on to note, however, that: "In a sense, the investigation of a case is the responsibility of the entire department, and not just a single investigator. Effective investigation often depends on many people and on the organizational structure that governs what they do."

In this chapter, when the term "investigator" is used, it may be interpreted as referring to either a patrol officer performing investigative duties or to a specialist assigned only investigative duties.

The Rand Corporation undertook an extensive study of the role of detectives in solving crimes. Waldron (1984, pp. 194–95) says of this study:

> *The single most important determinant of whether or not a case will be solved is the information the victim supplies to the immediately responding patrol officer. If information that uniquely identifies the perpetrator is not presented when the crime is reported, the perpetrator usually will not be subsequently identified. Of those cases that are ultimately cleared but in which the perpetrator is not identified at the time of the initial police incident report, almost all are cleared as a result of routine police proce-*

*dures. Differences in investigative training, staffing, workload, and proce-
dures have no appreciable effect on crime, arrest, or clearance rates.*

This same interpretation of the Rand Study of Detectives is made by
Klockars (1983, p. 131) who says the study shows that "all but about 5
percent of serious crimes that are solved by detectives are solved because
a patrol officer has caught the perpetrator at the scene, because a witness
tells the detective whodunit, or by thoroughly routine clerical procedures."

POLICE RESPONSE TIME

The Rand Study would seem to suggest that rapid response to a
report of crime is extremely important. A study conducted by the Forum
(Spelman and Brown 1981, pp. iii-xx) in Florida, Illinois, New York, and
San Diego, however, found that, in the cities studied, arrests could be
attributed to fast police response in only 2.9 percent of reported serious
crimes. Spelman and Brown indicate this is so because about 75 percent
of all serious crimes are discovery crimes, crimes discovered after they
have been committed. It is in only the remaining 25 percent, the
involvement crimes, that rapid response is critical. Klockars (1983,
p. 130) rather humorously suggests: "Police currently make on-scene
arrests in about 3 percent of the serious crimes reported to them. If they
traveled faster than a speeding bullet to all reports of serious crimes, this
on-scene arrest rate would rise no higher than 5 percent."

RESPONSIBILITIES OF THE INVESTIGATOR

To accomplish a successful investigation, police officers must (1)
take their time, (2) use an organized approach that is efficient and
methodical, because this may be their only chance to observe the scene,
(3) recognize the issues and find facts to settle these issues, and (4)
determine if a crime has been committed, and, if so, by whom and how.

Each of these investigator's responsibilities will be discussed in a
few pages, but first a distinction should be made between the preliminary
investigation and the follow-up investigation.

The *preliminary investigation* consists of actions performed immediately upon receiving a call to respond to the scene of a crime. This
preliminary investigation is usually conducted by patrol officers. When
patrol officers receive a call to proceed to a crime scene, they must
proceed to the scene promptly and safely; render assistance to anyone
who is injured; arrest the suspect if he or she is still at the scene; secure
the crime scene and protect any evidence; interview complainants,
witnesses, and suspects; collect evidence; and make careful notes of all
facts related to the case.

The International Association of Chiefs of Police (1970, p. 13) has
developed an acronym around the meaning of PRELIMINARY as follows:

P   *Proceed to the scene promptly and safely.*
R   *Render assistance to the injured.*
E   *Effect the arrest of the criminal.*
L   *Locate and identify witnesses.*
I   *Interview the complainant and the witness.*
M   *Maintain the crime scene and protect the evidence.*
I   *Interrogate the suspect.*
N   *Note conditions, events, and remarks.*
A   *Arrange for collection of evidence (or collect it).*
R   *Report the incident fully and accurately.*
Y   *Yield the responsibility to the follow-up investigator.*

The *follow-up investigation* may be conducted by the investigative services division, sometimes also known as the detective bureau. Therefore, the success of many criminal investigations relies on the cooperative, coordinated efforts of both the patrol and the investigative functions. In most smaller departments, however, the same officer handles both the preliminary and the follow-up investigations.

The primary responsibilities of the investigator are to:

- *assure that the crime scene is secure;*

- *record all facts related to the case for further reference;*

- *photograph and sketch the crime scene;*

- *obtain and identify evidence;*

- *interview witnesses and interrogate suspects;*

- *assist in the identification of suspects.*

SECURING THE CRIME SCENE

Any area that contains evidence of criminal activity is considered a crime scene, and it must be secured to eliminate contamination of the scene and outlying areas. The investigator in charge should limit the number of officers assigned to the crime scene, using only those required to do the work. Although some crimes do not have identifiable scenes (for example, embezzlement) or known scenes, the majority of crimes do; for example, bank robberies, burglaries, homicides, assaults, and bombings.

The suspect may have left evidence such as fingerprints, blood, footprints, a weapon, a tool, strands of hair, fibers from clothing, or some personal item, such as a billfold, which may contain identification. No evidence should be touched or moved until photographing, measuring, and sketching of the scene are complete.

Walton (1979, p. vii) emphasizes: "In both large and small communities, the first officer on the scene must know enough to protect the crime

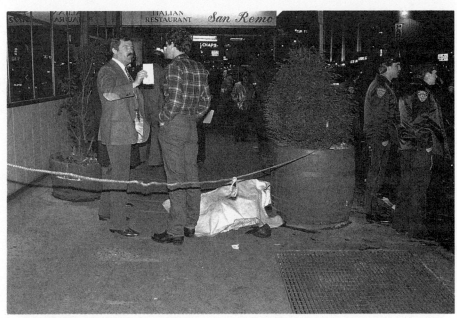

An investigator and officers at the scene of a crime.

scene from further change. Although this officer may have little or nothing further to do with the case, this single responsibility is a large one and may have far reaching effects on a final solution of the crime. It is essential that physical evidence be properly protected if it is to have legal and scientific validity."

RECORDING RELEVANT INFORMATION

Investigators do not rely upon memory; they record all necessary information by photographing, sketching, and taking notes to be used later in a written report of the investigation. Photographs, sketches, and notes are a permanent aid to memory and may be helpful not only in investigating the case and writing the report but also in testifying in court.

The notes should be written in a notebook, not on scraps of paper that might be lost or misplaced. They should be written in ink because they are a permanent record and also because pencil may smear and become unreadable over time. The notes should be written legibly and be identified by the investigator's name, the date, and the case number. They should contain all relevant facts, especially the names and addresses of victims, witnesses, and possible suspects.

Although each specific type of crime requires somewhat different information, most investigations require answers to such questions as the following: (Hess and Wrobleski, 1985)

> ***When:*** *did the incident happen? was it discovered? was it reported? did the police arrive on the scene? were suspects arrested? will the case be heard in court?*

Where: did the incident happen? was evidence found? stored? do victims, witnesses, and suspects live? do suspects frequent most often? were suspects arrested?

Who: are suspects? accomplices?

Complete descriptions would include the following information: sex, race, coloring, age, height, weight, hair (color, style, condition), eyes (color, size, glasses), nose (size, shape), ears (close to head or protruding), distinctive features (birthmarks, scars, beard), clothing, voice (high or low, accent), other distinctive characteristics such as walk.

Who: were the victims? associates? was talked to? were witnesses? saw or heard something of importance? discovered the crime? reported the incident? made the complaint? investigated the incident? worked on the case? marked and received the evidence? was notified? had a motive?

What: type of crime was committed? was the amount of damage or value of the property involved? happened (narrative of the actions of suspects, victims, and witnesses; combines information included under "how")? evidence was found? preventive measures had been taken (safes, locks, alarms, etc.)? knowledge, skill, or strength was needed to commit the crime? was said? did the police officers do? further information is needed? further action is needed?

How: was the crime discovered? does this crime relate to other crimes? did the crime occur? was evidence found? was information obtained?

Why: was the crime committed (was there intent? consent? motive?) was certain property stolen? was a particular time selected?

The investigator must obtain answers to the questions: who? what? where? when? how? and why?

Answers to these questions are obtained by observation and by talking to witnesses, complainants, and suspects. They are recorded in notes, photographs, and sketches or are in the form of actual physical evidence.

PHOTOGRAPHING, MEASURING, AND SKETCHING THE CRIME SCENE

In addition to taking notes, the investigator or crime-scene technician should photograph, measure, and sketch the crime scene. Photographic coverage of the scene must be done carefully. In addition to being technically competent and well equipped, the photographer must photograph objects that are related to the case and in such a way that no distortion occurs. The photographs should show the scene as it was found. They are usually taken in a series and "tell a story." In addition, they are usually taken from general to specific, that is, first an entire room, then one area of the room, then specific items within that area.

The evidence and location should be in their proper relationship and in a sequence that will orient a person unfamiliar with the scene. If a photograph is intended to show dimensional relationships, a suitable scale should be included. Photographs of evidence such as shoe prints, tire tracks, and tool marks must be done using close-up photography. DeAngelis (1980, p. 30) cautions:

> Unlike the studio photographer, the crime scene photographer has only one chance. If later he finds his photographs fail to show what is needed, then the opportunity is lost because the scene cannot be reconstructed. Crime scene photography is critical, with great consequences, and there are no arranged conditions. . . . All other processing of the crime scene must wait until the crime scene photographer's work is finished.

It is important that investigators not only know *how* to take photographs but that they know *what* to photograph. They should take enough photographs that the entire scene can be recreated for the jury.

In addition to traditional photography done at crime scenes, other types of photography such as ultraviolet, infrared, and aerial are also used. Videotaping has become increasingly common as a way to record a crime scene.

In addition to photographs, a sketch should be made of the crime scene before any evidence is moved. Sketches supplement photographs. They can be selective, and they can also show entire areas, for example, an entire layout of a home or business. The sketch need not be an artistic masterpiece as long as it includes all relevant details and is accurate and clear. The sketch should show the locations of all important evidence found during the crime-scene search. See figure 10.1 for some common types of sketches.

Both photographs and sketches are usually needed. The photographs include all detail and can show items close up. Sketches can be selective and can show much larger areas.

DeAngelis (1980, p. 9) stresses that "a crime scene sketch (drawn to scale) should usually be made because it can be a valuable aid in the presentation of most criminal cases."

O'Hara and O'Hara (1988, p. 66) define a crime-scene sketch as "a tool which is the simplest and most effective way of showing actual measurements and of identifying significant items of evidence in their locations at the scene."

Some rookie police officers do not see the need for sketches if photographs have been taken, but this is incorrect. Sketches and photo-

Figure 10–1   Types of Crime-Scene Sketches

graphs complement each other. According to Bennett and Hess (1987, p. 86):

> Photographs present an overview of the entire scene; sketches present a detailed yet selective picture of relevant objects, omitting those that clutter or confuse the scene. . . .
>
> Photographs alone are insufficient for a number of reasons. They are not selective, do not show objects behind other objects, do not show measurements or true distances between objects and evidence, and may distort the scene because of the camera angle. Problems such as poor lighting or incorrect film may also cause pictures to be inaccurate. And errors can occur in developing.

OBTAINING AND IDENTIFYING PHYSICAL EVIDENCE

A primary responsibility of the investigator is to obtain and identify physical evidence. All important decisions will revolve around the available evidence and how it was obtained.

Effective investigators understand their functions as finders of facts and suppliers of proof that have both a scientific and a legal basis for presentation in court. Items of evidence found at the crime scene are usually routinely taken and held pending apprehension of a suspect. Frequently evidence is sent to a crime laboratory for analysis and comparison.

In the preface to the *Laboratory Manual for Introductory Forensic Science*, Walton (1979, p. vii) notes: "Today, the successful prosecution of criminal cases rests less upon confessions or eyewitness accounts and more upon the use of physical evidence. Even so, it is commonly conceded that a pitifully small fraction—2 percent or less— of available evidence is properly recognized, collected, evaluated, and brought into court to tell its story to judge and jury." Walton contends that this is a "sorry situation" and that it must be corrected at the source, that is, the crime scene, "with properly trained and qualified personnel who know what to look for and how to collect, handle, and transport evidence so as to keep intact its legal and scientific integrity. At the crime laboratory the *criminalist* must evaluate what facts may be obtained from the evidence and be prepared to support his or her findings in a court of law."

The investigator must recognize, collect, mark, preserve, and transport physical evidence in sufficient quantity for analysis and without contamination.

Walton sees physical evidence as being the primary responsibility of two law enforcement agents: the crime-scene investigator (who may be a patrol officer, remember) and the criminalist. And he sees the single most important question in **criminalistics** as being related to identity: "Did this blood stain come from this victim? Did this automobile hit this pedestrian? Was this slug fired from this handgun?" Such questions are often answered by comparing one item to another, for example, fingerprints left at a crime scene with those taken from a suspect.

Physical evidence can be valuable in verifying that a crime has, in fact, been committed, identifying the person(s) who did it, and exonerating all other suspects. To realize its full potential, however, certain qualities of evidence must be attained and some minimum quantities collected before the crime lab can help. In the majority of cases, the police officers who protect and search the crime scene play a critical role in determining whether the evidence will be of value.

The kind of evidence to be anticipated is often directly related to the type of crime committed.

Crimes against the person include homicide, rape, robbery, assault, kidnapping, and sex crimes. These crime scenes frequently contain evidence such as blood, hair, fibers, fingerprints, footprints, and weapons.

Crimes against property include burglary, larceny, arson, and auto theft. These crime scenes are commonly characterized by forcible entry with tools leaving marks on doors, windows, safes, money chests, cash registers, and desk drawers.

Among the more common types of evidence found at the crime scene are fingerprints, blood, hair, fibers, documents, footprints or tire prints, tool fragments, tool marks, broken glass, paint, insulation from safes, firearms, and explosives.

Specific Evidence and Scientific Aids

Fingerprints are often found at crime scenes. Fingerprint identification is currently the most positive form of identification because the ridge arrangement on every finger of every person is different and unchanging, although as a person grows, the patterns enlarge slightly. According to Allison (1973, p. 123): "A temporary scar will alter the print during the time of healing, but when the healing process is completed, the pattern on the print will return to its former structure. Permanent scars may change the appearance of the print, but this is not to say that it cannot be identified." Experts in fingerprints look for nine basic patterns, which can occur in any combination (see figure 10.2). The classification system used today in most countries was developed in 1900 by Sir Edward R. Henry and is called the *Henry System.*

Latent fingerprints are made by sweat or grease that oozes out of the pores from little wells situated under the ridges at the ends of the fingers. When a person grasps an item with reasonable pressure, this grease takes

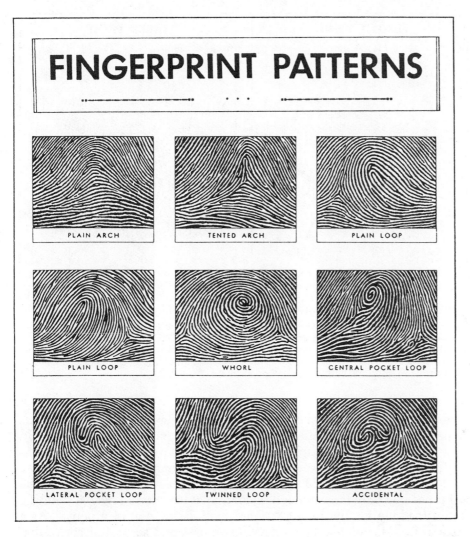

FINGERPRINT PATTERNS

PLAIN ARCH	TENTED ARCH	PLAIN LOOP
PLAIN LOOP	WHORL	CENTRAL POCKET LOOP
LATERAL POCKET LOOP	TWINNED LOOP	ACCIDENTAL

Source: Courtesy of Faurot, Inc. 26 Nepperhan Avenue, Elmsford, N.Y. 10523.

Figure 10–2   Fingerprint Chart

the pattern of the person's fingerprints. This usually happens if the item grasped has a highly polished surface such as glass, polished metalware, highly glazed fabrics, or paper. It usually will not occur if the item grasped is soft, spongy, or has a rough surface.

Fingerprints may be found in an infinite number of places and under varied circumstances. Most crime scenes contain fingerprints of the suspect. Usually articles such as weapons, tools, documents, glass, metal, or any other objects that might have been touched or handled by the perpetrators have latent fingerprints on them.

Finding fingerprints is only half the job; they must be matched with the actual (inked) fingerprints of a suspect to be valuable as evidence.

Figure 10–3 **Positive Identification of a Fingerprint**

Three men checked into a motel at 11:00 P.M. Shortly after midnight when a new desk clerk came on duty, the men went to the office and committed an armed robbery. Police investigating the scene went to the room occupied by the three men and found the latent fingerprint on an ashtray. This print was later matched up to one of the suspects, whose fingerprints were on file with the police department.

The basic points of comparison are shown in figure 10.3. Most experts require ten to twelve similar points to make a positive identification of a fingerprint, although no specific number is legally required. Any unexplainable difference, however, makes positive identification impossible.

Likewise, no set print size is required for positive identification. The print need be only large enough to contain at least ten to twelve points, a count that can be met by an area as small as the end of a pencil. As a general rule, if police officers develop an area and see a fingerprint that appears to have several ridges, regardless of the area size, the print should be lifted, marked, and submitted to the laboratory.

Points used for identification of fingerprints occur not only in the pattern area of the finger but also outside the pattern area, as well as on the first and second joints of the finger and the entire palm of the hand. Patterns are also present on the toes and the entire sole of the foot.

Although fingerprints are perhaps the most common form of physical evidence and certainly one of the most valuable, they do have limitations. It is impossible to determine the age of latent prints. It is also not possible to determine the age, sex, race, or occupation of the person leaving the print. Nonetheless, latent prints are such valuable evidence that great effort should be made to recover them, recognizing that they are fragile, susceptible to complete destruction, and difficult to find.

Blood can be classified as having come from humans or animals. Human bloodstains can be classified into one of the four international blood groups: A, B, AB, or O. Bloodstains may be valuable as evidence in assaults, homicides, burglaries, hit-and-run cases, and rape. Although blood cannot be identified as having come from a particular individual, race, or sex, it can be helpful in eliminating suspects.

In addition, the physical appearance of the blood can sometimes be of help. For example, whether it is in the form of a pool, drops, stains, or splashes can tell investigators important information about the crime. Sometimes the appearance can also help to establish the approximate time the crime occurred.

Hair can also be classified as having come from humans or animals. Technology has not yet progressed to the point where it can be stated that a hair definitely came from a specific person, however. Currently, hair found at a crime scene can be examined and have one of three results:

- Inconclusive—it is neither similar or dissimilar to the suspect's hair. This may result if the sample submitted was too small, if contamination or damage were present, or if there simply were not enough characterization.
- Exclusionary—the hair cannot be considered similar to the suspect's.
- Similarity—it is possible that the hair left at the scene came from the suspect. This result is corroborative only, never conclusive by itself.

It can be established that the hair was pulled out forcibly if the root end is present. In addition, the region of the body from which the hair was removed can be determined with considerable accuracy from the length, size, color, stiffness, and general appearance. Hair from the scalp, beard, eyebrows, eyelid, nose, ear, trunk, and limbs all have different characteristics. Hair from each racial group can be identified by its shape. The sex and age of a person cannot be determined from a hair examination with any degree of certainty except in the case of infant hair.

The possibility of hair evidence in any crime should never be overlooked. Hair is often valuable as a means of personal identification or as an investigative aid in cases such as hit-and-run, unusual death, and rape. Hair may be found from both the victim and the suspect on clothing, weapons, undergarments, blankets, sheets, seat covers, and the undercarriage of vehicles.

Fibers are excellent aids to investigators. It is possible to identify fibers as to type, such as wool, cotton, rayon, nylon, and so on. Sometimes it is possible to determine the type of garment from which the fibers came. In assault and homicide cases some contact usually occurs between the victim and the suspect causing clothing fibers to be interchanged. Fingernail scrapings and weapons may also contain fiber evidence. In burglaries, clothing fibers are frequently found where the burglar crawled through a window or opening. In hit-and-run cases, clothing fibers are often found adhering to the fenders, grill, door handle, or parts of the undercarriage of the automobile.

Document examination consists of a side-by-side comparison of handwriting, typewriting, or other written or printed matter. Age, sex, and race cannot be determined with certainty; however, in cases such as check forgery and alteration of wills, stocks, and bonds, conclusions based on examinations conducted by competent experts are positive and reliable. Such handwriting testimony has been accepted in United States courts for many years. Typewriter samples may also identify the manufacturer, make, model, and age of a typewriter.

A *shoe or tire impression* can be a "material witness" in locating a criminal and placing him or her at the scene of a crime. Such evidence is sometimes more reliable than an eyewitness. Impressions from shoes or tires are often found where the perpetrator of the crime hastily entered or left the scene of the crime and overlooked the impressions. After photographing, measuring, and sketching, investigators carefully preserve such evidence by making a plaster cast of it. It often serves as a vital link to a criminal.

Shoe and tire prints are of two types: contamination prints and impressions. Contamination prints result when the shoe or tire has a substance on it, such as dirt or blood, that leaves a print on a hard surface. Impressions, in contrast, are prints left on a soft surface such as sand or mud.

Whether dealing with a shoe or tire print, of prime importance are individual characteristics such as nicks and scars. It is important to

Pry tool used to open the rear door of a hardware store. Items 2 and 4 were found at the scene of the burglary. Item 3 was found in the suspect's car. This evidence led to the suspect's conviction for burglary.

remember that it may be necessary to make a cast or photograph approximately seven feet long of tire prints to have a complete surface available to compare with the suspect's tires.

Tool fragments may be found at the crime scene. These pieces may later be matched to a broken tool in the possession of a suspect.

Tool marks may be left where windows have been forced with screwdrivers or pry bars, locks have been snipped with bolt cutters, or safes have been attacked with hammers, chisels, and/or punches. All these tools leave marks that, under favorable conditions, can be identified as definitely as fingerprints. Tool marks are most commonly found in the crime of burglary and malicious destruction of property. They may be found on windowsills, frames, doors, door frames, cash register drawers, file cabinets, or cash boxes.

Tool marks are of two types: impressions and sliding or cutting marks. For example, a hammer that has been pounded on a surface does not hit directly, so it leaves both some sliding marks and an impression.

In the past tool marks were frequently of more use because variations in the manufacture of the tools made each somewhat unique. Modern technology, however, has progressed to the point where many tools are identical to one another.

Glass is also an aid to the laboratory crime investigator. Glass is an excellent source of positive identification because two pieces of glass rarely contain the same proportions of sand, metal, oxides, or carbonates.

Striation pattern of a sledge hammer used to open a safe. The white marks are safe insulation. The left half of the photograph is evidence obtained at the scene of the crime; the right half shows the actual hammer seized from the suspect. The marks were matched up under a comparison microscope and magnified.

Police officers frequently encounter glass from windows, automobiles, bottles, and other objects as evidence in burglaries, murders, assaults, and a large variety of other crimes.

When a criminal breaks a window, minute pieces of glass are usually found in his or her clothing, for example in pant cuffs, breast pockets, or, to a lesser extent, on the surface of clothing. Since these fragments are so small they should be removed with a vacuum. Larger fragments should be carefully collected. The area adjacent to the actual break in a glass is critical in the examination. Fragments should not be overlooked.

Microscopic examination of glass fragments by an expert can determine the following:

- Whether a tiny glass fragment probably or definitely came from a particular broken glass object.
- If a large fragment came from a particular glass object that was broken.
- If a fragment came from a particular kind of glass object such as a window pane, a spectacle lens, a bottle, etc.
- The origin of a fracture, its direction, and the direction of the force producing it.
- The order of occurrence of multiple fractures.

An investigator can determine whether glass was broken from the inside of a building by noticing where the fragments are.

DeAngelis (1980, p. 123) describes the process of breaking glass as follows:

1. *Pressure is applied to the surface of the glass.*
2. *The glass is pushed away from the direction of the pressure. As the elasticity of the glass reaches the maximum point, the glass starts to crack on the opposite side of the force.*
3. *A fracture results radiating away from the point of pressure. This is called a radial fracture.*
4. *If pressure continues, the glass then starts to break on the pie shaped portion, forming circular ridges around the point of pressure. This is called a concentric fracture.*
5. *Often there is significant backward fragmentation when glass fractures resulting from fragmentation on the force side of the breaking glass. Therefore, it is quite possible to find fragments on a suspect who has broken glass even though the glass flew in the opposite direction.*

Summing up, the first fracture is called a *radial fracture* (radiating out of the center). The second fracture is called a *concentric fracture,* and it forms a circular pattern around the point of force and between the radial lines. Radial fractures start on the opposite side of a force, and concentric fractures start on the same side as the original force.

Paint frequently is transferred from one object to another during the commission of a crime. Paint is often smeared on tools during unlawful

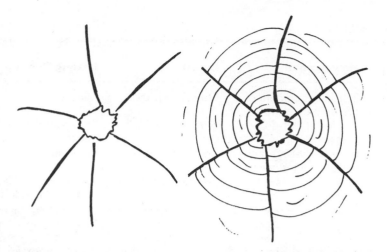

Figure 10–4 (a) Radial Fracture; (b) Concentric Fracture

entry. It may be chipped off surfaces during burglaries. It may flake off automobiles during hasty getaways following impacts. Paint has often proved to be a strong link in the chain of circumstantial evidence. It may have sufficient individual and distinct characteristics for significant examination or comparison. It often associates an individual with the crime scene, or it may eliminate innocent suspects.

Insulation from safes may also prove valuable as evidence. Insulations can be identified microscopically by composition, color, mineral content, and physical characteristics. Since few laypersons normally come into contact with this type of material, particles of safe or fireproof insulation material on the clothing or shoes of a suspect are a strong indication of guilt.

Bite marks are frequently overlooked in criminal investigations. According to DeAngelis (1980, p. 99): "Bite marks on the human body may last from a few seconds to several weeks, depending on the amount of pressure, the sharpness of the teeth, and the location of the bite. Also bite marks on a live body have different characteristics from those on a dead body." DeAngelis classifies bite marks into four degrees (see table 10–1). Bite or teeth marks have individual characteristics matching the size and configuration of the teeth.

Firearms left at a crime scene may be traced to their owner through the serial number, the manufacturer's identification, or the dealer who sold the gun. The firearm might also contain the suspect's fingerprints or other marks that could lead to identification.

The make of the weapon is usually determined by the riflings in the barrel, which are spiral grooves cut into the barrel of a gun in its manufacture. The riflings vary considerably from manufacturer to manufacturer.

In addition, the entry of a bullet can be determined by the hole it makes; the bullet produces a cone-shaped hole, entering from the small point of the hole and emerging through the large end.

Table 10–1   Classification of Bite Marks

Degree of Impressions	Defined	How Formed	Result	Lasting Damage
1	Clearly	Significant amount of pressure on skin	No cut or bruise	Minimal
2	Obvious	Increased first-degree pressure	Bruise	Lasts longer than first degree
3	Quite noticeable	Increased biting pressure; violent reaction	Breaks or cuts skin	Indefinite
4	Skin lacerated	Skin violently torn from body	Skin tissue missing	Unknown; medical treatment needed

In 1988 in the United States firearms were used in 384,000 reported crimes. This included approximately 11,000 murders and 192,000 aggravated assaults and 181,000 robberies (Uniform Crime Reports, 1988). In addition to these 384,000 crimes involving firearms, tens of thousands of suicides and accidents also involved firearms.

Before leaving the topic of firearms identification, it should be noted that sometimes the term *ballistics* is used to refer to this aspect of criminalistics, but this is not correct. Ballistics deals with the motion of the projectile, *not* with identification of the weapon from which it was fired.

Explosives may be of value as evidence in burglary; malicious destruction of property such as school buildings, churches, or public buildings; murder; or murder attempted by an explosive placed in an automobile or a home. The area around an explosion may contain such items as blasting caps, cap fragments, detonating wire, safety fuse, dynamite paper, cotton, soap, masking tape, primacord, or steel fragments. In some cases it is possible to find samples of unexploded materials.

DNA FINGERPRINTING

A new technique called *DNA fingerprinting* holds great promise for forensic investigations. According to Kelly, Rankin, and Wink (1987, p. 105):

> The strength of the DNA technique rests in the intrinsic properties of Dexoxyribonucleic Acid (DNA), the material of which chromosomes are made. Only tiny quantities are required for analysis, and each individual's DNA is unique. Under the correct circumstances DNA is remarkably stable and indeed has been extracted from Egyptian mummies.

An article entitled "Getting Personal in Hunt for Clues" (1986, p. 5) states:

> It's found in the blood, in the hair, in saliva, semen, fingernail clippings—indeed, no part of the body is without it. More importantly to

law enforcers, it may help revolutionize the identification of muggers, murderers and rapists as well as solve newborn baby mixups, aid in the identification of missing persons, alter immigration procedures, and establish parentage.

The article reports that researchers have made identifications from a four-year-old bloodstain and from several weeks-old semen stains.

Whereas other tests of human tissues and secretions can only eliminate suspects, DNA can positively identify an individual, with the exception of identical twins. The implications for law enforcement are tremendous. According to Dodenhoff (1989, p. 1) the DNA breakthrough "promises to revolutionize forensic science."

Development of this new technique started in 1985, when Dr. Alec Jeffreys, a British geneticist, developed a technique to analyze the genetic sequence of DNA—the "blueprint of life"—from blood and human tissue. He was joined by Dr. David J. Werrett, a British forensic scientist, and the two worked to apply the technique to criminal investigations.

Kelly, Rankin, and Wink (1987, pp. 108–109) describe some applications of the technique. In one instance in 1983 a young boy was refused entry into the United Kingdom because immigration officers doubted that his mother was a Ghanaian woman who held rights of

Courtesy of Federal Bureau of Investigation

Figure 10–5   **Restriction Fragment Length Polymorphism (RFLP); Multi and Single Locus DNA Probes**

settlement there. Immigrations officers believed the boy was her nephew, not her son. When DNA fingerprinting was done, however, statistical analysis established with virtual certainty that the boy was the woman's son. And in 1986 a youth who had been imprisoned for three months on a charge of murder was freed after DNA tests showed that he was not the murderer.

According to Dodenhoff (1989, p. 10): "In 1987 an Orlando jury convicted Tommie Lee Andrews of rape almost exclusively on the basis of DNA profiling. In late 1988, a state appellate court upheld the conviction and the use of the DNA evidence."

DNA fingerprinting uses the material from which chromosomes are made to positively identify individuals. No two individuals, except identical twins, have the same DNA structure.

Some disadvantages do exist, however. First, it is very expensive, costing an estimated $100,000 for a laboratory. At present only three labs exist: the FBI, Lifecodes Corporation, and Cellmark Diagnostics. These labs could be overwhelmed with business if DNA fingerprinting becomes popular in law enforcement. In addition it is very labor intensive and takes about two weeks to conduct each test. And, the technique has not yet received the "stamp of approval" from our justice system. Finally, the technique currently relies on a radioactive process, something scientists are trying to move away from.

PROTECTING AND STORING EVIDENCE

All evidence collected must be marked with the identifying mark of the investigator who collected it. It must be properly packaged and placed in the police evidence room until needed. If it is removed from the evidence room for any reason, strict check-out and check-in procedures should be followed.

As noted by Bennett and Hess (1987, pp. 173–74):

> Evidence is subject to chemical change, negligence, accident, intentional damage, theft, or alteration during handling. Protecting and storing evidence is often the weakest link in the chain of evidence. Some evidence requires more care than others.
>
> Improperly sealed containers can allow liquid evidence to evaporate or moisture to enter, causing rust. Envelopes can split open. Tags can fall off. Writing on labels can become smudged, blurred, or faded to the point of illegibility.
>
> Proper storage prevents theft, loss, tampering, contamination, and deterioration.

SUMMARY

A large part of an investigator's role centers around *objectively* obtaining and presenting information and evidence. The primary responsibilities of the investigator are to (1) assure that the crime scene is secure, (2) record all facts related to the case for future reference, (3) photograph, measure, and sketch the crime scene, (4) obtain and identify evidence, (5) interview witnesses and interrogate suspects, and (6) assist in the identification of suspects.

Investigators, be they patrol officers or detectives, are responsible for securing the crime scene, which includes any surrounding area that contains evidence of criminal activity. They must obtain answers to the questions: who? what? where? when? how? why? Usually they must obtain both photographs and sketches because although photographs include all details and can show items close up, sketches can be selective and can show much larger areas.

A primary responsibility of investigators is to recognize, collect, mark, preserve, and transport physical evidence without contamination in sufficient quantity for analysis. Such evidence may consist of fingerprints, blood, hair, documents, shoe prints or tire prints, tool fragments, tool marks, broken glass, paint, insulation from safes, firearms, and explosives.

A relatively new technique, DNA fingerprinting, uses the material from which chromosomes are made to positively identify individuals. No two individuals except identical twins, have the same DNA structure.

DISCUSSION QUESTIONS

1. What are the goals of an investigating officer?

2. What does a preliminary investigation consist of?

3. Name five relevant facts that may appear in an arson investigation?

4. What differences exist between a studio photographer and a crime scene photographer?

5. What are some characteristics of crimes against property?

6. How do fingerprints enhance criminal investigations?

7. If you had a choice to present any type of evidence you wanted in a burglary case, what convincing evidence would you choose?

8. What type of evidence might you find at the scene of an assault? A forcible rape? A homicide?

9. In what types of crimes might you find bite marks?

10. Why is DNA fingerprinting not more commonly used in criminal investigations?

References

Allison, H. C. *Personal Identification.* Boston: Holbrook Press, 1973.

Balazs, I., and Glassberg, J. "Application of Deoxyribonucleic Acid (DNA) Polymorphisms to the Analysis of DNA Recovered from Sperm." *Journal of Forensic Sciences.* April 1986, pp. 409–16.

Bennett, W., and Hess, K. M. *Introduction to Criminal Investigation.* 2nd ed. St. Paul, Minn.: West Publishing Company, 1987.

Crime in the United States, Uniform Crime Reports, Washington, D.C.: FBI, 1988.

DeAngelis, F. J. *Criminalistics for the Investigator.* Encino, Calif.: Glencoe Publishing, 1980.

Dodenhoff, P. "LEN Salutes Its 1988 Man-of-the-Year, Dr. David Werrett," *Law Enforcement News,* January 31, 1989, pp. 1, 10–11.

"Getting Personal in Hunt for Clues: Scientists Eye DNA as New Key to Identifications." *Law Enforcement News,* April 7, 1986, p. 5.

Hess, K. M., and Wrobleski, H. M. *For the Record: Report Writing in Law Enforcement.* Eureka, Calif.: Innovative Publications, 1985.

International Association of Chiefs of Police. *Criminal Investigation.* 2d ed. Gaithersburg, Md.: 1970.

Kelly, K. F.; Rankin, J. J.; and Wink, R. C.. "Method and Applications of DNA Fingerprinting: A Guide for the Non-Scientist." *Criminal Law Review,* February 1987, pp. 105–10.

Klockars, C. B. *Thinking about Police: Contemporary Readings.* New York: McGraw-Hill, 1983.

O'Hara, C. E., and O'Hara, G. *Fundamentals of Criminal Investigation,* 5th ed. Springfield, Ill.: Charles C. Thomas, 1988.

Spelman, W. G., and Brown, D. K. *Calling the Police: A Replication of the Citizen Reporting Component of the Kansas City Response Time Analysis.* Washington, D.C.: The Police Foundation, 1981.

Waldron, R. M. *The Criminal Justice System,* 3d ed. Boston: Houghton Mifflin, 1984.

Walton, G. *Laboratory Manual for Introductory Forensic Science.* Encino, Calif.: Glencoe Publishing, 1979.

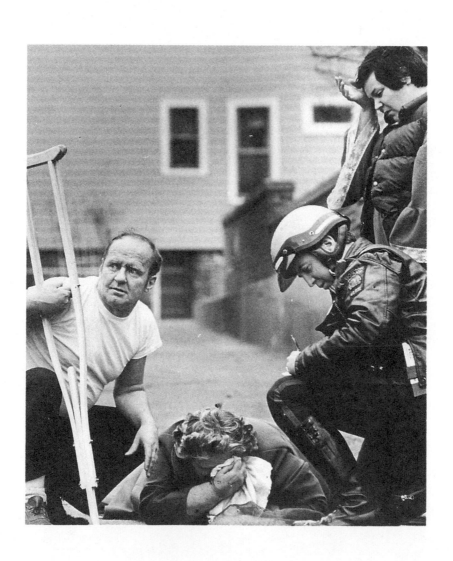

CHAPTER ELEVEN

Interviewing, Interrogating, and Identifying: The People Side of Investigation

You have the right to remain silent. Anything you say can and will be used against you in a court of law.—Miranda Warning

DO YOU KNOW

What the Miranda warning is and when it must be given?

What the public safety exception is?

Why two people may see the same event yet report it differently?

How witnesses may be aided in making an identification?

What the three basic types of identification are?

When each is appropriate?

What rights the suspect has during the identification process?

What instructions and precautions should be taken to assure the legality and admissibility of an identification in court?

What relevance the Wade decision has to identification of a suspect?

What should be done if a suspect refuses to participate in a lineup?

Introduction

Chapter 11

Police officers do not deal only with crime scenes and physical evidence. A large part of their investigative responsibilities is talking with people to obtain information. Sometimes people are very willing to talk, but other times they are very reluctant. In addition to gathering information about crimes that have been committed, police officers must determine the answer to the classic question: Who dunnit? Identifying suspects in a case is another critical investigative responsibility.

INTERVIEWING WITNESSES AND INTERROGATING SUSPECTS

The investigator must gain information by talking with victims, witnesses, friends, co-workers, neighbors, or immediate members of the family, as well as by talking with suspects in the case.

Witnesses

A **witness** is a person other than a suspect who has helpful information about a specific incident or a suspect. A witness may be a **complainant,** an accuser, a victim, an observer of the incident, a confidential or reliable **informant,** an expert, or a scientific examiner of physical evidence.

Most evidence at a trial is presented through witnesses. A person who is a qualified witness, who can perceive what was seen firsthand and can relate this experience, is an invaluable aid in the prosecution of the defendant.

Witnesses are valuable because they may have seen:

- the suspect actually committing the crime;
- a tool, gun, or instrument used in the commission of the crime in the suspect's possession before or after the crime's commission;
- property that was stolen in the suspect's possession after the crime's commission;
- the suspect making preparations to commit the crime, or heard the suspect threatening to commit the crime, or knew that he or she had a motive for committing it
- the suspect going to or leaving the scene of the crime about the time the crime was committed.

In cases such as robbery, assault, or rape, the eyewitness testimony of the victim or a witness may be all that is necessary for a conviction. It is always preferable, however, to have physical evidence to corroborate the eyewitness testimony.

Suspects

Before interrogating any suspect, the police officer should give the Miranda warning, as established in *Miranda v. Arizona*. The United States Supreme Court asserted that suspects must be informed of their rights to remain silent, to have counsel present, to a state-appointed counsel if they cannot afford one, and to be warned that anything they say might be used against them in a court of law. Many investigators carry a card that contains the Miranda warning to be read before interrogating a suspect.

On the evening of March 3, 1963, an eighteen-year-old girl was abducted and raped in Phoenix, Arizona. Ten days after the incident, Ernesto Miranda was arrested by Phoenix police, taken to police head-quarters, and put in a lineup. He was identified by the victim and shortly thereafter signed a confession admitting the offenses. Despite objections to the statement by the defense attorney, the trial court admitted the confession. Miranda was convicted and sentenced from twenty to thirty years on each account.

Miranda appealed on the grounds that he had not been advised of his constitutional rights under the Fifth Amendment. The Arizona Supreme Court ruled in 1965 that because Miranda had been previously arrested in California and Tennessee, he knowingly waived his rights under the Fifth and Sixth Amendments when he gave his confession to the Phoenix police. Justice McFarland of the Arizona Supreme Court ruled that because of Miranda's previous arrests, he was familiar with legal proceedings and individual rights and made an intelligent waiver.

In 1966, upon appeal, the United States Supreme Court reversed the Supreme Court of Arizona in a 5–4 decision and set up precedent rules for police custodial interrogation. Chief Justice Warren stated: "The mere fact that he signed a statement which contained a typed-in clause stating that he had 'full knowledge of his "legal rights"' does not approach the knowing the intelligent waiver required to relinquish constitutional rights."

Figure 11–1   **Miranda Warning Card**

Miranda Warning

1. You have the righ to remain silent.
2. If you give up the right to remain silent, anything you say can and will be used against you in a court of law.
3. You have the right to speak with an attorney and to have the attorney present during questioning.
4. If you so desire and cannot afford one, an attorney will be appointed for you without charge before questioning.

Waiver

1. Do you understand each of these rights I have read to you?
2. Having these rights in mind, do you wish to give up you rights as I have explained to you and talk to me now?

The United States Supreme Court mandated that any time a person was in police custody police officers must give the Miranda warning so that persons being questioned can intelligently waive their right not to incriminate themselves as provided by the Fifth Amendment. If the warnings are not given, the prosecution cannot prove an intelligent waiver against self-incrimination, and any statement or confession will not be admissible against the suspect.

The Miranda rule applies not only to in-custody situations but to any instance in which a suspect is questioned and the questioning results in the individual being deprived of a substantial portion of his or her liberty. When police officers attempt to obtain a statement or confession from a suspect, they should usually first advise that person of the Miranda warning. This applies whether a suspect is questioned in the police station, in a police car, or on a street corner.

When the probable cause builds to such a point that no reasonable person could deny that an arrest would be imminent, the police officer should at that point give the Miranda warning to the suspect if it has not already been given.

When the *Miranda* decision was handed down in 1966, there was much controversy. Many police officers and citizens complained that the court was "handcuffing the police," hampering them in their duties; however, the Federal Bureau of Investigation had been advising suspects of their constitutional rights for several years before the *Miranda* decision.

The Miranda warning must be given to a suspect who is interrogated in the custody of the police, that is, when the suspect is not free to leave.

Two terms are key in this situation: *interrogated* and *in custody*. The circumstances involved in an interrogation and whether it requires a Miranda warning were expanded in *Oregon v. Mathiason* (1977) when the court said:

> Any interview of one suspected of a crime by a police officer will have coercive aspects to it, simply by virtue of the fact that the police officer is part of a law enforcement system which may ultimately cause the suspect to be charged with a crime. But police officers are not required to administer Miranda warnings to everyone whom they question. Nor is the requirement of warnings to be imposed simply because the questioning takes place in the station house, or because the questioned person is one whom the police suspect. Miranda warnings are required only where there has been such a restriction on a person's freedom as to render him "in custody." It was that sort of coercive environment which Miranda by its terms was made applicable, and to which it is limited.

According to del Carmen (1987, p. 263): "A lot of confusion can be avoided if the officer simply remembers that 'custodial interrogation' takes place in two general situations: (1) when the suspect is under arrest and (2) when the suspect is not under arrest, but is 'deprived of his freedom in a significant way.' "

Sometimes both terms, *interrogation* and *in custody*, are issues, as was the case in *United States v. Mesa* (1980). In this case the FBI had an arrest warrant for a suspect charged with shooting his common-law wife and his daughter. The suspect barricaded himself in a motel room and was armed. Using a bullhorn, police tried to talk the suspect into coming out, but he refused. Finally he agreed to talk with them by phone. The FBI recorded the conversation, which included some incriminating statements by the suspect. The suspect finally surrendered peacefully and was arrested. The district court did not allow the statements made over the phone to be introduced, stating they were obtained in violation of the suspect's rights and that the Miranda warning should have been given. The circuit court of appeals reversed the decision, as noted by Inbau, Reid, and Buckley, (1986, p. 302):

> The chief judge concluded that "where an armed suspect who possibly has hostages barricades himself away from the police, he is not in custody (within) the meaning of the Miranda rule." Another judge was of the view that the agent's conversation with the suspect had not constituted an interrogation. The third judge dissented because he concluded that there had been both custody and interrogation.

Perhaps the best guideline is, when in doubt, give the Miranda warning.

del Carmen (1987, pp.(266–68) lists nine instances when Miranda warnings are not normally required:

> No questions asked.[This is not interrogation.]
> General questioning at the crime scene.
> Questioning witnesses.
> Volunteered statements.
> Statements made to private persons, for example, friends, cellmates.
> Questioning in an office or place of business.
> "Stop and frisk" cases.
> Before a Grand Jury.
> Noncustodial interrogations by a probation officer.

The *public safety exception* is an important consideration when discussing the *Miranda* decision. On June 12, 1984, in a landmark 5–4 decision in *New York v. Quarles*, the United States Supreme Court announced that in certain cases police may question suspects in custody without first advising them of their right not to incriminate themselves. Writing for the Court's majority, Justice Rehnquist cited the Supreme Court decision in *Michigan v. Tucker* (1974) and made the distinction that the Miranda warnings are: "Not themselves rights protected by constitution, but are measures to insure that the right against compulsory self-incrimination is protected. . . . On some facts there is a 'public safety' exception to the requirement that Miranda warnings be given before a suspect's answers may be admitted into evidence, and that the availability of that exception does not depend upon the motivation of the individual officers." Although the court set forth the "public safety exception," no attempt was made to determine in what situations this exception might apply.

Knowledge of the background in the *Quarles* case helps in understanding when the public safety exception is relevant. In 1980, a young woman stopped two police officers and told them she had been raped. She described her rapist, who, she said had just entered a nearby supermarket armed with a gun. The officers located the suspect, Benjamin Quarles, and ordered him to stop. But Quarles ran, and the officers momentarily lost sight of him. When they apprehended and frisked him, the officers found an empty shoulder holster. When the officers asked Quarles where the gun was, he nodded toward some cartons and said, "The gun is over there." The officers retrieved the gun, arrested Quarles, and read him his rights. Quarles waived his rights and answered questions.

At the trial, the court ruled that the statement, "The gun is over there," and the subsequent discovery of the gun resulting from that statement were inadmissible at the defendant's trial.

The United States Supreme Court, after reviewing the case, ruled that if Miranda warnings had deterred the response to the officer's question, the cost would have been more than just the loss of evidence, which might lead to a conviction. As long as the gun remained concealed in the store, it posed a danger to public safety.

The Court ruled that in this case the need to have the suspect talk took precedence over the requirement that the defendant be read his rights. The Court ruled that the material factor applying this public safety exception is whether a public threat could possibly be removed by the suspect making a statement. In this case the officer asked the question only to insure his and the public safety. He then gave the Miranda warning before continuing questioning.

The public safety exception allows police officers to question suspects without first giving the Miranda warning if the information sought sufficiently affects the officer's and the public's safety.

Waiving the Right   Suspects can *waive* their rights against self-incrimination and talk to police officers, but the waiver must be voluntary. Additionally, the suspect must fully understand what rights are being given up and the possible consequences.

If after hearing a police officer read the Miranda warning, suspects remain silent, this is *not* a waiver. To waive their rights, suspects must state, orally or in writing, that (1) they understand their rights and (2) they will voluntarily answer questions without a lawyer present.

Special care must be taken with individuals who do not speak English as their native language, who are under the influence of drugs or alcohol, who appear to be mentally retarded, or who appear to be hampered mentally in any way.

It is preferable to get the waiver in writing.

INTERVIEWING AND INTERROGATING TECHNIQUES

Witnesses who are pressured to give information may become antagonistic and refuse to cooperate. The following simple procedures (Hess and Wrobleski, 1985) may help make an **interview** with a witness or an **interrogation** of a suspect more productive:

- *Prepare for each interview in advance if time permits. Know what questions you need to have answered.*
- *Obtain your information as soon after the incident as possible. A delay may result in the subject's not remembering important details.*
- *Be considerate of the subject's feelings. If someone has just been robbed, or seen an assault, or been attacked, the individual may be understandably upset and emotional. Allow time for the person to calm down before asking too many questions. Remember that when emotions increase, memory decreases.*
- *Be friendly. Try to establish rapport with the subject before asking questions. Use the person's name; look at the person as you ask questions; respond to the answers.*
- *Use a private setting if possible. Eliminate as many distractions as you can, so that the subject can devote full attention to the questions you ask.*
- *Eliminate physical barriers. Talking across a desk or counter, or through a car window, does not encourage conversation.*
- *Sit rather than stand. This will make the subject more comfortable and probably more willing to engage in conversation.*
- *Encourage conversation. Keep the subject talking by:*
  Keeping your own talking to a minimum.
  Using open-ended questions, such as "Tell me what you saw."
  Avoiding questions that call for only a "yes" or "no" answer.
  Allowing long pauses. Pauses in the conversation should not be uncomfortable. Remember that the subject needs time to think and organize his thoughts. Give the subject all the time needed.
- *Ask simple questions. Do not use law enforcement terminology when you ask your questions. Keep your language simple and direct.*
- *Ask one question at a time. Allow the subject to answer one question completely before going to the next question.*
- *Listen to what is said, and how it is said.*
- *Watch for indications of tension, nervousness, surprise, embarrassment, anger, fear, or guilt.*
- *Establish the reliability of the subject by asking some questions to which you already know the answers.*
- *Be objective and controlled. Recognize that many persons are reluctant to give information to the police. Among the several reasons for this reluctance are fear or hatred of police, fear of reprisal, lack of memory, or unwillingness to become involved. Keep control of yourself and your situation. Do not antagonize the subject, use profanity or obscenity, lose your temper, or use physical force. Remain calm, objective, and professional.*

Table 11–1   **Interviewing Subjects**

Types of Individuals	Police Interviewing Behavior
Hostile Witness	Relieve anxiety and stress.
	Indicate what can and cannot be said.
	State the purpose of the interview.
	Exert control (nonthreatening).
	Develop trust and cooperativeness.
	Indicate potential outcomes of noninvolvement or silent behavior.
Nonhostile Witness	Listen closely to disclosures.
	Double-check all observations and perceptions.
	Avoid angering, confusing, frustrating, or silencing the interviewee.
	Reco.d all descriptions.
	Seek specific details.
Victims	Check their mental and physical health.
	Conduct the interview when the victim has stabilized from shock or trauma.
	Be patient. Forgotten or confused recall may be brought out with careful questions.
	Reassure, calm, relax, protect victim.
	Seek appropriate help where necessary.
	Keep initial questions to a minimum.
	Encourage cooperation.
Indirectly Involved or Uninvolved Subject	Be polite, patient, understanding.
	Thoroughly canvas frequented locales.
	Listen carefully.
	Be perceptive.
	Observe nonverbal signals.
	Avoid antagonizing the general public.
	Persuade reticent individuals to disclose.
Suspects	Safety first. Monitor the suspect's behavior and likelihood of possessing a weapon.
	Gather information; avoid initial interrogation.
	Inform a suspect of appropriate rights.
	Avoid forming prejudgments.
	Avoid giving a suspect cause for alarm.
	Avoid signaling nervousness or anxiety.
	Be honest. Do not make false promises.
	Do not bully or ridicule.
	Never underestimate a suspect's behavior or testimony.

The basic objective of an interview is to get the facts from a witness to eventually prove to the court that the suspect in question did, in fact, commit the crime. The interview itself must be carefully planned by the officer, with only relevant questions asked. In addition to seeking facts and evidence, the investigator is looking for honest witnesses, who demonstrate concern and cooperativeness.

Some witnesses are fearful, uninterested, or unwilling to get involved. With such witnesses, investigators must develop a rapport: be tolerant of the witness's position and thinking; eliminate misunderstanding,

Types of Individuals	Police Interviewing Behavior
Angry Witness	Assess the interviewee's mental stability. Check for weapon. Call for assistance where necessary. Gain control of the interview. Demonstrate neutrality. Never argue or disagree. Defuse anger with questions. Do not allow a shouting match to develop.
Excessively Verbal Subject	Redirect the interviewee's responses. Remind interviewee of the interview's purpose. Interrupt and ask closed-ended questions. Indicate specific topic areas for discussion.
Reticent Interviewee	Establish rapport. Compliment the interviewee. Reassure, reduce anxiety. Establish pleasant demeanor. Encourage talk. Avoid limiting response choices.
Uncooperative Interviewee	Exercise control. Remind interviewee of penalty for noncooperation. Reduce apprehension. Clarify unfounded fears. Provide incentives for disclosing.
Anxious and Stressed Interviewee	Direct stressed interviewee, when necessary, to professional counseling. Release tension in face and body. Establish a conversational climate. Clarify the nature of the interview. Allow opportunity for thinking. Do not rush responses.Double-check responses.
Interviewee of Different Race, Culture, Sex, or Ethnic Background	Be cognizant of how others communicate in interview situations. Understand the unique or specific verbal and nonverbal behaviors of people who differ from yourself. Repeat, reiterate, re-explain. Translate your meanings into the language of the interviewee.

Source: The Police Officers Guide to Better Communication by T. Richard Cheatham and Keith V. Erickson. Copyright © 1984 by Scott, Foresman and Company. Reprinted by permission.

mistrust, and suspicion; and induce confidence. They must recognize that each individual will have a somewhat different view of the same incident.

Tables 11–1 and 11–2 summarize interviewing techniques and the types of questions that might be asked.

Pena (1986, p. 206) suggests that police officers should avoid using police terminology while interviewing/interrogating people as it will "increase the incriminating atmosphere" of the questioning. He suggests the following:

Avoid	Better to Use
• Murder	• Death
• Mayhem	• Injury
• Robbery	• Property taken
• Burglary	• Entered
• Rape	• Have sex
• Assault	• Scuffle
• Kidnap	• Move
• Conspiracy	• Arrangement
• Embezzle	• Use
• Life imprisonment	• Some time

Witness Perception

Experience has illustrated time and again that no two people will view the same situation in exactly the same way. How a witness describes what has happened is affected by many factors, some subjective (within the individual) and some objective (inherent in the situation). Because these factors vary from person to person, two people looking at the same thing may see something different. Take, for example, figure 11–2. Whether the black surface projects toward the viewer or away depends completely upon the viewer's perception. In fact, the same person may see the black surface as projecting on first viewing, yet as receding on a second viewing.

Context, too, can alter how an object or event is perceived. For example, how do you "interpret" the following: 13

Now how do you interpret it? A 13 C   12 13 14

Another factor affecting perception is the amount of attention that is focused on an incident. When an incident barely catches the attention of a witness, perception is liable to be faulty. One reason for this is the human tendency to complete comprehension of a situation to make it meaningful. That is, people tend to organize their observations into a complete, meaningful picture. A witness may see a man with a mask on and his right hand extended as if holding a gun, and the witness may mentally *add* the gun in his perception of the incident, even though it did

Figure 11–2 Perception

Table 11–2   Interview Questions

Type of Question	Purpose	Characteristics	Example
Open-Ended	To elicit a variety of responses To provide interviewee response choices To break the ice To reduce apprehension	No set response expected of interviewee No specific topic Found in nondirected interviews Interviewee centered Nonthreatening	"How is the weather today?" "How have you been?" "Will it be a good football year?" "Life treating you well?" "What do you think of politics?" "How is the economy affecting you?"
Closed-Ended	To limit interviewee response choices To gather specific information from subject To facilitate use of time	One-to three-word replies Specific answers sought Authoritarian Frequently appears in a series of closed-ended questions Brusque	"What did he say?" "Did you do it?" "What is your name?" "Where do you work?" "What time is it?" "What did she wear?" "Was it red or green?"
Probing	To force replies Explanation Clarification Elaboration Confrontation Repetition	Seeks additional information Requires respondent to be responsive to interviewer Clears up misunderstandings Reveals sensitive/disguised information	"Explain what you mean?" "Tell me again what you said?" "How is that possible?" "You don't believe that do you?" "Why did you do that?" "More details, please."
Mirror	To keep interviewee talking Clarification Explanation	Repeats or paraphrases interviewee's remarks Places burden of talk on interviewee	"So, you took the bike, huh?" "And then you left town?" "You say you like it?" "Which job are you talking about?"
Leading	To lead interviewee to particular response To reveal discrepancies in testimony To facilitate admissions To force a stand	Suggests or implies an appropriate answer Places words in respondent's mouth Leaves little room for interviewee explanation of responses Placed in a series of questions	"You didn't like her, did you?" "Do you think that was right?" "Can you really say that was the correct thing to do?" "You won't act like that again, will you?"

Source: The Police Officers Guide to Better Communication by T. Richard Cheatham and Keith V. Erickson. Copyright © 1984 by Scott, Foresman and Company. Reprinted by permission

not actually exist. To overcome this tendency and obtain valid information, police officers must be aware of how and why people think and act in given situations. In other words, they should try to put themselves in the other person's position and use what is called "street sense" and empathy.

Perception of an incident is affected by the viewer's accuracy of observation, interpretation of what is seen, and attention paid to the incident.

As noted in the *Encyclopedia of Crime and Justice* (Yarmey, 1983 pp. 749–55):

> *Eyewitness identification is frequently much less reliable than the courts would generally believe. . . . Researchers have extensively investigated the perception and memory of faces. What is the application of this work to the criminal identification of suspects through the viewing of mug shots, artists' drawings, commercial composites, and corporeal lineups? Laboratory studies have indicated that subjects asked to identify faces in a recognition memory test did so accurately in about 75 percent of their selections. . . . More significantly, research is increasingly being con-*ducted outside the laboratory in more naturalistic settings, for example, *testing persons who witnessed mock crime performed in super markets and banks. . . As indicated in the United States v. Nobles* (1975), it is now for the courts to decide whether expert testimony on eyewitness identification should be taken to assist the jury in understanding the evidence, or whether such evidence should be excluded on the ground that it invades the province of the jury.

The Noncooperative Witness

A Witness Cooperation Study ("Witness Responses Misunderstood by Prosecutors" 1976) of almost three thousand randomly selected witnesses indicated that many citizens are incorrectly perceived as noncooperative. According to this study (p. 6): "Prosecutors were apparently unable to cut through to the true intentions of 23 percent or more of those regarded as noncooperative and recorded the existence of witness problems when this was a premature judgment at best and an incorrect decision at worst." The primary cause for this problem was attributed to faulty communication among police, prosecutor, and witness. Problems arise when witnesses are not contacted, when their role is not explained, when they are not told when and where to appear, when their participation is discouraged, and when they are given vague instructions.

The study showed that the police did not obtain the correct addresses for 23 percent of the witnesses at the time of the crime, that the prosecutors often did not ensure that witnesses knew when and where to appear, that police sometimes asked for witness identification within hearing of suspects, and that witnesses often had no understanding of their role in the judicial process.

OBTAINING IDENTIFICATION OF A SUSPECT

If police officers do not actually witness the commission of the crime, eyewitness indentification plays an important part in the arrest as well as in the trial proceedings.

Aids to Witness Identification of Suspects

Rather than simply asking a witness to describe a suspect, it is often helpful if the investigator asks specifically about such items as the following:

- Sex
- Race
- Age
- Height
- Weight
- Build—stout, medium, slim, stooped, square-shouldered
- Complexion—flushed, sallow, pale, fair, dark
- Hair—color, thick or thin, bald or partly bald, straight, kinky, wavy, style
- Eyes—color, close or far apart, bulgy or small
- Eyebrows—bushy or normal
- Nose—small, large, broad, hooked, straight, short, long, broken
- Beard—color, straight, rounded, chin whiskers only, goatee, long sideburns
- Mustache—color, short, stubby, long, pointed ends, turned-up ends
- Chin—square, broad, long, narrow, double and sagging
- Face—long, round, square, fat, thin, distinctive pimples or acne
- Neck—long, short, thick, thin
- Lips—thin, thick
- Mouth—large, small, drooping or upturned
- Teeth—missing, broken, prominent, gold, conspicuous dental work
- Ears—small, large, close to head or extended outward, pierced
- Forehead—high, low, sloping, bulging, straight
- Distinctive marks—scars, moles, amputations, tattoo marks, peculiar walk or talk
- Peculiarities—twitching of features, rapid or slow gait, eyeglasses or sunglasses, stutter, foreign accent, gruff or feminine voice, nervous or calm
- Clothing—mask: if so, color; did it have eye slits, ear openings, mouth openings? Did it cover the whole face, have any designs on it? Did the suspect wear a hat or cap (baseball, golf, etc)? Any markings on the hat? Shirt and tie, sport shirt only, scarf, coat or jacket? Gloves, color of trousers, shoes, stockings, dressed well or shabbily, dressed neatly or carelessly? Any monogram on shirt or jacket?
- Weapon used (if any)—shotgun, rifle, automatic weapon, handgun. Was weapon readily shown or concealed? Taken with or left at scene?
- Jewelry—any noticeable rings, bracelets, or necklaces, earrings, watch?

In addition to questions related to the suspect's appearance, the investigator might also assist the witness by using a description sheet.

Other information related to the suspect must also be obtained by the investigator. It is important to know how the suspect left the scene—running, walking, in a vehicle—and in what direction.

If the suspect escaped in a vehicle, the investigator should obtain information about the license number, make of the vehicle, number of passengers, direction of travel, the color and size of the car, as well as any other identifiable features such as racing stripes, hood ornaments, customized features, broken taillights or headlights, body damage, and so on. The car, if identified, may lead the investigator to the suspect.

If the witness knows the suspect, the investigator should ask about the suspect's personal associates, habits, and where he or she is likely to be found.

Very specific questions and use of an identification diagram may aid witnesses in their identification of suspects.

Usually, however, the witness does not know the suspect. If investigators can identify a suspect based on information given by the witness or on their own intuition as to who might be responsible for the crime, they must follow strict procedures in establishing that the individual is identified by the witness.

BASIC TYPES OF IDENTIFICATION

The three basic types of identification are field identification, photographic identification, and lineup identification. Each type of identification is used in specific circumstances, and each must meet certain legal requirements to be admissible in court. Frequently more than one type of identification is used.

The three basic types of identification are:

- *field identification;*
- *photographic identification;*
- *lineup identification.*

Field Identification

Field identification is at-the-scene identification and must be made within a reasonable time after a crime has been committed. Generally the suspect is returned to the crime scene for possible identification, or the witness may be taken to where the suspect is being held.

Field identification is generally used when a suspect matches the description given by a witness and is apprehended close to the scene of the crime. The critical element in a field identification is time.

Field identification is based on a totality of circumstances in which a witness identifies a suspect as being the person who committed a crime. Totality of circumstances takes into consideration the concentration a witness had upon the suspect at the time the crime was committed, the accuracy of the witness's description of the suspect, the certainty of the witness at the time of the confrontation, and the length of time between commission of the crime and the field identification.

Studies have shown a 60 percent probability of arrest if response time to crime calls was within one minute; however, the probability of arrest was considerably less when response time was longer. Rapid response greatly improves the officer's chances of apprehending suspects still at the scene. In such cases field identification is obviously justified. Even when the suspects have left the scene, however, if they are apprehended within a reasonable time (up to approximately fifteen minutes) after commission of the crime, immediate identification is justified. A reasonable basis for believing that immediate identification is needed must exist before using field identification, since the suspect does not have the right to have counsel present (*United States v. Ash, Jr.* 1973).

The suspect does not have the right to have counsel present at a field identification.

Photographic Identification

Most people are familiar with the procedure of having victims and witnesses go through mug books in hopes of finding a picture of the person they saw commit a particular crime. This type of identification is time consuming and is profitable only if the suspect has a record.

If a suspect is not known, witnesses may make identification through mug shots.

Mug shots are not the only types of photographs used in suspect identification. Frequently officers know, or have a strong suspicion about, who committed a given crime. If the suspect is not in custody, or if it is not possible to conduct a fair lineup, officers may present photographs of people of similar general descriptions to victims or witnesses, who may identify the suspect from among the photographs.

Photographic identification is reserved for times when the suspect is not in custody or it is not possible to conduct a fair lineup. Photographic identification should use people of comparable race, height, weight, and general description.

Photographs used for suspect identification should not contain labels that reveal that a certain suspect has a criminal record. The identification is to be impartial, based on the witness's view of the suspect, and untainted by the suspect's past record. Witnesses should be instructed that they are not obliged to identify anyone from the photographs.

Both the United States Supreme Court and several state supreme courts have issued decisions recognizing the hazards in identification from photographs. Some state prosecutors require a minimum number of photos; however, each has stated that every case must be considered on its own facts. Admissibility in court is more probable if the witness was shown the photographs when he or she was alone and had had no communications with any other witnesses.

Lineup Identification

The basic idea of the lineup is to provide the opportunity for witnesses to observe several individuals, one of whom is the suspect, to see if that suspect can be identified. As with photographic identification, the prosecutor may require a minimum number of participants in the lineup.

The witnesses not only can see the persons in the lineup, they also can hear them speak. A suspect may be asked to speak, walk, turn, assume a stance or a gesture, or put on clothing. If witnesses have described the suspect's clothing, then all persons in the lineup or none should wear that type of clothing. Obviously if only one dressed the way witnesses described, the tendency would be to pick that individual. Some police departments have a small inventory of clothing and personal effects such as sunglasses, masks, scarves, gloves, and coats that they have the participants in a lineup wear, depending upon the description of the witness(es).

A lineup is used when a suspect is in custody. It should contain persons of similar race, height, weight, and general description. Witnesses must be instructed that no identification need be made.

A number of important court decisions have been made regarding lineup identification. One of the most important is *United States v. Wade* (1967), which affirms a suspect's right to have counsel present when participating in a lineup.

Although requesting participation in a lineup is not considered a form of self-incrimination under the Fifth Amendment, the lineup is considered a "critical stage" in the legal process. The *Wade* decision was based on a case in which Wade was convicted of robbing a Texas bank. His case went to the United States Supreme Court, which reviewed the proceedings and then sent the case back to an appeals court. In its review, the Supreme Court said: "The Sixth Amendment of the Constitution guarantees that every citizen shall have the right to counsel in criminal prosecution. When a citizen is suspected of a crime and required to participate in a lineup where witnesses attempt to identify him, then he has a constitutional right to have his lawyer present." The United States Supreme Court stated that "a lineup is just as critical a stage of the prosecution as the trial itself." It should be noted, however, that this particular constitutional right does not apply to field identification or to photographic identification.

The Wade decision states that "prior to having a suspect participate in a lineup, the officer must advise the suspect of his constitutional right to have his lawyer present during the lineup." Requesting a suspect to participate in the lineup is not a violation of the person's civil rights.

When using lineup identification, the officer must know the legal requirements accompanying such an identification as well as the composition of the lineup itself. A legal lineup should assure that:

- the suspect has been advised of his or her right to a lawyer;
- a lawyer has been secured if requested;
- the witnesses have been given impartial prelineup advice;
- the lineup is conducted fairly;
- the individuals in the lineup meet the requirements previously specified.

Generally, when an officer talks about "reading a suspect his or her rights," the officer means the Miranda rights protecting the suspect from self-incrimination. For a lineup, however, the officer is talking about the suspect's Sixth Amendment right to have a lawyer present as specified in the *Wade* decision. The *Miranda* decision is not relevant here.

When a suspect is in custody a lineup should be used as long as it can be done without force and in a fair manner. If these conditions cannot be satisfied, photographic identification should be used.

If for any reason a suspect refuses to cooperate in a lineup, photographic identification may be used. The suspect's refusal to participate may be used against him or her in court.

If a lineup can be held, there is no reason to show pictures. If both are done in a short period of time, the officer destroys any doubt the witness might have that the person in the picture is the guilty party. A recent Midwest supreme court ruling reversed a guilty decision because a photo identification and lineup were held within minutes of each other.

Witnesses should not make photographic identification and then lineup identification within a short period of time.

SUMMARY

Investigators must interview witnesses and interrogate suspects. A witness may be a complainant, an accuser, a victim, an observer of the incident, a confidential or reliable informant, an expert, or a scientific examiner of physical evidence. A suspect, the person believed to have committed the crime, should not be interrogated without first being given the Miranda warning, which advises that he or she has the "right to remain silent . . . the right to speak with an attorney and to have the attorney present during questioning."

The Miranda warning must be given to a suspect who is interrogated in the custody of the police, that is, when the suspect is not free to leave. The public safety exception, however, allows police officers to question suspects without first giving the Miranda warning if the information sought sufficiently affects the officer's and the public's safety.

Information obtained from witnesses is usually critical to resolution of a case. Unfortunately, witnesses' perception of what happened often varies because perception is affected by the viewer's accuracy of observation, interpretation of what is seen, and attention paid to the incident.

In addition to physical evidence, eyewitness identification plays an important part in the arrest and in the trial proceedings. Very specific questions and use of an identification diagram may aid witnesses in their identification of suspects. Once this information has been obtained, the investigator may use three basic types of identification: (1) field identification, (2) photographic identification, or (3) lineup identification. Sometimes more than one type of identification is used.

Field identification is used when a suspect is temporarily detained or arrested. It is usually "at-the-scene" identification. Field identification is based on totality of circumstances in which a witness identifies a suspect as being the person who committed the crime. The suspect does not have the right to have counsel present at a field identification. The critical element in a field identification is time—it should usually occur within approximately fifteen minutes of the commission of the crime to be legally admissible.

Photographic identification may be of two types—mug shots or ordinary photographs. Mug shots are usually used when the suspect is not known to the witness or the police. Ordinary photographic identification is used when the police have a fairly good idea of who is involved in the crime and the suspect is not in custody or it is not possible to conduct a fair lineup. Photographic identification should use people of comparable race, height, weight, and general description.

A lineup is used when a suspect is in custody. The same legal requirements exist as for photographic identification: the lineup should contain persons of similar race, height, weight, and general description. Witnesses must be instructed that no identification need be made.

The *Wade* decision states that "prior to having a suspect participate in a lineup, the officer must advise the suspect of his constitutional right to have his lawyer present during the lineup." Requesting a suspect to participate in a lineup is not a violation of the person's civil rights. If for any reason the suspect refuses to cooperate in a lineup, however, photographic identification may be used and the suspect's refusal to participate may be used against him or her in court. If both photographic identification and lineup identification are used, they should not be done within a short period of time.

Discussion Questions

1. If there was a crime and the suspect was unusually tall or was a member of a minority group not common in the area, how could you hold a fair lineup?

2. In what crimes is eyewitness testimony all that is required for conviction?

3. Why would people not want to help put a stop to crime by being witnesses?

4. How do you convince witnesses to get involved when they really do not want to?

5. Can you force a witness to answer questions?

6. If two witnesses disagree on an identification, what happens?

7. If five witnesses are to identify a suspect in a lineup and four of them pick one person and one picks another, is it assumed that the majority are right, or is the lineup inconclusive?

8. How are participants in a lineup chosen?

9. Is it legal to put other suspects in a lineup with the prime suspect?

10. Why does the suspect not have the right to counsel at a field identification?

References

del Carmen, R. V. *Criminal Procedure for Law Enforcement Personnel.* Monterey, Calif.: Brooks/Cole Publishing, 1987.

Hess, K. M., and Wrobleski, H. M. *For the Record: Report Writing in Law Enforcement.* Eureka, Calif.: Innovative Publications, 1985.

Inbau, F. E.; Reid, J. E.; and Buckley, J. P. *Criminal Interrogation and Confessions,* 4th ed. Baltimore, Md.: Williams & Wilkins, 1986.

Pena, M. S. *Practical Criminal Investigation,* 2d ed. Sacramento, Calif.: Custom Publishing, 1986.

"Witness Responses Misunderstood by Prosecutors." *Target* (LEAA Newsletter) 5:1 (January 1976): 6.

Yarmey, A.D. "Eyewitness Identification." *Encyclopedia of Crime and Justice.* New York: The Free Press, 1983.

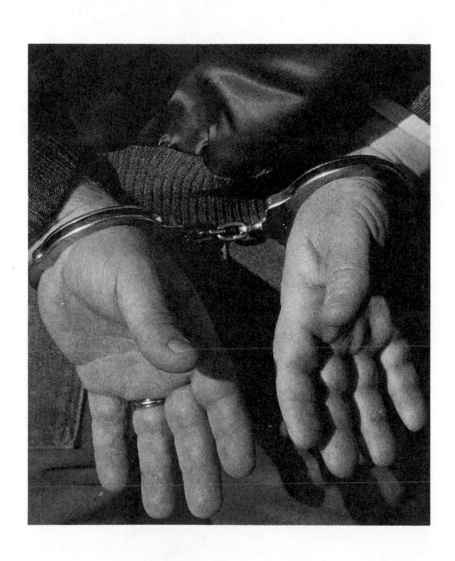

CHAPTER TWELVE

Searching and Arresting: Staying Within the Law

Police arrest powers are indeed awesome, and even while they protect society, they can destroy a citizen.—J.S. Creamer

DO YOU KNOW

The major provisions of the Fourth Amendment?

On what sources probable cause can be based?

The categories of informational probable cause?

What is established by the Exclusionary Rule?

What basic principles underlie stop and frisk and what differences distinguish them?

What significance the Terry case has in relation to the Fourth Amendment?

What the authorities for lawful arrest are?

What the justifications for a reasonable search are and what limitations are placed on them?

What a search warrant is and what it must contain?

When forcible entry is legal?

When night and no-knock warrants are justified?

How one can challenge a warrantless search?

What authorities and restrictions are provided by the following cases: Carroll, Chambers, Coolidge?

What special conditions apply to search of autos?

What is meant by plain view evidence?

Introduction

Chapter 12

Decency, security, and liberty alike demand that governmental officials shall be subjected to the same rules of conduct that are commands to the citizen. In a government of laws, existence of the government will be imperiled if it fails to observe the law scrupulously. Our government is the potent, the omnipresent teacher. For good or ill, it teaches the whole people by its example. Crime is contagious. If the government becomes a lawbreaker, it breeds contempt for the law; it invites every man to become a law unto himself; it invites anarchy. To declare that in the administration of the criminal law the end justifies the means—to declare that the government may commit crimes in order to secure the conviction of a private criminal—would bring terrible˙ retribution. Against this pernicious doctrine this court should resolutely set its face.

This synopsis was delivered by the Supreme Court justice Louis D. Brandeis in *Olmstead v. United States* (1928) and says, in effect, that government agents, including police officers, are subjected to certain restrictions in enforcing the laws. Those who are entrusted with the responsibility of protecting life and property must understand the principles of the federal and state constitutions and the duties that flow from their application as well as the numerous laws and statutes that have been enacted. In short, policing involves having to know the law without the benefit of having gone to law school.

THE FOURTH AMENDMENT

Arbitrary searches and/or seizures have no place in a democratic society. In fact, colonial grievances against unreasonable searches and seizures, in part, led to the revolt against English authority. The Fourth Amendment of the Constitution guarantees the right of citizens to be secure from such arbitrary searches and seizures.

The constitutional standards for searches and seizures, including arrests, are contained in the Fourth Amendment, which requires that searches and seizures be reasonable and based on probable cause.

The terms *reasonable* and *probable cause* provide a very fine, but significant, weight to balance the scales of justice, which measure the conduct of all people. Without what is referred to as probable cause, the laws that govern us might easily become unbalanced, that is, too permissive or too restrictive.

The second part of the Fourth Amendment, called the "warrant clause," states: "No warrant shall issue but upon probable cause." In other words, all warrants (search and arrest warrants) must be based on probable cause.

Reasonable

The rules for determining what constitutes a reasonable search or seizure result from interpretation of the first part of the Fourth Amendment, called the "reasonable search and seizure clause," which states, in part: "The right of the people to be secure in their persons, houses, papers, and effects, against unreasonable searches and seizures shall not be violated."

Reasonable means sensible, just, logical, possessing good sound judgment, well balanced. "Possessing good judgment" implies making decisions. Each case and situation is different from other cases and other situations; therefore, police officers must use their personal judgment as to what action to take. "Well balanced" applies to a built-in stability for justice. On the one hand there is the justification for an action, whether it be an arrest based on probable cause, or an arrest warrant, or stopping and frisking someone. On the other hand, the justification for the action must be balanced by observing the limitations on each action. When the limitations for any action are exceeded, we have gone beyond the reasonableness that made the action legal. Justification and limitation must always be considered together.

Reasonable means sensible, justifiable, logical, based on reason.

Probable Cause

According to Creamer (1980, p. 9):

Probable cause for an arrest is defined as a combination of facts or apparent facts, viewed through the eyes of an experienced police officer, which would lead a man of reasonable caution to believe that a crime is being or has been committed.

Probable cause for the issuance of a search warrant is defined as facts or apparent facts, viewed through the eyes of an experienced police officer, which would lead a man of reasonable caution to believe that there is something connected with a violation of law on the premises to be searched.

Probable cause requires more than mere suspicion; it requires facts or proof that would lead a person of reasonable caution to believe a crime has been committed or that premises contain evidence of a crime. Creamer goes on to note that according to Justice Rutledge (*Brinegar v. United States*, 1948): "The substance of all definitions of 'probable cause' is a reasonable ground for belief in guilt."

Further, in *Smith v. United States* (1949), probable cause is defined as: "The sum total of layers of information and the synthesis of what the police have heard, what they know, and what they observe as trained officers. We [the courts] weigh not individual layers but the laminated total."

Creamer also points out that the concept of probable cause is one of the oldest and most important in criminal law, having been in existence for more than two thousand years and occurring in both Roman law and the common law of England. According to Creamer (1980, p. 8): "This concept of probable cause has acquired its legal potency in the United States because it has constitutional dimensions and because it is interpreted in the final analysis by impartial judges rather than by the police. The severe penalty that the courts impose on police who fail to abide by the spirit of the Fourth Amendment is to declare the evidence they gathered inadmissible."

SOURCES OF PROBABLE CAUSE

Probable cause is "a state of facts that lead a man of ordinary care and prudence to believe and conscientiously entertain an honest and strong suspicion that the person is guilty of a crime." That strong suspicion may be founded on several sources: observation by officers, expertise of officers, circumstantial factors, or information communicated to officers.

More often than not, observational probable cause will be supplemented by expertise, circumstantial, or informational probable cause. In general, the officer has reason to believe a person is involved in a specific crime. For example, the officer sees a car weaving down the highway at 55 mph, the posted speed limit. Although the driver is not speeding, a car weaving from lane to lane would lead any reasonable person to entertain a strong suspicion that the driver was under the influence of alcohol or drugs. The officer not only has a right but also an obligation to stop the driver because the driver is jeopardizing his or her own life as well as the lives of other people on the highway.

Suppose the officer stops the weaving driver, and discovers that the driver is suffering from a sneezing attack caused by a gust of wind blowing a cloud of dust into the car. Obviously an arrest would not be justified even though the probable cause strongly suggested the driver was drunk. On the other hand, if the driver had shown signs of drinking, such as the odor of an alcoholic beverage on his or her breath, red eyes, slurred speech, or incoordination, the officer would need additional corroboration by administering a sobriety test at the scene and further evidence such as a breath or urine test at the time of booking.

Probable cause may be based on the following:

- *Observation by officers.*
- *Expertise of officers.*
- *Circumstantial factors.*
- *Information communicated to officers.*

Police officers first have to justify an arrest by proving to themselves that a crime has been committed and that sufficient evidence exists to convince a jury "beyond a reasonable doubt" that the suspect was involved in the crime. Probable cause to stop a person in reference to a specific crime does not always mean that an arrest will occur.

Observational Probable Cause

Observational probable cause is what the officer sees, hears, or smells, that is, evidence that is presented directly to the officer's senses. This is similar to eyewitness testimony, and it is the strongest form of probable cause. The courts have generally recognized certain types of events as being significant in determining probable cause.

Suspicious activities are generally regarded as contributing to probable cause. For example, a car being driven slowly can be suspicious when (1) the car has circled a block several times, (2) the people in the car are carefully observing a building, (3) the building is closed, and (4) the building is located in a high-crime area. All four factors contribute to probable cause.

Familiar criminal patterns are also generally recognized as contributing to probable cause. The conduct of a person can be indicative of a familiar pattern associated with the sale of stolen property or narcotics or of someone who is casing a building.

Officers assemble factors that contribute to probable cause for arrest. Any one factor by itself may not be sufficient to establish probable cause, but collectively they provide justification—probable cause.

Expertise and Circumstantial Probable Cause

Expertise and circumstantial probable cause are often tied to observational probable cause. Police officers' knowledge of criminal traits and their ability to "put the pieces together" may also contribute to probable cause. For example, two police officers questioned two men seen driving from an alley at 2:00 A.M. The officers noted the license number of the car and the occupants' names and questioned the driver and passenger. The two men were allowed to continue, but a short time later, when the officers learned there had been a burglary in a nearby town, they forwarded the description of the car and its occupants to the local law enforcement officers. The suspects were apprehended, and a search of the vehicle revealed burglary tools as well as the property taken in two burglaries.

In the original confrontation with the suspects, the two officers were not satisfied with the suspects' explanation of why they were there at such an early hour, and even though they did not have sufficient evidence to establish probable cause for an arrest, their investigation of the suspicious circumstances eventually led to the arrest and conviction of the suspects, who later pleaded guilty to seven prior offenses, all felonies.

Arrest and conviction in this case were based on the officers' decision as to when there was sufficient reason to act on probable cause.

To arrest without a warrant when a felony has been committed, the officers must have reasonable cause to believe that the person(s) arrested committed the crime.

Informational Probable Cause

Informational probable cause covers a wide range of sources. In the case previously described, the information about the two suspects forwarded by the police officers to the police in the nearby town constituted informational probable cause. In addition to official sources, victims of crime and citizen informants can be reliable sources of informational probable cause.

The major categories of reliable informational probable cause are (1) official sources, (2) victims of crimes, and (3) citizen informants.

Official sources include police bulletins, police broadcasts, and roll-call information. This information can be relied upon because it is received through official police channels. Information coming from official sources is, in itself, generally sufficient to justify arrest. Although the police officer may arrest on the basis of information received through official channels, this does not relieve the prosecution from establishing that the original source of information was reliable; that is, the original source of information was sufficient to establish probable cause to arrest.

It is the source of information, not the manner of transmission, that will be considered at a trial. Police officers may testify that the information on which they acted was sent over the police radio, but the defendant has the right to demand to know where the information originated and who passed it on to the dispatcher. In other words, as in any other case, the original source of the information must be reliable. For instances, if police officers make an arrest based on information obtained directly from other police officers, the original officers may be required to testify at the trial as to their sources of information, and it is that source which must establish probable cause to arrest. The source may be a victim of a crime, a witness to a crime, or an informant.

Victims of crimes are also usually reliable sources of informational probable cause. Officers can be and are entitled to rely on the information supplied by victims of crimes committed against their person or property and to use this information in making the decision to arrest suspects. Their statements to police officers can be the source of the officers' belief that they have probable cause to look for a person or persons involved in the commission of a crime.

Citizen **informants** quite often provide probable cause. Included in this category are citizens who actually witness a crime and openly aid in the apprehension of the suspect. Eyewitnesses are persons who have observed a crime, who expect no favors from the police, and who do not exchange information for protection or act out of motives for revenge. Complete and otherwise credible information from a citizen informant, based on his personal knowledge that a felony has been committed, is generally sufficient probable cause to justify a felony arrest or to obtain an arrest or search warrant.

Even though information from citizen informants, witnesses to the commission of a crime, is evidence to establish informational probable cause, it is not necessarily absolute evidence. With time permitting, police officers must evaluate as thoroughly as they can that they are, in fact, dealing with an actual witness to a crime. There would be little doubt if a customer was in a store when it was robbed, the owner was shot and killed, and the customer gave police a description of the assailant. The customer would still be at the scene of the crime when the police arrived.

But compare the authenticity of the above witness to the following. A man walked into a police station and identified himself as a serviceman on leave. He gave his address and telephone number and then informed the officers that he had just seen marijuana in the possession of and smoked by a number of people at a given address. The information proved to be accurate; the police went to the address, found people in possession of marijuana, arrested them, and charged them with possession. The judge ruled that the arrest was not justified because the officers had not established probable cause to arrest prior to going into the dwelling and finding the marijuana.

Why? Because they had not established the witness as a reliable informant, nor had they any reason to believe his information was reliable. The serviceman was unknown to them; in fact, the officers did not check his identity further than what he had provided. There were no other circumstances, no additional evidence that would corroborate his information and thus make it reliable.

THE EXCLUSIONARY RULE

Without procedures for enforcing the provisions of the Fourth Amendment, the impressive constitutional language would be meaningless. Consequently, the procedures and the power for their enforcement were vested in the courts. They must refuse to consider evidence obtained by unreasonable search and seizure methods, regardless of how relevant the evidence is to the case.

This rule, known as the **Exclusionary Rule,** is the direct result of the Supreme Court decision in the case of *Weeks v. United States* (1914). The Exclusionary Rule, defined in the *Weeks* case as a matter of judicial implications, was made applicable to the federal courts in 1914. In 1961 the Exclusionary Rule reached maturity when the Supreme Court, in the case of *Mapp v. Ohio*, extended the rule to every court and law enforcement officer in the nation.

Courts uphold the Fourth Amendment by use of the Exclusionary Rule, which demands that no evidence may be admitted in a trial unless it is obtained within the constitutional standards set forth in the Fourth Amendment. Weeks v. United States made the Exclusionary Rule applicable in federal courts. Mapp v. Ohio made it applicable to every court in the country.

On May 23, 1957, three Cleveland police officers arrived at Dolree Mapp's residence pursuant to information that a person wanted for questioning in connection with a recent bombing was hiding in Mapp's home and that there was also a large amount of gambling paraphernalia hidden there. After telephoning her attorney, Mapp refused to admit the officers without a search warrant. Three hours later the officers returned with reinforcements and again sought entrance. When she did not come to the door, the police officers gained entry by forcibly opening a door. Mapp demanded to see the search warrant. When a paper, claimed to be the warrant, was held up by one of the officers, she grabbed it and placed it in her bra. A struggle ensued in which the officers recovered the piece of paper and handcuffed Mapp. A thorough search was conducted of the entire apartment, including the basement of the building. Obscene materials, for the possession of which the defendant was ultimately convicted, were discovered as a result of that widespread search.

The state contended that even if the search were made without authority, it was not prevented from using the evidence at the trial because *Wolf v. Colorado* (1949) had authorized the admission of such evidence in a state court; furthermore, Ohio did not follow the Exclusionary Rule. After a discussion of other applicable cases, the Supreme Court decreed that henceforth evidence obtained by procedures that violated Fourth Amendment standards would no longer be admissible in state courts.

Since 1961 the Exclusionary Rule has applied to both the federal and state courts, and evidence secured illegally by federal, state, or local officers has been inadmissible in any court.

The Exclusionary Rule has important implications for the procedures followed by police officers, since neither the most skillful prosecutor nor the most experienced police officer can convince a jury of a defendant's guilt without adequate and lawfully obtained evidence. Police officers must obtain evidence that establishes that a crime has been committed, and they must obtain evidence that connects the defendant to the specific crime—usually long before the case comes to the prosecutor. Further, they must obtain such evidence without violating the rights of the defendant. Only if police officers obtain evidence that will be acceptable in court is there a probability of conviction.

STOP AND FRISK

One basic responsibility of police officers, and one heavily reliant on reasonableness and probable cause, is the responsibility to investigate suspicious behavior. Officers may simply talk to someone who is acting suspiciously and decide that no crime seems to be in progress or about to be committed. Or they may have their suspicions confirmed and decide to investigate further. The simple act of stopping someone may lead to a situation known in police terminology as a *stop and frisk*.

The courts have stated that suspicious circumstances impose upon police officers the duty to investigate, that is, to stop and question suspects. The procedure of stopping and questioning suspects is directly regulated by the justifications and limitations associated with lawful searches and seizures.

The basic legal considerations in a stop and frisk situation were set forth in the landmark United States Supreme Court decision in *Terry v. Ohio* (1968). This case resulted from the following situation: One afternoon in 1963 Detective McFadden saw two men standing near a jewelry store. For all practical purposes they just seemed to be talking to each other, but to McFadden, a man of thirty years of detective work (thirty-nine years of police experience), "they just didn't look right." He had never seen the two before and could not say what first drew his attention to them, but he decided to take a post in a nearby store entrance and watch for a while.

The two men repeated a ritual nearly a dozen times. One man would walk to the window, pause, look into the window for a while, and then walk toward the corner. He would come back to look into the same window and then rejoin his companion. After a short conference, the man would repeat the entire pattern: walk to the store window, up to the corner, back to the store, and then back to rejoin the first man.

While this was going on, Detective McFadden continued to watch the two. At one point a third man joined them, talked with them briefly, then left. When he left, the other two spent several more minutes repeating the routine.

By this time McFadden suspected they were casing the store for a "stickup." As he made this decision, he also feared they might have a gun. He had already decided to investigate their activity further when the two men walked toward the store where the third man was waiting. At this point, the detective's knowledge was confined to what he had observed. He didn't know any of the three men by name or sight, and he had received no information on them from any other source.

McFadden approached the three, identified himself as a police officer, asked for their names, and then decided to act. He turned one man, later identified as John Terry, around, putting Terry between himself and the other two men. McFadden then made a quick "pat down" of Terry's outer clothing. He could feel a pistol in one of Terry's pockets but was unable to remove the gun. Keeping Terry between himself and the others, he ordered all three men to enter the store. As they obeyed him,

McFadden removed Terry's coat and took a .38 caliber revolver from the pocket. Inside the store McFadden asked the owner to call for a police wagon while he patted the outer clothing of the others, taking another revolver from the coat of a man named Chilton. At the station Terry and Chilton were formally charged with carrying concealed weapons.

When Terry and Chilton were brought to court, their lawyers moved that the guns could not be used as evidence, claiming they were illegally seized. If the guns couldn't be used as evidence, there was no evidence and there was no charge or case.

The trial judge heard the two cases at the same time. He made two decisions that, at first, seemed to contradict each other. First, he rejected the defense motion that the evidence had been illegally seized. Then he rejected a prosecution contention that McFadden had established probable cause to arrest, and therefore, that officer had taken the guns in a search that was incidental to a lawful arrest. If neither theory applied, what did?

The judge said that on the basis of McFadden's experience, he had reasonable cause to believe that the defendants were conducting themselves suspiciously and some interrogation should be made of their actions. Purely for his own protection, the court added, McFadden had the right to frisk the men whom he believed to be armed. The judge said McFadden had stopped the suspects for the purpose of investigation, no arrest occurred at that point, and the "frisking of the outer clothing for weapons" was *not* a full search.

Both men appealed their conviction to the United States Supreme Court, but before the Court's decision was handed down in 1968, Chilton had died. Therefore, its review applied only to Terry.

The Court recognized Detective McFadden as a man of experience, training, and knowledge. McFadden was certainly "a man of reasonable caution." And, as a man of "**ordinary care** and prudence," he waited until he had strengthened his suspicions, making his move just prior to what he believed would be an armed robbery.

The United States Supreme Court upheld the Ohio court verdict; it said that McFadden had "acted reasonably" because (1) Terry's and Chilton's actions were consistent with McFadden's theory that they were contemplating a daylight robbery, (2) such a robbery would most likely involve the use of guns, and (3) nothing in the men's conduct, from the time the officer first noticed them until he confronted them, gave him any reason to doubt his theory.

The Court went on to say that McFadden had to make a quick decision when he saw the three gathered at the store and his actions were correct.

Although we associate a thoroughness to the terms *search* and *seizure* that does not seem to apply to the terms *stop* and *frisk*, the United States Supreme Court (*Terry v. Ohio*) says there is a **seizure** whenever a police officer restrains an individual's freedom to walk away; and there is a search when an officer makes an exploration of an individual's clothing even though it may be called a "pat down" or a "frisk."

A stop is a seizure if physical force or a show of authority is used. A frisk is a search.

Although stopping and frisking fall short of being a technical arrest and a full-blown search, they are definitely forms of search and seizure. Police officers stop citizens of their communities as part of their duties. This is daily practice, but most encounters cannot be considered "seizure of the person" because the officer does not restrain the individual's liberty. So an officer can stop a citizen without the action being considered a seizure of the person. Defining the term **frisk,** however, leaves no other alternative than to consider it a search.

The United States Supreme Court (Terry) had definite opinions about the type of search called a frisk: "It is simply fantastic," the court stated, "to urge that such a procedure, performed in public by a police officer, while the citizen stands helpless, perhaps facing a wall with his hands raised, is a 'petty indignity.' . . . It is a serious intrusion upon the sanctity of the person, which may inflict great indignity and arouse strong resentment, and it is not to be undertaken lightly." The Supreme Court gave its own definition of **stop and frisk** by calling it a "protective

Undercover officers stop and frisk a suspect.

search for weapons." As always, where there is a justification for taking specific action, there are also limitations. According to the Supreme Court, a protective seizure and search for weapons carries these limitations.

Stop and frisk is a protective search for weapons in which the intrusion must be limited to a scope reasonably designed to discover guns, knives, clubs, and other hidden instruments, which may be used for an assault of a police officer or others.

Since some states do not have stop and frisk laws, when this type of protective search and seizure for weapons is referred to, it is on the basis of the opinion of the United States Supreme Court.

The specific principles that arose from *Terry v. Ohio* (1968) can be applied to most stop and frisk situations.

1. Police officers have the right and duty to approach and interrogate persons to investigate crimes.
2. Police officers may stop and make a *limited* search of a suspect if they observe unusual conduct that leads them to reasonably conclude, in light of their experience, that criminal activity may be afoot and that the individual whose suspicious behavior the officers are investigating at close range is armed and probably dangerous.
3. The test of the officers' action is whether a "reasonably prudent man in the same circumstances would be warranted in the belief that his safety or that of others was in danger."
4. Officers may proceed to stop and frisk if nothing occurs to change the officers' theory that criminal activity may occur or that the suspect is armed.
5. The type of search in stop and frisk must be limited. It is a "protective seizure and search for weapons and must be confined to an intrusion which is reasonably designed to discover guns, knives, clubs, or other hidden instruments of assault."
6. If these conditions (principles 1–5) are met, the stop and frisk does *not* constitute an arrest.
7. Since stop and frisk actually involves a search and seizure, it must be governed by the intent of the Fourth Amendment of the Constitution, which forbids indiscriminate searches and seizures.

Seven principles applicable to stop and frisk came from the Terry case. It established that the authority to stop and frisk is independent of the power to arrest. A stop is not an arrest, but it is a seizure within the meaning of the Fourth Amendment and therefore requires reasonableness.

While it is true that both the stop and the arrest are seizures and both must be justified by a showing of reasonableness, there are some important differences between a stop and an arrest.

On January 8, 1985, the United States Supreme Court ruled unanimously that the police may act without a warrant to stop and briefly detain a person they know is wanted for investigation by police in another city. In *United States v. Hensley* (1965) the Court extended the warrantless stop and frisk rules that it established in the 1960s for police who suspect that a crime is about to be committed or is imminent. Police may now sometimes stop, question, and even search people when there is less than probable cause to believe they were involved in a past crime.

The Supreme Court's opinion on stop and frisk and the rights and limitations for this type of action are illustrated in the case of *Henry v. United States* (1959), which involved an arrest made by officers who had observed Henry and another man stop twice in an alley and load cartons into a car. When the officers saw the two men driving off, they waved Henry's car to a stop, searched it, took the cartons, and later made the formal arrest. The men were convicted in Illinois courts of unlawful possession of stolen radios. The Supreme Court overruled the Illinois verdict, saying that an actual arrest had taken place when the officers stopped the suspect's car. The problem in this case was that the officers observed the transaction from a distance of some three hundred feet and could not determine the size, number, or contents of the cartons. The suspects were formally placed under arrest some two hours after they were taken into custody.

The issue in this case was whether there was probable cause for the arrest leading to the search that produced the evidence on which the conviction rested. Since probable cause to arrest had not been established at that time, the Court said the stolen merchandise could not be accepted as evidence. Future cases in many states were decided on this 1959 case, and the accepted opinion was that stopping a vehicle or an individual constituted an actual arrest.

Just what constitutes a lawful arrest is the next topic of consideration.

REASONABLE SEIZURES—LAWFUL ARRESTS

Creamer (1980, p. 56) contends that an **arrest** is "the beginning of imprisonment, when a man is first taken by government and restrained of his liberty." *Black's Law Dictionary* defines arrest as follows: "The apprehension or detaining of the person in order to be forthcoming to answer an alleged or suspected crime." Laws of arrest are generally uniform in all fifty states and in federal criminal proceedings.

Statutes throughout the United States generally define arrest as the taking of a person into custody by the actual restraint of the person or by his or her submission to the custody of the officer that he or she may be held to answer for a public offense before a judge.

Brandstatter and Hyman (1971, p. 132) warn: "The legal definition of arrest has to do with control and detention; not with punishment. This is frequently overlooked or misunderstood. An arrest made for the purpose of punishing an individual is an invalid arrest. Not only will it not hold up in court, but the arresting officer may also face legal charges or departmental disciplinary action for misconduct."

Elements of Criminal Arrest

According to Creamer (1980, p. 56), the four elements of a criminal arrest are:

1. An *intent* by the peace officer to make an arrest.
2. Real or pretended *authority* to arrest.
3. A *seizure* or *restraint*, actual or constructive.
4. An *understanding* by the person being seized that he or she is being arrested.

Arrest Warrants

All states have a statute authorizing law enforcement officers to make arrests, but the Constitution stipulates that lawful arrests require an arrest warrant. Klotter and Kanovitz (1985, pp. 103–11) note: "Aside from constitutional considerations, there is a very practical reason why police officers should, wherever time permits, obtain a warrant before making an arrest. If the warrant is proper on its face and the officer does not abuse his authority in executing the arrest, he will be protected against civil liability for false imprisonment, even though it is later determined that the arrest was unjustified." Klotter and Kanovitz list eight requirements for a valid arrest warrant:

1. The warrant must be supported by probable cause. It will be up to the magistrate to determine if probable cause exists.

2. The affidavit for the warrant must be supported by oath or affirmation; that is, some individual must swear to the truth of the facts described in the affidavit.

3. The person to be seized (arrested) must be named.

4. The warrant must state the nature of the offense with sufficient clarity to advise the subject of the accusation.

5. The warrant must designate the officer or class of officers who are directed to carry out the court's order.

6. The warrant must be issued in the name of a state or the United States.

7. The warrant must be issued and signed by a neutral, detached judicial officer, including his/her title.

8. Additional state requirements may also be present.

Arrest without a Warrant

Lawful arrests require an arrest warrant. If, however, an emergency situation exists and the officers have probable cause to believe a person has committed a crime, they may make an arrest. The courts will determine its legality.

In *Draper v. United States* (1959) the United States Supreme Court stated: "Probable cause exists where the facts and circumstances within their (the arresting officers') knowledge and of which they had reasonable trustworthy information are sufficient in themselves to warrant a man of reasonable caution in the belief that an offense has been or is being committed."

Creamer (1980, p. 57) notes:

The exact moment when a warrantless arrest occurred is frequently the most important preliminary determination for a court. The legality of a warrantless arrest hinges, in large measure, on the probable cause or guilt-laden facts confronting the police officer up to and including, but never after, the actual moments of arrest. At the moment of arrest, probable cause ceases to build. Any after-the-arrest, guilt-laden facts that develop will not be considered by the courts as part of the probable cause necessary to justify the arrest.

If there is probable cause and an emergency situation exists, an officer may make an arrest without a warrant. The courts will determine whether the arrest was lawful.

Police officers may make lawful arrests without a warrant for felonies or misdemeanors committed in their presence or for felonies not committed in their presence if they have probable cause.

There are four authorities for arrest without a warrant. The first authority allows for an arrest for a public offense committed or attempted in the presence of an officer. Public offense includes both felonies and misdemeanors. To determine whether a public offense has been committed, ask this question: Would you be justified in seeking a complaint upon which an arrest warrant would be issued, and could you testify to all the elements of the crime?

"Committed or attempted in the presence of an officer" means the crime was apparent to the officer's senses, including sight, hearing, or smelling. A conversation over the telephone is within the officer's presence; therefore, a conversation lawfully overheard that might be indicative of criminal conduct is in the officer's presence. The odor of marijuana is evidence that a crime is being committed in the officer's presence and may constitute probable cause to effect an arrest. In most cases, however, the officer will actually see the crime committed, and this is where the first authority generally applies. A suspect can be arrested without a warrant for a misdemeanor only if the offense is committed in the officer's presence.

The remaining authorities allow an officer to arrest a suspect for a felony that was not committed in his or her presence. Any lawful arrest, with or without an arrest warrant, requires probable cause. Without an arrest warrant, police officers can arrest a suspect for a felony only if they have probable cause based on their own observations or on information provided to them. They cannot make this same type of arrest for a misdemeanor.

The four authorities for arrest without a warrant are as follows:

1. *When a public offense is committed or attempted in an officer's presence.*

2. *When a person arrested has committed a felony, although not in an officer's presence, for example, an all-points bulletin on a bank robber before a warrant is issued.*

3. *When a felony has in fact been committed, and the officer has reasonable cause to believe that the person has committed it; for example, an officer answers a shooting call and the suspect is still at the scene.*

4. *On a charge made upon probable cause of the commission of a felony; for example, a person observed running down the street as a burglar alarm sounds is a likely suspect for the crime.*

Creamer (1980, p. 64) emphasizes: "Police arrest powers are indeed awesome, and even while they protect society, they can destroy a citizen. The Fourth Amendment was designed to limit the chances of a citizen

Table 12–1 Stop and Arrest

	Stop	**Arrest**
Justification	Reasonable suspicion	Probable cause
Intent of Officer	To resolve an ambiguous situation	To make a formal charge
Search	Possibly a "pat-down" or frisk	Complete body search
Record	Minimal	Fingerprints, photographs, and booking

being harmed by an unjust arrest. The courts have the responsibility to make sure the Fourth Amendment works to protect the citizen and, at the same time, assure the security of society."

An arrest is not to be taken lightly. It has several important differences from a stop and frisk situation, as summarized in table 12–1. As can be seen, the search conducted in a frisk differs from that which can be conducted when a person is arrested. Focus your attention now on assuring that any search made is lawful.

LAWFUL SEARCHES

Creamer (1980, p. 58) defines a **search** as follows: "The looking into or prying into hidden places. The term search in the context of the Fourth Amendment involves a governmental invasion of privacy. Searchers are intrusions into the privacy for the purpose of obtaining incriminating evidence. . . . However, a search may never be justified by the incriminating evidence it turns up."

Guilty persons are convicted based on the facts that the court finds admissible. Police officers' reports must contain all the reasons for a search or seizure as proof of the reasonableness of their conduct. The questions most frequently asked by the prosecutor and the courts before admitting evidence are: Was the search reasonable? Was the arrest, if there was one, legal? There are rules to guide police officers in answering these questions on a day-to-day basis. The rules often seem contrary to what many people consider to be reasonable; however, these rules, contrary or not, *must* be considered when deciding whether a search or seizure is reasonable. The courts abide by these rules and base their decisions on them.

Since the word *unreasonable* is ambiguous, the courts have adopted guidelines to measure reasonableness and to assure law enforcement personnel that *if* certain rules are adhered to, their search or seizure will be acceptable—reasonable. The three principal justifications established by the court for the right to search are: (1) if the search is incidental to a lawful arrest; (2) if consent is given; (3) if a search warrant has been issued. These circumstances are the preconditions for a reasonable, legal search. A search that occurs under any one of these conditions is considered justified or reasonable.

The three principal justifications established by the court for the right to search are as follows:

1. If the search is incidental to a lawful arrest.

2. If consent is given.

3. If a search warrant has been issued.

Search Incidental to a Lawful Arrest

In a search incidental to a lawful arrest the search must be made simultaneously with the arrest and must be confined to the immediate vicinity of the arrest.

Chimel v. California (1969), involving a search incidental to an arrest, provides a definition of search of a person and a dwelling as well as the limitations of the search. Officers went to the Chimel home with a warrant to arrest Ted Chimel on a charge of burglarizing a coin shop. Mrs. Chimel admitted the officers, who then waited ten to fifteen minutes for her husband to come home. When the arrest warrant was handed to Chimel, he was told that the officers wanted to "look around." He objected but was informed that the officers had a right to search because it was a lawful arrest.

The officers opened kitchen cabinets, searched through hall and bedroom closets, looked behind furniture in every room, and even searched the garage. (Prior to this case, the courts had accepted fairly extensive searches incidental to an arrest.) On several occasions the officers had Mrs. Chimel open drawers and move the contents so they could look for items removed in the burglary. The search took nearly an hour and resulted in the officers finding numerous coins.

Chimel was convicted in a California court, but he appealed his conviction on burglary charges on the grounds that the evidence—the coins—had been unconstitutionally seized. The United States Supreme Court studied the principle of searches incidental to an arrest and determine the following:

> When an arrest is made, it is reasonable for the arresting officer to search the person arrested in order to remove any weapons that the latter might seek to use in order to resist arrest or effect his escape.
>
> It is entirely reasonable for the arresting officer to search for and seize any evidence on the arrestee's person in order to prevent its concealment or destruction and the area from within which the arrestee might gain possession of a weapon or destructible evidence.

The officers' justification for extending the search was based on the phrase that "It is entirely reasonable . . . to search . . . the area from within which the arrestee might gain possession of . . . destructible evidence."

In the *Chimel* case, the Supreme Court specified that the area of search could include only the arrestee's person and the area within his or her immediate control. The court defined **immediate control** as being that area within the person's reach.

Limitations on a search made incidental to an arrest are found in the Chimel Rule, which states that the area of the search must be within the immediate control of the suspect—that is, it must be within his or her reach.

The *Chimel* case resulted in a clear definition as to what, beyond the suspects themselves, could be searched when officers are using the authority of a search incidental to an arrest. The court pointed out that if an arrest is used as an excuse to conduct a thorough search, such as the search conducted in the *Chimel* case, the police would have power to conduct "general searches," which were declared unconstitutional by the Fourth Amendment over 200 years ago.

One can sympathize with the officers who had alerted Chimel's wife that they were looking for stolen coins and then felt they had to find them or face the possibility she would remove them. But the law allows only a limited search in this situation. Undoubtedly a magistrate would have issued a search warrant for the stolen coins if the officers had realized the limitations on their search and had requested the warrant.

Ironically, prior to the burglary, Chimel had wandered about the coin store, asked the owner where he kept his most valuable coins, inquired into the alarm system, and bragged that he was planning a robbery. Later he took exception to the owner's testimony that it was a "sloppy job," excitedly claiming that the burglary had been "real professional." But the Supreme Court reversed the California decision because the conviction had been based on evidence obtained in a search that was beyond reasonable limits.

An interesting sideline in the *Chimel* case is that three days after the initial search, officers again entered Chimel's house looking for evidence to support a separate charge of robbery. No evidence was seized on the second search, but Chimel was convicted and sentenced on the robbery charge.

Search with Consent

In a search where **consent** is given, the United States Supreme Court provides that the consent must be free and voluntary; therefore, it cannot be given in response to a claim of lawful authority by the officer to conduct the search at the moment. As with searches incidental to lawful arrest, a search with consent must be conducted only in the actual area for which the consent is given.

Consent must be free and voluntary, and the search must be limited to the area for which the consent is given.

As noted by the Maine Supreme Court in *State v. Barlow, Jr.* (1974): "It is a well established rule in the federal courts that a consent search is unreasonable under the Fourth Amendment if the consent was induced by deceit, trickery or misrepresentation of the officials making the search." A recognized exception to this general rule is when undercover operations are involved.

When a court is asked to determine if consent to search was "free and voluntary," it considers such things as the subject's age, background, mental condition, and education. The number of officers involved should not be a factor if no aggressiveness is displayed. As stated in *People v. Reed* (1975): "Where aggravating factors are not evident, the number of officers alone will not have an adverse effect on the consent. The presence of a large number of officers in an apartment does not present a situation which is per se coercive."

The time of day might also be a consideration. Officers should generally avoid seeking voluntary consent to search at night. In *Monroe v. Pape* (1961) Justice Frankfurter said: "Modern totalitarianisms have been a stark reminder, but did not newly teach, that the kicked-in door is the symbol of a rule of fear and violence fatal to institutions founded on respect for the integrity of man. . . . Searches of the dwelling house were the special object of this universal condemnation of official intrusion. Nighttime search was the evil in its most obnoxious form."

Perhaps most important is the way in which the request to search is made. It must, indeed, be a request, not a command.

Search Conducted with a Search Warrant

Recall the provision of the Fourth Amendment that the warrant must particularly describe "the place to be searched and the persons or things to be seized."

A search conducted with a warrant must be limited to the specific area and specific items delineated in the warrant.

We are all protected against unreasonable searches and seizures by the United States Constitution, which guarantees that probable cause, supported by **oath** or **affirmation,** shall be the basis for issuing a search warrant. Our courts have interpreted this guarantee to mean that any search or seizure other than one conducted with a warrant is technically unreasonable. The courts do, however, recognize that emergency situations will arise in which a police officer will not have the opportunity to secure a warrant.

A **search warrant** is an order issued by any court of record or by a justice of the peace in a county having no municipal court other than a probate court. The court must have jurisdiction in the area where the search is to be made.

The warrant must contain the reasons for requesting the search warrant; the names of the persons presenting affidavits, for example, the officer who applied for the warrant, his or her colleagues, or others who have information to contribute; what specifically is being sought; and the signature of the judge issuing it.

A search warrant is a judicial order directing a police officer to search for specific property, seize it, and return it to the court. Probable cause is required for issuance of all warrants. Technically, all searches are to be made under the authority of a search warrant issued by a magistrate.

The procedures for obtaining and executing search warrants vary from locality to locality, but the following example illustrates what may be involved. Generally a search warrant may be issued for the following reasons:

- The property or material was stolen or embezzled.
- The possession of the property or material constitutes a crime, for example, stolen property or drugs.
- The property or material is in the possession of a person with intent to use them to commit a crime, for example, possession of burglary tools with intent to use them.
- The property or material was used in committing a crime, for example, a gun, knife, or burglary tools.
- The items or evidence tend to show that a crime has been committed or that a particular person has committed a crime, for example, letters, clothing.

When police officers present an **affidavit** to a magistrate, their facts must be sufficiently detailed to enable the magistrate to determine that probable cause to search exists. The affidavit need not be as polished as an entry in an essay contest, but it should not skimp on the facts.

The Constitution does not require all necessary information to appear on the face of the complaint, as long as a sworn affidavit made at the time the warrant was issued contains those facts.

A police officer must present adequate evidence for a magistrate to determine probable cause. If sufficient facts are contained in the application and supporting affidavit or supplementary facts are presented during questioning of an officer who applies for a warrant, a magistrate will issue the search warrant.

The use of search warrants has increased since the *Chimel* decision, which restricted the area that could be searched incidental to a lawful arrest. Prior to the *Chimel* case, some courts allowed extensive searches incidental to a lawful arrest. The *Chimel* ruling, however, makes it necessary for police officers to obtain a search warrant as well as an arrest warrant if they want to search a suspect's house incidental to the execution of the arrest warrant.

What May Be Seized

A search warrant must clearly specify or describe the things to be seized. The prosecution or the state must accept the burden of proof when items are seized that are not specifically stated in the warrant. This does not mean such items cannot be seized. They can, if a reasonable relationship exists between the search and the seizure of materials not described or if officers discover **contraband**—anything that is illegal for a person to own or have in possession, such as heroin or a machine gun.

Police may seize items not specified in the search warrant if they are similar in nature to those items described, if they are related to the particular crime described, of if they are contraband.

Consider this example. On two separate occasions, officers arrived at a private dwelling with search warrants authorizing them to seize items taken from burglaries. On both occasions their knock was unanswered, so they entered through a living room window. They seized many items on the search warrants as well as other similar items not specifically mentioned in the warrants. When the case came to court, the defense challenged those items introduced as evidence of the burglaries that were not specifically mentioned in the warrants. The lower court allowed the evidence to be used, and the state supreme court upheld the decision. The high court said the items seized in addition to those mentioned in the warrants were similar to items that the stores had on hand when the burglaries occurred.

In addition, contraband discovered during a search authorized by a warrant may also be seized. It is not necessary that the contraband be connected to the particular crime described in the search warrant.

Gaining Entrance

Police officers are usually required to announce their authority and purpose before entering a home. This protects the citizen's rights and avoids needless destruction of property where the owner or occupant is willing to voluntarily admit a police officer. Sometimes, however, the suspect will not allow entrance, or there may be no one home.

Police officers who arrive to execute a search warrant and find the house unoccupied may forcibly enter the house to search it. If the dwelling is an apartment, they could probably get a passkey from a caretaker, but this would still be considered a **forced entry.** Opening a closed but unlocked door or window is also considered a forced entry. Officers who are denied entrance to execute a search warrant may break an inner or outer door or window to gain entry.

Generally police officers must announce themselves. They may enter a house by force to execute a search warrant if they are denied entrance or if there is no one home.

Nighttime and No-Knock Search Warrants

A search warrant will normally be issued to be served during daylight hours, that is, from sunrise to sunset. **Nighttime search warrants** may be justified and requested of the court by police officers. They must state the reasons, based on facts, for fearing that unless the search is conducted at night the objects of the search might be lost, destroyed, or removed.

Similarly, unannounced entries for the purpose of executing search warrants must also receive prior judicial authorization. The **no-knock search warrant** is reserved for situations where the judge recognizes that the normal cooperation of the citizen cannot be expected and that an announced entry may result in loss, destruction, or removal of the objects of the search; for example, surprise entries are often used in searches for narcotics and gambling equipment. In either of these instances, the court will usually acknowledge that evidence can easily be destroyed during the time required to give notice, demand admittance, and accept the citizen's denial of entry.

Two special types of search warrants, nighttime and no-knock, must be authorized by a magistrate as a special provision of a search warrant.

Emergency Situations/Extenuating Circumstances— Warrantless Search

When police officers follow the letter of the law and secure a search warrant, they receive an advance court decision that probable cause does exist. It was originally believed that the magistrate should be the sole judge of probable cause, but when **emergency situations** or **extenuating circumstances** became apparent, the courts decided there were times when reasonable searches and seizures could be based on the decisions of police officers.

In situations where police officers sincerely believe they have established probable cause and there is no time to secure a warrant, they can act on their own decisions. But it is here that the opportunity for a defense lawyer to challenge the legality of the search can be used. While a number of challenges can be raised, two occur most frequently. The defense may contend that a magistrate would not have issued a warrant had the officers presented the facts before the court (probable cause was not established), or that the officers had ample opportunity to secure a warrant and therefore had no justification to act without one.

If the defense raises one of these challenges in a case involving evidence seized as a result of a warrantless search, the burden of proof is on the officer and the prosecution. It must be proven that the officer was reasonable and prudent and had gathered sufficient facts to make the important decision that probable cause to search existed and that the search must be conducted immediately.

When police officers conduct a search without a warrant, they may be challenged on the basis that:

- *probable cause was not established;*
- *the officers had opportunity to secure a warrant and had no justification to act without one.*

The Fourth Amendment says a great deal in only fifty-four words. It guarantees that United States citizens will not be unjustly searched or arrested and that their property will not be unlawfully seized. With added historical court decisions, most of the language of our present laws governing search and seizure is represented.

The Fourth Amendment was intended to interpose a magistrate between the police and the citizen—requiring a magistrate to study the evidence presented by the police and decide whether a warrant should be issued. The Constitution is a product of a period when authority had been badly misused, and it was presumed magistrates would be more objective than officers.

A strict interpretation of the Constitution requires that a magistrate decide whether probable cause exists. When the officer presents the facts to a magistrate and is granted a warrant, the defense lawyer cannot attack the decision of the individual officer. When the search warrant is issued, it becomes an order from the court, as the Constitution intended it to be. It is no longer the prosecution who has to defend its actions, but it is the lawyer for the accused who has to prove that a magistrate erred in issuing the warrant.

While the laws are still intended to provide protection, they are also designed to meet emergency situations not considered in the original amendment. There are rules to be observed in such situations; each must fall within the guarantees in the Fourth Amendment. The key is to protect all citizens against unreasonable searches and seizures.

The individuals who drafted the Constitution understood that other reasonable measures would have to be accepted to uphold the laws of the nation. The Supreme Court, therefore, surveys cases brought before it to determine whether the action taken in a particular situation was reasonable according to the Fourth Amendment. What may be reasonable in one situation may not be reasonable in another. For instance, you could justify a warrantless search of a vehicle by stating the reasons you believed it would be gone if you waited to obtain a search warrant. This same logic, however, cannot be applied to a search of a house or any other fixed object.

You have already looked at three types of warrantless searches:

- Searches connected with stop and frisk (limited to a search for weapons).
- Searches incidental to an arrest.
- Searches when consent has been given.

Although Supreme Court approval of warrantless searches incidental to an arrest was established in cases prior to 1920, it was the *Chimel* opinion in 1969 that confined the search to an area within the immediate control of the person arrested. This opinion did not apply to automobiles, however.

As noted, searches may be conducted without a warrant even though the search is not associated with stop and frisk, incidental to an arrest, or with consent; but when it is conducted under these circumstances, police officers must prove that an emergency existed that did not allow them to secure a search warrant. Very frequently this involves automobiles and other conveyances having **mobility.**

Warrantless Searches of Automobiles and Other Conveyances

When a vehicle is involved, the rules of reasonableness, although within the boundaries of the Constitution, are quite different. The courts have long recognized the need for separate exemptions from the requirement of obtaining a search warrant where mobility is involved.

The precedent for a warrantless search of an automobile resulted from *Carroll v. United States* (1925), which established two basic principles justifying warrantless searches of automobiles: (1) there is probable cause, and (2) the automobile or other conveyance would be gone before a search warrant could be obtained.

Carroll v. United States set the precedent for warrantless searches of automobiles provided there is probable cause for the search and provided the vehicle would be gone before a search warrant could be obtained.

The *Carroll* case did not involve a search incidental to an arrest. The concern was with probable cause for a search, not for an arrest.

During Prohibition in the 1920s, some 1,500 agents pursued bootleggers, many of whom brought liquor down from Canada. In addition to the imports, there was so much local production that the 9,500 stills raided in the first six months of Prohibition were known to be only a small fraction of the total.

Visualize a scene in a Michigan "honky-tonk" during the 1920s. Four men were sitting at a table holding a meeting; two were supposed buyers, and two were bootleggers. The "buyers" were actually federal Prohibition agents. Although the meeting seemed to go well, the two bootleggers, George Carroll and John Kiro, were somewhat suspicious. They indicated that the liquor had to come from the east end of Grand Rapids, Michigan. They would get it and return in about an hour. Later that day, Carroll called and said delivery could not be made until the next day. But the two did not return the next day.

The agents returned to their normal duty of watching a section of road between Grand Rapids and Detroit known to be used by bootleggers. Within a week after their unsuccessful attempt to make the "buy," the agents recognized Carroll and Kiro driving by. They gave chase but lost the car near East Lansing.

Two months later they again recognized Carroll's car coming from the direction of Detroit. They pursued the car and this time were successful in overtaking it. The agents were familiar with Carroll's car, they recognized Carroll and Kiro in the automobile, and they had reason to believe the automobile would contain bootleg liquor. A search of the car revealed sixty-eight bottles of whiskey and gin, most of it behind the upholstery of the seats where the padding had been removed. The contraband was seized, and the two men were arrested.

George Carroll and John Kiro were charged with transporting intoxicating liquor and were convicted in federal court. Carroll's appeal, taken to the United States Supreme Court, resulted in a landmark decision defining the rights and limitations for warrantless searches of vehicles.

The agents' knowledge of the two men and their operation, as well as the fact that the car was believed to be used in the transportation of liquor, produced the probable cause necessary to justify a search. So the first principle establishing this as an exception to the rule requiring a search warrant was met.

The Carroll decision established that the right to search an automobile is not dependent on the right to arrest the driver or an occupant, but rather it is dependent upon the probable cause the seizing officer has for believing that the contents of the automobile violate the law.

Regarding the mobility of such a conveyance, the court amplified its opinion to include some of the key reasons why an automobile can be exempted while a house or fixed object cannot:

- A vehicle or conveyance can be quickly moved out of the jurisdiction or locality in which the warrant must be sought.
- The occupants of the vehicle are immediately alerted.
- The vehicle's contents may never be found again if a police officer has to wait to obtain a search warrant before searching the car.

The Supreme Court saw each of these possibilities in the case against George Carroll and, consequently, provided a basis for making a similar judgment in a situation where these circumstances might occur.

The requirement of mobility is also present in the case of *Chambers v. Maroney* (1970). This case involved the armed robbery of a service station. The station attendant described the two men who held guns on him, and two boys provided officers with a description of a vehicle they had seen the men in circling the block prior to the robbery and again speeding out of the area. Within an hour officers spotted the vehicle and identified the occupants as the men the three witnesses had described. They stopped the car and arrested the men. The evidence seized and later used to convict Chambers and the other man included two revolvers and a glove filled with change they had taken from the service station.

Chambers based an appeal on the fact that the officers took the car to the police station before searching it. The defense contended that the search was illegal because it was made incidental to rather than simultaneous with the arrest. The defense was right. As a search

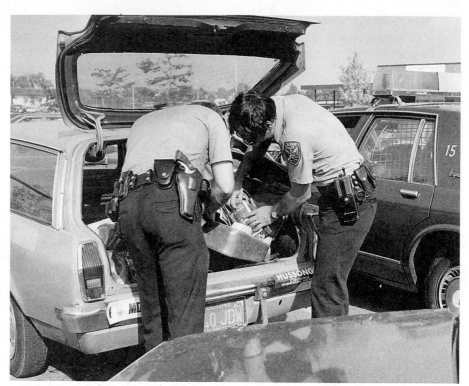

Officers can search a vehicle if they have probable cause to believe that its contents violated the law.

incidental to an arrest, it would have been illegal. But the Court observed the same set of circumstances in relation to the warrantless search of a vehicle; the seizing officers did have probable cause to believe that the contents of the automobile violated the law. Therefore, it was the right to search, not the right to arrest, that provided the officers with the authority for their actions.

The Supreme Court added another opinion to the *Chambers* case when it said that it was not unreasonable under these circumstances to take the vehicle to the police station to be searched. In other words, the probable cause to search at the scene continued to exist at the police station. Based on the facts, the Supreme Court said there was probable cause to search, and since it was a fleeing target, the Chambers vehicle could have been searched on the spot where it stopped. The Court reasoned that probable cause still existed at the police station, and so did the mobility of the car. The Court quickly pointed out that such actions must be confined to vehicles and other conveyances having mobility.

The Chambers case established that a car may retain its mobility even though it is impounded.

Yet another interpretation of mobility was provided in the case of *Coolidge v. New Hampshire* (1971). The *Coolidge* case, a homicide, tested the requirements of mobility. A fourteen-year-old girl disappeared in Manchester, New Hampshire, and her body was found eight days later. She had been shot. A number of errors were made in the case, including the fact that arrest and search warrants were drawn up and signed by the man who became the chief prosecutor.

A neighbor's tip led police to E. H. Coolidge, whom officers admitted was fully cooperative, even to the point of agreeing to a polygraph examination. The examination was conducted several days after Coolidge was first questioned. During the next two and a half weeks, evidence against Coolidge began to accumulate. The evidence included what the prosecution said was the murder weapon, which officers had obtained from Mrs. Coolidge. The arrest and search warrants were drawn up based on this evidence. The search warrant specifically designated Coolidge's car, which was in the driveway in plain view of the house at the time of the arrest. Mrs. Coolidge was told she was not allowed to use the car, and it was impounded prior to other officers dropping Mrs. Coolidge at a relative's home. During the next fourteen months the car was searched three times, and vacuum sweepings from the car were introduced as evidence.

Coolidge was convicted of the girl's murder. His appeal challenged the legality of the evidence seized from the car. Discounting the fact the warrants were invalid and the prosecution could not prove the search was incidental to an arrest, the prosecution contended the seizure of the car should be allowable based on the standards established by the *Carroll* and *Chambers* cases.

The Court considered the principles of the *Coolidge* case and weighed them against those of the precedent cases. Because testimony from witnesses and from Coolidge indicated that his car was at the scene of the murder, the Court accepted the fact that probable cause to search had been established. But was there sufficient cause to fear the automobile might be moved?

The Court said there was not. Coolidge could not have gained access to the automobile when the officers came to arrest him, and he had, in fact, received sufficient prior warning that he was a prime suspect to have already fled. The only other adult occupant, Mrs. Coolidge, was driven to a relative's home by other officers who were with her after the vehicle was actually taken to the station.

Coolidge v. New Hampshire *established that the rule of mobility cannot be applied unless there is actually a risk that the vehicle would be moved.*

Neither the *Carroll* nor the *Chambers* opinions could apply here because of the following differences:

- There appeared to be no criminal intent to flee.
- This was not a case of a fleeting opportunity to search on an open highway after a hazardous chase.
- There was no evidence of contraband, stolen goods, or weapons.
- There was no evidence of any friends of Coolidge's waiting to move the car and the evidence therein.
- The automobile in question was secured from intrusion when it was found.

Since the Coolidge premises were guarded throughout the night, and since Mrs. Coolidge was with officers until after the car had been towed in, the car was secure at all times.

The Court could not accept the prosecution's contention that the Coolidge vehicle was included in the category of mobility.

Vehicles may also be searched without a warrant when they are used in the commission of serious crimes such as felonies. Such **instruments of a crime** may be seized and searched if the vehicle is an integral part of the defendant's apparatus for the commission of the crime. This generally includes getaway vehicles as well as automobiles, trailers, or similar conveyances used to secrete or transport stolen items.

United States v. Ross (1982) held that the police may search a car, including containers, without a warrant as long as they have probable cause to believe contraband is somewhere in the car.

Vehicles or other conveyances used in a crime may be seized and searched if the vehicle is an integral part of the defendant's apparatus for the commission of the crime.

Table 12–2 summarizes the limitations on searching vehicles.

Plain View

Plain view refers to evidence that is not concealed and that is inadvertently seen by an officer engaged in a lawful activity. Several factors determine what constitutes plain view. First, the police officer must be engaged in lawful activity prior to the discovery of plain view evidence. Such circumstances might occur while the officer is executing a warrant to search for another object, while in pursuit of a suspect, during a search incidental to a lawful arrest, during stop and frisk, or any other legitimate reasons justifying an officer's lawful presence.

Second, the seized items must not be concealed. As the name implies, they must be in "plain view." Third, the discovery of the evidence in plain view must be inadvertent, by accident. Police officers cannot obtain a warrant to search an automobile and fail to mention a

Table 12–2 Searching Cars

Method of Search	Leading Case Authority	Justification for Search	Permissible Scope of Search	Time of Search	Purpose of Search
Stop-frisk	*Terry v. Ohio*, 392 U.S. 1 (1968)	Officer's reasonable fear for his own safety	Person and area in his immediate control	At time of stop	Self-protection of officer
Arrest-search	*Preston v. United States*, 376 U.S. 364 1964; *Chimel v. California*, 395 U.S. 752 (1969)	Probable cause to arrest someone in car	Person and area of car in his control	At time of arrest	Self-protection of officer and preservation of evidence
Search warrant	*Spinelli v. United States*, 393 U.S. 410 (1969)	Probable cause presented to judge	Entire car	Any time after warrant issued	Find and preserve evidence
Consent search	*Amos v. United States*, 225 U.S. 313 (1921)	Waiver of 4th Amendment rights by owner or driver	Entire car	Any time after consent	Find and preserve evidence
Custodial search of impounded car	*Cooper v. California*, 386 U.S. 58 (1967)	Police regulations to protect property in their custody	Entire car	Any time	Preserve car and contents
Probable cause search	*Chambers v. Maroney*, 399 U.S. 42 (1970)	Probable cause that car contains contraband, etc.	Entire car	Any time	Find and preserve evidence

Source: *The Law of Arrest, Search, and Seizure* by J. Shane Creamer. Copyright © 1980 by Holt, Rinehart and Winston. Reprinted by permission of CBS College Publishing.

particular object they are looking for and then justify its seizure pursuant to the plain view doctrine. If they were looking for it initially, it must be mentioned in the warrant. Fourth, plain view alone is not sufficient to justify the warrantless seizure evidence.

Plain view refers to evidence that is not concealed and that is inadvertently seen by an officer engaged in a lawful activity.

In the *Coolidge* case the Court could not accept the seizure of the car as being within plain view limitations because the officers intended to seize the car when they came onto Coolidge's property. So the rule that applied to *Coolidge* and to all plain view cases following is that the discovery of evidence in plain view must be inadvertent—by accident. The plain view doctrine applies even though the objects seized are not under immediate control of the suspect.

The Inevitable Discovery Doctrine

On June 11, 1984, the United States Supreme Court ruled that illegally obtained evidence may be admitted at trial if the prosecution can prove that the evidence would "inevitably" have been discovered by lawful means *(Nix v. Williams).* From this case the Supreme Court adopted what is now known as "the inevitable discovery exception to the Exclusionary Rule."

Chief Justice Warren E. Burger wrote in the majority opinion: "Exclusion of physical evidence that would inevitably have been discovered adds nothing to either the integrity or fairness of a criminal trial." The point of the inevitable discovery doctrine, he said, was to put the police in the same, not a worse, position than they would have been in if no police error or misconduct occurred.

Limitations on Searches

A **reasonable search** involves more than justification by an arrest, consent, a search warrant, or extenuating circumstances. **Limitations** on the search itself are set as you have seen. After establishing the right to search, police officers must determine the limitations on that right— limitations imposed by law and interpreted by the courts. General searches are unconstitutional.

The most important limitation imposed upon any search is that the scope must be narrowed. General searches are unconstitutional.

SUMMARY

The constitutional standards for searches and seizures, including arrests, are contained in the Fourth Amendment, which requires that searches and seizures be reasonable and be based on probable cause. As the word implies, *reasonable* means sensible, justifiable, logical, based on reason. Probable cause requires more than mere suspicion. It requires facts or proof that would lead a person of reasonable caution to believe a crime has been committed by a specific individual or premises contain evidence of a crime.

Probable cause may be founded on (1) observation, (2) expertise, (3) circumstantial factors, and (4) information conveyed to the officers, including official sources, victims of crimes, and citizen informants.

The Fourth Amendment is reasonable in protecting the rights of the people while allowing law enforcement the right to investigate crime. It is strong enough to protect citizens but also flexible enough to enable police officers to uphold the Constitution.

The standards established by the Fourth Amendment are enforced by use of the Exclusionary Rule, which states that no evidence can be admitted in a trial unless it is obtained within the standards established in the Fourth Amendment. The federal precedent for this rule is found in the case of *Weeks v. United States*. The state precedent is found in the case of *Mapp v. Ohio*.

Stop and frisk is a form of search and seizure and, as such, is governed by the intent of the Fourth Amendment, which demands that all searches and seizures be based on reason. A stop is not an arrest; the authority to stop and frisk is independent of the power to search or arrest. A frisk, however, is a search. The type of search allowed under stop and frisk is limited to a protective seizure and search for weapons and is not a search for evidence of a crime.

Citizens of the United States are protected against unreasonable arrest (seizure) by the Fourth Amendment. An arrest is usually defined as the taking of a person into custody by the actual restraint of the person or by his or her submission to the custody of the officer so that he or she may be held to answer for a public offense before a judge. Such arrests must be reasonable, and they must be predicated on probable cause.

The Fourth Amendment requires that arrests be made by having a magistrate issue an arrest warrant, but police officers may make an arrest without an arrest warrant in an emergency; for example, for a felony or misdemeanor committed in their presence or for a felony not committed in their presence if they have probable cause. A person can be arrested for a misdemeanor only if (1) there is an arrest warrant or (2) the crime was committed in the officer's presence. A person can be arrested for a felony if (1) there is an arrest warrant, (2) the crime is committed in the presence of an officer, or (3) there is probable cause that the person committed a felony.

Reasonable searches must also meet the standards set forth in the Fourth Amendment. The three principal justifications for a search are (1) it is incidental to a lawful arrest, (2) consent is given, or (3) a search warrant is obtained. The limitations placed on searches incidental to lawful arrest come from the case of *Chimel v. California*, which states that the scope of the search must be narrowed to the area within the suspect's immediate control. The limitations to a search made with consent are that the consent must be free and voluntary, not in response to an implied right to search, and the scope must be limited to the area for which consent has been given. The limitations to a search made with a warrant are stated within the warrant itself.

Most searches require a warrant. A search warrant is a judicial order directing a police officer to search for specific property, seize it, and return it to the court. Probable cause is required for issuance of all warrants. Technically, all searches are to be made under the authority of a search warrant issued by a magistrate. If a search is conducted with a warrant, the burden of proof as to admissibility of evidence seized is on the defense; if it is conducted without a warrant, the burden of proof is on the searching officer and the prosecution.

Police may seize items not specified in the search warrant if they are similar in nature to those items described, if they are related to the particular crime described, or if they are contraband.

When police officers execute a search warrant, they generally announce themselves. They may enter a home by force if they are denied entrance or if no one is home. Two special types of search warrants, nighttime and no-knock, may be requested if the officers fear the objects of the search might be lost, destroyed, or removed.

Warrantless searches, based on probable cause, have been justified in stop and frisk, incidental to a lawful arrest, with consent, in an emergency situation, and when mobility is involved.

The two most frequent challenges to such warrantless searches that may be raised by the defense are that (1) there was insufficient evidence to establish probable cause, so a search warrant would not have been issued by a magistrate, and (2) there was sufficient time to obtain a search warrant.

Special provisions have been made for warrantless searches of cars and other conveyances due to their mobility. Precedents for the warrantless search of an automobile were established by the *Carroll* case, which demonstrated that probable cause must exist along with mobility—the belief that the car or evidence would be gone by the time a search warrant was obtained. It also demonstrated that the right to search was not dependent on the right to arrest but rather on probable cause. The *Chambers* case demonstrated that a car may retain its mobility even though it is impounded. The *Coolidge* case demonstrated that the rule of mobility cannot be applied unless there is actually a risk the vehicle will be moved. A car may also be searched without a warrant if it is an instrumentality of a crime.

A special instance of legal seizure of evidence without a warrant exists in the plain view situation; that is, evidence that is not concealed is inadvertently seen by an officer engaged in lawful activity and is supported by other facts or evidence.

Even when the required conditions are met, certain limitations are placed on the search. The most important limitation imposed upon any search is that the scope must be narrowed. General searches are unconstitutional.

Discussion Questions

1. In popular television programs how are police officers portrayed in relation to protecting citizen's Fourth Amendment rights?

2. Why are the police not given total freedom to help stop crime? Why are they not allowed to use evidence that clearly establishes a person's guilt, no matter how they obtained this evidence?

3. In a state where stop and frisk is legal, can a police officer be sued for stopping and frisking someone?

4. According to Sir Arthur Conan Doyle, author of the Sherlock Holmes mystery stories: "When you have eliminated the impossible, whatever remains, however improbable, must be the truth." Discuss this quotation in light of what you know about lawful arrest.

5. What are the most important factors in determining if and when an arrest occurred?

6. Must all elements of probable cause exist prior to a lawful arrest?

7. Why is the presence of ten officers not considered intimidation when a request to search is made?

8. Have you ever been involved in a search and seizure situation? How was it handled?

9. From what you have learned about search and seizure, do you feel that the restrictions placed upon police officers are reasonable?

10. Why did the Court state that the search in *Coolidge v. New Hampshire* was not valid?

References

Brandstatter, A. F., and Hyman, A. A. *Fundamentals of Law Enforcement.* Beverly Hills, Calif.: Glencoe Press, 1971.

Creamer, J. S. *The Law of Arrest, Search, and Seizure,* 3d ed. New York: Holt, Rinehart, and Winston, 1980.

Klotter, J. C., and Kanovitz, J. R. *Constitutional Law,* 5th ed. Cincinnati: Anderson Publishing, 1985.

SECTION THREE
The Problems and
People Involved

Having looked at police operations in the 1990s and the responsibilities police officers face in the areas of community service, patrol, traffic, investigation, and preservation of civil rights, you are now ready to look at some of the very specific problems and people involved with law enforcement.

Robbery, murder, and rape, the common crimes against people and property, comprise only one area of criminal activity with which police officers deal. They are also involved with much less commonly known crimes such as white-collar crimes, computer crimes, bias crimes, and ritualistic crimes (chapter 13). They also can play a large role in combating the national threat of organized crime (chapter 14). Likewise, local law enforcement is key in dealing with the crisis-proportion drug problem facing the United States (chapter 15).

All these crimes are committed by people—criminals—who must be dealt with by law enforcement officers (chapter 16). A growing problem is the amount of crime committed by gangs (chapter 17). And, not only must law enforcement deal with those who break the law, they must also help those who are victimized (chapter 18).

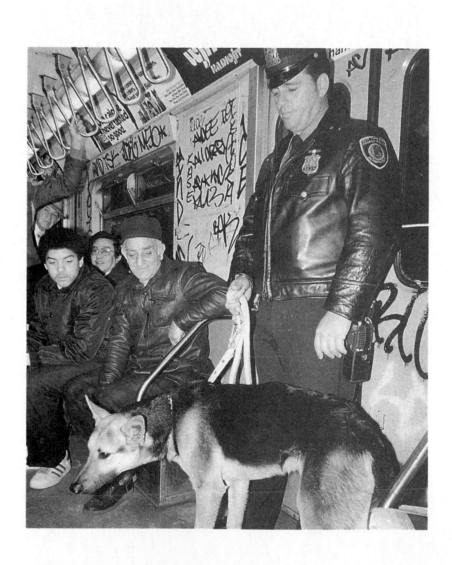

CHAPTER THIRTEEN

Crime in the United States: Special Problems Facing Law Enforcement

No man is above the law and no man is below it; nor do we ask any man's permission when we require him to obey it—Theodore Roosevelt

DO YOU KNOW

What white-collar crime is?

What the most common types of white-collar crime are?

What computer crime may involve?

What three key characteristics of computer-related crime are?

What types of computer-related crime are most frequently committed?

What bias crime is?

What types of bias may be involved?

What a ritual is?

What a ritualistic crime is and what must be investigated in it?

| Introduction | Chapter 4 discussed the major Index crimes, the crimes |

Chapter 4 discussed the major Index crimes, the crimes most familiar to law enforcement and to the general public. Each state has its own specific statutes to define these crimes and assess penalties for them. But a whole other arena of crime is pervasive in the United States, an arena where the laws and the procedures for law enforcement officers to follow are not so clear. This arena includes white-collar crime, computer-related crime, bias crime, and ritualistic crime.

WHITE-COLLAR CRIME

White-collar crime is an occupational or business-related crime. The Part I offense of larceny/theft and several of the Part II offenses can also be classified as white-collar crimes. These crimes often involve billions of dollars and pose an extremely difficult challenge to law enforcement officers.

White-collar crime is occupational or business-related crime.

A special Report of the Bureau of Justice Statistics (1987, p. 1) states:

Although white-collar offenses are less visible than crimes such as burglary and robbery, their overall economic impact may be considerably greater. Among the white–collar cases filed by U.S. Attorneys in the year ending September 30, 1985, more than 140 persons were charged with offenses estimated to involve over $1 million each, and 64 were charged with offenses valued at over $10 million each. In comparison, losses from all bank robberies reported to police in 1985 were under $19 million, and losses from all robberies reported to police in 1985 totaled about $313 million.

In a large southern city, a grand jury brought indictments on thirty-two counts against a vice-president of a bank for embezzling funds. Outstanding community leader, father of several children—a respectable individual in the community was suddenly disgraced. At the same time in a western city, a grand jury brought indictments on twelve counts against a warehouse employee who had taken merchandise from his employer's warehouse, loaded it on a friend's truck, sold it, and divided the profits. The warehouse employee, a family man who attended church regularly, was shunned by his friends and fired by his employer.

Although most people in business are honest, corruption does exist. Security abuses, tax frauds, embezzlements, bribes, and kickbacks frequently occur, often the result of a "look the other way" attitude of co-workers and employers. Not only do employees and employers frequently ignore dishonesty within their businesses, they frequently engage in such practices themselves, rationalizing that they are acquiring something to which they really were entitled. For example, employees who make long-distance calls on an employer's phone or who pad expense accounts may tell themselves that since they are underpaid, this is simply one way of getting what they have coming to them.

When stealing from the boss (company, firm, business), most employees do not consider what they are doing as theft but merely a fringe benefit of the job. Going across the street and taking the same thing from another firm would be considered dishonest—but not when taken from one's own employer.

Eldefonso, Coffey, and Grace (1974, p. 2) note that the existence of white-collar crime has an extremely demoralizing effect upon those who lack material possessions. Such individuals, while not having the opportunity to engage in white-collar crime, may follow the example of illegal means to obtain material gain.

White-collar crime includes: (1) securities theft and fraud, (2) insurance fraud, (3) credit card and check fraud, (4) consumer fraud, illegal competition, and deceptive practices, (5) bankruptcy fraud, (6) embezzlement and pilferage, (7) bribes, kickbacks, and payoffs, and (8) receiving stolen property.

Criminals involved in fraudulent schemes of all types are usually extremely mobile, moving from city to city and state to state, ruining individuals and small businesses.

Securities Theft and Fraud

Securities theft and fraud may be perpetrated by clerks acting independently, by individuals who rob messengers and steal from the mails, or by well-organized rings, one of which was reported as stealing approximately five million dollars worth of stock monthly. Most security thefts involve cooperation of dishonest employees ("inside" people) and may involve counterfeit and bogus securities as well.

Insurance Fraud

Insurance fraud losses lead to higher premiums for consumers. Since insurance is important to businesses and individuals, false claims for life, health, and accident benefits affect almost everyone.

Especially prevalent are fraudulent auto accident claims seeking compensation for treatments for personal injury, time lost from work, and automobile repairs.

Many white-collar crime experts exclude insurance fraud since it is not typically done in the course of a white-collar occupation.

Credit Card and Check Fraud

The billions of checks and millions of credit cards in circulation each year present limitless opportunity for crime. Unauthorized use of credit cards (found, stolen, or counterfeited) results in losses of millions annually.

Check fraud, including checks passed with insufficient funds or with no account, forged checks, counterfeit checks, stolen travelers' checks, money orders, and payroll checks, costs billions annually.

As with insurance fraud, many white-collar crime experts exclude credit card and check fraud since they are not typically done in the course of a white-collar occupation.

Consumer Fraud, Illegal Competition, and Deceptive Practices

Thousands of different schemes have been reported to defraud the public, including offers for "free" articles, advice, vacations, mailing or unordered merchandise, phony contests, recommendations for unneeded repairs, "going-out-of-business" sales, unqualified correspondence schools, and price fixing. Hundreds of other schemes undoubtedly exist but have not been reported because although the victims may realize the swindle, they do not want to admit having been "taken in."

Bankruptcy Fraud

Bankruptcy fraud, also called planned bankruptcy, scam, or bust-out, involves purchasing merchandise on credit from many different suppliers, selling the merchandise for cash that is "hidden," and then claiming bankruptcy, and not paying the creditors. A small business that has extended a large amount of credit to a company that declares bankruptcy (legitimately or not) may be forced out of business. Such an owner may then decide to use the same tactic, rationalizing the fraud as a justified effort to save his or her debt-ridden business.

Embezzlement and Pilferage

Many businesspeople consider embezzlement and pilferage to be their most serious problem. Both are, in effect, theft. To embezzle is to steal or use for oneself money or property entrusted to the person. To pilfer is basically the same, but on a much smaller scale. The pilferer usually takes such things as office supplies, spare parts, and materials rather than money, but the result is the same. Cumulatively, the losses from pilferage may be much greater than what some other dishonest employee might embezzle. Equally dishonest is unauthorized use of company equipment, personnel, and time.

Bribes, Kickbacks, and Payoffs

Bribes, kickbacks, and payoffs are pervasive in the business world and are frequently used to obtain new clients, to keep old clients, to influence decisions, or to obtain favors. They can involve anyone from the custodian to the company president, and they can occur in any aspect of a company's operation.

Receiving Stolen Property

Although classified as a white-collar crime, receiving stolen property frequently occurs in conjunction with crimes such as robbery and burglary. The individual who buys and sells stolen property is of vital importance to the success of most burglars, robbers, and hijackers. Criminals depend upon a "fence" (a professional receiver and seller of stolen property) to convert what they have stolen to cash.

Other Types of White-Collar Crime

Police officers may also be called upon to investigate such white-collar crimes as crimes by businesses, as well as violent white-collar crimes such as selling dangerous products or intentional violation of safety codes. Investigating such crimes is difficult because usually individuals in top management are suspects and, consequently, uncooperative.

Computer-Related Crime

Computer-related crime is a relatively new, yet highly profitable, type of white-collar crime. As noted in the *Washington Post*, December 6, 1976:

> *The federal government is becoming increasingly concerned with the growing misuse of computers to steal, defraud, embezzle, sabotage and blackmail people in private and public agencies. According to a study by the General Accounting Office, 69 computer crimes defrauded federal agencies of $2 million over the last two years. In addition, more than 400 crimes-by-computer cases have been documented over the last eight years with victims losing $200 million.*

The Bureau of Justice Statistics (1983, p. 3) states that "the dramatic growth in high technology has brought with it sensational accounts of computerized 'heists' by sophisticated felons seated safely behind computer terminals."

Computer fraud may involve the input data, the output data, computer time, or the program itself.

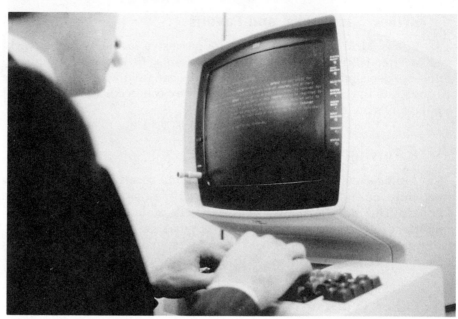

Computer-related crime is a growing type of white-collar crime.

Input data may be altered; for example, fictitious suppliers may be entered, figures may be changed, or data may be removed. Some universities have experienced difficulties with student grades being illegally changed. In a case cited by Dickey (1985, p. 29) the following occurred:

> *A fifteen-year-old hacker with an inexpensive personal computer (PC) and modem [telephone hook-up] accessed patient files in the database of a hospital in California. Purely for self-amusement, he altered case histories and prescriptions. As a result of his interference, a patient suffered a massive allergic reaction, went into shock and nearly died. Eventually the hacker was traced and apprehended. He was a brilliant student—much admired by his teachers—and the son of a bank vice president. When the hacker's case was heard in juvenile court, the judge said that, as serious as the consequences might have been, no one had actually died. He also said that the hospital should not have relied on its computer to the extent that it had. Consequently, the sentence was suspended; since juvenile court records are closed, the hacker has no criminal record.*

Output data may be obtained by unauthorized persons through such means as wiretapping, electromagnetic pickup, or theft of data sheets. An article in the *Las Vegas Review Journal* (March 2, 1986), cited the case of a Charles County, Maryland, teenage hacker who used a home PC to access a list of credit card account numbers and then charged $2,000 worth of computer equipment from seven computer firms in California, Georgia, Michigan, Minnesota, New York, Ohio, and Wisconsin. The crime was discovered when one of the computer firms became suspicious of fraud because several orders were received using different names but the same mailing address. The firm contacted the United States Secret Service in

Baltimore. The youth was subsequently charged with seven counts of theft. Typically, however, output data is misused by an employee, not an outsider.

Computer time may be used for personal use, an example of pilferage to be discussed shortly. Some employees have even used their employer's hardware and company time to set up their own computer services for personal profit.

The computer program itself might be tampered with to add costs to purchased items or to establish a double set of records.

According to Siegel (1983, pp. 332–33):

A number of common techniques are used by computer criminals. In fact, computer theft has become so common that experts have created their own jargon to describe theft styles and methods:

The trojan horse. One computer is used to reprogram another for illicit purposes. In a recent incident, two high-school-age computer users reprogrammed the computer at DePaul University, preventing that institution from using its own processing facilities. The youths were convicted of a misdemeanor.

The salami slice. An employee sets up a dummy account in the company's computerized records. A small amount—even a few pennies—is subtracted from customers' accounts and added to the account of the thief. Even if they detect the loss, the customers don't complain, since a few cents is an insignificant amount to them. The pennies picked up here and there eventually amount to thousands of dollars in losses.

Super-zapping. Most computer programs used in business have built-in antitheft safeguards. However, employees can use a repair or maintenance program to supersede the antitheft program. Some tinkering with the program is required, but the "super-zapper" is soon able to order the system to issue checks to his or her private account.

The logic bomb. A program is secretly attached to the company's computer system. The new program monitors the company's work and waits for a sign of error to appear, some illogic that was designed for the computer to follow. Illogic causes the "logic bomb" to kick into action and exploit the weakness. The way the thief exploits the situation depends on his or her original intent—theft of money, theft of defense secrets, sabotage, and so on.

Impersonation. An unauthorized person uses the identity of an authorized computer user in order to use the computer in his or her stead.

Data leakage. A person illegally obtains data from a computer system by leaking it out in small amounts.

Bennett and Hess (1987, p. 392) describe two classic examples of computer fraud:

Two computer programmers for an oil company plant who were responsible for the company's purchasing files created a fictitious supply company. They altered the company's computer database so that the oil company bought its supplies twice, once from the real supplier and once from the fictitious supply company, resulting in an embezzlement of several million dollars over a two-year period. The crime was discovered during a surprise audit, but the company declined to prosecute, not wanting to publicize how vulnerable its database was or how long it took to discover the embezzlement. Ironically, rather than being dismissed, the two embezzlers were promoted and placed in charge of computer security.

In another instance, a New York bank hired an outside consultant to work with its computer technicians on transferring funds electronically. In the course of his work the consultant observed the access code being used to transfer the funds. He later used this access code to transfer a large sum of money to his own bank account. When the loss was finally discovered, management insisted that everyone in the section take a polygraph test, including the consultant. All except the consultant complied, and all passed. Although management was convinced the consultant had stolen the money, they did not prosecute; they simply changed their access code.

These cases illustrate three key characteristics of computer crimes.

Characteristics of computer-related crime are as follows:

- *Computer crimes are relatively easy to commit and difficult to detect.*
- *Most computer crimes are committed by "insiders."*
- *Most computer crimes are not prosecuted.*

The Data Processing Management Association (DPMA) in Park Ridge, Illinois, conducted a study of one thousand data processing executives in *Fortune* 1000 companies and found that only 2 percent of discovered computer abuses were reported to management or the authorities. The survey also found that only 2 percent of these abuses were committed by people outside the firm (Dickey, 1985, p. 30).

As noted by Bennett and Hess (1987, p. 393):

> *Enormous sums of money and tremendous quantities of information are electronically transferred by computers throughout the nation daily. These transfers present a unique opportunity for the computer thief. In October of 1986, President Reagan signed a bill modernizing the federal wiretap law to protect the privacy of high tech communications. This bill makes it illegal to eavesdrop on electronic mail, video conference calls, conversations on cellular car phones, and computer-to-computer transmissions. Other federal statutes relevant to computer-related crimes include patent laws, espionage and sabotage laws, trade secret laws, the Copyright Act of 1976, and the Financial Privacy Act of 1978.*
>
> *At the state level, computer crime statutes exist in thirty-seven states (Dickey, 1985, p. 34), some being stringent. For example, disclosing the password of a computer system without the owner's consent is considered "unlawful use of a computer." Additionally, in many instances, existing state statutes are applicable to crimes involving computers. (See Table 13–1.)*

The DPMA survey (Dickey, 1985, p. 30) mentioned previously revealed the following:

Table 13–1 **Computer-Related Crime and Current Statutes**

Arson	Intentionally setting fire to a computer center
Burglary	Entering a computer center illegally with the intent to commit a crime therein
Extortion/Blackmail	Making threats against the operator(s) of a computer center to obtain money
Collusion	Working with others to commit a crime
Conspiracy	Several persons agreeing to commit an illegal act
Counterfeit	Copying or imitating computer documents
Embezzlement	Fraudulently converting property to personal use
Espionage	Stealing secret documents or information
Forgery	Issuing false documents
Fraud	Altering accounts or illegally transferring funds
Larceny	Theft of computer parts and materials
Malicious Destruction of Property	Destroying computer hardware or software
Murder	Tampering with life-sustaining computerized equipment resulting in the death of a patient
Receiving Stolen Property	Accepting any goods or information stolen by computer, knowing they were stolen
Sabotage	Intentionally destroying computer information, programs, or hardware
Theft	Stealing goods or money by use of a computer or stealing computer parts and materials

Misuse of computer services made up nearly half of all incidents . . . .
(Misuse could be anything from game playing or using the computer for
personal work to diverting funds or altering records.) Program abuse—
copying or changing programs—was the next most prevalent area (24 per-
cent). Data abuse—diverting information to unauthorized individuals—
was third (22 percent), and hardware abuse—damaging or stealing
computer equipment—was last (5 percent).

The most common types of computer-related crime are misuse of computer
services, program abuse, and data abuse.

Because use of computers in homes, small and large offices, businesses, and government installations will steadily increase, it can be expected that computer-related crimes will be a serious police investigative problem.

BIAS CRIMES

As noted by Lutz (n.d.):

Not a day has passed in the last seven years without someone in the
United States being victimized by hate violence. Harassment, vandalism,

arson, assault and murder motivated by racism, antisemitism or other forms of bigotry—such as homophobia—plague every section of our country. This violence is a largely unrecognized cancer eating away our communities and social institutions. . . .

Ku Klux Klan and neo-nazi groups have increasingly targeted gay and lesbian people for physical attack and intimidation. In addition, a largely spontaneous wave of homophobic violence appears to be sweeping the nation. . . .

The traditional targets of hate violence, black people and other people of color, as well as Jews, remain the single largest target of organized hate violence. . . .

Bigoted violence has become a critical criminal justice issue of the late 1980s.

The Center for Democratic Renewal has documented nearly three thousand acts of bigoted violence between 1980 and 1986.

Bias crimes are crimes motivated by bigotry and hatred against a specific group of people.

Randolph (1988, pp. 128–30) discusses the black student's battle against racism on college campuses: "Racial prejudice is a daily fact of college life. This reality is particularly chilling since black students are attending predominantly white colleges in record numbers, while those attending historically black colleges have declined from 44 percent to 16 percent between 1965 and 1985. . . . America's college campuses are witnessing one of their most turbulent and disturbing periods since the racial unrest of the '60s."

As noted, blacks are not the only target. An article in *Time* magazine, "Open Season on Gays" (Zuckerman 1988, p. 24), states: "AIDS sparks an epidemic of violence against homosexuals." The article claims that according to gay-rights groups, hate-motivated assaults have nearly tripled in recent years. As one person put it: "AIDS has provided a green light to the bashers and the bigots." The article suggests:

Victims who go to the police often find them insensitive or even hostile. . . .

A report released by the National Institute of Justice last fall concluded that "homosexuals are probably the most frequent victims" of hate-motivated violence, but the "criminal-justice system—like the rest of society—has not recognized the seriousness" of the problem.

Types of bias include racial, religious, national origin, sex, age, disability, and sexual orientation.

Offenses frequently involved in bias crimes include cross burning, swastika painting, bombing, hanging in effigy, disturbing a public meeting, graffiti, obscene letters or phone calls, or face-to-face oral abuse. Assault is becoming more frequent in bias crimes, some even resulting in death.

Neo-Nazi Skinheads

A special report of the Anti-Defamation League (ADL), *Young and Violent: The Growing Menace of America's Neo-Nazi Skinheads* (1988, p. 1) states:

> The Skinheads are shaven-headed youths who sport Nazi insignia and preach violence against Blacks, Hispanics, Jews, Asians and homosexuals. They range in age from about thirteen to twenty-five, with males outnumering females. The typical skinhead has either a shaved head or closely cropped hair; is tatooed with Nazi and/or Satanic symbols; wears jeans, suspenders and "Doc Martens," a heavy boot of British make, sometimes used to kick or stomp on victims.

According to an ADL survey conducted through its thirty-one regional offices, the number of racist Skinheads has risen to about two thousand, located in twenty-one states. The ADL contends: "The rise in the number of Skinheads has been paralleled by an increase in the amount of violent crime they have committed, including two homicides and numerous shootings, beatings and stabbings, mostly directed against members of minority groups."

Skinheads at a rally.

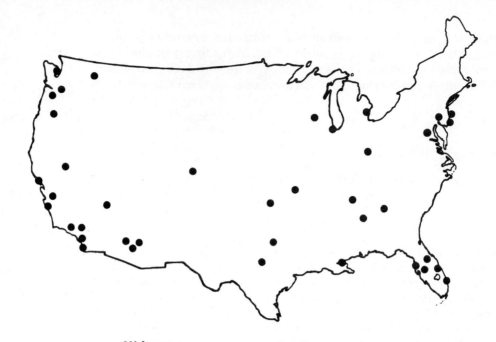

West	Midwest	South	East
Arizona Phoenix Scottsdale Tempe	**Illinois** Chicago	**Alabama** Birmingham	**Maryland** Baltimore Westminster Washington D.C. (suburbs)
California San Diego Riverside Orange County Ventura County Salinas Hollister San Francisco	**Michigan** Detroit Grand Rapids **Missouri** Springfield **Ohio** Cincinnati	**Georgia** Atlanta **Florida** Tampa Clearwater Miami Beach Pinellas County Broward County Orlando	**New Jersey** North Jersey Atlantic City **Pennsylvania** Philadelphia
Colorado Denver	**Wisconsin** Milwaukee	**Louisiana** New Orleans	
Nevada Las Vegas Reno		**Oklahoma** Oklahoma City Tulsa	
Oregon Portland Salem		**Texas** Austin Dallas	
Washington Seattle Spokane Vancouver		**Tennessee** Memphis	

Source: *Young and Violent: The Growing Menace of America's Neo-Nazi Skinheads,* Anti-Defamation League of B'nai B'rith, 1988.

Figure 13–1   **Locations Where Skinhead Groups Have Been Operating**

One hate group with close links with the Skinheads is WAR, headed by Tom Metzger, a television repairman from California and a former Grand Dragon of the California Ku Klux Klan. Metzger's twenty-year-old son John heads up WAR's affiliated Aryan Youth Movement (AYM). In addition to their links with Tom Metzger's organizations, Skinheads also participate in joint activities with other hate groups, especially the Ku Klux Klan.

The ADL (1988, p. 28) describes the Skinheads as "undisciplined, violence-prone, . . . obvious misfits. . . .Besides their tendency to commit violence against outsiders, the Skinhead gangs have severe internal problems. There is substantial evidence of drug use, Satanism, intragang violence, theft and all the other sociopathic tendencies to be found these days on the outer fringes of the youth culture." The ADL (1988, p. 29) states that Skinheads "typically promote their views through stickers, graffiti, the distribution of such hate publication as WAR, and records bearing lyrics of their 'white power' rock songs."

The ADL stresses that not all juveniles with shaved heads are neo-Nazis and that, in fact, some are very antiracist and have been targets of the neo-Nazi Skinheads.

RITUALISTIC CRIME

Ritualistic crimes include unlawful activities performed by people involved with the occult, witchcraft, vodoo, Satanism, and black magic.

Rituals have a rich heritage. The Egyptians used amulets for good luck charms to ward off evil or to bring about good fortune. The Greeks practiced several forms of ritual, including hydromancy, similar to our wishing wells. They would throw bread onto a body of water: if it sunk they would have good luck, and if it floated they would have bad luck. Little wonder we throw pennies rather than bread into wishing wells. They also put much faith in astrology and the signs of the zodiac.

The Romans, too, practiced rituals, primarily fertility rites, including eating partridge flesh and fish eggs. Later in Europe and in the United States, witchcraft became a focus. In Europe over 200,000 witches were killed for their beliefs.

Most people have some sort of superstition they believe in, for example, breaking a mirror, or walking under a ladder bringing bad luck, finding a four-leaf clover bringing good luck, and the like. And many of us grew up with "supernatural" beings in our lives such as the tooth fairy, the Easter Bunny, and even Santa Claus.

Indeed, all recognized religions have rituals meaningful to their members.

A ritual is a system of rites, a ceremonial act.

Satanic symbols spray-painted on a fence.

Rituals may include symbols, artifacts, words, gestures, costumes, music, almost anything imaginable. They are heavily linked to a belief system.

Whether this belief system is a formal religion or not, it is protected by the First Amendment right to worship as one wishes.

When the rituals of a group involve crimes such as desecration of cemeteries, grave robbing, cruelty to animals, child sexual abuse, and even murder, it becomes a problem for law enforcement.

As noted by Los Angeles Police Department Investigator Patrick Metoyer, "We don't investigate warlocks, satanists, vampires, Jews, Catholics, or Protestants. We investigate *crime*."

Satanic Cults

The Church of the Final Judgment is an umbrella satanic cult believed to have members across the country. The *Church of Satan* was organized in 1966 in San Francisco by Anton LaVey, a former circus performer and police photographer. LaVey, who calls himself the High Priest of Satan, published *Satanic Rituals* and *The Satanic Bible*, a book that outsells the Christian Bible in many bookstores. The Church of Satan has grown to over fifty thousand members nationwide.

Cults such as these have one strong leader to whom all members give allegiance. Often the leader is worshipped as an anti-God—the embodiment of Satan and evil. The cult meets the needs of people who feel they have no self-identity and no power. One major drawing point of Satanism is that anything goes. Whatever one wants, one does.

Young people become involved in Satanism because it gives them a feeling of belonging, worth, and power. Members are often youths who do

AC/DC	ANTI-CHRIST DEVIL CHILD
ZOSO	THREE HEADED DOG GUARDS GATE TO HELL
S	SATAN/STONER
MARKOŞ	ABRACADABRA
FFF	ANTI-CHRIST
666	ANTI-CHRIST
	ANTI-CHRIST
NATAS	SATAN REVERSED
6,9,13,XIII	OCCULT NUMBERS
	HORNS AND TAIL ADDED TO ANY LETTER
	LIGHTNING BOLT HEAVEN TO HELL STRENGTH
	SWASTIKA
	ANTI-CHRIST CROSS OF CONFUSION

PENTAGRAM WHITE MAGIC

PENTAGRAM UPSIDE DOWN STAR SIGN OF OCCULT

HEXAGRAM CIRCLE

INFINITY-CONTAINMENT CONTROL OF EVIL POWER

ANK

LUCIFER MORNING STAR

Source: Young and Violent: *The Growing Menace of Americas' Neo-Nazi Skinheads*, Anti-Defamation League of B'nai B'rith, 1988.

Figure 13–2   Signs of Satan

not fit in with their peers. In the cult they are accepted and given attention. They are often influenced by heavy metal music and may dress in a "punk" style. Members of cults frequently wear pentagrams and inverted crosses. Dark clothing is common, as is self-mutilation such as safety pins through nipples.

Chief Donald Story (1987, p. 81) warns that "ritualistic crimes are occurring with greater frequency in America. However, in many instances police officers do not realize that homicides, assaults, kidnappings, child abuse, animal mutilations or suicides are linked with the occult."

Satanic Rituals   Satanic rituals often include use of robes (red or black), daggers, candles, altars, and pentagrams. They often include chanting, occur at night, and are conducted in strict secrecy. According to Story (p. 83): "Satanists believe that there is a power of energy within the souls and bodies of animals and humans and that that power can be released and absorbed following rituals ranging from sexual activity to murder and cannibalism." He notes that the rituals often include sacrificing animals and that during the rituals the hearts, eyes, and tongues may be removed from goats, lambs, chickens, and doves. Drinking blood is also common.

Satanic rituals often include criminal actions. According to the National School Safety Center (1988, p. 21):

> Satanic references and symbols have been associated with the "Son of Sam" serial murders (New York, 1977), the McMartin Preschool child molestation case (Los Angeles, 1984), and, most recently, the "Night Stalker" homicides (Los Angeles and San Francisco, 1985). Animal mutilations, exhumation of bodies and church desecrations are becoming alarmingly prevalent.

Zorn (1986) states: "Devil worship was said to be involved in a series of multilation killings in Cook and DuPage Counties in 1981 and 1982, in which four men abducted and murdered up to eighteen young women. One of the men confessed to police that several parts of the women's bodies were used in sexual and cannibalistic rituals devoted to Satan."

And according to Stratford (1988, pp. 200–201), people who have escaped from satanic cults have "horror stories" to tell.

> One young man was a high priest in Satanism until he became a born-again Christian. On the "Oprah Winfrey Show" he said, "I started when I was at the age of five. I started out in what is known as the earth mother religion. Eventually I was told that it was Satan we were worshipping." He told about how four times a year his group performed human sacrifices. "The victims are easily picked up. They are wandering teenagers looking for a good time, runaways, skid-row bums, paper boys. . . ."
>
> On November 19, 1987, Geraldo Rivera interviewed a former Satanic priestess who identified herself only as Elain. "At seventeen, I saw my first sacrifice—a live baby," she said on the CBS network television program. "They carved the heart out of this child. I was told that if I said anything, I would be killed in such a manner or worse. These people mean what they say. They absolutely, totally control the children and the young, the teenagers, in absolute total fear."

Investigating Ritualistic Crime

Story (1987, p. 83) offers some specific suggestions for investigating ritualistic crime:

At the crime scene, look for indications of a mockery of Christian symbols—items such as inverted crosses, candles or candle drippings, vandalized Christian artifacts and unusual drawings or a non-discernable alphabet used in writings or graffiti.

Search for animal parts, blood, and books on Satanism. The presence of altars, bowls with colored salt, and skulls are very indicative.

In homicide cases, pay close attention to the position of the body. Missing body parts and bodily multilation are important characteristics to note. The location of wounds and the type of wounds may have a strong bearing on determining if the crime was satanic in nature.

Other indicators at a crime scene include oils or incense found on the body or close by, and human or animal feces found on the body, or in the body during a post mortem examination. The stomach contents can be of vital importance in determining what occurred just prior to death.

In summary, look for symbolism, animal mutilation, candles, bones or anything out of the ordinary.

Ritualistic Child Abuse

Of great concern to law enforcement is growing evidence of rather widespread ritualistic abuse of children. In a newsletter, ''Believe the Children,'' one ''survivor'' of ritualistic crime states:

I must speak, for the children no one will believe, for the adults wandering in utter pain and confusion not knowing why they are in such agony, and for the boy whose life was taken in front of me, an innocent, precious life destroyed at the hand of evil and ruthless forces.

Please, believe the children. This is no fantasy. It is happening, and it has been happening for many years. Satanic abusers are counting on the children never talking, and the adults not believing them if they do, which is why they make their rituals so bizarre.

Ritualistic crime is a problem law enforcement must become aware of and skilled at investigating.

A ritualistic crime is an unlawful act committed during a ceremony related to a belief system. It is the crime, not the belief system, that must be investigated.

Normal investigative techniques are not effective with ritualistic crime. Usually multiple victims and multiple suspects are involved, and often logic will not work. Horror stories of murders may in actuality be some sort of staged illusion to gain control of the cult members. Ritualistic crimes add yet another dimension to the challenge of law enforcement.

SUMMARY

White-collar crime—occupational or business-related crime—includes fraud involving securities, insurance, credit cards, checks, and bankruptcy, as well as illegal competition, deceptive practices, embezzlement and pilferage, bribes, kickbacks, payoffs, and receiving stolen property. White-collar crime involves billions of dollars annually.

Computer fraud may involve the input data, the output data, computer time, or the program itself. Computer crimes are relatively easy to commit and difficult to detect. Most are committed by "insiders," and most are not prosecuted. The most common types of computer crime are misues of computer services, program abuse, and data abuse.

Bias crimes are crimes motivated by bigotry and hatred against a specific group of people. Types of bias include racial, religious, national origin, sex, age, disability, and sexual orientation.

A ritual is a system of rites, a ceremonial act. A ritualistic crime is an unlawful act committed during a ceremony related to a belief system. It is the crime, not the belief system, that must be investigated.

DISCUSSION QUESTIONS

1. What are some of the reasons employees steal from employers?

2. Do you feel that employees who steal from employers should have the alternative of reimbursement rather than going to court?

3. Should misuse of a credit card be considered a hazard of doing business and not be classified in the criminal category?

4. Should all crimes committed through the use of a computer be violations of federal law?

5. Are there any methods police might educate computer owners about so that computer crime might be more preventable?

6. Should computer hackers pay a heavy penalty for their misdeeds?

7. Describe what a bias crime might consist of.

8. Should additional penalties be imposed on people found guilty of committing bias crimes?

9. How should people guilty of participating in ritualistic crimes be treated in the criminal justice system?

10. What evidence would lead you to believe a Satanic ritual may have taken place?

REFERENCES

Anti-Defamation League of B'nai B'rith/Civil Rights Division. An ADL Special Report. *Young and Violent: The Growing Menace of America's Neo-Nazi Skinheads.* New York, NY 1988.

Bennet, W., and Hess, K. M. *Criminal Investigation,* 2d ed. St. Paul, Minn.: West Publishing Company, 1987.

Dickey, S. "Is Getting in Getting out of Control?" *Today's Office,* September 1985, pp. 29–36.

Eldefonso, E.; Coffey, A.; and Grace, R. C. *Principles of Law Enforcement.* New York: John Wiley & Sons, 1974, 1983.

Lutz, C. "They Don't All Wear Sheets: A Chronology of Facist and Far Right Violence— 1980–1986" (pamphlet), Center for Democratic Renewal. Published by the Division of Church and Society of the National Council of the Churches of Christ in the U.S.A. (no date).

National School Safety Center. *Gangs in Schools: Breaking Up Is Hard to Do.* Malibu, Calif.: Pepperdine University Press, 1988.

Randolph, L. B. "Black Students Battle Racism on College Campuses," *Ebony*, December 1988, pp. 126–30.

Siegel, L.J. *Criminology.* St. Paul, Minn: West Publishing Company, 1983.

Story, D. W. "Ritualistic Crime: A New Challenge to Law Enforcement." *Law and Order*, September 1987, pp. 81–83.

Stratford, L. *Satan's Underground.* Eugene, Oreg.: Harvest House Publishers, 1988.

Terry, M. *The Ultimate Evil: An Investigation into America's Most Dangerous Satanic Cult.* Garden City, N.Y.: Doubleday, 1987.

"White Collar Crime," Bureau of Justice Statistics, Special Report, U.S. Dept. of Justice September, 1981, pp. 1–8.

Zorn, E. "Satan Worship Called Dangerous, Growing," *The Chicago Tribune*, April 27, 1986.

Zuckerman, L. "Open Season on Gays," *Time*, vol. 131, no. 19, March 7, 1988, p. 24.

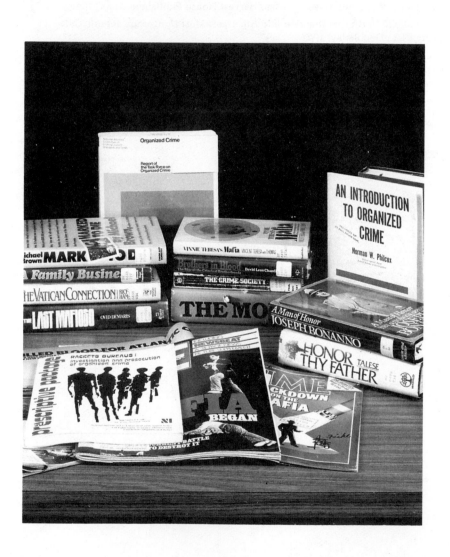

Organized Crime in the United States: A National Threat

Organized crime will put a man in the White House some day, and he won't know it until they hand him the bill.—Ralph Salerno

DO YOU KNOW

How organized crime is usually defined?

What two characteristics of organized crime set it apart from other crimes committed by a group of individuals?

What names organized crime is known by?

What types of crime are most frequently engaged in by members of organized crime?

What is organized crime's largest source of revenue?

What specific threats organized crime poses to the United States?

What special problems organized crime presents to law enforcement?

What major federal legislation has been enacted to deal with organized crime?

Chapter 14

According to the National Advisory Committee on Criminal Justice Standards and Goals (1976, p. 7):

> *Organized crime exists in both urban and rural areas. . . . Organized crime income is presently invested in a variety of businesses, including liquor establishments, nightclubs, health spas, travel agencies, massage parlors, motels, real estate agencies, nursing homes, and pornographic book stores and films. There are no "safe" enterprises, for organized crime may choose to infiltrate and take over wherever there is potential profit. Tactics adopted by organized crime include homicide, arson, and intimidation.*

ORGANIZED CRIME DEFINED

Definitions of **organized crime** vary from lengthy, detailed statements to simple eleven-word definitions. California's definition of organized crime is one of the more detailed (Committee on Criminal Justice Standards and Goals 1976, p. 214):

> *Organized crime consists of two or more persons who, with continuity of purpose, engage in one or more of the following activities:*
> *1. The supplying of illegal goods and services, that is, vice, loansharking, etc. . . .*
> *2. Predatory crime, for example theft, assault, etc. . . .*
> *Several distinct types of criminal activity fall within this definition of organized crime. The types may be grouped into five general categories:*
> *1. Racketeering.*
> *2. Vice operations (narcotics, prostitution, loansharking, gambling).*
> *3. Theft/fence rings (fraud, bunco schemes, fraudulent document passers, burglary rings, car thieves, truck hijackers).*
> *4. Gangs (youth gangs, outlaw motorcycle gangs, prison gangs).*
> *5. Terrorists.*

A New York Conference on Combatting Organized Crime (Office of the New York Counsel to the Governor 1966) defined organized crime as follows:

> *Organized crime is the product of a self-perpetuating, criminal conspiracy to wring exhorbitant profits from our society by any means—fair and foul, legal and illegal. Despite personnel changes, the conspiratorial entity continues. It is a malignant parasite which fattens on human weakness. It survives on fear and corruption. By one or another means, it obtains a high degree of immunity from the law. It is totalitarian in its organization. A way of life, it imposes rigid discipline on underlings who do the dirty work while the top men of organized crime are generally insulated from the criminal act and the consequent danger of prosecution.*

Rhodes (1984, p. 46) cites a 1967 Task Force Report that describes organized crime as a "society":

> *Organized crime is a society that seeks to operate outside the control of the American people and their governments. It involves thousands of*

criminals, working within structures as complex as those of any large corporation, subject to laws more rigidly enforced than those of legitimate governments. Its actions are not impulsive, but rather the result of intricate conspiracies, carried on over many years and aimed at gaining control over whole fields of activity in order to amass huge profits.

And, as noted by Rhodes (1984, p. 47), by 1971 the National Advisory Commission recognized the wide variety of types of organized crime in its definition.

Organized crime is a type of conspiratorial crime, sometimes involving the hierarchial coordination of a number of persons in the planning of illegal acts or in the pursuit of a legitimate objective by unlawful means. Organized crime involves continuous commitment by key members, although some individuals with specialized skills may participate only briefly in the ongoing conspiracies.

The Task Force on Organized Crime (National Advisory Council, p. 7) notes:

In nonlegal terms, organized crime has been called everything from nonexistent to a vast conspiracy. As one observer of the organized crime scene noted, "For most purposes the term 'organized crime' has no precise legal configuration, although some specific attributes of syndicated criminal operations can be accurately defined."

Another problem encountered in discussing the problem of organized crime and possible solutions to it is the fact that organized crime itself is not illegal. According to Cressey (1969, p. 229):

It is not against the law for an individual or group of individuals rationally to plan, establish, develop, and administer an organization designed for the perpetration of crime. Neither is it against the law for a person to participate in such an organization. What is against the law is bet-taking, usury, smuggling and selling narcotics and untaxed liquor, extortion, murder, and conspiracy to commit these and other specific crimes. Because "organized crime" is merely a social category, rather than a legal category, police and other governmental agencies cannot even routinely compile information on it as they do for other categories of crime.

Organized crime is a type of conspiratorial crime, sometimes involving the hierarchial coordination of a number of persons in the planning and execution of illegal acts or in the pursuit of a legitimate objective by unlawful means. Organized crime involves continuous commitment by key members, although some individuals with specialized skills may participate only briefly in the ongoing conspiracies.

Says Rowan (1986, p. 24):

Crime pays. Annual gross income from the rackets will probably exceed $50 billion this year. That makes the mob's business greater than all U.S. iron, steel, copper, and aluminum manufacturing combined, or about 1.1% of GNP. . . . They [the figures] do not include billions more brought in from the mob's diversification into such legitimate enterprises as entertainment, construction, trucking and food and liquor wholesaling . . . the mob's hold on the economy stifles competition and siphons off capital, resulting in a loss of some 400,000 jobs. . . . Since organized-crime members cheat on taxes, the rest of the population will pay an estimated $6.5 billion more to the Internal Revenue Service this year.

DISTINCTIVE CHARACTERISTICS OF ORGANIZED CRIME

All crime is a threat to our country, but organized crime poses a unique threat. Two features of organized crime, corruption and enforcement powers, set it apart from other types of crime and make it especially threatening, not only to police officers, but to our entire democratic process.

Organized crime is distinct from other forms of crime in that it is characterized by corruption and enforcement powers.

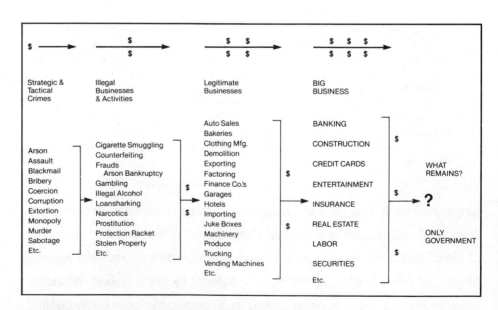

Source: *The Crime Confederation* by Ralph Salerno and John Tompkins. Copyright © 1969 by Ralph Salerno and John S. Tompkins. Used by permission of Doubleday & Company, Inc.

Figure 14–1   **The Classic Pattern of Organized Crime**

Corruption

The President's Commission on Law Enforcement and Administration (1967, p. 241) drew the following conclusions about organized crime in the United States:

> In many ways organized crime is the most sinister kind of crime in America. The men who control it have become rich and powerful by encouraging the needy to gamble, by luring the troubled to destroy themselves with drugs, by extorting profits from honest and hardworking businessmen, by collecting usury from those in financial plight, by maiming or murdering those who oppose them, by bribing those sworn to destroy them. Organized crime is not merely a few preying on a few. In a very real sense, it is dedicated to subverting not only American institutions, but the very decency and integrity that are the most cherished attributes of a free society. As the leaders of Cosa Nostra and their racketeering allies pursue their conspiracy unmolested, in open and continuous defiance of the law, they preach a sermon that all too many Americans heed: The government is for sale; lawlessness is the road to wealth; honesty is a pitfall and morality a trap for suckers.

Corruption poses an extremely serious threat to police professionalism, discipline, and efficiency, and the greatest source of that corruption is organized crime. (The types of corruption associated with organized crime are illustrated in table 14–1.)

Enforcement Powers

A second unique characteristic of organized crime is the use of enforcement activities. Perhaps the gravest threat of organized crime is this assumption of enforcement powers. In our society, only legitimate government has the power to coerce its citizens through due process and the criminal justice system. When another group, such as organized crime, usurps that coercive power, it nullifies our legitimate government.

Organized crime usually has one or more fixed positions for "enforcers," who maintain organizational integrity by arranging for the maiming and killing of recalcitrant members and those who oppose them.

Unfortunately, organized crime's violent tactics seem to have caught the public's fancy, as evidenced by the tremendous success of books and movies about the Mafia. The public interest in gangsters' activities implies an element of voyeurism in participating vicariously in something illegal, yet exotic and tacitly approved. Because of the popularity of books and movies concerning organized crime, many Americans are much more aware of its existence, but few realize the true threat it poses to our society.

Organized crime has many names including the mob, the syndicate, the rackets, the Mafia, and Cosa Nostra.

Table 14–1 A Typology of Organized Crime Payoffs

Participants	How Obligations Are Incurred	How the Debts Are Paid
Elected officials (federal)	Support in political campaigns. Trips, vacations on company expense accounts, cash through foundations, and cash bribes through lobbyists, etc.	Political appointments Contracts Personal favors Paroles, pardons
Appointed staff	Campaign workers Liaison with revenue sources Cash payoffs	Hired as staff worker Retains contact with revenue sources Conducts business for elected official
The elected official	*State* Campaign contributions Trips on private accounts Cash through lobbyists Tips on investments, i.e., public franchises and licenses *Local* Campaign contributions Promise to self-interest groups—gamblers, etc. Money to citizens' committees during preelection campaign Cash payoffs through lobbyists	Contracts Allocations of franchises Granting license such as liquor Contracts for local service—garbage, ambulance, towing, etc. Abstain from enforcing certain type of laws
The judge	*All Levels* Campaign contributions Cash payoffs	Favorable decisions Probation, parole and select court assignment
The lawyer	Client contacts and referrals Campaign workers Liaison with business and criminal clientele Cash payoffs (fees)	Appointments to positions to keep contacts with proper clients Consultants on contracts, crime commissions, etc.
The police	*All Levels* Political patronage Campaign contributions to elected offices Budget manipulation Cash payoffs	Select enforcement methods Preferential treatment in the degree of enforcement Lack of enforcement

Source: Denny F. Pace, Jimmie C. Styles, Organized Crime: Concepts and Control © 1975, p. 31. Reprinted by permission of Prentice-Hall, Inc., Englewood Cliffs, New Jersey.

THE STRUCTURE OF ORGANIZED CRIME

Each group of organized criminals is known as a family, with membership varying from as many as seven hundred to as few as twenty (President's Commission on Law Enforcement and Administration of Justice 1967, p. 193):

> *Each family can participate in the full range of activities in which orga-*
> *nized crime generally is known to engage. Family organization is ratio-*
> *nally designed with an integrated set of positions geared to maximize*
> *profits. Like any large corporation, the organization functions regardless*
> *of personnel changes, and no individual—not even the leader—is indis-*
> *pensable. If he dies or goes to jail, business goes on.*

The hierarchial structure of the families resembles that of the Mafia groups that have operated for almost a century on the island of Sicily. *Theft of the Nation* (Cressey 1969) describes in detail the national structure as well as the intricate structure of the family itself.

The **Commission,** also called the "High Commission," the "Grand Council," the "Administration," the "Roundtable," and the "Inner Circle," is a combination board of business directors, legislators, supreme court justices, and arbitrators, but its primary function is judicial.

The Commission is the ultimate authority on organizational disagreements and is made up of nine to twelve bosses of the most powerful families in the country. Some families do not have members on the Commission, but they usually have a specified Commission member to look after their interests. Commissioners are not equal in power and authority; informal understandings give one member authority over another.

Within the family itself, an intricate structure is established. Each family is headed by one person, a boss, who maintains order and maximizes profits. The boss is subject only to the national advisory group, the Commission; his authority in all family matters is absolute.

Each boss has an *underboss*, a vice-president or deputy director, who collects information, relays messages, passes instructions down to his own underlings, and acts for the boss in his absence.

The boss also has a *consigliere* (counselor or advisor) who is on the same level as the underboss but who operates in a staff capacity. He is often an elder member of the family, partially retired from a criminal career, who gives advice to family members including the boss and underboss; therefore, he has great influence and power.

Below the underboss are the *caporegime* (lieutenants), lower-echelon personnel. Some caporegime serve as buffers between the top members of the family and the law. To maintain their insulation from the police, the boss will usually insist that all commands, information, complaints, and money flow through a trusted go-between. A caporegima does not make decisions or assume any of the boss's authority.

Other caporegime are chiefs of operating units that vary with the size and activities of particular families. The caporegima often has one or two associates who work closely with him, carrying orders, information, and money to the people in his unit. The caporegima is similar to a plant supervisor or sales manager.

The lowest level members of the family are the *soldiers* or "button men" who report to the caporegima. Soldiers may operate illicit enterprises such as loansharking operations, dice games, bookmaking operations, smuggling operations, or vending machine businesses on a commission basis. Or they may "own" the business and pay a percentage to the organization for the right to operate. Frequently soldiers form partnerships with one another or with caporegime. Some soldiers and most upper-echelon family members are involved in more than one enterprise.

The soldiers oversee a large number of employees, not family members and not necessarily Italians. Employees do most of the actual work, but they have no buffers or insulation from the law. They take bets, answer phones, sell drugs, make book, and work in legitimate businesses. For example, in a major lottery business that operated in black neighborhoods in Chicago, the workers were blacks, the bankers for the lottery were Japanese-Americans, but the game, including the banking operation, was licensed for a fee by a family member.

The Chain of Command

The hierarchy or chain of command within a family is illustrated in figure 14–2. Notice that the soldiers are responsible for corruption of police and public officials as well as for exercising control (enforcing). Notice also the illegal activities as well as the legitimate businesses in which organized crime is involved. It should also be noted, however, that not all who study organized crime agree with this description of organized crime as a clear organizational hierarchy.

THE NATURE AND EXTENT OF ORGANIZED CRIME ACTIVITIES IN THE UNITED STATES

The diversified yet interrelated nature of organized crime activities is evident in the Task Force Report (National Advisory Council, pp. 10–12):

> Gambling has long been a traditional arena for organized crime, and is one area law enforcement officials fear that there may be attempts by organized crime elements to take over any gambling operations that may be legalized in the future. As for other activities, the drug business (notably cocaine trafficing) is growing; pornography also is showing astronomical distribution profits. Loansharking is found to be tied into several other activities, including gambling, and arson and fraud are tied into insurance irregularities.
>
> There are also large, organized hijacking rings, armed robbery groups, and increasing vehicle losses, including heavy equipment. Untaxed cigarettes are another major problem. Credit card and stock frauds, sale of stolen and counterfeit securities, and the manufacture and distribution of counterfeit money are among prevalent white-collar crimes.
>
> There apparently is a link between organized crime and street crime where drug operations, fencing, gambling, and certain burglaries are concerned.
>
> Drug addicts pose a major problem in terms of burglaries. Some law enforcement people believe that most established crime figures began their careers in street crime operations. They also point to ties between organized crime and thefts of credit cards, airline tickets, securities, and

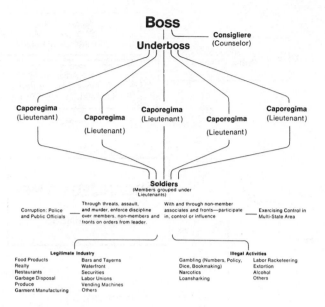

Source: *The Challenge of Crime in a Free Society.* 1967, p. 194, President's Commission on Law Enforcement and Administration of Justice.

Figure 14–2   An Organized Crime Family

money. They believe that channels controlled by organized crime are used to launder stolen money and to distribute stolen credit cards.

The relationship between corruption and street crime also is important, with elements creating a subculture in which certain people believe they are above the law. In some communities their impact is so strong that they in fact become the law, maintaining a well-insulated position and buying official protection.

Legitimate businesses are not only infiltrated or manipulated, but also are taken over by organized crime. For example, the liquor industry is a primary arena for organized crime operations—one often ignored in crime reports and one that benefits from weaknesses in law enforcement. Alcoholic beverage outlets are the underworld's retail market for all its goods and activities, and tax fraud is a frequent occurrence in connection with liquor operations.

Another vulnerable area is the vending machine industry—whether the machines are operated for services, entertainment, or other purposes. Because they involve large cash flows, these machines are a growing operational area for organized crime.

Organized crime figures are believed to have influence over the banking industries, grand juries, and some members of the legal profession.

Organized crime is heavily involved in gambling, drugs, prostitution, pornography, loansharking, and infiltration of legitimate businesses.

The web of organized crime, a portion of which is shown
above, reaches into every part of the nation and affects
all levels of society.

Source: Courtesy of the Federal Bureau of Investigation.

Figure 14–3   **The Web of Organized Crime**

Gambling

Illegal gambling (placing bets with bookmakers) is a billion-dollar
business in the United States. It occurs throughout the country, with
organized crime maintaining control by violence and by providing
services including protection, sharing of financial risk (layoffs), legal
assistance, and financial aid.

Wagers on football are most popular. Organized crime often either
controls gambling operations or takes a cut of someone else's operation.
The " street people" (bookies) are part of the organized crime network, but
they are not part of organized crime itself, and they know little about it.

Organized crime is also involved in legal gambling, such as the
casinos in Las Vegas, race tracks throughout the country, and even legal
charity games. Only lotteries seem to have escaped the infiltration of
organized crime.

Without participation of "law-abiding" citizens, organized crime would lose billions of dollars and much of its power. Unfortunately, countless millions of citizens contribute to the wealth and power of organized crime by making illegal bets. The benefits to the bettor are numerous, even when legitimate games are available. Illegal games offer greater variety, better odds, regular service, and a fast, guaranteed payoff. The bettor can phone in bets, charge them, preserve anonymity, and avoid having to pay taxes on winnings. These advantages offset the risks of getting caught or becoming indebted to organized crime.

Sports betting, supported by millions of American citizens, is organized crime's largest source of revenue.

Betting on Sports   Most bets are made on football, baseball, and basketball, both professional and college. Although the majority of bets are made between acquaintances, the vast majority of money wagered is bet through bookmakers. The bookie handles larger bets, which cannot comfortably be made between friends, and acts as a broker for those who want to bet large amounts of money on a given team.

Many bookmakers subscribe to a national handicapping service, which provides detailed information about the teams playing and a list of point spreads. The bookmaker begins the day on a telephone, with a call to the biggest book in town, getting the opening odds or point spreads on the day's games. In exchange, for this service, the bookmaker bets approximately $1,000 a month with the "big man," who has obtained the line from a syndicate in a distant city and who places at least $5,000 a month with the syndicate in exchange for its expertly calculated line.

The bookmaker often makes calls from public phone booths since federal authorities frequently check telephone bills to see who is being called and where they are located.

When the bettors call in, the bookie writes down the wagers on a single sheet of paper, which can be stuffed under a floorboard or into a slit in a door if raided. Some bookies use combustible paper treated chemically to vanish in a puff of smoke when touched with a cigarette or match, leaving no ashes. Other bookies use watersoluable paper, which disintegrates when dropped into a toilet or sink, leaving no evidence.

The Numbers Game   Betting on numbers is legal in a few states, but operating a numbers game is not legal. The most popular form of the numbers game consists of a player choosing any three-digit number from 0 to 999. The player has one in a thousand chances to win. The winning number is determined by betting totals or payoff odds on selected races at horse-racing tracks. The two most common systems are the Brooklyn System and the New York System.

The Brooklyn number is the last three digits of the track's total pari-mutuel handle for the day. The New York number is more complicated, combining the payoff odds for win, place, and show horses in the first seven races. Because the first digit is calculated after the third race, the second digit after the fifth race, and the last digit after the seventh race, the New York number is often referred to as playing 3-5-7.

Numbers are played in offices, factories, and residential areas. The numbers organization has three layers. At the bottom are many runners and collectors who report to a smaller number of controllers, who are the agents or associates of a relative handful of bankers at the top. The runner, controller, and banker are somewhat comparable to salesperson, district manager, and president in a legitimate business.

Illegal numbers game operators require several services, including access to large amounts of money in case they are heavily hit and protection from the law. Organized crime's capital and contacts put it in a position to provide the money and the protection. Since the numbers game is the most visible of organized crime's activities, it is peculiarly susceptible to police interference and requires an extensive network of contacts with public officials at many levels. Therefore, it provides an entry point to the law enforcement structure. Corruption related to the numbers game is pervasive, affecting arrests, investigations, prosecutions, and sentencing.

Drugs

Organized crime's involvement in drugs concentrates on heroin and cocaine, a trade made to order because of its large demand, substantial profit, and need for an efficient organization with a good deal of capital as well as street-level protection.

The sale of narcotics is usually organized like a legitimate import business. Organized crime purchases large quantities of drugs from Europe, Asia, or Mexico and then distributes it in smaller lots to middle-level wholesalers, who cut it further and sell it to dealers on the street.

Organized crime figures usually do not become directly involved beyond the middle level, thus protecting themselves from the authorities. They are primarily financiers, putting up capital for large-scale purchases. Frequently even import and distribution is taken over by others.

Organized crime may also be involved in the illegal production or distribution of prescription drugs. In the early 1970s the New Jersey State Commission on Investigation found evidence that organized crime and some newer black groups were financing illegal laboratories to produce "speed" in Newark, Atlantic City, Philadelphia, Detroit, and Canada.

Prostitution

Prostitution, one of organized crime's rackets since the turn of the century, reached its peak during the Depression but since that time has declined. The Organized Crime Task Force of the President's Commission on Law Enforcement (National Advisory Council 1976) quoted from the 1952 Second Interim Report of the United States Senate's Kefauver Committee, which investigated organized crime:

Before the First World War, the major profits of organized criminals were obtained from prostitution. The passage of the Mann White Slave Act, the changing sexual mores, and public opinion combined to make commercialized prostitution a less profitable and more hazardous enterprise. . . . Prostitution is difficult to organize and discipline is hard to maintain.

One form of prostitution—streetwalking—was probably too conspicuous and hard to regulate for organized crime. Not only do streetwalkers get arrested frequently, they also may be involved in prostitution-related crimes (robbery of customers, assault), and they frequently have pimps, individuals regarded with contempt by most organized crime members. When organized crime is involved in prostitution, it is usually in such forms as call girls, brothel trade, massage parlors, and encounter joints. Although organized crime takes a large share of the profits derived from prostitution and limits the prostitutes' independence, it also provides valuable services: housing, clients, and protection from the law.

Pornography

The pornography industry consists of films, magazines, books, sexual devices, and various "service" establishments. A number of recent studies indicate that pornography is organized crime's latest business. As with gambling and the drug trade, pornography is a prohibited product with a large market, requiring good organization, money, muscle, and lax law enforcement.

It is not known when organized crime became involved in pornography, but the Supreme Court decision in 1967, *Redrup v. New York*, may have been a contributing factor. This case left unclear what constitutes pornography, making it difficult for law enforcement officers to build

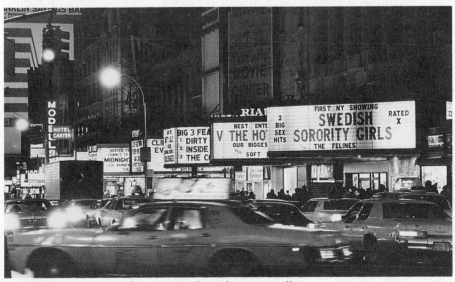

Organized crime is into the pornography industry as well.

cases. Although organized crime's links to the pornography industry are documented as early as the 1950s, it did not become heavily involved until the late 1960s. By 1969 it is estimated that organized crime controlled 60 percent of the pornographic movies in New York.

The Task Force Report on Organized Crime (National Advisory Council, p. 227) notes that organized crime's pornography operations cover the country, and that although no accurate figures exist on what profits organized crime receives, it must be good money or organized crime would not be involved. Especially insidious is organized crime's involvement in and promotion of "kiddie porn."

Supreme court decisions related to pornography have complicated the problem of law enforcement officers when dealing with the pornography industry. The court has not extended First Amendment protections to pornography, so it is not automatically legal, but the Court's decisions have left unclear what constitutes pornography. At present three somewhat vague critereia exist (*Miller v. California*, 1973):

1. The dominant theme of the material must appeal to prurient interests;
2. The material must be utterly without redeeming social, political, literary, or scientific value; and
3. The material must be patently offensive in its depiction of sexual matters, in terms of contemporary standards.

Each state must pass its own legislation defining the standards, but a jury representing the community decides on individual cases.

The pornography issue was further complicated by a 1969 Supreme Court ruling (*Stanley v. Georgia*), which held that pornography for private use in one's home is legal.

Some pornography laws have successfully withstood legal challenge; however, public display of pornography, mailing unsolicited material, and sale or distribution to minors are banned nationally. Additionally, the federal government bans using the mails or interstate commerce facilities for conveying pornographic material.

Loansharking

Loansharking, lending money at higher than legally prescribed rates, is the second largest source of revenue for organized crime. Gambling profits often provide the initial capital for loanshark operations. Many types of individuals became involved with loansharks: gamblers to pay off gambling debts, drug addicts to obtain needed drugs, businesspeople to buy goods or to close deals.

Interest rates may vary from 1 percent to 150 percent a week, depending on the relationship between the lender and the borrower, the intended use of the money, and the size of the loan. A common rate for the small borrower is 20 percent a week. The payments are usually due at a certain hour on a certain day, and failure to make payment may result in a rise in interest rate and/or physical brutality.

According to the President's Commission on Law Enforcement and Administration of Justice (1967, p. 189): "No reliable estimates exist of the gross revenue from organized loansharking; but profit margins are higher than for gambling operations, and many officials classify the business in the multi-billion dollar range."

Infiltration of Legitimate Business

Organized crime invests much of its money in legitimate business, thereby establishing a source of legal funds. Because business ownership is easily concealed, it is difficult to determine all the types of businesses that organized crime has penetrated. Control of businesses is usually acquired through one of four methods (Presidents' Commission on Law Enforcement and Administration of Justice, 1967, p. 190):

1. Investing concealed profits acquired from gambling and other illegal activities.
2. Accepting business interests in payment for the owner's gambling debts.
3. Foreclosing on usurious loans.
4. Using various forms of extortion.

The ordinary businessperson can seldom compete with organized crime, which has large amounts of ready cash, union connections, and "enforcers" to assure cooperation.

According to the Task Force Report: (National Advisory Council, p. 25)

Organized crime tends to engage in those legitimate businesses that can profit from political influence. Its profits are made possible, to a large extent, by its corruption of the public officials charged with regulating those businesses. The opportunity for corruption exists in every instance where government regulates business. The public officials charged with such regulatory activities are open to bribery in exchange for disregarding, for example, character requirements in the area of liquor licensing, zoning laws in the issuance of construction permits, and fire and health violations in building inspection.

THE THREAT OF ORGANIZED CRIME

The primary goals of organized crime, whether through illegal enterprises such as gambling or legitimate businesses, are making money and maximizing profit. Organized crime has found it expedient to invest large amounts of money in corrupting political figures from the local level to the federal level as well as figures within the law enforcement field. Cressey (1969) has stated that the goal of organized crime is "the nullification of government." Organized crime can flourish only if it can control police investigation, prosecutions, judicial proceedings, and the corrections process.

The direct national threat is that organized crime seeks to corrupt and control police officers, prosecutors, judicial proceedings, and the corrections process.

Police Corruption

Police officers' discretionary powers make them prime targets for corruption. (We will be discussing police discretion in depth later.) They can decide what laws to enforce, and organized crime may pay them handsomely not to enforce certain laws. Failure to arrest and prosecute those whom officers know have violated the law is only one form of police corruption. Goldstein (1975, pp. 16-18) lists several other forms of corruption:

> *Agreeing to drop an investigation prematurely.*
> *Agreeing not to inspect various locations where a violation may be occurring.*
> *Reducing the seriousness of a charge against an offender.*
> *Agreeing to alter testimony at a trial.*
> *Influencing departmental recommendations regarding the granting of licenses.*
> *Agreeing to alter departmental records of arrested persons.*

When police officers are corrupt, the entire department becomes less effective and honest police officers do not know whom they can trust within the department. Police corruption also erodes the public's confidence in them.

Corruption in the Judicial System

A study done in cooperation with the New York City Police Department between 1960 and 1970 (National Advisory Council, p. 25) covered 71 raids resulting in the positive identification of 99 persons who had a total of 356 arrests among them. Of these arrests, 198 were dismissed, 63 were acquitted, 12 were found guilty and given suspended sentences, 77 were fined, and 5 served jail sentences. The average fine was $113; the average jail sentence was 17 days. Although it is obvious from the preceding statistics that some judicial corruption exists, it is seldom proven.

Corruption in the Corrections System

Salerno and Tompkins (1969, p. 183) present convincing evidence that when organized crime figures do go to prison, they are usually quite comfortable:

> *Sam Giancana, for instance, frequently used the warden's office in the Cook County jail for business conferences, was permitted out of his cell after "lights out," and had easy access to liquor, special foods, and expensive cigars. And three weeks after Sam deStefano was moved by court order he was operating a loansharking business from his hospital room and enjoying fine foods, vintage wines, card games with underworld friends, and visits from women. Harold Koenigsberg, an enforcer and loanshark collector for Costa Nostra figures, was a Federal prisoner in Hudson county jail. Tracking down rumors, federal authorities found that Koenigsberg lived in a special room with a telephone and women and food sent in. At one point in the ensuing flap, Koenigsberg sent his lawyer to court to try and recover $1,000 he had lent the warden.*

THE POLICE OFFICER AND ORGANIZED CRIME

Organized crime is everyone's problem. Unfortunately many people believe that sole responsibility rests with law enforcement—that it is up to the police officer to apprehend those involved in organized crime. Here, more than in any other area of law enforcement, the police officer needs the help of the citizen and a judicial and political system free of corruption.

Among the special problems the law enforcement officer encounters when dealing with organized crime are as follows:

- *The lack of citizen cooperation.*
- *The code of ethics of organized crime members, which prevents them from giving information.*
- *The tremendous wealth, power, and organization behind them.*
- *The corruption of other police officers, politicians, judges, jury members, and corrections officers.*

Perhaps one of the most serious of the problems is lack of citizen cooperation. Citizens not only do not want to get involved. Many actually promote organized crime by engaging in illegal activities from which organized crime obtains its working capital, for example, illegal betting, buying stolen goods from fences, buying drugs, and so on.

The challenge is clear; however, it is also clear that law enforcement cannot do the job alone. A large part of the challenge rests in enlisting public support.

FEDERAL LEGISLATION REGARDING ORGANIZED CRIME

Siegel (1983, p. 392) points out that one of the first directly anti–organized crime measures was the Interstate and Foreign Travel or Transportation in Aid of Racketeering Enterprises Act (Travel Act—18 U.S. 1952 [1976]). This act prohibits travel in interstate commerce or use of interstate facilities for promoting, managing, establishing, carrying on, or facilitating any unlawful activity.

The Organized Crime Control Act

The Organized Crime Control Act was passed by Congress in 1970. It has several important provisions, including the following (National Advisory Council 1976, p. 18):

> *It provides for establishing a special grand jury in cities having major organized crime operations.*
> *It establishes a federal "use immunity" whereby witnesses can be ordered to testify in return for immunity from prosecution using any information so derived. Witnesses who fail to testify can be jailed for up to eighteen months.*
> *It provides protection for witnesses in organized crime cases and members of their families.*
> *It provides for perjury prosecution.*

The Organized Crime Control Act provides protection for witnesses in organized crime cases.

*It provides for taking and using pre-trial depositions when because of
"exceptional circumstances it is in the interest of justice."
It expands federal jurisdiction over illegal gambling operations.
It prohibits using illegal profit from racketeering activity to take over legitimate businesses and unions (RICO).
It provides for extended sentences for persons convicted of participating
in continuing illegal businesses or who are habitual criminals.*

RICO   The most important measure of the Organized Crime Control Act is
Title IX, The Racketeer Influenced and Corrupt Organization Act (RICO)
(Pub. L. No. 91-452, Title IX, 84 Stat. 922 [1970]). This act defines
racketeering activity as involvement in two or more acts prohibited by
twenty-four existing federal and state statutes. Siegel (1983, p. 392) states
that the offenses listed in RICO include state-defined crimes such as
murder, kidnapping, gambling, arson, robbery, bribery, extortion, and
narcotic violations, as well as federally defined crimes such as bribery,
counterfeiting, transmitting gambling information, prostitution, and mail
fraud. Siegel goes on to note that RICO is designed to limit patterns of
organized crime activity by defining racketeering as an act intended to:

1. derive income from racketeering or the unlawful collection of
   debts and to use or invest such income;
2. acquire through racketeering an interest in or control over any
   enterprise engaged in interstate or foreign commerce;
3. conduct business enterprises through a pattern of racketeering;
4. conspire to use racketeering as a means of making income,
   collecting loans, or conducting business.

Arson is included in the list of RICO offenses.

A person found guilty of violating RICO is subject to twenty years in prison and a fine of $225,000. In addition, the person so convicted forfeits to the United States government any investment in a business that violates RICO.

To enforce the legislation, the federal government created a Strike Force Program in eighteen cities. This program coordinates the efforts of several state and federal law enforcement officers and prosecutors to work as a team against racketeering and organized crime.

The Organized Crime Control Act was passed in 1970. Title IX of this act, the Racketeer Influenced and Corrupt Organization Act (RICO), created new categories of offenses in racketeering activity.

SUMMARY

Organized crime is a threat not only to its victims but to our entire society. Its two unique characteristics, use of corruption and strong-arm tactics, can destroy respectable citizens and eventually the country if allowed to go unchecked. Unfortunately, the severity of the threat is seldom recognized by the public and is sometimes not recognized by individuals within law enforcement. Until the elimination of organized crime becomes a priority for police departments and communities, it poses a direct threat to each of us and to our society.

Organized crime goes by many names including the mob, the syndicate, the rackets, the Mafia, and Cosa Nostra.

Organized crime is heavily involved in gambling, drugs, prostitution, pornography, loansharking, and infiltration of legitimate businesses. Its largest source of revenue is sports betting, particularly wagers on football games. Loansharking is its second largest source of revenue.

Not only does organized crime cost the nation billions of dollars annually and ruin hundreds of lives, it also poses a direct national threat because it seeks to corrupt and control police officers, prosecutors, judicial proceedings, and the corrections process. Nonetheless, many citizens actually promote organized crime by engaging in illegal activities, for example, buying stolen property, placing bets with bookies, and the like. Among the difficult problems the law enforcement officer encounters when dealing with organized crime are (1) lack of citizen cooperation, (2) the code of silence of family members, (3) their tremendous wealth, power, and organization, and (4) the corruption of other police officers, politicians, judges, jury members, and corrections officers.

In 1970 Congress passed the Organized Crime Control Act. Title IX of this act, the Racketeer Influenced and Corrupt Organization Act (RICO), created new categories of offenses in racketeering activity.

Although not a crime in itself, organized crime is truly a serious problem to be dealt with by law enforcement agencies.

Discussion Questions

1. Why would or could you blame a person for not testifying against organized crime?

2. A recent article described witnesses testifying against organized crime. After testifying they had their names changed and were moved with their families to a different location. After several moves and a promise of protection from the federal government, the witnesses were informed that due to lack of funds, they could not be protected any longer. How do you view this decision?

3. Why is it so difficult for the police to deal with organized crime on a local level?

4. Why is it dangerous to have the mob infiltrate legitimate businesses?

5. What are some ways the average citizen can help stop or slow down organized crime?

6. Should you fear organized crime? Is it truly a dangerous threat to society?

7. Why is more not being done to curb organized crime? What is being done?

8. Does your area have organized crime? If so, in what activities do they engage?

9. Is the disappearance of Jimmy Hoffa connected with organized crime?

10. Does sports betting influence the outcome of sporting events? If so, which sports?

References

Cressey, D. R. *Theft of the Nation: The Structure and Operations of Organized Crime in America.* New York: Harper & Row, 1969.

Goldstein, H. *Police Corruption.* New York: Police Foundation, 1975.

National Advisory Committee on Criminal Justice Standards and Goals. *Organized Crime: Report of the Task Force on Organized Crime.* Washington, D.C.: U.S. Government Printing Office, 1976.

Office of the New York Counsel to the Governor 1966.

Pace, D. F., and Styles, J. C. *Organized Crime: Concepts and Control.* Englewood Cliffs, N.J.: Prentice Hall, 1983.

President's Commission on Law Enforcement and Administration of Justice. *The Challenge of Crime in a Free Society.* Washington, D.C.: U.S. Government Printing Office, 1967.

Rhodes, R. P. *Organized Crime: Crime Control vs. Civil Liberties.* New York: Random House, 1984.

Rowan, Roy. "The 50 Biggest Mafia Bosses," *Fortune,* November 10, 1986, pp. 24–32, 34, 36, 38.

Salerno, R., and Tompkins, J. S. *The Crime Confederation: Cosa Nostra and Allied Operations in Organized Crime.* New York: Doubleday, 1969.

Siegel, L. J. *Criminology.* St. Paul, Minn.: West Publishing Company, 1983.

The Drug Problem: A Nation of Users

Trouble, with a capital T that rhymes with D, that stands for drugs.
—Law Enforcement News

DO YOU KNOW

What act made it illegal to sell or use certain narcotics and dangerous drugs?

What narcotics and "dangerous" drugs are and what results they produce?

What exactly federal law prohibits in relation to narcotics and dangerous drugs?

What the most commonly observed drugs on the street, in possession of users, and seized in drug raids are and what the most frequent drug arrest is for?

What the most widely abused drug in the United States is?

If drug use and alcohol abuse are linked to crime?

What approaches to the drug problem have been suggested?

Introduction

Chapter 15

"While police officials struggled to establish and maintain the innovations of recent years, such as community– or problem–oriented policing and the application of new technologies," says Rosen (1989, p. 1), "for the most part the criminal justice system found its attention [in 1988] riveted on three things: drugs, drugs, and more drugs." Rosen says that the "war on drugs" is "no longer a metaphorical catchphrase." Instead, it has "turned into an armed conflict of house–to–house fighting." According to Rosen, during 1988, "Prisons overflowed as an outgrowth of rising arrest rates, and police found themselves dealing more and more with recycled repeat offenders who carried increasingly powerful firearms." According to the director of the FBI, William Sessions (1989, p. 11):

> *Our nation is facing the greatest law enforcement crisis in its history. It is a crisis of drug trafficking and drug use—and the enormous amount of violent crime caused by drugs.*

An ABC documentary, "Drugs: Why This Plague," pointed out that American history is filled with drug use, including alcohol and tobacco. As the early settlers moved west, one of the first buildings in each frontier town was a saloon. Cocaine use was also common by the 1880s. At the turn of the century cocaine was the "drug of choice," said to cure everything from indigestion to toothaches. It was added to flavor soft drinks like Coca-Cola in 1886. In effect, cocaine became the "all-American" drug.

In 1909 a presidential commission reported to President Theodore Roosevelt that cocaine was a hazard, leading to loss of livelihoods and lives.

As the public became increasingly aware of the hazards posed by cocaine and other drugs, they pressed for legislation against the use of such drugs.

In 1914 the Harrison Narcotics Act was passed by the federal government, making it illegal to sell or use certain drugs.

In 1920 every state required that their students learn about the effects of narcotics. And in 1937, under President Franklin Delano Roosevelt, marijuana became the last of the drugs to be banned. For a quarter of a century the drug problem lay dormant.

Then came the 1960s, a time of youthful rebellion, a time of Haight Asbury and the flower children, a time to protest the war in Vietnam. A whole culture had as its theme: tune in, turn on, and drop out—often through marijuana and LSD.

By the 1970s, according to one survey, marijuana had been tried by 40 percent of eighteen to twenty-one-year-olds, and it was being used by many soldiers fighting in Vietnam. Many other soldiers, however, turned to heroin. At the same time, an estimated half a million Americans began using heroin back in the states.

The peak of the drug culture came in the mid-1970s, and with it came the emergence of heavy cocaine use.

As noted by Mann (1989, p. 103):

> From the mid-1960s through the 1970s, rock music, TV and films all made drug use seem fun, glamorous, a totally acceptable facet of life. The multimillion-dollar drug-paraphernalia industry was then completely legal.
>
> During those years, marijuana's proponents gained the support of some of the most respected and influential members of our society, from the White House on down. . . .
>
> Spearheading the movement was the National Organization for the Reform of Marijuana Laws (NORML). . . . President Carter himself backed decriminalization—but not legalization—of marijuana in a speech to the nation on drug abuse. . . .

During the '70s the United States became the most drug-pervaded nation in the world, with marijuana leading the way. One law enforcement student, in fact, wrote a term paper titled, "The United States: The World's Largest Drug Store."

The 1980s saw a turnaround in drug use, with celebrities advocating, "It's not cool to do drugs," and "Just say no to drugs." But at the same time other advertisements advocated that where alcohol and smoking are is where the "fun is at." And the United States remains a culture of pill poppers.

- Can't sleep?—take a pill.
- Want to lose weight?—take a pill.
- Want to quit smoking?—take a pill.
- Want to relax?—take a pill.
- Got a headache?—take a pill.
- Don't want children?—take a pill.

Just who is taking these drugs and why?

THE DRUG USERS

Authorities say that in New York City alone there are 400,000 drug addicts requiring an endless supply of drugs. Nationally there are about two million addicts out of forty million drugs users. The Federal Drug Enforcement Agency (FDEA) estimates that 5 percent of the population, or nearly ten million Americans, are involved in drug abuse of some sort.

Common symptoms of drug abuse include the following:

- Sudden and dramatic changes in discipline and job performance.
- Unusual degrees of activity or inactivity.
- Sudden and irrational flareups.
- Significant change in personal appearance for the worse.
- Dilated pupils or wearing sunglasses at inappropriate times or places.
- Needle marks or razor cuts, or long sleeves constantly worn to hide such marks.
- Sudden attempts to borrow money or to steal.
- Frequent association with known drug abusers or pushers.

Why???

People do drugs and drink alcohol primarily for the "high" they get from it, for the escape from the trouble and tensions of the everyday world. In addition, it is often a very sociable thing to do. Teenagers, in particular, are greatly influenced by peer pressure, although some teenagers say they got the idea to drink or do drugs from watching their parents. In fact, many parents serve wine to their very young children along with Sunday dinner. And many children under age twelve say they learned to drink or do drugs from older brothers and sisters.

Researchers have found that children of alcoholics are 70 percent more likely than of nonalcoholics to abuse drugs and alcohol at some point in their lives.

During the teenage years, fitting in is extremely important to most youth. They are growing fast, and some have what has been termed a "terminal case of the awkward." They are self-conscious and uncertain as to just who they are. Cocaine, especially, numbs such teenage anxieties. It helps anxious, awkward young people find an escape from a world that is frightening to them. It also gives them the illusion of membership, energy, and confidence.

THE DRUG DEALERS

American drug users pay drug traffickers an estimated $140 billion a year. Some dealers hand out free drug samples to hook new buyers. Illegal drugs are readily available, from marijuana to cocaine. Any buyer can find some kind of drug to meet his or her needs.

The core of the American drug business is primarily in our inner cities. Dealing drugs is a way of making a very profitable living.

Many decaying buildings are becoming crack "factories." In these buildings, powder cocaine is processed into rock cocaine, or crack, and pure heroin and cocaine are diluted with baking soda or sugar "stepped on" to increase the product, turning a thousand-dollar ounce of cocaine into two ounces worth two thousand dollars.

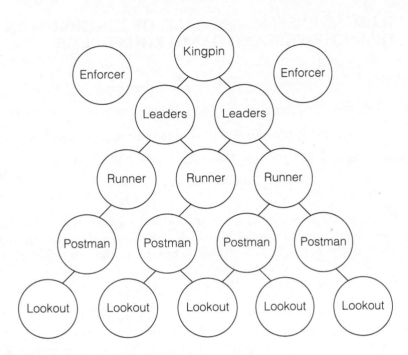

Figure 15–1   Street Drug Rings

Street drug rings can be quite sophisticated, as illustrated in figure 15–1. The kingpin runs the operation, purchasing narcotics from foreign smugglers. Under the kingpin are leaders who oversee the packaging and distribution of the illegal drugs. Runners take the drugs to the street sellers, called postmen. Lookouts get approximately two hundred dollars a day just looking out for the police.

Profits for the dealers are very high, with a good week netting them thirty thousand dollars. According to a Ford Foundation study, drugs are often sold openly in inner cities, with inner-city residents resigned to drug dealing as a way of life. In some cities drug dealers have actually bought the cooperation of neighborhoods. Drug dealers come into a neighborhood, offer residents money or cars, and, in turn, use their homes for drug deals.

The enforcers are, as the name implies, people who carry out the kingpin's orders, including killing people who get in the way of drug trafficking.

According to Kraar (1988, p. 19): "The illicit drug trade is probably the fastest-growing industry in the world and is unquestionably the most profitable. . . . The global drug trade may run up to $500 billion a year . . . . The drug trade has created a breed of shadowy billionaires who seem as canny in business as they are vicious."

ILLEGAL POSSESSION, SALE, OR DISTRIBUTION OF NARCOTICS AND DANGEROUS DRUGS

Narcotics are drugs that produce sleep, lethargy, or relief of pain, including heroin, cocaine, crack, and marijuana. Dangerous drugs are addicting, mind-altering drugs such as depressants, stimulants, and hallucinogens.

It is a crime in most states to use or sell narcotics and dangerous drugs without a prescription. Additionally, the abuse of these substances is often closely connected to other types of crime. Homicide, rape, burglary, armed robbery, and shoplifting have been connected with the use of narcotics and dangerous drugs and with the drug abuser's need for money to support his or her habit.

The misuse and abuse of drugs and their illegal sale and disposition have become a national problem not limited to slum areas or to the use of hard narcotics. Consequently, new amendments by Congress, laws by state legislatures, and ordinances by local political subdivisions provide stronger regulation of the manufacture, distribution, delivery, and possession of many narcotics, depressants, stimulants, and hallucinogens.

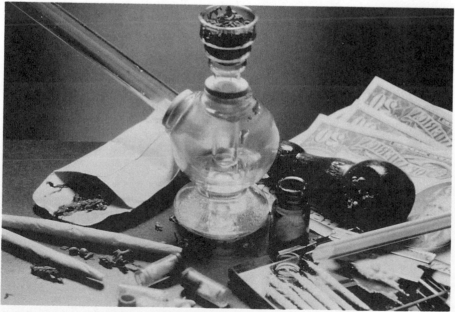

Cocaine, Marijuana, and Crack

In most states narcotics and dangerous drugs may not be used or sold without a prescription. Federal law prohibits sale or distribution not covered by prescription, but it does not prohibit possession for personal use.

Narcotics

Prohibited narcotics include heroin, cocaine, crack, and marijuana.

Heroin is a commonly abused narcotic. It is synthesized from morphine and is up to ten times more potent in its effects. Morphine comes from opium, which is derived from the dried resin from the base of the opium poppy grown in Afghanistan, Burma, Iran, Laos, Mexico, and Thailand. (See figure 15–2.) Heroin is physically addictive and expensive. It causes an easing of fears, followed by euphoria, and finally stupor. According to Kaplan (n.d., p. 1):

Source: Intelligence Trends

Figure 15–2   **Sources of Opiates/Heroin**

Although heroin can be smoked or eaten, injection into a vein is the pre-
ferred means by which addicts in the United States take the drug. . . .

A primary reason for concern about heroin addiction in the United
States today is the heroin addict's need to violate the law in order to
raise sufficient funds to support the habit. . . . A rough estimate is that
there are 500,000 addicts whose average daily consumption of heroin has
a retail cost of about sixty dollars per day. The best estimates suggest that
60 percent of this roughly fifteen billion dollars per year is obtained from
consensual crimes, such as prostitution and heroin sales, from welfare
payments, and from occasional work. Most of the remainder, approxi-
mately six billion dollars, comes from the commission of property crimes,
such as burglary, shoplifting, and other "hustles." . . .

In all, the best estimate is that addicts commit about six times as
many crimes while they are in a "run" of heroin use as when they are
abstinent or using the drug irregularly.

Cocaine

Cocaine hydrochloride is a central nervous system stimulant narcotic. It is derived from the Erythroxylon coca bush of South America.
Peruvian and Bolivian Indians chewed leaves of the coca bush for
pleasure and also to enable them to do strenuous work. Sigmund Freud
described the euphoric effects of cocaine and was supposedly one of its
first abusers.

Peru and Bolivia are presently the main sources of cocaine. Cultivation of the bush is legal in these countries, with most of the product sold
to flavor soft drinks and for medical uses. (See the map in figure 15–3.)

Coca leaves are soaked in a solution of water, potassium carbonate,
and a petroleum distillate such as kerosene. This produces a doughlike
sludge called *paste* that is dried and shipped to clandestine laboratories
throughout Latin America. The cocaine that is extracted from the paste
looks somewhat like rock sugar candy and is often called *rock*. Its purity
varies from 70 to 80 percent. A more refined form of cocaine is called
flake. It comes in flat crystals and is approximately 95 percent pure.

Cocaine smuggling is big business, run primarily by Colombians.
They often are assisted by tourists, students, and the like, called *mules*.
Larger quantities are brought in by professional smugglers, often using
private planes and boats.

Cocaine may be inhaled or injected, producing euphoria, excitation,
anxiety, a sense of increased muscular strength, talkativeness, and a
reduction in feelings of fatigue. The pupils frequently become dilated, and
the heart rate and blood pressure usually increase.

Physical dependence on cocaine is possible, and psychological
dependence can be extreme.

Crack

Crack is a relatively new form of cocaine first observed in Southern
California in 1981. Traditional "freebasing" of cocaine converts cocaine

Source: Cocaine Abuse. *Study Notes*, 1977, p. 2.

Figure 15–3   **The Chief Countries in Which the Coca Bush Is Grown and Cocaine is Processed**

hydrochloride (CH1) back to cocaine base for smoking. It uses solvents to remove dilutents, producing a powdery material. Danger of explosion or fire is high. In the crack procedure, only baking soda or ammonia and water are added to cocaine HC1. The mixture is heated and cooled, then filtered to collect the crystals. Eliminating use of flammable solvents eliminates risk of explosion and fire.

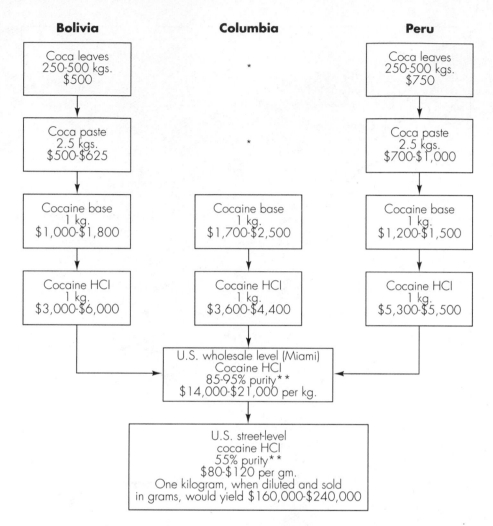

*Organizations or cooperative ventures apparently handle both leaf and paste production in Colombia. Neither is sold separately. In Peru and Bolivia, however, these commodities are bought and sold at different levels of trafficking and among different trafficking groups.
**All prices are in terms of undiluted product. Prevailing purities at distribution levels are indicated merely for convenience.
Source: Intelligence Trends, 1987, p. 6.

Figure 15—4   Cocaine

Crack is usually sprinkled on a marijuana or tobacco cigarette or mixed with marijuana or tobacco and then smoked in a pipe. It produces the same intense "rush" and euphoria that freebase cocaine does but at a greatly reduced cost.

According to Bennett and Hess (1987, pp. 462–463) the pellet-size bits or chunks of crack are often put into small plastic vials and sold for ten to twenty dollars per vial. This is much less than a similar amount of cocaine, which would cost one hundred dollars or more. They note: "In 1986 from 55 to 75 percent of all cocaine busts involved crack. The predominant users were twenty- to thirty-five-year-old men."

Marijuana

Marijuana is probably the most socially acceptable of the illegal drugs; legislation lessening penalties for its use has frequently been proposed. Although it has been known for nearly five thousand years, it is one of the least understood of all natural drugs, yet one of the most versatile. Marijuana is derived from the cannabis plant, which still grows wild in many parts of the United States. Figure 15–5 illustrates marijuana's sources.

Marijuana is a hardy weed adaptable to most climates. It grows best in moderate moisture and direct sunlight, but this hemp plant can survive in extremely adverse conditions.

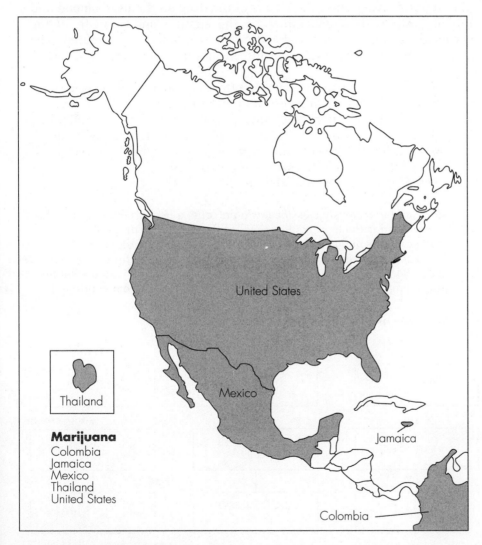

Source: Intelligence Trends, 1987, p. 4.

Figure 15–5   **Sources of Marijuana**

The Asian variety of marijuana provides the drug hashish, which has the same properties as marijuana but is four times more intoxicating.

The marijuana plant is distinctive, resembling a poinsetta. It grows at a phenomenal rate from a seedling to a twenty-foot plant in one year. The leaves are then picked and dried in the sun, a stove, or even a clothes drier.

Marijuana is frequently used in the form of cigarettes, which have a distinctive odor like that of burning alfalfa. Its scent is clearly different from tobacco.

Marijuana cigarettes, also called joints, are usually rolled with two cigarette papers and crimped at both ends. They are usually smoked with the aid of a holder, called a roach holder or alligator clip.

When smoked, marijuana enters the bloodstream quickly, causing rapid onset of symptoms. The effects of the drug on the user's mood and thinking vary widely, depending on the amount and strength of the marijuana as well as the social setting and the effects anticipated. The drug usually takes effect in about fifteen minutes and lasts from two to four hours.

"Social" doses of one or two cigarettes may cause an increased sense of well-being; initial restlessness and hilarity followed by a dreamy, carefree state of relaxation; alteration of sensory perceptions including expansion of space and time; a more vivid sense of touch, sight, smell, taste, and sound; a feeling of hunger, especially a craving for sweets; and subtle changes in thought formation and expression.

According to Bennett and Hess (1987, p. 464):

> Marijuana is variously classified as a narcotic, a depressant, and a hallucinogen and is the most controversial of the dangerous drugs. The use of marijuana was outlawed by the Federal Marijuana Tax Act of 1927.
>
> A wide spectrum of opinions exist regarding the harmfulness of marijuana. Some feel it should be legalized; others feel it is a very dangerous drug. Many surveys document psychological addiction from continued

Domestic marijuana

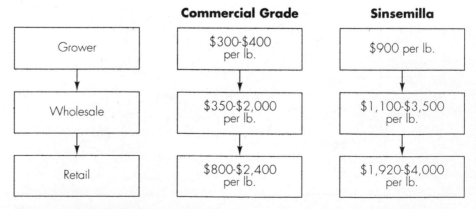

	Commercial Grade	**Sinsemilla**
Grower	$300-$400 per lb.	$900 per lb.
Wholesale	$350-$2,000 per lb.	$1,100-$3,500 per lb.
Retail	$800-$2,400 per lb.	$1,920-$4,000 per lb.

Figure 15–6   Selling Prices for One Pound of Marijuana at Successive Levels of Trafficking

Hashish

Since American cannabis users prefer marijuana, there is limited trafficking in hashish. When encountered, however, a pound of hashish at the retail level sells for $1,200 to $2,000; an ounce for $80 to $400. The probable sources of hashish available in the United States are Pakistan/Afghanistan, Lebanon, and Morocco.

Foreign source marijuana

Mexico

Interior price
$50-$100 per lb.

↓

Border point
$136-$455 per lb.

↓

U.S. wholesale
$325-$650 per lb.

Colombia

Cultivation site
$2-$4 per lb.

↓

Embarcation point
$6-$11 per lb.

↓

U.S. wholesale
$550-$900 per lb.

Thailand

Grower
$5-$10 per lb.

↓

Broker
$11-$33 per lb.

↓

U.S. wholesale
$850-$1,300 per lb.

Jamaica

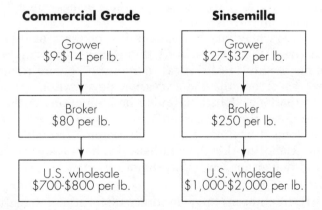

Commercial Grade

Grower
$9-$14 per lb.

↓

Broker
$80 per lb.

↓

U.S. wholesale
$700-$800 per lb.

Sinsemilla

Grower
$27-$37 per lb.

↓

Broker
$250 per lb.

↓

U.S. wholesale
$1,000-$2,000 per lb.

use of marijuana, as is true for most drugs. Research does not indicate that marijuana is physically addictive. However, some users claim withdrawal symptoms similar to those resulting from discontinuance of hard narcotics.

Whether marijuana abusers continue on to hard narcotics or other controlled substances has not been totally researched. It is known that the vast majority of hard narcotics users once used marijuana, but how many marijuana users proceed to hard drugs is unknown. Marijuana is frequently used with alcohol, barbituates, and amphetamines. The marijuana user may be more susceptible to experimenting with other drugs while under the influence of marijuana.

Although research does not clearly establish or disclaim harmful results from continued use, marijuana is an illegal drug in all states, except Alaska, making its use or sale a violation of the law.

Dangerous Drugs

Depressants (Barbiturates)   Depressants, or **barbiturates,** are sedatives taken orally as a small tablet or capsule to induce sleep or to relieve tension. Homemakers are the most common abusers of barbiturates.

Small amounts of barbiturates make the user relaxed, sociable, and good-humored. Heavy doses cause sluggishness, depression, deep sleep, or coma. A barbiturate addict usually takes ten to twenty pills a day and often shows symptoms of drunkenness: speech becomes slurred and indistinct, physical coordination is impaired, and mental and emotional instability occurs. Many barbiturate addicts are quarrelsome and have a "short fuse." Overdoses are common and frequently cause intentional or accidental death.

Stimulants (Amphetamines)   Stimulants, or **amphetamines,** are taken orally as a tablet or capsule, or intravenously, to reduce appetite and/or relieve mental depression. They are often taken by truck drivers, salespeople, college students, and businesspeople who want to stay awake for long periods and by people who want to lose weight.

Normal doses produce wakefulness, increased alertness and initiative, and hyperactivity. Large doses produce exaggerated feelings of confidence, power, and well-being.

Habitual users may take amphetamines for three or four days, eat nothing, and drive themselves until they black out from exhaustion. Heavy users may exhibit restlessness, nervousness, hand tremors, pupil dilation, dryness of mouth, and excessive perspiration. They may be talkative and experience delusions and/or hallucinations. Although small doses may produce cheerfulness and an unusual increase in activity, heavy and prolonged use may produce symptoms resembling paranoid schizophrenia. Handling this deviant behavior has always been a source of concern and danger for law enforcement officers.

Hallucinogens   **Hallucinogens** may produce distortion, intensify sensory perception, and lessen the ability to discriminate between fact and fantasy. The unpredictable mental effects include illusions, panic, psychotic or antisocial behavior, and impulses toward violence and self-destruction. Probably the best known hallucinogen is LSD, which gets its name from the colorless, odorless substance lysergic acid diethylamide from which it is made.

Although hallucinogens are usually taken orally as a tablet or capsule, their physical characteristics allow them to be disguised as various commonly used powders or liquids. LSD has been found on chewing gum, hard candy, crackers, vitamin pills, aspirin, blotting paper, and postage stamps.

Other hallucinogens include DMT (dimethyltryptamine), a powerful drug similar to LSD; mescaline, a chemical derived from the peyote cactus; and psilocybin, a natural ingredient in a species of Mexican mushroom.

PCP (phencyclidine), another hallucinogen, was developed as an anesthetic and is still used as such by veterinarians. It appeared in San Francisco in the 1960s and was called the "Peace Pill." As its use spread across the country it was called by various other names, including angel dust, mist, zoom, superweed, and angel weed. According to Police Services, Inc. (1979):

> PCP is extremely unpredictable. In low or moderate doses, it produces a "floaty" euphoria and a sense of detachment. Higher doses can create auditory hallucinations and feelings of impending doom. Chronic users sometimes have illusions of physical strength. They may then become violent and a source of danger to anyone who happens to be near them.
>
> The drug can be swallowed in a pill or capsule, sniffed like cocaine, or smoked. Smoking is usually done after the drug has been sprayed on marijuana, tobacco, parsley, catnip, oregano, or any other similar plant material.

A "bad trip" from any of the hallucinogens can be "more devastating than the most horrible nightmare." (Police Services, Inc., 1979)

Deliriants

Deliriants are volatile chemicals that include airplane glue, gasoline, lighter fluid, paint thinner, Freon, carbon tetrachloride, and other volatile commercial products. Although technically neither narcotics nor dangerous drugs, deliriants may be a prime cause of psychological dependency among young people.

Deliriants may be sniffed or inhaled either directly from a container or from a paper or plastic bag or cloth. Redness or irritation commonly occurs around the nostrils and lips. Other reactions vary according to the deliriant used and the amount inhaled; however, deliriants generally produce a "high" similar to that produced by alcohol.

Common Factors

In spite of numerous differences produced by use of various kinds of narcotics and dangerous drugs, certain common factors occur, the most important of which are (1) they are mind altering, (2) they may become addicting—either physically or psychologically, and (3) overdosage may result in convulsions and death.

Table 15–1 Controlled Substances Uses and Effects

Drug	Trade or Other Names	Methods of Usual Administration
Narcotics		
Opium	Dover's Powder, Paregoric, Parepectolin	Oral, smoked
Morphine	Morphine, Pectoral Syrup	Oral, smoked, injected
Codeine	Tylenol with Codeine, Empirin Compound with Codeine, Robitussan A-C	Oral, injected
Heroin	Diacetylmorphine, Horse, Smack	Injected, sniffed, smoked
Hydromorphone	Dilaudid	Oral, injected
Meperidine (Pethidine)	Demerol, Mepergan	Oral, injected
Methadone	Dolophine, Methadone, Methadose	Oral, injected
Other narcotics	LAAM, Leritine, Numorphan, Percodan, Tussionex, Fentanyl, Darvon, Talwin,* Lomotil	Oral, injected
Depressants		
Chloral Hydrate	Noctec, Somnos	Oral
Barbiturates	Phenobarbital, Tuinal, Amytal, Nembutal, Seconal, Lotusate	Oral
Benzodiazepines	Ativan, Azene, Clonopin, Dalmane, Diazepam, Librium, Xanax, Serax, Tranxene, Valium, Verstran, Halcion, Paxipam, Restoril	Oral
Methaqualone	Quaalude	Oral
Glutethimide	Doriden	Oral
Other **Depressants**	Equanil, Miltown, Noludar, Placidyl, Valmid	Oral
Stimulants		
Cocaine **	Coke, Flake, Snow	Sniffed, smoked, injected
Amphetamines	Biphetamine, Delcobese, Desoxyn, Dexedrine, Mediatric	Oral, injected
Phenmetrazine	Preludin	Oral, injected
Methylphenidate	Ritalin	Oral, injected
Other Stimulants	Adipex, Bacarate, Cylert, Didrex, Ionamin, Plegine, Pre-Sate, Sanorex, Tenuate, Tepanil, Voranil	Oral, injected
Hallucinogens		
LSD	Acid, Microdot	Oral
Mescaline and Peyote	Mesc, Buttons, Cactus	Oral
Amphetamine Variants	2,5-DMA, PMA, STP, MDA, MDMA, TMA, DOM, DOB	Oral, injected
Phencyclidine	PCP, Angel Dust, Hog	Smoked, oral, injected
Phencyclidine Analogs	PCE, PCPy, TCP	Smoked, oral, injected
Other **Hallucinogens**	Bufotenine, Ibogaine, DMT, DET, Psilocybin, Psilocyn	Oral, injected, smoked, sniffed
Cannabis		
Marijuana	Pot, Acapulco Gold, Grass, Reefer, Sinsemilla, Thai Sticks	Smoked, oral
Tetrahydrocannabinol	THC	Smoked, oral
Hashish	Hash	Smoked, oral
Hashish Oil	Hash Oil	Smoked, oral

*Not designated a narcotic under the CSA
**Designated a narcotic under the CSA

Table 15–1 (continued)

Possible Effects	Effects of Overdose	Withdrawal Syndrome
Euphoria, drowsiness, respiratory depression, constricted pupils, nausea	Slow and shallow breathing, clammy skin, convulsions, coma, possible death	Watery eyes, runny nose, yawning, loss of appetite, irritability, tremors, panic, chills and sweating, cramps, nausea
Slurred speech, disorientation, drunken behavior without odor of alcohol	Shallow respiration, clammy skin, dilated pupils, weak and rapid pulse, coma, possible death	Anxiety, insomnia, tremors, delirium, convulsions, possible death
Increased alertness, excitation, euphoria, increased pulse rate and blood pressure, insomnia, loss of appetite	Agitation, increase in body temperature, hallucinations, convulsions, possible death	Apathy, long periods of sleep, irritability, depression, disorientation
Illusions and hallucinations, poor perception of time and distance	Longer, more intense "trip" episodes, psychosis, possible death	Withdrawal syndrome not reported
Euphoria, relaxed inhibitions, increased appetite, disoriented behavior	Fatigue, paranoia, possible psychosis	Insomnia, hyperactivity and decreased appetite occasionally reported

Table 15–2 Indicators of Drug Abuse

Drug	Physical Evidence	Observable Conditions
Morphine	Burning spoon, candle, hypodermic needle, actual substance	Needle marks, euphoria
Heroin	Burning spoon, candle, hypodermic needle, razor blade, eyedropper, actual substance	Needle marks or razor cuts, euphoria, starry look, constricted pupils, profuse perspiration
Cocaine	White or colorless crystalline powder, hypodermic needle, pipe	Needle marks, dilated pupils, increased heart rate, convulsing
Crack	Pellets, glass pipes, plastic bottle	Depression, euphoria, convulsions
Stimulants	Pills of various shapes and sizes	Restlessness, nervousness, hand tremor, dilated pupils, dry mouth, excessive perspiration
Depressants	Pills of various shapes and sizes	Resembles drunkenness: slurred, indistinct speech and loss of physical coordination
Hallucinogens	Hypodermic needle, eyedropper, spoon, bottle caps, tourniquets, cotton balls, actual substance	Needle marks on inner elbow, extreme emotionalism, noticeable dilation of pupils, often causing persons to wear dark glasses even at night
Marijuana	Roach holder, pipe with fine screen stuck halfway down bowl, actual substance	Sweet smoke odor; resembles mild intoxication: staring off into space, glassy eyes, sometimes passing into semiconsciousness or falling asleep

The most commonly observed drugs on the street, in possession of users, and seized in drug raids are heroin, opium, morphine, codeine, cocaine, crack, and marijuana. Arrest for possession or use of marijuana is the most frequent drug arrest.

Drug Abuse, AIDS, and the HIV Virus

An estimated 50 percent of intravenous drug abusers are infected with the HIV virus. And intravenous drug abusers comprise 17 percent of AIDS victims. Among new reported cases of AIDS, approximately one-third were intravenous drug abusers. The Center for Disease Control [*Aids Policy and Law*, n.d.) estimates that almost 300,000 Americans will have developed AIDS by 1991. According to the Center, "Researchers now see intravenous drug abuse as the major vehicle for the AIDS virus to be spread to the general public." And, according to the United States Surgeon General, speaking before a Senate committee, without drastic, "innovative" measures, the number of affected people could reach into the millions by 1990.

Needle marks can be seen on the arms of intravenous drug users.

It is estimated that states have enacted more than six hundred pieces of AIDS-related legislation dealing with employment, health care, insurance liability, and criminal conduct. Some states are attempting to apply criminal punishment to those who spread AIDS.

Societal Effects

Although drug abusers may claim that it is their right to ingest, smoke, sniff, or inject whatever they want into their own bodies, the results of such actions do have serious implications for society. Users are no longer in control of what they think, say, or do and often pose a threat to other members of society.

The occasional user of marijuana may argue that no harm is being done to anyone, but researchers point out that a person predisposed to the abuse of one drug may be likely to abuse other, stronger drugs (U.S. Department of Justice n.d.). Also (U.S. Department of Justice n.d.) users of one drug may be exposed to a variety of other drug users and sellers and, through this association, may be encouraged to experiment with more potent drugs. More importantly, however, is the expense involved in supporting a drug habit. Frequently this expense causes the addict to turn to crime to obtain money with which to purchase the needed drugs.

ALCOHOL

Although drinking alcohol is not illegal, laws have been established that regulate the age at which it becomes legal to drink as well as the amount that a person can drink and then operate a vehicle. The problem of the drunk driver is well known to police officers. Drunk drivers are a

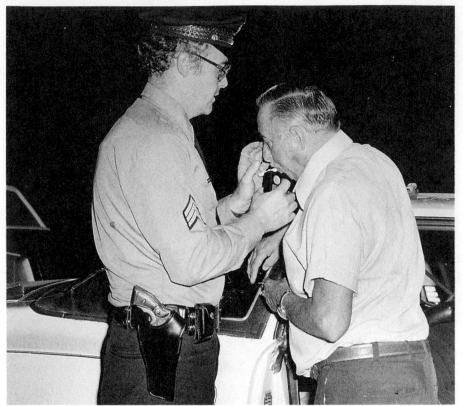

An officer administers a breath-test.

menace to themselves and to others. "Drinking is a factor in at least half of all fatal motor vehicle accidents." (National Safety Council 1984, p. 53).

Alcohol is the most widely abused drug in the United States.

The widespread abuse of alcohol is partly due to its legality but also to its social acceptance. Alcohol is the drug of choice among teenagers, as indicated in figure 15–7.

DRUG ABUSE AND CRIME

The National Institute of Justice has recently implemented a Drug Use Forecasting (DUF) system. Under this system they are able to detect and track drug-use trends among people arrested for serious crimes. This voluntary program is in place in twelve major cities. Four times a year samples of arrestees in each city are interviewed and asked to provide urine specimens, which are tested for illicit drugs.

Initial tests showed a high level of drug use among the arrestees, with 50 to 80 percent of those arrested for serious crime testing positive. Their research also showed that criminals commit four to six times as much crime when they are actively using drugs as they do when they are drug free.

Clearly drug use is linked to criminal activity.

According to the National Institute most of those tested were charged with street crimes such as burglary, grand larceny, and assault. The most frequently found drugs were marijuana, cocaine, heroin, PCP, and amphetamines.

Tests conducted in New York City showed that cocaine use almost doubled during the three-year period. It more than tripled in the District of Columbia. The National Institute estimates that these rates are from two to nine times higher than in the general population.

In addition, according to the Bureau of Justice Statistics (1983, p. 39), alcohol abuse is common among criminals, with more than a third of all prison inmates indicating they drank heavily. Approximately 10 percent of the offenders indicated they were "very drunk" at the time of the offense.

Table 15–3   Alcohol Usage Patterns: United States High School Seniors, 1986

	Lifetime Use	Annual Use	Last Month	Daily in Last Month
All Seniors	91.3	84.5	65.3	4.8
Sex				
Male	92.3	85.8	69.0	6.7
Female	90.6	83.4	61.9	2.8
College Plans				
None or under 4 years	92.2	85.1	66.6	6.8
Complete 4 years	91.1	84.6	64.8	3.5
Region				
Northeast	94.3	88.7	67.6	4.9
Midwest	93.5	88.4	71.3	4.9
South	88.0	78.4	58.2	4.9
West	89.7	82.9	64.5	4.2
Population Density				
Large SMSA	92.8	86.8	66.2	4.0
Other SMSA	91.0	84.1	64.8	4.5
Non-SMSA	90.6	83.0	65.2	5.8

Source: High School Senior Survey. National Institute of Drug Abuse, 1986 extrapolations by Metropolitan Life Insurance Company Health and Safety Education personnel, 1987

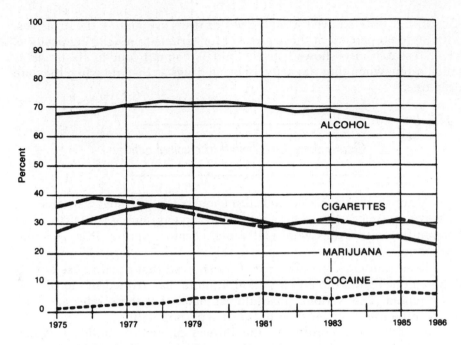

Source: High School Senior Survey. National Institute of Drug Abuse, 1986.

Figure 15–7   **Trends in Current Use of Cocaine and the Top Three Prevalent Drugs Mentioned by High School Seniors**

TYPES OF DRUG-INVOLVED OFFENDERS

Chaiken and Johnson (1988) studied the types of adolescent and adult drug-involved offenders, their typical drug use, problems, and contact with the justice system. Their results are summarized in tables 15–4 and 15–5.

COMBATING THE PROBLEM

Several options have been suggested as a way to combat the drug problem.

The drug problem might be approached by

- *legalization;*
- *increased law enforcement;*
- *a two-market approach;*
- *asset forfeiture programs;*
- *enlisting public support.*

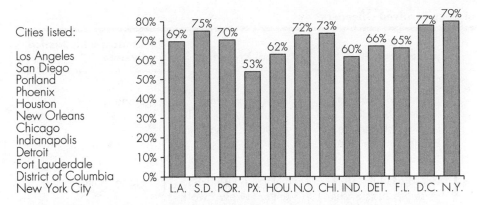

Figure 15—8   **Percentage of Male Arrestees Testing Positive for Any Drug, Including Marijuana (June–November 1987)**

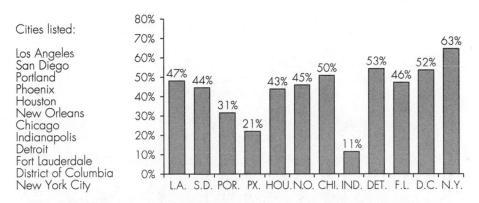

Figure 15—9   **Percentage of Male Arrestees Testing Positive for Cocaine (June–November 1987)**

Legalization

Some people advocate legalizing marijuana and other drugs just as alcohol is, claiming that this would reduce the cost of maintaining a drug habit and, consequently, reduce the amount of crime that might be committed to obtain money to support the habit.

Proponents of legalization say that the prohibition on drug use has created "huge profits for drug dealers, overcrowded jails, a distorted foreign policy and urban areas terrorized by bloodthirsty gangs" (Church, 1988, p. 12).

Church cites the following arguments for and against legalization: FOR:

- Costs. Some of the $8 billion spent on interdiction and local enforcement could be used for education and treatment, which receive less than $500 million.

Table 15–4   Types of Drug-Involved Offenders

Type of Offender	Typical Drug Use	Typical Problems	Contact with Justice System
Occasional users			
Adolescents	Light to moderate or single-substance, such as alcohol, marijuana, or combination use.	Driving under influence; truancy, early sexual activity; smoking.	None to little.
Adults	Light to moderate use of single substances such as hallucinogens, tranquilizers, alcohol, marijuana, cocaine, or combination use.	Driving under influence; lowered work productivity.	None to little.
Persons who sell small amounts of drugs			
Adolescents	Moderate use of alcohol and multiple types of drugs.	Same as adolescent occasional user; also, some poor school performance; some other minor illegal activity.	Minimal juvenile justice contact.
Adults	Moderate use of alcohol and multiple types of drugs including cocaine.	Same as adult occasional user.	None to little.
Persons who sell drugs frequently or in large amounts			
Adolescents	Moderate to heavy use of multiple drugs including cocaine.	Many involved in range of illegal activities including violent crimes; depends on subtype (see table 15–5).	Dependent on subtype (see table 15–5).
Adults	Moderate to heavy use of multiple drugs including heroin and cocaine.	Depends on subtype (see table 15–5).	Dependent on subtype (see table 15–5).

Table 15–5   **Types of Dealers Who Sell Drugs Frequently or in Large Amounts**

Type of Dealer	Typical Drug Use	Typical Problems	Contact with Justice System
Top-level dealers Adults (only)	None to heavy use of multiple types of drugs.	Major distribution of drugs; some other white-collar crime such as money laundering.	Low to minimal.
Lesser predatory Adolescents	Moderate to heavy drug use; some addiction; heroin and cocaine use.	Assaults; range of property crimes; poor school performance.	Low to moderate contact with juvenile or adult justice system.
Adult men	Moderate to heavy drug use; some addiction; heroin and cocaine use.	Burglary and other property crimes; many drug sales; irregular employment; moderate to high social instability.	Low to high contact with criminal justice system.
Adult women	Moderate to heavy drug use; some addiction; heroin and cocaine use.	Prostitution; theft; many drug sales; addicted babies; AIDS babies; high-risk children.	Low to moderate contact with criminal justice system.
Drug-involved violent predatory offenders: **The "losers"** Adolescents	Heavy use of multiple drugs; often addiction to heroin or cocaine.	Commit many crimes in periods of heaviest drug use including robberies; high rates of school dropout; problems likely to continue as adults.	High contact with both juvenile and adult criminal justice system.
Adults	Heavy use of multiple drugs; often addiction to heroin or cocaine.	Commit many crimes in periods of heaviest drug use including robberies; major source of income from criminal activity; low-status roles in drug hierarchy.	High contact with criminal justice system; high incarceration.
The "winners" Adolescents	Frequent use of multiple drugs; less frequent addiction to heroin and cocaine.	Commit many crimes; major source of income from criminal activity; take midlevel role in drug distribution to both adolescents and adults.	Minimal; low incarceration record.

- Organized crime. Cocaine and marijuana sales bring drug lords more than $20 billion each year. Legalization would wipe out their major source of funds.
- Foreign policy. The U.S. drug habit generates $2 billion in revenues for Latin American thugs. Crackdowns severely strain relations.
- Revenues. Treatment programs could be financed by taxes on drugs, like taxes on alcohol and tobacco.

AGAINST:

- Exposure. Cheap, available drugs would increase addiction; only 10 percent of drinkers become hooked, while an estimated 75 percent of regular drug users could become addicted.
- Exotics. Legalization could lead to the sale of synthetic drugs or derivatives like crack without any understanding of their effects.
- Medical costs. The health costs of drug abuse, estimated at $60 billion annually, would increase.
- Social mores. Removing the legal strictures could make drug use socially acceptable.

One strong argument against legalization has been set forth by John Lawn, head of the Drug Enforcement Administration, who says: "Drugs are not bad because they're illegal. They're illegal because they're bad. The legal production and sale of drugs would threaten all of society" (Church, 1988, p. 18).

Increased Law Enforcement

Efforts could be increased to stop illegal drugs from being produced in other countries, from being smuggled into the United States, and/or from being sold here.

Each approach has its problems. As far as preventing production of illicit drugs, Kaplan (n.d.) notes that preventing production of opium would require controlling poppy cultivation and international cooperation. Preventing smuggling is equally difficult. Kaplan suggests, for example, that the total heroin requirement of all American addicts for an entire year is probably less than 10 tons, yet 100 million tons of freight come into the United States yearly, and more than 200 million people cross American borders yearly.

Kraar (1988, p. 23) contends that "America's war on drugs is long on rhetoric and short on effectiveness. Busting drug dealers, as a Washington analyst puts it, 'is like trying to put General Motors out of business by knocking off used-car dealers.' "

A Two-Market Approach

Under this approach, addicts would be supplied at clinics or other types of health facilities, but illegal drugs would not be available for

This tank-like vehicle is being used by some police departments, like this one in Los Angeles, to bash into suspected "Crackhouses."

nonaddicts. Kaplan describes the "British system," where heroin is provided to addicts at clinics specifically set up for that purpose. In more recent years, however, they have switched to using methadone, a synthetic opiate, as a maintenance drug.

Asset Forfeiture Program

Burden (1988, p. 29) notes that in the last fiscal year, the United States Justice Department approved payment of $24.4 million to state and local law enforcement agencies as their share of cash and property seized from organized crime and drug traffickers.

The Asset Forfeiture Program was enacted in 1984 and allows the Justice Department to share seized assets with state and local law enforcement agencies that participated in the investigations and arrests. Such forfeitures have included a recording studio, a Chevrolet dealership, a one-thousand-acre plantation, a horse farm with 210 Appaloosas including a stud horse worth $1.5 million, luxury homes, cars, boats, and planes.

Enlisting Public Support

FBI Director William Sessions (1989, p.11) urges police officers and administrators to become community leaders in fostering public support for the war against drugs:

Police officials must use their skills and influence to help reshape public attitudes toward drug abuse. The fight against drugs is a war, and public support is needed for victory. . . .

Police have a special responsibility to become fully engaged with the public to obtain their unflagging support.

In their role as community leaders, the police must make the public recognize what is at stake—not only the hearts and minds of millions of adults and children, but their safety and lives, as well.

SUMMARY

In 1914 the Harrison Narcotics Act was passed by the federal government making it illegal to sell or use certain drugs, including narcotics and dangerous drugs. Narcotics are drugs that produce sleep, lethargy, or relief of pain, including heroin, cocaine, crack, and marijuana. Dangerous drugs are addicting, mind-altering drugs such as depressants, stimulants, and hallucinogens.

In most states narcotics and dangerous drugs may not be used or sold without a prescription. Federal law prohibits sale or distribution not covered by prescription, but it does not prohibit possession for personal use. The most commonly observed drugs on the street, in possession of users, and seized in drug raids are heroin, opium, morphine, codeine, cocaine, crack, and marijuana. Arrest for possession or use of marijuana is the most frequent drug arrest.

Although legal, alcohol is the most widely abused drug in the United States. Drug use and alcohol abuse have been linked to criminal activity. The drug problem might be approached by legalization, increased law enforcement, a two-market approach, an asset forfeiture program, and enlisting public support.

DISCUSSION QUESTIONS

1. Where does alcohol fall in the categories of drugs and crimes?

2. How does your city rank in the United States as far as occurrence of drug abuse?

3. Which drugs pose the greatest problem for law enforcement?

4. How effective is our court system in deterring sales and use of drugs?

5. Is imprisonment a good deterrent for those engaged in selling and using drugs?

6. If drugs were legalized, would law enforcement agencies benefit?

7. What can our government do to deal with the drug problem in the United States?

8. Should we establish trade embargoes on countries known to allow the transportation of drugs to the United States?

9. What is the best approach to combat drugs?

10. Should alcohol be banned in the United States?

REFERENCES

AIDS Policy & Law (letter to "Executives"). Washington, D.C.: Buraff Publications, A division of The Bureau of National Affairs, Inc., n.d.

Bennett, W., and Hess, K. M. *Criminal Investigation.* St. Paul, Minn.: West Publishing Company, 1987.

Burden, O. P. "Finding Light at the End of the Drug War Tunnel." *Law Enforcement News,* Vol. 14, No. 282, December 15, 1988.

Chaiken, M. R., and Johnson, B. D. *Characteristics of Different Types of Drug-Involved Offenders.* Washington, D.C.: U.S. Department Of Justice, National Institute of Justice, Office of Communication and Research Utilization, February 1988. NCH 108560.

Church, George J. "Thinking the Unthinkable," *Time.* May 30, 1988, pp. 12–16, 18–19.

Cocaine Abuse. *Study Notes.* Niles, Ill.: Police Science Services, 1977.

Crack. What It Is and What It Does. Department of Health & Human Services, Public Health Services. Alcohol, Drug Abuse, Mental Health Administrative Services, Rockville, Md., 1988, pp. 23–24.

Drug Use Forecasting (DUF): National Institute of Justice Report, March/April 1988. No. 208.

Hoover, R. David, editor. *Drugs of Abuse.* U.S. Department of Justice, Drug Enforcement Administration. Washington, D.C.: U.S. Government Printing Office. 1988.

Intelligence Trends, Special Report. *From the Source to the Street: Current Prices for Cannabis, Cocaine, and Heroin,* Vol. 14, No. 3. U.S. Department of Justice/Drug Enforcement Administration, 1987.

Jennings, P. "Why This Plague?" ABC Documentary, July 11, 1988.

Kaplan, J. *Heroin.* National Institute of Justice, Crime File Study Guide. U.S. Department of Justice. NCH 97225, n.d.

Kraar, Louis. "The Drug Trade." *Fortune,* June 20, 1988, pp. 27–29, 32, 33, 36–38.

National Safety Council. *Accident Facts.* Chicago 1984.

PCP and the Hallucinogens. *Study Notes.* Niles, Ill.: Police Science Services, 1979.

Report to the Nation on Crime and Justice, 2d ed. U.S. Department of Justice, Bureau of Justice Statistics, March 1988.

Rosen, M. S. "1988 in Review: Trouble, with a Capital T that Rhymes with D, that Stands for Drugs." *Law Enforcement News,* January 31, 1989, pp. 1–2.

Sessions, William, S. "Public Support Needed for Victory Against Drugs." *The Police Chief,* September 1989, p. 11.

U.S. Department of Justice. Drug Enforcement Administration. *Fact Sheet.* Washington, D.C. 1988.

CHAPTER SIXTEEN
Criminals: The Lawbreakers

The most conservative estimates suggest that thirty-six to forty million persons—16 to 18 percent of the total United States population—have arrest records for nontraffic offenses.—Report to the Nation on Crime and Justice

DO YOU KNOW

What the three major sources of information about crime are?

What juvenile delinquency is?

How serious the delinquency problem is?

What status offenses are?

Who is responsible for most crime?

What the classical and the positivist theories of crime causation state?

What are some causes of criminal behavior?

How our criminal justice system may actually be contributing to crime?

Introduction

Chapter 16

Just as since ancient times, society makes laws to protect its members, and there are those individuals who do not abide by the laws. Sometimes breaking the law is not considered criminal; for example, a person who breaks a traffic law by speeding would not be considered by most as a criminal. Other offenses, however, are serious enough that the person committing them is called a criminal or, if under legal age, a juvenile delinquent.

Sutherland and Cressey (1978, pp. 20–21) indicate that sociological criminologists take three different positions on who is a criminal. The first group is legally oriented, confident that statutes clearly describe criminal behavior and, consequently, anyone who violates a statute is a criminal, whether apprehended or not. A second group takes the opposite position, arguing that laws are irrelevant, that "persons of little power are criminals according to the law in action, but more powerful people are not." The third group takes a position in between, contending that statutory definitions are used as reference points by both ordinary citizens and criminal justice personnel. They note that most people, for example, know it is against the law to rob, even if they do not know the legal definition of robbery and often confuse it with burglary. This group of criminologists feels you can speak of "unapprehended criminals" and "criminals at large," even if no one has been arrested or even detected.

CRIMINALS—WHO COMMITS CRIME?

The Bureau of Justice Statistics (1983, pp. 31–34) answers the question, Who is the "typical" offender? with the following facts:

Most crimes are committed by men, especially by men under age twenty. Offenders described in arrest, jail, and prison data are disproportionately young, black, unmarried males. Violent offenders are typically low-income youth with a high likelihood of unemployment.

Serious crime arrests are highest in young age groups; participation in crime declines with age.

Property crimes are more typical of youths than of older offenders.

Violent juvenile offenders and adult felons have very similar characteristics.

Gang membership is a major difference between youth and adult criminals.

Relatively few offenders are career criminals.

Career criminals, though few in number, account for most crime.

Chronic violent offenders start out and remain violent.

Prior criminal behavior is one of the best predictors of future criminality.

Relatively few offenders are female.

A relatively large proportion of offenders come from minority groups.

Many offenders have backgrounds that include a turbulent home life, lack of family ties, and poor education. Most offenders were not married; yet most inmates had dependent children.

Prior to arrest many inmates had little or no legal income.

Drug and alcohol abuse is common among offenders. Two out of five prison inmates reported they were under the influences of drugs or were very drunk around the time of the offense.

Table 16–1 What Are the Characteristics of Arrestees and Offenders in Jails and Prisons?

	U.S. Population 1980	Index Crime Arrestees		Jail Inmates		State Prison Inmates	Federal Prison Inmates
		Violent	Property	Unconvicted	Convicted		
	226,545,805	443,686	1,707,434	88,120	132,620	405,312	31,926
Sex							
Male	49%	89%	78%	93%	93%	96%	95%
Female	51	11	23	7	7	4	5
Race							
White	86	51	66	54	61	51	65
Black	12	48	33	44	36	47	33
Other	2	1	2	2	3	3	3
Ethnic Origin							
Hispanic	6	12	11	15	14	8	23
Non-Hispanic	94	88	89	85	86	57	77
Unknown	0	0	0	0	0	35	0
Age							
Under 15	23	5	14	*	*	0	0
15–19	9	23	32	14	11	7	0
20–29	18	43	32	53	54	56	34
30–39	14	19	13	23	24	25	40
40–49	10	7	5	6	7	8	17
50–59	10	3	2	3	3	3	7
60 +	16	1	2	1	1	1	2

*Less than .5%.
Note: Percentages may not add to total because of rounding.
Sources: *Statistical Abstract of the United States 1981.* FBI *Crime in the United States 1983. Jail Inmates, 1983,* BJS Bulletin, November 1985. BJS Survey of Inmates of Local Jails 1983, unpublished data. BJS Prisoners in State and Federal Institutions year end 1983, unpublished data.

SOURCES OF KNOWLEDGE ABOUT WHO COMMITS CRIMES

Much crime is never reported. What is reported comes from three major sources.

The three major sources about crime are:

- *official records;*
- *self-report surveys;*
- *victim surveys.*

Official records include data collected by the FBI and reported yearly in their *Uniform Crime Reports* and data collected by the Department of

Table 16—2 Which Criminals Do We Know the Most About?

The major sources do not give uniformly complete information about every kind of offender. In particular they tell us much more about common criminals than they do about white-collar criminals.

Much of what we know about offenders and their traits is limited to the common criminals who commit the offenses of greatest concern to the public: predatory crimes such as robbery and burglary.

Offenses	Arrestees include many later released—most arrests are for less serious offenses	Jail inmates include those awaiting trial or sentencing and those serving short sentences for less serious crimes	Prison inmates are those sentenced to more than one year—generally for serious crimes
Murder/manslaughter	.15%	6%	18%
Sexual assault	.30	3	6
Robbery	1	11	25
Assault	8	8	6
Other violent crimes	. . .	2	3
Burglary	4	14	18
Larceny-theft	11	11	5
Forgery/fraud/embezzlement	4	5	4
Auto theft	1	2	2
Other property	3	5	2
Drugs	7	10	7
Public order	25	12	3
Driving while intoxicated	15	7	1
Number	11,945,200	223,552	274,564

. . . Not available.

Sources: FBI *Crime in the United States 1985. Jail Inmates, 1983,* BJS Bulletin, November 1985. BJS Survey of Inmates of State Correctional Facilities, 1979, unpublished data.

Justice, Bureau of Justice Statistics, and published in their *Report to the Nation on Crime and Justice.* Such data must be interpreted cautiously, however, because they represent only *reported* crimes.

Self-report studies include one-to-one interviews, surveys, and anonymous questionnaires. In these studies people are usually asked whether they have committed certain crimes and if they were apprehended or not. These findings must also be interpreted cautiously, however, because people often exaggerate, conceal, or forget. In addition, many self-report surveys are conducted with people in correctional facilities.

Victimization Data Victim surveys such as the National Crime Survey (NCS) seek information from people who have been the victims of crimes. The NCS is conducted by the Bureau of Justice Statistics and the United States Census Bureau. They have surveyed about 100,000 individuals each year for the past ten years. According to the NCS, about 34.2 million crimes occurred in the United States in 1986, a much higher figure than "official" sources indicated.

JUVENILE OFFENDERS

States vary as to the age of a juvenile, but most state statutes specify an individual under the age of sixteen or eighteen. **Juvenile delinquency** is behavior by a person not of legal age that violates a local, state, or federal law.

Kratcoski and Walker (1978, p. 261) note:

Delinquency encompasses a wide range of youthful behavior. It applies to juveniles who have committed rape or murder and those who have run away from home to escape intolerable or even threatening situations. Juvenile delinquency, in various jurisdictions, also includes having a fist fight; fishing without a license; taking a ride in a car without the owner's knowledge; buying beer, wine or liquor; drag racing; having sexual relations with a person of the opposite sex; skipping school; gambling for money in card games; or staying out after a certain hour at night.

Juvenile delinquency is behavior by a person not of legal age that violates a local, state, or federal law.

Juvenile delinquency presents a serious problem with an enormous number of youngsters involved. Self-report studies indicate that approximately 90 percent of all young people have committed at least one act for which they could be brought to juvenile court (President's Commission on Law Enforcement and Justice, 1967, p. 55); however, many of these offenses are minor (for example, fighting, truancy, and running away from home), and state statutes often define juvenile delinquency so broadly that virtually all youngsters could be classified as delinquent.

Even though many offenses are minor, and even though many juvenile offenders are never arrested or referred to juvenile court, alarming numbers are. The Children's Bureau estimates that one in every nine youths and one in every six male youths will be referred to juvenile court for a delinquent act (excluding traffic offenses) before his or her eighteenth birthday (President's Commission on Law Enforcement and Justice 1967, p. 56).

Arrest statistics point out the severity of the problem, although such statistics may be somewhat exaggerated as juveniles are often more easily caught than adults, and they often act in groups when committing the crimes, thereby producing a greater number of arrests than crimes committed.

Table 16–3, from the Uniform Crime Reports, indicates the type and extent of crimes in which youth are involved. The seriousness of the problem is evident in the amount of relatively serious property crimes: burglary, larceny, and motor vehicle thefts. In addition, although juveniles account for more than their share of arrests for several serious crimes, such arrests are only a small part of all juvenile arrests. Juveniles are most

Table 16–3   **Total City Arrests of Persons Under 15, 18, 21, and 25 Years of Age, 1988**

[6,919 agencies; 1988 estimated population 129,470,000]

Offense charged	Total all ages	Number of persons arrested				Percent of total all ages			
		Under 15	Under 18	Under 21	Under 25	Under 15	Under 18	Under 21	Under 25
TOTAL	7,938,517	456,722	1,381,909	2,512,306	3,825,324	5.8	17.4	31.6	48.2
Murder and nonnegligent manslaughter	12,575	172	1,514	3,714	6,069	1.4	12.0	29.5	48.3
Forcible rape	21,941	1,123	3,372	6,059	9,710	5.1	15.4	27.6	44.3
Robbery	99,438	6,066	22,535	39,886	58,892	6.1	22.7	40.1	59.2
Aggravated assault	240,212	9,719	32,769	60,584	100,274	4.0	13.6	25.2	41.7
Burglary	251,502	33,842	85,869	128,939	166,283	13.5	34.1	51.3	66.1
Larceny–theft	999,521	137,986	309,869	446,012	572,726	13.8	31.0	44.6	57.3
Motor vehicle theft	124,962	13,566	51,838	74,470	91,690	10.9	41.5	59.6	73.4
Arson	10,872	3,383	4,986	5,914	7,041	31.1	45.9	54.4	64.8
Violent crime[1]	374,166	17,080	60,190	110,243	174,945	4.6	16.1	29.5	46.8
Property crime[2]	1,386,857	188,777	452,562	655,335	837,740	13.6	32.6	47.3	60.4
Crime Index total[3]	1,761,023	205,857	512,752	765,578	1,012,685	11.7	29.1	43.5	57.5
Other assaults	550,997	31,828	84,003	145,020	240,682	5.8	15.2	26.3	43.7
Forgery and counterfeiting	54,730	795	5,027	13,663	24,264	1.5	9.2	25.0	44.3
Fraud	141,021	4,581	10,948	24,856	50,058	3.2	7.8	17.6	35.5
Embezzlement	7,791	106	822	2,364	3,943	1.4	10.6	30.3	50.6
Stolen property; buying, receiving, possessing	100,738	7,042	27,062	47,099	63,388	7.0	26.9	46.8	62.9
Vandalism	183,117	36,928	73,679	99,159	124,058	20.2	40.2	54.2	67.7
Weapons; carrying, possessing, etc.	133,557	6,222	23,911	45,711	68,918	4.7	17.9	34.2	51.6
Prostitution and commercialized vice	75,586	135	1,324	9,759	27,908	.2	1.8	12.9	36.9
Sex offenses (except forcible rape and prostitution)	59,559	4,955	9,792	15,131	23,221	8.3	16.4	25.4	39.0
Drug abuse violations	686,841	8,899	67,040	175,417	316,706	1.3	9.8	25.5	46.1
Gambling	15,496	107	721	1,612	2,919	.7	4.7	10.4	18.8
Offenses against family and children	27,579	635	1,962	4,601	9,262	2.3	7.1	16.7	33.6
Driving under the influence	805,047	286	11,920	82,202	230,383	(4)	1.5	10.2	28.6
Liquor laws	384,143	7,147	96,968	258,448	301,848	1.9	25.2	67.3	78.6
Drunkenness	500,891	1,729	15,131	56,114	128,813	.3	3.0	11.2	25.7
Disorderly conduct	513,303	23,417	80,503	157,781	255,946	4.6	15.7	30.7	49.9
Vagrancy	27,207	556	2,017	4,991	8,557	2.0	7.4	18.3	31.5
All other offenses (except traffic)	1,750,234	59,502	204,785	450,217	777,534	3.4	11.7	25.7	44.4
Suspicion	9,951	604	1,836	2,877	4,525	6.1	18.5	28.9	45.5
Curfew and loitering law violations	52,427	14,587	52,427	52,427	52,427	27.8	100.0	100.0	100.0
Runaways	97,279	40,804	97,279	97,279	97,279	41.9	100.0	100.0	100.0

[1]Violent crimes are offenses of murder, forcible rape, robbery, and aggravated assault.
[2]Property crimes are offenses of burglary, larceny–theft, motor vehicle theft, and arson.
[3]Includes arson.
[4]Less than one-tenth of 1 percent.
Source: Uniform Crime Reports, *Crime in the United States,* 1989.

often arrested for petty larceny, fighting, disorderly conduct, liquor-related offenses, and noncriminal conduct such as curfew violations, truancy, incorrigibility, or running away from home.

Youth is responsible for a substantial and disproportionate part of the national crime problem.

A special category of offenses has been established for juveniles, designating certain actions as illegal for any person under the state's defined juvenile age of sixteen or eighteen. These are **status offenses.**

Status offenses are violations of the law applying only to those under legal age. They include absenting from home, truancy, drinking alcoholic beverages, smoking, violating curfew, and incorrigibility.

According to the *Report to the Nation on Crime and Justice* (1988):

> Most juvenile delinquents do not go on to become adult criminals, but many do continue to commit crimes.
>
> In Marion County, Oregon, 30 percent of the juvenile boys convicted of serious crimes were later convicted of serious crimes as adults.
>
> In Chicago, 34 percent of the boys appearing in juvenile court later went to jail or prison as adults.
>
> The more serious the juvenile career, the greater the chances of adult criminality. In New York City, 48 percent of the juveniles who had only one year of juvenile activity had one or more adult arrests and 15 percent were serious adult offenders. In contrast, 78 percent of those with lengthy juvenile careers were arrested as adults and 37 percent were serious adult offenders.
>
> A few criminals commit many crimes. Studies in Philadelphia, Pennsylvania; Racine, Wisconsin; and Columbus, Ohio, show that 23 to 34 percent of the juveniles involved in crime are responsible for 61 to 68 percent of all crimes committed by juveniles. In a national sample of United States youths ages eleven to seventeen, the 7 percent who were the most active offenders committed about 125 crimes per year each, whereas the 55 percent who were the least active committed an average of fewer than 8 per year.

CAREER CRIMINALS

As noted by the *Report to the Nation:* "The term 'career criminal' has been used to describe offenders who

- have an extensive record of arrests and convictions
- commit crimes over a long period of time
- commit crimes at a very high rate
- commit relatively serious crimes
- use crimes as their principal source of income
- specialize (or are especially expert) in a certain type of crime
- have some combination of these characteristics.

Such criminals are often described as "chronic, habitual, repeat, serious, high-rate, or professional offenders."

As with juvenile offenders, a few adult criminals commit much of the nation's crime.

The Chaiken's study of nearly 2,200 offenders coming into California, Michigan, and Texas jails and prisons found that 50 percent of the robbers committed an average of fewer than 5 robberies per year, but a robber in the most active 10 percent committed more than 85 per year. And, while 50 percent of the burglars averaged fewer than 6 burglaries per year, the most active 10 percent averaged more than 232 per year.

A Washington, D.C. study reported that 24 percent of all the adult arrests were attributable to just 7 percent of the adults arrested. Similarly, a twenty-two-state study by the Bureau of Justice Statistics of young parolees revealed that about 10 percent of this group accounted for 40 percent of their later arrest offenses. (Report to the Nation)

A few criminals commit many crimes. Repeat offenders, juvenile and adult, are responsible for much of our crime.

Garmire (1982, pp. 172–73) stresses that "special attention should be given to the career criminal as a part of a police agency's total investigative effort." Garmire suggests that most police administrators feel that about 10 percent of the criminals are committing the majority of crimes, including robberies, burglaries, larcenys, car theft, forgeries, and fraud. He points out the following:

Often the career criminal is thought of as a member of organized crime—an invisible figure, highly sophisticated, possessing cunning and cleverness. Such is not, in fact, the case. The career criminal is often known to the police from prior offenses; he or she is most often an opportunist who will commit whatever crime is convenient. Often the career criminal is highly talented in one specialty, such as fraud, passing bad checks, or burglary. A single arrest is not sufficient to alter his or her pattern of crime.

WHY DO PEOPLE COMMIT CRIME?

The reason people commit crime has been debated since crime was first defined. Two philosophical theories have been set forth.

Classical versus Positivist Theory of Crime Causation

The **classical theory** was developed by the eighteenth-century Italian criminologist Cesare Beccaria.

This view is held by Thimmesch (1984): "Who breaks the law are those who have convinced themselves that they are special and superior and that what they are doing is not wrong." Reese (1981) puts it a little more forcefully: "Idiot liberals think every human being on earth has the same value system they do and those who don't must be sick. Hogwash!

There are a lot of perfectly rational people who see nothing wrong in cutting a throat or cracking a skull."

The classical theory sees people as free agents with free will. People commit crimes because they want to.

A refinement to the classical theory is the *routine activity theory* developed by Lawrence Cohen and Marcus Felson. This theory states that the volume and distribution of predatory crime (where the offender tries to steal an object directly) correlates highly with three variables found in everyday, routine American life:

1. The availability of suitable targets (homes/stores containing easily sold goods).
2. The absence of watchful guardians (homeowners, neighbors, friends, relatives, guards, security systems, etc.).
3. The presence of motivated offenders (unemployed individuals, drug abusers, etc.).

The presence of these three variables increases the chances of a predatory crime occurring. This theory gives equal weight to the role of victim and offender. It also suggests that the opportunity for criminal action depends on the victim's life-style and behavior.

The **positivist theory** was developed by Cesare Lombroso, an Italian criminologist, at the turn of the century.

The classic studies of Lombroso (1911) support a biological causation for deviant behavior and, in fact, suggest that individuals who do not conform to society's laws and regulations are biologically inferior. *Biological theorists* suggest that how a person acts is basically a result of heredity. Richard Speck, convicted of killing eight Chicago nurses, for example, showed an unusual genetic structure. He had one extra male chromosome. Speck is not the only convicted criminal to display such a genetic abnormality.

The positivist theory sees criminals as "victims of society" and of their own biological, sociological, cultural, and physical environments.

Further, Herrnstein and Wilson (1983, p. 19) state: "Criminologists have long known about the correlation between criminal behavior and IQ, but many have discounted it for various reasons." Nonetheless the correlation does exist, and IQ is thought to be greatly influenced by heredity.

A counterposition to the biological theory is the *behavioral theory,* which suggests that criminals are *made,* not born.

Siegel and Senna (1988, p. 92–96) suggest other possible causes of delinquency including biochemical factors and neurological dysfunction. As noted by Drowns and Hess (1990, p. xx):

> *Biochemical research focuses on the connection between youths' antisocial behavior and their biochemical makeup. Diet, blood chemistry, hormonal imbalances, and allergies all affect body function and the central nervous system. These physical factors can influence behavior and have, in fact, been linked to anti-social behavior. Diet is of particular interest because an unusually high consumption of artificial food colorings, milk, and sweets may negatively affect behavior.*
>
> *Neurological research focuses on the brain and nervous system. . . . A study of inmates on death row showed that a significant number had neurological handicaps due to head injuries they suffered as children.*

Raloff (1983) suggests that "inborn chemical imbalances may underlie some of the severest criminal violence."

Timnick (1983) suggests:

> *The classic criminal's callousness, lack of remorse, inability to learn from experience or punishment, failure to anticipate the consequences of certain acts and seeming inability to "feel" is mirrored by objective physical measurements such as skin conductance tests, pulse rates, chemical levels in the blood, and brain wave tracings—all of which suggest that his nervous system is different, if not deficient.*

It is likely that criminal behavior is the result of both heredity and life experiences.

Multiple Causes of Criminal Behavior

Rainwater (1974, p. 7) has identified five different perspectives on the causation of crime:

> *For the social pathologist, the problem is the defective character of individuals in society. . . . For the sociologist who focuses on social disorganization, the problem is in ineffectiveness of rules for organizing constructive social processes. For the value conflict theorist, the problem can be understood only as a result either of conflicts among groups in society or of conflicting interests held by a single individual. For the deviance theorist, the problem lies in the instigations to rule violation created by the unequal distribution of opportunities for self-realization in society. For the*

labeling theorist, the problem is very much in the eye of the beholder, and in the process by which society separates its members into the moral and the immoral, the conforming and the deviant.

Each perspective offers some insight into the complexity of the causations of crime, and each illustrates that there is no single factor responsible for the existence of crime, a fact long accepted by criminologists.

No definitive answer exists as to why people commit crimes. Of the several theories set forth, several suggest a combination of sociological, psychological, and biological factors.

According to the Bureau of Justice Statistics (1983, p. 30):

Historically, the causes of criminal behavior have included explanations ranging from the influences of evil spirits to the abnormal shape of the skull. Contemporary theories for the causes of crime still abound, but can be grouped into three general explanations:

The sociogenic—focuses on the environment's effect on the individual and places responsibility for crime on society. It identifies as the causes of crime such factors as poverty, ignorance, high unemployment, inadequate housing, and poor health. To these general environmental factors, it adds the impact of unstable homes, viewing their consequent discord, absence of affection and consistent discipline, and improper moral instruction as especially contributory to juvenile delinquency and youth crime. However, recent research has shown that these factors do not account for long-term fluctuations in crime. Moreover, these factors cannot explain why under certain circumstances, one individual commits a crime and another does not.

The psychogenic—focuses on psychological factors and understands crime to be the result of an individual's propensity and inducement toward crime. Propensity toward crime is determined by the individual's ability to conceptualize right and wrong, to manage impulse and postpone present gratifications, and to anticipate and take into account consequences that lie in the future as well as the individual's fondness of risk and willingness to inflict injury on others. Inducement relates to situational factors such as access and opportunity that may provide the individual with the necessary incentives to commit a crime. Under this explanation, while many environmental factors contribute to an individual's propensity to commit crime, the individual is responsible for his behavior. Further, inducement toward committing crime may be inherent in our technological age which, among other things, allows increased access through greater mobility.

The biogenic—focuses on biological functions and processes and relates human behavior, specifically criminal behavior, to such biological variables as brain tumors and other disorders of the limbic system, endo-

crine abnormalities, neurological dysfunction produced by prenatal and postnatal experience of infants, and chromosomal abnormalities (the XYY chromosomal pattern).

Further support for the multiplicity of causes for crime is presented by Hood and Sparks (1970), who note that numerous comparisons of groups of criminals with groups of noncriminals have failed to produce any single characteristic or "factor" that absolutely distinguishes the two groups. Further, since the concepts of crime, delinquency, deviant behavior, and the like apply to such a wide range of different kinds of behavior, having in common only the fact that they have been declared contrary to legal rules in various times and places, no single causal explanation can possibly cover this wide range of behaviors.

Many Americans have come to accept the existence of crime as a part of life, a price paid by a democratic society for its high standard of living where those who "have not" seek to get their fair share in any way possible.

Crime has always been a local problem and responsibility, yet it is a social problem that concerns the entire country. Its causative factors and effects have been studied by scientists and researchers for over a century. Its increase in the last quarter-century has so alarmed the country and cities that in the sixties and seventies politicians often dictated a "law and order" platform.

Many of the causative factors of crime are well beyond the control of the law enforcement officer. Included among these are the population, its density and size, that is, how many people live in a square mile; economics; the legal policies of prosecutors; the educational system of the community; the recreational areas and facilities available; and the religious characteristics of some communities. With a breakdown in discipline in many schools with open, permissive policies and a breakdown in the family value system, crime has become one of America's gravest social problems.

The high level of unemployment, especially among the young, increases the problem. With teenage unemployment in some large cities running 40 percent, attitudes and values may change considerably. The free enterprise system may appear to have little to offer a young person who cannot gain access to the system because no jobs are available. For some the logical alternative is to engage in crime. When frustration, emotional conflict, and desperation overcome individuals because of social and economic conditions, they frequently resort to a crime against property or persons. The result is that those individuals who have been able to cope with the stresses of the free enterprise system and are law abiding find themselves victimized by those who have turned to crime.

Others, such as Sviridoff and Thompson (1983) argue that employment does not stop crime: "They was making $200 a day in the street, $150 a day gambling, stealing. And now they gonna work, ten hours a day; seven days a week for $125?" Employment must be good enough (either pay enough or offer the promise of advancement) to compete with life on the street.

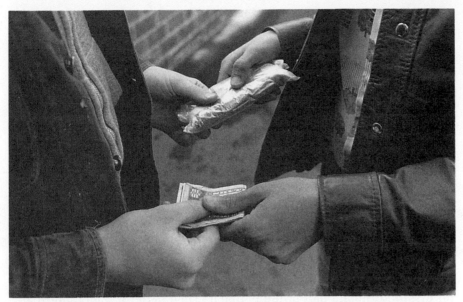

For some people, unemployment makes crime look like an attractive way to make money.

Likewise, many do not feel that poverty is a cause of crime. Says Morriss (1982): "Most poor people, in fact, do not steal; poverty does not compel criminality. During the Great Depression, the streets, homes, parks, and subways were safe—at a time when college professors sold apples on the street and all Americans were dreadfully deprived."

THE ROLE OF OUR CRIMINAL JUSTICE SYSTEM

Although our criminal justice system may not actually cause crime, several people feel that it promotes crime.

Our criminal justice system, including plea bargaining, low conviction rates, lack of prison space, and lenient juvenile justice, may promote crime.

According to Rosenblatt (1981):

There are specific reasons for the nation's incapacity to keep its street crime down. Almost all of these reasons can be traced to the American criminal justice system. . . . It is not that there are no mechanisms in place to deal with American crime, merely that the existing ones are impractical, inefficient, anachronistic, uncooperative, and often lead to as much civil destruction as they are meant to curtail. . . . The majority of criminals go untouched by it [the system]. . . . Even when a suspect is apprehended, the chances of his getting punished are mighty slim.

These sentiments are echoed by Dershowitz (1982):

Incredible disparity makes the system a roulette wheel. It depends on where you commit a crime, which judge hears the case and whether you're smart enough to follow the first rule of crime. Commit it with somebody more important than you so that you can turn them in and make a plea bargain for yourself. The net result is that, however tough we may be in theory, the average criminal does not think he's going to do time for serious crimes. Criminals are gamblers by nature. They say to themselves, "If there's any chance that I might get off, I'll probably get off."

SUMMARY

The three major sources about crime are official records, self-report surveys, and victim surveys. Crimes are committed by youths and adults.

Juvenile delinquency is behavior by a person not of legal age that violates a local, state, or federal law. Youth is responsible for a substantial and disproportionate part of the national crime pattern. Many youth are guilty of status offenses, violations of the law applying only to those under legal age. They include absenting from home, truancy, drinking alcoholic beverages, smoking, violating curfew, and incorrigibility.

A few criminals commit many crimes. Repeat offenders, juvenile and adult, are responsible for much of our crime. Why do they do so? Two philosophies exist. The classical theory sees people as free agents with free will. People commit crimes because they want to. The positivist theory, in contrast, sees criminals as "victims of society" and of their own biological, sociological, cultural, and physical environments. It is likely that criminal behavior is the result of both heredity and life experiences. No definitive answer exists as to why people commit crimes. Of the theories set forth, several suggest a combination of sociological, psychological, and biological factors.

In addition, our criminal justice system, including plea bargaining, low conviction rates, lack of prison space, and lenient juvenile justice, may promote crime.

Discussion Questions

1. What problems can arise in the legal definition of a juvenile delinquent and serious crimes such as murder?

2. Is there one single causative factor for crime today?

3. How can the personal biases of those in the criminal justice system be avoided in handling criminals in the community?

4. What are some high risk factors that contribute to a criminal career?

5. How long does one remain a criminal—until the crime has been "paid for" or for a lifetime?

6. What factors prevent most juvenile offenders from becoming adult criminals?

7. Why are more arrests among juveniles for theft than any other crime?

8. How reliable are self-report questionnaires given juveniles about their deviant behavior?

9. Are parents responsible for their children becoming criminals?

10. Have you ever known an adult convicted of a crime? If so, what was he or she like?

References

Bureau of Justice Statistics. U.S. Department of Justice. *Report to the Nation on Crime and Justice.* Washington, D.C.: U.S. Government Printing Office, 1983.

Dershowitz, *U.S. News World Report,* August 9, 1982.

Drowns, R., and Hess, K. M. *Juvenile Justice.* St. Paul, Minn.: West Publishing Company, 1990.

Gamire, B. L. (ed.) *Local Government Police Management,* 2d ed. Washington, D.C.: International City Management Association, 1982.

Herrnstein, R. J., and Wilson, J. Q. "Are Criminals Made or Born?" in *Encyclopedia of Crime and Justice.* Vol. 4, ed. S. H. Kadish. New York: The Free Press, 1983, pp. 17–20.

Hood, R., and Sparks, R. *Key Issues in Criminology.* New York: McGraw-Hill, 1970.

Kratcoski, P. C., and Walker, D. B. *Criminal Justice in America: Process and Issues.* Glenview, Ill.: Scott Foresman, 1978.

Lombroso, C. *Crimes: Its Causes and Remedies.* Montclair, N.J.: Patterson Smith, 1968. Originally published in 1911.

Morriss, F. "Lack of Virtue, Not Jobs, at Root of Social Unrest," *The Wanderer,* December 16, 1982.

President's Commission on Law Enforcement and Administration of Justice. *The Challenge of Crime in a Free Society.* Washington, D.C.: U.S. Government Printing Office, February 1967.

Rainwater, L. *Inequality and Justice.* Chicago: Adline Publishing, 1974.

Raloff, J. "Locks—A Key to Violence?" *Science News,* August 20, 1983.

Reese, C. *The Union Leader,* August 19, 1981.

Report to the Nation on Crime and Justice, 2d ed. U.S. Department of Justice, Bureau of Justice Statistics, March 1988.

Rosenblatt, R. "Why the Justice System Fails," *Time,* March 23, 1981.

Siegel, L. J., and Senna, J. J. *Juvenile Delinquency,* 3d ed. St. Paul, Minn.: West Publishing Company, 1988.

Sutherland, E. H. *The Professional Thief.* Chicago: University of Chicago Press, 1937.

Sutherland, E. H., and Cressey, D. R. *Criminology,* 10th ed. Philadelphia: Lippincott, 1978.

Sviridoff, M., and Thompson, J. W. *Crime and Delinquency,* April 1983.

Thimmesch, N. *Human Events,* February 25, 1984.

Timnick, L. *The Los Angeles Times,* June 26, 1983.

U.S. Department of Justice. Uniform Crime Reports. *Crime in the United States, 1988.* Washington, D.C.: U.S. Government Printing Office, Sept 9, 1989.

CHAPTER SEVENTEEN
Gangs: A Growing Menace

Gangs are now spreading through our society like a violent plague.—Jackson and McBride, L.A.P.D.

DO YOU KNOW

How a gang is defined?

Whether gangs are racially or ethnically mixed?

What the distinguishing characteristics of gangs are?

How gang members might be identified?

What the role of most female gangs is?

What the most common reasons for joining gangs are?

The *Encyclopedia of Crime and Justice*, (ECJ) (1983, p. 1) notes the following:

Much of the violent and predatory crime in the United States is committed by members of youth groups. Law-violating youth groups take many forms. The term most widely used to refer to such groups is gang. Youth gangs command considerable public attention and pose serious crime problems in many communities. The type of group designated as a gang varies from place to place, from time to time, and among agencies in particular localities.

GANGS DEFINED

The *ECJ* (1983, p. 1673) defines youth gangs as follows: "Youth gangs are self-formed associations of youths distinguished from other types of youth groups by their routine participation in illegal activities."

Jackson and McBride (1985, p. 20) define youth gangs this way:

A gang is a group of people that forms an allegiance for a common purpose, and engage in unlawful or criminal activity.

A definition commonly accepted by law enforcement is that a gang is any group gathered together on a continuing basis to commit antisocial behavior.

A BRIEF HISTORICAL PERSPECTIVE

Gangs have existed in nearly every civilization back through recorded history. Street gangs probably started in our country in Los Angeles about the turn of the century.

Hispanic Gangs

Davis (1982, p. 5) suggests that between 1910 and 1925 a great influx of immigrants from Mexico occurred. These immigrants tended to live with others from their native areas of Mexico, and rivalries developed that eventually resulted in the formation of gangs such as Bunker Hill, Mara Villa, and San Fernando. These Hispanic gangs lived in barrios that often could trace their heritage back several generations. They had a strong system of tradition and became known as "traditional" gangs.

The depression of the 1930s brought Latino families from Arizona, New Mexico, and Texas to Los Angeles. They fragmented into groups, each claiming its own territory and forming such gangs as Happy Valley, HoyoSoto, Alpine Hazard, and White Fence.

In the 1960s freeway displacement drove families from the central city eastward, where they created more new gangs such as Lomas and Bassett.

Black Gangs

Black street gangs also existed in the Los Angeles area for many years. They began as groups of young high school "thugs" who extorted money from students and terrorized teachers. One gang called itself the Crips. It had the reputation of being the toughest black gang in Los Angeles. Other gangs started incorporating the word "Crip" into their names. Although they shared a common name, they were in reality independent, and rivalries developed. The black gangs divided themselves into the Crips and the Non-Crips or Bloods. Since black gangs have not existed as long as Hispanic gangs, they do not have generations of tradition and, consequently, are often referred to as "nontraditional" gangs.

Other types of Gangs

Asian gangs known as Yu Li, Joes Boys, and Wah Chings exist in most of the major cities of the United States and Canada.

Filipino neighborhood street gangs are similar to Hispanic gangs and may gravitate toward Mexican gangs. The most common Filipino gangs are the Santanas, the Tabooes, and Temple Street.

The Korean community also has active gangs, the most well known being the Korean Killers.

Most gangs are racially or ethnically homogeneous.

Table 17–1 summarizes the origins and characteristics of the major youth gangs operating in the United States.

SPECIFIC CHARACTERISTICS OF YOUTH GANGS

Five general characteristics are often associated with gangs (*ECJ*, pp. 1671–73).

Distinguishing characteristics of gangs include leadership, organization, associational patterns, domain identification, and illegal activity.

Table 17–1   Youth Gangs Characteristic Groups

Black Gangs	Origins in Los Angeles, Chicago, New York, Miami, and other major urban ghettos. Crips, Bloods, Players, Untouchables, and Vice Lords are some of the more prominent gangs.
Jamaican Posses	Immigrant Jamaicans in the U.S. with roots in Jamaica. Groups have been identified in New York, Boston, Philadelphia, Washington, D.C., Houston, Atlanta, Detroit, Seattle, and Anchorage among other locations.
Hispanic Gangs	Origins in Los Angeles, valleys of California, New York (Puerto Rico), Miami (Mariel Cubans, Dominicans), Washington, D.C., and other urban barrios. Tend to use highly stylized graffiti lettering.
Asian Gangs	Origins among recent emigres from Viet Nam, Hong Kong, and Philippines. Activity centered in New York, New Orleans, Los Angeles and Orange County, California, Portland, Oregon, Seattle, San Francisco, and Houston.
Pacific Islander Gangs	Primarily Samoans who have migrated to Western urban areas, i.e., Los Angeles, San Francisco, Portland.
White "Stoner" Gangs	Caucasian groups identified with Heavy Metal and Punk Rock music preferences and with some British working class gangs. Sometimes involved with Satanic rites and symbols.
Neo-Nazi Gangs	Tend to articulate white supremacy, racism, and Nazi symbols. Some call themselves "skinheads" and sport close-cut hair or shaved heads.
Motorcycle Gangs	Dominantly caucasians, branches of Hells Angels and other notorious motorcycle groups. Tend to be heavily involved with the manufacture and sale of methamphetamine.

Source: Metropolitan Court Judges Committee Report: Drugs—The American Family in Crisis: A Judicial Response; 39 Recommendations, 8–4–88.

Leadership

Gang leadership is usually quite well defined and may be one of three types: key personality, chain of command, or collective. As the name suggests, in the key personality leadership gang one particular gang member, often older than the others, is a strong and influential leader. He becomes a role model for other gang members.

In a gang with a chain of command form of leadership, the gang functions like a military unit or even a police department. Each member within the group has a specific rank, with authority going from the top down. As noted by Vetter and Territo (1984, p. 518):

At the top is the "prez," who gains his or her position by being the most ruthless and violent member of the gang—and who remains on top only as long as he or she meets every challenge of authority. Under the "prez" is the "veep," who collects dues, supervises the recruitment and initiation of new members, and manages internal affairs.

In a gang with a collective leadership style, leaders change depending on the activity in which the gang is involved. If the gang is planning a crime, the best criminal mind is leader. If they are planning an attack on a neighboring gang, the best fighter is leader.

Organization

Gangs tend to be quite formally organized. One common organizational element is age. Gangs commonly have two to four age divisions. Another common organizational element is location, that is, two or more gangs may have localized versions of the same gang name, for example, the Southside Warriors and the Tenth Street Warriors.

Gangs also tend to have a hierarchical authority as described under leadership.

Associational Patterns

Gang members become very close to each other, hanging out together on street corners and in parks, school yards, and parking lots. They are, in effect, "family."

As noted in the *ECJ* (1983), gangs in many cases take the place of family, school, and church. Concepts such as loyalty, ego strength, and camaraderie are all-important. An attack on a gang member is an attack on the entire gang.

Gangs often have specific criteria for membership and special initiation ceremonies. Often a person wanting to become a member may have to commit a crime before being admitted into the gang. According to Davis (1982, p. 10):

One normally joins a street gang by either committing a crime or by being "jumped in." "Jumped in" is where the person being initiated is beaten, sometimes severely by fellow members to test his courage and fighting ability. The way to get out of a gang is not so easy as you have to be "jumped out." This is similar except they go to hurt you seriously, not to just see what you can do. This can discourage even the toughest gang member from leaving the gang.

Domain Identification

Typically gangs stake out a geographic territory, or "turf," as their domain. This may be a specific facility such as a school or it may be an entire neighborhood. If one gang "trespasses" on another gang's turf, gang violence is likely.

Some gangs claim exclusive control over certain activities in an area such as the right to collect fees from students for using the restrooms or "insurance" payments from local merchants in exchange for protection.

Criminal Activity

As noted in the *ECJ* (1983, p. 1672): "The most distinctive form of gang offense is gang-fighting."

Vetter and Territo (1984, pp. 571–18) claim: "Today, urban gangs are responsible for roughly one-quarter of all juvenile crimes committed each year. Gone are the knives, clubs, bicycle chains, and homemade 'zip' guns used as weapons in yesterday's 'rumbles.' The gang wars of today . . . feature sophisticated weaponry—AR-15s, M-16s, grenades, and plastic explosives— that would do credit to a military assault troop."

And according to Trojanowicz (1978, p. 402):

In some cities, gangs have gotten out of control to the point where regular activities in the community are disrupted. Armed bands of young gang members board buses and physically force passengers to give up wallets and other personal items. Gang members are getting so bold that not only do they show total disregard for their fellow man, but they have no fear of police or any formal consequences for their actions.

Acts of vandalism, arson, graffiti painting, stabbings, and shootings are common. Student extortion and teacher intimidation are also common.

Davis (1982, p. 1) warns that gang activity "is more lethal today than at any time in the twentieth century. . . . They have indeed become our most pervasive threat to date relative to criminal victimization. Epidemics of murders, stabbings, drug sales and 'rip' offs by groups begin to identify a pattern. . . . [They] develop a lifestyle characterized by extortion, shootings, knifings, and dope deals. . . . Mutual excitement comes from pistol whippings or committing armed robberies."

According to the *ECJ* (1983, p. 1674) liberals and conservatives have opposing ideas as to why gangs engage in crime:

Liberals generally ascribe gang crime to such unjust social conditions as poverty, inequality, bigotry, unemployment, discriminatory policies of criminal justice agencies, and inadequate resources for social services to the poor. Conservatives generally blame a progressive deterioration in social morality, including a weakening of self-discipline, individual responsibility, family solidarity, sexual restraint, and religion.

OTHER GANG CHARACTERISTICS

Other characteristics may help law enforcement officers identify gang members.

Gang members might be identified by their names, their symbols (clothing and tattoos), and how they communicate, including graffiti and sign language.

Gang *names* vary from colorful and imaginative to straightforward. They commonly refer to localities, animals, birds, royalty, and rebellion. As noted in the *ECJ* (1983, p. 1677):

> *Localities can be streets (for example, the Tenth Streeters), neighborhoods (The Southsiders), housing projects (the Alazones Courts), and cities or towns (the Johnstown Gang). Popular animal names are the Tigers, the Panthers, the Cougars, the Leopards, the Cobras, the Eagles, and the Hawks. Royal titles include the Kings, the Emperors, the Lords, the Knights, the Barons, and the Dukes. Names denoting rebellion or lawlessness include the Rebels, the Outlaws, the Savages, and the Assassins. Gangs may be designated by the name of a leader or other important member such as "Joey and Them Kids" or "Garcia's Boys." A common combination is a local designation coupled with another category, for example, the West Side Majestic Warlords, the Third Street Rangers, and the Spring Hill Savages.*

Gang *symbols* are also common. Clothing, in particular, can distinguish a particular gang. Perhaps best known is the typical attire of an outlaw motorcycle gang member: tattered Levis, scuffed boots, leather vests, and jackets with their own unique emblems. Sometimes "colors" are used to distinguish a gang, as dramatized in the film *Colors*. Gang members also use jerseys, t-shirts, and jackets with emblems.

Tattoos are also symbols used by some gangs, particularly outlaw motorcycle gangs and Hispanic gangs. Black gangs members seldom have tattoos.

Communications

Graffiti is a very common form of communication used by gang members. It is frequently used to stake out a gang's turf. Defacing, erasing, or substituting one gang's graffiti by a rival gang constitutes a challenge and usually results in violence and gang warfare.

A Los Angeles White Paper on gang activity suggests:

> *Much valuable information relative to police work may be gained from gang graffiti. For instance, one may be able to determine what gang is in control of a specific area by noting the frequency of the unchallenged graffiti because throwing a "placa" on a wall corresponds to claiming a territory. Writing left unchanged reaffirms the gang's control. As one moves away from the center or core area of a gang's power and territory, the more rival graffiti and cross-outs are observed.*
>
> *Contested areas are common when both gangs arrive at the same place at the same time. A confrontation occurs.*

The White Paper also notes that black and Latino styles of graffiti are vastly different, with the black gang graffiti lacking the flair and attention to detail evidenced by the Latino gang graffiti. Much of the black gang wall writing is filled with profanity.

Another form of communication typical of gang members is hand signals. These signs are often used to identify the person with a specific gang.

FEMALE GANGS

Female gangs are relatively rare.

Most female gangs are adjuncts or auxiliaries to a male gang.

A female gang may have a name affiliated with their male counterpart such as the Vice Ladies (from the Vice Lords). These auxiliaries usually consist of sisters and girlfriends of the male gang members. The females often assist the male gang, serving as decoys for rival gang members, as lookouts during the commission of crimes, or as carriers of weapons when a gang war is impending.

Campbell (1984, p. 266) studied the relationships among the girls in three New York gangs and found "intense camaraderie and strong dependency" on one another. According to Campbell, the "fundamental gang role of females has not altered substantially. Girl gangs exist as an adjunct to the male gang, and the range of possibilities open to their members is dictated and controlled by the boys."

WHY PEOPLE JOIN GANGS

The most frequently cited reason for people joining gangs is to *belong*. According to Sidney J. Harris, nationally syndicated columnist: "Gangs make martyrs of losers. . . . Gang members tend to be chronic losers, who can accomplish nothing individually, or who live in so depressed an environment that only by banding together can they exercise any influence over their lives."

The close ties of gang members is a major motive for membership. The membership provides both psychological and physical security. Most gang members are underachievers who come from broken homes or homes with no strong male authority figure. Davis (1982, pp. 9–10) cites four reasons people typically join gangs:

The most common reasons for joining a gang are for identity or recognition, for protection, for fellowship and brotherhood, or from intimidation.

Says Davis: (1982, pp. 9–10)

Most gang members visualize themselves as warriors or soldiers protect-ing their barrio (community or neighborhood) from what they perceive to be a hostile outside world. You can see this in the gang murals painted on the walls throughout L.A. County.

Many members join because they live in the gang area and are, there-fore, subject to violence by rival gangs. Joining guarantees support in case of attack and retaliation for transgressions.

To the majority of gang members, the gang is a substitute for a family cohesiveness lacking in the gang members' home environment. Many older brothers and relatives belong to or have belonged to the gang.

Some members are forced into joining by their peer group. Intimida-tions range from extorting lunch money to beatings. If a particularly vio-lent war is in progress, the recruitment tactics used by the gang can be extremely violent, even to the point of murdering one to cause others to conform.

According to the Los Angeles White Paper, family structure is probably the most important factor in formation of a gang member.

Investigators have found certain common threads running through most families having hardcore gang members. The family is quite often a racial minority on some form of government assistance. It often lacks a male authority figure. This male figure may be a criminal or drug addict and, therefore, represents a negative role model. Typically neither adult has more than an elementary school education. Children live with minimal adult supervision.

When one child first encounters law-enforcement authorities, the dominant figure (usually the mother) makes excuses for the child, often in the form of accusations against society. Thus, children are taught early that they are not responsible for their actions and are shown how to transfer blame to society.

A second common type of family structure is one that may have two strong family leaders in a mother and father. Usually graduates from gangs themselves, they see little wrong with their children belonging to gangs. This is known as an assembly-line production of gang members.

A third common family structure is where the parents are non–English speaking. The children tend to adapt rapidly to the American way of life and in doing so, lose respect for their parents and the "old ways." They become experts at manipulating their parents, and the parents lose all control.

Many of these structures overlap.

THE PROGRESSION

The continual process of criminal experience and living is illus-trated in figure 17–1.

A Continual Process of Criminal Experience and Learning

Killed
What to show for it?

2nd and 3rd Prison
Terms

Parole to Street Connections
from Prison

Prison to Gang Violence
from Gang Violence on
the street

Age: 23

Parole to Recycle Gang Activity

Arrests and Previous Record to CYA

Probation—Camp Setting then Back to
the community (Gang neighborhood).

Re-Arrest—All other probation alternatives
tried before or unavailable.

Age: 18 to 20

Gang Associations identified by police and other agencies
again . . . earlier crime has been gang related.

Re-Arrest for gang related crime-Probation in
custody status

Age: 15

Re-Arrest for gang related crime-Probation

Re-Arrest for gang related crime-Probation

Re-Arrest for gang related crime-Acquitted

Re-Arrest for gang related crime-Charges dropped

Re-Arrest for gang related crime-Probation

Age: 12 to 14

Some inappropriate behavior at school. Truancy record. Home is not appropriate
but there are no alternatives. Poor education skills (learning disabled. Brother is
poor model. Previous gang involvement. Father has some criminal record.
Parents separated. Neighborhood in socio-economically deprived area.

Age: 8 to 10   Has some Gang awareness

Doing alright in school but shows signs in picking up basic skills. May have a
learning impairment.

Age: 6   Starts school

Source: James R. Davis, *Street Gangs,* Dubuque, Iowa: Kendall/Hunt Publishing, 1982, p. 4. Reprinted by
permission.

Figure 17–1   **Symbolic Profile of a Gang Member's Life**

The challenge gangs present to law enforcement and the juvenile
delinquency problem it fosters is well put by Sgt. Jackson, Los Angeles
Police Department:

> *How can you tell a kid who's making $500 a week guarding a rock house
> that he really ought to be in school or that he ought to be getting up at 4
> a.m. every day to ride his bicycle around the neighborhood to deliver the
> morning papers?"* (National School Safety Center, 1988, p. 15)

RELATIONSHIP TO PRISON GANGS

Jackson and McBride (1985, p. 54) discuss the relationship between street gangs and prison gangs:

> Essentially there is no formal relationship between these two kinds of gangs, in the sense that one is an extension of the other. However, from the evidence available, it appears that the street gang members are potential raw material for the prison gang. The majority of prison gang members were at one time members of either barrio, ghetto, or motorcycle gangs. . . .
>
> Prison gang philosophy is very often diametrically opposed to that of the street gang. For example, although loyalty is a prime value for both groups, disagreements among prison gang members are many times settled by the murder of the offending member or members of his family. . . .
>
> The prison gang is cold, calculating, and purposeful. Individuals who break prison gang rules are punished ruthlessly and swiftly. The street gang, on the other hand, operates through pure emotion. Its planning is usually unsophisticated, its actions spontaneous.

THE EXTENT OF THE PROBLEM

Miller (1976) reports that there may be as many as 2,700 gangs in the nation's six largest cities: New York, Los Angeles, Chicago, Detroit, Philadelphia, and San Francisco. Membership in these gangs may be as high as 81,500.

The *ECJ* states that California alone has nearly 1,000 gangs and has suffered nearly 5,000 gang-related homicides since 1980. In over 100 cities there were gang-related murders last year.

Davis (1982, p 5) states: "In the Los Angeles County area today there are over 600 gangs with an estimated 25,000 to 70,000 members and associates."

Authorities say members of two rival drug gangs from Los Angeles, the Crips and the Bloods, have infiltrated cities from Alaska to Washington, D.C., selling cocaine and its derivative, crack. Last year, 387 people died in gang-related violence in Los Angeles, about half of them innocent bystanders.

And, as noted by Robbins (1988, p. 29A):

> With the entrepreneurial savy of MBAs, the Bloods and Crips are making their way across the United States, and officials say there are few states they haven't reached. . . . Two California gangs, fanning out along the interstate highway system, are spreading a sophisticated pattern of violence and drug-dealing across the country. . . . Humphrey [Minnesota Attorney General] said the arrival of the Bloods and Crips gangs makes tougher laws necessary. "These drug gangs are the organized crime families of the 1990s," he said.

And according to the findings of a California State Task Force on Youth Gang Violence (1986):

Youth gang violence and its threat to innocent citizens are increasing in California.

Heavy Metal, Punk Rockers and Satanic groups have emerged as new phenomena.

Youth gangs are responsible for a disproportionate and growing share of the violence and vandalism in schools.

California laws do not effectively deal with the violent crimes of youth gangs.

Victim and witness intimidation is a major threat to gang case investigations and prosecutions.

Narcotics involvement has become a major factor in gang violence and gang recruitment.

WHAT CAN BE DONE?

The State Task Force on Youth Gang Violence (1986) of the California Council on Criminal Justice suggests that both short- and long-term solutions are needed for dealing with gangs and gang violence. Short-term approaches would rely on law enforcement efforts, including stiffer penalties for hard-core gang members, and on special training for police, prosecutors, and judges. Long-term solutions would emphasize preventive and community-based counseling for both gang members and their parents.

The State Task Force (1986, p. 37) made the following long-term prevention and intervention solutions to youth gang problems:

Legislation should be enacted or policy should be established to
1. *design and develop a statewide gang information system and clearinghouse;*
2. *implement a school-based gang/narcotic prevention program to operate cooperatively with local law enforcement agencies;*
3. *provide technical assistance to local law enforcement agencies for gang crime analysis;*
4. *establish a model project within the Department of the Youth Authority to identify youth gang members and intensify parole supervision;*
5. *establish or expand special units in probation departments to supervise gang members;*
6. *establish a Southeast Asian youth gang prevention and intervention program;*
7. *establish statewide standards within custodial institutions to restrict any activity encouraging or condoning gang membership;*
8. *establish a model gang intervention program using ex-gang members and community street workers.*

SUMMARY

A gang is a group of people that forms an allegiance for a common purpose and engages in unlawful or criminal activity. Most gangs are racially or ethnically homogeneous.

Distinguishing characteristics of gangs include leadership, organization, associational patterns, domain identification, and illegal activity. Gang members might also be identified by their names, their symbols (clothing and tattoos), and how they communicate, including graffiti and sign language. Most female gangs are adjuncts or auxiliaries to a male gang.

The most common reasons for joining a gang are for identity or recognition, for protection, for fellowship and brotherhood, or from intimidation.

DISCUSSION QUESTIONS

1.   Are there gangs in your area? If so, in what are they involved?

2.   Do you think the gang problem is as serious as authorities claim?

3.   Are street gangs depicted realistically on television shows? In movies?

4.   Do you personally know a gang member?

5.   What do you think might be done to reduce the gang problem?

6.   What are some distinguishing characteristics of gangs?

7.   Do gangs have some value in society?

8.   Why do people join gangs?

9.   Is a hard or soft approach to gang activity the best approach to curtail criminal activity?

10.   Are gangs a threat to the quality of life in your area?

REFERENCES

Campbell, A. *The Girls in the Gang: A Report from New York City.* New York: Basil Blackwell, 1984.

Davis, J. R. *Street Gangs.* Dubuque, Iowa: Kendall/Hunt Publishing, 1982.

Drugs—The American Family in Crisis: A Judicial Response, 39 Recommendations. National Council of Juvenile and Family Court Judges, August 4, 1988.

Encyclopedia of Crime and Justice, vol. 4. New York: The Free Press, a Division of Macmillan, 1983.

Jackson, R. K., and McBride, W. D. *Understanding Street Gangs.* Sacramento, Calif.: Custom Publishing, 1985.

Miller, W. B. "American Youth Gangs: Past and Present," *Current Perspectives on Criminal Behavior: Original Essays on Criminology,* 2d ed. Edited by Abraham S. Blumberg. New York: Knopf, 1981.

Miller, W. B. *Violence by Youth Gangs and Youth Groups as a Crime Problem in Major American Cities.* Washington, D.C.: U.S. Government Printing Office, 1976.

National School Safety Center. *Gangs in Schools: Breaking Up Is Hard to Do.* Malibu, Calif.: Pepperdine University Press, 1988.

Robbins, W. "California Gangs Staking Claims across the U.S. *Star Tribune,* December 4, 1988, p. 29A.

State Task Force on Youth Gang Violence. *Final Report.* California Council on Criminal Justice, January 1986.

Street Gangs of Los Angeles County: A White Paper.

Trojanowicz, R. C. *Juvenile Delinquency: Concepts and Control.* Englewood Cliffs, N.J.: Prentice-Hall, 1978.

Vedder, C. B., and Somerville, D. B. *The Delinquent Girl.* Springfield, Ill.: Charles C. Thomas, 1970.

Vetter, H. J., and Territo, L. *Crime and Justice in America.* St. Paul, Minn.: West Publishing Company, 1984.

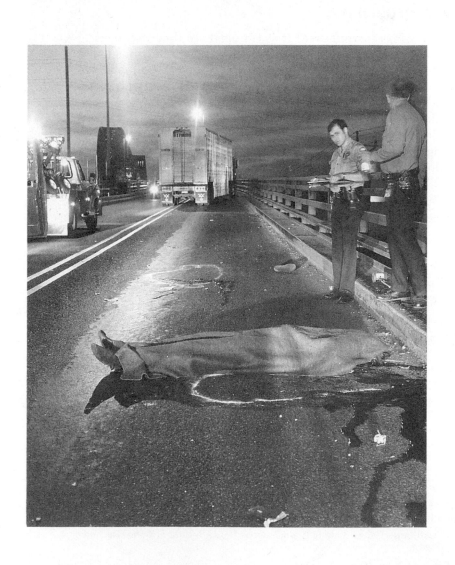

Victimization:
What Are the Risks?

Something insidious has happened in America: crime has made victims of us all. Awareness of its danger affects the way we think, where we live, where we go, what we buy, how we raise our children, and the quality of our lives as we age. The specter of violent crime and the knowledge that, without warning, any person can be attacked or crippled, robbed, or killed, lurks at the fringes of consciousness.—Statement of the Chairman, President's Task Force on Victims of Crime

DO YOU KNOW

What groups of people are most likely and least likely to become victims of crime?

What households are at greatest risk of violent crime?

If a person is more likely to be victimized by a stranger or by a relative or acquaintance?

How victims of violent crime protect themselves?

How crime affects its victims?

What percentage of all crimes against people and their households are not reported to police?

How many states have compensation programs to help victims of violent crimes and what these programs typically offer?

Introduction

Chapter 18

It is common knowledge that law enforcement officers must know how to deal with criminals. Even more important, however, is the officers' ability to deal with those who are victims of crime. This is critical, not only because personal concern and establishment of rapport will enhance communications, and consequently, result in the officers' ability to obtain more information related to the crime, but also because this will enhance the image of the police officer as a professional.

All of the material found in this chapter is contained in *Report to the Nation on Crime and Justice,* chapter 2, prepared by the Bureau of Justice Statistics of the U.S. Department of Justice. Unless otherwise noted, all information, statistics, figures, and tables are adapted from this reference. The report uses crime statistics from several different sources, including the National Crime Survey (conducted since 1973), the Uniform Crime Reports (analyzed for eleven years from 1979–88), and homicide statistics from coroners' reports to the National Center for Health Statistics (NCHS).

INDIVIDUAL RISK FACTORS

Certain individuals are at greater risk than others, as summarized in table 18–1.

As noted by the Bureau of Justice Statistics:

- Victims of crime are more often men than women.
- Younger people are much more likely than the elderly to be victims of crime. (But the elderly have a greater fear of crime and may restrict their lives in ways that reduce their chances of being victimized.)
- Blacks are more likely to be victims of violent crime than whites or members of other racial groups.
- The divorced or separated and the never married are more likely than the married or the widowed to be victims of crime.
- Violent crime rates are higher for lower-income people.
- Theft rates are highest for people with high incomes (more than $50,000 per year).
- Students and the unemployed are more likely than housewives, retirees, or the employed to be victims of crime.
- Rural residents are less often crime victims than are people living in cities.

Young, black, unemployed males living in the city have the highest victimization rates; elderly white females living in rural areas have the lowest victimization rates.

Table 18–1 Victimization Rates per 1,000 Persons Age 12 and Older

	Personal crimes of...			Personal crimes of...			Personal crimes of...	
	violence	theft		violence	theft		violence	theft
Total (U.S.)	30	69						
Sex			**Family income**			**Race, sex, and age summary**		
Male	39	75	Less than $7,500	52	68	White males		
Female	22	65	$7,500–$9,999	34	63	12–15	73	111
			$10,000–$14,999	32	65	16–19	92	134
Age			$15,000–$24,999	28	68	20–24	78	116
12–15	54	108	$25,000–$29,999	29	69	25–34	44	87
16–19	67	122	$30,000–$49,999	22	76	35–49	23	66
20–24	60	108	$50,000 or more	25	90	50–64	11	42
25–34	37	83				65 and older	5	22
35–49	20	63	**Education**			White females		
50–64	10	40	0–4 years	13	23	12–15	39	116
65 and older	5	19	5–7 years	35	59	16–19	47	129
			8 years	34	57	20–24	42	103
Race and origin			9–11 years	39	71	25–34	28	78
White	29	70	High school graduate	27	60	35–49	15	62
Black	38	63	1–3 years college	34	87	50–64	8	39
Other	25	73	College graduate	22	89	65 and older	3	17
Hispanic	30	60				Black males		
Non-Hispanic	30	70	**Employment status** (1984)			12–15	68	81
			Retired	5	20	16–19	69	74
Marital status by sex			Keeping house	14	35	20–24	67	103
Males			Unable to work	17	25	25–34	60	113
Never married	72	112	Employed	32	81	35–49	31	60
Divorced/separated	57	102	In school	45	110	50–64	27	48
Married	19	52	Unemployed	76	90	65 and older	*	21
Widowed	10	31				Black females		
Females			**Residence** (1984)			12–15	19	74
Never married	38	102	Central city	43	85	16–19	46	54
Divorced/separated	51	84	1,000,000 or more	45	80	20–24	58	70
Married	11	50	500,000–999,999	45	92	25–34	48	68
Widowed	7	21	250,000–499,999	37	88	35–49	20	54
			50,000–249,999	44	81	50–64	10	33
			Suburban	30	77	65 and older	*	12
			Rural	22	54			

Note: Personal crimes of violence include rape, robbery, and assault. Personal crimes of theft include larceny without contact, purse snatching, and pocket picking.

*Too few cases to obtain statistically reliable data.
Source: BJS *Criminal victimization in the U.S. 1984 and 1985.*

Violent crimes can be looked at in more detail by examining the incidence of robbery, assault, and rape, as summarized in table 18–2. Again, males are at higher risk than females. Risk of violent victimization drops significantly after age thirty-four. As might be expected risk is greatest in the central city and least in rural areas.

HOUSEHOLD RISK FACTORS

Certain types of households also are more likely to be victims of crime than others. Included in the high-risk category are Hispanics, blacks, renters, households headed by younger persons, households containing six or more people, and households in urban areas.

National Crime Survey data for 1984 and 1985 indicates that only 24 percent of all violent crimes occurred in and around the victim's home, but that 30 percent of all rapes occurred there.

Table 18–2   Victimization Rates for Robbery, Assault, and Rape

| | Rates per 1,000 persons age 12 and older | | |
	Robbery	Assault	Rape
Sex			
Male	7	32	*
Female	3	17	**
Age			
12–15	9	45	*
16–19	9	55	2
20–24	10	48	2
25–34	6	30	1
35–49	3	16	*
50–64	2	8	*
65 and older	2	3	*
Race and origin			
White	4	24	1
Black	11	26	2
Other	7	17	*
Hispanic	8	22	*
Non-Hispanic	5	24	1
Marital status			
Divorced/separated	9	42	2
Never married	10	45	1
Married	2	13	0
Widowed	3	4	*
Income			
Less than $7,500	9	41	2
$7,500–$9,999	7	25	1
$10,000–$14,999	5	26	1
$15,000–$24,999	5	23	*
$25,000–$29,999	5	24	*
$30,000–$49,999	4	18	1
$50,000 or more	3	21	*
Employment status (1984)			
Employed	6	26	1
In school	9	33	3
Keeping house	3	10	1
Retired	2	3	*
Unable to work	5	11	*
Unemployed	17	56	3
Residence (1984)			
Central city	11	31	1
Suburban	5	24	1
Rural	3	19	1

*There were too few cases to obtain statistically reliable data.
**This rate based on women only; the rate based on the total population is 1.
Source: BJS *Criminal victimization in the U.S., 1984 and 1985.*

Blacks are more often victims of household crimes than nonblacks.

• *Renters have higher household crime rates than home owners.*

• *Household crime more often affects households headed by younger people.*

• *Household crime rates are highest for households with six or more people.*

• *Households in cities have higher crime rates than suburban or rural households.*

Table 18-3 Victimization Rates for Theft

	Rates per 1,000 households		
	Household burglary	Larceny	Motor vehicle theft
Age of household head			
12–19	213	224	18
20–34	83	137	21
35–49	69	110	15
50–64	48	75	13
65 and older	33	41	5
Race or origin of household head			
White	60	95	13
Black	83	120	22
Other	45	88	17
Hispanic	85	127	23
Non-Hispanic	62	96	14
Income			
Less than $7,500	86	98	11
$7,500–$9,999	60	101	15
$10,000–14,999	67	101	14
$15,000–$24,999	59	104	14
$25,000–$29,999	54	95	13
$30,000–$49,999	58	99	16
$50,000 or more	56	104	21
Number of persons in household			
One	53	62	10
2–3	61	92	14
4–5	75	136	18
6 or more	78	173	17
Form of tenure			
Home owned or being bought	50	83	11
Home rented	84	123	19
Place of residence (1984)			
Central city	87	129	22
1,000,000 or more	85	97	35
500,000–999,999	81	138	20
250,000–499,999	90	144	22
50,000–249,999	91	142	13
Outside central city (suburban)	56	97	˙16
Nonmetropolitan (rural)	53	76	8

Source: BJS *Criminal victimization in the U.S., 1984 and 1985.*

HOMICIDE RATES

Both the Uniform Crime Reports and statistics from the Public Health Department indicate that the homicide rate has been rising since 1961. Reasons for the rise in the homicide rate include the fact that babies born during the baby boom reached age sixteen in the early 1960s. Since violent victimization is more prevalent among people under age thirty, it might be expected that the homicide rate would increase as a large proportion of the population reached the victimization-prone ages.

- Homicide victims are more often men than women.
- Persons aged twenty-five to thirty-four are the most likely to be homicide victims.
- Blacks are five times more likely than whites to be homicide victims.

Table 18—4   Homicide Rates

Victim characteristics	Homicides in 1985	Number per 100,000 inhabitants
Total including unknown characteristics	17,545	7
Sex		
Male	13,015	11
Female	4,511	4
Age		
Under 1 year	190	5
1–14	690	1
15–24	4,081	10
25–34	5,370	13
35–44	3,087	10
45–54	1,576	7
55–64	1,120	5
65 and older	1,048	4
Unknown age	383	
Race		
White	9,789	5
Black	7,294	24
Other	369	5

Sources: FBI *Crime in the United States 1985*, Estimates of the Population of the United States by Age, Sex, and Race, 1980–85, U.S. Bureau of the Census.

THE RELATIONSHIP BETWEEN VICTIM AND OFFENDER

When people worry about crime, they are most often worried about being attacked by strangers. This fear is frequently justifiable: with the exception of murder and rape, most violent crimes are committed by strangers. Males, blacks, and young people face the greatest risk of violent crime by strangers and are victimized by violent strangers at an annual rate almost triple that of women. Blacks are more than twice as likely as whites to be robbed by strangers.

Table 18—5   What Is Your Lifetime Risk of Being a Homicide Victim?

Lifetime risk of homicide

1 out of:	
179	White males
30	Black males
495	White females
132	Black females

Source: Updated data based on similar material from *The Risk of Violent Crime*, BJS Special Report, May 1985.

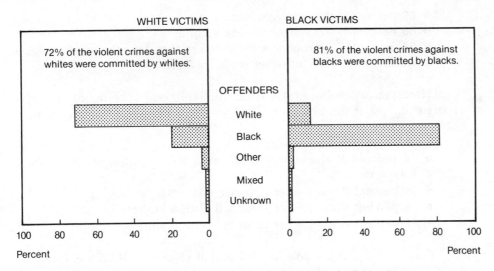

Victims and offenders are of the same race in three out of four violent crimes.

Figure 18–1   Race of Victims and Offenders

Most violent crimes except murder and rape are committed by strangers.

The risk of robbery is less for older people, but this may be because many older people are no longer physically able to move about outside their homes and many others may fear crime and, consequently, remain at home most of the time. It may be that older people who are active and mobile may be at as much risk as the general population.

Women are more vulnerable than men to assaults by acquaintances and relatives, with two-thirds of all assaults on divorced and separated women committed by acquaintances and relatives. Spouses or former spouses committed only 5 percent of the assaults by single offenders. In almost three-fourths of spouse versus spouse assaults, the victim was divorced or separated at the time of the incident.

More than half of all homicides are committed by someone known to the victim. Acquaintances commit more than 39 percent of all homicides; relatives commit 17 percent of all homicides.

It is of interest to note that victims and offenders are usually of the same race, as summarized in figure 18–1.

USE OF WEAPONS IN VICTIMIZATION

Except for homicide, most violent crimes do not involve the use of weapons (see table 18–6). When a weapon is used, the likelihood that a victim will lose property in a robbery attempt is greater. The likelihood of losing property is:

- 80 percent if the robber wields a gun;
- 60 percent if the robber wields a knife;
- 54 percent if the robber is unarmed or threatens the victim with a stick, bottle, club, or other such weapons.

However, according to statistics, the likelihood of being injured by a stranger is less if the stranger is armed. The likelihood of injury to a robbery victim is:

- 53 percent if the robber displays a stick, bottle, or other such weapon;
- 34 percent if the robber is unarmed;
- 25 percent if the robber is armed with a knife;
- 17 percent if the robber is armed with a gun.

One logical explanation for this is that victims will be less likely to resist a robber armed with a gun or knife.

Likewise, police officers assaulted by gun-bearing offenders sustained the lowest percentage of injuries (see table 18–7). This is not to imply that a gun-wielding offender is not a threat to citizens and law enforcement officers. Of the sixty-six law enforcement officers killed in the line of duty in 1986, three-quarters (fifty-one officers) were killed by handguns, eight by rifles and three by shotguns. Fifteen were shot with their own service weapons. Four were intentionally run down by automobiles.

HOW VICTIMS PROTECT THEMSELVES

Victims rarely respond by wielding a weapon. However, rape victims are more likely to use force, try a verbal response, or attract attention and are less likely than others to do nothing to protect themselves. In contrast, robbery victims are least likely to try to talk themselves out of being victimized and the most likely to do nothing, as summarized in table 18.8.

Table 18–6   Involvement of Weapons in Crime

Except for homicide, most violent crimes do not involve the use of weapons.

Weapon used	Homicide	Rape	Robbery	Assault**
Weapon used	93%	25%	49%	34%
Firearm	59%	11%	23%	12%
Knife	21	14	21	10
Other	13	5*	13	15
None used	7	75	51	66
Total	100%	100%	100%	100%

Note: Because some victimizations involve more than one type of weapon, detail may add to more than 100%.
*Estimate is based on ten or fewer samples and is therefore statistically unreliable.
**Includes simple assaults, which by definition do not involve the use of a weapon.
Source: BJS Special Report, January 1986, and FBI *Crime in the United States, 1985.*

Table 18–7   Use of Weapons in Assaults on Law Enforcement Officers

Means of assault	Percent of all assaults	Percent resulting in personal injury
Firearm	5	21
Knife	3	27
Other weapon	9	41
Hands, fists, feet, etc.	84	34
Total	100%	100%

Note: Totals add to more than 100% because of use of multiple weapons.

Source: FBI *Law Enforcement Officers Killed and Assaulted,* 1985.

Of all responses reported by victims to the National Crime Survey, physical force, trying to attract attention, and doing nothing to protect oneself or property resulted in the highest proportions of seriously injured victims (16 percent, 14 percent, and 12 percent, respectively). In contrast, those who tried to talk themselves out of the situation or took nonviolent evasive actions were less likely to incur serious injury (both 6 percent).

Table 18–8   How Do Victims of Violent Crime Protect Themselves?

Victim response*	Percent of victims who used self-protection by type of crime*		
	Rape	Robbery	Assault
Weapons use Used or brandished gun or knife	3%	4%	4%
Physical force Used or tried physical force	29	22	23
Verbal response Threatened, argued, reasoned, etc., with offender	19	10	16
Attracting attention Tried to get help, attract attention, scare offender away	18	13	10
Nonviolent evasion Resisted without force, used evasive action	13	14	23
Other	1	2	3
No self-protective actions	18	37	22
Total	100%	100%	100%
Number of victimizations	1,206,755	8,484,516	36,269,845

*Victim self-protective responses are listed in the table in order of assertiveness. If victims indicated that they took more than one type of action, only the most assertive action was used in the analysis. Percentages may not sum to 100% because of rounding.
Source: BJS National Crime Survey, 1979–85.

Victims of violent crime can protect themselves by returning physical force, by verbal response, by attracting attention, by nonviolent evasion, or by brandishing a weapon.

Use of Deadly Force

Each state distinguishes when citizens may legally use deadly force compared to physical force to protect their dwellings. **Deadly force** refers to any force intended to cause death or serious physical injury. Physical force, in contrast, refers to all force directed to another person but not intended to be lethal, including confinement.

In some states forced entry is enough to indicate that an inhabitant is in imminent, immediate danger justifying deadly force. In other states, the intruder must attack directly or threaten an inhabitant before deadly force is justified. Generally, a trespasser is not considered to pose a direct threat to life. Therefore, deadly force against trespassers is not usually justified.

If an assailant is attacking a third party, citizens are justified in using deadly force if the third party is in imminent, immediate danger of losing his or her life, provided the third party did not provoke the attack.

CRIME'S EFFECT ON ITS VICTIMS

National Crime Survey and UCR data suggests that losses from personal and household crime exceeded $13 billion in 1985 and that two million injuries or deaths resulted from violent crime.

Violent crime can affect its victim physically, economically, and emotionally.

The economic impact of crime must also take into consideration time lost from work, medical costs, and the introduction of security measures to prevent future victimization.

Rowan (1986, p. 24) estimated the total income for the "rackets" to be between $50 billion in 1986. The social cost of underground activity includes lost tax revenues, treatment programs for drug abusers, higher insurance premiums, and increased law enforcement efforts. In fact, the entire cost of the criminal justice system is an indirect cost of crime.

FEAR OF VICTIMIZATION

Public opinion polls have found that people do fear crime in general, but they generally feel their own neighborhoods are relatively safe. If

Table 18—9   **State Laws that Justify Deadly Force**

State	Even if life is not threatened, deadly force may be justified to protect:		Specific crime against which deadly force may be justified
	Dwelling	Property	
Alabama	Yes	No	Arson, burglary, rape, kidnaping, or robbery in "any degree"
Alaska	Yes	No	Actual commission of felony
Arizona	Yes	No	Arson, burglary, kidnaping, aggravated assaults
Arkansas	Yes	No	Felonies as defined by statute
California	Yes	No	Unlawful or forcible entry
Colorado	Yes	No	Felonies, including assault, robbery, rape, arson, kidnaping
Connecticut	Yes	No	Any violent crime
Delaware	Yes	No	Felonious activity
D.C.	Yes	No	Felony
Florida	Yes	No	Forcible felony
Georgia	Yes	Yes	Actual commission of a forcible felony
Hawaii	Yes	Yes	Felonious property damage, burglary, robbery, etc.
Idaho	Yes	Yes	Felonious breaking and entering
Illinois	Yes	Yes	Forcible felony
Indiana	Yes	No	Unlawful entry
Iowa	Yes	Yes	Breaking and entering
Kansas	Yes	No	Breaking and entering including attempts
Kentucky	No	No	—
Louisiana	Yes	No	Unlawful entry including attempts
Maine	Yes	No	Criminal trespass, kidnaping, rape, arson
Maryland	No	No	—
Massachusetts	No	No	—
Michigan	Yes	No	Circumstances on a case by case basis
Minnesota	Yes	No	Felony
Mississippi	Yes	—	Felony including attempts
Missouri	No	No	—
Montana	Yes	Yes	Any forcible felony
Nebraska	Yes	No	Unlawful entry, kidnaping, and rape
Nevada	Yes	—	Actual commission of felony
New Hampshire	Yes	—	Felony
New Jersey	Yes	No	Burglary, arson, and robbery
New Mexico	Yes	Yes	Any felony
New York	Yes	No	Burglary, arson, kidnaping, and robbery including attempts
North Carolina	Yes	No	Intending to commit a felony
North Dakota	Yes	No	Any violent felony
Ohio	—	—	
Oklahoma	Yes	No	Felony within a dwelling
Oregon	Yes	—	Burglary in a dwelling including attempts
Pennsylvania	Yes	—	Burglary or criminal trespass
Rhode Island	Yes	—	Breaking or entering
South Carolina	No	No	—
South Dakota	Yes	—	Burglary including attempts
Tennessee	Yes	No	Felony
Texas	Yes	No	Burglary, robbery, or theft during the night
Utah	Yes	—	Felony
Vermont	Yes	—	Forcible felony
Virginia	No	No	—
Washington	No	No	—
West Virginia	Yes	No	Any felony
Wisconsin	No	No	—
Wyoming	No	No	—

Note: This table provides a summary of state statutes and should not be used by citizens in planning their protection. Legal advice that considers the specific situation and the State statute is advised.
Source: BJS update as of December 1986 based on data from Ronald Cruit, ed., *Intruder in Your Home* (New York: Stein and Day, 1983).

someone in the neighborhood is victimized, however, the entire neighborhood may feel much more vulnerable.

Interestingly, the people who express the greatest fear of being victimized are females and the elderly, and, as previously stated, they are at lower risk than other segments of the population. Whether they are at lower risk because they take measures to reduce their chances of being victimized is not known. If the elderly, for example, restrict their activities because they are afraid of becoming victims of crime, this fear is, in itself, a sort of victimization.

REPORTING OF CRIMES TO THE AUTHORITIES

A great deal of crime is not reported to the police. Reporting rates have been found to vary by type of crime and by age and sex of the victim but not by the victim's race. In 1985 reporting rates were higher for violent crimes than for personal crimes (47 percent versus 26 percent), for female than for male victims of violent crimes (53 percent versus 45 percent), and for older than for younger victims. Reporting rates were also higher for motor vehicle theft than for burglary and for household larceny. Homeowners and high-income groups were more likely to report household crimes than renters and low-income groups.

Two-thirds of all crimes are not reported to the police.

Reporting rates can vary quite a bit.

Reasons for not reporting violent crimes to the police were varied, with the most common being a private/personal matter (see table 18–10).

VICTIM COMPENSATION PROGRAMS

As noted in the *Encyclopedia of Crime and Justice* (1983, p. 1606):

The use of public monies to aid persons victimized by crime has roots in antiquity. The policy goes back at least to the ancient Babylonian Code of Hammurabi which decreed communal responsibility when it proved impossible to establish individual blame for a crime. . . . Such compensatory approaches were also characteristic of Anglo-Saxon law, but they gave way in the thirteenth and fourteenth centuries to a system of state-operated criminal prosecution.

The encyclopedia goes on to say that during the nineteenth century several reformers advocated reviving the system of compensating crime victims, but it was not until the 1960s that the movement gained momentum. This momentum was initiated in large measure by an article in the London *Observer* written by Margery Fry, proposing that victims should no longer have to rely on civil lawsuits to recover losses sustained because of violent crimes. According to the encyclopedia: "Fry cited a

Table 18–10 **Reasons Given for Not Reporting Violent Crimes to the Police**

Many violent crimes were unreported because they were "private matters," and many crimes of theft were "not important enough to report."

Percent of victimizations not reported to the police, by reason for not reporting

	Private/ personal matter	Nothing could be done/ lack of proof	Not impor- tant enough	Reported to some- one else	Police wouldn't want to be bothered	Too inconve- nient	Fear of reprisal	All other reasons	Not given
Crimes of violence									
Rape	35%	18%	4%	8%	*%	2%	16%	42%	2%
Robbery	15	21	15	9	9	6	7	39	5
Aggravated assault	31	10	22	11	7	3	5	22	4
Simple assault	32	8	30	14	7	2	3	14	3
Crimes of theft									
Burglary	9	23	23	7	10	2	1	44	2
Larceny	8	23	39	3	10	2	1	32	2
Motor vehicle theft	12	18	16	8	8	3	*	52	1

Note: Percents add to more than 100% for each type of crime because some people gave more than one reason for not reporting.
*0 or less than 0.5%.
Source: BJS National Crime Survey, 1981.

1951 court award of £11,500 to a man blinded in an assault. The amount was to be paid at the rate of five shillings a week, which meant that it would take 442 years for the victim to recover the full amount." Fry wrote: "The logical way of providing for criminally inflicted injuries would be to tax every adult citizen . . . to cover a risk to which each is exposed."

In 1965 California initiated the first statewide victim compensation program. These programs supplement existing programs that assist victims, such as rape crisis centers and prosecutors' victim assistance programs.

According to the *United States Department of Justice* (1988) almost all states have established programs to assist crime victims and witnesses.

Forty-four states, the District of Columbia, and the Virgin Islands provide compensation for medical bills and lost wages for victims.

In general, victim compensation programs do the following:

- Provide financial assistance to victims and witnesses.
- Protect the rights of victims and witnesses.
- Complement existing efforts to aid special categories of victims such as rape victims and victims of family abuse.

Victim/witness services may also be provided by noncriminal justice agencies such as local or state departments of health or human resources. Additionally, many private organizations have developed programs such as rape crisis centers.

If a victim dies, payments may cover burial and related expenses, payable to dependent survivors. Often, people injured while trying to prevent a crime or apprehend an offender (Good Samaritans) are also eligible for payment.

Most states establish upper limits on payments, and most do not compensate for property losses. Usually payment can be made whether or not the offender is apprehended or convicted, but most states require that the crime be reported to the proper authorities.

The 1984 Federal Victims of Crime Act provides federal grants to help states with established qualifying victim compensation programs.

Many states also allow victims to recover crime-related losses, including property damages, if a court requires restitution by the offender as sentencing condition. Such payments are available only if the offender is convicted and is financially solvent.

Many states also require that any profits earned by an offender in publicizing details of a crime be escrowed and, if the offender is convicted, be used to cover crime-related costs incurred by the victim, including, in some cases, legal fees.

Table 18–11 summarizes characteristics of the existing victim compensation programs.

Table 18–11   **Victim Compensation Programs**

State	Victim compensation board location[a]	Financial award	To qualify, victim must—		
			show financial need	report to police within:	file claim within:
Alabama	Alabama Crime Victim Compensation Commission	$0–10,000	No	3 days	12 mos.
Alaska	Department of Public Safety	$0–40,000	Yes	5	24
Arizona	Arizona Criminal Justice Commission	**	Yes	3	**
California	State Board of Control	$100–46,000	Yes	*	12
Colorado	Judicial district boards	$25–10,000	No	3	6
Connecticut	Criminal Injuries Compensation Board	$100–10,000	No	5	24
Delaware	Violent Crimes Board	$25–20,000	No	*	12
D.C.	Office of Crime Victim Compensation	$100–25,000	Yes	7	6
Florida	Department of Labor and Employment Security, Workmen's Compensation Division	$0–10,000	Yes	3	12
Hawaii	Department of Corrections	$0–10,000	No	*	18
Idaho	Industrial Commission	$0–25,000	No	3	12
Illinois	Court of Claims	$0–25,000	No	3	12
Indiana	Industrial Board	$100–10,000	No	2	24
Iowa	Department of Public Safety	$0–20,000	No	1	6
Kansas	Executive Department	$100–10,000	Yes	3	12
Kentucky	Victim Compensation Board	$0–25,000	Yes	2	12
Louisiana	Commission on Law Enforcement	$100–10,000	No	3	12
Maryland	Criminal Injuries Compensation Board	$0–45,000	Yes	2	6
Massachusetts	District court system	$0–25,000	No	2	12
Michigan	Department of Management and Budget	$200–15,000	Yes	2	12
Minnesota	Crime Victims Reparation Board	$100–50,000	No	5	12
Missouri	Division of Workmen's Compensation	$200–10,000	No	2	12
Montana	Crime Control Division	$0–25,000	No	3	12
Nebraska	Commission on Law Enforcement and Criminal Justice	$0–10,000	Yes	3	24
Nevada	Board of Examiners and Department of Administration	$0–15,000	Yes	5	12
New Jersey	Executive Branch	$0–25,000	No	90	24
New Mexico	Executive Branch	$0–12,500	No	30	12
New York	Executive Department	$0–30,000+	Yes	7	12
North Carolina[b]	Department of Crime Control and Public Safety	$100–20,000		3	24
North Dakota	Workmen's Compensation Bureau	$0–25,000	No	3	12
Ohio	Court of Claims Commissioners	$0–25,000	No	3	12
Oklahoma	Crime Victims Board	$0–10,000	No	3	12
Oregon	Department of Justice/Workmen's Compensation Board	$250–23,000	No	3	6
Pennsylvania	Crime Victims Board	$0–35,000	No	3	12
Rhode Island	Superior court system	$0–25,000	No	10	24
South Carolina	Crime Victims Advisory Board	$100–3,000	No	2	6
Tennessee	Court of Claims Commission	$0–5,000	No	2	12
Texas	Industrial Accident Board	$0–25,000	No	3	6
Utah	Department of Administrative Services	$0–25,000	**	7	12
Virgin Islands	Department of Social Welfare	Up to $25,000	No	1	24
Virginia	Industrial Commission	$0–15,000	No	5	24
Washington	Department of Labor and Industries	$0–15,000+	No	3	12
West Virginia	Court of Claims Commissioner	$0–35,000	No	3	24
Wisconsin	Department of Justice	$0–40,000	No	5	12

[a]If location of the board is not indicated in the state statute, the board itself is noted.
[b]North Carolina's program is administratively established but not funded.
*Must report but no time limit specified.
**No reference in statute.
+Plus unlimited medical expenses.
Source: BJS 1987 update of *Victim/witness legislation: An overview*, BJS, July 1984 with assistance from National Organization for Victim Assistance.

State laws and the 1984 Federal Victim and Witness Protection Act also protect crime victims and witnesses against physical and verbal intimidation.

Many states also require that victims be notified of the progress in a case, that they be notified of the release or escape of an offender, and that they be advised of any scheduling changes as well as any available funds to cover court appearances.

In some states victims may participate in sentencing, parole, and other custody decisions. "Victim Impact Statements" describing the financial and emotional effects of a crime on the victim are required in many state and federal cases as part of the presentence investigation report.

Comprehensive "Victim's Bill of Rights" laws in some states may also ensure the victim's right to continued employment, provide medical or social support services, and appoint an "ombudsman" to protect the victim's rights during the trial.

THE RELATIONS BETWEEN THE POLICE AND VICTIMS

Garmire (1982, p. 172) contends: "An important part of the total criminal investigative process is the police relationship with victims of crime. It has been too common in the past for victims to be forgotten after

The preliminary investigation of a crime is a very important stage.

the crime, until they are needed to assist in the prosecution of the offender in court. Then in many cases, the victim either cannot be found or is unwilling to appear."

The first and all-important contact between the police and a victim is made during the preliminary investigation. It is critical that police officers be realistic with victims. If a police agency has an "early case closure system," victims should be told that nothing further can be done unless additional information comes to light. Victims should be given the case number and a phone number to call if they should obtain more information about the crime.

Victims should be told of any assistance that might be available to them and, if applicable, they should be reminded to call their insurance companies. If victims need legal advice, police officers should advise them about the legal aid office.

If a case continues under investigation or will go to court, police officers should maintain contact with victims (and witnesses). If property is recovered it should be returned to victims as soon as possible. If a case goes to court, victims should be briefed as to their roles and should be kept updated.

The President's Task Force on Victims of Crime, *Final Report* (1982) stresses:

> *The police are often the first on the scene; it is to them, the first source of protection, that the victim first turns. They should be mindful that, in ful- filling their obligation to solve the crime and apprehend the criminal, they must also treat victims with the attention due them. The manner in which police officers treat a victim affects not only his immediate and long-term ability to deal with the event but also his willingness to assist in a prosecution. The foundation of all interactions between police and victims should be the knowledge that it is these citizens whom the officer has sworn to serve.*

Recommendations

The President's Task Force (1982) made four very specific recommendations:

1. Police departments should develop and implement training programs to ensure that police officers are sensitive to the needs of victims and informed, knowledgeable, and supportive of the existing local services and programs for victims.
2. Police departments should establish procedures for the prompt photographing and return of property to victims, with prosecutor approval.
3. Police departments should establish procedures to ensure that victims of violent crime are periodically informed of the status and closing of investigations.
4. Police officers should give a high priority to investigation of reports by witnesses of threats or intimidation and forward these reports to the prosecution. Some use a card as in figure 18–2.

Figure 18—2 Informational Brochure for Victims and Witnesses

SUMMARY

Individuals having the highest victimization risk are young, black, unemployed males living in the city; those having the lowest victimization risk are elderly white females living in rural areas.

In 1985 almost a third (30 percent) of all households were victimized by violence or theft. Households at greatest risk are those rented by black people in central cities, headed by younger people, and having more than six people living in the same household.

Most violent crimes except murder and rape are committed by strangers. Victims of violent crime have protected themselves by returning physical force, by verbal response, by attracting attention, by nonviolent evasion, or by brandishing a weapon.

Violent crime can affect its victim physically, economically, and emotionally.

When people are victimized, they often do not report it to police. In fact, two-thirds of all crimes are not reported to police. If a person is seriously injured, a victim compensation program may be available. Forty-four states, the District of Columbia, and the Virgin Islands have such programs. Most provide for recovery of medical expenses and some for lost earnings.

Discussion Questions

1. Does your state have victim compensation laws? If so, how do they compare to those provided in other states?

2. Have you ever been victimized? Has a member of your family? A friend or neighbor? What were the effects?

3. Why is it so difficult for a victim of a crime to accept its consequences?

4. What one common concern do victim compensation programs all share?

5. How can prosecutors assist victims in their experiences with the criminal justice system?

6. Should victims be allowed to approve or disapprove any sentence the court places on those by whom they have been victimized?

7. When a suspect vandalizes while committing a burglary, what does that indicate to you?

8. Might a form of gun registration be beneficial in curbing crimes committed with the use of a gun?

9. Do you feel that in most cases the police in your area are sensitive to the needs of victims of crimes?

10. What type of crime victim is most likely to try to use force against a perpetrator?

References

Encyclopedia of Crime and Justice. New York: The Free Press, 1983.

Garmire, B. L. (ed.) *Local Government Police Management,* 2nd ed. Washington, D.C., International City Management Association, 1982.

President's Task Force on Victims of Crime. *Final Report.* Washington, D.C.: U.S. Government Printing Office, 1982.

Rowan, Roy. "The 50 Biggest Mafia Bosses," *Fortune.* November 10, 1986, pp. 24–32, 34, 36, 38.

U.S. Department of Justice. Bureau of Justice Statistics. *Report to the Nation on Crime and Justice,* 2d ed. Washington, D.C.: U.S. Government Printing Office, 1988.

SECTION FOUR

In Search of Justice:
The Police Officer and
the Criminal Justice System

According to Waldron (1984, p. 57): "Our system of criminal justice has three interrelated components staffed by more than 1.0 million people: *The law enforcement community* ... the *judicial community* ... and the *corrections community* ... Each of these components and its respective personnel in turn contributes to the criminal justice *process*, which is a well-defined legal continuum through which each offender may pass from detection and investigation of the criminal act; to arrest and accusation; to trial, conviction, sentencing, and possible incarceration; to eventual release."

This relatively brief section looks first at our courts and our corrections system (chapter 19) and then discusses our juvenile justice system (chapter 20), which has some important differences from the adult system. It concludes with a discussion of critical issues facing law enforcement in the 1990s (chapter 21).

CHAPTER NINETEEN
Courts and Corrections: Our Criminal Justice System in Action

Justice is truth in action.—Disraeli

DO YOU KNOW

How the police aid the criminal justice process?

What the adversary system requires?

What the critical criminal justice stages are?

What purpose a preliminary hearing serves?

What the discovery process is?

What some alternatives to trial are?

What plea bargaining is?

What the typical hierarchy is within the state court system? The federal court system?

How the defense attorney may attempt to discredit the testimony of a police officer?

What common sentencing schemes are?

What corrections is?

How jail differs from prison?

What negative characteristics are linked with jails?

What two philosophies are evident in U.S. prisons?

How parole differs from probation?

What reintegration methods have been used to facilitate the transition from prison to community?

Police officers are an integral part of the criminal justice

Introduction

Chapter 19

process. The criminal codes that guide police officers in enforcing laws are not a set of specific instructions, but rather they are rough maps of the territory in which police officers work and assist the criminal justice process. The officer's role in the criminal justice process include making legal arrests; legally obtaining accurate, relevant information and evidence; writing complete and accurate reports; identifying suspects and witnesses; and providing effective, truthful testimony in court. Regardless of how sketchy or complete the officers' education or experience, in reality they are interpreters of the law and may function as judge and jury at the start of every case. If the case reaches court, the court must subsequently approve or disapprove the police officers' actions by finding the person guilty or not guilty.

For example, police officers who stop a person for speeding make a judicial decision when they give out a ticket. They might simply warn the next offender. By shooting and killing a fleeing felon who is likely to kill someone while attempting to escape, the police officer delivers a capital penalty for a crime that may otherwise have netted probation or a prison term.

Police officers aid the criminal justice process by (1) making arrests, (2) obtaining information and evidence, (3) writing reports, (4) identifying suspects and witnesses, and (5) providing testimony in court.

Errors in any of these roles may seriously damage a case or even prevent a **conviction.** In today's society it is imperative that police officers become familiar with each step of the criminal justice process so they can intelligently bring about desired results.

Before looking at these critical steps in the criminal justice process, however, it is appropriate to consider the underlying assumption of the process—that it is an adversary system—and to consider who the adversaries are.

THE ADVERSARY SYSTEM

Our criminal justice system is based on an **adversary system**—the accuser versus the accused. The accuser must prove that the one accused is guilty.

The adversary criminal justice system requires that the accuser prove beyond a reasonable doubt to a judge or jury that the accused is guilty of a specified crime.

The assumption is that the accused is innocent until proof to the contrary is clearly established. Included on the side of the accuser is the citizen (or victim), the prosecutor, and the police officer. On the side of the accused is the defendant and the defense attorney. An impartial judge or jury hears both sides of the controversy and then reaches a decision as to whether the accuser has proven the accused guilty beyond a **reasonable doubt.**

As noted by Inbau, Thompson, and Fagel (1974, p. 229):

It [reasonable doubt] is a term often used, probably pretty well understood, but not easily defined. It is not mere possible doubt because everything relating to human affairs and depending on moral evidence is open to some possible or imaginary doubt. It is that state of the case which, after the entire comparisons and consideration of all evidence, leaves the minds of the jurors in that condition and they cannot say they feel an abiding conviction, to a moral certainty, of the truth of the charge. The burden of proof is upon the prosecutor. All the presumptions of law independent of evidence are in favor of innocence; and every person is presumed to be innocent until he is proved guilty. If upon such proof there is reasonable doubt remaining, the accused is entitled to the benefit of it by an acquittal. For it is not sufficient to establish a probability, though a strong one arising from the doctrine of chances, that the fact charged is more likely to be true than the contrary; but the evidence must establish the truth of the fact to a reasonable and moral certainty; a certainty that convinces and directs the understanding, and satisfies the reason and judgment of those who are bound to act conscientiously upon it. This we take to be proof beyond reasonable doubt; because if the law, which mostly depends upon considerations of a moral nature, should go further than this and require absolute certainty, it would exclude circumstantial evidence altogether.

Reasonable doubt means the juror is not morally certain of the truth of the charges.

The Suspect or Defendant

Until formally accused of a crime and brought to trial, a person accused is called a **suspect.** After formal accusation and court appearance, the person is called a **defendant.**

Everyone, including a person suspected of committing a crime, has certain rights that must be protected at all stages of the criminal justice process. Suspects have all the rights set forth in the Bill of Rights. They may waive these rights, but if they do, the waiver should be in writing because proof of the waiver is up to the police officer or the prosecution. The police officer must be able to show that all rights have been respected and that all required procedures have been complied with.

The Fourth Amendment forbids unreasonable search and seizure and requires probable cause. The Fifth Amendment guarantees due process; notice of a hearing, full information regarding the charges made, the opportunity to present evidence before an impartial judge or jury, and the right to refrain from self-incrimination. The Sixth Amendment establishes the requirements for criminal trials including the right to speedy public trial by an impartial jury and the right to have a lawyer. The Eighth Amendment forbids excessive bail and implies the right to such bail in most instances.

Since our system uses an adversary process to seek out basic truths, the right to counsel is fundamental. In *Faretta v. California* (1975), however, the United States Supreme Court held that the Sixth Amendment guarantees self-representation in a criminal case, but before the court can allow such self-representation, defendants must intelligently and knowingly waive their rights to the assistance of counsel when they formulate and conduct their own defenses. A record is usually made stating that counsel is available to the defendant to prevent subsequent claims of improper waiver of counsel or lack of counsel. It has often been said, however, that "one who defends himself has a fool for a client."

The purpose of the right to counsel is to protect the accused from a conviction that may result from ignorance of legal and constitutional rights. Although defendants in all criminal cases have basic constitutional rights, often they do not know how to protect them. The right to counsel is indispensable to their understanding of their other rights under the Constitution.

Although the criminal justice system is sometimes criticized when a defendant is found not guilty because of a technicality, such criticism is unfounded. Even though a person confesses to a hideous crime, if he or she was not first told of his or her rights and allowed to have a lawyer present during questioning, the confession should not be considered legal. As noted by the United States Supreme Court in *Escobedo v. Illinois* (1964):

> *No system of criminal justice can or should survive if it comes to depend for its continued effectiveness on the citizens' abdication through unawareness of their constitutional rights. No system worth preserving should have a fear that if an accused is permitted to consult with a lawyer, he will become aware of and exercise these rights. If the exercise of constitutional rights will thwart the effectiveness of a system of law enforcement, then there is something very wrong with that system.*

During the past several decades many landmark decisions of the Supreme Court have extended the rights of individuals accused of a crime to have counsel at government expense if they cannot afford to hire their own lawyers.

In *Powell v. Alabama* (1932) the Supreme Court ruled that in a capital case, where the defendants are indigent and are incapable of presenting their own defenses, the court must assign them counsel as part of the due process of the law.

Between 1932 and 1963 the United States Supreme Court heard a variety of "right to counsel" cases. The Supreme Court ruled in *Johnson v. Zerbst* (1938) that an indigent defendant charged with a federal crime had the right to be furnished with counsel; however, this case said nothing about indigents who appeared in state courts.

In *Betts v. Brady* (1942) the Supreme Court ruled that an indigent charged in a state court had *no* right to appointed counsel unless charged with a capital crime. Nineteen years later Clarence Gideon, a habitual criminal, was arrested in Florida for breaking and entering a poolroom. Gideon claimed to be an indigent and asked for appointed counsel. The court refused on the grounds that Florida statutes provide for appointment of counsel only in capital cases. Gideon made his request based on the *Betts* case, but he was turned down and subsequently sentenced to the state prison.

Gideon, in a handwritten petition, took his case to the Supreme Court. In the famous *Gideon v. Wainwright* case (1963) the United States Supreme Court overruled *Betts v. Brady* and unanimously held that state courts must appoint counsel for indigent defendants in noncapital as well as capital cases.

Expanding on the "fairness" doctrine in 1972 in the *Argersinger v. Hamlin* case (1972), the United States Supreme Court ruled that all defendants in court who face the possibility of a jail sentence are entitled to legal counsel, and that if the accused cannot afford counsel, the state must provide one.

The Defense Attorney

Lawyers who undertake to represent an accused have the same duties and obligations whether they are privately retained, serving as a legal aid in the system, or appointed by the court. They interview clients about their offenses, whether they are aware of any witnesses who might assist them, and whether they have given a confession. Lawyers investigate the circumstances of the cases and explore facts relevant to the guilt or innocence of their clients. They try to uncover evidence for their clients' defenses and organize the cases to present in court. The **defense attorney** represents the accused in court.

Although the role of the defense attorney has been glamorized by television series, in actuality over 99 percent of all criminal cases involve different kinds of lawyers and defense styles (Glick 1983, p. 155). Glick notes that criminal law is not emphasized in law school, which instead concentrates on business, property, and tax law, and that criminal law carries little prestige. Part of the reason for this is that clients are usually poor. In addition, the public generally has little sympathy for criminals and even less for a lawyer who "gets the criminal off."

The majority of criminal cases are assigned to public defenders or to a few private lawyers who handle such cases. Public defenders are full- and part-time lawyers hired by the state or county government to represent people who cannot afford to hire a lawyer. Like prosecutors, most public defenders see the position as a stepping-stone to private practice.

Not all cities have public defenders. In smaller cities, courts may appoint lawyers to represent poor people charged with crimes. In other cities the duty may be rotated among all lawyers practicing in the area as part of their professional obligation to society.

Most cities also have a small group of criminal lawyers who represent people who do not qualify financially for public defense. Known as "regulars," these lawyers do not intend to take these cases to court since few of the clients have much money. Instead they assist in plea bargaining with the prosecutors.

The Prosecutor

Prosecutors are officials elected to exercise leadership in the criminal justice system. They may be city attorneys, county attorneys, state attorneys, commonwealth attorneys, district attorneys, or solicitors.

Prosecutors are usually elected to a two- or four-year term at the state level. At the federal level they are appointed by the president. Eisenstein (1978, p. 40) notes: "United States attorneys also serve as lawyers for the federal government in civil cases, such as motor vehicle accidents involving postal vehicles. About 40 percent of their work involves noncriminal matters."

According to Jacob (1980, pp. 76-78): "Large cities may have dozens or even a hundred or more assistant prosecutors, a few of whom are interested in developing a political career, but most of whom want to gain experience before starting their own law practice."

Prosecutors are the legal representatives of the people and the police officers. They are responsible to the people who elected them, not to any other state or local official. They determine law enforcement priorities and are the key in determining how much, how little, and what types of crimes the public will tolerate. They serve the public interest and consider the public's need to feel secure, its sense of how justice should be carried out, and the community's attitude toward certain crimes. Sometimes a case becomes so well publicized that the prosecutor is forced to "do something about it" or face defeat in the next election.

Prosecutors are also the legal advisors for police officers; they are elected to decide what cases should be prosecuted and how. They rely heavily on the police officers' input in determining if a case should be brought to court or rejected. Often, however, misunderstanding and even ill will may result when a prosecutor refuses a police officer's request for a complaint because of insufficient evidence or some violation of a criminal procedure such as an illegal arrest. Plea bargaining may also cause ill will between a prosecutor and a police officer.

Since both police officers and prosecutors are striving for the same end—justice—they should be familiar with each other's problems. Police officers, for example, should understand what the prosecutor can and cannot do, which types of cases are worth prosecuting, and the need for and advantages of plea bargaining in certain situations. Prosecutors, on the other hand, should be sensitive to the police officers' objections to numerous legal technicalities and excessive paperwork and should include police officers in plea bargaining when possible, or, at the least, inform them when such bargaining has occurred.

Prosecutors perform one other critical function in the criminal justice process; they are responsible for protecting the rights of all involved, including the suspect. In essence they have a dual responsibility: on the one hand they are the leaders in the law enforcement community, the elected representatives of the public, and the legal advisors to the police officer; on the other hand, they are expected to protect the rights of persons accused of crimes. In *Berger v. United States* (1935) Justice Sutherland defined the prosecutor's responsibility as being "the representative not of an ordinary party to a controversy, but of a sovereignty whose obligation to govern impartially is as compelling as its obligation to govern at all; and whose interest, therefore, in a criminal prosecution is not that it shall win a case, but that justice shall be done.

Having looked at the nature of the adversary system and the key "contestants," now consider the critical steps normally involved in the criminal justice process.

CRITICAL STAGES IN THE CRIMINAL JUSTICE SYSTEM

The criminal justice system consists of several critical stages: the complaint or charge, the arrest, booking, preliminary hearing, grand jury hearing, the arraignment, the trial, and sentencing.

The Complaint or Charge

Usually the criminal justice process begins when a police officer or a citizen approaches the prosecutor to obtain a complaint. A **complaint** is a legal document drawn up by a prosecutor that specifies the alleged crime and the supporting facts providing probable cause.

The formal complaint, also called the *charge*, contains all necessary evidence and facts to enable a magistrate to independently determine that probable cause exists for believing the offense has been committed by the accused.

The Warrant

The police officer or citizen then presents the complaint to a magistrate and, in the magistrate's presence, swears to the accuracy of the content of the complaint and signs a statement to that effect. If the magistrate, after reading the complaint drawn up by the prosecuting attorney, concurs with the charge, he or she orders an arrest **warrant** (based on the probable cause established in the complaint) containing the substance of the complaint to be issued. If the magistrate does not concur, he or she dismisses the complaint.

An arrest warrant directs an officer to bring the suspect before the magistrate. The warrant is usually directed to the sheriff or constables of a county or to all police officers of the municipality within the court's jurisdiction. The officer specified then locates and arrests the suspect if not already in custody. The officer may execute the warrant in any part of the county where it is issued or in any part of the state.

The Arrest

Requirements for a legal arrest have been discussed. When making the arrest, officers must inform the suspect that they are acting on the authority of the warrant. The suspect is entitled to see it. If the officers do not have the warrant in their possession, they must show it to the suspect as soon as possible.

The arrest may occur at other points within the criminal justice process. In a misdemeanor case, it may have occurred without a complaint or warrant, provided the crime was committed in the presence of the arresting officer. Or, as will be discussed later, the prosecutor may choose to present the case to a grand jury for indictment prior to arresting a suspect.

Figure 19–1 illustrates the complexity of the criminal justice system.

The Booking

After a suspect is taken into custody, he or she is booked at the police station. The suspect is formally put into the police records system by the booking officer, who records on the booking sheet the suspect's name, date, time of arrest, charge, physical description, and physical characteristics. The suspect is photographed and fingerprinted. The prints are placed on file with the FBI in Washington, D.C., and the suspect has what is known as a Police Arrest Record.

Bail and Writ of Habeas Corpus

The Eighth Amendment forbids excessive bail and implies the right to bail in most instances.

One of the accused's rights is usually the right to be released from custody. Not only is this essential to the accused's immediate freedom, but it is in keeping with the premise that a person is innocent until proven guilty. After the formal booking process is completed, the suspect is usually entitled to be released on bail or on his or her own personal recognizance (**R.P.R.d**) if the crime is a misdemeanor or released on a writ of habeas corpus or bond if the crime is a felony.

The judges decide how much bail (money) is reasonable as a deposit to bring the defendant into court if released. Some statutes, however, allow a judge to set a schedule for the amount of bail required for specific

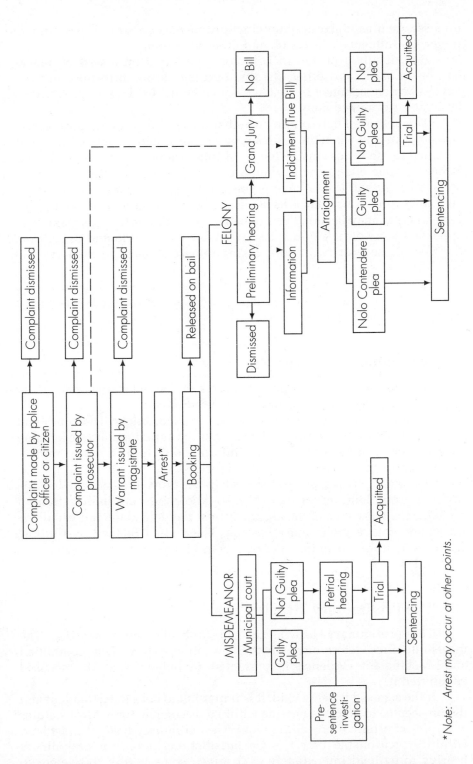

Figure 19–1   **The Criminal Justice System from Complaint to Disposition**

offenses such as violating municipal ordinances on shoplifting, driving under the influence of alcohol, and other violations.

Periodically a person in jail may be released on a **writ of habeas corpus**—a legal court order literally meaning "bring forth the body you have"—which commands that a person being held as a prisoner be brought forth immediately.

This means of determining whether the jailing of the suspect is legal is used primarily when the justice process moves slowly and a prisoner is detained for an unreasonable length of time before the court appearance. Habeas corpus often occurs when a person is arrested without a formal arrest warrant and the follow-up police investigation takes an unreasonably long time. Most states have adopted rules or guidelines as to how long a person may be jailed before being charged, released, or making an appearance in court. These rules are somewhat flexible and range from thirty-six to seventy-two hours, taking into consideration Sundays and holidays.

Up to this point in the criminal justice process, it makes little difference as to what type of crime—misdemeanor or felony—has been committed. The process is basically the same.

Misdemeanor versus Felony

Misdemeanors are usually disposed of by ticket, tab charge, or R.P.R.d, in which case the suspect is ordered to court.

Felony cases are more complex than misdemeanors. The complaint must be filed with the clerk of the district or the superior court. In a felony case the prosecutor may seek an "information" from the preliminary hearing or an indictment from a grand jury.

A formal written accusation, what has thus far been called the criminal complaint or charge, is also known as an **information.** It contains the substance of the charge against the defendant and usually is associated with a preliminary hearing. The United States Constitution, however, requires an indictment by a grand jury for most crimes against federal law.

The Preliminary Hearing

The **preliminary hearing** is the probable cause hearing. The magistrate first determines whether an offense has been committed and if sufficient evidence is presented to believe that the accused committed it.

If the accused is being held, it is important to both the defendant and the prosecutor to hold the hearing within a reasonable time. Most statutes and rules of criminal procedure require a preliminary hearing to be held within a "reasonable time." Some jurisdictions require a preliminary hearing to be held immediately after arrest, some within forty-eight to seventy-two hours, other within ten to thirty days.

The preliminary hearing seeks to establish probable cause to prevent persons from being indiscriminately brought to trial.

The magistrate in a preliminary hearing is not bound by the rules of evidence that ordinarily control a trial. A far broader range of evidence is usually admissible. The evidence need only show probable cause and reasonably and fairly tend to show the crime is as charged and that the accused committed it. The prosecutor only has to present the evidence; he or she need not prove the crime was committed beyond a reasonable doubt as long as probable cause is shown.

In reality the preliminary hearing is often a minitrial where the defense obtains as much information as possible to strengthen its case should it be bound over to a higher court. Both prosecution and defense often use this stage of the criminal justice process for tactical purposes. In some instances overwhelming evidence may lead to a guilty plea or to a request for plea bargaining.

The preliminary hearing is often a discovery tool for defendants as they hear the evidence presented. If the case went to the grand jury, the defendants would not be aware of this evidence. Some states have eliminated this element of surprise by including the **discovery process** in their rules of criminal procedure. The discovery process requires that all pertinent facts on both sides be made available prior to the time of the trial.

Used properly, the discovery process reduces questions of probable cause and other questions normally brought out in a preliminary hearing and encourages more final dispositions before trial, thereby saving court time. Available to both the prosecution and defense attorneys, it eliminates surprise as a legitimate trial tactic.

The discovery process requires that all pertinent facts on both sides be made available prior to the time of the trial.

The preliminary hearing does not determine who has won or lost. It merely determines whether further action should be taken. At this point the magistrate usually does not rule on complicated issues of evidence.

The main intent of the preliminary hearing is to add to the checks and balances of the criminal justice system by preventing the prosecutor from indiscriminately bringing someone to trial. The preliminary hearing, one of the critical stages of due process, is a very formal proceeding insuring that all accused persons are adequately informed and that all their constitutional rights are protected.

The outcome of a preliminary hearing may be to (1) dismiss the charges, (2) present an information and bind the defendant over to a higher court, or (3) send the case to a grand jury.

The Grand Jury

The United States Constitution requires an indictment by a federal grand jury before trial for most crimes against federal law. Grand juries frequently hear cases involving misconduct of public officials, violations of election laws, bankruptcy fraud, criminal conduct, and the like.

The consideration of a felony charge by a grand jury is in no sense of the word a trial. Only the prosecution's evidence is usually presented and considered. Contrary to the popular portrayal of grand juries on television and in movies, suspected offenders are usually not heard nor are their lawyers present to offer evidence in their behalf.

A **grand jury** is usually composed of twenty-three voting citizens of the county, selected by either the district or superior judges, jury commissioners, court officials, or some designated county supervisor. These juries may be called to duty any time the court is in session. Sixteen jurors constitute a quorum, and the votes of twelve members are usually necessary to return an indictment.

Grand juries meet in secret sessions and hear from witnesses and victims of crime. Because it meets in secret session, it is an accusatory body and determines only whether enough evidence exists to accuse a person or persons of a crime.

The prosecutor usually has considerable foundation for believing an offense has been committed before taking a case to the grand jury. The prosecutor is authorized to subpoena witnesses before the jury. Usually only one witness appears at a time before the jury and is questioned under oath by the prosecutor.

In some states, by statue, a grand jury can hear evidence from suspects. In order to testify, however, the persons being considered for indictment must sign a waiver of immunity and agree to answer all questions posed in the grand jury session even though their testimony might be incriminating and lead to an indictment. Their testimony also may be used against them in a criminal trial. Their lawyers are not allowed to be present in the grand jury room if they are testifying.

After the grand jury receives all testimony and evidence, it begins its deliberations. No one else is allowed in the room during these deliberations. Before an indictment can be reached, the jurors must agree that all the evidence presented leads them to believe probable cause exists that the person is guilty of a crime. If the majority of the grand jurors (or a specified number) agree, they instruct the prosecutor to prepare an **indictment** which specifies all the facts of the case and the names of those who appeared before the jury.

The indictment is signed by the grand jury foreman and presented to the district or superior court judge, who then orders the issuance of a bench warrant for the arrest of the defendant if not already in custody. If the defendant is indicted, until arrested or brought before the court, the fact that an indictment has been found must be kept secret; it is not public information.

Procedures are then implemented for the defendant's appearance in court, where a trial jury may be convened to hear the case.

Grand juries may also issue what is called a no bill. If, after hearing all the evidence presented and the witnesses, the jurors believe there is no criminal violation, the grand jury issues a no bill, which means they find no basis for an indictment and will no longer consider the matter unless further evidence is presented that may warrant an indictment.

Grand juries can also take action and conduct investigations on their own initiative. This is known as a presentment and in some jurisdictions is sufficient to support a prosecution. Some states, however, regard a presentment as mere instructions to the prosecutor to draw up a bill of indictment. If, when the grand jury reviews the bill of indictment, they agree it is a true bill, it becomes the basis for prosecution.

The Arraignment

When defendants are charged with a felony, they must personally appear at an **arraignment**. As in the preliminary hearing, the defendants are entitled to counsel. The procedures of the arraignment vary in some states, but generally defendants appear before the court, are read the complaint, information, or indictment, and, if they have not received a copy, they are given one. They then enter a **plea.**

Defendants have several alternatives when they appear for the formal arraignment. *Standing mute*, that is refusing to answer, is entered by the judge as a not guilty plea.

Nolo contendere means "no contest." By entering a plea of nolo contendere, defendants, in effect, throw themselves on the mercy of the court. This plea is often used when individuals know of some forthcoming civil actions against them and do not want their pleas to jeopardize their defenses in civil trials. (A guilty plea to any criminal offense could become a part of the civil trial.)

Guilty means the accused admits the actual charge or a lesser charge agreed to in a plea bargaining session. A guilty plea has many consequences: possible imprisonment, being labeled a criminal, and a waiver of constitutional rights of all defenses. Still, 90 percent of all criminal defendants plead guilty in the United States, but most plead guilty to offenses reduced from the original charges.

Not guilty means the accused denies the charge. He or she may have a valid defense for the charge such as intoxication, insanity, self-defense, or mistaken identity. Some states require defendants to automatically plead not guilty to capital crimes such as first-degree murder.

If defendants plead guilty or nolo contendere, a sentencing time is set. Usually a presentence investigation is ordered to determine if probation is warranted. If defendants make no plea or plead not guilty, they have the choice of a trial by a judge or by a jury, who weighs the facts of the case and makes the decision of guilt or innocence. If defendants wish a jury trial, the case will be assigned to the court docket and a date set.

Before looking at the trial itself, the court system within which it occurs, and the sentence that may result, first consider some alternatives to a trial.

ALTERNATIVES TO A TRIAL

Alternatives to a trial include diversion and plea bargaining.

Diversion

Before clients and their attorneys go to court, defense attorneys may explore the possibility of diverting the case from the criminal justice system by using a community agency if the circumstances warrant it; for example, in cases of mental incompetence an attorney may seek to divert the case to a mental institution. **Diversion** gives defendants an alternative to a trial, for example, to obtain help from a community agency or to make restitution to the victim of the crime.

Diversion is a discretionary decision that can occur at many points as the case progresses through the criminal justice system. For example, a police officer who assumes custody of an intoxicated person and releases that person to the custody of family or a detoxification center diverts. Likewise, a prosecutor who delays prosecution while a defendant participates in psychiatric treatment diverts. In both instances, a discretionary decision is made that there is a more appropriate way to deal with the defendant than to prosecute.

As might be expected, diversion has its opponents. Some individuals feel this is "letting criminals off easy." However, major benefits can result. According to the National Advisory Commission (1973, p. 27):

> *Many individuals come within the language of existing criminal statutes, but their conviction and punishment would not be consistent with the intent of the legislature. . . . By taking the offender out of the criminal justice process before conviction, diversion imposes no stigma of conviction, and unlike screening, prevents the offender from committing future harmful acts or requires him to make restitution. Only diversion provides a means of accommodating this compromise solution. If diversion programs were made available as sentencing alternatives, the objective of avoiding the stigma of a criminal conviction would be nullified.*

Another obvious benefit of diversion is economy, eliminating the necessity for what could be a costly court trial.

Plea Bargaining

The client and defense lawyer may also attempt to plea bargain their case. **Plea bargaining** is legal negotiation between the prosecutor and the defense lawyer or the client to reach an agreement that avoids a court trial. The prosecutor is seeking a conviction without going through the formality of a court trial. The defense is looking for some concessions by the prosecutor to reduce the punishment for the defendant.

Plea bargaining is a compromise between defense and prosecution that prearranges the plea and the sentence, conserving time and expense.

Basically, plea bargaining involves promises and compromises. From the prosecutor it may mean that if a series of charges are filed, the defendant would be charged with only one; the other charges would be dismissed. Or it might mean that the prosecutor would reduce a charge if only one charge is filed; for example, a charge of burglary might be reduced to breaking and entering which carries a lesser penalty.

A hazard of the plea bargaining system is that it may cause police officers to feel isolated. Throughout the criminal procedures system police officers are valued; the prosecutor, the complainants, the witnesses, and society depend upon them. But when it comes to plea bargaining sessions, they are left out. Often officers will inquire about the disposition of a case of vital interest to them only to find that it has been disposed of in plea bargaining. If officers are to be part of the total system, they should have some input into the disposition of the cases or, at the least, be informed of the disposition. As criminals are placed back into society, the police officers' problems in dealing with crime grow. If police officers are to deal with these problems, they should be consulted.

The Coroner's Jury

Coroners investigate violent deaths where suspicion of foul play exists. By law, coroners may conduct autopsies as to the cause of death, and they may conduct inquests. The **coroner's jury** usually consists of six members. In some states the coroner's jury system has been abandoned and its functions performed by a professional medical examiner, usually a pathologist or a forensic expert.

THE COURT SYSTEM

At the beginning of this chapter you were introduced to the adversary nature of our criminal justice system and to the key individuals in conflict with each other. For an adversary system to be truly fair and

The United States Supreme Court is the highest constitutional court.

impartial, certain safeguards must be in place. To this end, a highly structured court system has been established. And the key individuals within this system are the judges and, in some cases, members of a jury.

Judges

Although most people think of trial judges when they hear the word *judge*, many different kinds of judges exist. In fact, if a person comes to trial he or she will already have encountered certain levels of the court system and judges acting within that system.

Glick (1983, p. 163) suggests that judges have many important functions throughout the entire judicial process:

> *One of their most important jobs is to decide in preliminary hearings whether a prosecutor has sufficient evidence to justify prosecution. . . . Another important early decision for judges is whether to grant bail, if money bail is required and how much, or if the defendant can remain free without money bail before trial. Judges also make decisions to grant delays to give one side or the other additional time to prepare their case, to attend to other legal business, or to give a defense lawyer time to persuade a client to plead guilty or even to pay part of the lawyer's fee.*

In many instances the judge has the key role in imposing the sentence to be served if a defendant is found guilty. And, as noted by Glick (1983, p. 177): "Judges have special status and receive great respect from everyone in court . . . their lofty position gives them an opportunity to lead others. If judges choose to exert themselves, they have practically unchallenged opportunites to influence the outcome of cases."

The various types of judges and the functions they serve depend on the court to which they are appointed. At this point a brief review of the justice system, from a somewhat different vantage point, may help to clarify the hierarchy within our court system. The progression depicted in figure 19.2 can be repeated from a lower court to a higher court, one or more times.

Organizational Structure of the Courts

The courts in the United States operate within a highly structured framework that may vary greatly from state to state. Numerous dualities exist within this framework, the most obvious of which is the dual system of state and federal courts. These two systems will be discussed momentarily, but first some other dualities should be understood. Among the most important are those having to do with a court's jurisdiction—its authority to try a case or to hear an appeal. Technically it does not refer to a geographic area.

As noted by Waldron (1984, p. 283): "Jurisdiction should not be mistaken for the concept of *venue*, the requirement that the trial for an offense be held in the same area in which the offense occurred. The point to remember is that jurisdiction refers to a court's authority to take notice of and decide a case."

Another duality within the organizational structure of the courts and their jurisdiction is that of *original* versus *appellate* jurisdiction. A court with original jurisdiction has the authority to try cases, whereas a court with appellate jurisdiction has the authority to hear an **appeal** to set aside a conviction. In some cases a court has both types of jurisdiction, for example, the United States Supreme Court.

A court with the authority to try a case is often called a *trial* court, and since such courts are frequently the first to record the proceedings, they are also referred to as a *court of record*. A court that uses the record from a previous trial in considering an appeal, without calling a new trial, automatically identifies the court below as a court of record.

A *court of last resort* refers to the highest court to which a case may be appealed.

The State Court System   Each state's constitution and statutory law establish the structure of its courts. Consequently, great variety exists in the types of courts established, the names by which they are known, and the number of levels in the hierarchy. For example, until recently, Pennsylvania had eleven different types of courts, each having jurisdiction over a specific kind of case.

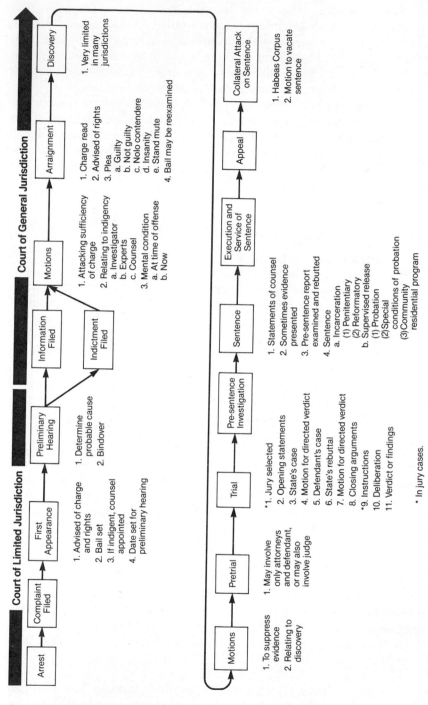

Figure 19–2   Typical Progression of Criminal Felony Litigation

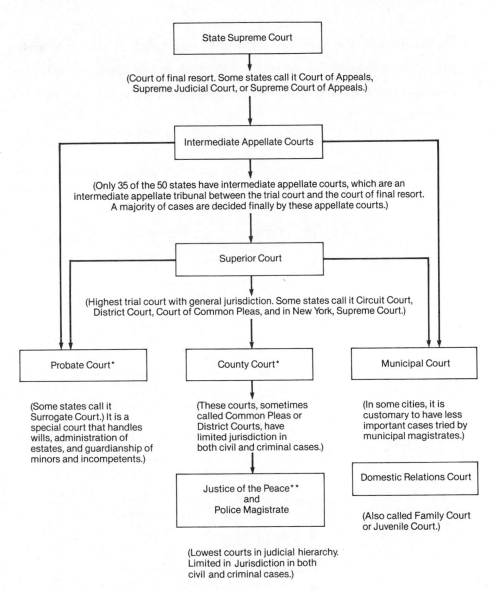

*Courts of special jurisdiction, such as probate, family, or juvenile courts, and the so-called inferior courts, such as common pleas or municipal courts, may be separate courts or part of the trial court of general jurisdiction.

**Justices of the peace do not exist in all states. Where they do exist, their jurisdictions vary greatly from state to state.
Source: American Bar Association, *Law and the Courts* (Chicago: American Bar Association, 1974), p. 20. Updated information provided by West Publishing Company.
Source: Joseph J. Senna and Larry L. Siegel, *Introduction to Criminal Justice*, 3d ed. St. Paul, Minn.: West Publishing Co., 1984.

Figure 19–3   **State Judicial System**

The hierarchy at the state level often goes from courts of special or limited jurisdiction called justice of the peace (J. P.) courts, to trial courts or original and general jurisdiction courts, to intermediate appellate courts, to the state supreme court.

The Federal Court System   Within the federal court system a further duality exists: constitutional courts and legislative courts. The constitutional

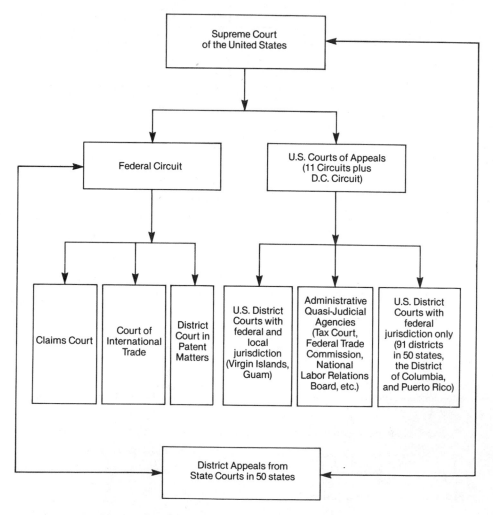

Source: American Bar Association, *Law and the Courts* (Chicago: American Bar Association, 1974), p. 21. Updated information provided by the Federal Courts Improvement Act of 1982 and West Publishing Company.
Source: Joseph J. Senna and Larry J. Siegel, *Introduction to Criminal Justice*, 3d ed., St. Paul, Minn.: West Publishing Co., 1984.

Figure 19–4 **Federal Judicial System**

courts include the United States Supreme Court as well as "such inferior Courts as the Congress may from time to time ordain and establish" (article III, section 1). These inferior courts include the courts of appeals, the district courts, and numerous specialized courts. Legislative courts are lower in the hierarchy and include trial courts in the United States territories, specialized courts, and the Military Court of Appeals.

The federal court system is three tiered: district courts, appellate courts, and the United States Supreme Court.

The United States **Supreme Court** is presided over by nine justices appointed by the president of the United States, subject to Senate confirmation. The president also appoints a chief justice, who assigns the cases to the other justices. Most have been lawyers and are from the upper class, white, male, protestant, and graduates of prestigious universities. Over half were judges prior to their appointments as United States Supreme Court Justices.

As noted by Glick (1983, p. 105):

> *Becoming a federal judge requires political visibility, involvement in political activity, party loyalty, and, depending on the court, sharing the political values or ideology of the administration making the appointments. . . . The occasional appointment of Jewish, Catholic, or black justices is a recent and rare event. President Reagan's appointment of Sandra D. O'Connor is the most recent change to occur in recruitment to the Supreme Court.*

The Constitution established tenure for "life on good behavior"; therefore the only way to remove a justice is through impeachment unless voluntary retirement can be obtained.

The Trial

When police officers enter the courtroom they realize that the trial is the climax in the criminal justice procedure. All previously made decisions now merge in one finality. The test of how well the police officers have investigated the case, compiled evidence and reported it, and dealt with the victim and witnesses are weighed in the courtroom.

The key figures in the trial are the judge, members of the jury, the defendant and defense attorney(s), the prosecuting attorney(s), police officer(s), and witnesses.

The judge has charge of the trial and decides all matters with respect to the law. He or she also assures that all the rules of trial procedure are followed. The jury decides all matters of fact. The advocates are the prosecuting attorney(s) and the defense attorney(s). The trial begins with the jury selection.

Jury Selection   Safeguards built into the jury selection process not only protect the rights of the defendant but also assure the public that justice is done. Trial jurors are selected at random by district or superior court judges or the commissioners of the county board. The judges or the commissioners randomly select a large group of prospective jurors and, when the trial is about to begin, call these people to the court and inform them of their duties in the particular case for which they may serve.

It is then up to the attorneys trying the case to decide which six or twelve of these individuals will be the jurors in the case. The clerk of courts draws the names of six or twelve jurors from the jury list, and these individuals take their seats in the regular jury box in the order in which their names were drawn. The defense attorney and then the prosecuting attorney question each individual as to his or her qualifications to be a juror in this case. The judge may also question the prospective jurors. The random selection of potential jurors and the careful questioning of each helps insure selection of six or twelve fair and impartial jurors.

The National Advisory Commission on Criminal Justice Standards and Goals (1975, p. 101) suggests that the twelve-person jury requirement for criminal trials that exists in most jurisdictions is an "accident of history," and that "juries of less than 12 can provide a reliable and competent fact-finding body." In *Williams v. Florida* (1970) the Court stated that the touchstone should be whether the group is "large enough to promote group deliberation, to be free from outside attempts at intimidation, and to provide a fair possibility for obtaining a representative cross-section of the community." In this same case the Supreme Court held that Florida's use of a six-person jury did not violate the defendant's Eighth and Fourteenth Amendment rights to trial by jury.

Opening Statements   After the jury is selected and instructed by the judge, opening statements are presented. The prosecutor informs the jury of the state's case and how he or she intends to prove the charges against the defendant. The defense lawyer makes an opening statement in support of the accused or may waive this opening statement.

Evidence and Testimony   The prosecutor then presents evidence and the testimony of the witnesses, attempting to prove that a crime had been committed and that the defendant did it. The prosecutor does so by using direct and indirect evidence, a confession, the testimony of witnesses, or the testimony of the police officers whose initial investigation brought the case to trial.

Through cross-examination, the defense attorney tries to discredit prosecution witnesses, the evidence, and the testimony of the police officers.

The Police Officer in Court   Almost all officers have a day in court. Because of overloaded court dockets, cases usually come up well after the officers' investigation; therefore, officers must refer to their reports and their original notes to refresh their memories. The notes may remind them that it was a cloudy day, a light rain had fallen and the streets were still wet,

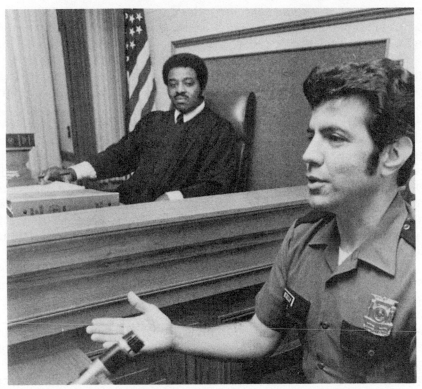

One way police officers aid the criminal justice system is by testifying in court.

that it was midafternoon, and that clearly visible bloodstains trailed out the back door.

A court appearance is an important part of any police officer's duty. All elements of the investigation are brought together at this point: the report, the statements of the witnesses, the evidence collected, and possibly even a confession from the defendant.

The prosecution needs to establish the corpus delicti of the crime, which means it has to establish the elements of the crime by testimony of witnesses, physical evidence, documents, recordings, or other admissible evidence. This information usually comes from police officers, their recollections, their notes, and their reports. The prosecutor works with police officers in presenting the arguments for the prosecution. On the opposing side is the defense attorney.

Defense attorneys use several different techniques for which police officers should be prepared. One frequently used technique is *rapid-fire questioning* with the intent of confusing the officer to obtaining inconsistent answers. To counter this tactic, officers should be deliberate and take their time in answering questions. They may ask the defense attorney to repeat the question to slow him or her down and thus thwart this effort at rapid-fire questioning.

The trial of a criminal case is a very serious contest. Someone wins and someone loses. The prosecution wins if it establishes the guilt of the defendant. It must prove the defendant is guilty beyond a reasonable doubt. The defendant wins if the prosecution fails in its obligation of proof.

Proof consists of two basic elements: the evidence itself and, equally important, presentation of this evidence. No matter how much evidence exists, if improperly presented, the prosecution will fail. Presenting evidence involves credibility and believability.

In a criminal case, the defense rarely expects to gain helpful information from police officers. The main intent is usually to discredit the officers or their testimony. One common approach is to establish a motive for officers' testimony, to show the officers have a personal interest in the case, to question their candor: Is the officer being open or holding back? Is the testimony consistent? Does it contain errors? Is the officer confident and relaxed or nervous, upset, and seemingly afraid? What is the officer's general appearance? Is it the appearance of a professional doing an important, serious job?

Defense attorneys also attack a police officer's credibility by focusing on the assumptions or inferences of the officer. Assumptions and inferences are natural. We spend our whole lives making assumptions, usually reasonable ones. The law recognizes the validity of assumptions and inferences. As a matter of fact, the court will instruct the jury to make reasonable inferences. From time to time, however, a defense attorney will try to discredit police officers' testimony by asking them if they are making assumptions. If officers have, in fact, drawn inferences or made assumptions, they should not attempt to deny it.

Another cross-examination tactic used by defense counsel from time to time is to present to the jury police officers' reluctance to relinquish their notes. The police officers' notes and their reports, as a general rule, are available to the defense counsel in making cross-examination. When police officers use their notes to testify, they are also available to the defense counsel.

The defense attorney may try to confuse or discredit a police officer by (1) rapid-fire questioning, (2) establishing that the officer wants to see the defendant found guilty, (3) accusing the officer of making assumptions, or (4) implying that the officer does not want anyone else to know what is in his or her notes.

Closing Statements   After the advocates have concluded their presentations, the jury hears the closing statements—a contest in persuasion first by the prosecution, stating the jury should render a guilty verdict, then by the defense attorney, concluding the client is surely innocent or at least not proven guilty beyond a reasonable doubt.

Jury Deliberation and Decision   With the closing of the case, the judge reads the instructions to the jury. This includes an explanation of the crime, what elements constitute the crime, alternate charges, and the concepts of presumption of innocence and reasonable doubt. The jury then retires behind closed doors to deliberate their findings. They can return one of three findings: guilty, not guilty, or no verdict. No verdict simply means that no agreement can be reached; this is also sometimes referred to as a "hung jury."

After the jury has come to a decision, the judge is notified and the jury returns to the courtroom. With everyone present, the jury foreman announces the verdict. Each juror is then polled as to how he or she voted and is asked if the verdict that the foreman has read is the verdict of the juror. If the finding is guilty, the defendant may either be sentenced immediately or may be given a sentencing date. If found not guilty, he or she is set free. If a hung jury results, the defendant may be retried at the discretion of the prosecutor.

Sentencing

Sentences for individuals convicted of crimes vary considerably from lenient to extremely severe penalties. For one convicted of a crime this may mean the difference between probation and several years in prison.

In many jurisdictions the court has the authority to set, within limits established by state statute, both maximum and minimum sentences. Common characteristics of these schemes are summarized in table 19–1.

Common sentencing schemes include indeterminate, indefinite, definite, determinate, mandatory, and presumptive.

Case Review and Appeal

To assure that justice is served, the court system provides for a review of cases and for a person convicted to appeal the conviction in most instances. The National Advisory Commission on Criminal Justice Standards and Goals (1975, pp. 122–25) states: "Determining guilt and fixing punishment should not be left to a single trial court. The interests of both society and the defendant are served by providing another tribunal to review the trial court proceedings to insure that no prejudicial error was committed and that justice was done." The commission goes on to note: "Review also provides a means for the ongoing development of legal doctrine in the common law fashion, as well as a means of insuring evenhanded administration of justice throughout the jurisdiction. Functionally, review is the last stage in the judicial process of determining guilt and fixing sentence. Like the trial proceeding, it should be fair and expeditious."

Table 19–1 **Common Sentencing Schemes**

Indeterminate	Minimum and maximum terms prescribed by legislature; place and length of sentence controlled by corrections and parole; judge has little discretion over time served; goal is rehabilitation; sentence to fit offender; uncertainity and disparity in sentencing are major problems.
Indefinite	Similar to indetermine sentence in some states; minimum and-maximum terms, or only maximum terms prescribed by legislature; sentence to match offender's needs; judge has some sentencing discretion; wide disparity in sentences imposed; parole used for early release.
Definite	Fixed period prescribed by legislature and imposed by judge; goal to punish and deter offender from further crime; allows for same sentence to apply to all convicted of particular offenses; eliminates disparity; judge has no discretion over length of sentence, only over choice of sentence; offender required to serve entire sentence; no parole, inflexibility, and rigidity are major problems.
Determinate	Similar to definite sentence; has one fixed term of years set by judge; offender required to serve entire sentence where no parole exists.
Mandatory	Fixed term set by legislature for particular crimes; sentence must be imposed by judge; judge has no discretion in choice of sentence; goal is punishment and deterrence; contrary to individualized sentence; no sentencing disparity; no parole.
Presumptive	Legislatively prescribed range of sentences for given crimes; minimum and maximum terms with judge setting determinate sentence within these bounds; judge maintains some discretion; guidelines and use of mitigating and aggravating circumstances established by legislature; goal is justice, deterrence, and individualization in sentencing; "just deserts."

Source: Reprinted by permission from *Introduction to Criminal Justice* by Joseph J. Senna and Larry J. Siegel. Copyright © 1984 by West Publishing Co. All rights reserved.

Corrections is that portion of the criminal justice system that carries out the court's orders. It consists of our probation and parole systems as well as our jails, prisons, and community-based programs to rehabilitate offenders.

CORRECTIONS

The final stage in the administration of the criminal justice system in the United States is corrections.

According to Eldefonso (1974, p. 4): "Corrections is America's prisons, jails, juvenile training schools, probation and parole machinery, and, as such, is the part of the criminal justice system that the public sees the least of and knows the least about. It seldom gets into the news, unless there is a prison riot, jail break, or a sensational scandal involving corruption or brutality in an institution or by an official."

Eldefonso (1984, p. 5) also suggests that the underlying philosophy of corrections is to serve and protect society by rehabilitating offenders: "The purpose of any correctional program is to make services available, within a client-restrictive status designed to protect society, which will enable the offender to become a useful, productive citizen." The National Advisory Commission on Criminal Justice Standards and Goals (1973, p. 222) points out, however: "Public protection is not always the sole objective of correctional programming. Some kinds of offenders, especially the most notorious, often could perfectly well be released without jeopardizing public safety. But their release will not be countenanced because public demands for retribution have not been satisfied."

The primary purpose of a correctional program is to make services available—within a restricted environment—which enable an offender to become a useful, productive citizen. Secondary purposes of a correctional program are individual deterrence, general deterrence, incapacitation, retribution, or expression of moral outrage.

Probation

A person who is found guilty of a crime may be placed on probation. Probation is the most frequent alternative to a jail or prison sentence. Probation is the conditional suspension of a sentence of a person convicted of a crime but not yet imprisoned for that crime. The defendant is placed under the supervision of a probation officer for a set period of time and must meet specific conditions.

Probation is most frequently used with first offenders and with crimes that are not considered heinous by society, such as many of the white-collar crimes. A first-time embezzler of high standing in the community might be given probation, avoiding the stigma of a prison record. Probation operates on a "second-chance" philosophy. Consequently, if a person is convicted a second time for a crime, that person is very unlikely to receive probation.

Correctional Institutions

The first truly correctional institution in the United States opened in Philadelphia in 1790 and was called the Walnut Street Jail. This jail, unlike existing workhouses, prisons, and jails, was used exclusively for the "correction" of convicted felons.

Not until the nineteenth century was the use of correctional institutions common in the United States. The primary goal of correctional institutions is to protect society. Secondary goals may be to deter, rehabilitate, and reintegrate offenders into society.

Although corrections attempts to rehabilitate offenders, conditions cannot be such that the prison is a pleasant place to be. Inmates should dread a return. Unfortunately, however, too often our correctional institutions do not rehabilitate but actually contribute to and reward criminial behavior.

Table 19–2   **Current Sentencing Alternatives Reflect Multiple Objectives**

What types of sentences usually are given to offenders?

Death penalty—In most states for the most serious crimes such as murder, the courts may sentence an offender to death by lethal injection, electrocution, exposure to lethal gas, hanging, or other method specified by state law.

- As of 1985, 37 states had laws providing for the death penalty.
- Virtually all death penalty sentences are for murder.
- As of yearend 1985, 50 persons had been executed since 1976, and 1,591 inmates in 32 states were under a sentence of death.

Incarceration—The confinement of a convicted criminal in a federal or state prison or a local jail to serve a court-imposed sentence. Confinement is usually in a jail, administered locally, or a prison, operated by the state or federal government. In many states offenders sentenced to 1 year or less are held in a jail; those sentenced to longer terms are committed to a state prison.

- More than 4,200 correctional facilities are maintained by federal, state, and local governments. They include 47 federal facilities, 922 state-operated adult confinement and community-based correctional facilities, and 3,300 local jails, which usually are county-operated.
- On any given day in 1985 about 503,000 persons were confined in state and federal prisons. About 254,000 were confined in local jails on June 30, 1985.

Probation—The sentencing of an offender to community supervision by a probation agency, often as a result of suspending a sentence to confinement. Such supervision normally entails specific rules of conduct while in the community. If the rules are violated a sentence to confinement may be imposed. Probation is the most widely used correctional disposition in the United States.

- State or local governments operate more than 2,000 probation agencies.
- At yearend 1985, nearly 1.9 million adults were on probation, or about 1 of every 95 adults in the nation.

Split sentences, shock probation, and intermittent confinement—A penalty that explicitly requires the convicted person to serve a brief period of confinement in a local, state, or federal facility (the "shock") followed by a period of probation. This penalty attempts to combine the use of community supervision with a short incarceration experience. Some sentences are periodic rather than continuous; for example, an offender may be required to spend a certain number of weekends in jail.

- In 1984 nearly a third of those receiving probation sentences in Idaho, New Jersey, Tennessee, Utah, and Vermont also were sentenced to brief periods of confinement.

Restitution and victim compensation—The offender is required to provide financial repayment or, in some jurisdictions, services in lieu of monetary restitution, for the losses incurred by the victim.

- Nearly all states have statutory provisions for the collection and disbursement of restitution funds. A restitution law was enacted at the federal level in 1982.

Community service—The offender is required to perform a specified amount of public service work, such as collecting trash in parks or other public facilities.

- Many states authorize community service work orders. Community service often is imposed as a specific condition of probation.

Table 19–2   Current Sentencing Alternatives Reflect Multiple Objectives   (*Continued*)

Fines—An economic penalty that requires the offender to pay a specified sum of money within limits set by law. Fines often are imposed in addition to probation or as alternatives to incarceration.

● The Victims of Crime Act of 1984 authorizes the distribution of fines and forfeited criminal profits to support state victim-assistance programs, with priority given to prgrams that aid victims of sexual assault, spousal abuse, and child abuse. These programs, in turn, provide assistance and compensation to crime victims.

● Many laws that govern the imposition of fines are being revised. The revisions often provide for more flexible means of ensuring equity in the imposition of fines, flexible fine schedules, "day fines" geared to the offender's daily wage, installment payment of fines, and the imposition of confinement only when there is an intentional refusal to pay.

● A 1984 study estimated that more than three-fourths of criminal courts use fines extensively and that fines levied each year exceed $1 billion.

U.S. Dept. of Justice. Bureau of Statistics. Washington, D.C., U.S. Gov't Printing Office, 1988.

The type of correctional institution an offender is sentenced to usually depends on the type of crime committed and the offender's past record. Alternatives include local and county jails and state and federal prisons.

The Jail   The jail is an important part of the criminal justice system in the United States.

Jail differs from prison in that its inmates are there for shorter terms, usually for less serious crimes.

The court's decisions directly affect the number and type of persons sentenced to jail. The court's decisions also dictate how much involvement the jail personnel must have with rehabilitative programs. If, for example, the court specifies that an offender must participate in a work program, the jail must provide such a program.

As part of the corrections segment of the criminal justice system, the jail has an advantage over prison because it is frequently located in the community and can coordinate its services with that of the community. In addition, its offenders are usually more likely to be rehabilitated than prison inmates, many of whom are habitual offenders.

Because jails are such an important part of the corrections program and the total criminal justice system, it is imperative that they be of high quality. Unfortunately, however, as noted by Pursley (1980, p. 416): "The jail has traditionally operated below standard." Pursley (1980, p. 420) contends: "The harsh reality is that most jails remain a serious problem in the system of American justice."

Clearly, one of the greatest problems is the variety of offenders either awaiting trial or serving sentences in our jails. Each needs different types of programs and requires different kinds of security. In most instances, the physical facility and lack of personnel make such individualization next to impossible.

Negative characteristics of jails in the United States include the following: the wide variety of backgrounds of the offenders in our jails; the problems of local control and politics; inadequate personnel; demeaning physical facilities; inept administration; failure to adopt alternative programs and dispositions.

The Prison   The word *prison* usually conveys an image of rows of cagelike cells, several levels high, crowded mess halls, a "yard" where prisoners engage in physical activities, organized and not so organized, all patrolled by tightlipped, heavily armed guards.

The physical facility itself reflects the philosophy regarding the purpose of imprisonment. Two basic physical designs developed in the United States. The first design consisted of fortresslike structures containing solitary cells, each with a tiny walled-in courtyard. Prisoners were, in effect, in solitary confinement for the duration of their sentences. The second design consisted of cells built back to back and facing a corridor. Meals were eaten in large rooms, and prisoners were expected to work at hard labor. This design, often referred to as the Auburn design because it was first used in the Auburn Penitentiary constructed in 1818 in Auburn, New York, is most frequently used in the United States today.

Both of the early philosophies influencing prison design were basically punitive. Throughout the decades, however, efforts at prison

The San Quentin prison in California.

Table 19–3 Philosophies of Imprisonment

Punitive Oriented	Treatment Oriented
Authority pattern based only on rank. For example, guards obey warden.	Authority pattern based on technical knowledge.
Very specific, measurable rules, with strict emphasis on obedience.	More general goals, more flexibility, more individualized.
Guards have limited decision-making authority, limited discretion.	Guards are encouraged to make their own decisions, use their own discretion.
Communications with inmates is very formal, usually restricted to orders.	Communications is less formal and is encouraged.
Incentives used are usually negative, for example, force and coercion, removal of privileges, solitary confinement, and the like.	Incentives used are usually positive, for example, granting of special privileges, better living quarters, furloughs, and the like.

Source: *Social Psychology of the Criminal Justice System*, A. S. Greenberg and R. B Rubeck. Monterey, Calif.: Brooks/Cole Publishing, 1982.

reform have lead to a change in emphasis, seeking to rehabilitate prisoners rather than to punish them.

As Greenberg and Rubeck (1982, p. 214) note: "All prisons are custodial (and therefore punitive, as custody implies the loss of rights and the denial of certain comforts), but some are more oriented toward treating and rehabilitating offenders than others." They go on to cite several important differences between these two orientations. (See table 19–3)

Greenberg and Rubeck (1982, p. 215) conclude: "Although both punitive/custodial prisons and treatment-oriented prisons exist in the United States and although most prisons have elements of both types, most lack the physical and human resources necessary for an effective treatment orientation and, therefore, are primarily of the punitive/custodial type."

Prisons may be punitive or treatment oriented. Punitive-oriented prisons are more formal and rigid, with an emphasis on obedience. Obedience is sought through negative incentives. Treatment-oriented prisons are more informal and flexible, with positive incentives for good behavior.

Parole

Parole is the most frequent type of release from a correctional institution. Parole differs from probation in that a person who is paroled has spent some time serving a prison sentence. It is similar to probation in that both require supervision of the offender and set up certain conditions that must be met by the offender.

Factors influencing whether a person serving a sentence is eligible for or, indeed, is granted a parole include the type of offense committed, the offender's prior record, and state statutes. In some jurisdictions, parole is prohibited by statute for certain crimes. In other jurisdictions, however, people sentenced to prison are immediately eligible for parole.

Parole differs from probation in that a person who is paroled has spent some time serving a prison sentence. It is similar to probation in that both require supervision of the offender and set up certain conditions that must be met by the offender.

Community-Based Institutional Programs

In some instances, jail or prison is not the best alternative for an offender.

Community-based institutional programs aimed at reintegration of the offender into society include halfway houses and restitution centers.

Halfway Houses   As the name implies, halfway houses are community-based institutions for individuals who are halfway into prison, that is, on probation, or halfway out of prison, that is, on or nearing parole.

Halfway houses have existed for centuries, with one of the earliest being in sixth-century France, founded by St. Leonard, who secured the release of convicts and let them live in his monestery. Williams, Formby, and Watkins (1982, p. 460) note that the first modern halfway house in the United States was founded in 1954 by the Reverend James G. Jones, Jr., chaplain of the Cook County Jail in Chicago. Since that time many halfway houses have been opened in the United States.

Halfway houses typically provide offenders with a place to live, sleep, and eat. Counselors are provided to help with reintegration into society, including help with finding a suitable job and sometimes with transportation to a job.

As noted, halfway houses may serve those who are halfway into prison, such as the misdemeanant—a person convicted of a crime requiring no more than a one-year sentence. Or they may serve persons who are halfway out of prison—those who are nearing parole or who have actually been paroled but who still need support services. Halfway houses serving those nearing parole or actually discharged from prison are sometimes called "prerelease centers."

Restitution Centers   A new variation of the halfway house is the restitution center. A restitution center differs from a halfway house in that in the restitution center offenders work to partially repay their victims. Like the halfway house, restitution centers offer an alternative to prison, either for those who are halfway into prison or those who are halfway out of prison.

For restitution to be a viable alternative, the amount of money to be repaid must be within reason and the offender must not pose an escape risk. Since persons convicted of crimes typically cannot obtain high-paying jobs, frequently some type of compromise is reached between the victim and the offender, with the agreement put into a signed contract.

Many sociologists suggest that restitution centers offer advantages to both the victim and the offender. For the victim they provide not only partial repayment, but also a sense that the criminal justice system is indeed fair and that it is as concerned with the victims of crime as it is with the perpetrators of crime. On the other hand, restitution centers may also benefit the offenders, not only as an alternative to jail or prison, but also as a means of coming to know the victim as an individual who has suffered from the crime committed. Often offenders do not think about their victims as people with the same feelings as themselves. If they can see the harm they have caused, it may assist in their reform.

Other Reintegration Methods

Several methods of reintegration into society have been used, with varying degrees of success. The most common are furloughs, work release, and study release. In all instances the possibility of escape from the directives of the criminal justice system must be considered.

Three common reintegration methods are furloughs, work release, and study release.

Furloughs   Furloughs are short, temporary leaves from a prison or jail. They may be supervised or unsupervised, although generally they are the latter. Furloughs are often used as positive motivators for good behavior. They may be granted for family emergencies, for a weekend with a spouse, or for job interviewing. Many experts feel that the use of conjugal furloughs for good behavior not only is a positive motivator, but it may also reduce homosexual activity within the correctional facility.

Work and Study Release   Another positive motivator for good behavior that also serves as a means to reintegrate offenders into society is release for either a job or a course of study. Often such programs are conducted through halfway houses. They may also be conducted through local jails. One problem associated with such programs is that those who are released may smuggle contraband back into the correctional facility.

The rules in work release and study release programs are usually very explicit and rigid. For example, a strict curfew may be established; going into a bar may be prohibited; and association with known criminals may be forbidden.

Individuals on work programs usually have their pay closely controlled. They may be required to pay a portion of their room and board, and, if married, to send part of their earnings to their dependents.

The Community   Traditionally correctional institutions were isolated from other human service agencies and were required merely to hold prisoners and to provide some form of nominal supervision for individuals on probation and parole. More recently, however, as already noted, it is expected that corrections take a more positive approach, seeking rehabilitation whenever possible. These revised expectations make it necessary to link corrections to the community in every phase of operation.

Community-based corrections require a complicated interplay among judicial and correctional personnel from related public and private agencies, citizen volunteers, and civic groups. It also requires leadership.

Table 19–4   More than 2.6 Million Adults Are Under Some Form of Correctional Care, Custody, or Supervision

Regions and States	Number of adults				Regions and States	Number of adults			
	On probation	In jail	In prison	On parole		On probation	In jail	In prison	On parole
United States, total	1,870,132	218,995	503,315	277,438	South				
Federal	55,217	*	40,223	16,860	Alabama	16,520	4,452	11,015	2,425
State	1,814,915	218,995	463,092	260,578	Arkansas	9,268	1,540	4,611	3,830
					Delaware	7,103	*	2,553	864
Northeast					District of Columbia	11,777	*	6,404	2,340
Connecticut	36,805	*	6,149	597	Florida	130,767	14,313	28,600	4,214
Maine	4,451	542	1,226	68	Georgia	94,461	10,213	16,014	8,538
Massachusetts	24,637	3,304	5,390	4,496	Kentucky	14,887	3,652	5,801	3,471
New Hampshire	3,096	469	683	453	Louisiana	26,638	8,501	13,890	3,718
New Jersey	48,466	5,956	11,335	13,385	Maryland	67,138	4,572	13,005	7,308
New York	100,816	15,877	34,712	25,279	Mississippi	6,636	2,482	6,392	3,392
Pennsylvania	65,286	10,167	14,227	12,200	North Carolina	56,207	3,474	17,344	3,184
Rhode Island	7,536	*	1,307	402	Oklahoma	20,310	2,164	8,330	1,625
Vermont	5,298	*	677	236	South Carolina	17,964	2,674	10,510	3,261
					Tennessee	24,648	5,975	7,127	7,499
Midwest					Texas	269,909	15,176	37,532	47,471
Illinois	74,156	8,819	18,634	11,421	Virginia	17,236	5,616	12,073	5,641
Indiana	39,121	3,466	9,904	2,797	West Virginia	3,905	1,015	1,725	638
Iowa	12,063	828	2,832	1,971					
Kansas	15,473	1,305	4,732	2,282	West				
Michigan	75,162	7,627	17,799	6,639	Alaska	2,606	34	2,329	155
Minnesota	32,986	1,941	2,343	1,364	Arizona	18,176	2,906	8,531	1,717
Missouri	26,760	3,761	9,915	4,534	California	210,449	41,656	50,111	33,983
Nebraska	10,720	817	1,814	364	Colorado	17,612	2,739	3,369	2,003
North Dakota	1,569	236	422	166	Hawaii	7,986	*	8,111	716
Ohio	61,465	7,087	20,864	6,509	Idaho	3,414	566	1,294	483
South Dakota	2,249	310	1,047	415	Montana	2,712	394	1,129	694
Wisconsin	24,288	3,003	5,442	3,850	Nevada	5,365	928	3,771	1,313
					New Mexico	4,185	1,324	1,324	1,115
					Oregon	22,377	2,304	4,454	2,010
					Utah	6,330	906	1,633	1,174
					Washington	44,248	3,595	6,909	6,039
					Wyoming	1,678	309	758	329

Note: Jail data are for June 30, 1983. All other are for December 31, 1985.
*Jail populations in states with consolidated jail/prison systems are included in prison population counts.
Source: *Probation and Parole 1985*, BJS Bulletin, January 1987.

Community-based corrections includes any activities in the community aimed at helping offenders become law-abiding citizens. The oldest community-based correctional program is supervision under probation, a foundation on which to build a wide range of community-based services. The use of control and surveillance is basic to a sound community corrections system.

Community-based corrections includes all correctional activities that occur in the community as an alternative to confinement of an offender at any point in the correctional process. A community-based approach to corrections has three significant advantages: humanitarian, restorative, and managerial. The humanitarian aspect is obvious because no one should be subjected to custodial control unnecessarily. To help a person avoid the unfavorable consequences of prison, even though the result of the offender's own criminal actions, is humanitarian. Second, restorative measures should help an offender achieve a position in the community in which he or she does not violate the law. The accomplishment of this objective can be measured by recidivism.

Additionally, the managerial goal of cost effectiveness can often be obtained from a community-based program. Any shift from custodial control saves money; however, the primary criterion is *not* fiscal. The public must be protected. If offenders can be shifted from custodial control to community-based programs without loss of public protection, a managerial objective can be accomplished.

Further, community-based correctional programs cannot succeed without the understanding and cooperation of the police because individuals within these programs *will* come in contact with the police, and the nature of that contact will directly affect the offender's adjustment. The police can and must make affirmative contributions to community-based corrections programs. They know the resources available as well as the pitfalls to be avoided. In essence, the police are an integral part of any successful corrections program, from using good judgment in making arrests to assisting those on parole or probation to reenter the community.

SUMMARY

Police officers aid the criminal justice process by (1) making legal arrests, (2) legally obtaining accurate, relevant information and evidence, (3) writing complete, accurate reports, (4) identifying suspects and witnesses, and (5) providing effective, truthful testimony in court.

Our criminal justice system is based on the adversary system, which requires that the accuser prove beyond a reasonable doubt to a judge or jury that the accused is guilty of a specified crime.

The adult criminal justice system has several critical stages including the complaint or charge, the arrest, the booking, the preliminary hearing, the grand jury, the arraignment, and the trial.

The preliminary hearing is the probable cause hearing. It seeks to prevent persons from being indiscriminately brought to trial. The discovery process requires that all pertinent facts on both sides be made available prior to the time of the hearing.

Not all cases go to court. Alternatives to a trial include diversion or plea bargaining. Diversion provides the defendant with an alternative to a trial, for example, obtain help from a community organization or make restitution to the victim. Plea bargaining is a compromise between defense and prosecution that prearranges the plea and the sentence, conserving time and expense. The case may or may not go to trial, depending on the circumstances.

Our judicial system operates at both the state and federal level. The hierarchy at the state level often goes from courts of special or limited jurisdiction called justice of the peace (J. P.) courts, to trial courts or original and general jurisdiction courts, to intermediate appellate courts, to the state supreme court. The federal court system is three tiered: district courts, appellate courts, and the United States Supreme Court. Police officers' testimony at the trial is of great importance. They should be aware of tactics frequently used by defense attorneys to confuse or discredit a police officer who is testifying: (1) rapid-fire questioning, (2) establishing that the officer wants to see the defendant found guilty, (3) accusing the officer of making assumptions, or (4) implying that the officer does not want anyone else to know what is in his or her notes.

Although the police officer and the prosecutor represent the accuser, in effect, their ultimate responsibility is to see that justice is done—not to see that a conviction is obtained. If a conviction is obtained, common sentencing schemes include indeterminate, indefinite, definite, determinate, mandatory, and presumptive.

Corrections is that portion of the criminal justice system that carries out the court's orders. It consists of our probation and parole system as well as our jails, prisons, and community-based programs to rehabilitate offenders.

Many offenders, especially repeat offenders, are sentenced to correctional institutions, jails or prisons. Jail differs from prison in that its inmates are there for shorter terms, usually for less serious crimes. Negative characteristics of jails in the United States include: (1) the variety of the offenders, (2) the problems of local control and politics, (3) inadequate personnel, (4) demeaning physical facilities, (5) inept administration, and (6) failure to adopt alternative programs and dispositions.

Prisons may be punitive oriented or treatment oriented. Punitive-oriented systems have authority patterns based only on rank; rules are very specific and are emphasized; guards have limited decision making; communication with inmates is very formal and restricted to orders; and incentives are usually negative. In contrast, treatment-oriented systems stress an authority pattern based on technical knowledge; goals are more general, flexible, and individualized; guards are encouraged to make their own decisions and to communicate with the inmates; and incentives are usually positive.

The vast majority of people sentenced to jail or prison become eligible for parole. Parole differs from probation in that a person who is paroled has spent some time serving a prison sentence. It is similar to probation in that both require supervision of the offender and set up certain conditions that the offender must meet. Parole and probation often involve community-based institutional programs aimed at reintegrating offenders into society, including halfway houses, restitution centers, furloughs, work release, and study release programs.

Discussion Questions

1. Is the jury system really fair?

2. What alternatives to the jury system are there?

3. What is the best kind of notebook for police officers to use for testifying in court?

4. Can the defense attorney examine the officer's entire notebook even if it contains notes on other cases?

5. Should the victim of a crime be consulted when plea bargaining is used?

6. How can police officers be sure a person they have just arrested understands the Miranda warning?

7. Is our system truly an adversary system when the prosecutor also has to protect the accused's rights?

8. Do you feel the public accepts community-based corrections programs?

9. What are some justifications to support monetary restitution in corrections?

10. What are some obstacles in establishing prison or jail reforms?

11. Are the systems of probation and parole effective tools in dealing with law violators?

12. In our modern society, with its constant changes in corrections philosophy, do you feel that parole boards serve a useful function?

References

Eisenstein, J. *Counsel for the United States,* Baltimore: Johns Hopkins University Press, 1978.

Eldefonso, E. *Issues in Corrections: A Book of Readings.* Beverly Hills, Calif.: Glencoe Press, 1974.

Glick, H. R. *Who Are Federal Judges.* New York: McGraw-Hill, 1983.

Greenberg, M. S., and Ruback, R. B. *Social Psychology of the Criminal Justice System.* Monterey, Calif.: Brooks/Cole Publishing, 1982.

Inbau, F. E.; Thompson, J. R.; and Fagel, J. B. *Criminal Law and Its Administration.* Mineola, N.Y.: The Foundation Press, 1974.

Jacob, H. *Crime and Justice in Urban America.* Englewood Cliffs, N.J.: Prentice-Hall, 1980.

National Advisory Commission on Criminal Justice Standards and Goals, *Corrections.* Washington, D.C.: U.S. Government Printing Office, 1973.

National Advisory Commission on Criminal Justice Standards and Goals. *The Courts.* Washington, D.C.: U.S. Government Printing Officer, 1975.

Pursley, R. D. *Introduction to Criminal Justice,* 3d ed. New York: Macmillan, 1980.

Waldron, R. J. *The Criminal Justice System, An Introduction,* 3d ed. Boston: Houghton Mifflin, 1984.

Williams, V. L.; Formby, W. A.; and Watkins, J. C. *Introduction to Criminal Justice.* Albany, N.Y.: Delmar Publishing, 1982.

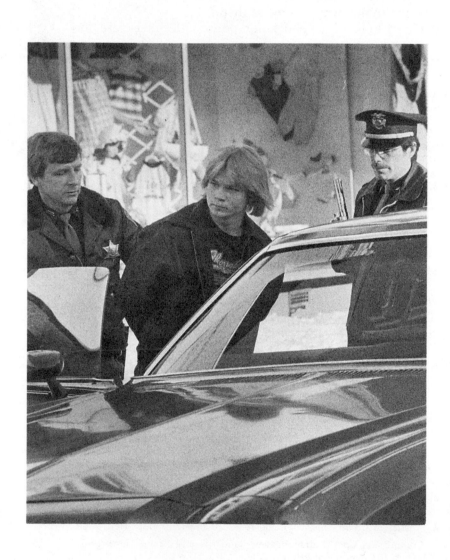

_____

CHAPTER TWENTY

The Juvenile Justice System: Caring for Our Nation's Youth

There is evidence, in fact, that there may be grounds for concern that the child receives the worst of both worlds: that he gets neither the protections accorded to adults nor the solicitious care and regenerative treatment postulated for children.—Supreme Court Justice Abe Fortas

DO YOU KNOW

What four phases of development the juvenile justice system has gone through?

What is meant by the principle of parens patriae?

What was established by the Kent, Gault, Winship, and McKiever decisions?

What balance the juvenile justice system seeks?

How much discretion police have with juveniles?

What procedural safeguards should be followed if detaining or arresting a juvenile?

If youth can be fingerprinted or photographed?

What services police often provide juveniles?

How police affect the juvenile justice system?

How juvenile court differs from adult court?

What correctional facilities juvenile delinquents have?

What a school liaison program is?

What police-community relations programs have been implemented?

Introduction	This chapter presents concepts related to how patrol

Introduction

Chapter 20

This chapter presents concepts related to how patrol officers or, in larger departments, officers assigned to the juvenile division deal with not only juvenile delinquents but also law-abiding juveniles. The Constitution guarantees that all citizens be presumed innocent until proven guilty. This applies to juveniles as well. The majority of the juveniles in our country are not delinquents and do not deserve to be treated as such merely because they are underage. If good relations can be established between the police and our youth, everyone will benefit.

In addition, police officers must investigate and intervene on behalf of children who are neglected and/or abused.

HISTORICAL OVERVIEW

Our juvenile justice system has had its own unique development from the time of the colonists to the 1990s. According to McCreedy (1975), our juvenile justice system has its roots as far back as the feudal period in England when the crown assumed the protection of the property of minors. When the feudal period ended, supervision of the duties previously assumed by the overlord was transferred to the king's court of chancery. This chancery court operated on a principle known as *parens patriae*. Under this doctrine, the king, through the chancellor, was responsible for the general protection of all people in the realm who could not protect their own interests. This included the children of the realm. Consequently, the king, by means of the chancery court and chancellor, assumed supreme guardianship over the persons and property of minors. McCreedy (1975, p. 1) notes: "In effect, the chancellor acted as a substitute father for those children who were abandoned, neglected, or destitute."

The doctrine of equity was used when dealing with children; that is, decisions were made based on the spirit of the law and on an attempt at fundamental fairness rather than on strict interpretation of the law. This gave much more flexibility in deciding a case.

Another principle in English common law that influenced our juvenile justice system was the belief that children younger than seven years old were considered incapable of criminal intent. Between the ages of seven and fourteen they were presumed to still be incapable of criminal intent unless it could be shown differently. After age fourteen, children, like adults, were held responsible for their acts and treated according to a strict interpretation of the law. In effect, age had a direct bearing on how someone who broke the law was treated.

The four major phases of the juvenile justice system have been (1) a Puritan emphasis, (2) an emphasis on providing a refuge for youth, (3) development of the separate juvenile court, and (4) emphasis on juvenile rights.

The Puritan Emphasis

The concept of *parens patriae* and the notion that there was an age below which there can be no criminal intent were brought by the colonists to America. From the time the colonists first arrived in the United States until the nineteenth century, however, emphasis was on Puritan values, which held that the child was basically evil. Parents were considered responsible for controlling their children who were, in effect, their property. The law dealt very severely with children who broke the law. McCreedy (1975) points out as an example that in 1828 in New Jersey, a boy of thirteen was hanged for an offense committed when he was twelve. This Puritan emphasis lasted until the 1820s.

Providing a Refuge

By the 1820s several states had passed laws to protect children from the punishments associated with criminal laws. According to McCreedy (1975, p. 2): "The first changes came in the area of institutional custody. Central to the reform effort in this area was a recognition of the brutality of confining children in the same institutions with adults convicted of crime. This awareness resulted in attempts to separate children from adult criminal offenders."

The first American institution that isolated children convicted of crimes from adult criminals was New York City's House of Refuge, established in 1825. This was, in effect, the first juvenile reformatory in the United States.

In 1869 Massachusetts became the first state to pass a law requiring an agent from the State Board of Charity to investigate all cases involving children coming to court, to attend their trials, and to make recommendations to the judge. In 1870 Massachusetts passed legislation that established separate trials for children in Suffolk County, and by 1872 this means of handling juvenile cases extended throughout the state.

Another major development in the mid-1800s was probation, instituted in 1841 by John Augustus, the first probation officer, who was authorized by judges in Boston, Massachusetts, to take into his custody adults and children convicted of crimes.

In 1884 New York passed legislation allowing a trial judge to place a child under the age of sixteen convicted of a crime under the supervision of any suitable person or institution willing to accept him or her.

During this period of development of the juvenile justice system, the state took over the parents' role of responsibility for their children but not to the degree that this attitude continued into the next phase of the system's development.

The Juvenile Court

According to Vetter and Territo (1984, p. 497):

The establishment (by statute) of the first juvenile court in [Chicago] Illinois in 1899 marked the beginning of an era of "social jurisprudence."

Table 20—1   **Antecedents of the Juvenile Court**

1825	New York House of Refuge was opened, followed by houses in Boston (1826), Philadelphia (1828), and New Orleans (1845).
1831	Illinois passed a law that allowed penalties for certain offenses committed by minors to differ from the penalties imposed on adults.
1841	John Augustus inaugurated probation and became the nation's first probation officer.
1854	State industrial school for girls opened in Lancaster, Massachusetts (first cottage-type institution).
1858	State industrial school for boys in Lancaster, Ohio, adopted a cottage-type system.
1863	Children's Aid Society founded in Boston. Members of the organization attended police and superior court hearings, supervised youngsters selected for probation, and did the investigation on which probation selection was based.
1869	Law enacted in Massachusetts to direct State Board of Charities to send agents to court hearings that involved children. The agents made recommendations to the court that frequently involved probation and the placement of youngsters with suitable families.
1870	Separate hearings for juveniles were required in Suffolk County, Massachusetts. New York followed by requiring separate trials, dockets, and records for children; Rhode Island made similar provisions in 1891.
1899	In April, Illinois adopted legislation creating the first juvenile court in Cook County (Chicago). In May, Colorado established a juvenile court.

Source: Reprinted by permission from *Crime and Justice in America: A Human Perspective,* by Harold J. Vetter and Leonard Territo. Copyright © 1984 by West Publishing Company. All rights reserved.

> *Although the juvenile court was a bona fide court, its procedures were dramatically different from adult court proceedings. Prior to the establishment of juvenile court, children, like adults, were required to furnish bail or be placed in jail; they were indicted by grand juries; they were tried according to adult criminal procedure; and they were sentenced to prison or required to pay fines.*

In contrast, according to Vetter and Territo (1984, p. 497):

> *The court's major objective was to help the wayward child become a productive member of the community. The determination of guilt or innocence, using standard rules of evidence, was not of primary importance. Instead, . . . court procedures were to be more diagnostic than legal in nature, giving major consideration to the information obtained on the youngster's environment, heredity, as well as his physical and mental condition.*

The Juvenile Court Act not only created the first juvenile court, it also had as a central purpose to regulate the treatment and control of *dependent, neglected, and delinquent* children. In effect, it equated poor and abused children with criminal children and provided that they be treated in essentially the same way. Most juvenile courts in the 1990s have this same multiple charge.

Judge Benjamin Lindsey, left, is generally recognized as the founder of the U.S. juvenile court system.

During this period of the development of the juvenile justice system, the philosophy of *parens patriae* was in full effect. The Chicago legislation grew out of the efforts of civic-minded citizens who saw the inhumane treatment of children who were confined in police stations and jails. The legislation, entitled "An Act to Regulate the Treatment and Control of Dependent, Neglected and Delinquent Children," included many of the characteristics of our modern-day juvenile courts, such as a separate court for juveniles, separate and confidential records, informal proceedings, and the possibility of probation.

The Chicago legislation also required that children be given the same care, custody, and discipline that parents should give them. The major goal was to save the child. This was also the first basic principle of the juvenile court—that of *parens patriae*. The state not only acts as a substitute parent to abandoned, neglected, and dependent children, but it also acts as a "superparent" for delinquent children. As noted by McCreedy (195, p. 7): "In this role, the state can take legal control of a child away from the child's natural parents or guardians. For example, the state acts as a superparent whenever it commits a child to an industrial school or other correctional facility. The juvenile system symbolizes the state's parenthood."

The parens patriae *doctrine made the state legally responsible for the children within that state, providing a legal foundation for state intervention in the family.*

McCreedy (1975, p. 7) goes on to note:

> The state, as the child's substitute parent, was not supposed to punish the child for his misconduct, but to help him. To reach this noble goal, many of the procedures used in adult criminal proceedings were abandoned or replaced with procedures commonly used in non-criminal (civil) court proceedings. A whole new legal vocabulary and new methods of operation were developed to reflect the new philosophy and procedures used in the juvenile justice system.
>
> Instead of a complaint being filed against the child, a petition was filed. No longer was the child to be arrested in the strict sense of the term. Instead, the child was given a summons. A preliminary inquiry or initial hearing replaced an arraignment on the charge. The child was not required to plead either guilty or not guilty to the alleged misconduct. Instead of being found guilty of a crime, the child was found delinquent. Moreover, adjudication of delinquency was not to be considered a conviction. None of the liabilities attached to a criminal conviction were to apply to a child found delinquent; for example, disqualification from future civil service appointments, the inability to be licensed by the state or the right to vote.

Table 20–2 **The Language of Juvenile and Adult Courts**

Juvenile court term	Adult court term
Adjudication: decision by the judge that a child has committed delinquent acts.	Conviction of guilt
Adjudicatory hearing: a hearing to determine whether the allegations of a petition are supported by the evidence beyond a reasonable doubt.	Trial
Adjustment: the settling of a matter so that parties agree without official intervention by the court.	Plea bargaining
Aftercare: the supervision given to a child for a limited period of time after he or she is released from training school but while he or she is still under the control of the juvenile court.	Parole
Commitment: a decision by the judge to send a child to training school.	Sentence to imprisonment
Delinquent act: an act that if committed by an adult would be called a crime. The term does not include such ambiguities and noncrimes as "being ungovernable," "truancy," "incorrigibility," and "disobedience."	Crime
Delinquent child: a child who is found to have committed an act that would be considered a crime if committed by an adult.	Criminal
Detention: temporary care of an allegedly delinquent child who requires secure custody in physically restricting facilities pending court disposition or execution of a court order.	Holding in jail
Dispositional hearing: a hearing held subsequent to the adjudicatory hearing to determine what order of disposition should be made for a child adjudicated as delinquent.	Sentencing hearing

Table 20–2   The Language of Juvenile and Adult Courts   (*Continued*)

Hearing: the presentation of evidence to the juvenile court judge, his or her consideration of it, and his or her decision on disposition of the case.	Trial
Juvenile court: the court that has jurisdiction over children who are alleged to be or found to be delinquent. Juvenile delinquency procedures should not be used for neglected children or for those who need supervision.	Court of record
Petition: an application for a court order or some other judicial action. Hence, a "delinquency petition" is an application for the court to act in a matter involving a juvenile apprehended for a delinquent act.	Accusation or indictment
Probation: the supervision of a delinquent child after the court hearing but without commitment to training school.	Probation (with the same meaning as the juvenile court term)
Residential child care facility: a dwelling (other than a detention or shelter care facility) that is licensed to provide living accommodations, care, treatment, and maintenance for children and youth. Such facilities include foster homes, group homes, and halfway houses.	Halfway house
Shelter: temporary care of a child in physically unrestricting facilities pending court disposition or execution of a court order for placement. Shelter care is used for dependent and neglected children and minors in need of supervision. Separate shelter care facilities are also used for children apprehended for delinquency who need temporary shelter but not secure detention.	Jail
Take into custody: the act of the police in securing the physical custody of a child engaged in delinquency. The term is used to avoid the stigma of the word "arrest."	Arrest

Source: Reprinted by permission from *Crime and Justice in America: A Human Perspective,* by Harold J. Vetter and Leonard Territo. Copyright © 1984 by West Publishing Company. All rights reserved.

The second major principle underlying the juvenile justice system, in addition to *parens patriae,* is the individualization of justice. According to McCreedy (1975, p. 8): "This principle stems from the belief that children, like adults differ from one another. Each person has a different family background, mentality, physical capability, and personality. . . . As the purpose of the court is to save the child and not to punish him, it is necessary for those individuals involved in the juvenile justice system to consider the background of the child in order to treat him."

Although the establishment of juvenile courts was a tremendous advancement in our juvenile justice system, it did present some major problems as well. Because children were no longer considered "criminals," they lost many of the constitutional protections of due process in criminal proceedings. In many instances, for example, delinquents were not given notice of the charge, were not provided with a lawyer, and were not given the chance to cross-examine witnesses.

Justification for the informal procedures used in the juvenile justice system prior to 1960 was set forth half a century ago in *Commonwealth v. Fisher* (1905):

To save a child from becoming a criminal or from continuing in a career in crimes . . . the Legislature may surely provide for the salvation of such a child . . . by bringing it into one of the courts of the state without any process at all, for the purpose of subjecting it to the state's guardianship and protection. The natural parent needs no process to temporarily deprive his child of its liberty by confining it in his own home, to save it from the consequences of persistence in a career of waywardness: nor is the state, when compelled as parens patriae, to take the place of the father for the same purpose, required to adopt any process as a means of placing its hands upon the child to lead it to one of its courts.

By the 1960s, however, the United States Supreme Court began to seriously question the use of *parens patriae* as the sole reason for denying the child many constitutional rights extended to adults charged with a crime, leading into the fourth phase in the development of the juvenile justice system—juvenile rights.

Juvenile Rights

In 1956 a landmark federal case was the first of a series of cases that resulted in drastic changes in the juvenile justice system. In *Shioutakon v. District of Columbia* (1956) the courts established the role of legal counsel in juvenile court. In essence, if a juvenile was to have his or her liberty taken away, that juvenile had the right to be represented by a lawyer in court. If the parents could not afford a lawyer, the court was to appoint counsel.

A second case establishing juvenile rights was *Kent v. United States* (1966). This case involved Morris Kent, a juvenile with a police record who was arrested at age sixteen in Washington and charged with housebreaking, robbery, and rape. Kent confessed to the charges and was held at a juvenile detention facility for nearly a week. The judge then decided to transfer jurisdiction of his case to an adult criminal court. Kent received no hearing of any kind; the transfer was completely at the judge's discretion and was based on several reports written by probation staff.

In reviewing the *Kent* case, the Supreme Court decreed: "As a condition to a valid waiver order, petitioner (Kent) was entitled to a hearing, including access by his counsel to the social records and probation or similar reports which are presumably considered by the court, and to a statement of the reasons for Juvenile Court's decision."

Kent v. United States established that if a juvenile court transfers a case to adult criminal court, juveniles are entitled to a hearing, their counsel must be given access to probation records used by the court in reaching its decision, and the court must state its reasons for waiving jurisdiction over the case.

According to Arnold and Brungardt (1983, p. 24): "The impact of the Kent case went far beyond the relatively narrow legal issue—conditions of waiver to criminal court—that it addressed. It served as a warning to the juvenile justice system that the juvenile court's traditional laxity toward procedural and evidentiary standards would no longer be tolerated by the highest court in the land."

An appendix to the *Kent* decision contained the following criteria established by the United States Supreme Court for states to use in deciding on transfer of juveniles to adult criminal courts for trial:

1. the seriousness of the alleged offense and whether the protection of the community requires waiver;
2. whether the alleged offense was committed in an aggressive, violent, premeditated, or willful manner;
3. whether the alleged offense was against persons or against property, greater weight being given to offenses against persons, especially if personal injury resulted;
4. the prospective merit of the complaint;
5. the desirability of trial and disposition of the offense in one court when the juvenile's associates in the alleged offense are adults who will be charged with crimes in the adult court;
6. the sophistication and maturity of the juvenile as determined by consideration of his or her home, environmental situation, emotional attitude, and pattern of living; and
7. the record and previous history of the juvenile.

The following year, another landmark Supreme Court ruling in the *Gault* case (1968) resulted in additional major changes in our juvenile justice system. Gerald Gault was fifteen years old and on probation when he was taken into custody for allegedly making obscene phone calls to a neighbor. At 10:00 A.M., when Gerald was picked up at home, his mother and father were working. No notice was left at the home that Gerald was being taken into custody nor were any steps taken to notify his parents. Mrs. Gault arrived home about 6:00 P.M. to find Gerald missing. An older brother accidentally discovered that Gerald had been taken into custody.

Mrs. Gault went to the detention home, and the probation officer told her why Gerald was there and that a hearing would be held the next day, June 9. On June 9 the officer filed a petition with the juvenile court making only general allegations of "delinquency." No particular facts of Gerald's behavior were stated.

The hearing was held in the judge's chambers. The complaining witness was not present, no one was sworn in, no attorney was present, and no transcript of the proceedings was made. At the hearing Gerald admitted to making a less obnoxious part of the phone call in question. At the conclusion of the hearing, the judge said he would take the matter under advisement.

Gerald was returned to the detention home for another two days and then released. After the release Mrs. Gault was informed by note from the probation officer that on June 15 further hearings would be held on Gerald's delinquency. The June 15 hearing was also without benefit of complaining witnesses, sworn testimony, transcript, or counsel. The probation officer made a referral report that listed the charge as lewd phone calls and filed it with the court, but it was not made available to

Gerald or his parents. At the conclusion of the hearing the judge committed Gerald as a juvenile delinquent to the State Industrial School until age twenty-one. Gerald, only fifteen years old at the time, received a six-year sentence for an action for which an adult would receive a fine or a two-month imprisonment.

The United States Supreme Court overruled Gerald's conviction on the grounds that:

- Neither Gerald nor his parents had notice of the specific charges against him.
- No counsel was offered or provided to Gerald.
- No witnesses were present, thus denying Gerald the right of cross-examination and confrontation.
- No warning of Gerald's privilege against self-incrimination was given to him, thus no waiver of that right took place.

The Gault decision requires that the due process clause of the Fourteenth Amendment apply to proceedings in state juvenile courts, including the right of notice, the right to counsel, the right against self-incrimination, and the right to confront witnesses.

Justice Fortas delivered the opinion of the Court:

Where a person, infant or adult, can be seized by the State, charged and convicted for violating a state criminal law, and then ordered by the State to be confined for six years, I think the Constitution requires that he be tried in accordance with the guarantees of all provisions of the Bill of Rights made applicable to the States by the Fourteenth Amendment. Undoubtedly this would be true of an adult defendant, and it would be a plain denial of equal protection of the laws—an invidious discrimination—to hold that others subject to heavier punishments could, because they are children, be denied these same constitutional safeguards. I consequently agree with the Court that the Arizona law as applied here denied to the parents and their son the right of notice, right to counsel, right against self-incrimination, and right to confront the witnesses against young Gault. Appellants are entitled to these rights, not because "fairness, impartiality and orderliness—in short, the essentials of due process"—require them and not because they are "the procedural rules which have been fashioned from the generality of due process," but because they are specifically and unequivocally granted by provisions of the Fifth and Sixth Amendments which the Fourteenth Amendment makes applicable to the States.

It is clear that juveniles are to be afforded all the same rights and privileges as adults in the criminal process. The logical implications of the *Gault* decision require safeguards in the prehearing stage as well as use of the Miranda warning for juveniles, whether at the station house, in the squad car, or on a street corner.

The Supreme Court refused to rule on two questions raised on Gault's behalf: the right to an appeal and the right to a record of court proceedings.

In 1970 another Supreme Court decision expanded juvenile rights. In *In Re Winship* (1970) the United States Supreme Court examined the standard of proof in a 1967 New York case against a twelve-year-old boy who allegedly had stolen $112 from a woman's purse. The New York judge acknowledged that he had operated on the civil court principle of "preponderance of evidence," a standard of proof much weaker than the "proof beyond a reasonable doubt" required in a criminal court. In the review of the *Winship* case, the Supreme Court ruled that if adjudication might result in deprivation of liberty for the juvenile, the juvenile court must use the same standards of proof as are required in adult criminal trials.

The Winship *decision established a juvenile defendant must be found guilty beyond a reasonable doubt.*

One right of adults charged with crimes that is not afforded to juveniles charged with crimes is the right to a trial by jury.

McKiever v. Pennsylvania *established that a jury trial is not a constitutional right of juveniles.*

McKiever v. Pennsylvania (1971) involved a Pennsylvania youth charged with robbery, larceny, and receiving stolen goods. According to Arnold and Brungardt (1983, p. 24), in this case:

> The Supreme Court slowed its march toward reshaping the juvenile court to impose stronger due-process standards and formal procedures. In McKiever, the Court, fearing that jury trials would bring delay and increased formality to the juvenile court, supported noncriminal juvenile hearings and ruled that a jury trial is not a constitutional right of juveniles . . . . The court felt strongly that if the formalities of the criminal adjucative process are to be superimposed upon the juvenile court system, there is little need for its separate existence.

Arnold and Brungardt (1983, p. 24) go on to note:

> These Supreme Court decisions, taken as a whole, clearly indicate the Court's support of stronger due-process and evidentiary standards for juvenile court proceedings. However, by declining to rule on the questions of the right to a jury trial and the right to records of the proceedings in Gault, and in issuing the McKiever decision, the Court has pointed to a

fundamental dilemma it faces in its juvenile court decisions. On the one hand, the Supreme Court is alarmed by the denial of constitutional rights in juvenile courts; on the other hand, it wants to maintain something of the informality and protectiveness long characteristic of the juvenile court. It appears the movement to bring justice to the juvenile court system has been successful, although the degree to which the orientation of actual court practice has changed is highly visible.

The juvenile justice system seeks to balance the informal and protective emphasis of the parens patriae doctrine with the constitutional rights of juveniles charged with crimes.

See table 20–3 for the evolution of our juvenile justice system.

THE JUVENILE JUSTICE SYSTEM IN THE 1990s

Just as within the adult criminal justice system, the juvenile justice system has three separate but integrally related components: the police, the court, and corrections—referred to as "Youth Authority." The normal progression of youth within the juvenile justice system is diagrammed in figure 20–1.

ENFORCING THE LAWS

One critical aspect of the juvenile justice system is the initial contact with the law. Trojanowicz (1978, pp. 175–76) notes:

> *The intake and screening process is an important aspect of the juvenile justice system. When used properly, it can effectively curtail or interrupt much delinquent behavior before it becomes serious. The intake process can also stimulate community agencies to help parents to better understand their children's behavior and the measures needed to prevent further delinquent acts.*
>
> *If the child is released at intake and no further processing takes place, there should still be a follow-up after any referral to a community agency by either the police or the intake unit. Follow-up facilitates not only the rendering of services to the child, but also promotes closer cooperation between the agencies involved. . . . The police have a great deal of discretionary power, ranging all the way from the option of releasing the juvenile at initial contact in an unofficial manner to referring him to the juvenile court, which may result in detention.*

Within this range are other options such as referring the juvenile to a community agency.

Whether a juvenile is actually arrested usually depends on a number of factors, the most important of which is the seriousness of the offense. Other factors that enter into the decision include the following (Trojanowicz 1978, p. 419):

Table 20–3   Juvenile Justice Developments: 1646 to Present

System (period)	Major developments	Influences	Child-state relationship	Parent-state relationship	Parent-child relationship
Puritan (1646–1824)	Massachusetts Stubborn Child Law (1646).	Christian view of child as evil; economically marginal agrarian society.	Law provides symbolic standard of maturity; support for family as economic unit.	Parents considered responsible for and capable of controlling child.	Child considered both property and spiritual responsibility of parents.
Refuge (1824–1899)	Institutionalization of deviants, New York House of Refuge established (1824) for delinquent and dependent children.	Enlightenment; immigration and industrialization.	Child seen as helpless, in need of state intervention.	Parents supplanted as state assumes responsibility for correcting deviant socialization.	Family considered to be a major cause of juvenile deviancy.
Juvenile court (1899–1960)	Establishment of separate legal system for juvenile—Illinois Juvenile Court Act (1899).	Reformism and rehabilitative ideology; increased immigration, urbanization, large-scale industrialization.	Juvenile court institutionalizes legal irresponsibility of child.	Parens patriae doctrine gives legal foundation for state intervention of family.	Further abrogation of parents' rights and responsibilities.
Juvenile rights (1960-present)	Increased "legalization" of juvenile law—*Gault* decision (1966). Juvenile Justice and Delinquency Prevention Act (1974) calls for deinstitutionalization of status offender.	Criticism of juvenile justice system on humane grounds, civil rights movements by disadvantaged groups.	Movement to define and protect rights as well as provide services to children.	Reassertion of responsibility of parents and community for welfare and behavior of children.	Attention given to children's claims against parents. Earlier emancipation of children.

Adapted from U.S. Department of Justice, Reports of the National Juvenile Assessment Centers, *A Preliminary National Assessment of the Status Offender and the Juvenile Justice System* (Washington, D.C.: U.S. Government Printing Office, 1980) p. 29, by permission of the U.S. Department of Justice.
Source: Reprinted by permission from *Crime and Justice in America: A Human Perspective,* by Harold J. Vetter, Leonard Territo. Copyright © 1984 by West Publishing Company. All rights reserved.

The appraised character of the youth, which in turn is based on such facts as his prior police record, age, associations, attitude, family situation, the conduct of his parents, and the attitude of other community institutions such as his school. The external community may exert pressure on the police department which may affect the disposition of any case. Here attitudes of the press and the public, the status of the complainant or victim, the status of the offender, and the conditions which prevail in the available referral agencies (the length of the waiting list, the willingness of the social agencies to accept police referrals) are all of consequence. Internal police department pressure such as attitudes of coworkers and supervisors and the personal experience of the officer may also play an important part in determining the outcome of any officially detected delinquent offense. These factors also indirectly determine the officially recorded police and court delinquency rates.

Figure 20–1   From Arrest to Disposition

The amount of discretion available to police officers and the lack of criteria by which to make a decision were noted several years ago by the President's Commission on Law Enforcement and Administration of

Justice, Task Force on Juvenile Delinquency and Youth Crime, when it stated (1967a, p. 14):

> In sum, the range of police dispositions is considerable, and the criteria for selection of a disposition are seldom set forth, explicitly, ordered in priority, or regularly reviewed for administrative purposes. Inservice training designed to assist police in exercising their discretionary functions is unusual.

The police have a considerable amount of discretionary power when dealing with juveniles.

Detaining or Taking into Custody

If police officers determine that the offense is serious enough to warrant detention or that the juvenile is a threat to self or the general public, they should exercise certain safeguards.

In most jurisdictions it is mandatory that the parents of a juvenile who is detained be notified as soon as possible and that questioning of the juvenile be delayed until the parents are present.

In addition to notifying the parents, police officers are also required to notify juveniles of their rights, the direct result of the *Gault* decision.

If a juvenile is detained or taken into custody the parents should be notified. In addition, as a result of the Gault decision, the juvenile must be told of his or her rights.

After questioning the juvenile, the police officers must determine whether the juvenile should be referred to the court or returned to his or her parents. Usually, if the offense is relatively minor, the juvenile's attitude and past record are good, and the parents are willing to provide adequate supervision and guidance, the juvenile will be returned to the parents with no further legal action taken.

If the offense is judged to be serious, if the youth has a past record of criminal activity, or if the parents appear unconcerned or nonsupportive of the police's position, the juvenile may be taken to a detention facility and may be referred to the court for a hearing. In such instances all records related to the case should be provided to the judge.

Fingerprinting and Photographing

Whether juveniles should be fingerprinted or photographed is an important issue. Some states allow one or the other but not both.

Questions are often raised as to who should have access to these records and for how long. Some states have laws that require the police to purge all juvenile records when the youngster reaches age eighteen.

Some states prohibit fingerprinting or photographing of juveniles. Others permit fingerprinting and photographing, but the records are kept by the department and not released to any other agency.

POLICE SERVICES FOR JUVENILES

The police are also responsible for some specific services involving children.

Police services involving children include helping to locate missing or runaway children, conducting fingerprinting programs, and investigating reports on neglected or abused children.

Missing Children

A missing child is an extremely traumatic experience for parents. In contrast, police officers know that the vast majority of missing children show up safe and well. Frequently they have stopped at a friend's home and forgotten about the time. Despite the fact that most missing children do show up or are found, police officers must not be casual about the situation. It is a critical circumstance in the eyes of the parents.

A complete description of the child and the clothing worn should be obtained, as should a recent picture. Details regarding where the child was last seen and favorite hideaways should also be obtained.

Sometimes it is necessary to call in additional help, for example, if a child wandered off into a forest. Local Boy Scout troops can sometimes be called on to assist in such situations. Dogs may also be of help.

Time is an important factor because the more time that elapses, the more likely it is that the child will wander farther away or come to harm.

On October 12, 1982, President Reagan signed into law the Missing Children Act, requiring the attorney general to "acquire, collect and preserve any information which would assist in the location of any missing person (including children . . .) and provide confirmation as to any entry (into FBI records) for such a person to the parent, legal guardian or next of kin." What this means, in effect, is that parents, legal guardians, or the next of kin may have access to the information in the FBI National Crime Information Center's (NCIC) Missing Person File.

The law does not, however, require that the FBI investigate the case. It can undertake a preliminary inquiry if an indication exists that a crime has been committed and the child has been transported out of the state.

Because of this law, it is even more important that children be fingerprinted. Many schools have instituted such a program in conjunction with the local police department.

Runaway Children

The same procedures used to search for a missing child might be used to locate a runaway child. Here much depends on the child's age and reason for running away. If the child is a teenager with good reasons for running away, it may be futile to conduct a search.

Runaway children who are found should not automatically be returned to their homes. An investigation should be conducted to see if conditions there are such that they led to the youth leaving. It may be that the youth would be better off in a foster home or even staying with friends for a time.

Neglected or Abused Children

Police are sometimes called upon to investigate reports of neglected or abused children. Eldefonso (1983, p. 12) notes: "Most jurisdictions define as a crime parental abuse or neglect of children, but vary in their criteria for defining what constitutes abuse or neglect. In general, some degree of failure to feed and clothe a child is usually defined as a crime, along with some degree of failure to provide adequate shelter. Most jurisdictions establish discretionary or judgmental statutes with respect to the degree of cleanliness required in homes for children." He lists five conditions that indicate, separately or collectively, the need for action (p. 388):

- Lack of physical care and protection
- Lack of supervision, guidance, and discipline
- Exploitation
- Lack of protection from degrading conditions
- Abuse and fear of physical cruelty

Eldefonso (1983, p. 392) suggests: "The line between neglect and abuse is sometimes difficult to draw, but the two can generally be distinguished in the following way: neglectful parents usually do not consciously intend to harm their children, but through failure to meet children's health, nutritional, comfort and emotional needs, they expose their children to severe risk."

When a law enforcement agency receives a report of child neglect or abuse it may investigate on its own or with personnel from the Welfare Department. No matter what the source of the report or who does the investigating, the primary responsibility of those investigating is the welfare of the child. Any child who appears to be in danger should be removed to protective custody.

According to the Metropolitan Court Judges Committee Report (*Deprived Children* 1985–86, p. 6): "It is estimated that as many as four or five million children are neglected or physically or sexually abused each year, with an additional two million vulnerable as runaways or missing."

THE POLICE AND THE JUVENILE JUSTICE SYSTEM

The police usually are the youth's initial contact with the juvenile justice system. They have broad discretion and may release juveniles to their parents, refer them to other agencies, place them in detention, or refer them to a juvenile court. The police may also temporarily detain juveniles, either for their own protection or to assure that they do appear in court.

As noted by Eldefonso (1974, p. 3): "Generally juveniles are referred to local authorities after arrest . . . . In juvenile matters, probation departments provide most of the services for the court from initial screening and filing of a petition in behalf of the juvenile through termination of wardship (i.e., supervision and control)."

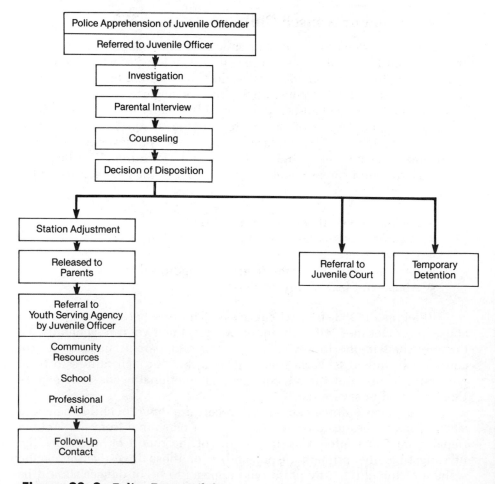

Figure 20–2 **Police Responsibility**

The police usually are the youth's initial contact with the juvenile justice system. They have broad discretion and may release juveniles to their parents, refer them to other agencies, place them in detention, or refer them to a juvenile court.

The probation department may or may not be part of a juvenile division. Carey et al. (1967, p. 26) have diagrammed the decision points in police handling of juveniles (see figure 20–3).

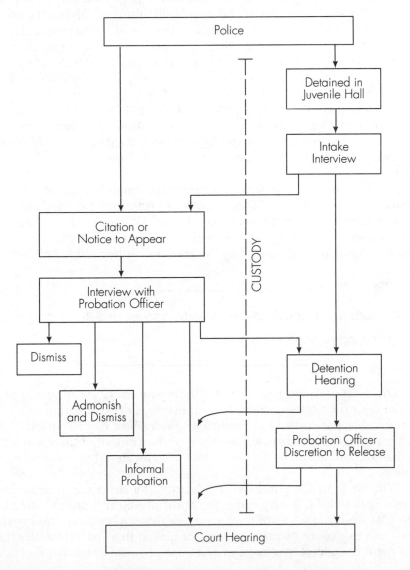

Figure 20–3   **Decision Points in Probation Handling of Juveniles**

THE COURTS AND THE JUVENILE JUSTICE SYSTEM

Laws relating to juvenile courts attempt to secure care and guidance for each minor under the jurisdiction of the court, preferably in the minor's own home. The laws seek to protect the spiritual, emotional, mental, and physical welfare of the minor as well as the best interests of the state. Laws related to juveniles attempt to preserve and strengthen family ties whenever possible, removing minors from parental custody only when the minor's welfare or safety or protection of the public cannot be adequately safeguarded without such removal. When minors are removed from their own families, the courts seek to provide them with custody, care, and discipline as nearly equivalent as possible to that usually given by competent parents.

Juvenile court also has jurisdiction over neglected and dependent children who may suffer from abuse, malnutrition, or unsanitary conditions in the home or who may have been abandoned by their parents. The court also has jurisdiction over those persons who encourage, cause, or contribute to a child's delinquency. Because of the court's scope and clientele, laws relating to juveniles are frequently liberally construed.

Juveniles are subjected to a conglomerate of laws and restraints that do not apply to adults. For example, juveniles are frequently arrested for liquor law violations, curfew violations, absenting from home, truancy, smoking, suspicion, and incorrigibility (these are called status offenses). The courts in which such offenses are judged differ greatly from adult courts.

Juvenile courts are more concerned with rehabilitation of the juvenile than with punishment. These courts are informal, private, and often do not follow formal judiciary procedures. Although adult courts are based on the adversary system, juvenile courts, in contrast, are nonadversary systems, even though they do have the authority of confinement.

Juvenile courts are informal, private, nonadversary systems that stress rehabilitation rather than punishment of youth.

The court may counsel children, their parents, or guardians or place them in their own homes under the supervision of a probation officer or other suitable person under conditions prescribed by the court. These conditions might include rules for their conduct or that of their parents or guardian designed for the physical, mental, and moral well-being of the children.

When it is in the child's best interests, the court can transfer legal custody of the child. It may order the child placed in a foster home or a child-placing agency, committed to a youth conservation commission, transferred to a county welfare agency, or placed in a special facility if the child requires special treatment and care for physical or mental health. As

The establishment of juvenile courts advanced the juvenile justice system.

noted by Trojanowicz (1978), diversion, a popular method of solving juvenile problems in recent times, shows great promise of success.

Juvenile courts vary from state to state, but most begin with some sort of intake, which usually begins as a petition against the child. Frequently the petition originates with a law enforcement agency, but it can come from another source such as a school, which can refer truancy or vandalism cases, or parents who may feel they cannot control their children. The intake or initial screening is usually controlled and supervised by the juvenile court. As noted by the historic President's Commission on Law Enforcement (1967a, p. 14):

> *Intake is essentially a screening process to determine whether the court should take action and, if so, what action or whether the matter should be referred elsewhere. Intake is set apart from the screening process used in adult criminal courts by the pervasive attempt to individualize each case and the nature of the personnel administering the discretionary process. In adult proceedings at the post-arrest stage, decisions to screen out are entrusted to the grand jury, the judge, or usually to the prosecutor. The objective is screening as an end in itself: attempts to deliver service to those screened out are rare. . . . At intake in the juvenile courts, screening is an important objective, but referral is an additional goal. Thus, the expressed function of intake is likely to be more ambitious than that of its criminal law counterpart and the function is performed chiefly by persons who are neither legally trained or significantly restricted in the exercise requirements comparable to those of the criminal law.*

Most referrals to juvenile court are for property crimes, but 17% are for status offenses.

Table 20—4   **Reasons for Referrals to Juvenile Courts**

11% **Crimes against persons**	
Criminal homicide	1%
Forcible rape	2
Robbery	17
Aggravated assault	20
Simple assault	59
	100%
46% **Crimes against property**	
Burglary	25%
Larceny	47
Motor vehicle theft	5
Arson	1
Vandalism and trespassing	19
Stolen property offenses	3
	100%
5% **Drug offenses**	100%
21% **Offenses against public order**	
Weapons offenses	6%
Sex offenses	6
Drunkenness and disorderly conduct	23
Contempt, probation, and parole violations	21
Other	44
	100%
17% **Status offenses**	
Running away	28%
Truancy and curfew violations	21
Ungovernability	28
Liquor violations	23
	100%
100% Total all offenses	

Note: Percents may not add to 100 because of rounding.
Source: *Delinquency in the United States 1983*. National Center for Juvenile Justice, July 1986.

In addition, the National Advisory Commission on Criminal Justice Standards and Goals (1973, p. 296) recommends that intake units should do the following:

1. *Make the initial decision whether to place a juvenile referred to the court in detention or shelter care.*
2. *Make the decision whether to offer a juvenile referred to the court the opportunity to participate in diversion programs.*
3. *Make, in consultation with the prosecutor, the decision whether to make a formal petition in the court alleging that the juvenile is delinquent and ask that the family court assume jurisdiction over him.*

At the adjudication hearing, considered to be part of the preliminary hearing, the youth is questioned about the alleged offense. The National Advisory Commission on Criminal Justice Standards and Goals (1973, pp. 302, 474) recommends the following procedures for adjudicatory hearings:

At the adjudicatory hearing, the juvenile alleged to be delinquent should be afforded all of the rights given a defendant in adult criminal prosecution, except that trial by jury should not be available in delinquency cases.

In all delinquency cases a legal officer representing the state should be present in court to present evidence supporting the allegation of delinquency.

The defense counsel should use all methods permissible in a criminal prosecution to prevent determination that the juvenile is delinquent. He should function as the advocate for the juvenile, and his performance should be unaffected by any belief he might have that a finding of delinquency might be in the best interests of the juvenile. As advocate for the juvenile alleged to be delinquent, counsel's actions should not be affected by the wishes of the juvenile's parents or guardian if those differ from the wishes of the juvenile.

At the adjudication hearing, the petition may be dismissed, or, if there is enough evidence that the child is delinquent, a court date is set for the *disposition hearing.*

Ideally, enough time should be allowed between the adjudication and disposition hearings for the probation officer to make a thorough investigation of the case, including an evaluation of the child's home and

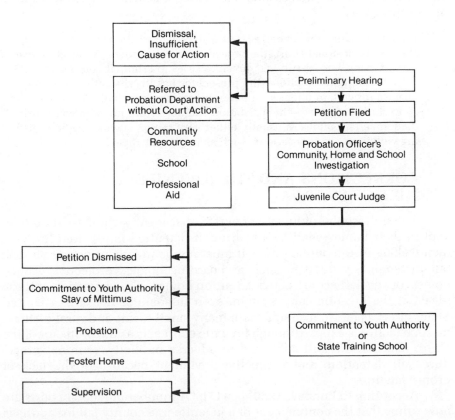

Figure 20–4 **Juvenile Court Responsibility**

school environment, the child's attitude and behavior at home and in the neighborhood, school, and community, and the amount of supervision provided at home. Often, however, the disposition hearing is the second half of the adjudication hearing.

At the disposition hearing the judge has several alternatives. Based on the findings of the investigation, the judge may put the youth on probation, place the youth in a foster home, release the child to the parents, commit the child to an institution, or make the child a ward of the court so as to receive the required supervision. The National Advisory Commission on Criminal Justice Standards and Goals recommends that the procedures followed at the disposition hearing be identical to those followed in sentencing adult offenders.

More serious juvenile offenders have been committed to mental institutions, reformatories, prisons, and county and state schools for delinquents. Some cities, such as New York and Chicago, have set up youth courts that are adult courts using the philosophy of juvenile courts. These youth courts usually confine their hearings to misdemeanors. When a juvenile has committed a series of serious crimes, juvenile courts have the legal power to adjudicate anyone under their jurisdiction as an adult. The juvenile is then charged and required to appear in an adult court.

According to the Bureau of Justice Statistics (1984, p. 61): "All states allow juveniles to be tried as adults in criminal courts." This may occur in one of three ways:

> *Judicial waiver*—the juvenile court waives its jurisdiction and transfers the case to criminal court (the procedure is also known as "binding over," "transferring," or "certifying" juvenile cases to criminal courts).
>
> *Concurrent jurisdiction*—the prosecutor has the discretion of filing charges for certain offenses in either juvenile or criminal courts.
>
> *Excluded offenses*—the legislature excludes from juvenile court jurisdiction certain offenses, usually either very minor, such as traffic or fishing violations, or very serious, such as murder or rape.

CORRECTIONS AND THE JUVENILE JUSTICE SYSTEM

The philosophy of juvenile court is that ideally children should be kept in their homes pending a hearing. If detention is required for their own welfare or the public safety, it must not be in jails or police stations but in temporary quarters such as boarding homes, protective agency homes, or specially constructed detention homes. The realization of these ideals of the juvenile court system, even in some of the largest United States cities, is far from complete. In many small towns and rural districts no such facilities exist. Although juvenile court acts as the protector of the child, children are still subjected to adverse publicity, criminal procedure, jail detention, and ineffective treatment because of the lack of proper facilities.

According to Pursley (1980, p. 417): "A number of federal courts are now ruling that the confinement of a juvenile in a county jail for adults is in violation of the provision against 'cruel and unusual punishment' of the Eighth Amendment."

Table 20–5   Age at Which Criminal Courts Gain Jurisdiction of Youth

Age of offender when under criminal court jurisdiction	States
16 years	Connecticut, New York, North Carolina
17	Georgia, Illinois, Louisiana, Massachusetts, Missouri, South Carolina, Texas
18	Alabama, Alaska, Arizona, Arkansas, California, Colorado, Delaware, District of Columbia, Florida, Hawaii, Idaho, Indiana, Iowa, Kansas, Kentucky, Maine, Maryland, Michigan, Minnesota, Mississippi, Montana, Nebraska, Nevada, New Hampshire, New Jersey, New Mexico, North Dakota, Ohio, Oklahoma, Oregon, Pennsylvania, Rhode Island, South Dakota, Tennessee, Utah, Vermont, Virginia, Washington, West Virginia, Wisconsin, Federal districts
19	Wyoming

Source: "Upper Age of Juvenile Court Jurisdiction Statutes Analysis," Linda A. Szymanski, National Center for Juvenile Justice, March 1987.

Twelve states authorize prosecutors to file cases in the juvenile or criminal courts at their discretion.

This procedure, known as concurrent jurisdiction, may be limited to certain offenses or to juveniles of a certain age. Four states provide concurrent jurisdiction over juveniles charged with traffic violations. Georgia, Nebraska, and Wyoming have concurrent criminal jurisdiction statutes.

As of 1987, thirty-six states excluded certain offenses from juvenile court jurisdictions.

Eighteen states excluded only traffic, watercraft, fish, or game violations. Another thirteen states excluded serious offenses; the other five excluded serious offenses and some minor offenses. The serious offenses most often excluded are capital crimes such as murder, but several states exclude juveniles previously convicted in criminal courts.

Forty-eight states, the District of Columbia, and the federal government have judicial waiver provisions.

Youngest age at which juvenile may be transferred to criminal court by judicial waiver	States
No specific age	Alaska, Arizona, Arkansas, Delaware, Florida, Indiana, Kentucky, Maine, Maryland, New Hampshire, New Jersey, Oklahoma, South Dakota, West Virginia, Wyoming, Federal districts
10 years	Vermont
12	Montana

Table 20–5   Continued

Youngest age at which juvenile may be transferred to criminal court by judicial waiver	States
13	Georgia, Illinois, Mississippi
14	Alabama, Colorado, Connecticut, Idaho, Iowa, Massachusetts, Minnesota, Missouri, North Carolina, North Dakota, Pennsylvania, South Carolina, Tennessee, Utah
15	District of Columbia, Louisiana, Michigan, New Mexico, Ohio, Oregon, Texas, Virginia
16	California, Hawaii, Kansas, Nevada, Rhode Island, Washington, Wisconsin

Note: Many judicial waiver statutes also specify offenses that are waivable. This chart lists the states by the youngest age for which judicial waiver may be sought without regard to offense.
Source: "Waiver/Transfer/Certification of Juveniles to Criminal Court: Age Restrictions: Crime Restrictions," Linda A. Szymanski. National Center for Juvenile Justice, February 1987.

A small proportion of juvenile cases are referred to criminal court.

Recent studies found that most juveniles referred to criminal court were age seventeen and were charged with property offenses. However, juveniles charged with violent offenses or with serious prior offense histories were more likely to be adjudicated in criminal court. Waiver of juveniles to criminal court is less likely where court jurisdiction extends for several years beyond the juvenile's eighteenth birthday.

Juveniles tried as adults have a very high conviction rate, but most receive sentences of probation or fines.

More than 90 percent of the judicial waiver or concurrent jurisdiction cases in Hamparian's study resulted in guilty verdicts, and more than half the convictions led to fines or probation. Sentences to probation often occur because the criminal courts view juveniles as first offenders regardless of their prior juvenile record. However, serious violent juvenile offenders are more likely to be institutionalized. In a study of twelve jurisdictions with Habitual Serious or Violent Juvenile Offender Programs, 63 percent of those convicted were sentenced to prison and 14 percent to jail. The average prison sentence was 6.8 years.

Correctional activities for juveniles tried as adults in most states occur within the criminal justice system.

In 1978, in more than half the states, youths convicted as adults and given an incarcerative sentence could only be placed in adult corrections facilities. In eighteen jurisdictions, youths convicted as adults could be placed in either adult or juvenile corrections facilities, but sometimes this discretion was limited by special circumstances. Only six jurisdictions restricted placements of juveniles convicted as adults to state juvenile corrections institutions. Generally, youths sentenced in this manner will be transferred to adult facilities to serve the remainder of their sentence on reaching majority.

Figure 20–5   **Youth Authority Responsibility**

The disposition of juveniles and the problem of the juvenile can be partially gauged by the number of facilities existing in the United States to care for wayward youth.

Reception and diagnostic centers screen juvenile court commitments and assign them to appropriate treatment facilities.

Detention centers provide temporary care in a physically restrictive environment for juveniles in custody pending court disposition and often for juveniles who have been adjudicated delinquent or are awaiting return to another jurisdiction.

Training schools provide strict confinement and instruction in vocational skills. They serve delinquent juveniles committed to them by juvenile courts or placed in them by an agency with such authority.

Shelters provide temporary care similar to that of detention centers but in a physically unrestrictive environment.

Ranches, forestry camps, and farms are residential treatment facilities for juveniles who do not require strict confinement such as in training schools. These ranches, camps, and farms allow juveniles greater contact with members of the community.

Group homes are residences that allow juveniles extensive contact with the community through jobs and schools. Seldom are juveniles placed in group homes on probation or parole.

Halfway houses provide nonrestrictive residential group living where 50 percent or more of the juveniles are on probation or parole. The juveniles are allowed extensive community contact through jobs and schools.

Facilities other than punitive correctional institutions for juveniles include reception and diagnostic centers; detention centers; training schools; shelters; ranches, forestry camps, and farms; group homes; and halfway houses.

In addition to providing facilities for juveniles who have already become delinquent, many communities are attempting to meet the problem of juvenile delinquency by programs that stress prevention rather than rehabilitation, for example, police-school liaison programs.

These juveniles are in a prison boot camp at the Sumter Correctional Institution in Florida.

REDUCING JUVENILE DELINQUENCY

Traditionally the police officer's role was clearly defined: arrest lawbreakers and preserve the peace. Although historically the police have been viewed as punitive and authoritarian, this view is changing. Rather than simply apprehending and punishing offenders, police officers now also seek to educate and to promote prevention of crime. Modern

Table 20–6   Selected Characteristics of Public Juvenile Facilities, 1985

	Long-term, state-operated, institutitonal facilities	All other long-term facilities*	Short-term facilities†
Number of facilities	199	360	481
Number of residents	23,823	11,548	16,031
Number of annual admissions	49,610	44,570	433,579
Average size	120	32	33
Average percent occupied	91%	81%	66%
Percent of residents who were committed	92%	89%	14%
Percent of residents who were status offenders	1%	8%	7%

*Includes locally operated facilities with institutional or open environments and state-operated facilities with open environments.
†Includes state or locally operated facilities with institutional or open environments.
Source: Bureau of Justice Statistics, U.S. Dept. of Justice, Special Report, Survey of Youth in Custody, 1987, Washington, D.C., 1987.

Police seek to educate children and promote cooperation.

Table 20—7   Use of Illegal Drugs by Youth in Institutions, Year-end 1987

Type of drug	Total			Less than 18 years old			18 years and older		
	Ever used drugs	Used regu-larly*	Under influ-ence at time of of-fense	Ever used drugs	Used regu-larly	Under influ-ence at time of of-fense	Ever used drugs	Used regu-larly	Under influ-ence at time of of-fense
Any drug	82.7%	63.1%	39.4%	80.6%	59.7%	39.1%	88.2%	72.3%	40.3%
Marijuana-/hashish	81.2%	59.0%	30.0%	79.4%	59.6%	31.7%	85.9%	65.4%	25.4%
Cocaine	46.1	21.5	12.8	42.6	19.6	12.9	55.3	26.7	12.6
Amphet-amines.	36.3	15.5	6.0	37.8	15.6	6.4	32.5	15.2	4.9
LSD	28.9	11.9	6.5	26.7	11.5	7.3	34.7	13.2	4.2
Barbiturates	27.3	8.9	2.7	28.4	9.3	2.8	24.4	7.9	2.4
PCP	22.6	8.9	4.9	18.7	6.4	3.4	33.0	15.5	9.0
Quaaludes	14.6	3.0	.7	14.9	3.1	.9	13.7	2.7	.3
Heroin	13.0	5.2	3.4	11.9	4.5	2.9	16.0	7.0	4.7

Note: Percents do not add to total using any drug because of multiple drug use.
*Used once a week or more for at least a month.
Source: Bureau of Justice Statistics, U.S. Dept. of Justice, Special Report, Survey of Youth in Custody, 1987, Washington D.C., 1987.

approaches to juvenile delinquency take several forms, but all have in common a goal of preventing juvenile delinquency.

Knowledge of Indicators of Potential for Delinquent Behavior by Juveniles

Certain factors may indicate that a youngster has the potential for or actually is involved in delinquent behavior. Police should learn to recognize these factors and take appropriate actions, considering community resources and school and police department policies.

Police officers are in a unique position to help juveniles because they are usually the first persons of authority to confront the juvenile offender during or following a delinquent act. Additionally, police officers are often familiar with the youngsters in their patrol area whose behavior marks them as potential delinquents, and they have the authority to reprimand, release, or refer youngsters to court.

Environmental factors potentially contributing to delinquency include broken homes, criminal parents, incompetent parents, erratic discipline, economic insecurity, impoverished neighborhoods, transient populations, and racial and other tensions.

Personal factors or behavior indicating potential delinquency include unsociability, cheating, lying, fighting, temper tantrums, anxiety, guilt feelings, hostility and aggression, laziness, truancy, running away from home, and a rebellious attitude.

The environmental and personal factors may be complicated by misuses of alcohol, narcotics, and drugs, by economic factors, by physical disabilities, by sexual problems, or by numerous other factors. The result is frequently youths who show overwhelming symptoms of weakness and inadequacy. They cannot accept life as it is, cannot conform, cannot get along, cannot compete, or cannot exercise self-control.

The sooner a police officer recognizes such youngsters and attempts to work with them, the greater the chance that the juveniles will not become delinquents.

Police-School Liaison Programs

Prevention programs in juvenile delinquency began in the early twentieth century when a wave of social reform swept through the Western world. The earliest documented program, established in 1905 in Portland, Oregon, was designed to protect young girls. In 1918 New York City assigned "welfare officers" to each precinct, the beginning of a program that expanded into a comprehensive community program called "The Juvenile Aid Bureau," a forerunner of the more modern police-school liaison programs.

Although police participate in many different types of school programs, such programs do not exist in a large number of police jurisdictions. Where they do exist, they have evolved gradually in response to community requests. Formal programs frequently result from surveys conducted by forward-looking police departments.

Recognizing factors that contribute to juvenile delinquency is important.

The need for specialized training of juvenile officers in understanding children and their problems has also been recognized. The importance of special training for officers appointed to juvenile units and the need for close police-school relationships is supported by the Flint Michigan Program, the first publicized, comprehensive, formalized police-school liaison effort in the United States (Morrison 1968, p. 62). Cooperatively developed between 1958 and 1960 by school, police, court, social agency, and community personnel interested in decreasing juvenile delinquency in Flint, the program has been a model for many police-school programs.

A police-school liaison program places a police officer within a school as a cooperative effort of the schools and the law enforcement agencies to develop an understanding of law enforcement functions and to prevent juvenile delinquency and crime.

PROGRAMS TO PROMOTE SAFETY AND GENERAL WELFARE

In addition to programs that seek citizen cooperation in reducing juvenile delinquency, many police departments have implemented community service programs to provide juveniles with information and guidance in protecting their general safety and welfare.

Community service programs emphasize drug abuse prevention, bike safety, or general safety.

Drug Abuse Prevention

Drug abuse prevention is a responsibility of local law enforcement agencies. They have attacked the problem of drug abuse and narcotics by attempting to apprehend the illegal distributor, by educating and seeking voluntary compliance by industries producing and distributing narcotics and dangerous drugs, and by educating the public on the hazards of drugs and narcotics.

Through various programs with civic groups and the schools, law enforcement officers can make citizens aware of the hazards of narcotics and dangerous drugs. By presenting factual information through pamphlets, speeches, films, and displays to a variety of organizations, especially the schools, law enforcement personnel may heighten the local citizen's concern and install cooperation in combating the problem of drug abuse in the community.

Bike Safety

Bike safety programs are found throughout the country. The Minnesota Highway Department, for example, has a "talking" bike that presents safety rules to the children through a tape-recorded message.

Mike the Talking Bike has all the necessary safety features for a bike to be used in traffic: reflectors on the spokes, the sidewalls of the tires are a luminous white, the new pedals reflect, and a tall yellow flag is on the rear. Throughout the presentation the children are reminded to be visible when riding bicycles, to ride on the proper side of the road, and to stop and yield the right-of-way before crossing streets. They are cautioned always to be careful—to watch for traffic and to drive defensively. Even if in the right, a bike rider usually is the loser if an accident occurs.

An earlier version of the Minnesota Highway Patrol talking bike was Spike, an old battered bike that told the children all the bad things he did to get into trouble. He also told them about the little boy who was riding him and was killed when hit by a car. A combination of these two bikes might make a very effective presentation for youngsters.

Other bike safety programs include police officers going into grade schools, conducting safety inspections of the children's bicycles, licensing them, and sponsoring bike rodeos that concentrate on both knowledge about bike safety and demonstration of safe bike-riding skills.

General Safety

Some community service programs emphasize general safety and welfare. An example of one such program is the Safety City program in Eden Prairie, Minnesota.

Safety City is a scaled-down city with houses, businesses, church, school, park, movie theater, fire station, and police station. Twice a year Safety City is set up for one week to give area school children ages five to nine a controlled, realistic environment in which to learn or review community safety rules.

SUMMARY

The juvenile justice system has developed through four phases in the United States: (1) a Puritan emphasis with severe penalties for juvenile crime (1776–1823), (2) an emphasis on providing a refuge for youth (1824–1899), (3) development of a separate juvenile court (1899–1960), and (4) emphasis on juvenile rights (1960 to present). Important in the evolution of the juvenile justice system has been the *parens patriae* doctrine, which makes the state legally responsible for the children within that state, providing a legal foundation for state intervention in family control.

The most recent phase, that emphasizing juvenile rights, has included several landmark Supreme Court decisions. *Kent v. United States* established that as a valid waiver order to adult criminal court, juveniles are entitled to a hearing, their counsel must be given access to probation records used by the court in reaching its decision, and the court must state its reasons for waiving jurisdiction over the case.

The *Gault* decision required that the due process clause of the Fourteenth Amendment be applied to proceedings in state juvenile courts, including the right of notice, the right to counsel, the right against self-incrimination, and the right to confront witnesses.

The *Winship* decision established that a juvenile defendant must be found guilty beyond a reasonable doubt. And *McKiever v. Pennsylvania* established that a jury trial is not a constitutional right of juveniles.

In the 1990s the juvenile system is continually seeking to balance the informality and protective emphasis of the *parens patriae* doctrine with the constitutional rights of juveniles charged with crimes.

When dealing with juveniles, the police have a great deal of discretionary power, ranging from the option of releasing the juvenile at initial contact in an unofficial manner to referring him or her to the juvenile court, which may result in detention. If a juvenile is detained or taken into custody the parents should be notified. In addition, as a result of the *Gault* decision, the juvenile must be told of his or her rights. An additional precaution is that in some states, fingerprinting or photographing juveniles is prohibited.

In addition, police are often responsible for providing other services involving children, including helping to locate missing or runaway children, conducting fingerprinting programs, and investigating reports of neglected or abused children.

The police usually are the youth's initial contact with the juvenile justice system. They have broad discretion and may release juveniles to their parents, refer them to other agencies, place them in detention, or refer them to juvenile court. Juvenile courts are informal, private, nonadversary systems that stress rehabilitation rather than punishment of youth. Facilities other than punitive correctional institutions for juveniles include reception and diagnostic centers; detention centers; training schools; shelters; ranches, forestry camps, and farms; group homes; and halfway houses. In addition to providing facilities for juveniles who have already become delinquent, many communities are attempting to meet the problem of juvenile delinquency by programs that stress prevention, for example, police-school liaison programs.

One means to deter juvenile delinquency is through a police-school liaison program. Such programs place a police officer in a school as a cooperative effort of the schools and the law enforcement agencies to develop an understanding of law enforcement functions and to prevent juvenile delinquency and crime.

Community service programs may emphasize drug abuse prevention, bike safety, or general safety, such as the Safety City program.

Discussion Questions

1. Do juvenile courts too often stress rehabilitation and keeping youngsters in the home?

2. Are parents required to testify against their children in court?

3. What correctional facilities are available for juvenile delinquents in your area? Your state?

4. Do you feel the process of justice should be the same for juveniles as it is for adults?

5. Do you feel juveniles should have the right to a jury trial?

6. In what noncriminal matters does the juvenile court become involved?

7. Should police officers have as much discretionary power as they have with juveniles? Why or why not?

8. Does your community have a police-school liaison program? If so, how effective does it seem to be? How popular does it seem to be?

9. What other community relations programs are offered by your police department for juveniles?

10. Does your police department have a separate juvenile division or do police officers have the responsibility for dealing with juveniles?

References

Arnold, W. R., and Brungardt, T. *Juvenile Misconduct and Delinquency.* Boston: Houghton Mifflin, 1983.

Bureau of Justice Statistics. *Report to the Nation on Crime and Justice.* Washington, D.C.: U.S. Government Printing Office, 1984.

Carey, J. T.; Goldfarb, J.; Rowe, M. H.; and Lohman, J. D. *The Handling of Juveniles from Offense to Disposition.* U.S. Department of Health, Education, and Welfare. Washington, D.C.: U.S. Government Printing Office, 1967.

Deprived Children: A Judicial Response. Metropolitan Court Judges Committee Report, National Council of Juvenile or Family Court Judges, 1985–86.

Eldefonso, E. *Law Enforcement and the Youthful Offender,* 4th ed. New York: John Wiley and Sons, 1983.

McCreedy, K. R. *Juvenile Justice—System and Procedures.* Albany, N.Y.: Delmar Publishers, 1975.

Morrison, J. "The Controversial Police-School Liaison Programs." *Police* (November-December 1968): 60–64.

National Advisory Commission on Criminal Justice Standards and Goals. *Corrections.* Washington, D.C.: U.S. Government Printing Office, 1973.

President's Commission on Law Enforcement and Administration of Justice. *Task Force Report: Juvenile Delinquency and Youth Crime.* Washington, D.C.: U.S. Government Printing Office, 1967a.

Pursley, R. D. *Introduction to Criminal Justice,* 3d ed. New York: Macmillan, 1980.

Trojanowicz, R. C. *Juvenile Delinquency, Concepts and Control,* 2d ed. Englewood Cliffs, N.J.: Prentice-Hall, 1978.

Vetter, H. J., and Territo, L. *Crime and Justice in America: A Human Perspective.* St. Paul, Minn.: West Publishing Company, 1984.

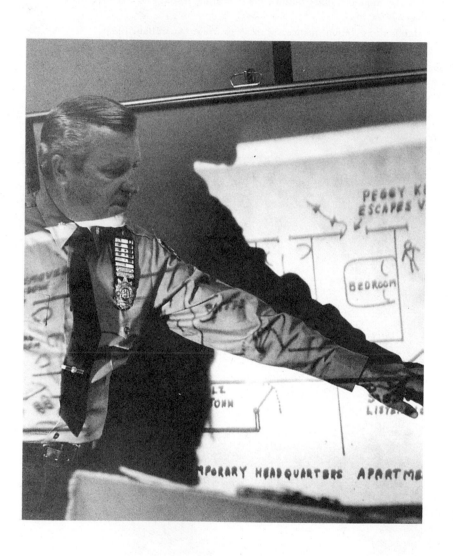

Critical Issues in Law Enforcement/Criminal Justice: Challenges of the 1990s

He who will not reason, is a bigot; he who cannot is a fool; and he who dares not is a slave.—William Drummond

DO YOU THINK

Some provisions of the Bill of Rights are controversial?

Some crimes might be decriminalized?

Plea bargaining is in the best interests of society?

Police departments should be unionized?

Police departments should be accredited?

Police officers face ethical issues in carrying out their responsibilities?

Police officers are justified in using deadly force?

Police have an image problem?

Law enforcement is a profession?

Introduction

Chapter 21

The criminal justice system has several vital issues facing it in the last part of the twentieth century. The issues encompass law enforcement, the courts, and corrections. Several issues affect all three. Although this chapter concentrates on those issues that directly affect law enforcement, issues related to the courts and corrections that may also affect law enforcement are also discussed briefly.

INTERPRETING THE BILL OF RIGHTS

The law is a living reality that encourages the opening of new avenues of human conduct. As Oliver Wendell Holmes put it: "The life of the law has not been logic; it has been experience." People who view the Bill of Rights as an outdated document fail to see that it is the best structure so far in history for a growing society with changing institutions.

Controversial issues related to the Bill of Rights include:

Gun control—The Second Amendment.

The Exclusionary Rule and the Miranda decision—The Fourth and Fifth Amendments.

Capital punishment—The Eighth Amendment.

The Second Amendment is a continuing source of controversy. Those who oppose gun control state that outlawing handguns would arm criminals and disarm law-abiding citizens. They say the criminals will get guns anyway. The question revolves around whether the government should regulate handguns—the number-one weapon of killers. Some eighteen thousand murders occur every year in the United States, often committed by "law-abiding" people shooting other "law-abiding" people. In addition, an average of more than ninety police officers are slain by handguns every year.

Some polls consistently show that the majority of Unites States citizens support sensible handgun legislation. When Massachusetts held a referendum proposing to ban handguns, however, it was defeated by a 70 percent majority. Possibly they realized what New York's tough gun law has shown: if only one state outlaws guns, a person can easily get one in another state.

Controversy also exists over the Exclusionary Rule and the *Miranda* decision. Recall that the Exclusionary Rule disallows the introduction of illegally seized evidence in a trial, and the *Miranda* decision forbids confessions as evidence if the suspects have not been informed of their constitutional rights. The Exclusionary Rule has been regularly challenged in our courts. Opponents of the rule say that it penalizes society and rewards the defendant for any mistakes made by the police. When the *Miranda* decision was handed down in 1966, many people felt the criminals were decidedly given the upper hand; consequently the Supreme Court came under blistering attack from some police, prosecutors, and citizens. Since 1966 twenty-two states have sought to overturn the *Miranda* decision through the Supreme Court, but to no avail. Today's police officers are functioning and performing their jobs better than before *Miranda*; they are not hindered by it. Police officers, above all others, ought to obey the laws. Further, withdrawal of the rights provided by the Fourth and Fifth Amendments could lead to a police state.

Another controversial amendment is the Eighth Amendment, which forbids "cruel and unusual punishment." The question of capital punishment has been in the courts for the past quarter-century. In 1976 the Supreme Court ruled that states that used certain guidelines could pass laws allowing them to execute convicted murderers, but the Court reserved any decision on whether the death penalty is constitutional for any other crime. Still unresolved are such questions as how far prosecutors can go in making emotional charges in their closing arguments to a jury in a capital punishment case and whether rape can be punished by death.

DECRIMINALIZATION

The basic issues involved in decriminalization are: If a crime is victimless, is there really a crime? Can you legislate morality?

According to Williams, Formby, and Watkins (1982, p. 336): "The overreach of modern American criminal law is notorious. We have for years operated under a 'pass a law' syndrome regarding the criminalization of behavior deemed distasteful or dangerous by the lawmaking branch of government. Such a state of affairs has placed an enormous strain on all segments of the criminal justice establishment."

Obviously, the criminal justice system has limited resources. Should it not concentrate those resources on the Part I offenses such as murder, robbery, and rape?

Unfortunately, the crime-related portion of most police officers' responsibilities is devoted to lesser offenses such as prostitution or gambling. Decriminalization of certain offenses would allow concentration of resources on serious crime and might also legalize certain actions, such as gambling and prostitution, that are major revenue sources for organized crime. The acts now considered criminal may be engaged in more frequently by law-abiding citizens if they were decriminalized, however, thus lowering our country's moral standards.

Williams, Formby, and Watkins (1982, p. 337) say if "the offense so repealed is one that has heretofore created and sustained a major underground or blackmarket operation, a repeal may mean that such endeavors will ultimately cease operation because of the now legal nature of the enterprise." Legalization of drugs such as cocaine, heroin, and crack falls within this area.

Law-Abiding Citizens Select the Laws They Obey

Many good citizens disobey the law every day and justify it as "not hurting anyone else." For example, countless citizens break speed laws, drive after drinking, and pilfer from their employers. Even more serious, many citizens, although abhorring organized crime in general, foster, promote, and support it daily by gambling and using its many other "services." Perhaps the deeply entrenched force of organized crime has gone beyond the comprehension of the general public. Many notorious criminals of the present era wear the mantle of respectability because they have bought into legitimate businesses with their illegal money or have simply strong-armed their way in. These criminals have gained social prominence and often community acceptance.

Decriminalization would likely focus on those crimes that are now selectively enforced and would return emphasis to the more serious crimes. Offenses that would be candidates for decriminalization include prostitution, sexual activities between consenting adults, gambling, public drunkenness, certain types of juvenile delinquency (status offenses), narcotics and drug offenses, vagrancy, and disorderly conduct. This would conserve resources that have come to be overextended in many communities.

Nearly two decades ago, the National Advisory Commission on Criminal Justice Standards and Goals (1973a) recommended that the states "reevaluate laws on gambling, marijuana use and possession for use, pornography, prostitution, and sexual acts between consenting adults in private. Such reevaluation should determine if current laws best serve the purpose of the state and the needs of the public."

This recommendation is reiterated by Williams, Formby, and Watkins (1982, p. 339): "Criminal justice policymakers in the 1980s and beyond must come to grips with the criminal laws' overreach. Until such is done, we will continue to have a system of criminal law enforcement in the United States that is administratively cumbersome, selectively unjust, and economically wasteful."

Offenses that would be candidates for decriminalization include prostitution, sexual activities between consenting adults, gambling, public drunkenness, certain types of juvenile delinquency (status offenses), narcotics and drug offenses, vagrancy, and disorderly conduct.

The following extracts from the National Advisory Committee on Criminal Justice Standards and Goals (1976, pp. 230–32) summarize the arguments for and against reform or decriminalization.

General Arguments for Reform

It is not the proper function of government or the criminal justice system to regulate private morality or behavior through criminal laws; that is the role of nonlegal institutions.

The laws are ineffective. They do not deter involvement in the proscribed activities, either by organized crime or the public. Neither fines or jail rehabilitate or alter the behavior of offenders.

The laws are unenforceable. The volume of activity is too great, public support is lacking and criminal justice systems resources are inadequate.

There is no evidence that legalization/decriminalization will lead to a harmful increase in immoral behavior. The activities are already easily accessible to anyone who wants them.

The rights of individuals to live as they want, so long as they do not harm others, is a fundamental principle on which this nation was founded.

There is no proof that the moral standards of the country are declining, or that the nation as a whole is being negatively affected by victimless crimes.

The burden of proof that harm results from these crimes should rest with those wishing to impose sanctions, not with participants in the activities.

Society cannot morally declare persons to be victims when they do not see themselves as such.

Even if the law's function is to provide symbolic guidance for a correct standard of behavior, it is questionable that the laws against victimless crimes guide people in the right direction. Instead, they may engender cynicism and disrespect for the criminal justice and legal systems and for government in general.

The laws are hypocritical. They allow some activities while proscribing others that are comparable; they penalize some people involved in an activity, but not others.

More realistic and well-founded policies must be developed. Current policies are based on emotion, outdated moral norms and values, and inaccurate information. Using up-to-date information on the effects of an activity, and bearing in mind the many priorities to be met, policymakers must weigh the costs of an activity against the costs of ineffective laws. Goals and effective approaches must then be developed.

The laws have many hidden costs: creation of a class of criminals who would not otherwise be considered criminals; discriminatory, arbitrary, and selective application of the laws; unsavory and often degrading tactics employed by the police to obtain evidence or make arrests; increase in crime associated with victimless crimes; creation of subcultures of criminals who reinforce one another's behavior; overburdening the criminal justice system; creation of antagonism among minority youth toward police as a result of enforcement that hits the inner city hardest; and fail-

ure to afford constitutional rights to the accused because of efforts to process cases quickly.

There is a lack of public support for the laws.

Overemphasis on the law blunts efforts to find other solutions to abuses of the proscribed activities.

The basis on which the laws were originally promulgated no longer apply; social mores and values have changed, and new information on the effects of the activities contradicts previously held theories and assumptions.

General Arguments against Reform

The activities known as victimless crimes are antithetical to Christian beliefs and the principles on which the nation was founded.

Modification of the sanctions against these activities will result in a disastrous increase in their occurrence. This in turn will lead to a moral decline of society. The nation will become a second class power. Both the Greek and Roman civilizations were destroyed by the decadence of their citizenry.

Because morality affects the viability of a nation, it is a proper function of government to regulate morality by the use of criminal laws.

Laws are a reflection of social values and should be used, even symbolically, as a guide to proper behavior.

There has never been a serious, sustained effort to enforce the laws, so it is inaccurate to say the statutes are ineffective. A reform government backed by the public can wipe out organized crime, vice, and corruption.

Better law enforcement in terms of other crimes will not necessarily result from freeing resources by modifying the victimless crime laws, for "There is no empirical evidence that the police do a better job of protecting persons and property." (Goldberg, p. 56, 1972) Perhaps there is a limit to the amount of resources a police department can effectively spend.

There are better ways to combat corruption than eliminating the victimless crime laws. Legalization will not eliminate the temptation to corrupt, because it will involve new regulations.

It is traditional in this country for government to protect individuals from themselves. For example, the state requires motorcycle drivers and riders to wear helmets.

The fact that a law seems unenforceable is no reason to abolish it. For example, murder and theft laws are not 100 percent enforceable but are nevertheless needed. A preferable alternative to abolishing the victimless crime laws is providing more resources to implement them.

The laws do not serve as deterrents because they are not strictly enforced and the sanctions are not strong enough.

If the criminal justice system is overburdened, the answer is not to eliminate certain laws. It is to increase the resources available to it.

If the laws result in more related crime, enforcement efforts should be stepped up.

There are not enough hard facts on the impact of victimless crimes to justify modifying the laws.

THE PLEA BARGAINING CONTROVERSY

As previously discussed, plea bargaining is a system whereby a defendant pleads guilty to a crime in exchange for a reduced punishment. According to Levine, Husheno, and Palumbo (1980, p. 214): "In many courts, more than 90 percent of criminal convictions are not obtained by the verdict of a jury or the decision of a judge. Rather, they are based upon the defendant's own plea of guilty." The prevalence of plea bargaining is also noted by Glick (1983, p. 164): "In 1971, the U.S. Supreme Court also acknowledged plea bargaining as a fact and a necessity of judicial life (*Santobello v. New York*, 104 U.S. 257). But, many people oppose plea bargaining and argue that it provides few benefits for courts, criminal defendants, or the public. Since nearly all cases are settled short of a trial, plea bargaining is a central feature of the judicial process and we need to evaluate carefully its place in American justice."

Glick (1983, pp. 164–65) also notes:

Once a prosecutor decides to pursue a case and a judge refuses to grant motions to dismiss, the chances of conviction are overwhelming. Usually the crimes involved are serious or the evidence against defendants is so clear that the chances of being acquitted of a crime are extremely remote. Some readily plead guilty because they recognize the odds are against them and want to put an end to the stress and disruption. They simply want to get out of the system. Others plead guilty because they expect leniency or have negotiated specific bargains with prosecutors and judges.

The mechanics and details of bargained guilty pleas vary considerably. Arrangements may involve reducing criminal charges to less serious crimes, dropping certain charges altogether, promising light sentences for guilty pleas to original charges, and possible combinations. Whatever the arrangements, the key element to any bargain is that in return for pleading guilty and avoiding a trial, cooperative defendants expect to receive lighter sentences. Through plea bargaining, almost all cases end with convictions, but not with trials.

Plea bargaining not only involves avoiding a trial, but it also involves the defendant surrendering such constitutional rights as the right to take the witness stand, the right to confront witnesses against him or her, the right to trial by jury, and the right to be assumed innocent until proven guilty by proof beyond a reasonable doubt. Levine, Husheno, and Palumbo (1980, p. 42) warn: "A system that encourages the waiver of such fundamental rights is defensible only if it deals justly with the person waiving those rights. On the other hand, plea bargaining also affects the police, who have accumulated evidence of guilt; the victim, who has suffered at the hands of the offender; and the public at large, who demand protection against future offenses. These interests also must be dealt with justly in the plea negotiation process, or the process is as indefensible as if it violated the rights of the offender."

A high percentage of cases are settled through plea bargaining. While plea bargaining is acknowledged to be a central part of the judicial process, some critics warn that it might not be in the best interests of society at large.

The case *Bordenkircher v. Hayes* (1978) expanded the power of plea bargaining from the prosecution's side, upholding the prosecutor's right to threaten criminal defendants with more serious charges if they refuse to plead guilty to the charges offered. In this case Hayes was indicted by a grand jury for forging an $88.30 check. In pretrial meetings the prosecutor told Hayes and his lawyer that if Hayes pleaded guilty, making a trial unnecessary, the prosecution would recommend a five-year sentence. (The sentence under Kentucky law, where the case was being tried, would have carried a sentences of two to ten years.) The prosecutor also said that since Hayes had two previous felony convictions, if he refused to plead guilty, prosecution would seek a new indictment—a habitual offender charge, which would bring a life sentence. Hayes refused to plea bargain, was convicted, and was sentenced to life. His appeal to the United States Circuit Court of Appeals was that the prosecutor's "reverse plea-bargaining" violated Hayes's due process rights. This appeal was granted, but then overturned by the United States Supreme Court, which said prosecutors must have broad discretionary powers in plea bargaining.

Glick (1983, pp. 165–67) sets forth numerous arguments for and against plea bargaining, as summarized in table 21–1.

UNIONISM

According to Cole (1983, p. 214): "For much of this century, police employee organizations were mainly fraternal associations that existed to provide opportunities for fellowship, to serve the welfare needs (death benefits, insurance) of police families, and to promote charitable activities." He notes that the 1950s saw a dramatic rise in membership in police unions, partly due to job dissatisfaction, particularly regarding pay and working conditions; the perception that other public employees were improving their positions through collective bargaining; the feeling that the public was hostile to police needs; and an influx of younger officers with less traditional views on police-employee relations. In addition, during this time organized labor was making strong recruitment efforts.

Most police officers are members of local employee organizations. Cole (1983, p. 216) feels the police unions are locally based because the key decisions related to law enforcement are made at this level. And, although most police officers have joined local organizations rather than become affiliates of the AFL-CIO or other national unions, the strength of police unions has increased in many cities.

Table 21–1   **Arguments for and against Plea Bargaining**

Pro: Allows courts to move cases quickly and efficiently.

Lightens the burden on judges, prosecutors, lawyers, and other court employees.

Spares victims the stress and possible humiliation of public trial.

Cooperative defendants are screened from the system and receive reduced penalties for not requiring everyone to prepare for a trial.

Allows the punishment to fit the crime and the individual criminal. Few professional, hardened criminals are allowed to go free.

Con: Cheapens the image of justice by using hurried, secret negotiations to obtain convictions.

The prosecutor comes out ahead by the guilty plea and the defendant gets the best deal he or she can on the sentence.

Places pressure on defendants to plead guilty.

Forces defendants to give up constitutional protections and safeguards.

Legal errors made by police, prosecutors, or trial judges can rarely be reviewed by an appellate court.

Amounts to a coerced confession, which violates the Fifth Amendment.

Produces sentences that are too lenient.

Most police officers are currently members of local employee organizations and are not directly enrolled in a national labor union.

One common objection to unionism is the tactics commonly employed, including slowdowns, "sickouts," and strikes. Although it is usually illegal for most public employees to strike, strikes by law enforcement officers have occurred in San Francisco, California; Tucson, Arizona; Oklahoma City, Oklahoma; Las Cruces, New Mexico; and Youngstown, Ohio (Gentel and Handman 1980, p. 5). Some of the strikes lasted only a few days, but others lasted weeks. In some instances strikers lost their jobs, but in other instances they obtained raises.

Other objections raised against unionism include the fear of law enforcement administrators and public officials that unionized police employees could abuse their collective bargaining power, and that specific aspects of administration such as transfers and promotions could become bound up in arbitration and grievance procedures. Cole (1983, p. 214) states: "Many administrators view the union as interfering with their law enforcement leadership and with the officers in the ranks." In addition, police unions have resisted changes in law enforcement organizations and techniques that affect their membership. According to Juris and Feuille (1974, p. 206), the unions opposed attempts to shift from two-person to one-person patrol cars in at least two of the twenty-two cities studied. Unions have also objected to efforts to hire civilians in clerical positions, and they have resisted affirmative action efforts, seeking to maintain the status quo rather than to increase recruitment of women and minorities into law enforcement.

In discussing the future of police unions, Cole (1983, p. 217) suggests:

> *Clearly, collective bargaining is a concept whose time has come, and police officials are going to have to recognize this new influence on law enforcement administration. At the same time, note that in a public sector of diminished resources, state and local governments may not have the funds to increase salaries to meet inflation. Already New York City and Boston have reduced the size of their police force as one way of reducing budget deficits. But in other cities, particularly those in expanding regions of the country and in the more affluent suburbs, police unions are making greater headway and can be expected to retain their influence. There are still, however, crucial questions about the role that unions should play in determining police department policies and the methods that they can use to influence bargaining agreements.*

LAW ENFORCEMENT ACCREDITATION

The Commission on Accreditation for Law Enforcement Agencies was formed in 1979 to develop a set of law enforcement standards and to establish and administer an accreditation process to which law enforcement agencies could voluntarily apply to demonstrate that they met professional criteria.

The commission is the combined effort of the International Association of Chiefs of Police (IACP), the National Organization of Black Law Enforcement Executives (NOBLE), the National Sheriffs' Association (NSA), and the Police Executive Research Forum (PERF). Members of these four organizations direct approximately 80 percent of the law enforcement community in the United States.

The standards address six major areas:

- The law enforcement role and responsibilities, and relationships with other agencies
- Organization, management, and administration
- Personnel administration
- Law enforcement operations, operational support, and traffic law enforcement
- Prisoner and court-related services
- Auxiliary and technical services

The standards were developed to help law enforcement agencies: (1) increase agency capabilities to prevent and control crime, (2) enhance agency effectiveness and efficiency in the delivery of law enforcement services, (3) improve cooperation and coordination with other law enforcement agencies and with other components of the criminal justice system, and (4) increase citizen and employee confidence in the goals, objectives, policies, and practices of the agency.

The Commission on Accreditation for Law Enforcement Agencies was formed to develop a set of professional standards and to establish and administer a voluntary accreditation process.

Any "legally constituted governmental entities having mandated responsibilities to enforce laws and having personnel with general or special law enforcement powers" are eligible to apply. If accepted, the accreditation fee is contingent upon the size of the agency, based on the number of full-time employees. In 1989 the rates ranged from $5,500 for an agency with fewer than ten full-time employees to $20,900 for agencies with more than three thousand full-time employees. This accreditation lasts five years. Whether this cost is justifiable is strongly debated in many departments.

Supporters of national accreditation suggest that it is one way to raise law enforcement into a professional status and to assure that certain standards are met. An overview of the accreditation program (Commission Update, 1984) lists the following benefits

- *Nationwide recognition of professional excellence.*
- *Continued growth and improvement.*
- *Community understanding and support.*
- *Employee confidence; esprit.*
- *State and local government officials' confidence.*
- *State-of-the-art, impartial guidelines for evaluation, and change, when necessary.*
- *Proactive management systems; policies and procedures documented.*
- *Liability insurance costs contained or decreased.*
- *Liability litigation deterred.*
- *Coordination with neighboring agencies and other parts of the criminal justice system.*
- *Access to the latest law enforcement practices.*

Not all police departments and agencies support accreditation, however. According to Gavzer (1984, pp. 3–4):

New York and Los Angeles are in states whose police chiefs' associations have reservations about the accreditation commission. "We object to a national commission as an intrusion on local government," says Joe Dominelli, executive director of the New York police chief's outfit. "We go along with standards and accreditation but want it done on a statewide basis.'' The California chiefs' group says standards of the Peace Officers Standards and Training Commission (POST) are good enough. It expresses a fear that the accreditation commission could lead to having to deal with a Big Brother out of Washington.

Further information regarding accreditation can be obtained by writing to The Commission on Accreditation for Law Enforcement Agencies, Inc., 4242B Chain Bridge Road, Fairfax, Virginia 22030.

POLICE ETHICS AND CORRUPTION

According to Walker (1980, p. 19): "Corruption is the oldest and most persistent problem in American policing. The history of law enforcement agencies is the story of repeated scandals over corrupt practices.'' Numerous definitions have been set forth for police corruption. One very plausible definition has been stated by Goldstein (1975, p. 3): "Police corruption consists of acts involving the misuse of authority by a police officer in a manner designed to produce personal gain for himself or for others.''

The two key elements in the definition are: (1) the misuse of authority and (2) personal gain. Both elements must be present. The officer must be acting as a police officer, for example, using the authority of the badge to gain entrance to a building and then committing a theft. The act must also result in personal gain. Illegal acts of police officers such as excessive use of force or an illegal search do not constitute police corruption because they do not result in personal gain.

Walker (1983, p. 174) notes: "Police corruption is a problem of enormous magnitude.'' He contends that to deal with the problem effectively, it is necessary to understand the types of corruption that exist, why it exists, and how it might be controlled.

Police corruption is the misuse of authority by an officer for personal gain. It includes accepting gratuities and bribes as well as committing theft or burglary. The most common and extensive type of corruption is accepting small gratuities or tips.

Walker notes that a great difference exists between the officer who accepts a free meal and one who accepts, perhaps even encourages, a cash payment. In fact, many cities do not consider gratuities as corruption. A restaurant owner may sincerely want to do something extra for those who "serve and protect" and may also feel that police cars parked in the lot may deter crime in the area.

Although discounts and free service are usually not regarded as important, cash payments to police officers are quite another matter. The

Knapp Commission (1973, p. 4) distinguished between "grass eaters" and "meat eaters," with the grass eaters being officers who passively accepted gratuities offered to them, in contrast to meat eaters who aggressively solicited payments.

Even more serious are outright bribes to avoid arrest or a fine. The most common instance of this occurs in traffic violations, particularly speeding. All too often a person who has been stopped for speeding may include a ten or twenty dollar bill along with the requested driver's license and end up with a warning rather than a ticket. In some instances, officers may actually suggest that a bribe be made, perhaps in the form of buying tickets to a police benefit.

Another form of extremely serious police corruption is appropriating material or money that comes into their possession in the line of duty. For example, according to Daley (1978), New York detectives regularly divided their "scores" of narcotics and cash, sometimes amounting to thousands of dollars. Or property may be taken from the property room and then mysteriously "disappear."

The seriousness of the problem cannot be ignored. According to Walker (1983, p. 187): "Corruption undermines the basic law enforcement function of the police. Whether the corrupt act involves a small bribe to ignore a traffic violation or a sizable and regular payoff to protect a gambling operation, illegal activity is being tolerated." And this communicates the message that criminal activity is acceptable behavior, undermining the basic mission of the police and damaging the reputation of the entire police department.

Chapter 6 introduced you to the Law Enforcement Code of Ethics, a very idealistic code, but often extremely difficult to follow. The following listing of police values illustrates what is often encountered in real life (Sherman, 1982):

1. **Discretion A:** *Decisions about whether to enforce the law, in any but the most serious cases, should be guided by both what the law says and who the suspect is. Attitude, demeanor, cooperativeness, and even race, age and social class are all important considerations in deciding how to treat people generally, and whether or not to arrest suspects in particular.*
2. **Discretion B:** *Disrespect for police authority is a serious offense that should always be punished with an arrest or the use of force. The "offense" known as "contempt of cop" or P.O.P.O. (pissing off a police officer) cannot be ignored. Even when the party has committed no violation of the law, a police officer should find a safe way to impose punishment, including an arrest on fake charges.*
3. **Force:** *Police officers should never hesitate to use physical or deadly force against people who "deserve it," or where it can be an effective way of solving a crime. Only the potential punishments by superior officers, civil litigation, citizen complaints, and so forth should limit the use of force when the situation calls for it. When you can get away with it, use all the force that society should use on people like that—force and punishment which bleeding-heart judges are too soft to impose.*
4. **Due Process:** *Due process is only a means of protecting criminals at the expense of the law abiding and should be ignored whenever it is safe*

to do so. *Illegal searches and wiretaps, interrogation without advising suspects of their Miranda rights, and if need be (as in the much admired movie, Dirty Harry), even physical pain to coerce a confession are all acceptable methods for accomplishing the goal the public wants the police to accomplish: fighting crime. The rules against doing those things merely handcuff the police, making it more difficult for them to do their job.*

5. Truth: *Lying and deception are an essential part of the police job, and even perjury should be used if it is necessary to protect yourself or get a conviction on a "bad guy." Violations of due process cannot be admitted to prosecutors or in court, so perjury (in the serious 5 percent of cases that ever go to trial) is necessary and therefore proper. Lying to drug pushers about wanting to buy drugs, to prostitutes about wanting to buy sex, or to congressmen about wanting to buy influence is the only way, and therefore a proper way, to investigate these crimes without victims. Deceiving muggers into thinking you are an easy mark and deceiving burglars into thinking you are a fence are proper because there are not many other ways of catching predatory criminals in the act.*

6. Time: *You cannot go fast enough to chase a car thief or traffic violator, nor slow enough to get to a "garbage" call; and when there are no calls for service, your time is your own. Hot pursuits are necessary because anyone who tries to escape from the police is challenging police authority, no matter how trivial the initial offense. But calls to nonserious or social-work problems like domestic disputes or kids making noise are unimportant, so you can stop to get coffee on the way or even stop at the cleaner's if you like. And when there are no calls, you can sleep, visit friends, study, or do anything else you can get away with, especially on the midnight shift, when you can get away with a lot.*

7. Rewards: *Police do very dangerous work for low wages, so it is proper to take any extra rewards the public want to give them, like free meals, Christmas gifts, or even regular monthly payments (in some cities) for special treatment. The general rule is: take any reward that doesn't change what you would do anyway, such as eating a meal, but don't take money that would affect your job, like not giving traffic tickets. In many cities, however, especially in the recent past, the rule has been to take even those rewards that do affect your decisions, as long as they are related only to minor offenses—traffic, gambling, prostitution, but not murder.*

8. Loyalty: *The paramount duty is to protect your fellow officers at all costs, as they would protect you, even though you may have to risk your own career or your own life to do it. If your colleagues make a mistake, take a bribe, seriously hurt somebody illegally, or get into other kinds of trouble, you should do everything you can to protect them in the ensuing investigation. If your colleagues are routinely breaking rules, you should never tell supervisors, reporters, or outside investigators about it. If you don't like it, quit—or get transferred to the police academy. But never, ever, blow the whistle.*

A conflict between the code of police ethics and the values often found within the police culture is evident. One of the most widely recognized and publicized areas of concern is corruption. As noted by Pollock–Byrne (1989, p. 85):

Police routinely deal with the seamier side of society—not only drug addicts and muggers, but middle-class people who are involved in dishon-

esty and corruption. The constant displays of lying, hiding, cheating, and theft create cynicism and threaten even the strongest code of ethics, especially when these behaviors are carried out by judges, prosecutors, superiors, and politicians. The following are some rationales that might easily be used by police to justify behavior. (Murphy & Moran, 1981, p. 3).

The public thinks every cop is a crook—so why try to be honest?

The money is out there—if I don't take it, someone else will.

I'm only taking what's rightfully mine; if the city paid me a decent wage, I wouldn't have to get it on my own.

I can use it—it's for a good cause—my son needs an operation, or dental work, or tuition for medical school, or a new bicycle.Given constant exposure to others' misdeeds, peer pressure to conform, and previously vague or nonexistent ideas about right and wrong, the question is not why some officers engage in corrupt practices but rather why more don't.

USE OF DEADLY FORCE

"The authority to use deadly force," says Waldron (1984, p. 198), "is the most critical and awesome responsibility that will ever be placed on a police officer. No other single government official has the right or the means to lawfully take another human life."

Waldron goes on to caution:

Make no mistake, a decision to use deadly force is irreversible. After the fact, the decision is final. . . . Similarly, a decision not to use deadly force may also result in an irreversible situation. A police officer who hesitates or decides not to employ deadly force may suffer his or her own death or the death of another person the officer is sworn to protect.

The amount of force police departments use and condone directly affects the public's attitudes toward the police. Excessive use of force has been a chronic complaint of minorities, particularly in the 1960s and the 1980s.

Pursley (1984, p. 244) notes: "An issue that has grown in importance in recent years has been the use of deadly force by the police. This issue is usually tied inextricably to the broader issues of police-minority relations and the supporting issues of police violence and/or police brutality." Pursley also cities an extensive analysis of police use of deadly force conducted by the Police Foundation, the research findings of which are summarized as follows (Milton et al., 1977, pp. 10–11):

1. Police departments differ widely in their policies and review procedures relating to the use of deadly force. There is no universally accepted standard dictating when an officer should use a firearm.

2. There is a clear national trend in police departments toward the enactment of written policies governing the use of firearms. Often, however, these policies are not set forth in any single document, but are scattered among several department orders or bulletins. Many of these policy statements are poorly organized and confusing.

3. Many departments appear to shy away from adopting firearms policies that are much more restrictive than state law, for fear of increasing their vulnerability to civil suits. In addition, police administrators have *to cope with increasing police union opposition to the adoption of more restrictive standards.*

4. The rates of shootings by police officers vary widely among jurisdictions, and it is impossible (within the limits of the study) to say what specific factors are responsible for these differences.

5. Many departments are beginning to develop record-keeping procedures designed to identify and monitor officer conduct involving the use of excessive and repeated involvement in shooting incidents.

6. It is difficult, after the fact, to categorize certain shootings as "justified" or "unjustified." Some shootings are clearly and unequivocally acts of self-defense. Some manifestly fail to meet the requirements of law and local policy, or appear to have served no compelling purpose, in that no lives were saved and no dangerous felons apprehended. Many incidents, however, fall into a middle ground where the officer's word may be pitted against that of a friend or friends of the victim, or where one or two facts appear to be inconsistent with the officer's version of events.

7. Most shootings are called "justified" by departments, and very few are referred to criminal charges. When an officer is formally charged in connection with an incident occurring in the line of duty, juries generally do not convict, perhaps because most witnesses are themselves participants and not impartial observers. Department discipline in such cases rarely goes beyond a verbal or written reprimand to the officer involved.

8. The formal review of shooting incidents by a civilian or part-time civilian body does not in itself guarantee a fairer or more systematic resolution.

9. The number of blacks and other minorities shot by police is substantially greater than their proportion in the general population, but is not inconsistent with the number of blacks arrested for serious (Part I) crimes. Shootings of minority juveniles, in particular, have been responsible for increased tensions and occasionally violent disturbances in ghetto neighborhoods.

10. The review of shooting incidents in the cities surveyed for this study indicates that a sizable percentage involved out-of-uniform officers (both on duty in plainclothes and off duty), perhaps because out-of-uniform officers are less conspicuous and thus more able to intervene in situations in which criminal or suspicious activity is still going on.

When considering the justifiable use of deadly force, two interrelated rights are important: the legal right to use such force and the moral right compelling the officer to do so.

State legislators have generally given the police very broad discretion in this area, with most politicians fearful of being labeled as "soft on criminals" if they did otherwise. Many state statutes authorize use of deadly force to prevent the commission of a felony or to prevent a fleeing felon from escaping. In fact, in one state, it is a felony to run from the police, thus making it legal for police to shoot the person. Although this is legally right, is it morally right?

To balance the legal and moral rights involved, several states have adopted penal codes that do not rely solely on a crime being classified as a felony. They focus instead on the danger posed by the suspect to the officer and society.

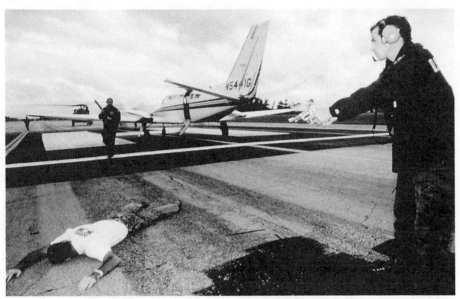

The use of deadly force is a critical issue that police must deal with.

Justification for use of deadly force must take into consideration not only the legal right, but also the need to apprehend the suspect compared to the safety of the arresting officer and compared to the value of human life.

Pursley (1984, p. 245) concludes: "Like so many other concerns surrounding crime and criminals, discussion of such issues tends to be more emotional rather than logical. To minorities it is simply a means to further oppress and show disregard for Blacks or Chicanos; for many white Americans it is simply giving the robbers, the rapists, the murderers what they deserve—after all, they say, it's not our problem that a disproportionate number of them are Black or Chicanos. For the police themselves, it's an issue of perceived safety, and they naturally feel at 'greater risk' when confronting the more perceived prevalence of violence among minorities."

A landmark Supreme Court ruling, *Tennessee v. Garner* (1985), is of extreme importance in the issue of use of deadly force. This ruling bars police from shooting to kill fleeing felons unless there is an imminent danger to life. This ruling invalidates laws in almost half the states that allow police officers to use deadly force to prevent the escape of a suspected felon. According to Nislow (1985, p. 1):

The current ruling sprang from a 1974 incident in which a Memphis police officer fatally shot an unarmed fifteen-year-old, fleeing from police after having stolen ten dollars in money and jewelry from an unoccupied house. . . . The police officer who fired the fatal shot testified that he had fired because he believed the suspect would otherwise escape and because he had been trained that Tennessee state law permitted him, in such situations, to shoot a suspected fleeing felon.

The Supreme Court ruled that the Tennessee "fleeing felon" statute was unconstitutional insofar as it authorized the use of deadly force against fleeing suspects who are unarmed and pose no threat to the officer or third parties.

In effect, since taking a life is a "seizure" protected by the Fourth Amendment, any use of deadly force must be *reasonable*.

THE POLICE IMAGE

Recognize that each police officer is an individual. Police officers are fathers, mothers, sons, daughters, uncles, aunts, coaches of Little League teams, church members, and neighbors. As people, they like to be liked, but often their profession requires that they take negative actions against those who break the law. As a result, they are often criticized and berated for simply doing their jobs.

Although police officers are individuals just like those in the community they have sworn to "serve and protect," their behavior is very public. As noted by More (1976, p. 126): "Policemen may simply be very ordinary people who happen to be extraordinarily visible."

Still, the public's image of the police varies greatly. Some see police officers as saviors; others see them as militaristic harassers. The sight of a police officer arouses feelings of respect, confidence, and security in some citizens; fear, hostility, and hatred in others; and indifferences in yet others.

The image of the police officer frequently portrayed on television has not been very helpful. The "Dirty Harry" tactics, with much violence and disregard for civil rights, are often presented as *the* way a police officer should behave.

The effects of television on both the police image and the fight against crime cannot be accurately measured. Certainly, it has an impact. Hardly an hour passes without an illegal search, a coerced confession, police brutality, and general violence dealt out by the police officers. Many modern-day police "heroes" are shown blatantly indulging in illegal and unconstitutional behavior, which in effect instills in the public the opinion that police misconduct is acceptable and, in fact, sometimes the only way to apprehend criminals. The same criticisms may be applied to our movies.

In spite of what is written in books or portrayed on television and in movies, the abstraction we call the "police image" is primarily the result of day-to-day contacts between police and citizens. It is the behavior of police officers at the patrol level rather than at the command level that is of greatest importance in establishing the police image. In turn, the individual behavior of the police officer who creates the police image is the result of several factors including length of service, the community served (ghetto or exclusive suburb), training, and experience.

The police image results from everyday contacts between individual police officers and citizens.

In addition to easily identifiable and predictable factors such as experience, training, and locality served, numerous subtle factors influence police behavior and image, including the nature of police work itself, a confusion of identity, the police officer's unique relation to the criminal justice system, the democratic nature of our society, and the individual officer's personality.

The Nature of Police Work   Numerous demands are placed upon the police officer. Police officers are under constant pressure and faced with rapidly changing conditions, sometimes life-threatening situations, with few guidelines and little supervision; they frequently must "play it by ear." Skolnick (1967) describes two principal variables of the police officer on the beat—danger and authority. He cautions that these variables must be interpreted in the light of constant pressure to appear efficient.

The stressfulness of the situation in which police officers are placed is described by More (1976, p. 33):

> It is obviously difficult and often impossible for police officers to respond in an appropriate manner to the numerous incidents called to their attention. They are under constant pressure, especially in highly congested areas, to handle a volume of cases that is beyond their capacity—forcing them to develop short-cut responses to run-of-the-mill situations. They lack adequate training with respect to some of the more complex social problems. And there has been little effort to provide individual officers with the guidelines which they require if they are expected to make more effective and judicious decisions in disposing of the incidents which come to their attention. In the absence of adequate resources, training, and guidance, the tendency is for individual police officers to attempt to meet largely by improvisation the varied demands made upon them.

In addition to the need to improvise in many situations, police officers must deal with people from all walks of life who are involved in criminal and noncriminal activities and must use broad discretion in a wide variety of situations with little supervision. They deal with crimes already committed, with people who are hurt, confused, angry, and upset; yet they must remain neutral, calm, and objective. They may appear indifferent or unsympathetic, but, much like physicians, they cannot become personally involved and still do a professional job. They must remain detached and objective.

The image resulting from the nature of police work might easily be compared to the image of a football referee. It is readily accepted that referees are necessary to the game. Without them chaos would reign. Despite their criticality, however, their image is frequently negative. No matter what call they make, a great many people are unhappy with them. They are usually perceived as being on the opponent's side. Defeats are frequently blamed on referees; however, seldom is a referee given credit for a team's victory. It is often a thankless, sometimes dangerous job. Fans have thrown pop bottles at and attempted to physically assault referees. Likewise, abusive names are frequently hurled at the referee. It often makes one wonder what type of individual could continue to work under such pressures.

Role Conflict   The role conflict faced by many police officers has a direct influence on the image projected (More, 1976, p. 180):

> *He wants to function as a crime fighter, but does not. He is not trained or rewarded for being a peace keeper or community service agent. His quasi-judicial role is poorly differentiated. He works on the one hand in an autonomous situation on the street, but on the other hand is supposed to be highly responsive to a chain of command. All these issues engender role conflict in the police officer.*

Most police officers feel they are law enforcement officers, not social workers. They did not create nor can they control the social problems that exist and that prompt numerous service calls. When they do respond to such calls, their help is often perceived as interference; they may be berated or even assaulted.

Unique Relationship to the System   Another factor influencing the police image is the officers' relationship to the law. Although police officers frequently initiate the criminal justice system by investigating and apprehending criminals, they often feel like outsiders in the judicial system. They may feel their investigation and apprehension of criminals is hampered by legal restrictions and that the suspect has more rights than the victim of the crime.

Although police officers are frequently blamed for rising crime rates, their participation in the legal system is often minimized. They may be made to feel as if they were on trial during the court proceedings as the defense attorney cross-examines them. They are seldom included in any plea bargaining. And frequently defendants are found not guilty because of loopholes or legal technicalities. When a confessed robber is acquitted on a technicality or a known rapist is not brought to trial by the prosecutor, police officers may take this as a personal affront, as a criticism of their investigative expertise. In addition, citizens of the community may also blame the police officers for the unsuccessful prosecution of the suspect. Further, legal technicalities may even result in the police officer being sued for false arrest.

The Police Personality—Reality or Myth?

Popular and scientific literature related to the police image often identifies several personality traits of the "typical" police officer.

Police officers are frequently described as being suspicious, cynical, bigoted, indifferent, authoritarian, and brutal.

Suspicious Police work requires a police officer to be wary of situations that are out of the ordinary, for example, a person with an umbrella on a sunny day or a person wearing sunglasses at midnight. Not only is keen observation critical to effective investigation and crime prevention, it is critical to self-defense. Danger is always possible in any situation. Skolnick (1967, pp. 45–46) believes that the police officer "develops a perceptual shorthand to identify certain kinds of people as symbolic assailants, that is, as persons who use gesture, language, and attire that the policeman has come to recognize as a prelude to violence. This does not mean that violence by the symbolic assailant is necessarily predictable. On the contrary, the policeman responds to the vague indication of danger suggested by appearance."

Cynical Because police officers deal with criminals, they are constantly on guard against human faults. Police officers see people at their worst. they know that people lie, cheat, steal, torture, kill. They deal with people who do not like police, who even hate them, and they feel the hatred. Additionally, they may see persons they firmly believe to be guilty of a heinous crime freed by a legal technicality. Neiderhoffer (1967) asserts that "the kind of cynicism that is directed against life, the world, and people in general. . . is endemic to policemen of all ranks and persuasions." This cynicism may also lead to paranoia.

Bigoted Police are frequently victims of problems they have nothing to do with and over which they have no control. They are not to blame for the injustices suffered by members of minority groups: housing, educational, and employment discrimination. Yet often members of minority groups perceive the police officers as a symbol of the society that has denied them its privileges and benefits. Tension between minority group members and any representatives of "authority" has become almost a way of life in many parts of large cities. The minority group members vent their anger and frustration on the police, and some police, understandably, come to feel anger and dislike for them.

Indifferent When police officers are called to the scene of a homicide, they are expected to conduct a thorough, impartial investigation. Their objectivity may be perceived by grieving relatives of the victim as indifference or coldness. Police officers must remain detached, however; one of the grieving relatives might well be the murderer. Further, a certain amount of distancing is required to work with difficult situations. Ellison and Genz (1978, p. 4) state that officers who must deal with assignments involving mutilation and death develop coping mechanisms: "These defenses, which permit one to do an important job well, often prevent him from doing the work which involves interacting with others."

Authoritarian   Effective law enforcement requires authority; authoritarianism comes with the job. Without authority and respect, the police officer could not effectively compel citizens of the community to obey the law. As noted by the French philosopher Pascal: "Justice without force is powerless; force without justice is tyrannical." The physical appearance of the police officer adds to this authoritarian image. The uniform, gun, club, and handcuffs project an image to which most people respond with uneasiness or even fear. Yet this image projects the right of the police to exercise the lawful force of the state in serving and protecting as well as in enforcing laws. The difficulty arises when the power that comes with the position is transferred to "personal power."

Brutal   Sometimes force is required to subdue suspects. Unfortunately, the crime-related aspects of a police officer's job are what frequently draw public attention. When police officers have to physically subdue a suspect, people notice. When they help individuals get into their locked cars, few notice. Sometimes, however, more force is used than is required. This, too, is easier to understand if one thinks of the other personality traits that often become part of the police "personality," particularly cynicism and authoritarianism. Police officers may use excessive force with a rapist if they believe that the probability is great that the rapist will never be brought to trial because of the prosecutor's policies on rape cases. They may also erroneously believe that violence is necessary to obtain respect from individuals who seem to respect nothing but force and power.

The eyes of the beholder determine how a police officer's actions will be interpreted or described. A person who dislikes police officers will probably perceive a specific behavior negatively, while the same behavior might be perceived positively by an individual who has a high regard for police officers. Consider, for example, the actions listed in table 21–2 and the way each is described by an individual who feels negatively about the police and one who feels positively about the police.

POLICE PROFESSIONALISM

Throughout this text the field of law enforcement has been referred to as a profession; however, whether law enforcement technically qualifies as a profession is extremely controversial. Several years ago, Wilson (1973, p. 283) called the police "subprofessionals" and "members of the craft." But changes have occurred since then.

Table 21–2 Police Actions Seen Negatively and Positively

Action by officer	Negative person	Positive person
Steps in to stop a fight in a bar.	Interference.	Preserving the peace.
Questions a rape victim.	Indifferent, cold.	Objective.
Uses a baton to break up a violent mob.	Brutal.	Commanding respect.
Steadily watches three youths on a corner.	Suspicious.	Observant.

Part of the problem is that definitions of professionalism vary. To some, professional means simply an important job. Sociologists, however, have identified certain elements that qualify an occupation as a profession. Moore (1970, pp. 3–22) summarized the key elements of a profession as professional knowledge, professional autonomy, and the service ideal.

The three key elements of professionalism are (1) professional knowledge, (2) professional autonomy, and (3) the service ideal.

Professional Knowledge The time when someone could walk into a police department, fill out an application, and be hired are gone in most parts of the country. Many departments now require a two-year college degree, and some require a four-year degree. In addition to a college degree, many departments require that applicants complete some kind of "skills" training. And, as noted, most larger departments also have their own "rookie schools" where new police officers learn what is expected in a particular agency.

As technology advances and as criminals become more sophisticated, more knowledge and training can be expected to be required.

Professional Autonomy Professional autonomy refers to the ability to control entrance into the profession, to define the content of the knowledge to be obtained, and to be responsible for self-monitoring and disciplining.

In addition, the autonomy of a profession is usually authorized by the power of the state; for example, physicians, dentists, lawyers, and teachers are licensed by the state. These professions are, in effect, legalized monopolies.

Law enforcement does fit the criterion of professional autonomy in that requirements to be a police officer are usually set by the legislature. The growth of Peace Officers Standards and Training (POST) boards throughout the country to oversee the profession attests to this fact.

Issues like the gun control controversy involve interpretation of the Bill of Rights.

A Service Ideal   The third element of a profession, the service ideal, requires that members of the profession follow a formal code of ethics and be committed to serving the community. In this area, police officers qualify as professionals provided the department stresses the public servant aspects of police work.

SUMMARY

Numerous issues are important in law enforcement in the 1990s. Some issues in law enforcement involve interpretation of the Bill of Rights, including the Second Amendment and gun control controversies; the Fifth and Sixth Amendments and the associated Exclusionary Rule and *Miranda* decision; and the Eighth Amendment and the use of capital punishment as cruel and unusual.

Controversy also exists as to whether certain offenses should be decriminalized. Such decriminalization would allow concentration of resources on serious crime and might also legalize certain actions such as gambling and prostitution, which are major revenue sources for organized crime. On the other hand, acts now considered criminal may be engaged in more frequently by law-abiding citizens if they were decriminalized, thus lowering our country's moral standards. Offenses that would be candidates for decriminalization include prostitution, sexual activities between consenting adults, gambling, public drunkenness, certain types of juvenile delinquency, narcotics and drug offenses, vagrancy, and disorderly conduct.

Heated controversy surrounds the practice of plea bargaining. In many courts more than 90 percent of criminal convictions are not obtained by the verdict of a jury or the decision of a judge. Rather, they are based upon the defendant's own plea of guilty. Convincing arguments exist both for and against plea bargaining; however, there is general agreement that it is practiced extensively.

Other issues involve whether police departments should be unionized and whether they should be accredited. The Commission on Accreditation for Law Enforcement Agencies was formed in 1979 to develop a set of law enforcement standards and to establish and administer an accreditation process to which law enforcement agencies could voluntarily apply to demonstrate that they met professional criteria. Whether the cost is justifiable is a strongly contested issue in many departments. Most police officers are currently members of local employee organizations and are not directly enrolled in a national labor union.

Another issue is police corruption and what can be done about it. Police corruption consists of acts involving the misuse of authority by a police officer in a manner designed to produce personal gain for oneself or for others. It is a problem of enormous magnitude and takes several forms, including accepting gratuities and bribes as well as committing theft or burglary. The most common and extensive type of corruption is accepting small gratuities or tips.

Yet another important question is when police are justified in using deadly force. Any such use must take into consideration not only the legal right, but also the moral right to use deadly force—the need to apprehend the suspect compared to the safety of the arresting officer and compared to the value of human life.

Another critical issue is whether police officers have an image problem. The police image results largely from everyday contacts between individual citizens and individual police officers. The police officer's behavior and the resulting image conveyed are influenced by the nature of police work, by the frequent confusion of identity and role conflict, by the police officer's unique relation to the criminal justice system, by the democratic nature of our society with its emphasis on civil rights and civil liberties, and by the police officer's personality.

Police officers are frequently described as being suspicious, cynical, bigoted, indifferent, authoritarian, and brutal. Sometimes, however, the fault is not in the behavior of the police officer but in the way it is perceived by the citizen.

A final issue is whether law enforcement qualifies as a profession. According to sociologists, the three key elements of professionalism are (1) professional knowledge, (2) professional autonomy, and (3) the service ideal.

Discussion Questions

1. Will police departments be totally professionalized?
2. Unions have played a vital role in the economic development of this country. Do they have a place in police work?
3. How serious is police corruption?

4. What role should police officers play in the plea bargaining process, if any?

5. How do police officers deal with their own lives when they spend so much time with the worst of people?

6. How can police get away from the superhuman image?

7. What are some societal factors interfering with police work?

8. Why is the police officer on the street responsible for the success of police-community relations programs and the police image?

9. Has the police image changed in the past ten years? The past hundred years?

10. What do you think is the general image of the police in your community?

References

"Accreditation Program Overview." Fairfax, VA: Commission on Accreditation for Law Enforcement Agencies. 1984.

Cole, G. F. *The American System of Criminal Justice*, 3d ed. Monterey, Calif.: Brooks/Cole Publishing, 1983.

Daley, R. *Prince of the City: The True Story of a Cop Who Knew Too Much.* Boston: Houghton-Mifflin, 1978.

Gavzer, Bernard. "Can Your Department Pass Muster?" *Parade*, December 30, 1984.

Gentel, W. D., and Handman, M. L. *Police Strikes: Causes and Prevention.* U.S. Department of Justice. Washington, D.C.: U.S. Government Printing Office, 1980.

Glick, H. R. *Courts, Politics, and Justice.* New York: McGraw-Hill, 1983.

Goldberg, W. I., "Victimless Crimes: Should Police Preserve Community Morals." *Tennessee Law Enforcement Journal*, p. 56, reprinted from *Police Law Quarterly*, April 1, 1972.

Goldstein, H. *Police Corruption: A Perspective on its Nature and Control.* Washington, D.C.: Police Foundation, 1975.

Juris, H. A., and Feuille, P. "Employee Organizations." In *Police Personnel Administration*, edited by O. G. Stahl and R. A. Staufenberger. Monterey, Calif.: Duxbury Press, 1974.

Knapp Commission. *Report on Police Corruption.* New York: George Braziller, 1973.

Levine, J. P.; Husheno, M. C.; and Palumbo, D. J. *Criminal Justice, a Public Policy Approach.* New York: Harcourt Brace Jovanovich, 1980.

Milton, C. H.; Halleck, J. W.; Lardner, J.; and Abrecht, G. L. *Police Use of Deadly Force.* Washington, D.C.: Police Foundation, 1977.

Moore, W. E. *The Professionals: Rules and Roles.* New York: Russell Sage, 1970.

Murphy, Paul, and Moran Kenneth T. "The Continuing Cycle of Systemic Police Corruption." In *The Social Basis of Criminal Justice: Ethical Issues for the 80s*, ed. F. Schmalleger and R. Gustafson, Washington, D.C.: University Press, 1981, pp. 87–101.

National Advisory Committee on Criminal Justice Standards and Goals. *Organized Crime: Report of the Task Force on Organized Crime.* Washington, D.C.: U.S. Government Printing Office, 1976.

Nislow, "Fleeing-Felon Rule Cut Down." *Law Enforcement News* XI, no. 8, April 22, 1985: 1.

Pollock-Byrne, Joycelyn M. *Ethics in Crime and Justice: Dilemmas & Decisions.* Pacific Grove, CA: Brooks/Cole Publishing Company, 1989.

Pursley, R. D. *Introduction to Criminal Justice*, 3d ed. New York: Macmillan, 1984.

Sherman, L., "Learning Police Ethics." *Criminal Justice Ethics* 1, no. 1, 1982: 10–19. Copyright 1982 by the John Jay College of Criminal Justice. Reprinted by permission.

Walker, S. *The Police in America: An Introduction*. New York: McGraw-Hill, 1983.

Walker, S. *Popular Justice*. New York: Oxford University Press, 1980.

Waldron, R. J. *The Criminal Justice System*, 3d ed. Boston: Houghton Mifflin, 1984.

Williams, V. L.; Formby, W. A.; and Watkins, J. C. *Introduction to Criminal Justice*. Albany, N.Y.: Delmar Publishers, 1982.

Wilson, J. Q. *Varieties of Police Behavior*. New York: Atheneum, 1973.

EPILOGUE
Why Become a Police Officer Today?

With violence a constant threat in communities and to individuals in the form of hijackings, murders, assaults, rapes, and kidnappings, police officers must be true professionals dedicated to the American creed of justice and liberty.

It is evident that the general public has become somewhat suspicious of the rhetoric of politicians, and many citizens want simple solutions to the crime problem where none exist. Police agencies themselves have become more militant and political; some ambitious administrators have even used a police agency to launch themselves into high political offices. Many police departments have problems with poor image, low status, and limited training, while at the same time they are asked to perform the most skilled, important, and dangerous police work.

What leads us to believe that the next ten years will be much better? Not much, on the surface. Only 1.5 percent of the convicted criminals are ever imprisoned. The odds are ninety-nine to one that you could commit a crime and never go to jail for it. Besides, if we were to imprison every convicted criminal, we would have to build thousands more jails, and the public simply would not stand the cost.

The question today is whether our citizens can succeed in controlling crime by resurrecting the determined pioneering spirit exhibited by our "heroes" in history. Seldom have city dwellers been as apprehensive about their safety as they are today, even though statistics show there is more fear of crime than actual crime itself.

Our forefathers fought to gain liberty for us; today we struggle to maintain and perpetuate that liberty. The police must enforce the law, but citizens must help. They must express their outrage at crime by reporting it. They must cooperate fully in its investigation and prosecution. They must give full support to law enforcement and criminal justice programs. As citizens see for themselves the correction of inequities in their communities, crime will start to be contained.

We need to rekindle the spirit of self-esteem in America, and police officers can provide the leadership. It will take intelligence, courage, and determination.

So why does anyone want to be a police officer today? Because, despite all that is terribly wrong with our country, the majority of citizens do not commit crimes, and they need protection. Law violators are a minority. Most people in our country are honest and good, and among them are many men and women who, although realizing that no one ever said being a police officer is easy, nonetheless want the challenge of service to their community, which is implicit in being a law enforcement officer.

GLOSSARY

Administrative services—those services such as recruitment, training, planning and research, records and communications, and crime laboratories and facilities including the police headquarters and jail.

Affidavit—a statement reduced to writing, sworn to before an officer or notary having authority to administer an oath.

Affirmation—usually related to an oath.

Aggravated assault—an unlawful attack upon a person for the purpose of inflicting severe bodily injury or death.

Aggravated rape—having sexual intercourse through use of force, threats or immediate use of force, or taking advantage of an unconscious or helpless woman or a woman incapable of consent because of mental illness or a defect reasonably known to the attacker.

Amphetamine—a stimulant taken orally as a tablet or capsule or intravenously to reduce appetite and/or to relieve mental depression.

Appeal—to ask a higher court to review the actions of a lower court to correct mistakes or injustice.

Arraignment—a court procedure whereby the accused is read the charges against him or her and is then asked how he or she pleads.

Arrest—to deprive a person of liberty by legal authority. Usually applied to the seizure of a person to answer before a judge for a suspected or alleged crime.

Arson—intentionally damaging or destroying, or attempting to damage or destroy, by means of fire or explosion the property of another without the consent of the owner or one's own property, with or without the intent to defraud.

Assault—an unlawful attack by one person upon another for the purpose of inflicting bodily harm.

Ballistics—a science dealing with the motion and impact of projectiles such as bullets and bombs.

Barbiturate—a depressant usually taken orally as a small tablet or capsule to induce sleep and/or to relieve tension.

Bill of Rights—the first ten amendments to the Constitution.

Bow Street Runners—the first detective unit; established in London by Henry Fielding in 1750.

Burglary—an unlawful entry into a building to commit a theft or felony.

Case law—a collection of summaries of how statutes have been applied by judges in various situations; the precedents that have been established by the courts.

Chief of police—the chief law enforcement officer at the local level.

Civil law—all restrictions placed upon individuals that are noncriminal in nature; seeks restitution rather than punishment.

Civil liberties—an individual's immunity from governmental oppression.

Civil rights—claims that the citizen has to the affirmative assistance of government.

Commission—the highest ruling body of the Mafia.

Common law—in England, the customary law set by the judges as disputes arose; the law in force before and independent of legislation.

Complainant—a person who makes a charge against another person.

Complaint—a legal document drawn up by a prosecutor that specifies the alleged crime and the supporting facts providing probable cause.

Consent—to agree; to give permission; voluntary oral or written permission to search a person's premises or property.

Constitution—the basic instrument of government and the supreme law of the United States; the written instrument defining the power, limitations, and functions of the United States government and that of each state.

Contraband—any article forbidden by law to be imported or exported; any article of which possession is prohibited by law and constitutes a crime.

Conviction—finding a person guilty of a criminal charge.

Coroner's jury—an inquest, usually before a jury of six members, to establish cause of death occurring under unusual circumstances.

Crack—a relatively new form of cocaine available at greatly reduced cost.

Crime—an action that is harmful to another person and/or to society and that is made punishable by law.

Criminal intent—a resolve, design, or mutual determination to commit a crime, with full knowledge of the consequences and exercise of free will.

Criminalistics—the scientific study of evidence in a criminal case and of individuals involved in such cases.

Criminal law—the body of law that defines crimes and fixes punishments for them.

Dangerous drugs—addicting, mind-altering drugs such as depressants, stimulants, and hallucinogens.

Data privacy act—the regulation of confidential and private information gathered by governmental agencies on individuals in the records, files, and processes of a state and its political subdivisions.

Deadly force—any force intended to cause death or serious physical injury.

Defendant—the person accused in a criminal proceeding.

Defense attorney—the representative of the accused in court.

Deliriant—a volatile chemical that can be sniffed or inhaled to produce a "high" similar to that produced by alcohol.

Deposition—a written statement made by a witness under oath to be used in court.

Discovery process—a system that requires all pertinent facts be available to the prosecutor and the defense attorney prior to the time of trial.

Diversion—bypassing the criminal justice system by assigning an individual to a social agency or other institution rather than bringing to trial.

Emergency situation—circumstances where a police officer must act without a magistrate's approval (without a warrant).

Equity—a concept that requires that the "spirit of the law" take precedence over the "letter of the law."

Evidence—all the means by which any alleged matter or act is either established or disproved.

Exclusionary Rule—a United States Supreme Court ruling that any evidence seized in violation of the Fourth Amendment will not be admissible in a federal or state trial.

Executive—the administrative branch of government that carries out the laws.

Extenuating circumstances—requiring immediate action; an emergency situation.

Felony—a major crime, for example, murder, rape, arson; the penalty is usually death or imprisonment for more than one year in a state prison or penitentiary.

Field services—the operations or line divisions of a law enforcement agency such as patrol, traffic control, investigation, and community services.

First-degree murder—willful, deliberate, and *premeditated* (planned) taking of another person's life.

Forced entry—an announced or unannounced entry into a dwelling or a building by force for the purpose of executing a search or arrest warrant to avoid the needless destruction of property, to prevent violent and deadly force against the officer, and to prevent the escape of a suspect.

Frisk—a patting down or minimal search of a person to determine the presence of a dangerous weapon.

Grand jury—a group of citizens, usually twenty-three, convened to hear testimony in secret and to issue formal criminal accusations (indictments) based upon probable cause if justified.

Habeas corpus—a judicial order to bring a person being held in custody to court.

Hallucinogen—a drug whose physical characteristics allow it to be disguised as a tablet, capsule, liquid, or powder; hallucinogens produce distortion, intensify sensory perception, and lessen the ability to discriminate between fact and fantasy.

Heroin—a commonly abused narcotic synthesized from morphine. Physically addictive and expensive.

Homicide—the willful killing of a human being by a another human being; also *Murder*.

Immediate control—within a person's reach.

Indictment—a written accusation based on probable cause, returned by a grand jury charging an individual with a specific crime.

Informant—a person who furnishes information concerning accusations against another person or persons.

Information—a formal written accusation of a crime resulting from a preliminary hearing; a charging document.

Informational probable cause—statements made to officers that can be relied upon and are generally sufficient in themselves to justify an arrest.

Instruments of a crime—the means by which a crime is committed or the suspects and/or victims transported; for example: gun, knife, burglary tools, car, truck.

Intent—*see* Criminal intent.

Interrogation—the questioning of a suspect.

Interview—the questioning of a witness.

Jury—a group of persons selected by law and sworn in to look at certain facts and determine the truth.

Justification—a sufficiently lawful reason why a person did or did not do the thing charged.

Juvenile delinquency—behavior by a person not of legal age (usually under age eighteen, but in a few states under age twenty-one) that violates a law or an ordinance.

Larceny/theft—the unlawful taking and removing of the property of another with the intent of permanently depriving the legal holder of the property.

Law—a body of rules for human conduct that are enforced by imposing penalties for their violation.

Lawful arrest—lawfully taking a person into custody (with or without a warrant) for the purpose of holding that person to answer for a public offense; all legal standards must be satisfied, particularly probable cause.

Legal—authorized by law.

Leges Henrici—a document that made law enforcement a public matter and separated offenses into felonies and misdemeanors.

Liability—a broad word for legal obligation, responsibility, or debt.

Limitation—a legal restriction of time or authority relating to an offense.

Loansharking—lending money at higher than legally prescribed rates.

Mafia—an Italian word referring to the lawless, violent bands of criminals who engaged in kidnapping and extortion in Sicily in the nineteenth and twentieth century; used today to refer to organized crime.

Magna Carta—a decisive document in the development of constitutional government in England that checked royal power and placed the king under the law (1215).

Manslaughter—accidentally causing the death of another person. No malice or intent is involved.

Marijuana—the most socially acceptable of the illegal drugs, derived from the cannabis plant, a hardy weed adaptable to most climates. Variously classified as a narcotic, a depressant, and a hallucinogen. Usually smoked.

Misdemeanor—a minor offense, for example, breaking a municipal ordinance, speeding; the penalty is usually a fine or a short imprisonment, usually less than one year, in a local jail or workhouse.

Mobility—movable; not firm, stationary, or fixed; for example, an automobile that is capable of being moved quickly with relative ease.

Motor vehicle theft—the unlawful taking or stealing of a motor vehicle without the authority or permission of the owner. Includes automobiles, trucks, buses, motorcycles, motorized boats, and aircraft.

Murder—*see* Homicide.

Narcotic—a drug that produces sleep and lethargy or relieves pain; usually an opiate.

NCIC (National Crime Information Center)—the computerized files of the Federal Bureau of Investigation containing records of stolen property and wanted persons.

Negligence—failure to exercise a reasonable amount of care in a situation that causes harm to someone or something.

Negligent homicide—an accidental death that results from the reckless operation of a motor vehicle, boat, plane, or firearm.

Nighttime warrant—a search or arrest warrant issued by a magistrate that authorizes a police officer to execute the warrant during the night.

Nolo contendre—"I will not contest it." A defendant's plea of "no contest" in a criminal case. It means he or she does not directly admit guilt, but submits to sentencing or other punishment.

No-knock search warrant—authorization by a magistrate upon the issuance of a search warrant to enter a premise by force without notification to avoid the chance that evidence may be destroyed if the officer's presence were announced.

Oath—a legal attestation or promise to perform an act or make a statement in good faith and under a responsibility to God.

Offense—an act prohibited by law, either by commission or omission.

Offense report—a preliminary report filled out by the responding officer for all crimes, attempts, investigations, and incidents to be made a matter of record.

Ordinary care—such degree of care, skills, and diligence as a person of ordinary prudence would employ under similar circumstances.

Organized crime—conspiratorial crime involving a hierarchy of persons who coordinate, plan, and execute illegal acts using enforcement and corruptive tactics.

Parens patriae—the right of the government to take care of minors and others who cannot legally take care of themselves.

Parish constable—an early system of law enforcement used primarily in rural areas of the United States.

Pennsylvania Constabulary—organized in 1905 and considered the first modern state police agency.

PCP—phencyclidine, also known as Angel dust, a hallucinogen.

Plain view—evidence that is not concealed and that is inadvertently seen by an officer engaged in a lawful activity; what is observed in plain view is not construed within the meaning of the Fourth Amendment as a search.

Plea—the accused's answer to formal charges in court.

Plea bargaining—a compromise between the defense and prosecuting attorneys that prearranges the plea and the sentence, conserving time, effort, and court expense.

Police authority—the right to direct and command.

Police power—the power of the federal, state, or municipal governments to pass laws regulating private interests, to protect the health and safety of the people, to prevent fraud and oppression, and to promote public convenience, prosperity, and welfare.

Preliminary hearing—a court process to establish probable cause to continue the prosecution of the defendant.

Probable cause—reasonable grounds for presuming guilt; facts that lead a person of ordinary care and prudence to believe and conscientiously entertain an honest and strong suspicion that a person is guilty of a crime.

Prosecutor—an elected or appointed official who serves as the public's lawyer.

Rape—carnal knowledge of a woman or man through the use of force or the threat of force.

Reasonable—sensible; just; well-balanced; good, sound judgment; that which would be attributed to a prudent person.

Reasonable doubt—when a juror is not morally certain of the truth of the charges.

Reasonable force—force not greater than that needed to achieve the desired end.

Reasonable search—a search conducted in a manner consistent with the Fourth Amendment.

Reasonable seizure—the seizure of evidence or persons according to constitutional standards set forth in the Fourth Amendment.

Relevant—having a direct relationship to the issue in question.

Restraint—to restrain; to prohibit; to bar further movement; to limit freedom.

Robbery—the stealing of anything of value from the care, custody, or control of a person in his or her presence, by force or by the threat of force.

Roll call—the briefing of officers prior to their tour of duty to update them on criminal activity and calls for service.

Rookeries—criminal areas of London.

R.P.R.d—released on own recognizance.

Scandinavian-type law—prohibits driving with blood-alcohol concentrations exceeding specific levels and establishes severe penalties for disobedience.

Search—examination of a person or property for the purpose of discovering evidence to prove guilt in relation to a crime.

Search warrant—a judicial order directing a peace officer to search for specific property, seize it, and return it to the court; it may be a written order or an order given over the telephone.

Second-degree murder—the unpremeditated but intentional killing of another person.

Seizure— a forcible detention or taking of a person or property in an arrest.

Sentence—the punishment, such as time in jail, given to a person convicted of a criminal offense.

Sheriff—the principal law enforcement officer of a county.

Simple assault—an unlawful attack by one person upon another, but without the intention of causing serious, permanent injury.

Simple rape—misleading a victim into having sexual intercourse.

Sir Robert Peel—often referred to as the "Father of Police Administration," his efforts organized the Metropolitan Police of London (1829).

Spoils system—a political system whereby "friends" of politicians were rewarded with key positions in the police department.

Status offense—a crime restricted to persons under the legal age, for example, smoking, drinking, breaking curfew, absenting from home, truancy, incorrigibility.

Statutory law—law passed by a legislature.

Stop and frisk—a protective search for weapons that could be used to assault police officers and others, for example, knives, guns, and clubs.

Submission—placing of one's person or property under the control of another; yielding to authority.

Subpoena—a written legal document ordering the person named in the document to appear in court to give testimony.

Supreme Court—the highest court in the United States and the only court established by the Constitution.

Tithing—in Anglo-Saxon England, a unit of civil administration consisting of ten families; established the principle of collective responsibility for maintaining law and order.

Tort—a civil wrong for which the court seeks a remedy in the form of damages to be paid.

United States Attorney General—the head of the Department of Justice and the chief law officer of the federal government.

Warrant—a written order issued by an officer of the court, usually a judge, directing a person in authority to arrest the person named, charged with the named offense, and to bring that person before the issuing person or court of jurisdiction.

Watch and Ward—a system of law enforcement that was used to protect citizens twenty-four hours a day; the day shift was called the "ward" and the night shift the "watch."

White-collar crime—occupational or business-related crime.

Witness—a complainant, an accuser, a victim, an observer of an incident, a source of information, or a scientific examiner of physical evidence.

Writ of habeas corpus—*see* Habeas corpus.

Index

F

T